The Letters and Legacy of Paul

The Letters and Legacy of Paul

FORTRESS COMMENTARY ON THE BIBLE
STUDY EDITION

Margaret Aymer

Cynthia Briggs Kittredge

David A. Sánchez

Editors

Fortress Press
Minneapolis

THE LETTERS AND LEGACY OF PAUL
Fortress Commentary on the Bible Study Edition

Excerpted from the *Fortress Commentary on the Bible: The New Testament*
(Minneapolis: Fortress Press, 2014); Margaret Aymer, Cynthia Briggs Kittredge, David A. Sánchez, volume editors.

Fortress Press Publication Staff:
Neil Elliott and Scott Tunseth, Project Editors
Marissa Wold, Production Manager
Laurie Ingram, Cover Design.

Copyeditor: Jeffrey A. Reimer

Typesetter: PerfecType, Nashville, TN

Proofreader: David Cottingham and Linda Maloney

Library of Congress Cataloging-in-Publication data is available

ISBN: 978-1-5064-1591-8

eISBN: 978-1-5064-1592-5

The paper used in this publication meets the minimum requirements of American National Standard for Information Sciences—Permanence of Paper for Printed Library Materials, ANSI Z329, 48-1984. Manufactured in the U.S.A.

CONTENTS

PUBLISHER'S NOTE

About the Fortress Commentary on the Bible Study Editions

In 2014 Fortress Press released the two-volume *Fortress Commentary on the Bible*. See the Series Introduction (pp. 1–3) for a look inside the creation and design of the Old Testament/Apocrypha and New Testament volumes. While each comprehensive commentary volume can easily be used in classroom settings, we also recognized that dividing the larger commentaries into smaller volumes featuring key sections of Scripture may be especially helpful for use in corresponding biblical studies courses. To help facilitate such classroom use, we have broken the two-volume commentary into eight study editions.

Please note that in this study edition the page numbers match the page numbers of the larger Fortress Commentary on the Bible volume in which it first appeared. We have intentionally retained the same page numbering to facilitate use of the study editions and larger volumes side by side.

The Letters and Legacy of Paul was first published in Fortress Commentary on the Bible: The New Testament.

ABBREVIATIONS

General

AT	Alpha Text (of the Greek text of Esther)
BOI	Book of Isaiah
Chr	Chronicler
DH	Deuteronomistic History
DI	Deutero-Isaiah
Dtr	Deuteronomist
Gk.	Greek
H	Holiness Code
Heb.	Hebrew
JPS	Jewish Publication Society
LXX	The Septuagint
LXX B	Vaticanus Text of the Septuagint
MP	Mode of production
MT	Masoretic Text
NIV	New International Version
NRSV	New Revised Standard Version
OAN	Oracles against Nations (in Jeremiah)
P.	papyrus/papyri
P	Priestly source
PE	Pastoral Epistles
RSV	Revised Standard Version
TI	Trito-Isaiah

Books of the Bible (NT, OT, Apocrypha)

Old Testament/Hebrew Bible

Gen.	Genesis
Exod.	Exodus
Lev.	Leviticus
Num.	Numbers
Deut.	Deuteronomy

Josh.	Joshua
Judg.	Judges
Ruth	Ruth
1 Sam.	1 Samuel
2 Sam.	2 Samuel
1 Kgs.	1 Kings
2 Kgs.	2 Kings
1 Chron.	1 Chronicles
2 Chron.	2 Chronicles
Ezra	Ezra
Neh.	Nehemiah
Esther	Esther
Job	Job
Ps. (Pss.)	Psalms
Prov.	Proverbs
Eccles.	Ecclesiastes
Song.	Song of Songs
Isa.	Isaiah
Jer.	Jeremiah
Lam.	Lamentations
Ezek.	Ezekiel
Dan.	Daniel
Hosea	Hosea
Joel	Joel
Amos	Amos
Obad.	Obadiah
Jon.	Jonah
Mic.	Micah
Nah.	Nahum
Hab.	Habakkuk
Zeph.	Zephaniah
Hag.	Haggai
Zech.	Zechariah
Mal.	Malachi

Apocrypha

Tob.	Tobit
Jth.	Judith
Gk. Esther	Greek Additions to Esther
Sir.	Sirach (Ecclesiasticus)

Bar.	Baruch
Let. Jer.	Letter of Jeremiah
Add Dan.	Additions to Daniel
Pr. Azar.	Prayer of Azariah
Sg. Three.	Song of the Three Young Men (or Three Jews)
Sus.	Susanna
Bel	Bel and the Dragon
1 Macc.	1 Maccabees
2 Macc.	2 Maccabees
1 Esd.	1 Esdras
Pr. of Man.	Prayer of Manasseh
2 Esd.	2 Esdras
Wis.	Wisdom of Solomon
3 Macc.	3 Maccabees
4 Macc.	4 Maccabees

New Testament

Matt.	Matthew
Mark	Mark
Luke	Luke
John	John
Acts	Acts of the Apostles
Rom.	Romans
1 Cor.	1 Corinthians
2 Cor.	2 Corinthians
Gal.	Galatians
Eph.	Ephesians
Phil.	Philippians
Col.	Colossians
1 Thess.	1 Thessalonians
2 Thess.	2 Thessalonians
1 Tim.	1 Timothy
2 Tim.	2 Timothy
Titus	Titus
Philem.	Philemon
Heb.	Hebrews
James	James
1 Pet.	1 Peter
2 Pet.	2 Peter
1 John	1 John

2 John	2 John
3 John	3 John
Jude	Jude
Rev.	Revelation (Apocalypse)

Journals, Series, Reference Works

ABD	*Anchor Bible Dictionary*. Edited by David Noel Freedman. 6 vols. New York: Doubleday, 1992.
ACNT	Augsburg Commentaries on the New Testament
AJA	*American Journal of Archaeology*
AJT	*Asia Journal of Theology*
ANET	*Ancient Near Eastern Texts Relating to the Old Testament*. Edited by J. B. Pritchard. 3rd ed. Princeton: Princeton University Press, 1969.
ANF	*The Ante-Nicene Fathers*. Edited by Alexander Roberts and James Donaldson. 1885–1887. 10 vols. Repr., Peabody, MA: Hendrickson, 1994.
ANRW	*Aufstieg und Niedergang der römischen Welt: Geschichte und Kultur Roms im Spiegel der neueren Forschung*. Edited by Hildegard Temporini and Wolfgang Haase. Berlin: de Gruyter, 1972–.
ANTC	Abingdon New Testament Commentaries
AOAT	Alter Orient und Altes Testament
AbOTC	Abingdon Old Testament Commentary
AOTC	Apollos Old Testament Commentary
A(Y)B	Anchor (Yale) Bible
BA	*Biblical Archaeologist*
BAR	*Biblical Archaeology Review*
BDAG	Bauer, W., F. W. Danker, W. F. Arndt, and F. W. Gingrich. *Greek-English Lexicon of the New Testament and Other Early Christian Literature*. 3rd ed. Chicago: University of Chicago Press, 1999.
BEATAJ	Beiträge zur Erforschung des Alten Testaments und des Antiken Judentum
Bib	*Biblica*
BibInt	*Biblical Interpretation*
BJRL	*Bulletin of the John Rylands University Library of Manchester*
BJS	Brown Judaic Studies
BNTC	Black's New Testament Commentaries
BR	*Biblical Research*
BRev	*Bible Review*
BSac	*Bibliotheca sacra*
BTB	*Biblical Theology Bulletin*
BZAW	Beihefte zur Zeitschrift für die alttestamentliche Wissenschaft
CAT	Commentaire de l'Ancien Testament

CBC	Cambridge Bible Commentary
CBQMS	Catholic Biblical Quarterly Monograph Series
CC	Continental Commentaries
CH	*Church History*
CHJ	*Cambridge History of Judaism.* Edited by W. D. Davies and Louis Finkelstein. Cambridge: Cambridge University Press, 1984–.
ConBNT	Coniectanea biblica: New Testament Series
ConBOT	Coniectanea biblica: Old Testament Series
CS	Cistercian Studies
CTAED	*Canaanite Toponyms in Ancient Egyptian Documents.* S. Ahituv. Jerusalem: Magnes, 1984.
CTQ	*Concordia Theological Quarterly*
CurTM	*Currents in Theology and Mission*
ExpTim	*Expository Times*
ETL	*Ephemerides Theologicae Lovanienses*
ExAud	*Ex auditu*
FAT	Forschungen zum Alten Testament
FC	Fathers of the Church
FRLANT	Forschungen zur Religion und Literatur des Alten und Neuen Testaments
HAT	Handbuch zum Alten Testament
HBT	*Horizons in Biblical Theology*
HNTC	Harper's New Testament Commentaries
HR	*History of Religions*
HSM	Harvard Semitic Monographs
HTKAT	Herders Theologischer Kommentar zum Alten Testament
HTR	*Harvard Theological Review*
HTS	Harvard Theological Studies
HUCA	*Hebrew Union College Annual*
HUCM	Monographs of the Hebrew Union College
HUT	Hermeneutische Untersuchungen zur Theologie
IBC	Interpretation: A Bible Commentary for Teaching and Preaching
ICC	International Critical Commentary
Int	*Interpretation*
JAAR	*Journal of the American Academy of Religion*
JAOS	*Journal of the American Oriental Society*
JBL	*Journal of Biblical Literature*
JBQ	*Jewish Bible Quarterly*
JECS	*Journal of Early Christian Studies*
JJS	*Journal of Jewish Studies*
JNES	*Journal of Near Eastern Studies*

JNSL	*Journal of Northwest Semitic Languages*
JQR	*Jewish Quarterly Review*
JRS	*Journal of Roman Studies*
JSem	*Journal of Semitics*
JSJ	*Journal for the Study of Judaism in the Persian, Hellenistic, and Roman Periods*
JSNT	*Journal for the Study of the New Testament*
JSOT	*Journal for the Study of the Old Testament*
JSOTSup	Journal for the Study of the Old Testament Supplement Series
JSQ	*Jewish Studies Quarterly*
JSS	*Journal of Semitic Studies*
JTI	*Journal of Theological Interpretation*
JTS	*Journal of Theological Studies*
JTSA	*Journal of Theology for Southern Africa*
KTU	*Die keilalphabetischen Texte aus Ugarit.* Edited by M. Dietrich, O. Loretz, and J. Sanmartín. AOAT 24/1. Neukirchen-Vluyn: Neukirchener, 1976.
LCC	Loeb Classical Library
LEC	Library of Early Christianity
LHB/OTS	Library of the Hebrew Bible/Old Testament Studies
LW	*Luther's Works.* Edited by Jaroslav Pelikan and Helmut T. Lehmann. 55 vols. St. Louis: Concordia; Philadelphia: Fortress Press, 1958–1986.
NAC	New American Commentary
NCB	New Century Bible
NCBC	New Cambridge Bible Commentary
NedTT	*Nederlands theologisch tijdschrift*
Neot	*Neotestamentica*
NICNT	New International Commentary on the New Testament
NICOT	New International Commentary on the Old Testament
NIGTC	New International Greek Testament Commentary
NovT	*Novum Testamentum*
NPNF[1]	*The Nicene and Post-Nicene Fathers,* Series 1. Edited by Philip Schaff. 14 vols. 1886–1889. Repr., Grand Rapids: Eerdmans, 1956.
NTL	New Testament Library
NTS	*New Testament Studies*
OBT	Overtures to Biblical Theology
OTE	*Old Testament Essays*
OTG	Old Testament Guides
OTL	Old Testament Library
OTM	Old Testament Message
PEQ	*Palestine Exploration Quarterly*
PG	Patrologia graeca [= Patrologiae cursus completus: Series graeca]. Edited by J.-P. Migne. 162 vols. Paris, 1857–1886.

PL	John Milton, *Paradise Lost*
PL	Patrologia latina [= Patrologiae cursus completus: Series latina]. Edited by J.-P. Migne. 217 vols. Paris, 1844–1864.
PRSt	*Perspectives in Religious Studies*
QR	*Quarterly Review*
RevExp	*Review and Expositor*
RevQ	*Revue de Qumran*
SBLABS	Society of Biblical Literature Archaeology and Biblical Studies
SBLAIL	Society of Biblical Literature Ancient Israel and Its Literature
SBLDS	Society of Biblical Literature Dissertation Series
SBLEJL	Society of Biblical Literature Early Judaism and Its Literature
SBLMS	Society of Biblical Literature Monograph Series
SBLRBS	Society of Biblical Literature Resources for Biblical Study
SBLSCS	Society of Biblical Literature Septuagint and Cognate Studies
SBLSP	*Society of Biblical Literature Seminar Papers*
SBLSymS	Society of Biblical Literature Symposium Series
SBLWAW	SBL Writings from the Ancient World
SemeiaSt	Semeia Studies
SJT	*Scottish Journal of Theology*
SNTSMS	Society for New Testament Studies Monograph Series
SO	Symbolae osloenses
SR	*Studies in Religion*
ST	*Studia Theologica*
StABH	Studies in American Biblical Hermeneutics
TD	*Theology Digest*
TAD	*Textbook of Aramaic Documents from Ancient Egypt.* Vol. 1: *Letters.* Bezalel Porten and Ada Yardeni. Winona Lake, IN: Eisenbrauns, 1986.
TDOT	*Theological Dictionary of the Old Testament.* 15 vols. Edited by G. Johannes Botterweck, Helmer Ringgren, and Heinz-Josef Fabry. Translated by David E. Green and Douglas W. Stott. Grand Rapids: Eerdmans, 1974–1995.
TJT	*Toronto Journal of Theology*
TNTC	Tyndale New Testament Commentaries
TOTC	Tyndale Old Testament Commentaries
TS	*Theological Studies*
TZ	*Theologische Zeitschrift*
VE	*Vox evangelica*
VT	*Vetus Testamentum*
VTSup	Supplements to Vetus Testamentum
WBC	Word Biblical Commentary
WSA	Works of St. Augustine: A Translation for the Twenty-First Century
WUANT	Wissenschaftliche Untersuchungen zum Alten und Neuen Testament

WUNT	Wissenschaftliche Untersuchungen zum Neuen Testament
WW	*Word and World*
ZAW	*Zeitschrift für die alttestamentliche Wissenschaft*
ZBK	Zürcher Bibelkommentare
ZNW	*Zeitschrift für die neutestamentliche Wissenschaft und die Kunde der älteren Kirche*

Ancient Authors and Texts

1 Clem.	*1 Clement*
2 Clem.	*2 Clement*
1 En.	*1 Enoch*
2 Bar.	*2 Baruch*
Abot R. Nat.	*Abot de Rabbi Nathan*
Ambrose	
Paen.	*De paenitentia*
Aristotle	
Ath. Pol.	*Athēnaīn politeia*
Nic. Eth.	*Nicomachean Ethics*
Pol.	*Politics*
Rhet.	*Rhetoric*
Augustine	
FC 79	*Tractates on the Gospel of John, 11–27.* Translated by John W. Rettig. Fathers of the Church 79. Washington, DC: Catholic University of America Press, 1988.
Tract. Ev. Jo.	*In Evangelium Johannis tractatus*
Bede, Venerable	
CS 117	*Commentary on the Acts of the Apostles.* Translated by Lawrence T. Martin. Cistercian Studies 117. Kalamazoo, MI: Cistercian Publications, 1989.
Barn.	*Barnabas*
CD	Cairo Genizah copy of the Damascus Document
Cicero	
De or.	*De oratore*
Tusc.	*Tusculanae disputationes*
Clement of Alexandria	
Paed.	*Paedogogus*
Strom.	*Stromata*
Cyril of Jerusalem	
Cat. Lect.	*Catechetical Lectures*
Dio Cassius	
Hist.	*Roman History*

Dio Chrysostom
    Or.   *Orations*
Diog. Diognetus
Dionysius of Halicarnassus
    Thuc.   *De Thucydide*
Epictetus
    Diatr.   *Diatribai (Dissertationes)*
    Ench.   *Enchiridion*
Epiphanius
    Pan.   *Panarion (Adversus Haereses)*
Eusebius of Caesarea
    Hist. eccl.   *Historia ecclesiastica*
Gos. Thom.   *Gospel of Thomas*
Herodotus
    Hist.   *Historiae*
Hermas, *Shepherd*
    Mand.   *Mandates*
    Sim.   *Similitudes*
Homer
    Il.   *Iliad*
    Od.   *Odyssey*
Ignatius of Antioch
    Eph.   *To the Ephesians*
    Smyr.   *To the Smyrnaeans*
Irenaeus
    Adv. haer.   *Adversus haereses*
Jerome
    Vir. ill.   *De viris illustribus*
John Chrysostom
    Hom. 1 Cor. *Homiliae in epistulam i ad Corinthios*
    Hom. Act.   *Homiliae in Acta apostolorum*
    Hom. Heb.   *Homiliae in epistulam ad Hebraeos*
Josephus
    Ant.   *Jewish Antiquities*
    Ag. Ap.   *Against Apion*
    J.W.   *Jewish War*
Jub.   *Jubilees*
Justin Martyr
    Dial.   *Dialogue with Trypho*
    1 Apol.   *First Apology*

L.A.E.	*Life of Adam and Eve*
Liv. Pro.	*Lives of the Prophets*
Lucian	
Alex.	*Alexander (Pseudomantis)*
Phal.	*Phalaris*
Mart. Pol.	*Martyrdom of Polycarp*
Novatian	
Trin.	*De trinitate*
Origen	
C. Cels.	*Contra Celsum*
Comm. Jo.	*Commentarii in evangelium Joannis*
De princ.	*De principiis*
Hom. Exod.	*Homiliae in Exodum*
Hom. Jer.	*Homiliae in Jeremiam*
Hom. Josh.	*Homilies on Joshua*
Pausanias	
Descr.	*Description of Greece*
Philo	
Cher.	*De cherubim*
Decal.	*De decalogo*
Dreams	*On Dreams*
Embassy	*On the Embassy to Gaius (= Legat.)*
Fug.	*De fuga et inventione*
Leg.	*Legum allegoriae*
Legat.	*Legatio ad Gaium*
Migr.	*De migratione Abrahami*
Mos.	*De vita Mosis*
Opif.	*De opificio mundi*
Post.	*De posteritate Caini*
Prob.	*Quod omnis probus liber sit*
QE	*Quaestiones et solutiones in Exodum*
QG	*Quaestiones et solutiones in Genesin*
Spec. Laws	*On the Special Laws*
Plato	
Gorg.	*Gorgias*
Plutarch	
Mor.	*Moralia*
Mulier. virt.	*Mulierum virtutes*
Polycarp	
Phil.	*To the Philippians*

Ps.-Clem. Rec.	*Pseudo-Clementine Recognitions*
Pss. Sol.	*Psalms of Solomon*
Pseudo-Philo	
L.A.B.	*Liber antiquitatum biblicarum*
Seneca	
Ben.	*De beneficiis*
Strabo	
Geog.	*Geographica*
Tatian	
Ad gr.	*Oratio ad Graecos*
Tertullian	
Praescr.	*De praescriptione haereticorum*
Prax.	*Adversus Praxean*
Bapt.	*De baptismo*
De an.	*De anima*
Pud.	*De pudicitia*
Virg.	*De virginibus velandis*
Virgil	
Aen.	*Aeneid*
Xenophon	
Oec.	*Oeconomicus*

Mishnah, Talmud, Targum

b. B. Bat.	*Babylonian Talmudic tractate Baba Batra*
b. Ber.	*Babylonian Talmudic tractate Berakhot*
b Erub.	*Babylonian Talmudic tractate Erubim*
b. Ketub.	*Babylonian Talmudic tractate Ketubbot*
b. Mak.	*Babylonian Talmudic tractate Makkot*
b. Meg.	*Babylonian Talmudic tractate Megillah*
b. Ned.	*Babylonian Talmudic tractate Nedarim*
b. Naz.	*Babylonian Talmudic tractate Nazir*
b. Sanh.	*Babylonian Talmudic tractate Sanhedrin*
b. Shab.	*Babylonian Talmudic tractate Shabbat*
b. Sotah	*Babylonian Talmudic tractate Sotah*
b. Ta'an.	*Babylonian Talmudic tractate Ta'anit*
b. Yev.	*Babylonian Talmudic tractate Yevamot*
b. Yoma	*Babylonian Talmudic tractate Yoma*
Eccl. Rab.	*Ecclesiastes Rabbah*
Exod. Rab.	*Exodus Rabbah*
Gen. Rab.	*Genesis Rabbah*

Lam. Rab.	*Lamentations Rabbah*
Lev. R(ab).	*Leviticus Rabbah*
m. Abot	*Mishnah tractate Abot*
m. Bik.	*Mishnah tractate Bikkurim*
m. Demai	*Mishnah tractate Demai*
m. 'Ed.	*Mishnah tractate 'Eduyyot*
m. Git.	*Mishnah tractate Gittin*
m. Pesaḥ	*Mishnah tractate Pesaḥim*
m. Šeqal.	*Mishnah tractate Šeqalim (Shekalim)*
m. Shab.	*Mishnah tractate Shabbat*
m. Sotah	*Mishnah tractate Sotah*
m. Ta'an.	*Mishnah tractate Ta'anit*
m. Tamid	*Mishnah tractate Tamid*
m. Yad.	*Mishnah tractate Yadayim*
m. Yebam.	*Mishnah tractate Yebamot*
m. Yoma	*Mishnah tractate Yoma*
Num. Rab.	*Numbers Rabbah*
Pesiq. Rab.	*Pesiqta Rabbati*
Pesiq. Rab Kah.	*Pesiqta Rab Kahana*
S. 'Olam Rab.	*Seder 'Olam Rabbah*
Song Rab.	*Song of Songs Rabbah*
t. Hul.	*Tosefta tractate Hullin*
Tg. Onq.	*Targum Onqelos*
Tg. Jer.	*Targum Jeremiah*
y. Hag.	*Jerusalem Talmudic tractate Hagiga*
y. Pesaḥ	*Jerusalem Talmudic tractate Pesaḥim*
y. Sanh.	*Jerusalem Talmudic tractate Sanhedrin*

Dead Sea Scrolls

1QapGen	*Genesis apocryphon* (Excavated frags. from cave)
1QM	*War Scroll*
1QpHab	*Pesher Habakkuk*
1QS	*Rule of the Community*
1QSb	*Rule of the Blessings* (Appendix b to 1QS)
1Q21	*T. Levi*, aramaic
4Q184	Wiles of the Wicked Woman
4Q214	Levi[d] ar (*olim* part of Levi[b])
4Q214b	Levi[f] ar (*olim* part of Levi[b])
4Q226	psJub[b] (4Q *pseudo-Jubilees*)
4Q274	Tohorot A

4Q277	Tohorot B^b (*olim* B^c)
4Q525	*Beatitudes*
4QMMT	*Miqsat Ma'aśê ha-Torah*
4QpNah/4Q169	4Q Pesher Nahum
4Q82	*The Greek Minor Prophets Scroll*

Old Testament Pseudepigrapha

1 En.	*1 Enoch*
2 En.	*2 Enoch*
Odes Sol.	*Odes of Solomon*
Syr. Men.	*Sentences of the Syriac Menander*
T. Levi	*Testament of Levi*
T. Mos.	*Testament of Moses*
T. Sim.	*Testament of Simeon*

INTRODUCTION

The *Fortress Commentary on the Bible*, presented in two volumes, seeks to invite study and conversation about an ancient text that is both complex and compelling. As biblical scholars, we wish students of the Bible to gain a respect for the antiquity and cultural remoteness of the biblical texts and to grapple for themselves with the variety of their possible meanings; to fathom a long history of interpretation in which the Bible has been wielded for causes both beneficial and harmful; and to develop their own skills and voices as responsible interpreters, aware of their own social locations in relationships of privilege and power. With this in mind, the *Fortress Commentary on the Bible* offers general readers an informed and accessible resource for understanding the biblical writings in their ancient contexts; for recognizing how the texts have come down to us through the mediation of different interpretive traditions; and for engaging current discussion of the Bible's sometimes perplexing, sometimes ambivalent, but always influential legacy in the contemporary world. The commentary is designed not only to inform but also to invite and empower readers as active interpreters of the Bible in their own right.

The editors and contributors to these volumes are scholars and teachers who are committed to helping students engage the Bible in the classroom. Many also work as leaders, both lay and ordained, in religious communities, and wish this commentary to prove useful for informing congregational life in clear, meaningful, and respectful ways. We also understand the work of biblical interpretation as a responsibility far wider than the bounds of any religious community. In this regard, we participate in many and diverse identities and social locations, yet we all are conscious of reading, studying, and hearing the Bible today as citizens of a complex and interconnected world. We recognize in the Bible one of the most important legacies of human culture; its historical and literary interpretation is of profound interest to religious and nonreligious people alike.

Often, the academic interpretation of the Bible has moved from close study of the remote ancient world to the rarefied controversy of scholarly debate, with only occasional attention to the ways biblical texts are actually heard and lived out in the world around us. The commentary seeks to provide students with diverse materials on the ways in which these texts have been interpreted through the course of history, as well as helping students understand the texts' relevance for today's globalized world. It recognizes the complexities that are involved with being an engaged reader of the Bible, providing a powerful tool for exploring the Bible's multilayered meanings in both their ancient and modern contexts. The commentary seeks to address contemporary issues that are raised by biblical passages. It aspires to be keenly aware of how the contemporary world and its issues and perspectives influence the interpretation of the Bible. Many of the most important insights of contemporary biblical scholarship not only have come from expertise in the world of antiquity but have also been forged in modern struggles for dignity, for equality, for sheer survival, and out of respect for those who have died without seeing justice done. Gaining familiarity with the original contexts in which the biblical writings were produced is essential, but not sufficient, for encouraging competent and discerning interpretation of the Bible's themes today.

Inside the Commentary

Both volumes of *The Fortress Commentary on the Bible* are organized in a similar way. In the beginning of each volume, **Topical Articles** set the stage on which interpretation takes place, naming the issues and concerns that have shaped historical and theological scholarship down to the present. Articles in the *Fortress Commentary on the Old Testament* attend, for example, to the issues that arise when two different religious communities claim the same body of writings as their Scripture, though interpreting those writings quite differently. Articles in the *Fortress Commentary on the New Testament* address the consequences of Christianity's historic claim to appropriate Jewish Scripture and to supplement it with a second collection of writings, the experience of rootlessness and diaspora, and the legacy of apocalypticism. Articles in both volumes reflect on the historical intertwining of Christianity with imperial and colonial power and with indexes of racial and socioeconomic privilege.

Section Introductions in the Old Testament volume provide background to the writings included in the Torah, Historical Writings, Wisdom, Prophetic Writings, and a general introduction to the Apocrypha. The New Testament volume includes articles introducing the Gospels, Acts, the letters associated with Paul, Hebrews, the General Epistles, and Revelation. These articles will address the literary and historical matters, as well as theological themes, that the books in these collections hold in common.

Commentary Entries present accessible and judicious discussion of each biblical book, beginning with an introduction to current thinking regarding the writing's original context and its significance in different reading communities down to the present day. A three-level commentary then follows for each sense division of the book. In some cases these follow the chapter divisions of a biblical book, but more often contributors have discerned other outlines, depending on matters of genre, movement, or argument.

The three levels of commentary are the most distinctive organizational feature of these volumes. The first level, "The Text in Its Ancient Context," addresses relevant lexical, exegetical, and literary aspects of the text, along with cultural and archaeological information that may provide additional insight into the historical context. This level of the commentary describes consensus views where these exist in current scholarship and introduces issues of debate clearly and fairly. Our intent here is to convey some sense of the historical and cultural distance between the text's original context and the contemporary reader.

The second level, "The Text in the Interpretive Tradition," discusses themes including Jewish and Christian tradition as well as other religious, literary, and artistic traditions where the biblical texts have attracted interest. This level is shaped by our conviction that we do not apprehend these texts immediately or innocently; rather, even the plain meaning we may regard as self-evident may have been shaped by centuries of appropriation and argument to which we are heirs.

The third level, "The Text in Contemporary Discussion," follows the history of interpretation into the present, drawing brief attention to a range of issues. Our aim here is not to deliver a single answer—"what the text means"—to the contemporary reader, but to highlight unique challenges and interpretive questions. We pay special attention to occasions of dissonance: aspects of the text or of its interpretation that have become questionable, injurious, or even intolerable to some readers today. Our goal is not to provoke a referendum on the value of the text but to stimulate reflection and discussion and, in this way, to empower the reader to reach his or her own judgments about the text.

The approach of this commentary articulates a particular understanding of the work of responsible biblical interpretation. We seek through this commentary to promote intelligent and mature engagement with the Bible, in religious communities and in academic classrooms alike, among pastors, theologians, and ethicists, but also and especially among nonspecialists. Our work together has given us a new appreciation for the vocation of the biblical scholar, as custodians of a treasure of accumulated wisdom from our predecessors; as stewards at a table to which an ever-expanding circle is invited; as neighbors and fellow citizens called to common cause, regardless of our different professions of faith. If the result of our work here is increased curiosity about the Bible, new questions about its import, and new occasions for mutual understanding among its readers, our work will be a success.

Fortress Commentary on the Old Testament

Gale A. Yee
Episcopal Divinity School

Hugh R. Page Jr.
University of Notre Dame

Matthew J. M. Coomber
St. Ambrose University

Fortress Commentary on the New Testament

Margaret Aymer
Interdenominational Theological Center

Cynthia Briggs Kittredge
Seminary of the Southwest

David A. Sánchez
Loyola Marymount University

READING THE CHRISTIAN NEW TESTAMENT IN THE CONTEMPORARY WORLD

Kwok Pui-lan

On Ascension Sunday in May 2012, the faculty and students of my school who were taking part in a travel seminar to China attended the worship service at the Shanghai Community Church. We arrived half an hour before the service began, and the church, which can accommodate about two thousand people, was already filled to capacity. Another two thousand people who could not get into the sanctuary watched the worship service on closed-circuit TV in other rooms in the church building. Through this experience and while visiting churches in other cities, we learned about and encountered the phenomenal growth of the Chinese churches in the past twenty-five years. The official statistics put the number of Chinese Christians at around 30 million, but unofficial figures range from 50 to 100 million, if those who belong to the unregistered house churches are counted. China is poised to become the country with the highest number of Christians, and China has already become the largest printer and user of the Bible in the world. In 2012, the Amity Printing Company in Nanjing celebrated the publishing of 100 million Bibles since its inception in 1987 (United Bible Societies 2012).

Besides China, sub-Saharan Africa has also experienced rapid church growth, especially among the African Independent Churches, Pentecostal churches, and Roman Catholic churches. By 2025, Africa will be the continent with the greatest number of Christians, at more than 670 million. At the turn of the twentieth century, 70 percent of the world's Christians were European. By 2000, that number had dropped to 28 percent (Flatow). The shift of Christian demographics to the South and the prospect of Christianity becoming a non-Western religion have attracted the attention of scholars and popular media (Sanneh 2003; Jenkins; Johnson and Ross). According to the *World Christian Encyclopedia*, almost two-thirds of the readers of the Bible are Christians from Africa, Asia, Latin America, and Oceania (around 1.178 billion) as compared to Europe and America (around 661 million) and Orthodox Eastern Europe (around 158 million) (Patte, xxi).

These changing Christian demographics have significant implications for reading the Bible as global citizens in the contemporary world. To promote global and intercultural understanding, we can no longer read the Bible in a narrow and parochial way, without being aware of how Christians in other parts of the world are reading it in diverse linguistic, cultural, and social contexts. In the past decade, biblical scholars have increasingly paid attention to global perspectives on the Bible to prepare Christians to live in our complex, pluralistic, and transnational world (Patte; Wicker, Miller, and Dube; Roncace and Weaver). For those of us living in the Global North, it is important to pay attention to liberative readings from the Global South and to the voices from the majority world. Today, the field of biblical studies has been enlivened and broadened by scholars from many social locations and culturally and religiously diverse contexts.

The New Testament in Global Perspectives

The New Testament touches on many themes highly relevant for our times, such as racial and ethnic relations, religious pluralism, social and political domination, gender oppression, and religious movements for resistance. The early followers of Jesus were Jews and gentiles living in the Hellenistic world under the rule of the Roman Empire. Christianity developed largely in urban cities in which men and women from different linguistic, cultural, and religious backgrounds interacted and commingled with one another (Theissen; Meeks). Christians in the early centuries lived among Jews and people devoted to emperor cults, Greek religion, and other indigenous traditions in the ancient Near East. Jesus and his disciples spoke Aramaic, the common language of Palestine. The New Testament was written in Koine Greek, the lingua franca of much of the Mediterranean region and the Middle East since the conquest of Alexander the Great. Living under the shadow of the Roman Empire, early Christians had to adapt to the cultures and social structures of empire, as well as resist the domination of imperial rule.

From its beginning in Palestine and the Mediterranean, Christianity spread to other parts of the Roman Empire and became the dominant religion during Constantine's time. Some of the notable early theologians hailed from northern Africa: Origen (c. 185–254) and Athanasius (c. 300–373) from Alexandria, Tertullian (160–225) from Carthage, and Augustine (354–431) of Hippo. While Christianity was persecuted in the Roman Empire prior to 313, it found its way to the regions east of the Tigris River possibly as early as the beginning of the second century. Following ancient trade routes, merchants and missionaries brought Christianity from the Mediterranean to the Persian Gulf and across central Asia all the way to China (Baum and Winkler, 8). In the early modern period, Christianity was brought to the Americas and other parts of the world, with the help of the political and military power of colonizing empires. Even though Christianity was a world religion, the study of church history in the past tended to focus on Europe and North America and to marginalize the histories in other parts of the world. Today, scholars of world Christianity have contested such Eurocentric biases. They have produced comprehensive accounts that restore the peoples of Africa, the Near East, and Asia to their rightful place in the rich and multilayered Christian tradition (Hastings; Irvin and Sunquist 2001; 2012; Sanneh 2007).

The translation of the Bible, especially the New Testament, into the native and vernacular languages of different peoples was and remains an important strategy of Christian missions. The United Bible Societies (2013) report that the complete Bible has been translated into at least 451 languages and the New Testament into some 1,185. The Bible is the most translated collection of texts in the world. There are now 2,370 languages in which at least one book of the Bible has been produced. Although this figure represents less than half of some 6,000 languages and dialects presently in use in the world, it includes the primary means of communication of well over 90 percent of the world's population.

Most Christians are more familiar with the New Testament than the Hebrew Bible. The New Testament is read and preached throughout the world in liturgical settings and worship services, taught in seminaries and church Sunday schools, studied in private devotions, and discussed in Bible study groups, women's fellowships, college campuses, and grassroots religious organizations and movements. Christians, Jews, Muslims, and atheists debate the meaning of Jesus and the gospel in books, mass media, and on the Internet. The life and the story of Jesus Christ have been depicted and interpreted in popular culture, such as films, songs, music videos, fiction, blogs, websites, photographs, paintings, sculpture, and other forms of art. The study of the New Testament is not limited to the study of the biblical text, but includes how the text is used in concrete contexts in Christian communities, popular media, and public spheres.

The Bible is taken to mean many things in our contemporary world. Christian communities regard the Bible as *Scripture*, and many Christians think that it has authority over their beliefs and moral behavior. In the academy, the Bible is treated more as a *historical document*, to be studied by rigorous historical criticism. Increasingly, the Bible is also seen as a *cultural product*, embedded in the sociocultural and ideological assumptions of its time. The meaning of the Bible is not fixed but is continually produced as readers interact with it in different contexts. The diverse understanding of what the Bible is often creates a clash of opinions. For example, Christians may think Lady Gaga's "Judas" video (2011) has gone too far in deviating from orthodox teaching. There is also a wide gap in the ways the Bible is read in the church and academy. The experts' reading may challenge the beliefs of those sitting in the pews.

In the field of biblical studies, Fernando F. Segovia (34–52) delineates three stages in the development of academic biblical criticism in the twentieth century. The historical-critical method has been the dominant mode of interpretation in academia since the middle of the nineteenth century. The meaning of the text is seen as residing *behind* the text—in the world that shaped the text, in the author's intention, or both. The second stage is literary criticism, which emerged in the middle of 1970s in dialogue with literary and psychoanalytic theory. The literary critics emphasize the meaning *in* the text and focus on genre, plot, structure, rhetoric, levels of narration, and characterization as depicted in the world of the text. The third stage is cultural studies or ideological criticism of the Bible, which developed also in the 1970s, when critics from the two-thirds world, feminist theologians, and racial and ethnic minority scholars in North America began to increase their numbers in the guild. They have increasingly paid attention to the flesh-and-blood readers *in front of* the text, who employ different methods, such as storytelling and reader-response criticism, in their interaction with the text to construct meaning in response to concerns arising from their communities.

The shift to the flesh-and-blood reader contests the assumption that there is a "universal" reader and an "objective" interpretation applicable to all times and places. The claim of an "objective" and "scientific" reading is based on a positivistic understanding of historiography, which presumes that historical facts can be objectively reconstructed, following established criteria in Western academia. But the historical-critical method is only one of the many methods and should not be taken as the "universal" norm for judging other methodologies. Its dominance is the result of the colonial legacy as well as the continued hegemony of Eurocentric knowledge and cultural production of our time. Nowadays, many methods are available, and biblical critics have increasingly used interdisciplinary approaches and a combination of theories and methods, such as postmodern theory, postcolonial theory, and queer studies, for interpretation (Crossley; Moore 2010).

What this means is the democratization of the study of the Bible, because no one group of people has a monopoly over the meaning of the Bible and no single method can exhaust its "truths." To understand the richness of the biblical tradition, we have to learn to listen to the voices of people from multiple locations and senses of belonging. Eleazar S. Fernandez (140) points out, "real flesh-and-blood readers assume a variety of positions—in relation to time, geography, geopolitics, diaspora location, social location, religion, ethnicity, gender, sexuality, and so on—in the power-knowledge nexus that inform their readings and cultural or religious discursive productions in the global market." Interpreting the Bible in global perspectives requires us to pay attention to the contextual character of reading and the relationships and tensions between the global and the local.

Reading the New Testament in Diverse Contexts

The shift from the author and the text to the reader means that we need to understand the ways the Bible functions in diverse sociolingusitic contexts (Blount 1995). Our critical task must go further than analyzing the text and the processes for production and interpretation, to include the cultural and social conditions that influence the history of reception. Let us go back to the examples of reading the Bible in the Chinese and African contexts. When Christianity arrived in China, the Chinese had a long hermeneutical tradition of interpreting Confucian, Buddhist, and Daoist texts. The missionaries and biblical translators had to borrow from indigenous religious ideas to translate biblical terminologies, such as God, heaven, and hell. The rapid social and political changes in modern China affected how the Bible is read by Christians living in a Communist society (Eber, Wan, and Walf). When the Bible was introduced to the African continent, it encountered a rich and complex language world of oral narratives, legends, proverbs, and folktales. The interpretation of oral texts is different from that of written ones. In some instances, the translation of the Bible into the vernacular languages has changed the oral cultures into written cultures, with both positive and negative effects on social development (Sanneh 1989). And if we examine the history of translation and reception of the English Bible, we will see how the processes have been affected by the rise of nationalism, colonial expansion, and the diverse forms of English used in the English-speaking world (Sugirtharajah 2002, 127–54).

Some Christians may feel uneasy about the fact that the Bible is read in so many different ways. For the fundamentalists who believe in biblical inerrancy and literal interpretation, multiple ways of reading undermine biblical authority. Even liberals might wonder if the diversity of readings will open the doors to relativism. But as James Barr has pointed out, the appeal to the Bible as authority for all doctrinal matters and the assumption that its meaning is fixed cannot be verified by the Bible itself. Both Jesus and Paul took the liberty to repudiate, criticize, and reinterpret parts of the Hebrew Bible (Barr, 12–19). Moreover, as Mary Ann Tolbert has noted, since the Reformation, when the doctrine of *sola scriptura* was brought to the forefront, the invocation of biblical authority by various ecclesiastical bodies has generally been negative and exclusive. "It has been used most often to *exclude* certain groups or people, to *pass judgment* on various disapproved activities, and to *justify* morally or historically debatable positions [such as slavery]" (1998, 142). The doctrinal appeal to biblical authority and the insistence on monocultural reading often mask power dynamics, which allow some groups of people to exercise control over others who have less power, including women, poor people, racial and ethnic minorities, and gay people and lesbians.

Multiple readings and plurality of meaning do not necessarily lead to relativism, but can foster deeper awareness of our own interpretive assumptions and broaden our horizons. In his introduction to the *Global Bible Commentary*, Daniel Patte (xxi–xxxii) offers some helpful suggestions. (1) We have to acknowledge the contextual character of our interpretation. There is no context-free reading, whether in the past or in the present. (2) We have to stop and listen to the voices of biblical readers who have long been silenced in each context. (3) We have to learn the reading strategies and critical tradition developed in other parts of the world, such as enculturation, liberation, and inter(con)textuality. Contextual readings do not mean anything goes or that interpreters may proceed without self-critique. (4) We have to respect other people's readings and assume responsibility for our own interpretation. (5) Other people's readings often lead us to see our blind spots, and invite us to notice aspects of the Bible we have overlooked. (6) We have to learn to read *with* others in community, rather than reading *for* or *to* them, assuming our reading is superior to others.

We can use the different readings of the story of the Syrophoenician woman (Matt. 15:21-28; Mark 7:24-30) to illustrate this point. Many Christians have been taught that the story is about Jesus' mission to the gentiles, because Jesus went to the border place of Tyre and Sidon and healed the gentile woman's daughter and praised her faith. Japanese biblical scholar Hisako Kinukawa (51–65), however, does not emphasize gentile mission but Jesus' crossing ethnic boundaries to accept others. She places the story in the cultic purity and ethnic exclusion of first-century Palestine and draws parallels to the discrimination of Koreans as minorities living in Japan. We shall see that the generalization of first-century culture may be problematic. Nevertheless, Kinukawa argues that the gentile woman changed Jesus' attitude from rejection to affirmation and created an opportunity for Jesus to cross the boundary. Jesus has set an example, she says, for Japanese people to challenge their assumptions of a homogeneous race, to overcome their prejudice toward ethnic minorities, and to respect other peoples' dignity and human rights.

On the African continent, Musa W. Dube, from Botswana, emphasizes the importance of *reading with* ordinary readers. She set out to find out how women in the African Independent Churches in Botswana read the Matthean version of the story (2000, 187–90). She found that some of the women emphasized that Jesus was testing the woman's faith. They said the meaning of the word "dog" should not be taken literally, as Jesus often spoke in parables. Several women did not read the story as if Jesus had insulted the woman by comparing the Canaanites as "dogs" to the Israelites as children. Instead, they saw the Canaanite woman as one of the children because of her faith, and the "dogs" referred to the demonic spirits. This must be understood in the context of the belief in spirits in the African religious worldview. The women interpreted the woman's answer to Jesus, that even the dogs eat the crumbs from the master's table (Matt. 15:27), to mean that no one is permanently and totally undeserving. The women believed that Jesus had come for all people, without regard for race and ethnicities.

These two examples show how social and cultural backgrounds affect the interpretation of the story and the lessons drawn for today. The majority of interpreters, whether scholars or ordinary readers, have focused on the interaction between Jesus and the woman. I would like to cite two other readings that bring to the forefront other details of the text that have been overlooked. Laura E. Donaldson reads the story from a postcolonial Native American perspective and places the "demon-possessed" daughter at the center of her critical analysis. In the text, the daughter does not speak, and her illness is considered taboo and stigmatizing. Donaldson challenges our complicity in such a reading and employs the insights of disabilities studies to demystify the construction of "able" and "disabled" persons. She then points out that the Canaanites were the indigenous people of the land, and the daughter might not be suffering from an illness pejoratively identified as "demon possession" by the Christian text. Instead, the daughter may be in an altered state of consciousness, which is a powerful form of knowing in many indigenous spiritual traditions. For Donaldson, the daughter may "signify a trace of the indigenous," who has the power to access other sites of knowledge (104–5).

While many commentators have noted the lowly position of dogs in ancient Mediterranean and Near East culture, Stephen D. Moore, who grew up in Ireland and teaches in the United States, looks at the Matthean story through the prism of human-animal relations. He contrasts the construction of the son of man with the dog-woman in Matthew. While the son of man is not an animal and asserts power, sovereignty, and self-control, following the elite Greco-Roman concept of masculinity, the dog-woman of Canaan embodies the categories of savages, women, and beasts. Jesus said that he was sent to the lost sheep of the house of Israel and it was not fair to take the children's food and throw it to the dogs. The problem of the dog-woman is that she is not a sheep woman. The image of Canaan as heathen, savage, and less than human justified the colonization of non-Christian people in Africa, the Americas, and other regions. Moore notes that the image of "heathens" in nineteenth- and twentieth-century biblical commentary conjured up the reality of "unsaved" dark-skinned people in need of Christ and in need of civilizing, and hence in need of colonizing (Moore 2013, 63). Moore's reading points out that mission to the gentiles may not be benign, and might mask colonial impulses.

These diverse interpretations of the Syrophoenician woman's story illustrate how reading with other people can radically expand our imagination. We can see how a certain part of the story is emphasized or reinterpreted by different readers to address particular concerns. Sensitivity to contextual and cross-cultural interpretation helps us to live in a pluralistic world in which people have different worldviews and assumptions. Through genuine dialogue and listening to others, we can enrich ourselves and work with others to create a better world.

Interpretation for Liberation

In the second half of the twentieth century, people's popular movements and protests led to the development of liberation theologies in various parts of the world. In Africa and Asia, anticolonial struggles resulted in political independence and people's demand for cultural autonomy. In Latin America, theologians and activists criticized the dependence theory of development, which continues to keep poor countries dependent on rich countries because of unequal global economic structures. Women from all over the globe, racial and ethnic minorities, and lesbian, gay, bisexual, and transgender people have also begun to articulate their theologies. People who are multiply oppressed began to read the Bible through the intersection of gender, race, class, sexuality, religion, and colonialism. I focus on liberative readings from the Global South here.

Following Vatican II (1962–1965), Latin American liberation theology began to develop in the 1960s and focused on social and economic oppression and the disparity between the rich and the poor. Using Marxist analysis as a critical tool, liberation theologians in Latin America argued that the poor are the subjects of history and that God has a preferential option for the poor. They insisted that theology is a reflection of social praxis, which seeks to change the oppressive situation that the majority of the people find themselves in. Juan Luis Segundo (9) developed a hermeneutical circle that consists of four steps: (1) our way of experiencing reality leads to ideological suspicion, (2) which we apply to the whole ideological superstructure, and especially theology, (3) being aware of how prevailing interpretation of the Bible does not take important data into account, resulting in (4) the development of a new hermeneutic.

Latin American theologians contested the formulation of traditional Christology and presented Christ as the liberator. The gospel of Jesus Christ is not about saving individual souls, without import for our concrete lives. In *A Theology of Liberation*, Gustavo Gutiérrez (102–5) argues that Christ is the liberator who opts for the poor. Jesus' death and resurrection liberates us from sin. Sin, however, is not private, but a social, historical fact. It is the absence of fellowship of love in relationship among persons and the breach of relationship with God. Christ offers us the gift of radical liberation and enables us to enter into communion with God and with others. Liberation, for Gutiérrez, has three levels: political liberation, liberation in the course of history, and liberation from sin and into communion with God.

Latin American women theologians have criticized their male colleagues' lack of attention to women's issues and *machismo* in Latin American culture. Elsa Tamez, from Mexico, is a leading scholar who has published extensively on reading the New Testament from a Latin American feminist perspective (2001; 2007). She has raised questions about Jesus' relation with women in the Gospels and the class difference between rich and poor women in the early Christian movement. The discussion of the Bible in the base Christian communities and women's groups helped spread the ideas of liberation theology among the populace. A collection of discussions of the gospel by Nicaraguan peasants who belonged to the Christian community of Solentiname was published as *The Gospel in Solentiname* (Cardenal). The peasants approached the Bible from their life situation of extreme poverty, and they connected with Jesus' revolutionary work in solidarity with the poor of his time. Some of the peasants also painted the scenes from the Gospels and identified biblical events with events leading to the 1979 Sandinista revolution (Scharper and Scharper). In response to the liberation movement, which had spread to the whole continent, the Vatican criticized liberation theology and replaced progressive bishops with conservative ones. But second-generation liberation theologians continue the work of their pioneers and expand the liberation theological project to include race, gender, sexuality, migration, and popular religions (Petrella).

Unlike in Latin America, where Christians are the majority of the population, Christians in many parts of Africa and Asia live among people of other faith traditions. Here, interpretation of the Bible follows two broad approaches. The liberation approach focuses on sociopolitical dimensions, such as the fight over poverty, dictatorship, apartheid, and other social injustice. The enculturation or the indigenization approach brings the Bible into dialogue with the African or Asian worldviews, popular religion, and cultural idiom. The two approaches are not mutually exclusive, and a holistic transformation of society must deal with changing the sociopolitical structures as well as the culture and mind-sets of people.

One of the key questions for those who read the Bible in religiously pluralistic contexts is how to honor others who have different religious identities and cultures. Some of the passages in the New Testament have been used to support an exclusive attitude toward other religions. For example, Jesus said that he is the way and no one comes to the Father except through him (John 14:6) and charged his followers with the Great Commission, to "make disciples of all nations" (Matt. 28:19). But as Wesley Ariarajah (1989) has said, the universality of Christ supports the spirit of openness, mutual understanding, and interfaith dialogue with others. In Acts 10:9-16, Peter is challenged in a vision to consider nothing unclean that God has made clean. He crosses the boundary that separates Jews and gentiles and meets with Cornelius, the Roman centurion, which leads to his conversion. When Paul speaks to the Athenians, he says that they are extremely religious, and he employs a religious language different from that when he speaks to the Jews (Acts 17:22-31). Ariarajah argues that openness to others and dialogue does not contradict Christian witness.

In their protests against political oppression and dictatorship, Asian Christians have reread the Bible to empower them to fight for human rights and dignity. *Minjung* theology arose in South Korea during the 1970s against the dictatorship of the Park Chung Hee government. The word *minjung* comes from two Chinese characters meaning the masses of people. New Testament scholar Ahn Byung Mu points out that in the Gospel of Mark, the *ochlos* ("crowd or multitude") follows Jesus from place to place, listens to his teachings, and witnesses his miracles. They form the background of Jesus' activities. They stand on Jesus' side, against the rulers of Jerusalem, who criticize and challenge Jesus (Mark 2:4-7; 3:2-22; 11:8; 11:27; 11:32). Jesus has "compassion for them, because they were like sheep without a shepherd" (6:34). Jesus proclaims to them "the kingdom of God has come near" (1:15). He identifies with the suffering *minjung* and offers them a new hope and new life. *Minjung* theology developed a political hermeneutics not for the elite but for the people, and spoke to the Korean reality at the time.

In India, the caste system has subjected the Dalits—the "untouchables"—to the lowest rank of society. Dalits are the oppressed and the broken. They are discriminated against in terms of education, occupation, social interaction, and social mobility. The prejudice against the Dalits is so deep-seated that they face a great deal of discrimination even in Indian churches. Dalit theology emerged because of the insensitivity of the Indian churches to the plight of the Dalits and to give voice to Dalits' struggle for justice. In constructing a Dalit Christology, Peniel Rajkumar (115–26) finds Jesus' healing stories particularly relevant to the Dalit situation. Jesus touches and heals the leper (Mark 1:40-45), and transcends the social norms regarding purity and pollution. Afterward, Jesus asks the man to show his body to the priest (Mark 1:44) to bear witness that he has been healed and to confront the ideological purity system that alienates him. Jesus is angry at the system that maintains ritual purity to alienate and classify people. In coming to ask for healing, the leper also shows his faith through his willingness to break the cultural norm of purity. Again, we will find that the generalization of Jewish culture and purity taboo may be open to criticism. Jesus' anger toward injustice and his partnership with the leper to create a new social reality would help Dalits in their present struggles. The emphasis of Jesus' crossing boundaries is a recurrent theme in other Dalit readings (Nelavala). Many of the Dalit women from poor rural and urban areas are illiterate and do not have access to the written text of the Bible. The use of methods such as storytelling and role-play has helped them gain insights into biblical stories (Melanchthon).

In Africa, biblical scholars have addressed poverty, apartheid, religious and ethnic strife, HIV and AIDS, and political oppression, all of which have wreaked havoc in the continent. During apartheid in South Africa, a black theology of liberation was developed to challenge the Western and white outlook of the Christian church and to galvanize people to fight against apartheid. Itumeleng J. Mosala developed a historical-materialist reading of the Bible based on black history and culture. Mosala and his colleagues from Africa have asserted that Latin American liberation hermeneutics has not taken seriously the history of the blacks and Indians. His reading of Luke 1 and 2 brings out the material condition of the text, focusing on the colonial occupation of Palestine by Rome and the imperial extraction from peasants and the poor. He then uses the history, culture, and struggle of black people as a hermeneutical tool to lay bare the ideological assumptions in Luke's Gospel, showing it to be speaking for the class interest of the rich and eclipsing the experiences of the poor. He charges that some of the black theologians have continued to use Western and white hermeneutics even as they oppose the white, dominant groups. What is necessary is a new hermeneutics based on a black working-class perspective, which raises new questions in the interpretative process and enables a mutual interrogation between the text and situation.

In order to develop this kind of hermeneutics, biblical scholars must be socially engaged and read the Bible from the underside. With whom one is reading the Bible becomes both an epistemological and an ethical question. Several African biblical scholars emphasize the need for socially engaged scholars to read the Bible with ordinary poor and marginalized "readers." Gerald O. West maintains that if liberation theology begins with the experience of the poor and the oppressed, then these persons must be invited and included in the dialogical process of doing theology and reading the Bible. He describes the process of contextual Bible study among the poor, the roles of engaged biblical scholars, and lessons gleaned from the process. In the contextual reading of Luke 4:16-22, for instance, the women living around Pietermaritzburg and Durban related the meaning of setting the prisoners free, healing of the blind, and the relief of debts to their society. They discussed what they could do following the insights from the story to organize their community and create social change.

The Circle of Concerned African Women Theologians, formed in 1989, has encouraged Christian women from the African continent to produce and publish biblical and contextual hermeneutics. Some of the contributions have been published in *Other Ways of Reading: African Women and the Bible* (Dube 2001). The authors discuss storytelling methods, reading with and from nonacademic readers, toward a postapartheid black feminist reading, and the divination method of interpretation. The volume demystifies the notion of biblical canon, showing how women of the African continent have read the Bible with the canon of various African oral cultures. Aspects of African cultures serve as theories for analyzing the Bible. The volume is also conversant with feminist readings from other parts of the world, and in particular with African American women's hermeneutical approaches.

The HIV and AIDS epidemic brings enormous loss of life and suffering in the African continent, and the virus has spread mostly among heterosexual people. There is an increasing concern that in the sub-Saharan region, HIV infects more women than men. Musa Dube has played a key role in helping the African churches and theological institutions in addressing HIV and AIDS issues. In *The HIV and AIDS Bible* (Dube 2008), she implores scholars to develop biblical scholarship that is prophetic and healing. She challenges patriarchy and gender justice, and urges the churches to move beyond their comfort zone to respond to people affected by the virus. The church is HIV positive, she claims. Reading with people living with AIDS allows her to see the potential of the Bible to liberate and heal. She brings new insights to reading the miracles and healing stories of Jesus, such as the healing of Jairus's daughter (Mark 5:21-45). Her reading breaks the stigma and silence around HIV and AIDS while calling for adequate and compassionate care, and placing the HIV and AIDS epidemic within the larger context of other social discrimination.

The biblical readings from the Global South contribute to a global scholarship that takes into account other religious texts and classics in what is called intercultural and cross-textual reading (Lee). It is also interpreted through the lens of oral texts and retold and performed through storytelling, role-play, and skits. The exploration of these methods decentralizes Eurocentric modes of thinking that have gripped biblical studies for so long. It allows us to see the Bible and the world with fresh perspectives and new insights.

Contemporary Approaches to the New Testament

Books that introduce the wide array of contemporary methods used to interpret the New Testament are readily available (Anderson and Moore; Crossley). I have selected a few approaches that have global significance, as scholars from both the Global North and the Global South have used them and commented on them to illustrate current discussions shaping biblical scholarship. We will look at feminist approaches, social scientific approaches, racial and ethnic minority approaches, and postcolonial approaches.

Feminist Approaches

The New Testament was written by authors who lived in a patriarchal world with androcentric values and mind-sets. For a long time, churches have used parts of the Bible to deny women's full participation and treat them as second-class citizens in church and society. For example, churches have denied women's ordination based on the argument that all of Jesus' disciples were male. People have also cited the household codes (Col. 3:18—4:1; Eph. 5:21—6:9; 1 Peter 2:18—3:7) to support wives' submission to their husbands. Paul's teaching that women should be silent in the church (1 Cor. 14:34-35) has often been used to deny women's religious leadership. It is little wonder that some Western feminists have concluded that the Bible is irredeemably sexist and have become post-Christian. But feminist interpreters around the globe have developed ingenious ways to read against the grain and to find the Bible's liberating potential.

Christian feminists in many parts of the world have focused on stories about women in the Gospels. They have shown that women followed Jesus, listened to his preaching, and were healed because of their faith. Even when the disciples deserted Jesus at the cross, women steadfastly showed their faith. Scholars have drawn from some of these Gospel stories of women to illuminate how the gospel may speak to women's liberation of our time (Kinukawa; Tamez 2001). Christian women have also reclaimed and retold these stories, imagining dialogues, and supplying different endings. For example, I have heard from Christian women that the ending of Mary and Martha's story (Luke 10:38-42) should not end in Jesus' praising Mary over Martha, but the sisters' inviting Jesus to help in the kitchen so that all could continue the dialogue.

Other scholars find that the focus on biblical women is rather limited, for it does not provide a comprehensive framework to interpret the whole New Testament and still gives primacy and authority to the biblical text. Elisabeth Schüssler Fiorenza's influential book *In Memory of Her* (1983) presents a feminist historical-reconstructionist model, which places women at the center of the reconstruction of the Jesus movement and early Christianity. She shows that women were apostles, prophets, missionaries, as well as founders of household churches. She suggests that the radical vision of Jesus' movement was the praxis of inclusive wholeness and "discipleship of equals" (105–59). But women's leadership was increasingly marginalized in the second century, as patriarchalization set in when the church became more institutionalized. Schüssler Fiorenza's feminist model of critical interpretation insists that women should have the authority to judge whether a particular text is liberating or oppressive in the context of its reception.

Another approach is to use historical data and social theories to investigate the social world of early Christianity and to present a feminist social history. These studies look at women's marriage, status in the family, work and occupation, slave women and widows, and women's resistance in the Roman Empire (Schottroff; Yamaguchi). The parable of the leaven, for instance, makes visible women's work and uses a woman baking bread to describe the kingdom of God (Matt. 13:33; Luke 13:20-21). These works examine the impact of Roman persecution on women, the exploitative economic system, and Jewish resistance movements to provide a wider context to read the New Testament. Influenced by liberation theology, Elsa Tamez (2007) employs class analysis to study the Pastoral Letters. She describes how the rich people had challenged the leadership of the elders and presbyters in the church to which 1 Timothy was addressed. The injunction that women should be silent and submissive (1 Tim. 2:11-12) targeted the rich women, who used their power and status to cause troubles in the church.

Feminist scholars have also used literary and rhetorical approaches. For example, Ingrid Rosa Kitzberger uses a literary approach to examine the women in the Gospel of John, paying attention to the characterization of the Samaritan woman, Mary Magdalene, Mary and Martha, and the mother of Jesus, the intention of the narrator, narrative devices and rhetorical strategies, and the sequential perception of the reader in the reading process. Her goal is to present a reading against the grain—a feminist hermeneutics that empowers women. Antoinette Clark Wire reconstructs a picture of the women prophets in the church of first-century Corinth by analyzing Paul's rhetoric in 1 Corinthians. She suggests that the Corinthian women prophets claim direct access to resurrected life in Christ through the Spirit. These women sometimes conflicted with Paul, but they were known for proclaiming God's thought in prophecy and responding for the people to God (11:5; 14:1-38). Others use rhetorical criticism not to reconstruct historical reality but to focus on the persuasive power of the text to motivate action and shape the values and ethos of the community. Schüssler Fiorenza (1992, 40–50) has suggested a rhetorical approach that unmasks the interlocking system of oppression because of racism, classism, sexism, and colonialism. She coins the term *kyriarchy* (from *kyrios*, the Greek word for "lord" or "master") to describe these multiple systems of domination and subordination, involving more than gender oppression. Her goal is to create an alternative rhetorical space that respects the equality and dignity of women and is defined by the logic of radical democracy. She uses the term *ekklēsia gynaikōn* or "wo/men church" to denote this political hermeneutical space. The Greek term *ekklēsia* means the democratic assembly, and "wo/men" signifies not the feminine gender (as ladies, wives, mothers, etc.) but full decision-making political subjects. She argues that "one can theorize *ekklēsia* of wo/men not only as a virtual utopian space but also as an already partially realized space of radical equality, as a site of feminist struggles to transform social and religious institutions and discourses" (2007, 73). Feminist biblical scholars have also begun to unpack the structures of masculinity in the ancient world and how they were embedded in the biblical text (Moore and Anderson).

Social-Scientific Approaches

As mentioned above, biblical interpreters have used social sciences to learn about the social and cultural world of New Testament texts. One of the early important figures is Gerd Theissen, who studied the sociology of early Palestinian Christianity by focusing on the three roles of the Jesus movement: the wandering charismatics, their supporters in local communities, and the bearers of revelation. The use of social scientific methods has broadened the scope and sources of the third quest or newest quest of the historical Jesus since the 1980s. Billed as interdisciplinary research, scholars claim to possess at their disposal the latest archaeological knowledge, sociological analysis, cultural anthropology, and other newest social-scientific tools. Scholars have employed theories from the study of millennial movements, Mary Douglas's theory of purity and pollution, and non-Western medicine, magic, and charismatic religion to scrutinize the Jesus movement (e.g., Gager; Crossan 1991; Borg).

Schüssler Fiorenza has criticized the social-scientific quest of Jesus. She notes that the emergence of this third quest coincided with conservative politics of the Reagan and Thatcher era and with growing right-wing fundamentalist movements. She chastises the restoration of historical positivism as corresponding to political conservatism and the proliferation of the historical Jesus books as feeding "into literalist fundamentalism by reasserting disinterested scientific positivism in order to shore up the scholarly authority and universal truth of their research portrayal of Jesus" (2000, 46). While these Jesus books are written for popular consumption with their authors featured in mass media, the works of feminist scholars are sidelined and dismissed as being too "political" and not "objective" enough.

From a South African perspective, Mosala asks whether the social-scientific approaches to the Bible are "one step forward, two steps back" (43). On the one hand, the social-scientific approaches are useful, he says, because they help us to see biblical texts as ideological products of social systems and power relations. Far too often, middle-class Christians have the tendency to psychologize or use an individualist lens while reading the Bible. On the other hand, the social-scientific approaches as practiced in the white, liberal, North American and European academy often reflect bourgeois interests. Many scholars, for example, have adapted interpretive sociology and structural-functionalist analysis to study the social world of the New Testament. The structural-functionalist approach looks at how social systems are related to one another so that society can function as a whole. Focusing more on integration, stability, and unity, it is less prone to analyze social confrontation and conflict. Using Theissen's study of Palestinian Christianity as an example, Mosala points out that Theissen fails to provide an adequate structural location of the Jesus movement in the political economy of the Roman Empire and does not deal with the real economic and political contradictions of the time (64–65). As such, Theissen's study will be of limited use for the black South Africans struggling against apartheid and other social oppression. Mosala challenges biblical scholars to be open about their own class interest and the limitations of their methods.

One of the important dimensions of social-scientific criticism is the introduction of models from social and cultural anthropology. In addition to the ancient Jewish, Hellenistic, and Roman cultures that biblical scholars have been studying, Bruce J. Malina, Jerome H. Neyrey, and others suggest a pan-Mediterranean culture, with values and ethos markedly different from those in North American culture. The pivotal characteristics of Mediterranean culture in the first century included honor and shame, patronage and clientele, dyadic personality, and rules of purity. They apply the study of Mediterranean culture to interpret the group development of the Jesus movement and Paul's Letters. Scholars have questioned whether it is appropriate to impose models of contemporary societies onto the ancient Mediterranean. They remain doubtful whether the pivotal values of honor and shame are so different from the values in North American and northern European cultures. James G. Crossley also notes that "the Mediterranean frequently blurs into the contemporary Arab world, an area of renewed interest in American and European politics and media in the past forty years" (27).

As a discipline, anthropology emerged during the colonial time and often served the interests of empire. The hypothesis of a distinct Mediterranean culture and personality as contrasted with those in Western society reinforces a binary construction of the colonizers and the colonized. Malina and others have imported twentieth-century anthropological studies to the study of first-century Galilean and Judean society, assuming that Mediterranean cultures had remained unchanged over the years. Furthermore, the honor and shame code is attributed to a strong division of sexual and gender roles in the region and to the anxiety of Mediterranean men over their manhood. Female scholars such as Marianne Sawicki have voiced concerns that the study of honor and shame has largely followed a masculinist script and that women's experiences are overlooked and different. She suggests that the honor-shame sensibility might simply be an ethnocentric projection of the Euro-American male researchers onto the people they are studying (77).

R. S. Sugirtharajah, from Sri Lanka, has criticized Orientalism in the work of biblical scholars who use social-scientific methods. In *Orientalism*, Edward W. Said questions the representation of the Middle East as inferior, exotic, and stagnant in Western scholarship. Sugirtharajah notes prevalent Orientalist tendencies and the recycling of Orientalist practices in biblical scholarship, especially in the study of the social and cultural world of Jesus. He surmises that designations such as "Israel," "Judah," "the Holy Land," "Mediterranean," "world of Jesus," and "cultural world of Jesus" are "ideologically charged rhetoric and markers of Eurocentric and Christian-centric conceptualizations of that part of the world" (2012, 103). New Testament scholars have reinscribed Orientalist messages by suggesting the idea of a static Orient, by generalizing and reducing complex Mediterranean cultures to a few essentials, by gender stereotyping, and by highlighting the contrast between the East and the West. Jesus is depicted as one who is secure in his culture and yet critical of it through redefining honor culture and rearranging Mediterranean values. Since the publication of Said's work, many disciplines have become cautious about Orientalist methods and tendencies. But such methods have resurfaced in biblical studies and books that display Orientalist biases. Sugirtharajah points out that some of them have even become best sellers in mainstream culture (102–18).

Racial and Ethnic Minority Approaches

Racial and ethnic minorities in the United States began to develop their hermeneutical approaches to the Bible during the struggles of the civil rights movement in the 1960s. The development of black theology, Hispanic/Latino theology, and Asian American theology in the United States could not be separated from the ferment and protest against imperialism and apartheid in the Global South. Tat-siong Benny Liew (2013) characterizes racial and ethnic minority readings of the New Testament as "border crossing"—transcending the border of theology and biblical studies and the border between biblical studies and other disciplines. He also succinctly delineates the different stages of the development of such readings. In the first stage, racial and ethnic minority theologians and biblical scholars interpreted the biblical message through their social realities and experiences. For example, James Cone's black theology (1969; 1973) relates the gospel of Jesus to black power and freedom and argues that Christ is black, because Christ identifies with the powerless in society. Mexican American theologian Virgilio Elizondo relates the story of the marginalized Galilean

Jesus who came from the borderland area of Galilee to the story of Hispanic/Latino people as a new *mestizo* people. Asian American Chan-Hie Kim sees parallels between the Cornelius story in Acts 10–11 and Asian immigrant experience because both Cornelius and Kim are outsiders. Other scholars began to find minority subjects in the Bible and presented positive images of them or more complex pictures, such as the Ethiopian eunuch in Acts 8:26-40 (C. J. Martin 1989), and discussed slavery in early Christianity and modern interpretations (Lewis; Martin 1991).

In the current, second stage, racial and ethnic minority scholars do not simply employ different methods of biblical criticism with a racial inflection; they are more thoroughly informed by scholarship in ethnic studies and cultural studies. Their interpretation of the New Testament no longer begins with the biblical texts but with their experience as racial and ethnic minorities living in the United States. Liew characterizes this shift of emphasis as the move from "reading Scripture reading race" to "reading race reading Scripture" (2013, 183). Instead of finding "race" in the biblical text, new frameworks and paradigms of engaging with the Bible are sought. This shift can clearly be seen in *African Americans and the Bible* (Wimbush), which considers the Bible in contemporary African American culture, including poetry, aesthetics of sacred space, gospel music and spirituals, rap music, folk oratory, and many other contexts. Liew's own volume *What Is Asian American Biblical Hermeneutics?* (2008) reads all the major genres of the New Testament with Asian American literature, ethnic studies, and current events. David A. Sánchez's study of Revelation includes significant resources from Latino/a studies and Chicana/o studies.

Another significant development in the second stage is the move beyond a unified and essentialized notion of race to an acknowledgment of internal diversity within each racial and ethnic minority group. African American women articulate the issues of womanist interpretation of the Bible, placing gender at the intersection of race, class, and other anthropological referents. Demetrius K. Williams examines the biblical foundation of understanding of gender in black churches, while Rachel Annette Saint Clair presents a womanist reading of Mark's Gospel. Within the Asian American community, heterogeneity can be seen not only in the addition of women's voices but also in readings by diverse ethnic groups, intergenerational interpretations, and readings by Asian American adoptees and queer people (Foskett and Kuan; Cheng). Likewise, the diversity of the Hispanic/Latino people has been highlighted, and notions of borderland and *mestizaje* differ among different ethnic groups. Manuel Villalobos has combined the insights from feminist and queer theories to read the Ethiopian eunuch in Acts to bring hope and affirmation to Latino queer bodies.

Moving into the third stage, racial and ethnic minority theologians and biblical scholars have begun collaboration across minority groups. The move from articulating minority experience vis-à-vis the white dominant culture to conversing with other racial and ethnic minorities signals a new awareness, which is much needed to prepare for 2040, when, if current trends continue, there will be no racial and ethnic majority in the United States. An important example of such endeavor is the volume *They Were All Together in One Place? Toward Minority Criticism*, coedited by African, Asian, and Hispanic Americans (Bailey, Liew, and Segovia). This collaboration shows a desire for mutual learning and communication across color lines. In the future, more attention needs to be paid both to engaging Native American readings and, given our transnational world, to linking minority criticism with readings in the Global South.

Postcolonial Approaches

Emerging in the late 1970s, postcolonial studies has had significant influence in the fields of the humanities and social sciences. The prefix *post-* does not simply signify the period after colonialism in a chronological sense, but also refers to reading and social practices that aim at contesting colonialism and lifting up the voices of the suppressed and formerly colonized. Postcolonial criticism has drawn from many disciplines and was introduced to biblical studies in the 1990s, particularly through the works and encouragement of R. S. Sugirtharajah (1998; 2002). Other scholars have included a postcolonial optic in the study of the New Testament; for example, Tat-siong Benny Liew (1999), Fernando F. Segovia, Musa W. Dube (2000), Laura D. Donaldson, Stephen D. Moore (2006), and me (2005).

During Jesus' time, Galilee was under Roman imperial occupation and ruled by Herod Antipas (4 BCE–39 CE), and the early Christian communities lived under the whims of empire. Postcolonial critics of the New Testament share common interests with those contributing to the emerging subfield of "empire studies," promoted enthusiastically by Richard A. Horsley (1997; 2002) and other scholars (e.g., Carter; Crossan 2007). This subfield consists of books and articles with the recurrent words *empire* or *imperial* in their titles and with the intention of using the theme of empire to reframe New Testament interpretation. While the authors of works in empire studies are interested in the ancient imperial contexts, and some have related their work to contemporary contexts, they may or may not use postcolonial studies to aid their research and few have shown particular interest in affixing the label "postcolonial" to their works (Moore 2006, 14–19).

Postcolonial critics emphasize that biblical texts are not innocent. Sugirtharajah, for instance, understands postcolonial criticism as "scrutinizing and exposing colonial domination and power as these are embodied in biblical texts and in interpretations, and as searching for alternative hermeneutics while thus overturning and dismantling colonial perspectives" (1998, 16). Postcolonial criticism shares similarities with liberation hermeneutics, but also diverges from it because postcolonial critics are more suspicious of the historical-critical method that many liberation critics use. Postcolonial critics see biblical texts as more complex and multilayered and do not construct rich/poor, colonizer/colonized, and oppressor/oppressed in binary and dichotomous ways, as some liberation theologians do. Liberation theologians from Latin America tend to be Christocentric, while postcolonial critics engage more fully with religious pluralism and popular religions (Sugirtharajah 2002, 103–23).

Applying postcolonial criticism to the Gospels, Sugirtharajah (2002, 86–91) finds that there is no mention of Jesus' explicit resistance against the colonial occupiers. Yet Jesus' critique of local profiteers who colluded with the Romans and some of his sayings about earthly rulers (Matt. 11:8; Luke 7:25; 13:32) suggest that his alternative vision was against those in power. Horsley (2002) takes a stronger stance that Jesus was against empire. He places the Jesus movement within the context of popular resistance movements in Judea and Galilee, and says that the anti-imperial nature of Jesus' movement can provide a basis for theological critique of the Roman Empire in the past and the American empire in the present. Postcolonial studies of Paul's letters have also appeared; for example, Joseph A. Marchal applies feminist and postcolonial theories to the study of Philippians. The 2011 volume *The Colonized Apostle: Paul through Postcolonial Eyes* (Stanley) is the most comprehensive study to date, discussing Pauline agency, Paul's supposed social conservatism, hybrid identity and ethnicity, gender and colonialism, and Paul's relation to struggles in South Korea and the Philippines, among other topics. Moore (2006) uses postcolonial theorist Homi Bhabha to read apocalypse in Mark and John and the book of Revelation and argues that these texts mimic to a certain extent Roman imperial ideology, even when resisting and eroding it. *A Postcolonial Commentary on the New Testament Writings* (Segovia and Sugirtharajah), published in 2007, showcases the diversity of approaches and is an invaluable resource for further studies.

Postcolonial feminist interpretation challenges white male and female metropolitan readings for ignoring the issues of colonialism and imperialism and shows how their readings might collude with empire (Dube 2000). As we have discussed, Dube has lifted up the readings of ordinary female readers in African Independent Churches. Other critical concerns of postcolonial feminist criticism include the investigation of how the deployment of gender and symbolization of women relate to class interests and colonial domination in the Bible and studying women in the contact zones and the borderlands, such as Rahab, Ruth, and the Syrophoenician woman (Kwok, 81–85).

The publication of *Postcolonial Perspectives in African Biblical Interpretations* (Dube, Mbuvi, and Mbuwayesango) in 2012 pushes the envelope of postcolonial criticism even further. It raises the possibilities of "unthinking Eurocentrism" in biblical studies and developing Afrocentric criticism. The volume discusses the politics of translation of the Bible, the Bible as read in and through African creative writings, the relation of the Bible and "the scramble of Africa," HIV and AIDS, and the roles of socially engaged biblical scholars. The volume offers much insight and food for thought for interpreters in other parts of the Global South as well as in metropolitan areas who want to decolonize their minds and their methods when approaching the Bible.

Contemporary Issues

In this final section, I would like to take up some contemporary issues to see how they have led to new readings of the New Testament from fresh angles. First, the Holocaust has prompted many scholars to be conscious of the long history of anti-Jewish and antisemitic biases in the history of biblical interpretation. Scholars have proposed new ways to interpret New Testament texts so that they will not be construed as anti-Jewish. Second, the vigorous debates on same-sex marriage in the United States and elsewhere require us to reexamine the teachings on marriage, family, and same-gender relationships in the New Testament. Third, the study of "Gnosticism" and other writings in early Christianity has made us keenly aware of the politics of inclusion and exclusion surrounding the New Testament canon. A group of scholars has produced a new version of the New Testament combining both traditional and newly discovered texts.

Anti-Judaism and Antisemitism

Anti-Jewish attitudes and prejudices have contributed to antisemitism and the tragic genocide in modern times of Jewish people in Europe. Jews have been blamed for killing Jesus. Jesus' accusations against the scribes and Pharisees as hypocrites and his polemical sayings about the Jews in

John's Gospel have been used to cast Jewish people as the other, who did not accept the good news of Jesus Christ. Jesus has been seen as the founder of a new religion, separate from his Jewish background. Paul's contrast of law and gospel has been taken as the foundational difference between the covenant of the old and the new. Christianity has often been hailed as a universal religion, accepting gentiles into its mix, while Judaism has been cast in a negative light as a religion belonging to a particular group. Many Christians continue to harbor a supersessionist viewpoint, believing that Christianity ultimately triumphs over Judaism.

Interpreters sensitive to the charges of anti-Judaism and antisemitism have presented alternative views and interpretations different from those often taught in Christian churches. New Testament scholars have emphasized Jesus' Jewishness and interpreted Jesus' movement as a movement *within* Judaism. For example, Géza Vermes regards Jesus as a Jewish Galilean charismatic, while E. P. Sanders sees Jesus as an eschatological prophet who believed that the promises to Israel would soon be fulfilled and restoration would be at hand. Jewish New Testament scholar Amy-Jill Levine (2011) calls Jesus "the misunderstood Jew," and her work helps Jews and Christians understand the Jewish context of the first century. In *The Jewish Gospels*, Daniel Boyarin, a professor of talmudic culture, argues that Jesus' teachings can be found in the long-standing Jewish tradition and the coming of the Messiah was imagined in many Jewish texts. Many also point out that Jesus' arguments with the Pharisees and Jewish leaders were not conflicts between Christian and Jews, but intra-Jewish arguments (Wills, 101–32).

Jewish scholars such as Judith Plaskow and Levine (2000) have cautioned against the blanket generalizations of Jewish culture as misogynist in order to construct Jesus as a feminist over against his cultural background. Sometimes, Christian feminists have used Jesus' critique of his culture to support their challenge of patriarchy in their own cultures. To heed these scholars' call, we must avoid generalization and not imagine "the Jews" as the same transhistorically and transculturally. Some of the characterizations of "purity" discussed earlier would seem to fall under this criticism. More attention must be paid to local practices, regional history, and religious views and political ideologies of different groups and factions in first-century Judaism. Levine also suggests reading in community so that we can be exposed to our biases and blind spots in our reading.

An exciting development is the publication of the volume *The Jewish Annotated New Testament* (Levine and Brettler) in 2011, a collaborative effort of an international team of fifty Jewish scholars, which presents Jewish history, beliefs, and practices for understanding the New Testament. The New Testament is interpreted within the context of the Hebrew Bible and rabbinic literature. Each book of the New Testament is annotated with references, and the volume includes thirty essays covering a wide range of topics, including the synagogue, the law, food and table fellowship, messianic movements, Jewish miracle workers, Jewish family life, divine beings, and afterlife and resurrection. It also addresses Jewish responses to the New Testament and contemporary Jewish-Christian relations. The book will facilitate Jewish-Christian dialogue because it helps Christians better understand the Jewish roots of the New Testament and offers Jews a way to understand the New Testament that does not proselytize Christianity or cast Judaism in a negative light.

It should be pointed out that there is a difference between antisemitism and the critique of the policies of the state of Israel and its unequal treatment of Palestinians. Some Jewish thinkers and leaders, such as Judith Butler and Rabbi Michael Lerner, have criticized political Zionism, the dispossession of land, and hard-line policies of the Israeli state. Palestinian liberation theologian Naim Stifan Ateek has challenged Christian Zionism, adherents of which believe that the Jews must return to the Holy Land as a prerequisite for the second coming of Christ. Ateek draws from the example of Jesus to discuss the relation between justice and peace, nonviolent resistance, and the peacekeeping imperatives of the church.

Same-Sex Marriage

Debates on same-sex marriage in United States, Europe, Latin America, and Asia saw both supporters and opponents citing the Bible to support their positions. In the United States, the influential conservative Christian leader James Dobson defends what he calls the biblical definition of marriage, and blames homosexuality and gay marriage for all kinds of social decline. A cursory search on the Internet can find numerous posts citing biblical passages to defend heterosexual marriage and label homosexual passions and acts as unnatural, shameful, and contrary to God's will. These posts usually cite the creation of Adam and Eve in Genesis and the views of Jesus and Paul on marriage and sexuality as support.

Many Christians believe that the modern nuclear family represents the Christian ideal, but the current focus on heterosexual nuclear family dates back only to the 1950s. Dale B. Martin argues that there are more sources in the New Testament to criticize the modern family than to support it. Jesus was not a family man, and the Gospels present Jesus as living in alternative communities that shared his vision of divinely constituted family. He refused to identify with his natural family, saying, "Whoever does the will of God is my brother and sister and mother" (Mark 3:35; cf. Matt. 12:50; Luke 8:21). Jesus forbade divorce, even though Mosaic law allowed it (Matt. 19:4-9; Mark 10:6-12). But Matthew follows this with the saying about those who have "made themselves eunuchs for the sake of the kingdom of heaven" (Matt. 19:12), which might imply that the avoidance of marriage and of procreation is preferable. Jesus also says in the Gospels that in the resurrection, marriage will be obsolete (Matt. 22:30; Mark 12:26).

Paul in 1 Corinthians 7 did not promote marriage or traditional family and preferred Christians to follow his example and remain single and celibate. He thought that marriage would become a distraction from the life of faith "in Christ." But he allowed marriage for those who were weak and could not control their passions, saying "it is better to marry than to be aflame with passion" (1 Cor. 7:9). In Paul's time, passion and sexual desires were associated with the body and had to be put under severe control. The letters to the Colossians and Ephesians contain the household codes, which propose the hierarchy and order of a patriarchal family. But these letters are generally considered deuteropauline and were written during the increasing patriarchal institutionalization of the church.

Opponents to same-sex marriage often cite Rom. 1:23-27 to support their claims that homosexual acts are unnatural. Scholars have offered different explanations of the context of this text to argue that it is not against homosexual relations as we have come to know them in the present day (Goss, 198–202). Some suggest that homosexual acts were considered part of unclean gentile culture and were condemned by Paul for that reason. Others claim that Paul was not speaking about adult homosexual relations but pederasty in the Greco-Roman world. Some even proffer that Paul might have in mind oral or anal sex as unnatural sexual intercourse, among opposite-sex partners as well. Bernadette J. Brooten comments that Paul's injunction against female homosexual relations was due to his understanding of gender roles. Paul did not want women to exchange their supposedly passive and subordinate desire for an active role (216). Feminist scholars have challenged the androcentric mind-set and patriarchal ideologies of Pauline and other New Testament writings.

The New Testament thus cannot be easily enlisted to support a reductionistic understanding of "Christian marriage" or "family values," as if these have not changed over time. While same-sex marriage has become a rallying cry for marriage equality and recognition of human rights, some lesbians and gay men have also expressed concerns that the legislation of marriage would give too much power to the state, which can legitimize one form of sexual relationship while excluding others. Dale B. Martin belongs to this latter group and encourages queer Christians to expand their imaginations to "allow scripture and tradition to inspire new visions of Christian community free from the constraints of the modern, heterosexual, nuclear family" (39). Tolbert (2006) adds that same-sex couples can find the ideals of friendship in the New Testament supportive of their relationship. In John, Jesus told the disciples that they were his friends and shared with them his deepest knowledge of God. The New Testament, Tolbert says, does not promote marriage, heterosexual or not, as the bedrock of Christian community, but rather values friendship; as Jesus says, "No one has greater love than this, to lay down one's life for one's friends" (John 15:13). Even though the notion of friendship in the ancient world might be quite different from ours, the shift from promoting marriage to friendship opens new horizons.

A "New" New Testament

In 1945, local peasants in Nag Hammadi in Egypt discovered papyrus codices in a clay sealed jar consisting of fifty-two gnostic writings that were previously unknown. Though the papyrus dated back to the fourth century, some of the texts in the manuscripts can be traced back to as early as the first or second century. The Nag Hammadi library contains texts such as the *Gospel of Thomas*, the *Gospel of Philip*, the *Gospel of Truth*, and writings attributed to Jesus' followers, such as the *Secret Book of James*, the *Apocalypse of Paul*, and the *Apocalypse of Peter* (Pagels). The discovery of these texts greatly expanded our knowledge of religious writings in the early centuries.

Just as Jewish scholars have challenged us to reexamine our assumptions about Christian origins and the Jewish roots of Christianity, the discovery and study of the Nag Hammadi library raised new issues about the conceptualization of the history of the early church. Before the discovery, all we knew about "Gnosticism" was that the orthodox heresiologists, especially Irenaeus and Tertullian, vilified it. Karen L. King (2003) argues that these polemicists had constructed the category "heresy" as part of their project of identity formation and to exclude Jews and pagans as outsiders. The Nag Hammadi writings show what scholars have called "Gnosticism" as highly pluralistic and the boundary between Christianity and "Gnosticism" as more permeable than previously assumed. Both the so-called orthodox and the heretical writings belonged to a common body of tradition and represented "distinct varieties of Christianity developed in different geographical areas, at a time when the boundaries of orthodox and heresy were not at all fixed" (152). Moreover, certain texts were excluded from the

New Testament canon because of ideological reasons, such as to marginalize women's authority and leadership. For example, the *Gospel of Mary*, which was excluded, depicts Mary Magdalene as having received special knowledge from Jesus and serving as a leader among the disciples after Jesus' resurrection. This portrait of Mary should be considered together with the depiction of her as one of Jesus' followers and a key witness to his resurrection in the New Testament (King 1998).

In addition to the Nag Hammadi library, other texts have been discovered in the nineteenth and twentieth centuries and scientifically verified to be almost as old as the manuscripts of the traditional New Testament. A group of scholars, pastors, and church leaders under the leadership of Hal Taussig have produced a New Testament for the twenty-first century that includes with the established canon a selection of some of the texts outside the canon and called it "a new New Testament." The newly added documents include ten books, two prayers, and the *Odes of Solomon*, which consists mostly of prayers. Now, within the same volume, we can read about Mary Magdalene in the traditional Gospels as well as in the *Gospel of Mary*. In contrast to the traditional book of Revelation, the *Secret Revelation of John* offers a different picture of how Christ rescues the world, not through apocalyptic battles, but by teaching about God's light and compassion. Taussig hopes that this new New Testament can offer readers a chance to form new opinions about the earliest traditions of Christianity and be inspired by the teachings, songs, prayers, letters, and meditations of Jesus' early followers (xviii–xix).

Conclusion

The New Testament has shaped human cultures for millennia and is read by Christians, people of other religious traditions, and secular people in different tongues, cultural backgrounds, social contexts, and life circumstances. As global citizens living in the twenty-first century, we have to remember how the gospel of Jesus Christ has been misused to oppress and construct the other, whether the other is Jewish people, women, racial and ethnic minorities, colonized people, or queer people, so that history will not be repeated. The availability of so many new resources and methods in New Testament studies and the addition of underrepresented voices from all over the world are cause for celebration. New Testament reading in the contemporary world has become more global, multicentered, and plurivocal, and contributes to interreligious understanding. The interpretation of the New Testament has also been brought to the public square, as people look for insights from the Bible to address problems of our day. I hope that those among the younger generation who profess that they are "spiritual but not religious" will also appreciate the wisdom in the New Testament, as one of the most fascinating and influential religious and spiritual literatures of humankind.

Works Cited

Ahn, Byung Mu. 1981. "Jesus and the Minjung in the Gospel of Mark." In *Minjung Theology: People as the Subjects of History*, edited by Kim Yong Bock, 136–52. Singapore: Commission of Theological Concerns, Christian Conference of Asia.

Anderson, Janice Capel, and Stephen D. Moore, eds. 2008. *Mark and Method: New Approaches in Biblical Studies*. 2nd ed. Minneapolis: Fortress Press.

Ariarajah, Wesley. 1989. *The Bible and People of Other Faiths*. Maryknoll, NY: Orbis.

Ateek, Naim Stefan. 1989. *Justice, and Only Justice: A Palestinian Theology of Liberation*. Maryknoll, NY: Orbis.

Bailey, Randall C., Tat-siong Benny Liew, and Fernando F. Segovia, eds. 2009. *They Were All Together in One Place? Toward Minority Biblical Criticism*. Atlanta: Society of Biblical Literature.

Barr, James. 1983. *Holy Scripture: Canon, Authority, Criticism*. Oxford: Clarendon.

Baum, Wilhelm, and Dietmar W. Winkler. 2003. *The Church of the East: A Concise History*. London: RoutledgeCurzon.

Blount, Brian K. 1995. *Cultural Interpretation: Reorienting New Testament Criticism*. Minneapolis: Fortress Press.

Borg, Marcus J. 1994. *Jesus in Contemporary Scholarship*. Valley Forge, PA: Trinity Press International.

Boyarin, Daniel. 2012. *The Jewish Gospels: The Story of the Jewish Christ*. New York: New Press.

Brooten, Bernadette J. 1996. *Love between Women: Early Christian Responses to Female Homoeroticism*. Chicago: University of Chicago Press.

Butler, Judith. 2012. *Parting Ways: Jewishness and the Critique of Zionism*. New York: Columbia University Press.

Cardenal, Ernesto. 1976–1982. *The Gospel in Solentiname*. Translated by Donald D. Walsh. 4 vols. Maryknoll, NY: Orbis.

Carter, Warren. 2001. *Matthew and Empire: Initial Explorations*. Harrisburg, PA: Trinity Press International.

Cheng, Patrick S. 2002. "Multiplicity and Judges 19: Constructing a Queer Asian Pacific American Biblical Hermeneutic." *Semeia* 90–91:119–33.

Cone, James H. 1969. *Black Theology and Black Power*. New York: Seabury.

———. 1975. *God of the Oppressed*. New York: Seabury.

Crossan, John Dominic. 1991. *The Historical Jesus: The Life of a Mediterranean Jewish Peasant*. San Francisco: HarperSanFrancisco.

———. 2007. *God and Empire: Jesus against Rome, Then and Now*. New York: HarperCollins.

Crossley, James G. 2010. *Reading the New Testament: Contemporary Approaches*. London: Routledge.

Dobson, James C. 2004. *Marriage under Fire: Why We Must Win This War*. Sisters, OR: Multnomah.

Donaldson, Laura E. 2006. "Gospel Hauntings: The Postcolonial Demons of New Testament Criticism." In *Postcolonial Biblical Criticism: Interdisciplinary Intersections*, edited by Fernando F. Segovia and Stephen D. Moore, 97–113. London: Continuum.

Dube, Musa W. 2000. *Postcolonial Feminist Interpretation of the Bible*. St. Louis: Chalice.

———, ed. 2001. *Other Ways of Reading: African Women and the Bible*. Atlanta: Society of Biblical Literature.

———. 2008. *The HIV and AIDS Bible: Selected Essays*. Scranton, PA: University of Scranton Press.

Dube, Musa, Andrew M. Mbuvi, and Dora R. Mbuwayesango, eds. 2012. *Postcolonial Perspectives in African Biblical Interpretations*. Atlanta: Society of Biblical Literature.

Eber, Irene, Sze-kar Wan, and Knut Walf, eds. 1999. *The Bible in Modern China*. Nettetal, Germany: Steyler.

Elizondo, Virgilio. 1983. *Galilean Journey: The Mexican-American Promise*. Maryknoll, NY: Orbis.

Fernandez, Eleazar S. 2013. "Multiple Locations-Belongings and Power Differentials: Lenses for Liberating Biblical Hermeneutic." In *Soundings in Cultural Criticism: Perspectives and Methods in Culture, Power, and Identity in the New Testament*, edited by Francisco Lozada Jr. and Greg Carey, 139–49. Minneapolis: Fortress Press.

Flatow, Sheryl. 2009. "Christianity on the Move." *Bostonia*. http://www.bu.edu/bostonia/fall09/christianity.

Foskett, Mary F., and Jeffrey Kah-Jin Kuan, eds. 2006. *Ways of Being, Ways of Reading: Asian American Biblical Interpretation*. St. Louis: Chalice.

Gager, John G. 1975. *Kingdom and Community: The Social World of Early Community*. Englewood Cliffs, NJ: Prentice-Hall.

Goss, Robert E. 2002. *Queering Christ: Beyond Jesus Acted Up*. Cleveland: Pilgrim.

Gutiérrez, Gustavo. 1988. *A Theology of Liberation: History, Politics, and Salvation*. Translated by Caridad Inda and John Eagleson. Rev. ed. Maryknoll, NY: Orbis.

Hastings, Adrian, ed. 1999. *A World History of Christianity*. Grand Rapids: Eerdmans.

Horsley, Richard A., ed. 1997. *Paul and Empire: Religion and Power in Roman Imperial Society*. Harrisburg, PA: Trinity Press International.

———. 2002. *Jesus and Empire: The Kingdom of God and the New World Disorder*. Minneapolis: Fortress Press.

Irvin, Dale T., and Scott W. Sunquist. 2001. *History of the World Christian Movement*. Vol. 1, *Earliest Christianity to 1453*. Maryknoll, NY: Orbis.

———. 2012. *History of the World Christian Movement*. Vol. 2, *Modern Christianity from 1454 to 1800*. Maryknoll, NY: Orbis.

Jenkins, Philip. 2007. *The Next Christendom: The Coming of Global Christianity*. Rev. ed. New York: Oxford University Press.

Johnson, Todd M., and Kenneth R. Ross. 2009. *Atlas of Global Christianity, 1910–2010*. Edinburgh: Edinburgh University Press.

Kim, Chan-Hie. 1995. "Reading the Cornelius Story from an Asian Immigrant Perspective." In *Reading from This Place*. Vol. 1, *Social Location and Biblical Interpretation in the United States*, edited by Fernando F. Segovia and Mary Ann Tolbert, 165–74. Minneapolis: Fortress Press.

Kinukawa, Hisako. 1994. *Women and Jesus in Mark: A Japanese Feminist Perspective*. Maryknoll, NY: Orbis.

King, Karen L. 1998. "Canonization and Marginalization: Mary of Magdala." In *Women's Sacred Scriptures*, edited by Kwok Pui-lan and Elisabeth Schüssler Fiorenza, 29–36. London: SCM.

———. 2003. *What Is Gnosticism?* Cambridge, MA: Harvard University Press.

Kitzberger, Ingrid Rosa. 1998. "How Can This Be? (John 3:9): A Feminist Theological Re-Reading of the Gospel of John." In *What Is John?* Vol. 2, *Literary and Social Readings of the Fourth Gospel*, edited by Fernando F. Segovia, 19–41. Atlanta: Society of Biblical Literature.

Kwok Pui-lan. 2005. *Postcolonial Imagination and Feminist Theology*. Louisville: Westminster John Knox.

Lady Gaga. 2011. "Judas." Posted on May 3. http://www.ladygaga.com/media/?meid=6765.

Lee, Archie C. C. 1998. "Cross-Textual Interpretation and Its Implications for Biblical Studies." In *Teaching the Bible: The Discourses and Politics of Biblical Pedagogy*, edited by Fernando F. Segovia and Mary Ann Tolbert, 247–54. Maryknoll, NY: Orbis.

Levine, Amy-Jill. 2000. "Lilies of the Field and Wandering Jews: Biblical Scholarship, Women's Roles, and Social Location." In *Transforming Encounters: Jesus and Women Re-viewed*, edited by Ingrid Rosa Kitzberger, 329–52. Leiden: Brill.

———. 2006. *The Misunderstood Jew: The Church and the Scandal of the Jewish Jesus*. San Francisco: HarperSanFrancisco.

Levine, Amy-Jill, and Marc Z. Brettler, eds. 2011. *The Jewish Annotated New Testament*. New York: Oxford University Press.

Lewis, Lloyd A. 1991. "An African American Appraisal of the Philemon-Paul-Onesimus Triangle." In *Stony the Road We Trod: African American Biblical Interpretation*, edited by Cain Hope Felder, 232–46. Minneapolis: Fortress Press.

Liew, Tat-siong Benny. 1999. *The Politics of Parousia: Reading Mark Inter(con)textually.* Leiden: Brill.

———. 2008. *What Is Asian American Biblical Hermeneutics?* Honolulu: University of Hawai'i Press.

———. 2013. "Colorful Readings: Racial/Ethnic Minority Readings of the New Testament in the United States." In *Soundings in Cultural Criticism: Perspectives and Methods in Culture, Power, and Identity in the New Testament,* edited by Francisco Lozado Jr. and Greg Carey, 177–89, Minneapolis: Fortress Press.

Malina, Bruce J. 1981. *The New Testament World: Insights from Cultural Anthropology.* Atlanta: John Knox Press.

Marchal, Joseph A. 2008. *The Politics of Heaven: Women, Gender, and Empire in the Study of Paul.* Minneapolis: Fortress Press.

Martin, Clarice J. 1989. "A Chamberlain's Journey and the Challenge of Interpretation for Liberation." *Semeia* 47:105–35.

———. 1991. "The *Haustafeln* (Household Codes) in African American Interpretation: 'Free Slaves' and 'Subordinate Women.'" In *Stony the Road We Trod: African American Biblical Interpretation,* edited by Cain Hope Felder, 206–31. Minneapolis: Fortress Press.

Martin, Dale B. 2006. "Familiar Idolatry and the Christian Case against Marriage." In *Authorizing Marriage? Canon, Tradition, and Critique in the Blessing of Same-sex Unions,* edited by Mark D. Jordan, 17–40. Princeton: Princeton University Press.

Meeks, Wayne A. 1983. *The First Urban Christians: The Social World of the Apostle Paul.* New Haven: Yale University Press.

Melanchthon, Monica Jyotsna. 2010. "Dalit Women and the Bible: Hermeneutical and Methodological Reflections." In *Hope Abundant: Third World and Indigenous Women's Theology,* edited by Kwok Pui-lan, 103–22, Maryknoll, NY: Orbis.

Moore, Stephen D. 2006. *Empire and Apocalypse: Postcolonialism and the New Testament.* Sheffield: Sheffield Phoenix Press.

———. 2010. *The Bible in Theory: Critical and Postcritical Essays.* Atlanta: Society of Biblical Literature.

———. 2013. "The Dog-Woman of Canaan and Other Animal Tales from the Gospel of Matthew." In *Soundings in Cultural Criticism: Perspectives and Methods in Culture, Power, and Identity in the New Testament,* edited by Francisco Lozada Jr. and Greg Carey, 57–71. Minneapolis: Fortress Press.

Moore, Stephen D., and Janice Capel Anderson, eds. 2003. *New Testament Masculinities.* Atlanta: Society of Biblical Literature.

Mosala, Itumeleng J. 1989. *Biblical Hermeneutics and Black Theology in South Africa.* Grand Rapids: Eerdmans.

Nelavala, Surekha. 2006. "Smart Syrophoenician Woman: A Dalit Feminist Reading of Mark 7:24-31." *ExpTim* 118, no. 2: 64–69.

Neyrey, Jerome H. 1990. *Paul, in Other Words: A Cultural Reading of His Letters.* Louisville: Westminster John Knox.

Pagels, Elaine. 1979. *The Gnostic Gospels.* New York: Random House.

Patte, Daniel. 2004. Introduction to *Global Bible Commentary,* edited by Daniel Patte, xxi–xxxii. Nashville: Abingdon.

Petrella, Ivan. 2005. *Latin American Liberation Theology: The Next Generation.* Maryknoll, NY: Orbis.

Plaskow, Judith. 1980. "Blaming the Jews for the Birth of Patriarchy." *Lilith* 7:11–12, 14–17.

Rajkumar, Peniel. 2010. *Dalit Theology and Dalit Liberation: Problems, Paradigms, and Possibilities.* Burlington, VT: Ashgate.

Roncace, Mark, and Joseph Weaver, eds. 2013. *Global Perspectives on the Bible.* Upper Saddle River, NJ: Pearson.

Said, Edward W. 1978. *Orientalism.* New York: Pantheon.

Saint Clair, Rachel Annette. 2008. *Call and Consequences: A Womanist Reading of Mark*. Minneapolis: Fortress Press.

Sánchez, David A. 2008. *From Patmos to the Barrio: Subverting Imperial Myths*. Minneapolis: Fortress Press.

Sanders, E. P. 1985. *Jesus and Judaism*. Philadelphia: Fortress Press.

Sanneh, Lamin O. 1989. *Translating the Message: The Missionary Impact on Culture*. Maryknoll, NY: Orbis.

———. 2003. *Whose Religion Is Christianity? The Gospel beyond the West*. Grand Rapids: Eerdmans.

———. 2007. *Disciples of All Nations: Pillars of World Christianity*. New York: Oxford University Press.

Sawicki, Marianne. 2000. *Crossing Galilee: Architectures of Contact in the Occupied Land of Jesus*. Harrisburg, PA: Trinity Press International.

Scharper, Philip, and Sally Scharper, eds. 1984. *Gospel in Art by the Peasants of Solentiname*. Maryknoll, NY: Orbis.

Schottroff, Luise. 1995. *Lydia's Impatient Sisters: A Feminist Social History of Early Christianity*. Translated by Barbara Rumscheidt and Martin Rumscheidt. Louisville: Westminster John Knox.

Schüssler Fiorenza, Elisabeth. 1983. *In Memory of Her: A Feminist Theological Reconstruction of Christian Origins*. New York: Crossroad.

———. 1992. *But She Said: Feminist Practices of Biblical Interpretation*. Boston: Beacon.

———. 2000. *Jesus and the Politics of Interpretation*. New York: Continuum.

———. 2002. "The Ethos of Biblical Interpretation: Biblical Studies in a Postmodern and Postcolonial Context." In *Theological Literacy for the Twenty-First Century*, edited by Rodney L. Petersen, 211–28. Grand Rapids: Eerdmans.

———. 2007. *The Power of the Word: Scripture and the Rhetoric of Empire*. Minneapolis: Fortress Press.

Segovia, Fernando F. 2000. *Decolonizing Biblical Studies: A View from the Margins*. Maryknoll, NY: Orbis.

Segovia, Fernando F., and R. S. Sugirtharajah, eds. 2007. *A Postcolonial Commentary on the New Testament Writings*, New York: T&T Clark.

Segundo, Juan Luis. 1976. *Liberation of Theology*. Translated by John Drury. Maryknoll, NY: Orbis.

Stanley, Christopher D., ed. 2011. *The Colonized Apostle: Paul through Postcolonial Eyes*. Minneapolis: Fortress Press.

Sugirtharajah, R. S. 1999. *Asian Biblical Hermeneutics and Postcolonial Criticism: Contesting the Interpretations*. Maryknoll, NY: Orbis.

———. 2002. *Postcolonial Criticism and Biblical Interpretation*. Oxford: Oxford University Press.

———. 2012. *Exploring Postcolonial Biblical Criticism: History, Method, Practice*. Malden, MA: Wiley-Blackwell.

———, ed. 1998. "Biblical Studies after the Empire: From a Colonial to a Postcolonial Mode of Interpretation." In *The Postcolonial Bible*, edited by R. S. Sugirtharajah. Sheffield: Sheffield Academic Press.

Tamez, Elsa. 2001. *Jesus and Courageous Women*. New York: Women's Division, General Board of Global Ministries, United Methodist Church.

———. 2007. *Struggles for Power in Early Christianity: A Study of the First Letter to Timothy*. Translated by Gloria Kinsler. Maryknoll, NY: Orbis.

Taussig, Hal, ed. 2013. *A New New Testament: A Bible for the Twenty-First Century Combining Traditional and Newly Discovered Texts*. Boston: Houghton Mifflin Harcourt.

Theissen, Gerd. 1978. *Sociology of Early Palestinian Christianity*. Translated by John Bowden. Philadelphia: Fortress Press.

Tolbert, Mary Ann. 1998. "Reading the Bible with Authority: Feminist Interrogation of the Canon." In *Escaping Eden: New Feminist Perspectives on the Bible*, edited by Harold C. Washington, Susan Lochrie Graham, and Pamela Thimmes, 141–62. Sheffield: Sheffield Academic Press.

———. 2006. "Marriage and Friendship in the Christian New Testament: Ancient Resources for Contemporary Same-Sex Unions." In *Authorizing Marriage? Canon, Tradition, and Critique in the Blessing of Same-Sex Unions*, edited by Mark D. Jordan, 41–51. Princeton: Princeton University Press.

United Bible Societies. 2012. "Celebrating 100 Millions Bibles printed in China!" November 12. http://www.unitedBiblesocieties.org/news/2902-celebrating-100-million-Bibles-printed-in-china.

———. 2013 "About UBS Translation Work." http://www.ubs-translations.org/about_us.

Vermes, Géza. 1973. *Jesus the Jew: A Historian's Reading of the Gospels*. London: Collins.

Villalobos, Manuel. 2011. "Bodies *Del Otro Lado* Finding Hope in the Borderland: Gloria Anzaldúa, the Ethiopian Eunuch of Acts 8:26–40, *y Yo*." In *Bible Trouble: Queer Reading at the Boundaries of Biblical Scholarship*, edited by Teresa Hornby and Ken Stone, 191–221. Atlanta: Society of Biblical Literature.

West, Gerald O. 1999. *The Academy of the Poor: Towards a Dialogical Reading of the Bible*. Sheffield: Sheffield Academic Press.

Wicker, Kathleen O'Brien, Althea Spencer Miller, and Musa W. Dube, eds. 2005. *Feminist New Testament Studies: Global and Future Perspectives*. New York: Palgrave Macmillan.

Williams, Demetrius K. 2004. *An End to This Strife: The Politics of Gender in the African American Churches*. Minneapolis: Fortress Press.

Wills, Lawrence M. 2008. *Not God's People: Insiders and Outsiders in the Biblical World*. Lanham, MD: Rowman & Littlefield.

Wimbush, Vincent L., ed. 2000. *African Americans and the Bible: Sacred Texts and Social Textures*. New York: Continuum.

Wire, Antoinette Clark. 1990. *The Corinthian Women Prophets: A Reconstruction through Paul's Rhetoric*. Minneapolis: Fortress Press.

Yamaguchi, Satoko. 2002. *Mary and Martha: Women in the World of Jesus*. Maryknoll, NY: Orbis.

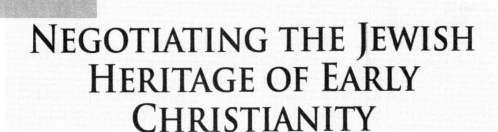

NEGOTIATING THE JEWISH HERITAGE OF EARLY CHRISTIANITY

Lawrence M. Wills

Any discussion of the dialogue between Jews and Christians in the twenty-first century must begin with some historical perspective as to what the traditional Christian view has been concerning the relations of Jews and followers of Jesus in the first century. In the first half of the twentieth century, for instance, the dominant Christian view was the following: on the one hand, there was one clear Judaism—viewed through the lens of Paul's critique of the law and represented by the Pharisees as depicted in Matthew—and on the other hand, one clear Christianity as a new entity that had separated from Judaism. If there was any disagreement among the first Christians, it was only that between the "correct" party—those who followed Paul—and the "incorrect" party—those who followed James in retaining Jewish law. How the divorce between Judaism and Christianity took place is treated in the book of Acts, which was taken as a historically accurate record of the intransigence of Jews in the face of Paul's preaching of the message of Christ. True, there were ambiguous passages throughout the Gospels, such as:

> When Jesus saw that he [the scribe] answered wisely, he said to him, "You are not far from the kingdom of God." (Mark 12:34)
>
> Jesus said to them, "The scribes and the Pharisees sit on Moses' seat; therefore, do whatever they teach you and follow it." (Matt. 23:2-3)

But these could be explained away by interpreting them in light of Paul's letters and Acts.

Over the last century, scholars have moved away from this simple view of the relation of ancient Judaism and early Christianity to a much more complex view, questioning almost every part of the description above. In the first half of the twentieth century, some Christian scholars argued that the variety of early Christian groups did not evolve out of one unified body of followers of Jesus, or even from the two divergent paths of "Paul Christians" and "James Christians." Rather, from the earliest period, there were already widely divergent practices and beliefs, without any clear sense of an agreed-on center. This challenge to a trunk-with-branches view of early Christian groups gave more weight to the "branches," groups formerly regarded as smaller, marginal, too Eastern, or heretical. Walter Bauer was a leading figure in this development; more recent scholars who exemplify this approach include James Robinson and Helmut Koester; Jack Sanders; and Stephen Wilson.

For instance, whereas it was traditionally assumed that the four Gospels were narrative depictions of a Jesus who taught essentially what Paul said in his letters using different language, now one had to take seriously the differences among the authors and audiences of these texts. The varied emphases that were found among the four Gospels, or between Paul's letters and Revelation, or between Acts and Jude, or between canonical texts and early Christian texts from outside the canon, came to be seen as reflective of widely divergent movements and eddies in this new religious movement. Scholars might retain the theological preferences of their own traditions, but in colleges and universities, and even in seminaries, the historical narrative no longer seemed like a tree with a clear trunk and branches, but followed the pattern of tubers and vines—widely propagating members with little clear order or lines of development.

In this process, Christian texts from outside the New Testament canon, even those that had been considered "heretical," came to be viewed as having an equal claim in the *historical* reconstruction of early Christianity, regardless of their theology. There was a larger and larger patchwork of groups, and a clear history of origins and development became ever more difficult to reconstruct. Very basic questions about the history of Judaism and Christianity were also introduced: Has the early Eastern history of Judaism and Christianity, all the way from Syria to India and later to China, been ignored as a result of the Western focus of much of the Christian church and of Judaism? To be sure, the Eastern church also included Paul in its canon, but was the relation between eastern Christians and Jews vastly different from that of their Western counterparts (Foltz)?

But another, parallel shift was also underway. In the last half of the twentieth century, scholars proposed a similar proliferation in the number of Jewish groups as well. Before about 1960, many scholars would have described Judaism in the first century as divided into three parties—Sadducees, Pharisees, and Essenes—based on a description of Judaism by the first-century Jewish historian Josephus (*J. W.* 2.117–66). But the discovery of the Dead Sea Scrolls, a new appreciation for the differences among the many Jewish texts of the period, and a growing realization that early rabbinic views were not authoritative for all Jews compelled scholars to recognize the wide variety of Jewish groups, beliefs, and practices (see Cohen 2006; J. J. Collins; Nickelsburg). The classic nineteenth-century history of the Judaism of this period by Emil Schürer (1886–1890) was enlarged in each of the many subsequent editions by the inclusion of more variety in terms of texts, theology, and practices.

Jewish scholars were also motivated by a desire to participate fully in the public discourse on the nature of religions. Judaism, they argued, should be studied in our colleges and universities as an important religious tradition alongside Christianity and other world religions. After World War II and the Shoah, or Holocaust—the genocide of six million Jews—there was an added motivation for both Jews and Christians: a more searching engagement about the origins of Jewish-Christian relations in the ancient world. If the historical assumptions behind a presumed Christian superiority could be challenged, then Christians, Jews, and others would have a chance of living in peace in the twentieth century and afterward without the corrosive effects of stereotypes derived from a misreading of ancient evidence.

Corresponding to the recognition of ancient variety was a new variety among the modern scholars who were studying it as well. During the twentieth century, there arose a full participation of Christian scholars in the study of Judaism and Jewish scholars in the study of Christianity—along with scholars from other religious backgrounds or with no religious affiliation at all. By the second half of the twentieth century, it came to be quite expected that New Testament scholars would know something about rabbinic literature and that Jewish historians of the Roman period would know something about the New Testament and early church. By the end of the twentieth century, there was not just one or two but a number of important studies on the New Testament by Jewish scholars and a number of important studies on rabbinic Judaism by Christians.

The situation at the end of the twentieth century, then, was drastically different from that at the beginning. Influenced by challenges in the social sciences, philosophy, and literary criticism, new issues came to be raised that only made the comparison more complicated, but in many cases, more interesting to modern audiences. Formerly, scholars compared Judaism and Christianity as two clearly defined bodies of people with separate identities, but increasingly many scholars realized that more elite voices within Judaism—for instance, the chief priests, Josephus, or Philo—were being unfairly compared to the less elite forms of Christianity—Mark or the sayings source of Matthew and Luke. The nonelite layers of the Christian movement seemed more revolutionary when compared with the aristocratic voices within Judaism, yet a comparison of Jewish prophetic movements (such as those reported in Josephus) to more elite Christian texts like Hebrews would look very different. Which is the "proper" comparison? Should popular movements among Christians be compared with popular movements among Jews, and more elite texts among Christians with elite Jewish authors, say, Hebrews with Philo? And further, would a female Christian who was the slave of a Christian master have had more in common with her master, or with a Jewish woman who was the slave of a Jewish master, or a female worshiper of Isis who was the slave of a master who worshiped Isis? The effects of geographical distance were also relevant, as both Jews and followers of Jesus were found in communities stretching well over a thousand miles, from Spain to the East, assimilating in each case to vastly different local customs. It was becoming increasingly difficult to define clearly separate bodies of "Jews" and "Christians."

The earlier consensus, then, might have compared the "three parties" of Judaism—Sadducees, Pharisees, and Essenes—and the "two parties" within Christianity—Pauline Christians and "Jewish Christians"—a comparison that could be depicted in this way:

Jewish groups: 1 1 1
Followers of Jesus: 1 1

But by the end of the twentieth century, in recognition of the great variety of subgroups, the comparison would appear more like this:

Jewish groups: 1 1 1 1 1 1 1 1 1 1 1 1 1
Followers of Jesus: 1 1 1 1 1 1 1 1 1 1 1

If many Jewish groups maintained strict observance of Torah, so did many followers of Jesus. If many followers of Jesus believed that the end of time was near, so did many Jewish groups. If many followers of Jesus believed that the community of believers was bathed in the holiness of God in a way that made the Jewish temple superfluous, so did some Jews. And finally: If the death of Jesus was the theological affirmation that supposedly separated Christians from Jews, what do we make of the fact that some followers of Jesus did not emphasize his death and some Jewish texts (for example, 4 Maccabees) did emphasize the death of Jewish heroes? Similarities and differences among the groups in *both* rows above introduced new challenges for comparing "Judaism" and "Christianity." The Gospel of Matthew, for instance, was clearly critical of Pharisees—*one* of the Jewish groups in the row above—but was it possible that Matthew was actually more similar to Pharisees than he was to Paul? The simple question of the relation of "Jews" and "Christians" could no longer be answered without pressing a more specific question: *Which* Jews? *Which* Christians?

Incorporating this new consensus concerning a variety of groups among Christians and among Jews, some scholars toward the end of the twentieth century began charting the history of the "partings of the ways" or the "divorce" between Judaism and Christianity (e.g., Dunn 1991; Townsend). A title that exemplified the new consensus of variety was James D. G. Dunn's *The Partings of the Ways* (1991), but challenges to the "new consensus" were, of course, inevitable. Dunn's title was countered by a collection of conference papers called *The Ways That Never Parted* (Becker and Reed; see also Boyarin). This volume asked: At what point were the followers of Jesus thoroughly parted from "Judaism" or "Israel"? True, differences among Jewish or Christian subgroups could be discerned, but could the line above of Christian subgroups really be clearly distinguished from the Jewish line? Thus it is somewhat ironic that, after a century of new studies emphasizing the distinctions among different Jewish groups and different Christian groups, some of the heirs of that consensus would amend it by deemphasizing the boundary line *between* Judaism and Christianity. As more and more subgroups were divided off, they began to fill out the *overall* circle of "Judaism and Christianity" approximately equally. It is even suggested that texts that seem at first to affirm a clear, separate identity are in some cases overstating the distinction, or even creating the illusion of separation, imposing distinctions that may barely exist, in order to instill a clearer sense of identity. (This may be true, for example, of Matthew.) As we learn from modern identity studies, the strongest assertions of difference, or the strongest assertions of a good "We" and an evil "Other," often appear between groups that are similar to each other, and almost indistinguishable by outsiders (Wills). Although this newest development appears at first to undo the previous consensus about variety and difference, it actually carries it forward by demonstrating that there is a wide, overlapping spectrum of beliefs and practices among Jews *and* followers of Jesus, and yet the differences that we perceive among groups and subgroups does not result in one clear line *between* Jews and followers of Jesus. Some Christian groups would admittedly be more clearly separated from Judaism—for example, the implied audience of the Letter to the Hebrews—but others would be more ambiguous in their separation than once thought. Again, it is as if the two lines of groups above should be merged into one indistinct set.

The Continuing Demand for Comparison, Despite the Complexity of the Data

While recognizing all of these challenging new questions, the effort to draw general conclusions about the relations of Jews and Christians continues, and is indeed necessary for a dialogue between Jews and Christians in the twenty-first century. The demands of modern Jews and Christians for dialogue have required some general observations about the first century in order to proceed. Some of the older conclusions still inform the present, more complex discussions among Jews, Christians, and others, and can be used as starting points.

Douglas R. A. Hare, for instance, divided the different assessments of Judaism found in the New Testament into three types. Some polemic in the Gospels is simply a critique of Jewish institutions by people who were, after all, also Jews. This he termed "prophetic anti-Judaism," the critique by a prophetic figure of his or her own institutions. (Even this use of the term *anti-Judaism* seems to separate the prophet from the people and imply that the prophet is *not* Jewish; it is tantamount to referring to Martin Luther King's "anti-Americanism." George Michael Smiga [12–13] tried to address this terminological problem.) According to Hare, Jesus himself would have fit in this category, and might be compared to figures such as Socrates, who, although he criticized his fellow Athenians, was not "un-Greek" or "anti-Greek." Nor did his students suggest that they must create a new entity in which to explore his philosophy (though Plato did eventually leave Athens to advise the king of Syracuse in a failed experiment to establish a "philosopher's state"). Other polemic in the New Testament, however, became progressively harsher, and pronounced a final condemnation on those Jews who did not accept Jesus as the Messiah. Hare termed this "Jewish-Christian anti-Judaism." Unlike the previous category, this type represents a division of groups within Judaism that is at the point of divorce, and the polemical language reflects the tension of being "mid-divorce" (Townsend). A third type is "gentilizing anti-Judaism," and is truly postdivorce: the critique of Judaism as a whole by gentile Christians (Wilson, 110–42, 258–84). Authors in this category are no longer realistically concerned with the conversion of Israel. It can be debated which texts of the New Testament or the early church would fall into these categories, but many scholars would consider the Gospel of Matthew as the first type, a prophetic critique of some (or even most) Jews from within Judaism; the Acts of the Apostles as a text of the second type, which condemns Jews for not accepting the message of Jesus as Messiah; and the Epistle to the Hebrews as an example of gentilizing anti-Judaism. But any of these might be and have been debated. Only if we could interrogate the authors could we be sure where they stood on key questions of the relations of the subgroups in a constantly differentiated Judaism.

In addition to historians and biblical scholars, theologians also entered into the dialogue and introduced terminology to define the various positions that Christians have taken in regard to their relation to Judaism. "Supersessionism" describes the traditional Christian view that in Jesus and Paul we find the belief that Judaism was superseded by God's new dispensation in Christ and the church. (Some New Testament scholars use the compound term rejection-replacement.) But even a doctrine of supersessionism can be more or less negative about the validity of the Jewish covenant. Does the old covenant have any continuing role in God's dispensation, or is it simply the precursor to Christianity (Novak; see also Soulen)? A so-called dual-covenant theology has arisen among liberal Christians, which is the notion that God's new dispensation in Christ did not cancel out the existing covenant with Jews. In this view, there are still two covenants operative, and thus there is no supersessionism, but rather a continuing coexistence of parallel covenants. Some passages from early Christian authors might be adduced in support of this position (see below concerning Paul).

Yet this overture only calls forth new questions. Even if Christians developed a benign view of the continuing validity of God's covenant with Jews, that does not begin to address the relations of Christians with religions other than Judaism. Jewish-Christian dialogue is an important beginning, but only a beginning, to dialogues with other faiths, and this should not be forgotten in discussions of the history of Jewish-Christian relations. Although it is understandable that Jewish leaders have often engaged in dialogue with Christian leaders in order to ameliorate the effects of antisemitism, for many Jews it would be unacceptable to achieve a recognition of God's continuing covenant with Jews if other religions still remained in a less favored status. In the twenty-first century, a broader notion of religious acceptance, beyond a "dual-covenant theology," has often arisen.

With these and similar analyses in mind, in the late twentieth century, scholars of the New Testament, including many Jewish scholars, proposed sweeping changes in regard to how the New Testament texts themselves evaluated Judaism. Vermes, Fredriksen, and Levine (17–52) returned to the Gospel accounts and Acts and argued that recoverable evidence about the historical Jesus depicts a teacher who may have *argued* about Jewish law—not surprising for a Jewish teacher—but who probably remained fairly observant to the end. A great deal of consensus has gathered around this view. If Jesus did reject certain aspects of Jewish law that were advocated by others, such as the Pharisees—again, not surprising for any non-Pharisaic Jew—he never made a blanket rejection of the markers of Judaism. Otherwise, why would Paul have been forced to argue so strongly with the disciples who actually knew Jesus (Galatians 1–2)? Some of Jesus' claims in the Gospels might actually constitute a *stricter* than usual observance of Jewish law, an "ultraorthodox" position! (These cases are sometimes ambiguous, and identifying something or someone as more or less orthodox is always a relative question—who defined the norm? Yet Jesus' rejection of divorce in Mark 10:2-12, or his constraints on accepted Jewish law in Matt. 5:17-48, could be considered a stricter "fence around the Torah" than that which became the norm in rabbinic literature. See also Vermes [80–81], and on the apparent exception in Mark 7:19, see below.)

It is likely that any observer in the year 30 CE would not have considered Jesus a "Reform" Jew (admittedly an anachronistic term), but more probably, a "strict" or "pious" Jew. As noted above, a compelling argument was also made that the Gospel of Matthew, although formerly viewed as "anti-Jewish" ("Scribes and Pharisees, hypocrites!" Matt. 23:13), was actually more anti-*Pharisaic* (Harrington, 1–3; Wills, 101–32). That is, Matthew does not perceive the movement of the followers of Jesus as opposing Judaism, but as opposing some within Judaism, especially Pharisees. To be sure, it is stated in Matthew that at the end, the gentiles will come in (28:19), but that is true of many Jewish texts as well. Matthew does not betray a "Pauline" critique of Jewish law and remains observant to the end.

Even if Jesus and the Gospel of Matthew assumed a continuing adherence to Jewish law, it has been assumed that Paul had irrevocably altered this situation by instituting a mission to gentiles without the law. But now this assumption as well has come in for a major reevaluation. The so-called new perspective on Paul has questioned the chasm that Christians have traditionally perceived between this apostle and the Judaism of his day (Dunn 1983). For the new-perspective scholars, Paul was more a missionary theologian than an abstract theologian or a psychologist of the human condition, and was rarely setting up an opposition between "Jews" and those in Christ. Rather than critiquing and rejecting Judaism as a form of legalism and "works righteousness" at odds with God's plan, almost all of Paul's apparent references to "Jews" are more likely referring to those *in the Jesus movement*, whether originally Jewish or gentile, who oppose his mission to gentiles without the law. This raises a challenging question: If gentiles had been allowed to enter freely into his churches without adhering to Jewish law, would Paul have voiced any reservations about the law for Jews at all?

The debate over the new perspective has been significant. The new perspective represents a direct challenge to strongly held tradition, and yet has achieved a large following. Still, conservative Protestant theologians have opposed it, and even those scholars who have self-identified as part of the new perspective can be divided into two groups, a moderate new perspective and a radical new perspective (Wills, 179–82). The distinction is based on how far they would push the questioning of the older consensus. The moderate new-perspective scholars hold that Paul was much less critical of Judaism than once thought. Says E. P. Sanders (552), whom we might consider a moderate new-perspective scholar: "In short, this is what Paul finds wrong in Judaism: it is not Christianity." That is, God (in Paul's view) is not "displeased" with Jews, Judaism, or Jewish law, but has simply, by the death of Christ, created a new door for all, both Jews and gentiles, to enter into the graces of God. The *discontinuity* between Judaism and Christianity is thus drastically reduced. This shift alone unsettled much Protestant tradition.

But the radical new-perspective scholars go further and argue a version of the dual-covenant theology mentioned above. For Paul, the death of Christ did indeed open a new door of access for gentiles that did not require Jewish law, but the old door for Jews remained open as well—without Christ and with the law still in effect! God was not closing one door to open a new one, but was opening an option for gentiles parallel to the one for Jews (Eisenbaum). Paul's letters are ultimately unclear on this question, but Eisenbaum's conclusions may be correct. However, as above with dual-covenant theology, the same demurral still applies: even if Paul envisioned a two-door access, for gentiles in Christ without the law and for Jews with the law only, he is quite explicit that gentile religion (apart from belief in Christ) is degraded and alienated from God (Rom. 1:2; Gal. 4:8; see

Wills, 179–82). There is no "newer perspective" on Paul that could soften his condemnation of the gentile religions, and in the twenty-first century this becomes a fundamental challenge for interfaith dialogue. (It would be speculative to try to imagine what Paul's views of Islam might have been, although the parallels to Paul's theology are significant. In Islam, Jesus is the Messiah of God, born of a virgin, who performed miracles, and the revelation in Islam came to a prophet who was also "last of all, as to one untimely born" [cf. 1 Cor. 15:8]. But even if, continuing this imaginative exercise on the analogy of the "two-covenant" understanding described above, we were to imagine Paul countenancing a third covenant, with Islam, what would we say of the status of other religions?)

Now, many passages in Paul, especially in Romans, would appear to fly in the face of the radical new-perspective scholars, but in each case an alternative interpretation is possible that would at least make this dual-covenant reading a plausible option. Consider the much-discussed case of Rom. 10:4: "For Christ is the end [*telos*] of the law so that there may be righteousness for everyone who believes." Like the English "end," *telos* can be translated as either "point of cessation" or "goal"; does Paul mean that Christ will bring the covenant of law to an end, or that Christ will constitute the goal of that law *for gentiles*? The interpretation of individual passages sometimes also comes down to whether Paul is speaking principally about Christ or God. For example, in Rom. 9:33, Paul quotes Isa. 8:14-15; 28:16.

> See, I am laying in Zion a stone that will make people stumble, a rock that will make them fall, and whoever believes in him will not be put to shame.

Is Paul referring here to Christ, as Christian tradition has generally held, or, like the Isaiah passages he quotes, to *God's* role in establishing Jerusalem? Note here that the Greek pronoun for "him" could equally be "*it*," that is, the stone (a masculine noun in Greek). Which is the center of Paul's vision, Christ or God? Is it necessary for Jews to have faith *in Christ*, or faith *in the promises of God for gentiles*? The radical new-perspective scholars point out that in Romans, Paul speaks of both.

Quite often, we see that the debate narrows to a microanalysis of individual verses. Indeed, interpretation can only proceed one passage at a time, and yet, if at each stop alternative understandings are possible, then the decision about the whole becomes more difficult to adjudicate. But for this, as for any important and difficult issue, the positions of scholars and of laypeople will likely not be based on "decoding" one or two passages, but rather on general dispositions to the texts. However, it is possible that the undisputed letters of Paul, really only about seventy-five pages in the English translations, simply do not unambiguously reveal Paul's view on this question. That in itself would still be news. If the supersessionist position were really so central to Paul's theology, should it not be easy to establish it in the letters without question? If the overall impression of ambiguity is sustained, does that not at least suggest that the assurance with which earlier interpreters spoke of Paul in supersessionist ways was unwarranted? If one sets aside the *later* Christian tradition on supersessionism, does the same view disappear in Paul's letters?

The issues found in the Gospel of John have also come under scrutiny. Unlike Matthew, which focuses its polemic stridently on the Pharisees, John equally insistently refers to opponents as "Jews"—*Ioudaioi* in Greek—which can also be translated "Judeans" (that is, those from Judea, where

Jerusalem was located). How does one explain the intense anti-Judaism of John, where it is stated that *Ioudaioi* are the "children of the devil" (8:44)? Was the audience of John an "introversionist sect," which turned the promise of salvation inward to a small group of followers who no longer identified with the *Ioudaioi*, meaning Jews who revered the temple authorities in Judea (Wills, 133–66; Reinhartz, 25; Kittredge, 49–63)? Or is the Galilean origin of the Gospel of John at play here, and should *Ioudaioi* be translated not as "Jews" but as "Judeans," those members of Israel who lived in Judea and exercised some control over the members of Israel (which may include Samaritans) who lived in Galilee and Samaria? Whatever sociological theory is asserted to explain the *Ioudaioi* in the Gospel of John, the text seems to express a polemical separation that is different from Matthew on one hand or Paul on the other. The distinction between good and bad people, or even good and evil people, is even stronger in John than in Paul or Matthew.

For twenty-first-century audiences, it is difficult to come to terms with the strong polemics voiced in our sacred texts. Should modern readers, both Christian and Jewish, simply conclude that the ancient writers of the now-sacred texts took group identity too far? Consider a passage from the Hebrew Bible and a passage from the New Testament.

> When the Lord your God brings you into the land that you are about to enter . . . and he clears away . . . the Hittites, the Girgashites, the Amorites, the Canaanites, the Perizzites, the Hivites, and the Jebusites, . . . then you must utterly destroy them. (Deut. 7:1-2)

> You [Jews] are from your father the devil, and you choose to do your father's desires. He was a murderer from the beginning and does not stand in the truth. . . . He is a liar and the father of lies. (John 8:44, referred to above)

One can imagine asking, "If you knew a Hittite well (or a Jew well), would you say that?" (On the ambiguity of these designations, see Wills, 21–51, 133–66.) But the many varieties of early followers of Jesus means that *different* lines were being drawn in the sand to differentiate groups, and while they defined the fissures between most Jews and followers of Jesus, they also defined serious breaches among different followers of Jesus. Would Paul, Matthew, or John have placed *each other* among the saved, or among the damned?

The Gospel of Mark as a Test Case

At the same time that bold new assessments were being raised in regard to the relations of Jews and followers of Jesus in Matthew, Paul, and John, there was relatively little rethinking of the situation in the Gospel of Mark, and this Gospel could become a test case for the *old* view. It has long been assumed that, *regardless of the original meaning of Paul's letters*, Mark understood Paul as Paul's followers did. The following assumptions seemed secure:

1. Mark was influenced by Paul and inherited a Pauline doctrine of faith.
2. Mark reflected a mission that was like Paul's; in Mark, Jesus moved into gentile territory to demonstrate an openness to gentile converts (Mark 7–9).

3. Mark must have been a gentile, because there are inaccuracies in regard to Jewish practice in the passion narratives and elsewhere, and Mark explains basic Jewish practices, often inaccurately (7:3-4).

4. Jesus is depicted as rejecting kosher laws across the board (7:19).

Now, however, these conclusions have also been challenged. First, it is not at all clear that Mark knew Paul's theology of faith *in contrast to law*. Faith was a constant element in the Hebrew Bible and also in the Jewish discourse of the period. The Hebrew word *'aman* ("to believe, have faith") and its related forms (in Aramaic as well) can be found behind the use of "amen" in liturgy and are related to the word truth (*'emet*, derived from *'aman*), and to the "faithful ones" (*ne'emanim*) among the Pharisees (*m. Demai* 4:6). In Neh. 9:38, the restored community in Jerusalem joins in a "faith covenant" (*'amanah*). The use of this root by Jews speaking Hebrew or Aramaic, and of the *pist-* root by those speaking Greek, only increases in the Hellenistic period. Thus, although the use of the language of "faith" and "believing" in Mark is pronounced, *it was also common in Judaism*, a fact that is almost totally ignored in assessments of Jewish-Christian relations in the first century. Further, the language of "faith" and "believing" in Mark is not explicitly contrasted with law as Paul would have it; it is used in the same way as other Jews were using it. (Parallels between Mark and Paul are often listed, but the Pauline passages are almost all found in Romans. Were Paul's words in this letter carefully chosen to respond to the *Jewish* discourse on faith in which that community would have been schooled?)

Second, although in Mark, Jesus does move into territories occupied by gentiles, these were also (with one exception, 7:1) part of the ancient borders of Israel. The Maccabees and their descendants had already conquered these lands in order to reestablish the boundaries of ancient Israel; so might we regard Jesus' itinerary in Mark as also reconstituting "Israel"? Jesus also heals gentiles, but so had the prophet Elisha (2 Kings 5); was the latter also "gentilizing" Israel? Third, Mark's Gospel does seem to include many *apparent* inaccuracies concerning Jewish practices, but these, too numerous to mention, are in some cases found in other Jewish texts or taken over in the "Jewish" Gospel Matthew, and other cases are much less clear than once thought (A. Y. Collins).

Last, we come to the argument that has often seemed conclusive: Mark's apparent cancellation of all kosher laws in Jesus' debate with the Pharisees and scribes at 7:1-23. The relevant verses are displayed here side by side with the equivalent section of Matthew. The parallel columns allow one to read Mark's words closely while at the same time noting the differences found in Matthew's treatment of this important issue. (Luke and John do not include this passage.)

Mark 7:1-23 (in part)	Matthew 15:1-20 (in part)
[1] When the Pharisees and some of the scribes who had come from Jerusalem gathered around him, [2] they noticed that some of his disciples were eating with defiled hands, that is, without washing them. [3] For the Pharisees, and all the Jews, do not eat unless they thoroughly wash their hands, thus observing the tradition of the elders; [4] and they do not eat anything from the market unless they wash it; and there are also many other traditions that they observe, the washing of cups, pots, and bronze kettles.	[1] Then Pharisees and scribes came to Jesus from Jerusalem,
[5] So the Pharisees and the scribes asked him, "Why do your disciples not live according to the tradition of the elders, but eat with defiled hands?" [Several scriptural and legal arguments follow here.]	and said, [2] "Why do your disciples break the tradition of the elders? For they do not wash their hands before they eat?" [Several scriptural and legal arguments follow here.]
[14] He called the people to him again and said, [15] "There is nothing outside a person which by going in can defile, but the things which come out are what defile.	[10] He called the people to him and said, [11] "It is not what goes into the mouth that defiles a person, but what comes out of the mouth, this defiles.
[18] Do you not see that whatever goes into a person from outside cannot defile, [19] since it enters not the heart, but the stomach, and goes out into the sewer?" Thus he declared all foods clean [literally, "Thus he cleansed all foods"].	[17] Do you not see that whatever goes into the mouth enters the stomach, and goes out into the sewer?
[20] And he said, "It is what comes out of a person that defiles. [21] For it is from within, from the human heart, that evil intentions come: fornication, theft, murder, [22] adultery, avarice, wickedness, deceit, licentiousness, envy, slander, pride, folly.	[18] But what comes out of the mouth proceeds from the heart, and this is what defiles. [19] For out of the heart come evil intentions, murder, adultery, fornication, theft, false witness, slander.
[23] All these evil things come from within, and they defile a person."	[20] These are what defile a person, but to eat with unwashed hands does not defile."

Mark's words here are traditionally interpreted in a "Pauline" way, that is, that Jewish law now no longer applies among the followers of Jesus. However, challenges to that interpretation of this passage have also arisen. Jesus' debate with Pharisees about eating food with unwashed hands may not be a rejection of Jewish law but a debate *within* Judaism. Mark here may actually have Jesus endorse the majority Jewish position against the stricter Pharisees. Was the view Mark attributes to Jesus actually more typical of Jewish practice in the first century than the Pharisees'? One also notices that the run-on sentence in 7:3-4 may have resulted from the combination of a simple, and accurate, statement about Pharisees and additional comments about practices of "all the Jews" that were added later. (Note that these verses are not present in Matthew.) But Mark's explanation of Jewish customs may also not be as out of place in Jewish discourse as once thought (A. Y. Collins, 345; Regev 2000, 180–81, 188–89). To be sure, the passage indicates (if it was not inserted later in its entirety) that Mark is including gentiles in the audience of the Gospel, but it does not neces-sarily reveal a gentile *author*. Mark's reference to the practices of "all the Jews" certainly seems to distance himself from them, but we encounter here a hidden problem with English that affects interpretation. An English-speaking Jew might say, "All Jews do such-and-such," but not "All *the* Jews do such-and-such." The English definite article has the power in this construction to separate off the group in question and to distance the speaker from the group. In Greek, however, usage of the definite article is often quite different from English, and it is not clear that it would distance the speaker in this way. Did Mark mean, "All Jews wash their hands"—which could include Mark—or "All *the* Jews wash their hands"—which seems to distance the Markan Jesus from the Jews?

The last half of this passage has also been reassessed. The central statement—"There is nothing outside a person which by going in can defile, but the things which come out are what defile"—may not be a rejection of purity concerns, as long supposed, but simply an insistence that *moral* purity is as important, or even more important, than *ritual* purity. The prioritizing of moral motives over observance was well known in the Jewish background (Mic. 6:6-8, Hosea 6:6), but the insistence that Jewish observance remains in effect as well is also found in New Testament texts: "You Phari-sees tithe mint and rue and herbs of all kinds, and neglect justice and the love of God. It is these you ought to have practiced, *without neglecting the others*" (Luke 11:42; Klawans, 147–48).

But Mark also broadens the discussion by the insertion of 7:19c, "thus he declared all foods clean" (*katharizōn panta ta brōmata*). This awkward and intrusive phrase, which does not appear in Matthew (the section as a whole, as noted, is lacking in Luke and John), may have been inserted later in the textual history of Mark (Booth, 49–50, 62–65), but even if these were Mark's own words, it is also possible that this clause has an entirely different meaning. The Greek literally says, "Jesus *cleansed* all foods," but translators, stumped by what that would mean, have chosen a paraphrasing translation that made perfect sense in the twentieth-century consensus: "Jesus declared all foods clean." This translation means that the "Pauline" Jesus was instituting a new policy canceling all kosher laws. However, in the ancient period, it was sometimes stated, in both Jewish and Christian texts, that at the end of time, for the special, saved community, there would be a *cleansing* of foods, vessels, or people. From Ezekiel (36:22-31) to Zechariah (14:16, 20-21) to *1 Enoch* (10:17—11:2) to Qumran (1QS 4:20-21), there are discussions of a shower of purity on the saved community, however that community is described (see also *Jub.* 1:17, 23; 4:26; 50:5; *Abot R. Nat. B* 42; *b. Erub.*

100b; Regev 2000; 2004). Indeed, with this notion in mind, one may look at other passages in Mark as well. Consider Jesus' healing of a leper, phrased in terms of "cleansing" (the *kathar* root in Greek).

> A leper came to him begging him, and kneeling he said to him, "If you choose, you can cleanse me [*katharisai*, cf. 7:19, discussed above]." Moved with pity, Jesus stretched out his hand and touched him, and said to him, "I do choose. Be cleansed [*katharistheti*]!" Immediately the leprosy left him, and he was cleansed [*ekatharisthe*]. After sternly warning him he sent him away at once, saying to him, "See that you say nothing to anyone; but go, show yourself to the priest, and offer for your cleansing [*katharismos*] what Moses commanded, as a testimony to them." (Mark 1:40-44)

Although this passage is often understood, from the perspective of *later* Christianity, as the rejection of purity laws about leprosy, a close reading reveals that Jesus miraculously returns the leper to a state of being clean, but does nothing to alter the Jewish laws concerning purity. In fact, the man is instructed to go to the temple to make the offering that Moses commanded (Leviticus 14). The point is important. Technically, in Jewish law, a leper is not pure until after the temple offering is made, but the point of Mark's story is that purity is now made miraculously available as an eschatological event (see Regev 2000; 2004). In the similar but not identical case in the Hebrew Bible mentioned above (2 Kings 5), the prophet heals Naaman the Syrian from his leprosy. But just as it is not generally suggested in Jewish or Christian tradition that Elisha is opening Israel to gentiles, it is also not suggested that he is canceling Jewish purity laws concerning leprosy. And Mark is not the only Christian text to describe an end-time cleansing of the saints; in an otherwise puzzling passage, Paul finds a new cleansing in the community members themselves; note the juxtaposition of "cleansing" with holiness language (the *hag-* root in Greek):

> The unbelieving husband is made holy [*hegiastai*] through his wife, and the unbelieving wife is made holy through her husband. Otherwise, your children would be unclean [*akatharta*], but as it is, they are holy [*hagia*]. (1 Cor. 7:14; see Johnson Hodge)

So just as the leper in Mark 1:40-45 is *cleansed*—purity rules are *not* abrogated—and in 1 Corinthians 7 an unbelieving spouse is made holy and the children cleansed, so in Mark 7 it is likely that in anticipation of an eschatological change, Jesus *cleanses* foods, as the Greek actually states. Thus, even if this verse was in Mark's original text, it may not have meant that Jewish kosher laws were being rejected, but that for this community, there is at the end of time a dispensation of purity that overwhelms impurity, and also defeats "impure spirits," Mark's more Jewish term for "demons." If, as Zech. 14:20 says, all vessels can be rendered pure at the end of time, and if, as 1 Corinthians 7 says, spouses can be rendered holy, why not lepers in the community, and foods? At the end of time, all heaven breaks loose, but only on the holy community, the *hagioi* ("saints"). There is a division of humanity for a simultaneous cleansing and judgment. The canceling of Jewish food laws, which is how Acts 10, for instance, has been traditionally interpreted, has been too hastily read back into Mark (see also Rom. 14:20).

This passage, then, which had been treated by scholars as a clear confirmation of the Pauline theology at the center of Mark, is much more ambiguous than was once supposed. Paul's letters were often used to justify a gentile mission and identity, but was Mark part of that development (as were Luke and Acts), or was it, like Matthew, part of that segment of the movement, perhaps the larger part, that had not abrogated Jewish law? What was once considered unlikely in regard to Mark now seems quite possible.

Conclusion

A common theme here is that Matthew, Paul, John, and Mark were likely much more rooted in Jewish tradition than Christians have generally assumed. The net effect of these newer investigations is to make discussions among Jews, Christians, and others much more unsettled, but also much richer. Much uncertainty has arisen about each old consensus, and this may seem daunting to contemporary audiences. But there is now a possibility of a wholly *new* dialogue, one that goes back to both the Jewish and Christian sources and asks again what the texts might have meant and what the relations were—both within each body and between the two bodies. The seeds of modern anti-Judaism and the Holocaust can still be seen in some of the ancient texts, but the varied relations also reveal the truth that the story is complex, and it includes many alternative visions of how religious subgroups could respond to each other. There is not just one blueprint for "the relations of Judaism and Christianity" in the first century.

Works Cited

Bauer, Walter. 1934. *Rechtgläubigkeit und Ketzerei im ältesten Christentum.* Tübingen: Mohr. Translated as *Orthodoxy and Heresy in Earliest Christianity.* Philadelphia: Fortress Press, 1979.

Becker, Adam H., and Annette Yoshiko Reed, eds. 2007. *The Ways That Never Parted: Jews and Christians in Late Antiquity and the Early Middle Ages.* Minneapolis: Fortress Press.

Booth, Roger P. 1986. *Jesus and the Laws of Purity: Tradition History and Legal History in Mark 7.* Sheffield: JSOT Press.

Boyarin, Daniel. 2004. *Border Lines: The Partition of Judaeo-Christianity.* Philadelphia: University of Pennsylvania Press.

Cohen, Shaye J. D. 2006. *From the Maccabees to the Mishnah.* 2nd ed. Louisville: Westminster John Knox.

Collins, Adela Yarbro. 2007. *Mark: A Commentary.* Hermeneia. Minneapolis: Fortress Press.

Collins, John J. 2000. *Between Athens and Jerusalem: Jewish Identity in the Hellenistic Diaspora.* 2nd ed. Grand Rapids: Eerdmans.

Dunn, James D. G. 1983. "The New Perspective on Paul." *BJRL* 65:95–122.

———. 1991. *The Partings of the Ways: Between Christianity and Judaism and Their Significance for the Character of Christianity.* London: SCM.

Eisenbaum, Pamela. 2009. *Paul Was Not a Christian: The Real Message of a Misunderstood Apostle.* New York: HarperOne.

Foltz, Richard. 2010. *Religions of the Silk Road: Premodern Patterns of Globalization.* 2nd ed. New York: Palgrave Macmillan.

Fredriksen, Paula. 1995. "Did Jesus Oppose Purity Laws?" *BR* 11:18–25, 42–48.

Hare, Douglas R. A. 1967. *The Theme of Jewish Persecution of Christians in the Gospel according to St. Matthew.* Cambridge: Cambridge University Press.

Harrington, Daniel J. 1991. *The Gospel of Matthew*. Sacra pagina. Collegeville, MN: Liturgical Press.

Johnson Hodge, Caroline. 2007. *If Sons, then Heirs: A Study of Kinship and Ethnicity in the Letters of Paul*. Oxford: Oxford University Press.

———. 2010. "Married to an Unbeliever: Households, Hierarchies, and Holiness in 1 Corinthians 7:12-16." *HTR* 103:1–25.

Kittredge, Cynthia Briggs. 2007. *Conversations with Scripture: The Gospel of John*. Harrisburg, PA: Morehouse.

Klawans, Jonathan. 2000. *Impurity and Sin in Ancient Judaism*. Oxford: Oxford University Press.

Levine, Amy-Jill. 2006. *The Misunderstood Jew: The Church and the Scandal of the Jewish Jesus*. San Francisco: HarperSanFrancisco.

Nickelsburg, George W. E. 2005. *Jewish Literature between the Bible and the Mishnah: A Historical and Literary Introduction*. 2nd ed. Minneapolis: Fortress Press.

Novak, David. 2004. "The Covenant in Rabbinic Thought." In *Two Faiths, One Covenant? Jewish and Christian Identity in the Presence of the Other*, edited by Eugene B. Korn, 65–80. Lanham, MD: Rowman & Littlefield.

Regev, Eyal. 2000. "Pure Individualism: The Idea of Non-Priestly Purity in Ancient Judaism." *JSJ* 31:176–202.

———. 2004. "Moral Impurity and the Temple in Early Christianity in Light of Ancient Greek Practice and Qumranic Ideology." *HTR* 97:377–402.

Reinhartz, Adele. 2001. *Befriending the Beloved Disciple: A Jewish Reading of the Gospel of John*. New York: Continuum.

Robinson, James M., and Helmut Koester. 1971. *Trajectories through Early Christianity*. Philadelphia: Fortress Press.

Sanders, E. P. 1977. *Paul and Palestinian Judaism: A Comparison of Patterns of Religion*. Philadelphia: Fortress Press.

Sanders, Jack T. 1993. *Schismatics, Sectarians, Dissidents, Deviants: The First One Hundred Years of Jewish-Christian Relations*. London: SCM.

Schürer, Emil. 1886–1890. *Geschichte des jüdischen Volkes im Zeitalter Jesu Christi*. 2 vols. Leipzig: Hinrichs.

Smiga, George Michael. 1992. *Pain and Polemic: Anti-Judaism in the Gospels*. Mahwah, NJ: Paulist.

Soulen, R. Kendall. 1996. *The God of Israel and Christian Theology*. Minneapolis: Fortress Press.

Townsend, John. 1979. "The Gospel of John and the Jews: The Story of a Religious Divorce." In *Antisemitism and the Foundations of Christianity*, edited by Alan T. Davies, 72–97. New York: Paulist.

Vermes, Géza. 1991. *Jesus the Jew: A Historian's Reading of the Gospels*. Philadelphia: Fortress Press.

Wills, Lawrence M. 2008. *Not God's People: Insiders and Outsiders in the Biblical World*. Lanham, MD: Rowman & Littlefield.

Wilson, Stephen G. 1995. *Related Strangers: Jews and Christians, 70–170 C.E.* Minneapolis: Fortress Press.

ROOTLESSNESS AND COMMUNITY IN CONTEXTS OF DIASPORA

Margaret Aymer

Rootlessness wanders through Christian imagination today as it has for thousands of years. Even today, hymns proclaiming "this world is not my home," and "I am a poor pilgrim of sorrow, I'm lost in this wide world alone," are sung by women and men whose families can trace their ancestry on any given land mass back multiple generations. Often, the Hebrew Scriptures are credited as the origin of themes of rootlessness, wandering, pilgrimage, and dispersion. However, the New Testament also contains themes of rootlessness and of the creation of community in times of diaspora.

Perhaps it takes an uprooted soul to notice these themes, this ongoing trope in the New Testament. Perhaps it takes the eyes of a woman between cultures, not fully American, and unquestionably not Caribbean—except when I unquestionably am—who emigrated as a child and has functioned as an interpreter of cultures for both my home and host cultures. Some Asian Americans call this the phenomenon of being "the 1.5 generation," the generation that stands between the deep memory of the first-generation immigrant who grew to adulthood in the country of origin and the deep acculturation of the second generation, born in the country of migration. As 1.5-generation people, we stand between homelands, always on a journey, negotiating when possible, turning away when endangered, forging a third way when necessary, and always being in the midst of creating and re-creating culture in ways that are at once rooted in the old, transplanted into a strange land, and bearing hybrid, sometimes nourishing fruit that may at times be unrecognizable as the result of transplantation.

I often read the New Testament with 1.5-generation eyes, eyes not only of an immigrant but also of an immigrant of color. And when I do, I notice that many of these New Testament texts bear marks of migration: evidence of negotiating one's way between home and host cultures, and of the work of forging culture and making meaning in the midst of displacement.

(Re)Considering the History and Rhetoric of New Testament Writings

To argue that the New Testament writings bear marks of migration is to make both a historical and a rhetorical argument. The historical argument is grounded in the accepted historical reconstruction of the creation of these writings by the majority of scholars. The rhetorical argument is grounded in the way in which the authors describe their displacement, their own rootlessness, and that of their community; and how they use that rhetoric to construct strategies of interaction with the wider world. Take, for example, the general consensus that Mark is the oldest canonical Gospel, written after the siege of Jerusalem (of which Mark 13 is understood as description after the fact rather than foretelling), and that it was not written in Judea or Galilee. Already that history suggests displacement, the Gospel narrative written in migration. This would not be the case if the story were an invention out of the imagination of "Mark" the Gospel writer. But if, as biblical scholars have claimed, "Mark" uses oral sources as well as written ones to construct a narrative that he believes to be factually true at least in part, then the ultimate origin of those oral sources would have had to be persons from Judea or Galilee whose bodies, or stories, had migrated to Mark's location. Thus we know with some certainty that at the very least, the stories are migratory.

Mark gives us more clues to suggest that the cultural home of his narrative is not his current audience. He includes and, of even more importance, he *translates* a number of Aramaic sayings of Jesus, among them *Talitha kum* (5:41), *Ephphatha* (7:34), and the cry from the cross, *Eloi, Eloi, lama sabachthani* (15:34). That there is Aramaic in Mark should come as no surprise. After all, Aramaic was one of the languages of Judea and the Galilee. The surprise is Mark's need to translate the Aramaic. This suggests, first, that either Mark or his oral source knows Aramaic, for the short passages are translated correctly. This makes Mark at least bilingual; the Gospel of Mark was composed in Greek. Second, it suggests that Mark is writing to an audience that is, at most, only partially literate in Aramaic.

All of these are traces, hints of the possible origins of the Gospel of Mark, which are, in reality, largely lost. However, these traces suggest a Gospel written in displacement and a writer bridging the distance between a story perhaps told in Aramaic and one written in Greek with Aramaic traces, translating the first generation to the second generation. If this is the case, Mark's Gospel not only tells the good news of Jesus Christ but also, like the older exilic writings of the Hebrew Scriptures, tells a story about a homeland and a home culture no longer accessible to a generation that may be in danger of forgetting. It is an immigrant's tale, a tale of which, if Mark 16:8 can be believed, Mark alone is the only faithful teller.

The other Gospels and the Acts of the Apostles might take issue with Mark's monopoly on faithful discipleship. As second- and third-generation readers (see Luke 1:1-2), they take the traditions of the migrants and rework them for their contemporaries, not unlike the transformation of English plum pudding into Caribbean Christmas cake or the twenty-first-century hip-hop recensions of Bob Marley's twentieth-century reggae hits. Some translation still needs to take place. Some original language still remains in place. And depending on the nature of the community, more of the home culture (Matthew) or more of the host culture (Luke) is emphasized. But the history remains the same: communities of persons outside of Judea and Galilee, and distant from the events of Jesus' life, inheriting a story told and retold in migration, a story possibly even recounted and written by migrants.

With the writings of Paul, one can demonstrate a case for their historical marks of migration much more simply. Paul is, after all, a wandering preacher writing to assemblies in cities and villages outside of his natal Tarsus. This alone is enough to make these writings migrant writings. But Paul, too, is engaging in translation: in this case, not translation from Aramaic to Greek, but the cultural work of translating a primarily Jerusalem-based, Jewish sect into an assembly that denies the distinctiveness between Jew and Greek, slave and free, perhaps even man and woman (Galatians 3). This is an assembly not just for gentiles, but even more powerfully for Diaspora Jews, those who for generations have lived away from but never completely separated from Jerusalem and Galilee. This group would have maintained some traditions and let others go, particularly others that would have made them peculiar or abhorrent to their majority-gentile neighbors. Indeed, by the time he writes to Philippi, Paul radically begins to imagine these assemblies not merely as bodies of believers gathered to pray but also as political entities in which those assembled had status, citizenship, and inheritance (Phil. 3:20). Paul's writing bears marks not only of his own migrant life but also of the diasporic migrant lives of his communities, and of a migrant imagination that forms new communities of migrants—persons living in one place with their citizenship in another.

Paul's interpreters, those who wrote the deuteropauline and Pastoral Epistles, are similarly involved in a work of translation: translation as cultural accommodation of the majority culture. Once Paul's apocalyptic insistence on the imminent return of Christ proves to be premature, these interpreters, perhaps a generation removed from Paul's migrant fervor, use their second-generation status to re-create a Christianity less dangerous to the empire in which it must survive.

Like Paul, John of Patmos seems to be a migrant, perhaps an involuntary migrant, if we take his self-description in Revelation 1:9 as evidence that he is in exile. His epistolary apocalypse then takes on the work of migrant writing, a writing both in migration (he is on Patmos) and to migrant communities. The letter does what John can no longer do, moving from place to place encouraging communities to hold fast and to remember that their final dwelling place is not the place where they currently abide and that their allegiances are not to the beasts of land and sea or to the dragon who gives them power. Rather, their allegiances are to the lion/slaughtered lamb on the throne and their true home is the new Jerusalem, which will come down from the new heaven on the new earth. They are thus to live as citizens of "an-other" place, as migrants in an evil world, waiting, like the souls under the altar, until all is accomplished and their nomadic God migrates to the new Jerusalem and pitches the divine tent among them (Rev. 21:3).

The writings attributed to John the Gospel writer and his community (the Gospel and the three pseudonymous epistles) betray a similar orientation to the world in which the community lives.

John 9, famously, has been held up by Raymond Brown and others as a narrative of the community's forced exile, its forced (e)migration from its community of origin (the synagogue/formative Judaisms) to an-other place, a location somehow outside of both "world" and "home" (John 1). Those who leave this other place are castigated in the first of the Johannine Epistles as antichrists. Within the Johannine community, forced migration on the basis of belief is virtuous; voluntary migration out of the community is satanic.

Migration as an underlying physical and/or rhetorical concern is thus evident in many of the New Testament writings. However, only two make it explicit: James and 1 Peter. James may well be a letter to, rather than by, migrant communities. Indeed, James's letter, addressed "to the twelve tribes in the Diaspora," strongly resembles other such Jerusalem-to-Diaspora missives sent by the Sanhedrin contemporary with this writing (Bauckham, 19–20). James's sermon-in-a-letter, or homiletic epistle, reminds those outside of the immediate influence of Jerusalem of the particular ethics expected of those who gather in synagogues (James 2), claim to follow the "royal law" (2:8), and consider themselves to be followers of the Lord Jesus Christ (2:1). Primarily, these communities should not resemble the stain of the world, but should be separate entities marked by an ethical concern for the workers, the widows and orphans, and the poor (1:27). However, they are not to consider their status permanent. They will continue in their involuntary migration only until the Parousia of the Lord (5:7). At that time, the injustices experienced in their exile will be adjudicated by the Lord of Sabaoth (5:4).

First Peter takes a similar tack. Writing specifically to those Diasporan exiles in Asia Minor, the advice of 1 Peter to these migrant communities is twofold. First, the author insists on the identity of these migrants as displaced royalty, exiled priests, and a people belonging to God (1 Peter 2). Their dispersal does not change their identity. Rather, it requires prudent interaction with the dominating culture of their exile until they can regain their inheritance as heirs to the kingdom of God. Second, the author requires that the migrant congregation act in ways that would be considered blameless during the time of their exile. For this author, this means that the community of faith must adopt even the norms of the kyriarchy of their community of exile. "Kyriarchy," a neologism coined by Elisabeth Schüssler Fiorenza, describes "the rule of the emperor, lord, slave master, husband, or the elite freeborn, propertied, educated gentleman to whom disenfranchised men and all wo/men were subordinated" (Schüssler Fiorenza, 9). Acceptance of such norms moved 1 Peter's Christian community away from less hierarchical structures such as those intimated by Galatians 3 and toward the more accommodationist stance of the second generation of the Pauline school. It was, among other things, a way for these migrants to "fit in." This kyriarchy-as-camouflage was, of course, counseled uncritically by a member of the literate class (or at least one who could pay for an amanuensis). Those who bore its burden most profoundly were the migrant community's least powerful members: women, children, and slaves.

Other New Testament writings give us far fewer clues about their migrant status. Yet even these reference comings, goings, and their impact on community identity. The pseudonymous letters of 2 Peter and Jude, for example, are unlikely to be of Galilean or Judean origin, although this is impossible to know. As such, they would also be migrant writings, strictly speaking. However, their discourse focuses less on the community's migrant nature and more on the danger of the immigration of other people—with other ideas about Christian identity—into their communities (2 Pet. 2:3; Jude 4). Even without a specific focus on the community's movement or clear evidence of displacement, these writings seek to create and strengthen communities that are outside the general population (e.g., not pagan, not Jewish, not licit), and there is still a sense of migration about them.

Hebrews, of course, stands as the New Testament enigma, giving its readers very few clues about authorship, dating, placement, or any other historical data. Yet even if one argues for Hebrews as an early Judean or Galilean document (as does DeSilva in this volume), there is still an overlay of migration in its rhetoric. For even if one depicts Hebrews as a letter/sermon written to, by, and in Judea or the Galilee, one cannot escape the trope of community-as-migrants and the rhetorical journey toward rest that wends its way through the homiletics of the unknown preacher. Hebrews too, although less explicit, bears the marks of migration.

Thus a phenomenon often overlooked marks at least a significant plurality of New Testament literature. The bulk of it, and perhaps all of it, could be categorized as migrant writing. As a result, although rootlessness is most frequently considered a concern of James and 1 Peter, and perhaps to a lesser extent of the rhetorics of Hebrews and Philippians, in truth, underlying all of the New Testament canon is a sense of rootlessness, of dispersion, and of the need to survive in a place that is not home, whether physically or culturally. The rest of this essay seeks to explore the implications of this underlying rootlessness, both in the New Testament writings and for those who appropriate these writings as Scriptures.

New Testament Writings as Diaspora Spaces

What difference might it make if the New Testament writings were considered to be migrant writings? Here, a brief consideration of theory about "diaspora spaces" might be helpful. Sociologist Avtar Brah proposes that diaspora space is that place

> where multiple subject positions are juxtaposed, contested, proclaimed or disavowed; where the permitted and the prohibited perpetually interrogate; and where the accepted and the transgressive imperceptibly mingle even while these syncretic forms may be disclaimed in the name of purity and tradition. [It is a space where] *tradition is itself continually invented even as it may be hailed as originating from the mists of time.* (Brah, 208, emphasis added)

This thick description reflects the struggle and promise of diaspora spaces, those spaces where migrants and host communities enter into the never-ending dance of self-definition. But what does it have to do with the New Testament? Simply this: If the New Testament writings are, indeed, migrant writings, these migrant rhetorics might be expected to create texts that are diaspora spaces, texts/spaces in which migrant writers and migrant communities struggle with the nature of faithfulness to their understanding of the new Christian movements while living in a majority-pagan world.

So, if the New Testament writings are migrant writings, one might expect to note the juxtaposition, contestation, proclamation, and/or disavowal of multiple subject positions (Brah, 208). Perhaps the quintessential example of such struggle is bound up in the person and history of Saul/Paul of Tarsus. He names himself a Jew, born of the tribe of Benjamin, circumcised and a Pharisee (Phil. 3:5). However, he is also named a citizen of the pagan, primarily Greek-speaking Roman Empire, and claims that status by birth rather than through financial or military transaction (Acts 22:25-28). He is Saul, named after the first king of Judea, but without fanfare becomes Paul as he begins his gentile evangelism, no doubt because his Hebrew name is transliterated *saulos* in Greek (Acts 13:9), and *saulos* is an adjective that describes "the *loose, wanton* gait of courtesans or Bacchantes" (Liddell and Scott, s.v. "*saulos*"). This is a person who claims to himself and to his entire community, Jew and Greek, the promises of the particularly Jewish Abrahamic covenant (Gal. 3:1-9). This same person claims to become "all things to all people" for the sake of his Christian evangelism (1 Cor. 9:22).

Of course, Paul is not alone in this place of juxtaposition, of negotiation between cultures. Other characters carry two names, two identities: consider Tabitha/Dorcas and John/Mark (Acts 9; 12). Neither is Paul alone is standing between cultures and negotiating different subject positions: consider Joanna, the wife of Chuza, Herod's steward, who stands between Roman client privilege in Herod's household and her support of Jesus—who would, no doubt, have been understood as a wandering Jewish prophet and social critic, and who was killed for sedition against the Roman Empire (Luke 8). However, not every New Testament figure makes the same choices that Paul makes when faced with this negotiation between cultures. The author of the Epistle of James, for instance, in his counsel to the "twelve tribes of the diaspora" (James 1:1), calls for withdrawal and self-preservation (1:27). Similarly, the seer on Patmos island, echoing the prophet's jeremiad, calls his people to "come out" of Babylon (Rev. 18:4, cf. Jer. 51:45). In a different response to the same question of positionality with respect to one's own culture and to "the world," John's Gospel suggests a third way, a way that is neither of the world nor of the home culture of the migrant outsiders. This way is signified by the Johannine phrase, "sons of God," and represents the formation of an-other position in society (John 1).

In addition to matters of the subject's positionality, New Testament writings also reveal the ongoing interrogation of permitted and prohibited, the mingling of accepted and transgressive, and ultimately the creation of syncretic forms that Brah describes as characteristics of diaspora space. Perhaps the most obvious New Testament example of the interrogation of the permitted and prohibited is the conflict regarding the inclusion of gentiles into the early churches without requiring of them the rite of circumcision. This early church-dividing conflict emerges in many of the undisputed Pauline writings, and differently in the Acts of the Apostles. Paul is usually the anticircumcision champion in his own writings; but the author of Luke-Acts makes Peter the standard-bearer after a theophany and an encounter with a gentile named Cornelius (Acts 10; 15). However, circumcision is not the only New Testament example of the interrogation and re-creation of traditions and forms. The "healing on the Sabbath" crisis seen in many of the Gospels is also part of this ongoing interrogation of what is and is not permitted to be done by faithful people during the Sabbath rest. Table fellowship is yet another example of the New Testament interrogation of permitted and prohibited: not merely who was admitted to the table (thus the Syrophoenician woman's protest in Mark 7) but even more the question of whether meat was to be served (1 Corinthians 8; Revelation 2). After all, meat was almost always sacrificed to the gods, whom Christians and Jews saw as idols. Should, then, Christians eat meat at their symposia, or was this a tacit acceptance of idolatry

(Taussig)? These discussions and debates about the interaction between the permitted and transgressive likely preceded the advent of Christianity among the Jewish migrants in Diaspora around the greater Mediterranean world. However, a new urgency in response to these questions would have been felt after the Roman destruction of the Jerusalem temple in 70 CE. After this destruction of the ritual and political center of Judaism, all claimants to the traditions of Abraham and Moses were in ongoing debates regarding what it might mean to be Jewish in a post-temple diasporic reality. This was not specific to the Gospel writers—or even to Christian writers. The rabbis, too, were beginning to argue about the nature of faithfulness after the fall of the temple.

Circumcision, Sabbath observance, and table fellowship were some of the more blatant ways in which this kind of cultural interrogation between permitted and transgressive took place. Other questions also arose, even if they were more subtly addressed. Should slavery persist in the Christian community, and how could one argue for slavery and yet argue that all have one master (see Col. 3:22-23)? What is the appropriate role of women, particularly of wives, in the early church and how might that intersect with the wider society's understanding of Christians (1 Cor. 7:12-13)? The answers are not straightforward. There are clear moves, particularly among the later Christian writings, to preserve kyriarchy, but the rationale for it is often a subtle rebuke of the dominating structures of the society, even if that rebuke does nothing to alleviate the distress of women, children, or slaves. In Colossians, for example, the command that slaves should obey their masters is followed by counsel to these slaves to perform their tasks "as for the Lord and not for your masters" and a promise that "the wrongdoer will be paid back for whatever wrong has been done" (3:23-25). When there is no rebuke, often there is a call for kyriarchal structuring of society as a mark of purity of the church, purity that makes the otherwise illicit church gathering unassailable by the pagan majority. Thus in 1 Timothy, slaves are told to obey their masters "so that the name of God and the teaching may not be blasphemed" (6:1).

Ultimately, as Brah posits, these ancient migrant writings represent the invention of a new tradition, a tradition we have come to call Christianity. For an example of this, one need look no further than to the name given to this ancient collection of writings: "New Testament." New Testament is an appropriation of the language of the Christian meal found in 1 Cor. 11:25 and Matt. 26:28. While most contemporary translations present this as a "new covenant," the Greek word *diathēkē* can be used either for "covenant" or "testament" (as in "last will and testament," see Galatians 3). So, "New Testament" also means "new covenant," and this in turn cannot be understood without reference to the "old covenant," as the early Christians would have understood it.

For many of these migrant groups, the "old" or Abrahamic covenant between God and God's people functioned not only as tradition but also as a fundamental identifier of the people (*ethnos*—the basis for the concept "ethnic group"). This identifier was traced primarily through the Abrahamic bloodline but could be extended to those who adhered to the identity markers of the covenant, among which were circumcision and the keeping of *kashrut*. So, when Paul and the Gospel writers, quoting the oral tradition that both trace to Jesus, speak of the table meal of the early church as a "new covenant" or "new testament," they are not only relating an important story in the birth of the church but also reinventing tradition, reinventing, not exorcising it. To speak of these stories and letters as a "new *diathēkē*" is both to invent a new way of being a covenant people in the world and to appropriate to the church—made increasingly of people from outside of the Abrahamic bloodline and covenant practices—the ancient *diathēkē* of the Abrahamic era.

Paul and the author of Luke-Acts do not explicitly value the new covenant as superior to the old covenant. However, for the writer to the Hebrews, the "new covenant" or "new testament" clearly supersedes the older. As the author of Hebrews argues, "if that first covenant had been faultless, there would have been no need to look for a second one" (Heb. 8:7). Yet even this assertion is premised on a reinterpretation of the received Scriptures of the people, the "Old Testament." The author to the Hebrews would probably not be claiming to invent tradition any more than would Paul or the author of Luke-Acts. Instead, he would assert that this new covenant is the real, heavenly variety—and thus ultimately more ancient than the human copy. And yet he, like Paul and Luke-Acts, is engaging in that diaspora-space activity of inventing, and claiming ancient provenance for, traditions (Brah).

All of this briefly suggests that, as a collection of primarily migrant writings, the writings of the New Testament can be shown to be diaspora space. The examples above are intended to be representative rather than exhaustive, and self-evident rather than nuanced. The struggle with subject positionality, juxtaposition of the permitted and transgressive, and (re)invention of tradition all appear in some of the most important theological discussions in the collection: discussions around identity, around who and what these Christians will be. However, to say that the New Testament writings constitute a kind of literary diaspora space is not to claim some uniformity of migrant reaction to their host cultures or their home culture. Rather, in the next section, four such possible migrant reactions will be explored, both for their presence or absence within the New Testament canon of writings and for their implications for the migrants who hold them.

New Testament Migrant Strategies

Just because one can argue that the New Testament writings constitute a kind of literary diaspora space, this does not mean that their migrant strategies for life as Christians in migration were identical. Psychologist John Berry's work proves helpful for unpacking these strategies. Berry outlines four migrants' strategies for interacting in their places of migration. He calls these four categories marginalization, separation, assimilation, and integration (Berry, 619).

Three of these strategies are readily observable in the New Testament writings. However, the strategy of assimilation is absent. Assimilation requires that migrants reject their home culture in favor of the host culture in which they find themselves. In twenty-first-century terms, this is the immigrant who intentionally loses her accent, forgets her native language, and claims only the nationality and culture of the nation in which she finds herself. Such assimilation does not exist in the New Testament canon; for, if it did, the writings would be pagan, extolling the virtues of the goddess Roma or the God Zeus/Jupiter. Indeed, an assimilationist of this time would have been found marching with the silversmiths of Ephesus crying out, "Great is Artemis of the Ephesians" (Acts 19:28).

In retaining their monotheistic theologies, both Jews and Christians set themselves apart from the majority-pagan polytheism of the ancient world in ways that were seen as misanthropic by their neighbors, regardless of how much else they mimicked the cultural norms of their host country. There seem to have been some Christians who did aspire to assimilate. To do so, they claimed a higher knowledge that allowed them to participate in pagan religiosity in all of its forms (including eating meat sacrificed to pagan gods) while at the same time claiming the faith of the early Christian church (see 1 Corinthians 7; Revelation 2). Such practices were condemned by those whose writings are preserved in the New Testament as misguided at best and satanic at worst. In fact, no New Testament writing counsels migrant assimilation; none offers a theology of assimilation. In the face of migration, each of the New Testament writings, regardless of how much they appear to mimic the greater society, preserves some separation from that society.

Liminal, or as Berry calls them, "marginalized" migrants take as their response to migration the rejection of both their home culture and their host culture. To determine that a migrant writing counsels such a stance for its audience, one must show *both* its rejection of the home culture, which in the case of early Christianity is Judaism and/or temple culture, *and* its rejection of the host culture in which it finds itself, which in many New Testament writings is simply called "the world." The Gospel according to John contains both of these kinds of counsel for its audience. Consider first this quotation:

> Then Jesus said to the Jews/Judeans who had believed in him, "If you continue in my word, you are truly my disciples; and you will know the truth, and the truth will make you free." They answered him, "We are descendants of Abraham and have never been slaves to anyone. . . .
> . . . Jesus said to them, "If you were Abraham's children, you would be doing what Abraham did, but now you are trying to kill me, a man who has told you the truth that I heard from God. This is not what Abraham did. You are indeed doing what your father does." They said to him, "We are not illegitimate children; we have one father, God himself." Jesus said to them, "If God were your Father, you would love me, for I came from God and now I am here. . . . You are from your father the devil, and you choose to do your father's desires." (John 8:31-33a, 39b-42b, 44a)

In this quotation, part of Jesus' longer diatribe against the "Jews" or the "Judeans," the author of John's Gospel, through Jesus, is disavowing any cultural consonance with those who would seem to be his own people, his home culture. There is no plea, here, that those who self-identify as Jews/ Judeans are of the same family tree as the community to which John is writing. Raymond Brown posits that John's community has been forcibly removed from the synagogue worship out of which it sprang because of its assertion of the messianic nature of Jesus. This seems to suggest that the audience of John's Gospel has separated itself from its home culture.

However, in turning from its home culture, John's audience has not uncritically embraced its host culture. To the contrary. As part of the symposium dialogue in the fifteenth chapter, the Gospel of John records the following teaching of Jesus:

> If the world hates you, be aware that it hated me before it hated you. If you belonged to the world, the world would love you as its own. Because you do not belong to the world, but I have chosen you out of the world—therefore the world hates you. (John 15:18-19)

Here, John's Gospel is depicting Jesus, and through Jesus, his community, as rejected by its host culture, "the world."

In all fairness, a careful reader of John realizes this at the very outset of the Gospel. In the first chapter, John describes the incarnate Word (*logos*) and the community of those who accepted him this way:

> He [the Word/*logos*] was in the world, and the world came into being through him; yet the world did not know him. He came to what was his own, and his own people did not accept him. But to all who received him, who believed in his name, he gave power to become children of God, who were born, not of blood or of the will of the flesh or of the will of man, but of God. (John 1:10-13)

Perhaps no verse better illustrates John's liminality, the stance of a community leader—and thus of a community—rejected both by the world (host culture) and by his own people (home culture). The audience shaped by John's Gospel reflects such a liminality, neither being part of the world nor part of the home culture, a stance that requires the community of faith to strike out into unknown territory, creating an ostensibly brand-new culture apart from either of these cultural anchors.

The Gospel according to John is joined by the Johannine Epistles (1, 2, and 3 John) and possibly the Gospel according to Mark in this liminal stance. However, most New Testament writings do not use this migrant strategy to interact with their home and host cultures. The Epistle of James is illustrative of a more popular strategy: separation. Consider the following:

> Religion that is pure and undefiled before God, the Father, is this: to care for orphans and widows in their distress, and *to keep oneself unstained by the world.* (James 1:27, emphasis added)

and

> Those conflicts and disputes among you, where do they come from? Do they not come from your cravings that are at war within you? You want something and do not have it; so you commit murder. And you covet something and cannot obtain it; so you engage in disputes and conflicts. You do not have, because you do not ask. You ask and do not receive, because you ask wrongly, in order to spend what you get on your pleasures. [Adulterous women]! Do you not know that *friendship with the world is enmity with God?* Therefore whoever wishes to be a friend of the world becomes an enemy of God. (James 4:1-4, emphasis added)

Like the Gospel of John, the Epistle of James stands firm in its dismissal of the world. As in the Gospel of John, so here also the host culture is rejected. However, unlike John, James also says this:

> Do not speak evil against one another, brothers and sisters. Whoever speaks evil against another or judges another, speaks evil against the law and judges the law; but if you judge the law, you are not a doer of the law but a judge. (James 4:11)

Law, in this case, must be understood as Torah, the law of James's own people and community. James thus is not advocating a liminal migrant strategy. Instead, James is advocating a strategy of separation.

Luke Timothy Johnson has demonstrated that James is very possibly a letter written from the earliest Christians in Jerusalem, through the brother of Jesus, to the earliest diasporic communities of Jews/Judeans who have accepted Jesus as the Christ and son of God. From Jerusalem, James writes to migrant Christ-communities still worshiping in synagogues (James 2). He counsels the earliest believers to adopt a migrant strategy of separation: not to adopt gentile ways in their time of migration. Rather, they are to continue their adherence to the law, to be wary of accepting worldly ways, and to keep themselves unstained from the world.

The Epistle of James is not alone in this counsel. The Gospel of Matthew provides a similar strategy to its readers, almost until the Great Commission at the end; and even that commission is less about befriending the world and more about recruiting it to the "home culture" (Matthew 28). Likewise, the enigmatic book Hebrews, with its focus on Christian endurance, seems to counsel separation from the things of the world in favor of the "race that is set before us" (Hebrews 12). Jude, the often overlooked polemic toward the end of the canon, embraces this sort of strategy; and it is central to the theology of the Revelation to John with its admonition to "come out of" Babylon (Revelation 18). In each of these cases, the migrant strategy of separation calls the community of faith back to its roots and away from the world.

Liminality and separation define strategies in some of the more pivotal New Testament writings. However, the predominant migrant strategy within the literary diaspora space called the New Testament is accommodation. Consider, for example, these quotations from the writings of Paul of Tarsus:

> As many of you as were baptized into Christ have clothed yourselves with Christ. There is no longer Jew or Greek, there is no longer slave or free, there is no longer male and female; for all of you are one in Christ Jesus. And if you belong to Christ, then you are Abraham's offspring, heirs according to the promise. (Gal. 3:27-29)

and

> To the Jews I became as a Jew, in order to win Jews. To those under the law I became as one under the law (though I myself am not under the law) so that I might win those under the law. To those outside the law I became as one outside the law (though I am not free from God's law but am under Christ's law) so that I might win those outside the law. To the weak I became weak, so that I might win the weak. I have become all things to all people, that I might by all means save some. (1 Cor. 9:20-22)

These writings indicate a shift in strategy. Paul's overt inclusion of persons both from within and outside his own migrant culture, and his willingness to accommodate gentile inclusion in his ministry, suggests that he does not advocate a total avoidance of the gentile world. However, Paul simultaneously claims that his mixed community of Jews/Judeans and gentiles, a community comprising migrant Jesus-believers, somehow inherits the benefits reserved specifically for the Jews/Judeans: the covenant blessings of Abraham (Galatians 3). Paul thus not only invites "the world" in but also continues to embrace some of his home culture, a culture steeped in the Abrahamic covenant and the Mosaic law.

This Pauline migrant strategy I have termed accommodation, following sociologist Margaret Gibson, rather than using Berry's term *integration* (Berry, 618; Gibson, 20). According to Gibson, accommodation is marked by "the deliberate preservation of the homeland culture, albeit in an adapted form more suitable to life in the host country" (Gibson, 20–21). To argue that Paul is engaged in accommodation and not integration is to argue that he has deliberately preserved the Jewish narrative while adapting it so that faith communities may include gentiles. The result is an uneasy tension of a migrant strategy that both accepts and critiques home and host cultures. This uneasy tension is most clearly evident in Romans 12 and 13. In chapter 12, Paul famously counsels, "Do not be conformed to this world, but be transformed by the renewing of your minds, so that you may discern what is the will of God—what is good and acceptable and perfect" (Rom. 12:2). However, in Romans 13, this same Paul calls for a certain amount of conformity to the world *as a way to fully comply with the requirements of the Mosaic law.* Here, I quote Paul at length:

> Let every person be subject to the governing authorities; for there is no authority except from God, and those authorities that exist have been instituted by God. Therefore whoever resists authority resists what God has appointed, and those who resist will incur judgment. For rulers are not a terror to good conduct, but to bad. Do you wish to have no fear of the authority? Then do what is good, and you will receive its approval; for it is God's servant for your good. But if you do what is wrong, you should be afraid, for the authority does not bear the sword in vain! It is the servant of God to execute wrath on the wrongdoer. Therefore one must be subject, not only because of wrath but also because of conscience. For the same reason you also pay taxes, for the authorities are God's servants, busy with this very thing. Pay to all what is due them—taxes to whom taxes are due, revenue to whom revenue is due, respect to whom respect is due, honor to whom honor is due. Owe no one anything, except to love one another; for the one who loves another has fulfilled the law. The commandments, "You shall not commit adultery; You shall not murder; You shall not steal; You shall not covet"; and any other commandment, are summed up in this word, "Love your neighbor as yourself." Love does no wrong to a neighbor; therefore, love is the fulfilling of the law. (Rom. 13:1-10)

Despite the counsel in Rom. 12:1-2, one must read Romans 13 as advice to conform to the world—at least in part—even as you also attempt to conform to the law. Here Paul, deliberately holding to the law, counsels the Romans to adapt a form of his adherence better suited to accommodate the host culture in which they find themselves and the home culture to which they must cling.

Paul is not alone in his use of the migrant strategy of accommodation. Along with the thirteen writings written either by him or by imitators of him, this strategy is adopted by the writer of the Gospel of Luke and the Acts of the Apostles, and by the authors of the Petrine letters. This constitutes the majority of the New Testament writings, both by number of writings and by size of corpus.

These three migrant strategies—liminality, separation, and accommodation—reflect three competing New Testament canonical responses to the historical reality of migration and the literary trope of displacement encoded in this canon. It would be a mistake to read this description as though it were intended to denote some kind of progression from "unrealistic" to "realistic"; nor a decline from "purity" to "admixture." Liminality, separation, and accommodation are survival strategies in the face of displacement and dispersion adopted by these different migrant writings. Each adds to the Pentecost-like cacophony (Acts 2) of the diaspora space called the New Testament.

Migrant Writings as Twenty-First-Century Scriptures

Considering the extent to which New Testament writings may also be migrant writings is certainly of interest for the historical study of these texts, as well as for their academic and, perhaps, theological interpretation. But how might this information allow us better to understand the role of these writings in the twenty-first century? To respond, one must first consider the nature of Scriptures themselves: specifically, one must consider what makes certain cultural productions (writings, recitations, songs, etc.) into Scriptures.

Here, the work of Wilfred Cantwell Smith will be a helpful conversation partner. Smith's seminal work *What Is Scripture? A Comparative Analysis* traces the human activity of Scripture-making and Scripture-using across a variety of religious communities and traditions. He finds that

> scripture is a human activity. . . . The quality of being scripture is not an attribute of texts. It is a characteristic of the attitude of persons—groups of persons—to what outsiders perceive as texts. *It denotes a relation between a people and a text.* Yet that too is finally inadequate. . . . at issue is the relation between a people and the universe, in the light of their perception of a given text. (Smith, 18, emphasis added)

Smith's definition makes explicit that those who consider New Testament writings to be Holy Scripture are living in a particular relationship with these ancient texts. This relationship involves more than just a people and their Scripture. The relationship stretches "between a people and the universe, in light of their perception of a given text" (Smith, 18). To use another metaphor, for people of faith, their Scriptures function as a lens through which all things are considered. Scripture helps people of faith to clarify their proper relationships with one another, with the God of their understanding, and with the world.

For the New Testament, an added complication is that not every person of faith has considered every text as equally scriptural, or as scriptural at all. This conflict between what is and is not truly "Scripture" dates as far back as the early second century CE, when Marcion of Sinope rejected those Scriptures he considered "Jewish." Later Christians have had similar reactions to particular books. Reformers like John Calvin and Martin Luther had no love for the Revelation to John and the Epistle of James, respectively. As twentieth-century theologian Howard Thurman revealed, among African Americans descended from US chattel slavery, New Testament writings in favor of slavery were held in low esteem, and even "read out" of the Bible (Thurman, 30–31). In *Jesus and the Disinherited*, Thurman tells a story of his grandmother who would not let him read from the Pauline Epistles, with the exception, on occasion, of 1 Corinthians 13. Thurman recounts:

> What she told me I shall never forget. "During the days of slavery," she said, "the master's minister would occasionally hold services for the slaves. . . . Always the white minister used as his text something from Paul. At least three or four times a year, he used as a text: 'Slaves be obedient to them that are your masters as unto Christ.' Then he would go on to show how it was God's will that we were slaves, and how, if we were good and happy slaves, God would bless us. I promised my Maker that if I ever learned to read and if freedom came, I would not read that part of the Bible." (Thurman, 30–31)

Thurman's grandmother's quite candid assessment of the New Testament caused her to determine not to treat the proslavery writings of the New Testament as Scripture, even if she had to omit almost every word attributed to the apostle Paul. She refused, in so doing, to use the proslavery New Testament writings as Scripture—as lenses to help her negotiate her relationship to the universe.

Like Marcion, Luther, Calvin, and even Thurman's grandmother, Christian practitioners still very often select which among the New Testament writings they will treat as Scripture, although they may not do so consciously. More commonly, even among those who claim inerrant divine inspiration for all of the biblical writings, certain texts are seen as "favorites," or as "the heart of the gospel." As noted above, each of these writings is also a migrant writing. As a result, unsurprisingly, people of faith very often also end up incorporating into their scriptural lenses not only the theological concepts that the texts propose but also the migrant strategies toward home and host cultures embedded in them. Those for whom John's Gospel is paramount might find themselves valuing liminality as the ideal interaction with their world. Those who privilege the Revelation to John might find themselves valuing separation. Those who hold to Paul's letters might find themselves valuing accommodation. These migrant strategies become inseparable from scriptural lenses. As a result, Christians of the dominant culture of a particular country, whose families may not have experienced migration for many generations, may still interact with that culture as though they were migrants in a host culture because of their scriptural lenses.

Within twenty-first-century civic life, this adaptation of migrant strategies may take the form of groups that stay to themselves and are viewed with suspicion because they privilege a separate migrant strategy. In a society in which every detail of human life is readily accessibly through the Internet, the choice of such groups to distance themselves from society at large may be seen as inviting or, by contrast, quite suspicious. Alternatively, it may take the form of groups that vilify both Christian religion as it is typically practiced and the society at large, turning instead to an alternative way of being entirely. Certainly such practices might go unnoticed. On the other hand, when in positions of power, Christians adopting liminal migrant strategies might have profound impact on schools, political parties, and social policy—whether they are found on the left or right wing of the political spectrum. This may seem oxymoronic. However, the liminality in this case is not actual societal power. Rather, these persons adopt a liminal stance toward society because of the Scriptures through which they refract their world, and which counsel them regarding their appropriate interaction with the world.

However, perhaps the migrant strategy that has had the strongest historical stance and still continues to be heard from among Christian practitioners is that of accommodation. In the United States and the Western north, this is in part due to the outsize influence of the writings of Paul in the Protestant churches. It is this strategy that brings us the abolitionist and civil rights movements among African Americans and many other movements for social justice. It is also this strategy that brings us the proslavery movement within the church and the twenty-first-century church's willingness to accommodate unjust policies regarding poverty and human rights. In each of these opposing cases, Christian interaction with the world is governed not only by what the Scriptures say but also by the scriptural stance of holding on to tradition while finding a way to engage the "world," which may appear to be hostile. Thus an abolitionist holds on to one set of scriptural sayings and a slaveholder to another set; however, both take the Pauline tack that both holds to the tradition and engages the society. At stake is the argument over what aspects of the dominant culture shall be accommodated and what resisted. Faithful Christians have, over time, responded very differently to these questions.

Each of these strategies persists today, strengthened by the migrant strategies in these ancient writings that continue to be Scripture for twenty-first-century Christians. As students of these texts, paying attention to these strategies may help us to unpack some of the Christianity-related arguments in our civic commons. Pay attention, also, to the sense of rootlessness that undergirds some of the music and culture, particularly of the United States: the sense that "there's no place like home," but also that "we're not in Kansas anymore" that can emerge in the rhetoric even of people whose families have been resident since the days of European colonialism. For this is not simply a product of changing times; times have always changed. In a culture so steeped in these migrant writings, this literary diaspora space called the New Testament, surely some of that rootlessness, some of those uncritically employed migrant strategies can be traced back to these ancient writings, these migrant Scriptures of the Christian church.

Works Cited

Bauckham, Richard. 1999. *James*. New Testament Readings. New York: Routledge.

Berry, John W. 2001. "A Psychology of Immigration." *Journal of Social Issues* 57, no. 3:615–31.

Brah, Avtar. 1996. *Cartographies of Diaspora: Contesting Identities*. New York: Routledge.

Brown, Raymond. 1979. *The Community of the Beloved Disciple: The Lives, Loves, and Hates of an Individual Church in New Testament Times*. Mahwah, NJ: Paulist.

Gibson, Margaret A. 2001. "Immigrant Adaption and Patterns of Acculturation." *Human Development* 44:19–23.

Johnson, Luke Timothy. 2004. *Brother of Jesus, Friend of God: Studies in the Letter of James*. Grand Rapids: Eerdmans.

Schüssler Fiorenza, Elisabeth. 2009. "Introduction: Exploring the Intersection of Race, Gender, Status, and Ethnicity in Early Christian Studies." In *Prejudice and Christian Beginnings*, edited by Laura Nasrallah and Elisabeth Schüssler Fiorenza. Minneapolis: Fortress Press.

Smith, Wilfred Cantwell. 1993. *What Is Scripture? A Comparative Approach*. Minneapolis: Fortress Press.

Taussig, Hal. 2009. *In the Beginning Was the Meal: Social Experimentation and Early Christianity*. Minneapolis: Fortress Press.

Thurman, Howard. 1976. *Jesus and the Disinherited*. Boston: Beacon.

THE APOCALYPTIC LEGACY OF EARLY CHRISTIANITY

David A. Sánchez

a•poc•a•lyp•tic (adj): of, relating to, or involving terrible violence and destruction: of or relating to the end of the world

leg•a•cy (noun): something transmitted by or received from an ancestor or predecessor or from the past

(Merriam-Webster Dictionary, 2003)

Introduction: The Problem of a Suppressed Legacy

We twenty-first-century Christians find ourselves in a strange place in relationship to our apocalyptic biblical inheritance. In many of our churches, apocalyptic literature, especially the Revelation to John, is treated with benign neglect, yet its images continue to fascinate us, as witness the tremendous success of novels like the *Left Behind* series. This is especially true from my perspective as a Roman Catholic: the book of Revelation remains liturgically peripheral in my tradition (with the exception of December 12—the Feast of the Virgin of Guadalupe, when Revelation 12 is a focal reading—and, on occasion, during the Lenten season). Yet Roman Catholics, like most twenty-first-century Christians, remain remarkably vulnerable to conjuring apocalyptic scenarios, under the right circumstances.

Meanwhile, over the last several decades, a great deal of ink has been spilled by scholars attempting to specify matters like the genre, form, and content of those ancient texts that qualify as "apocalyptic" and thus have contributed to this legacy. As one might expect, the book of Revelation has been the most obvious focal point in those conversations. Indeed, according to the most learned biblical specialists, this is the *only* writing in the New Testament that meets the scholarly criteria regarding the form of the genre apocalypse. I, for one, am in total agreement with this assessment, but I remain unsatisfied with the emphases of the scholarly conversation because something tells me, deep in my soul, that there is more to our Christian apocalyptic legacy than is addressed by such formal considerations.

In this essay, I would like to suggest an alternative point of entry, other than the Revelation to John, for discussing our apocalyptic inheritance. I would like initially to consider the Synoptic Gospels, not, however, as we usually read them, conflated together, as if they are telling roughly the same story; that keeps us from seeing something important—that from the very beginning, Christians have struggled with the troubling legacy of a genuinely apocalyptic vision. The Gospel tradition has embedded within it, specifically within the Gospel of Mark, what functions as a genuinely apocalyptic text. By examining how Matthew and Luke altered that text, we see how early Christians negotiated the first apocalyptic legacy in their tradition by altering its eschatological moorings. More precisely, Matthew and Luke demonstrate how a Christian *apocalyptic* moment was turned into an ecclesiastical movement with the alteration to a less imminent expectation of the Parousia of Jesus Christ.

To start with, this less obvious biblical apocalyptic moment serves several purposes. (1) It prevents us from isolating the book of Revelation as if it were the only example of an apocalyptic worldview in the Christian canon, and from sequestering it in the category of prophetically anomalous literature, rendering it so much easier to ignore. (2) It demonstrates that Matthew and Luke believed they needed to domesticate the apocalyptic agenda of the Gospel of Mark in the wake of the delayed return of Jesus Christ. And (3) it challenges us to bring to consciousness, in a cultural-psychoanalytic sense, the way other scriptural sources, in addition to Revelation, are embedded in our psyches and contribute to our perduring fascination with apocalyptic solutions, prompting us to "act out" apocalyptically under the right circumstances.

Apocalypticism

At this point it is critical to be clear how I am employing the term *apocalyptic*, especially because much scholarly ink has been spilled on the contentious question of categorization. I rely on David Aune's summary in an illuminating 2005 article.

> "Apocalyptic eschatology" is the narrative theology, characteristic of apocalypses, centering in the belief that (1) the present world order, regarded as both evil and oppressive, is under temporary control of Satan and his human accomplices, and (2) that the present evil world order will shortly be destroyed by God and replaced by a new and perfect order corresponding to Eden before the fall. During the present evil age, the people of God are an oppressed minority who fervently expect God, or his specially chosen agent the Messiah, to rescue them. The transition between the old and the new ages will be introduced with a final series of battles fought by the people of God

against the human allies of Satan. The outcome is never in question, however, for the enemies of God are predestined for defeat and destruction. (Aune, 236)

What I find most compelling in this definition—for the purposes of this essay and for my own personal relationship to apocalypticism—are the notions of cosmological dualism (with a war of heavenly proportions affecting, and afflicting, human actors), the introduction of the messianic agent (i.e., Jesus Christ), and the sense of temporal urgency. The present world order will be destroyed *soon*. It is this temporal consideration that I find most compelling when looking at an apocalyptic text like the Gospel of Mark—and at the Matthean and Lukan responses to Mark's acute temporality.

Excavating Mark as Another Example of Christian Apocalyptic

With this working definition of apocalypticism in mind, how does the Gospel of Mark function apocalyptically? Our first consideration is the moment in history when the Gospel of Mark was written. The majority of New Testament scholars date the Gospel between 66 and 70 CE, that is, squarely during the Jewish War with Rome, or shortly after the destruction of the Jerusalem temple. Thus Mark was written during a time of *real* political and cultural crisis (cf. Adela Yarbro Collins's language of *perceived* crisis; A. Y. Collins, 84–110) that may have indeed been an impetus for an apocalyptic response. Second, the Christology of the Gospel of Mark foregrounds the messiahship of Jesus. This is made explicit in the very first verse of the Gospel: "The beginning of the gospel of Jesus Christ" (i.e., Messiah). This christological emphasis is maintained throughout the Gospel (e.g., in the messianic secret motif: see the commentary on Mark). The relationship of a messianic figure to different apocalyptic scenarios is still under scholarly debate. I defer to Aune's assessment, noted above, which highlighted the expectation of God's oppressed people that an agent of God would act on their behalf at the critical and ultimate moment.

Other features of the Gospel of Mark that add to its apocalyptic tenor include its explicit cosmological dualism, as represented in the temptation of Jesus, after his baptism, by Satan (1:12-13) and the multiple exorcisms in the Gospel (e.g., 1:21-28; 5:1-20; 9:14-29). In comparison, the Gospel of John, arguably the least apocalyptic of the four canonical Gospels—has not one exorcism.

The Gospel of Mark also maintains a unique relationship to time. It is by far the most compressed of the four Gospels, narrating the ministry of Jesus from baptism to empty tomb. The Gospels of Matthew and Luke each begin with narratives of Jesus' birth, and end with accounts of his ascension into heaven. The Gospel of John goes even further, beginning "in the beginning" and ending with an ascension account. The Gospel of Mark employs the phrase "and immediately" some forty-one times in its narrative, twelve times in the first chapter alone. (The Greek phrase *kai euthys* occurs only nineteen times in the rest of the New Testament.) The phrase gives the reader/hearer the impression of a story moving very rapidly, and may remind the reader, ancient and modern alike, of the initial words uttered by Jesus in the Gospel: "The time is fulfilled, and the kingdom of God has come near" (1:15). Further, aspects of Mark's story reveal aspects of sectarian groups, as identified by modern theory: the requirement of severance of ties with one's biological family (e.g.,

1:16-20; 2:13-14; 10:28), the creation of a new eschatological family (3:31-35), and the mandatory renunciation of personal wealth for the benefit of the group (6:7-13; 10:17-27).

These observations crystallize the argument that Mark has apocalyptic features. This "excavation" goes beyond the usual characterization of Mark 13 as the "Little Apocalypse" to reveal that an apocalyptic character pervades the Gospel, and thus to foreground another apocalyptic moment in early Christian history; the Revelation to John does not stand in isolation. But consider next how both Matthew and Luke, unsatisfied with Mark's apocalyptic moorings some ten to fifteen years after the fact, chose to domesticate Mark when they incorporated his Gospel into their own. By means of this domestication, the legacy of Christian apocalypticism has been canonically offset, if not altogether suppressed, by the consequent conflated readings of the Gospel narratives.

Domesticating Mark: Matthew and Luke-Acts

I often imagine Matthew and Luke separately clinging to their manuscripts of Mark's Gospel and wondering just what on earth they were going to do with such an apocalyptically urgent Gospel. It is a humorous scene in my mind's eye, considering that apocalyptic movements have a short shelf life. How long can a preacher and/or teacher keep saying that deliverance is just around the corner? Thus I imagine Matthew and Luke questioning the validity of Mark's Gospel and how their Christian movements should proceed. In the wake of the delayed Parousia, with its delayed fulfillment of prophecy, do they quit the movement? Weren't the words of imminence placed on the very lips of Jesus himself (see esp. Mark 9:1; 13:30)? Perhaps they should bring about their own apocalypse, as subsequent Christian groups have done throughout the Christian era? Surely even slight provocation of Roman might accomplish that end. Or what if they took Mark's expected imminent Parousia and moved it into the distant future (by what scholars call "reserved eschatology")? If, as I contend here, this last was the option they chose, what were they to do with the rest of Mark, and even more acutely, what were they to do in the interim before the deferred Parousia?

These are fascinating questions that require some parsing. Note, first, that almost 90 percent of the Gospel of Mark is absorbed into Matthew's account. But how could one domesticate so apocalyptic a Gospel while absorbing so much of the original? Perhaps the best approach to this question is to assess how Matthew employed his sources. Arguably, the Gospel of Matthew can be reduced to three source-rich divisions. Chapters 1–2 are composed of material known as special M, biblical material unique to Matthew. This special source includes the (Matthean) birth narrative, the visitation of the magi, and the holy family's escape to Egypt in the wake of Herod's execution of Jewish male infants. This material accomplishes various purposes for Matthew, but most importantly for my point here, it expands the story of Jesus' life by almost three decades. Recall that the Gospel of Mark begins at Jesus' baptism, approximately one year before his death in his early thirties. Thus Matthew expands narrative time.

Matthew also proceeds in a much less rushed manner. The next section of the Gospel is made up primarily of materials gleaned from the sayings source Q. (See the essay on Jesus and the Gospels.) Embedded in this layer is a collection of words and teachings of Jesus apart from his deeds. In this material, we find the Sermon on the Mount, which takes up three chapters of Matthew's Gospel (chapters 5–7), and includes the Beatitudes and the Lord's Prayer. This saturation of Jesus' teachings in the middle of Matthew shifts the focus from Mark's apocalyptic Jesus to a more refined, rabbinic Jesus, one who certainly has much more time to teach and instruct his disciples on how to interact with the world in the interim before the Parousia.

We are finally introduced to the bulk of the Markan material as it is embedded in Matthew 12–28 (esp. after ch. 16). However, we have already been lulled into a more tranquil state of consciousness by the birth narrative and teaching discourse, so already the apocalyptic materials appear much more distant and future. The apocalyptic predictions imported from chapter 13 of the "Markan apocalypse" (Matthew 24) will come to pass (i.e., the destruction of the Jerusalem temple, wars and rumors of wars, persecution of the faithful, the desolating sacrilege, the appearance of false prophets, astronomical chaos, and the return of the son of man), but without the imminent tones of Mark's composition. This is also the case in the Lukan parallel to Mark 13 (Luke 21).

Even more brilliantly, Matthew incorporates ascension materials (28:16-20) to place Jesus back in heaven in the interim, thus overcoming what is, to Matthew, the more than slightly problematic lack of any indication where Jesus is during the interim according to the original ending of Mark (Mark 16:8, which, in my estimation, is a perfect ending for an *apocalyptic* Gospel). By conjoining it to the "Great Commission" in 28:18-20, Matthew has reframed Mark's apocalypticism into a template for a fledgling church movement that has much to accomplish before Christ's return. It is a brilliant piece of editorial work that simultaneously honors the primacy of Mark, by using so much of it as a source, *and* shifts Mark's emphasis from crisis and end-time speculation to an expanded story of the life of Jesus, with an emphasis on Jesus as aphoristic teacher and founder of a church. However, the point must not be overlooked that Matthew also felt the need for a complete eschatological overhaul of the Gospel of Mark, one that would privilege an emerging church. In my view, this was perhaps the most compelling reason for Matthew's privileged position in the New Testament canon. To place Mark at the beginning of the canon—noting its primacy among the Gospels—would have created an apocalyptic inclusio for the New Testament that would begin with Mark and end with the book of Revelation! The rhetorical brilliance of the canon as it now stands, however, is that the apocalypticism of the book of Revelation is now viewed as a futuristic culmination of the age of Matthew's developing and spreading church.

Luke, like his Synoptic cousin Matthew, had to make a tough decision regarding what to do with Mark's Gospel. I have always found it fascinating that both Luke and Matthew chose to retain and employ material from the Gospel of Mark. Surely, one avenue each author could have taken was to ignore the Gospel of Mark altogether and start from scratch. But neither did. Luke, as did Matthew, also employed special materials unique to his own Gospel, identified today as special L, and employed the 235 sayings of Jesus from Q. Unlike Matthew, however, the author of the Gospel of Luke used approximately one-half of the Gospel of Mark in the composition of his own Gospel (a large percentage even in relation to Matthew). Like Matthew, Luke also expanded the narrative time frame by introducing narratives of Jesus' birth and ascension. However, unlike any of his Gospel counterparts, Luke wrote a second contribution that would find its way into the New Testament canon, the Acts of the Apostles, which maps out the earliest years of the post-Easter church and the spread of the gospel from the Jewish world (foregrounding the apostleship of Peter) to the worldwide spread of the gospel to the gentiles (foregrounding the apostleship of Paul). In Lukan terms, this was the interim age of the Holy Spirit. The Parousia was delayed and Luke was prepared to encounter the delay, not as an unfulfilled prophecy, but as an opportunity to spread the gospel to the world. As in Matthew, the Gospel of Mark is relegated to the apocalyptic drama that would occur in the eschaton in the indeterminate future (again, reserved eschatology). Luke even hinted at an eschatology that we find most pronounced in the Gospel of John (that is, realized eschatology) when he hints at the benefits of the Parousia being accessible already, in the present, in Luke 17:20-21.

> Once Jesus was asked by the Pharisees when the kingdom of God was coming, and he answered, "The kingdom of God is not coming with things that can be observed; nor will they say, 'Look here it is!' or 'There it is!' For, in fact, the kingdom of God is among you."

It is evident from this brief analysis of both Matthew and Luke that both Gospel writers thought enough of the tradition of Mark to incorporate it into their literary productions while simultaneously toning down Mark's apocalyptic sensibilities to make it more palatable for Christians living in the 80s or later. Both spent much intellectual energy doing so. Matthew and Luke found themselves at least a decade removed from Mark's imminent apocalyptic prediction. The apocalyptic rhetoric had to shift because you cannot be an imminent apocalyptic preacher or sustain an apocalyptic community year after year after year.

Thus the Gospels present us with this curious combination of competing eschatologies. Because it has been a Christian interpretive practice to conflate our readings of the Gospels, emphasizing their presumed unity, the apocalypticism of Mark has been absorbed into the grander "gospel story." It is lost, or ignored, or projected into the undetermined future. The Markan legacy is a painful one, to be sure, because embedded within it is an unfulfilled prophecy of the imminent second coming of Christ, and so we can understand the energy that wants to avoid or defer it. But the presence of Mark among the Gospels means that even if we sequester the book of Revelation as some sort of apocalyptic anomaly, the intellectual fodder for subsequent apocalyptic movements and imaginings remains. Apocalypticism is embedded in our Gospel tradition itself, right in front of us, even if we choose not to acknowledge it. We may suppress it—and then act entirely surprised when apocalyptic inklings manifest themselves in us, like any other neurosis or psychosis would, given the right circumstances.

Expanding the Apocalyptic Landscape: The Pauline Tradition

Even the Pauline tradition—where scholars have long recognized the strength of apocalyptic influence on the apostle's thought—is not immune from a similar apocalyptic suppression. Paul's response to the church in Thessalonica regarding the fate of deceased Christians is illuminating:

> But we do not want you to be uninformed, brothers and sisters, about those who have died, so that you may not grieve as others do who have no hope. For since we believe that Jesus died and rose again, even so, through Jesus, God will bring with him those who have died. For this we declare to you by the word of the Lord, that we who are alive, who are left until the coming of the Lord, will

by no means precede those who have died. For the Lord himself, with a cry of command, with the archangel's call and with the sound of God's trumpet, will descend from heaven, and the dead in Christ will rise first. Then we who are alive, who are left, will be caught up in the clouds together with them to meet the Lord in the air; and so we will be with the Lord forever. (1 Thess. 4:13-17)

Here, Paul speaks to the faithful in Thessalonica in no uncertain terms—imminent apocalyptic terms. Paul expects to be at the Parousia of Jesus Christ. And just as we saw in the Synoptic tradition, Paul faced a period of time (approximately five or six years, if we accept the dating of 1 Thessalonians c. 49 CE and Romans c. 55 CE) in which he personally was confronted with the delayed Parousia. Although Romans was written to a different congregation on a completely different set of issues, it is nevertheless surprising how completely lacking are apocalyptic tones in the letter. If we regard Pauline Christianity as an apocalyptic movement like other apocalyptic groups throughout history, we should expect apocalypticism to be the theological lens through which all things are assessed. How could it be otherwise? But then the absence of apocalyptic elements in Romans is altogether curious.

It appears, then, that any assessment of the apocalyptic legacy of early Christianity must begin with an expansion of the scriptural materials we delegate as apocalyptic. To continue to focus our consideration of apocalyptic material solely on the book of Revelation allows us to compartmentalize our assessment of early Christian apocalyptic wholly on the last book of the Christian canon. Thus any subsequent appropriation of apocalyptic worldviews by Christian groups is easily marginalized by placing the hermeneutic blame on simplistic and/or overly literal readings of the book of Revelation. The first step in recovery is acknowledgment: in this case, acknowledgment that our apocalyptic roots run much deeper than the book of Revelation. Therefore, the work of intellectually excavating texts such as the Gospel of Mark and Paul's First Letter to the Thessalonians is a positive first step in parsing how and why Christian apocalypticism has endured over two millennia. It is in our biblical DNA, present in the earliest letter from the apostle Paul and in the first Gospel ever written. And indeed, it is there, in all of its pure genre form, in the book of Revelation. It is more pervasive than we choose to admit, and scholarly discussions on matters of proper form have only distracted us from that fact. But Matthew, Luke, and Paul have left evidence not only of the prevalence of apocalyptic expectation but also of some measure of its unsustainability: that is, evidence that they tried to distance themselves from a perspective that had such a short shelf life. It appears that individuals and communities simply can't be perpetually apocalyptic. Nevertheless, our apocalyptic memories are short, and we Christians find ourselves bouncing to and fro, from postures of apocalyptic fervor to more tranquil, reserved eschatological expectation. It is a rhythmic dance that has played out over two Christian millennia.

The Book of Revelation and the Explicit Legacy of Christian Apocalypticism

Acknowledgment of the comprehensive influence of the book of Revelation on the Western Christian imagination goes unchallenged even with attempts by some denominations to altogether suppress it. It is, according to both form and content, the only true apocalypse in the New Testament (Collins 1979, 9; see the commentary on Revelation). Its rich imagery, full of beasts, martyrs, heavenly interlocutors, plagues, mysterious gematria, natural disasters, whores, and a great descending city is almost too much for the senses to comprehend, yet simultaneously hypersensual enough to draw even the casual reader into a hypnotic state of attention. It is like the car wreck on the highway that simultaneously repels and irresistibly attracts at least a momentary gaze as we cautiously pass by. It has been the source of Christian apocalyptic ambivalence and anxiety for the last two millennia. A summary of that interpretive history will bear out the alternating rhythm described above, in which our collective traditions have tried to come to terms with the last entry in the New Testament.

The apocalyptic legacy of the book of Revelation began early in the second century of the Common Era. According to Robert M. Royalty Jr. and Arthur W. Wainwright, proto-orthodox Christians like Justin Martyr (c. 100–165) and Irenaeus (c. 130–200) represented an interpretive position known as chiliasm (i.e., millenarian, from the Greek *chilia*, "thousand"). Chiliasm, which represented a literal interpretation of the book of Revelation, was theologically "mainstream" in the early second century. This position is best defined as the theological system that "believed literally in the thousand-year reign of the saints in Rev. 20:4 and the actual, physical new Jerusalem in Rev. 21–22" (Royalty, 285). Wainwright argues that "the chiliasts lived in an age of persecution. It was for such an age that they believed the Apocalypse was written. . . . During this period Chiliasm provided an antidote to the fear of persecution. When people are oppressed, they find consolation in dreams of a better life and focus their anger on the institutions and leaders that threaten them" (Wainwright, 22). Thus Wainwright makes the interpretive assumption that the Apocalypse functioned as a rhetorical call for endurance during times of persecution.

One of the first challenges to literal chiliastic readings of the book of Revelation came from Phrygia in Asia Minor. The "New Prophecy" (c. 150–175), or Montanism (as it was called by its opponents), was founded by Montanus, Prisca, and Maximilla. According to the New Prophecy, the new kingdom would be inaugurated by Christ—but in Pepuza, the geographical epicenter of the New Prophecy movement, and not Jerusalem. The New Prophecy thus challenged "normative" chiliastic expectations through a very selective literal approach to the text by its protagonists (including Tertullian, c. 160–220).

The chiliastic certainty of the of the mid-second century was also countered by emerging late second-century and early third-century allegorical interpretations of the book of Revelation forwarded by the likes of Dionysius, bishop of Alexandria (third century), Clement of Alexandria (c. 150–215), and Origen (c. 185–254). These allegorical readings came to full fruition under Augustine of Hippo (ca. 354–430), who himself was first a proponent of chiliasm until his "eschatological conversion" later in his career. Dionysius, Clement, and Origen began to challenge aspects of chiliasm, especially the literal interpretation of the new Jerusalem as a *physical* and earthly place where "the redeemed would eat, drink, marry, have children, and exercise dominion over other people" (Origen, *De princ.* 2.11.2–3). Thus the early challenges to the literal interpretations focused primarily on the location of the new Jerusalem (New Prophecy) and its physical nature, as depicted in Revelation 21–22. These challenges were just enough to begin to dislodge the mainstream chiliastic interpretations that nevertheless prevailed until the reign of Constantine, in the fourth century of the Common Era. That is a fascinatingly long tenure for literal apocalyptic musings. In some ways, the first three centuries of the Christian era mirror the apocalyptic tension that existed in the now emerging canon, representing both movements with apocalyptic sensibilities and those that countered them. Our ambivalence regarding apocalypticism and the variety of divergent interpretive possibilities were beginning to take shape in these earliest Christian centuries.

It could be argued, if one follows the logic of Wainwright, that the fourth century, with the shift in Rome's relationship to Christianity from one of indifference to persecution, then to tolerance and ultimately acceptance, also marked a shift in the Christian rhetorical posture toward apocalyptic literature in general, and the book of Revelation in particular. Violently imaginative and passive-aggressive fantasies of revenge of the Apocalypse were no longer necessary with Christianity's new and prominent relationship to the empire. This was especially the case after 381, when Emperor Theodosius endorsed orthodox Nicene Christianity over Christian Arianism and banned all pagan religious ritual. What was once peripheral was now central, and the Christian relationship to its apocalyptic legacy needed to be reevaluated. On this matter, Royalty notes, "after the Roman emperors moved from tolerance to acceptance and promotion of orthodox Christianity, millenarian views were even more strongly challenged. No imperial ruler, political or ecclesiastical, eagerly anticipated the destruction of the empire they now controlled" (Royalty, 286).

The influence of Augustine's allegorical reading of the Apocalypse was comprehensive and dominated orthodox circles from the fifth through thirteenth centuries of the Common Era. Perhaps the greatest challenge to traditional readings of the Apocalypse was Augustine's hesitance in speculating about the date of the end. Recall that Aune's working definition of apocalypse (see above) identified one of the key elements of literal apocalyptic readings as the expectation of the imminent end. This was not the case for Augustine, however, and in essence, by his very hesitation, he lowered the expectation of what is probably the most important aspect of apocalyptic eschatology: imminence. To challenge literal chiliastic views on the imminent apocalypse, derived from Revelation 20,

> Augustine offered two key interpretive points in the *City of God*, Book 20. First, the thousand year period is symbolic of "the whole duration of the world," the earthly fullness of time. Thus Augustine tried to put an end to speculations about dates and times for this millennium to start and end, a point for which he had plenty of biblical proof texts. Second, this symbolic millennium has already begun in the time of the church for that is what binds Satan until the final end. . . . And as for the final, *final* end, do not count the days, for the thousand year period is symbolic. (Royalty, 286–87)

Thus, with one powerful, stunning theological gesture, Augustine succeeded in shifting the emphasis from literal readings of the apocalypse to spiritual and nonmillennial readings that would last through the thirteenth century—until a Calabrian abbot named Joachim of Fiore (c. 1135–1202) would once again shift our relationship and understanding of the Apocalypse.

In contrast to Augustine's symbolic reading of the Apocalypse, Joachim of Fiore insisted on what he believed was a historical reading of the text. Joachim alleged that the persecution of Christians in his lifetime was evidence that the signs predicted in the book of Revelation were being realized.

Thus Joachim countered the allegorized reading promoted by Augustine by renewing a historicized reading of the Apocalypse similar to those first endorsed by Justin and Irenaeus. After his spiritual conversion and time spent in the Holy Land on pilgrimage, Joachim returned to Calabria and became a recluse, devoting his study and prayer time to deciphering the book of Revelation. Completely frustrated with his attempt to come to terms with the text, he reported that upon awakening one Easter morning, the meaning of the Apocalypse was revealed to him. Thus, unlike Augustine, Joachim is best understood—like John of Patmos—as an apocalyptic seer.

Joachim's primary contribution as a mystical seer was formulating a system (*concordia*) that divided human history into three historical epochs or states (*status* in Latin). The first *status* was the period from Adam to Jesus Christ, which Joachim called the period of God the Father, corresponding to the Hebrew Scriptures (and to the layperson's church). The *status* from Jesus Christ to 1260 was the period of God the Son and of the Christian Testament (corresponding to the papal church). This was the period in which Joachim himself lived. The third and final *status* began in 1260 and was the period of the Holy Spirit. This third epoch corresponded to the Friars' church. This age, according to Joachim, was the age of the new millennial kingdom:

> [The third epoch] was to be inaugurated by a new Adam or a new Christ who would be the founder of a new monastic order. The transition between the Papal Church of the second age and the Spiritual Church of the third age would be a time of great troubles during which the period of the Papal Church was to endure all the sufferings that corresponded to Christ's passion. The Papal Church would be resurrected as the Spiritual Church in which all men would live the contemplative life, practice apostolic poverty, and enjoy angelic natures. To this level Joachim's ideas were debased and popularized during the thirteenth century by a series of pseudo-Joachimite writings, which probably originated amongst the spiritual Franciscans themselves. St. Francis was identified with the messiah that Joachim prophesied. During the later Middle Ages Joachimism and the Apocalypse preserved their ideological union. (Phelan, 14)

Again, in contrast to Augustine's more domesticating and spiritual reading of the Apocalypse, Joachim revisited subversive interpretations of the text that were more at home in a historical interpretive framework. On this matter, Royalty notes, "Joachim reenergized historicized and potentially politically subversive readings of the Apocalypse, with one result being ideological challenges to ecclesiological and civil authorities in Europe within some monastic and mendicant religious communities" (Royalty, 289). And like the historicized readings of the first century, Joachim employed the powerful rhetoric of persecution. The echoes of his historicized reading reverberated most prominently from the thirteenth through the sixteenth centuries in Western Christendom and, in a few select traditions, are palpable even today (Sánchez).

The Protestant Reformation was also not immune from the perduring legacy of the Apocalypse to John. The onetime Roman Catholic German monk Martin Luther (1483–1546) also had an ambivalent relationship with the book of Revelation. In his early career, Luther remarked,

> I miss more than one thing in this book, and this makes me hold it to be neither apostolic nor prophetic . . . there is one sufficient reason for me not to think highly of it—Christ is neither taught nor known in it. (Luther 1960a, 399)

On a disenchanting trip to Rome, Luther felt betrayed by the "corruption" of the Catholic Church. This initiated an intense search of the Scriptures, which led him to conclude that salvation was a function of his own personal faith rather than derived from any corporate church entity—especially a church that he now found so dismaying. Luther set his own course with the posting of his Ninety-Five Theses in Wittenberg, Saxony, which ultimately led to his excommunication from the Roman Catholic Church.

One of the most significant appropriations of the book of Revelation among Protestant Reformers, including Luther, was the equating of the papacy with the beast(s) of the Apocalypse. Wainwright notes that Luther himself promoted "that . . . the papacy was the beast of the land [Rev. 13:11-18], [and] the empire was the beast of the sea [Rev. 13:1-10]. But the pope, he [i.e., Luther] argued, had control over the empire" (Wainwright, 61). Luther was not the first or the only critic of the papacy who employed negative apocalyptic accusations at Rome: "Some of the sharpest criticism came from Bohemia and England. In Bohemia John Milicz (d. 1374), Mathias of Janow (d. 1394), and John Hus (1369–1415) implied the pope was Antichrist" (Wainwright, 59).

Roman Catholicism in general and the papacy in particular came under a severe Protestant challenge. The need for a swift Catholic response was clear. In some circles, the Catholic response was simply to employ the same apocalyptic polemic against the Protestants. Catholic bishops like Bertold Pürstinger (1463–1543), bishop of Chiemsee (Germany), "explained that the locusts of the sixth trumpet vision [Rev. 9:13-19] were Lutherans. Serafino da Fermo described Luther as the star falling from heaven [Rev. 9:1] and the beast from the land [Rev. 13:11-18]" (Wainwright, 61).

Two other lines of interpretation employed by Catholics against Protestant antipapal interpretations were futurism, championed by the Spanish Jesuit Francisco Ribera (1537–1591), and preterism, developed most fully by the Portuguese Jesuit Luis de Alcazar (1554–1613). "Futurists contended that most of the prophecies in the Apocalypse were still unfulfilled, Preterists argued that most of them had been fulfilled already" (Wainwright, 63). Both methods of interpretation were effective. Futurism was attractive to Catholics, "because it dissociated the pope from Antichrist. It was cogent because it recognized the connection of the beast and the harlot of Rome, although it was a Rome of the future. Futurism challenged both the antipapal interpretation and the assumption that the Apocalypse provided a survey of church history" (Wainwright, 63). Preterism, by arguing that most of the prophecies of the Apocalypse had already been fulfilled, "was congenial to Catholics because it rejected the suggestion that the pope was Antichrist and it gave honor to the Roman Catholic Church" (Wainwright, 63).

One interesting offshoot of the Reformation era was the contemporary emergence of a group known as the Anabaptists. The name Anabaptist was not claimed by the group itself but rather came from other Christian groups opposed to their rejection of infant baptism (a common practice in Roman Catholic circles). The name is derived from the Greek *anabaptismos*, which is loosely translated as "being baptized (over) again." The Anabaptists were part of a movement classified today as the Radical Reformation, and it should be noted that both Protestant and Catholics persecuted Anabaptists. Beyond their baptismal practices, Anabaptists rejected organized religious hierarchies in favor of an idealized theocratic state. This ideology led to a faction of their membership occupying the German city of Münster, which they likened to the new Jerusalem (Revelation 21), to await the return of the heavenly Christ. Within the Anabaptist ranks, a Dutch national named Jan Bockelson declared himself the Messiah of the end times, and coins were minted that referenced the imminent apocalypse. The siege of Münster ended violently in 1535.

In the nineteenth century, three religious movements emerged that also took a historical interpretive approach to the Apocalypse. Those groups are the Church of Jesus Christ of Latter-Day Saints (Mormons) founded by Joseph Smith (c. 1830) shortly after the publication of the Book of Mormon; the Seventh-Day Adventists (Millerites), founded by William Miller (c. 1833); and the Jehovah's Witnesses, founded by Charles Russell (c. 1872). These three US-born movements are relevant for the current discussion because all three movements predicted an imminent apocalypse in their initial years, survived those unrealized predictions, and continue to remain with us today. Therefore, all three movements are interesting examples of how to negotiate an evolving apocalyptic expectation.

Latter-Day Saints (LDS) are an interesting example of a religious group that expanded on the Christian canon by including the Book of Mormon, *The Pearl of Great Price*, and the *Doctrine and Covenants* as church Scripture. LDS members also accept the prophecies of their church leadership as authoritative. (The head of the LDS Church at any given time in its history is recognized as prophet.) This combination of Scriptures and "[prophetic] pronouncement of their leaders has led them to expect both the rebuilding of Jerusalem in the old world and the erection of the New Jerusalem [Revelation 21] in North America. They look forward to the return of Christ to inaugurate his millennial reign over the earth" (Wainwright, 99). This bifurcated manner of dividing the old and new worlds is consistent with the LDS belief that Jesus Christ also visited the Americas shortly after his resurrection, in the first century CE.

Seventh-Day Adventists, like the earliest apocalyptic Christians, also had to deal with their own version of the delay of the Parousia. Their founder, William Miller, predicted that Christ would return in 1843. When his prophecy was not fulfilled, he changed the date to 1844, but that too was not realized. This unrealized prophecy was cause for the earliest Adventists to reconsider and reconfigure their intense apocalyptic hopes. What does an apocalyptic group do when their dated expectation is not realized? As noted above, these groups can abandon their expectations, they can initiate their own (violent) apocalypse (see below for modern examples of this option), or they can adjust the anticipated date—thereby adjusting their imminent expectation much as Matthew and Luke adjusted the Markan apocalyptic time frame. Such was the case with the Adventists; and the denomination still thrives today, some 170 years after the original apocalyptic prophecy. The rhetorical shift they made was to the notion that "another divine event, invisible to human eyes, had occurred in 1844. Christ, they said, had entered the heavenly sanctuary (Heb. 9:24-28)" (Wainwright, 99; cf. Froom, 889–99).

Note that the domesticating of apocalyptic imminence among Adventists did not sway the denomination away from their allegiance to the Apocalypse itself. Wainwright notes, "In arguing for the observance of Saturday as the holy day, they quoted the statement that those who did not keep God's commandments have the mark of the beast (Rev. 14:9-12). The Adventist John Nevis Andrews (1829–83) identified the beast from the land with the United States, whose two horns were civil and religious liberty. The beast from the sea and the whore of Babylon represented the papacy" (Wainwright, 99–100). Thus the continued Adventist appropriation of the Apocalypse shifted away from imminent temporal concerns toward an applied cosmological dualism, a trait common in most apocalyptic literature (as expressed, e.g., in the explicit distinction of insiders from outsiders, saved from unsaved, sinners from righteous).

At the forefront of Jehovah's Witness appropriations of the Apocalypse is their privileging of the 144,000 elect referenced in Revelation 7 and 14. Revelation 7:4-8 reads:

Then I heard the number of those who were sealed: 144,000 from all the tribes of Israel.

> From the tribe of Judah, 12,000 were sealed,
> from the tribe of Reuben 12,000,
> from the tribe of Gad 12,000,
> from the tribe of Asher 12,000,
> from the tribe of Naphtali 12,000,
> from the tribe of Manasseh 12,000,
> from the tribe of Simeon 12,000,
> from the tribe of Levi, 12,000,
> from the tribe of Issachar 12,000,
> from the tribe of Zebulun 12,000,
> from the tribe of Joseph 12,000,
> from the tribe of Benjamin 12,000.

And Rev. 14:1 again refers to the 144,000: "Then I looked, and there before me was the Lamb, standing on Mount Zion, and with him 144,000 who had his name and his Father's name written on their foreheads." According to Jehovah's Witnesses, "the United Nations and the world's religious leaders will be on Satan's side in the Battle of Armageddon. Against them will be ranged the 144,000 and the other sheep, but Christ's heavenly army will actually win the victory, and the only survivors of the battle will be the Jehovah's Witnesses" (Wainwright, 100). This position is consistent with founder Charles Russell's original teaching that the 144,000 will constitute the foundation of God's people during the Christian millennium and will do battle with people marked with the mark of the beast (Wainwright, 100). Again, the acute dualism of this apocalyptic appropriation is evident in this end-time narrative. And like the Adventist Church, Jehovah's Witnesses have survived the crisis of unrealized apocalyptic prophecy.

> Mistaken prophecies have not daunted the Jehovah's Witnesses. Joseph Franklin Rutherford, who succeeded Russell as their leader, predicted that Abraham, Isaac, Jacob and other faithful Israelites would return to earth in 1925. More recent Witnesses have entertained the hope that the millennium might begin about 1975. In spite of the failure of these expectations, the organization continues to thrive. (Wainwright, 101)

The Apocalyptic Legacy Today

Looking back on this succinct review of how the apocalyptic legacy has endured over the Christian centuries, I, for one, am perplexed—yet not surprised—by the apocalyptically saturated culture in which we continue to live today. Over the last several decades, myriad films on the imminent end have been produced. Examples include *The Seventh Seal* (1958), *Fail Safe* (1964), *Planet of the Apes* (1968), *The Omega Man* (1971), *The Omen* (1976), *Apocalypse Now* (1979), *Pale Rider* (1985), *The Seventh Sign* (1988), the *Terminator* series (1984, 1991, 2003, 2009, and possibly a fifth episode in the series in 2015), *Independence Day* (1996), *The Matrix* series (1999, 2003, 2003), *Apocalypto* (2006), *Knowing* (2009), *The Road* (2009), *The Book of Eli* (2010), and *The Colony* (2013). At best, this is just a small representation of the hundreds of films produced in the recent past on an apocalyptic and catastrophic "end."

A great deal of apocalyptic music has also emerged over the same period: *The End*, by the Doors, 1967; *Burn,* by Deep Purple, 1974; *It's the End of the World as We Know It (And I Feel Fine)*, by R.E.M., 1987; *Idioteque*, by Radiohead, 2000; *When the Man Comes Around*, by Johnny Cash, 2002; and *Radioactive*, by Imagine Dragons, 2013.

From the literary world, one need look no further than Hal Lindsey and Carla C. Carlson's best-selling *The Late Great Planet Earth* (1970) and Tim LaHaye and Jerry B. Jenkins's sixteen books in the *Left Behind* series (1995–2007). Both pairs of authors were greatly influenced by another form of futurism known as dispensationalism, a term coined by British author John Nelson Darby (1800–1882) that "refers to the idea that all time can be divided into [seven] separate periods known as dispensations. The present dispensation spans the time between the first and second comings of Christ, and the next great dispensation will be the millennium" (Koester, 275). The reading and composition strategy of Lindsey and Carlson was to cut and paste a series of biblical passages to give the reader a comprehensive view of the end-time scenario. According to Craig Koester, "Hal Lindsey's *Late, Great Planet Earth* . . . linked the biblical text used in Darby's system [esp. Genesis 15; Daniel 9; 1 Thessalonians 4; 2 Thessalonians 2; 1 John 2; and the entirety of Revelation] to current newspaper headlines, giving readers the impression that scripture had predicted the dominant political trends of the Cold War. The *Left Behind* novels . . . present Darby's system through the medium of fiction" (Koester, 275).

Examples of Lindsey and Carlson's interpretation of current events as correlative of apocalyptic biblical scenarios include, but surely are not limited to examples like these:

> The seal visions . . . predict the outbreak of war in the Middle East. . . . They tell of economic distress, shortage of food, and the death of a quarter of the human race as a result of these disasters. . . . The sixth seal vision may describe the beginning of nuclear war, and the trumpet visions may foretell the disasters of that war. . . . The bowl visions describe the fearful punishment that will be inflicted on those who reject the Christian Gospel. (Wainwright, 84)

Unrealized scenarios, in Lindsey and Carlson's schema, are considered "still yet to come" rather than failed. Jack Van Impe, a popular apocalyptic and "historical" dispensationalist preacher on the Trinity Broadcasting Network, is another outstanding example of the ongoing hermeneutic tradition initiated by Darby and executed by Lindsey and Carlson. He too postpones unfulfilled prophetic expectations and continues to look to contemporary events as potential signs of imminent fulfillment.

The *Left Behind* series, as noted above, correlates apocalyptic biblical themes with fictional events (although the narrative can include real-world entities). For example, the first novel

> opens against a context of international food shortages, inflation (Rev. 6.5-6) and conflict (Rev. 6.4) in the Middle East. Amidst the upheaval, the rapture occurs. Children and Christian adults are taken up, but a few of those left behind appreciate what has occurred; most prefer the explanations offered by United Nations Secretary General Nicolae Carpathia, who promises a solution to the world's problems, heads a new ten-member (evoking the "ten crowns" of Rev. 13.2) Security Council, and brokers a peace deal for Israel. Carpathia is hailed as a great leader and replaces the United Nations with a totalitarian Global Community, as nations seeking peace and security willingly surrender their sovereignty. (Rev. 13; Wright, 2009, 81)

The popularity of the *Late Great Planet Earth* and the *Left Behind* series cannot be overstated. Combined sales of the books are well into the tens of millions. These books are, for many Christians, the primary source for their understanding of Christian apocalyptic. As Koester has noted, "The view of the future presented in [*Left Behind*] affirms that God is sovereign despite ominous world conditions. . . . The novels show that simple believers, who know the biblical script, are far better informed about global developments than the commentators on television" (Koester, 278). An appealing script for the apocalyptically inclined, indeed.

No survey of the apocalyptic legacy of Christian Scripture is complete without an acknowledgment of three of the most sensational and horrific demonstrations of that legacy in recent memory: Jonestown (1978), the Branch Davidians (1993), and Heaven's Gate (1997). As noted in the beginning of this essay, one generalized way to categorize the trajectories of apocalyptic groups is according to their responses when initial prophecies of an imminent event have been delayed. The group in question can disband; they can move the date of the end into the undefined future; or they can initiate a violent end within the parameters of their apocalyptic rhetoric. The three groups just named all chose the last option, under different circumstances. These three groups (and several others like them) pique our imaginations when we discuss modern apocalyptic groups. They represent the most extreme cases.

It may very well be that my own interest in apocalyptic groups began with the images I witnessed, as an eighteen-year-old, of the Jonestown debacle. The photos and film sent over the newswire were shocking: piles of bodies (many of whom were children) stacked up and grouped together in a jungle in Guyana, a dead US Congressman and reporters executed point blank lying on an airstrip, and syringes and vats of cyanide-laced, purple Kool Aid. Over 900 people died on a single day, March 18, 1978.

What we learned about the group and its leaders after the mass suicide was equally sensational. Pastor Jim Jones (1931–1978) had led his flock from its roots in Indianapolis, Indiana, to Redwood Valley, California, then to San Francisco, and ultimately to their final "utopian" location in Jonestown, Guyana. The group's migration to Jonestown began in 1977 and was executed in several stages: survey, development, occupation. Dominant in the group's rhetoric were themes of persecution, suffering, and potential martyrdom for the cause. The echoes of Christian apocalyptic are not difficult to discern in this rhetoric. Jones and his flock were committed to fighting what they perceived as "the injustices of a racist, classist, and capitalistic society" (Moore, 95). Jones believed that the group's new location in the jungles of Guyana would allow for the free exercise of their religion and the development of a socialist utopia.

The utopian beginnings of the relocated group were hounded by reports as early as 1972—the San Francisco years—"when a religion reporter for the *San Francisco Chronicle* wrote that a member wanting to leave the group had died under suspicious circumstances" (Moore, 97). Moore also reports that "the apostate group called the Concerned Relatives publicized an 'accusation of Human Rights Violations,' which detailed abuses that they believed were occurring in Jonestown" (Moore, 97). These accusations were the impetus for the visit of US Congressman Leo Ryan's visit to Jonestown in 1978. These accusations, combined with some current members desiring to leave Jonestown in conjunction with Jones's elevated paranoia (which may have included an increasing dependence on narcotics), fueled the volatile mix of the rhetoric of persecution and suffering and perceived external pressures. The pressure and paranoia became so acute that the infamous "white nights" (actual rehearsals of mass suicide) became more common in the latter stages of the group's existence. The actual performance was executed on the evening of March 18, 1978. In the words of the self-proclaimed messiah Jones, it was an act of "revolutionary suicide," an act no doubt influenced by apocalyptic ideation.

Fifteen years after the events of Jonestown, another apocalyptic group, the Branch Davidians, appeared on our apocalyptic landscape. The forensic analysis of the global press and the emerging World Wide Web allowed us our closest and most detailed look at an apocalyptic group and its violent end. Led by David Koresh (Vernon Howell, born 1959), another self-proclaimed messiah (Koresh is the Hebrew transliteration of Cyrus, a reference to the Persian king proclaimed messiah by the prophet Isaiah in Isa. 45:1), the Branch Davidians—an offshoot of the Seventh-Day Adventists Church—engaged in a lethal gun battle with US federal agents on April 19, 1993, in which their compound was destroyed by fire and seventy-six Davidians lost their lives. The source of the fire is still under debate: the two competing theories are that federal tear-gas canisters started the fire in the compound, or that members of the Davidians started the fire from within.

What is especially fascinating about this group was their explicit employment of the book of Revelation to map out their perceived apocalyptic destiny. Kenneth Newport argues, "The text [i.e., the book of Revelation] was at the very least an important factor . . . in the decision of the Branch Davidians to self-destruct (or 'act out their biblical destiny' as they would more probably have seen it)" (Newport, 213). He continues, "The community read the Book of Revelation (together with numerous other parts of the Bible, especially the Psalms) and what they read there, I suggest, together with the context in which they read it, led to the group's planned for and well executed apocalyptic self-destruction" (Newport, 213). Certainly texts like Rev. 10:7 were used by Koresh to depict himself as the seventh angel of the Apocalypse. The description of a lamblike beast in Rev. 13:11-18 was used to demonize the US government. Such passages were vital to group awareness. Thus, for the Branch Davidians, "the arrival of the ATF and then the FBI on the morning of 28 February, 1993, was highly significant and prophetically charged" (Newport, 219). For the Davidians (especially Koresh), as for Jonestown, all pressures from outside the group were biblically prophesied signs of the apocalyptic times. So when the *Waco Tribune-Herald* began publishing a critical exposé on Koresh, called "The Sinful Messiah," the day before the first day of the siege on the Davidian compound, all signs pointed to their impending end.

An interesting variation on the modern apocalyptic group coming to an abrupt end is Heaven's Gate. Founded in 1972 by Marshall Applewhite (1932–1997) and Bonnie Lu Nettles (1928–1985), the group chose to end their lives via ritualistic suicide by consuming a lethal combination of Phenobarbital (an anticonvulsant barbiturate) mixed with applesauce and chased with vodka. After law-enforcement authorities received an anonymous tip, thirty-nine bodies were discovered in a mansion in Rancho Santa Fe (an affluent suburb of San Diego), twenty-one women and eighteen men of various ages from twenty-six to seventy-two. The ritualistic suicides were performed over several days in 1997: fifteen on March 22, fifteen on March 23, seven on March 24, and the final two somewhere between March 24 and their eventual discovery on March 26.

The bodies (known as "vessels" by Heaven's Gate members) were all dressed in black shirts and trousers, black Nike sneakers, and a purple cloth covered their upper torsos. Each had an armband with the words "Heaven's Gate Away Team" embroidered on the band. The majority of the deceased had in their possession a five-dollar bill and three quarters.

The impetus for this ritualistic suicide is uniquely different from the rhetoric of persecution, suffering, and martyrdom commonplace in Jonestown and in Waco, Texas, among the Branch Davidians. Benjamin Zeller concludes that "while the movement surely experienced a sense of persecution and failure . . . these conditions are not in themselves sufficient to cause self-violence" (Zeller, 175). What motivated this group ritualistically to end their lives was their belief (according to their still-active website: heavensgate.com) that humanity needed to move beyond human existence to their rightful place at the "next level above human," the realm of God. For the members, the imminent timing of this transition was critical because it was their belief that the earth was soon to be "recycled."

It should be noted, however, that ritualistic suicide was not always a part of the group's theology. Rather, "for the first decade of the group's history it flatly rejected the very notion of suicide, arguing instead for the need to transition into the heavens while still embodied" (Zeller, 175). So what mechanism triggered the shift from embodied to disembodied transformation? The matter is still up for debate, but it should be noted that the death of cofounder Bonnie Lu Nettles of liver cancer in 1985 caused some cognitive dissonance among the membership. This period also marked the beginning of the group's devaluation of the body (from this point on, referred to as "vessels") that may have been a first step in their formulation of ritual suicide as spiritual release to the next level above human. This new understanding of the body, in combination with the belief that the earth was soon to be "recycled," played out when the comet Hale-Bopp manifested itself in the late-March skies of 1997. For Applewhite and the members of the Heaven's Gate group, this was *the sign*. A hypothesis was promoted by the group that located behind this comet was a spaceship that would gather the "elect" for the trip to the level above human. Although Zeller argued (as mentioned above) that the experienced sense of persecution and failure was not sufficient to explain the ritualistic violence that the group enacted, members were convinced in the days leading up to their end of "a massive government conspiracy to hide an extraterrestrial flying saucer trailing the comet" (Zeller, 177).

Epilogue

This essay began by questioning whether the book of Revelation was the sole source for the rich apocalyptic legacy in Western Christendom. It is, according to this essay, no doubt a tour de force in that history. Yet the history also reveals that Western Christians have had an ambivalent relationship with Revelation. The post-Augustinian shift from historical to spiritual readings is demonstrative of that point. That shift was, like Matthew and Luke's appropriation of Mark, a domestication of the apocalyptic tradition. And from roughly that point in history, Christians have both foregrounded and retreated from that position based on our interpretive agendas. The biblical tradition and the interpretive legacy have embedded within them *both* potentialities, for historicizing or for spiritualizing readings, and we are their inheritors.

With this inheritance comes great responsibility. History shows how easy it is for those enthusiastic for a final, definitive ending to risk actions that bring about lesser, still devastating ends. Today, however, more is at stake than the welfare of the members of an apocalyptic group. Apocalyptic scripts and a highly weaponized world make for a volatile mixture. As Catherine Wessinger observes, for example,

> In the 1980s Americans learned that President Reagan (Republican, served 1981–1989) had been influenced by [Hal] Lindsey's predictions about the roles of Israel and nuclear war in the final events. Throughout the Reagan administration Americans who did not believe in these apocalyptic prophecies contemplated the danger of having a Dispensationalist President as commander of the American nuclear arsenal. (Wessinger, 428; cf. Boyer, 140–43)

Apocalyptic scripts also make it much too easy to separate the world into sheep and goats, "axes of evil" and "elect nations"—perpetually seeking to identify antichrists for destruction. For example, George W. Bush's war on terror was often framed in the totalizing language of good versus evil. Again, Wessinger notes that the Bush administration's response to the attacks of 9/11 by Islamic jihadists was an act of "apocalyptic mirroring" (see Rosenfeld) in which "the radical dualism of the Bush administration matched that of jihadists, and Bush's apocalyptic war rhetoric mirrored that of bin Laden and colleagues" (Wessinger, 436). In a speech delivered on September 14, 2011, Bush declared that it was America's responsibility "to answer these attacks *and rid the world of evil*" (italics added; see Räisänen, 155). It should also be noted that the lyrics of hymns such as "Onward Christian Soldiers" and "The Battle Hymn of the Republic"—the musical selections for the Day of Prayer and Remembrance for the victims of 9/11 on September 14, 2001—reflect the anticipation of some fully to participate in the apocalypse on their time rather than God's. But all such appropriations are irrational and zealous impositions on the biblical texts—*all* of the texts we have identified as apocalyptic within the Christian canon (Jewett).

Perhaps it is our role as scholars, theologians, ministers, priests, and simply as rational human beings to remind those in our midst of the consequences of such human impositions on our sacred texts. The models of Jonestown, the Branch Davidians, and Heaven's Gate are just a few examples of the potential for disaster when we set the apocalyptic clock on our time. One could readily add other events and groups to an ever-expanding list (e.g., the Manson Family, Aum Shinrikyo, and the Solar Temple). Against the reflex to expedite the apocalyptic clock, we would do well to heed what the biblical texts actually have to say about the time frame of the end; for example, Jesus' words in Mark 13:32: "But about that day or hour no one knows, not even the angels in heaven, nor the Son, but only the Father." What is most tragic, however, is that our self-imposed acceleration of the apocalyptic clock has also accelerated the dangers of which the seer John issues an awesome warning against anyone who adds to his prophecy.

> I warn everyone who hears the words of the prophecy of this scroll: If anyone adds anything to them, God will add to that person the plagues described in this scroll. And if anyone takes words away from this scroll of prophecy, God will take away from that person any share in the tree of life and in the Holy City, which are described in this scroll. (Rev. 22:18-19)

The reflex to accelerate an apocalyptic schedule has actualized the calamities of which John warns. With or without explicit appeal to apocalyptic texts, the effort to determine the course of history through force has already begun to inflict plagues of biblical proportions on our world: the plague of war, the plague of famine, the plague of disease, the plague of a deteriorating ecosystem, and the plague of abject poverty are just a few prime examples. The time has come to stop and recognize the gravity, both explicit and implicit, of the scriptural inheritances that inform our apocalyptic legacy. Only then will we be able to begin to neutralize it.

Works Cited

Aune, David E. 2005. "Understanding Jewish and Christian Apocalyptic." *WW* 25, no. 3:233–45.

Boyer, Paul. 1992. *When Time Shall Be No More: Prophecy Belief in Modern American Culture.* Cambridge, MA: Harvard University Press.

Cameron, Averil, ed. 1989. *History as Text: The Writing of Ancient History.* Chapel Hill: University of North Carolina Press.

Chilton, Bruce. 2013. *Visions of the Apocalypse: Receptions of John's Revelation in Western Imagination.* Waco, TX: Baylor University Press.

Collins, Adela Yarbro. 1984. *Crisis and Catharsis: The Power of the Apocalypse.* Philadelphia: Westminster.

Collins, John J. 1979. "Introduction: Towards the Morphology of a Genre." *Semeia* 14:1–20.

———. 1984. *The Apocalyptic Imagination: An Introduction to Jewish Apocalyptic Literature.* New York: Crossroad.

Froom, LeRoy E. 2009. *The Prophetic Faith of Our Fathers.* Vol. 4. Hagerstown, MD: Review and Herald Publishing Association.

Hanson, Paul. 1979. *The Dawn of Apocalyptic: The Historical and Sociological Roots of Jewish Apocalyptic Eschatology.* Philadelphia: Fortress Press.

Jones, Ken Sundet. 2005. "The Apocalyptic Luther." *WW* 25, no. 3:233–45.

Koester, Craig R. 2005. "Revelation and the *Left Behind* Novels." *WW* 25, no. 3:274–82.

Kovacs, Judith L. 2005. "The Revelation to John: Lessons from the History of the Book's Reception." *WW* 25, no. 3:255–63.

Moore, Rebecca. 2011. "Narratives of Persecution, Suffering, and Martyrdom: Violence in Peoples Temple and Jonestown." In *Violence and New Religious Movements,* edited by J. R. Lewis, 95–111. Oxford: Oxford University Press.

Jewett, Robert. 1973. *The Captain America Complex: The Dilemma of Zealous Nationalism*. Philadelphia: Westminster.

Luther, Martin. 1960a. "Preface to the Revelation of John [I]." In *LW* 35.

———. 1960b. "Preface to the Revelation of John [II]." In *LW* 35.

Newport, Kenneth. 2009. "Be Thou Faithful Unto Death (cf. Rev. 2.10): The Book of Revelation, The Branch Davidians and Apocalyptic (Self-)Destruction." In *The Way the World Ends? The Apocalypse of John in Culture and Ideology*, edited by W. J. Lyons and Jorunn Økland, 211–26. Sheffield: Sheffield Phoenix.

Perkins, Judith. 1995. *The Suffering Self: Pain and Narrative Representation in the Early Christian Era*. London: Routledge.

Phelan, John Leddy. 1970. *The Millennial Kingdom of the Franciscans in the New World*. Berkeley: University of California Press.

Räisänen, Heikki. 2009. "Revelation, Violence, and War: Glimpses of a Dark Side." In *The Way the World Ends? The Apocalypse of John in Culture and Ideology*, edited by W. J. Lyons and Jorunn Økland, 211–26. Sheffield: Sheffield Phoenix.

Rosenfeld, Jean E. 2011. "Nativists Millennialism." In *The Oxford Handbook of Millennialism*, edited by Catherine Wessinger, 89–109. New York: Oxford University Press.

Royalty, Robert M., Jr. 2005. "The Dangers of the Apocalypse." *WW* 25, no. 3:283–93.

Sánchez, David A. 2008. *From Patmos to the Barrio: Subverting Imperial Myths*. Minneapolis: Fortress Press.

Wainwright, Arthur W. 1993. *Mysterious Apocalypse: Interpreting the Book of Revelation*. Nashville: Abingdon.

Wessinger, Catherine. 2014. "Apocalypse and Violence." In *The Oxford Handbook of Apocalyptic Literature*, edited by John J. Collins, 422–40. New York: Oxford University Press.

Wright, Melanie J. 2009. "Every Eye Shall See Him": Revelation and Film. In *The Way the World Ends? The Apocalypse of John in Culture and Ideology*, edited by W. J. Lyons and Jorunn Økland, 76–94. Sheffield: Sheffield Phoenix.

Wright, Stuart A. 2011. "Revisiting the Branch Davidian Mass Suicide Debate." In *Violence and New Religious Movements*, edited by J. R. Lewis, 113–31. Oxford: Oxford University Press.

Zeller, Benjamin E. 2011. "The Euphemization of Violence: The Case of Heaven's Gate." In *Violence and New Religious Movements*, edited by J. R. Lewis, 173–89. Oxford: Oxford University Press.

Situating the Apostle Paul in His Day and Engaging His Legacy in Our Own

Neil Elliott

After Jesus of Nazareth, the apostle Paul is the most significant figure in the New Testament. The letters he wrote, other letters attributed to him, and the portion of the Acts of the Apostles dedicated to him together account for about a third of its pages. In Christian churches that read the Bible according to lectionary cycles, Paul's is the single voice more often heard than any other, as his epistles are read in all three years of a cycle. Throughout Christian history, Paul has been revered as one of the chief witnesses of the risen Christ (1 Cor. 15:3-8) and as his "apostle to the nations" (Rom. 1:1-5, 13; 11:13; 15:16-18; Gal. 2:8). (The Greek word *apostolos* means one "sent," as on a mission; the translation "nations" will be discussed below.)

It is customary in modern scholarship (and in this commentary) to distinguish the letters whose authenticity has only rarely been questioned from other letters that appear under his name but are regarded by many scholars as pseudepigrapha—"falsely attributed" writings by others, after Paul's death, who traded on his name to win acceptance for their ideas. The genuine (or "unquestioned") letters are Romans, 1 and 2 Corinthians, Galatians, Philippians, 1 Thessalonians, and Philemon. (This is their order of appearance in our New Testament, based originally on decreasing length; one reconstruction of their probable chronological order is indicated in the timeline below.) The disputed letters include Colossians, Ephesians, 2 Thessalonians, and the Pastoral Epistles (see the discussions in the introductions to those letters). The genuine letters are premiere sources for understanding the beginnings of Christianity, but they are nonetheless puzzling and paradoxical sources, for reasons to be discussed below. The New Testament collection, however, makes no distinction between "genuine" and pseudepigraphic letters, presenting all alike as "Pauline Epistles" and as Scripture. As a consequence, not only are letters widely regarded as pseudepigrapha routinely read, especially in churches, as if they were from Paul himself, but also ambiguous passages in the unquestioned letters are frequently understood as if Paul "must have" meant the same thing that the disputed letters say.

A Basic Chronology of Paul's Life and Career (after Taylor, 35–40)

33	Crucifixion of Jesus
34	Paul's "conversion" (or better, call)
35–38	Missionary activity in Arabia (including escape from Damascus and from the ethnarch Aretas IV)
38	First visit to Jerusalem
38–48	Missionary activity in Syria and Cilicia
48	Second visit to Jerusalem (the "Apostolic Council")
48–52	Missionary activity in Asia Minor (Galatia), northern Greece (Philippi, Thessalonica, and Beroea), and Achaia (including Corinth)
50–56	Writing of 1 Thessalonians
51–52	Hearing before Gallio
52–55	Missionary activity centered in Ephesus; writing of Galatians, 1 Corinthians, portions of 2 Corinthians, Philemon, perhaps Philippians
55–57	Final missionary activity in Greece (Macedonia and Achaia); writing of other portions of 2 Corinthians and, from Corinth, Romans
57–59	Journey to Jerusalem with offering; arrest and imprisonment
59–60	Journey to Rome as prisoner
60–62	Imprisonment in Rome; perhaps writing of Philippians and Philemon
c. 62	Execution under Nero

Although Paul has been revered down the centuries, he was also opposed from the beginning, and today he is held by many men and women in suspicion, within the churches as much as outside them. Paul has been reviled—and not only in the modern age!—as a religious huckster who betrayed the teaching of Jesus, concocted a mythology of heavenly redemption through his death, and, in his enthusiasm for that religion, imposed on his converts a harsh doctrine of subordination to gender and social hierarchies (famously, Kazantzakis, 473–77). His detractors have regarded him as a spiritual charlatan at worst, a deeply flawed personality at best, and have regarded his letters as a toxic residue still leaching into contemporary culture with harmful consequences. Even in churches where his figure elicits deep devotion, Paul also evokes wariness, even antipathy, among men and women who have suffered real injuries under the invocation of his name.

To the historian of Christian origins, and of the relationship between early Christianity and Judaism in particular, Paul's letters are indispensable. But because the information they provide is partial and far less than the historian would like in producing a convincing picture, we are compelled to fill in the blanks with educated but nonetheless imaginative reconstructions. Not surprisingly, historians draw different conclusions, due to the different weights they give to various aspects of the evidence and to their assumptions about the scope and significance of their subject—assumptions shaped as much by their own social locations as by the scientific aura of historiography.

Paul's letters also present considerable challenges to readers seeking spiritual inspiration or theological clarity. They may be surprised how uninterested Paul actually appears to have been in elaborating metaphors or themes that have subsequently proven important for Christian doctrine. The obvious explanation is that Paul wrote his letters for others, far removed from us in historical circumstance and cultural presuppositions, and simply did not explain what he presumed his readers would understand. But because Paul himself repeatedly declares that Scripture (by which he meant Israel's Scripture) was "written for our sake" and that it provides examples "for us" (1 Cor. 9:8; 10:1-11), and a later Pauline letter declares that "all scripture is inspired by God and is useful for teaching, for reproof, for correction, and for training in righteousness" (2 Tim. 3:16), the rehearsal of such phrases has encouraged many modern readers to expect that his words (which, after all, are "Scripture" for many in our day) should be completely transparent and self-explanatory to the spiritually discerning. These readers will often be disappointed. Christian clergy—who are often familiar with the critical issues involved—would do well not only to mention these issues in their preaching and teaching but also to cultivate an awareness in their communities that reading Paul's letters is a complicated affair.

Beyond the confines of Christian churches as well as within them, statements from Paul's letters have come to be woven into the fabric of social roles and expectations in contemporary life—in the public sphere and domestic spaces alike. Modern readers may well find ourselves chafing against those statements. Much of the contemporary interest in Paul—in scholarly circles as well as beyond them—is driven by concerns to address the sometimes ambivalent, sometimes acutely painful legacy of his remarks, most often by seeking to set them into one or another historical context in Paul's life or the life of one or another assembly. None of these efforts have yet won universal acceptance, however, for reasons that cannot be attributed solely to the agendas—or the obstinacy—of the apostle's various interpreters. Paul's letters themselves present a confounding array of puzzles and problems. Even if a particular reconstruction of the past should prove convincing, its significance for the present would remain a conundrum, for Paul's letters are accorded very different levels of authority in different churches, let alone in a putatively secular society.

This essay will not attempt to resolve these interpretive questions or to set out a definitive portrait of Paul. To the contrary, one of its themes will be the remarkable variety of alternative interpretations on offer today. The task will instead be to identify some of the most important questions raised in the encounter with Paul and to discuss the sorts of decisions readers must make in the attempt to answer them. We will proceed in an order corresponding to the sequence in commentary entries in this volume. First, we will explore aspects of Paul's letters and of his apostolic work in their ancient context. Next, we will consider some of the varied ways Paul has been remembered, and appropriated, through history. And last, we will turn to questions of Paul's legacy and the interpreter's responsibility today.

Historical Puzzles in the Letters

Paul's letters are important to the historian for several reasons. They offer the only direct access to a first-person voice in the New Testament. (Jesus left behind no writings; the Gospel narrators are anonymous; and the epistles that appear under the names of Peter, James, and John are considered by many scholars to be pseudonymous: see the introductions to those writings.) They are also the earliest writings from the nascent movement of believers in Christ (with the possible exception of the hypothetical document Q: see the introduction to the Gospels).

But it is the powerful story that lies implicit behind Paul's letters that attracts and intrigues the historian, no less than the Christian believer. It is the story of a Pharisee, "zealous" for the law and ardent in his opposition to the earliest followers of Jesus, who was caught up short when "God revealed his son" to him and "called" Paul to be Christ's apostle (Gal. 1:13-17). That language evokes Israel's prophets, who were "called" and "sent" to deliver God's word; and if Jeremiah could speak of the word of the Lord like a fire "burning" irrepressibly in his bones (Jer. 20:8-9), Paul could declare that he had been "crucified with Christ; and it is no longer I who live, but it is Christ who lives in me" (Gal. 2:19-20). The intensity of the experience to which Paul repeatedly alludes has long attracted the attention of theorists of religion, whether or not they are sympathetic to Christian belief (Ashton; Meeks and Fitzgerald). Further, Paul's sharp juxtaposition of his "earlier life in Judaism" (Gal. 1:13-14) with his newfound life "in Christ" has long been read as evidence of his "conversion," his abrupt and total reversal from life under Torah to life in a new reality, though that understanding has been challenged and largely undermined, at least in scholarly circles, in the last half of the twentieth century (Stendahl; but see Kim).

Whatever its nature (a question to which we return below), the intensity of Paul's experience is echoed in the intensity of concern he expresses for "all the churches" (2 Cor. 11:28), the assemblies that he founded in various cities in Asia Minor, Macedonia, and Achaia. (The Greek word *ekklēsia* is usually translated "church" in English Bibles, and the Latin loanword *ecclesia* gives us the adjective "ecclesiastical" for all things churchly, but *ekklēsia* was also used in Paul's day for a civic assembly in a Greek city, and so a growing minority of interpreters prefer the translation "assembly.") The letters provide us tantalizing glimpses onto landscapes of community life in very different congregations, landscapes that defy easy description or even harmonization with each other. Because Paul addresses a bewildering assortment of issues in his correspondence with the Corinthian believers, our 1 and 2 Corinthians, which probably represent a compilation of earlier, more fragmentary letters (see the entries for each letter), are irresistible to the historian, and have often been used as the primary evidence for generalizations about "Pauline Christianity" (see Meeks; Theissen). But what situation should we imagine prompted these letters: a rift between Paul and the (more law-observant) Jerusalem apostles and their adherents (Barrett)? The impulses of an incipient Gnosticism among the

Corinthians (Schmithals)? Differences in economic status, reflected in theological conflicts (Theissen)? Tension between Paul's social experience and that of inspired women in the congregations (Wire)? Each of these answers (and there are more!) grasps at real clues in the letters, but none has won universal recognition for its capacity to explain the whole. And the issues Paul encountered in Corinth are quite different from those he addressed in letters to other cities.

And how should we understand Paul himself? To take a single question as an example, Paul tells the Romans that the horizon of his concern for the assemblies is not just the calling to secure "the obedience of faith among all the nations" (Rom. 1:5, my translation): that obligation is based in a deeper anguish for his "own people," that is, "Israelites" (Rom. 9:1-5). It is the clashing juxtaposition of what generations of readers have taken as Paul's "conversion," or from another perspective, his apparent *apostasy* from Judaism, with such expressions of abiding *loyalty* to the people Israel that generates some of the liveliest controversies in biblical scholarship today. Should we understand Paul as having left central aspects of his former life in Judaism behind, or, as a matter of principle, should we interpret his work and thought *within* Judaism? (See Nanos and Zetterholm.)

Stories We Tell about Paul

In the mid-twentieth century, Rudolf Bultmann wrote what stands as a crisp summary of Paul's place in early Christianity:

> Standing within the frame of Hellenistic Christianity, he raised the theological motifs that were at work in the proclamation of the Hellenistic church to the clarity of theological thinking; he called to attention the problems latent in the Hellenistic proclamation and brought them to a decision; and thus—so far as our sources permit an opinion on the matter—became the founder of Christian theology. (Bultmann, 187)

This summary makes clear that Paul did not develop his views from nothing, as some sort of theological genius: he joined a movement already in the lively process of developing beliefs and practices, and he received its most important traditions (see 1 Cor. 11:2, 23-26; 15:3-7). Scholars differ, however, among themselves and with Bultmann, regarding the key phrase in this summary. What *were* "the problems latent in the Hellenistic proclamation"? Bultmann recognized that Paul did not invent a movement that welcomed non-Jews without requiring Torah observance of them; that is, he already stood "within the frame of Hellenistic Christianity." But as Bultmann understood it, that frame appeared more a strategy of opportunity than a theological principle, and talk of freedom from the law could easily be construed by one or another Hellenistic church as mere libertinism. For Bultmann (as for many Protestant interpreters before and after him), Paul's grappling with the Hellenistic church required him to resolve tensions between the characteristically Jewish understanding of the human before God—which *had* been Paul's own understanding—and the understanding to which Paul had been brought "in Christ," especially regarding the role of the law in the human's obedience to God's claim. Even "within the frame of Hellenistic Christianity," then, the apostle was preoccupied in letter after letter by an implicit debate *with Judaism*. The eventual prevalence of a law-free "gentile" church is not a historical accident or an aberration, but the triumph of Paul's own ideas. Thus, although he did not write the Letter to the Ephesians, its calm assurance of the Torah's irrelevance to those who are "in Christ" could be regarded, on this view, as "the quintessence of Paulinism" (Peake).

Here a note on the translation of a Greek term *ethnē* is important. The word, a plural, literally means "peoples" or "nations," and is used throughout Jewish Scripture to mean the nations *other than Israel.* In many English New Testament translations, however, it is rendered "Gentiles." The capitalized form is potentially misleading since it suggests a coherent ethnic identity, like "Scythian" or "Egyptian," though no individuals in the ancient world called themselves "Gentiles." Furthermore, the same word is sometimes translated two different ways in the same Bible. For example, the NRSV uses "nations" in Isaiah, but "Gentiles" in Romans 15:9-12, *even where Paul is quoting the same passages from Isaiah.* The effect is subtle, but meaningful: it suggests that Paul imagines two sorts of people in the world, "Jews" and "everyone else," and is preoccupied with the boundary line that distinguishes them.

Just this understanding of Paul has been hotly contested in the late twentieth and early twenty-first centuries, however. We may broadly distinguish three "stories" that interpreters now tell about the apostle.

Paul as Convert from Judaism

The first story prevailed in Bultmann's day, as it still does today in much of Christianity. Paul received a preeminent education as a Jew. (Acts names him "Saul" in this period and makes him a student of the famed Rabbi Gamaliel II: 5:34; 22:3.) Indeed, his self-professed credentials, "as to the law, a Pharisee; as to zeal, a persecutor of the church; as to righteousness under the law, blameless" (Phil. 3:5-6), "zealous for the traditions of my ancestors" (Gal. 1:14), are an accurate self-appraisal as an exemplary Jew. It is as a representative Jew that he sought "a righteousness of [his] own that comes from the law" (Phil. 3:9), for all Israel characteristically strove for "the righteousness that is based on the law . . . as if it were based on works" (Rom. 9:31-32). On this view, Paul (Saul) the Pharisee persecuted the early believers in Jesus because they had, in some way he found intolerable, flouted or ignored the law. The reversal occasioned by the "revelation" of Christ to him was nothing less than a conversion, a personal about-face from one who now abandoned any effort at achieving his own righteousness through works of law and accepted instead the righteousness "on the basis of faith," meaning trust in Jesus (Rom. 9:32).

From this point on, Paul was opposed by other Jews because he adamantly insisted the law had no positive role in salvation: it provided only the knowledge of sin (Rom. 7:7). His resolve to approach those outside the law "as one outside the law" (1 Cor. 9:19-21) and his judgment that "nothing is unclean in itself" (Rom. 14:14) show his rejection of the Torah's binding authority. Even the Jerusalem apostles (and their delegates) fought Paul on these points, refusing to accept shared meals between Jews and "Gentiles" at Antioch (Gal. 2:11-14; for the view that the law forbade even social "associations" between Jews and gentiles, see Acts 10:28). Paul saw this failure as hypocrisy on the part of the apostles (Gal. 2:14), and could only regard with anguish his fellow Jews' stubborn insistence on that righteousness "as if based on works." Though Paul (in Gal. 2:1-9) and

Acts (15:1-29) agree that the Jerusalem apostles accepted his mission to the "uncircumcision," they apparently acquiesced when Paul was accused by other Jews of flouting the law himself and teaching other Jews to do the same (see Acts 21:17-36). Jewish antagonists further accused Paul (falsely, according to Luke) of bringing gentiles into the temple court, a capital offense—but James and the other apostles play no further role in the narrative. Paul's subsequent pleas before kings and Roman magistrates are eloquent arguments that he represents the true legacy of Israel's Scriptures, but by the end of the story he has convinced only a minority of Jews who hear him. The "parting of the ways" between Judaism and Christianity is already evident in the response to Paul. The anguish he expressed for his "kindred according to the flesh" (Rom. 9:1-4) was his response to their final failure to obey his gospel.

This is the account most familiar to readers today, and it still predominates in Christian preaching. Since the last quarter of the twentieth century it has been challenged, however, because of several landmark developments. One is the discovery in the 1940s and 1950s of the Dead Sea Scrolls, which bore abundant witness to a form of Judaism that could not be identified with the "works-righteousness" Paul presumably opposed, and that often sounded "Pauline," as in its insistence that "by [God's] righteousness alone is a human righteous" (e.g., 1QH 5.18; 8.12). Because the scrolls also included multiple copies of some Jewish texts that had previously been known, but marginalized in biblical interpretation (e.g., *Jubilees, 1 Enoch*), they sparked renewed interest in such "pseudepigraphic" writings and a growing awareness that Second Temple Judaism was a far richer and more complex array of religious expressions than the traditional account had allowed.

Second, in the wake of the mass murder of European Jews (the Shoah or "Holocaust"), many European and US churches turned to processes of institutional soul-searching, seeking to identify and repudiate aspects of Christian teaching that traded in stereotype and caricature of Jews and Judaism (see, notably, the Roman Catholic document *Nostra Aetate*). In this changed environment, older Jewish objections to Paul's rhetoric suddenly gained new attention from Christian and other interpreters.

Third, these developments provided the space in which new and innovative scholarly monographs appeared that reconfigured the relationship of Paul, Judaism, and the origins of Christianity (Ruether; Stendahl; Sanders). E. P. Sanders's demonstration that the traditional understanding of "works-righteousness" was *not* current in Paul's day issued in a changed climate, sometimes called the "post-Sanders era," in which a "new perspective on Paul" began to take shape (Dunn 1983; 1998).

Paul as the Champion of a Law-Free Church

The "new perspective" (now more than thirty years old) actually includes a variety of different interpretations, united by their acceptance of the agenda posed by Sanders. We may nevertheless sketch the outlines of a coherent second narrative in this array of new-perspective readings. Here, Paul is *not* assumed to have been a representative Jew, but (taking him at his word) is seen to have persecuted the early churches out of an extreme hyperobservance, having been "*far more* zealous for the traditions of my ancestors" than his peers (Gal. 1:13-14, emphasis added). Paul did not suffer the sort of introspective anguish regarding his own salvation that would later preoccupy Martin

Luther and subsequent Western interpreters; rather than being "converted" to a new understanding of redemption, Paul experienced a "call" similar to the call of Israel's prophets (Stendahl). This calling was specifically to bring a *biblical*, that is, *Jewish* message of salvation to the nations (or "gentiles"). The proper focus of interpretation, on this view, is thus not "soteriology" (the salvation of individuals) but the sociological behavior of groups. The "works of law" against which Paul repeatedly inveighed (Gal. 2:16; 3:2, 5, 10; Rom. 3:27-28; 4:2, 4-6; 9:32; 11:6) are now relieved of the burden of summarizing a Jewish theology of redemption; they should instead be identified with specific "boundary-maintaining" practices that distinguished Jews from their non-Jewish neighbors, especially circumcision, kosher diet, and Sabbath observance. Rather than opposing a Jewish understanding of "redemption" or "justification from works," Paul was defending the "gentile church" from Jewish opponents who sought to incorporate Paul's converts into Jewish life according to more traditional channels—the acceptance of circumcision and observance of Torah. The difference between Paul and other Jews, then, involved a question of the scope of salvation, rather than its mechanism. Was the covenant people limited to Israel (and "converts" or proselytes to Judaism), or did it, on Paul's innovation, include non-Jews as full members?

Challenges have been raised to this second narrative as well. Except for a few voices who have concluded that Paul's own thought was "inconsistent" or "incoherent" (Sanders; Räisänen), many new-perspective interpreters still put Paul forward as the pioneer of an intelligible and appropriately inclusive faith—the indispensable ancestor of contemporary Christianity. But this also means that Paul is not infrequently contrasted with negative characterizations of Jewish "ethnocentrism" or exclusivism. His identity as a Jew is affirmed, and his conflicts with other Jews are regarded as "inner-Jewish" controversies, but the often unavoidable implication is that Paul and his associates *alone* represented the open, inclusive, "right" legacy of Judaism, in contrast to the narrow and ill-fated insistence of the rest of his Jewish contemporaries on ethnic boundaries of the covenant people. The "parting of the ways" between Christianity and Judaism still appears here to be foreshadowed in Paul's controversies with other Jews.

Paul as a (Non-Christian) Jew

A third narrative has emerged from a small group of interpreters—many of them Jewish scholars of the New Testament—who seek thoroughly to interpret Paul's work and thought within Judaism, without appeal to a dramatic interruption (Paul's vision of Christ) that somehow set him on a course that necessarily led him away from it. On this account, Paul the Pharisee persecuted the early *ekklēsiai* not because of any deviation on their part from Jewish observance, but because their (thoroughly Jewish) proclamation of a messiah who had been crucified by Rome was potentially threatening to the precarious stability of other Jewish communities under Roman rule (Fredriksen, 133–76). As Alan F. Segal shows, Paul's vision of the crucified Jesus in heaven (as obliquely reported in 2 Corinthians 12) was formally similar to other Jewish visionary experiences. While Segal himself did not pursue the implications, we can extrapolate what such a vision might have meant for Paul, on purely Jewish terms, by examining the consequences for earthly life that other Jewish apocalypses drew from comparable visions of heaven. The confirmation of God's sovereignty in heaven generally informed how the apocalyptists understood the possibilities for living under oppressive Hellenistic or Roman rule (Portier-Young). Similarly, the vision of the crucified Jesus as heavenly Christ likely would have had immediate political implications for Paul (Elliott 1994, 140–80). This vision involved no halakhic "conversion": Paul remained a Jew (and never became a "Christian": Eisenbaum). These interpreters (in his essay in this volume, Lawrence M. Wills calls their view a "radical new perspective") point out that there is no evidence anywhere in his letters that Paul himself relinquished observance of Torah or taught other Jews to do so. (Paul's comment about acting "as one outside the law" in 1 Cor. 9:19-21 does not mean apostasy, on this view, but only a tactical choice to socialize with non-Jews.)

Paul's vision did involve Paul's perception of non-Jewish adherents to the proclamation of Jesus as the fulfillment of biblical prophecy. They were the "nations" who would turn to Israel and Israel's Messiah at the last day. (Note here that the term *ethnē* is given its more natural meaning "nations": Paul's concern is not with the un-Jewish ethnic identity of individuals but with relations between the world's nations and Israel, and with the biblical vision of international harmony to be achieved in the messianic age.) That is, Paul's resistance to the pressure to "normalize" these converts by making them Jews had nothing to do with any perceived insufficiency in Judaism or the law. It had everything to do with his expectation that *morally* converted non-Jews—rare enough, in Diaspora Jewish eyes—*united around obedience to Israel's Messiah, and in solidarity with Israel*—would be as clear a signal to other Jews as they were to him that the messianic age had dawned. His organization of a collection for "the poor among the holy ones" in Jerusalem (Rom. 15:25-28), which he perceived both as a gesture of reciprocity and as a sacred "offering" that he presented as a priestly service (Rom. 15:14-16, 27), was motivated by this expectation.

On this interpretation, already foreshadowed in some ways by Johannes Munck, Paul's disagreements with the Jerusalem apostles (e.g., in Antioch: Galatians 2) are not deep theological fissures but tactical or rhetorical differences (see Nanos 1996; 2002). His differences from Jews outside the assemblies arose, on one side, from his belief that the messianic age has arrived, and on the other, from the concern of Jews who did not share that belief to protect their communities from scrutiny or suspicion—the sort of unwanted attention that messianic agitation on the part of Paul's non-Jewish newcomers might prompt. As to the question of justification from works of law, interpreters in this third perspective hew methodologically to the principle that any of Paul's statements regarding the law *made in letters addressed primarily to non-Jews* should be read narrowly as statements about the significance of the law *for non-Jews*, rather than generalized statements about the Torah's role in salvation. The nature of *Jewish* opposition to Paul is less the focus of attention here than in the preceding two perspectives; on the other hand, the possible motivations of *non-Jews* in Paul's assemblies to adopt *some* Torah observances—but not all (see Gal. 5:2-3)—is a paramount consideration. Here, interpreters explore possible reasons for anxiety on the part of non-Jews who may have seen in the Torah the promise of achieving the goal of "self-mastery" (*enkrateia*) so highly prized in post-Augustan culture (Stowers 1994), or (in Galatia) might have sought to "pass" in Roman society, taking on some of the mystique of the synagogue in order to make their refusal of customary Roman worship ("idolatry") more palatable to their Roman neighbors (Gaston; Nanos

2002, 257–71; Kahl 2010). Paul's resistance to "Judaizing" is seen here as his thoroughly Jewish reaction to aberrant behavior on the part of non-Jews.

Similarly, the Letter to the Romans has been read as an admonitory warning to non-Jews not to show disdain or contempt for Jews. That warning is evident enough in Rom. 11:13-32, but in earlier interpretation, that passage was often seen as an isolated aside. When chapters 9–11 are read as the "climax" of the letter and the whole letter is read as rhetoric directed to a primarily non-Jewish audience, the brief address to a hypothetical Jew in Romans 2–3 is no longer seen as an attempt to "explode Jewish privilege"; rather it supports the overarching purpose of the letter to correct non-Jewish error. Here, too, Paul appears to offer a fundamentally Jewish response to aspects of the emerging Hellenistic church (Elliott 1990; 2008).

Paul against Roman Imperial Ideology

If, in service of the last-named narrative, interpreters have tried in different ways to understand Paul within Judaism, that effort seems also to have involved understanding Judaism not just as a *religion* or an *ethnic identification* (it was, of course, both in Paul's day), but also as participation in an identity construed in different ways by outsiders. The experience of Jews *under Roman rule*—as a minority population seeking civic recognition in different Roman cities and under different imperial regimes—becomes a central concern of such interpretation of Paul (Smallwood). A new field of study has sprung up since the late 1980s around the relationship between "Paul and empire." That scholarship initially sought to challenge the apolitical character of previous "theological" interpretation and to wrest Paul from what had become a fairly tight grip on his legacy on the political right, where Paul was routinely presented as an advocate of political quietism and social conservatism (points to which we return below). "Paul and empire" scholarship and the adjacent field of postcolonial study of Paul have now become themselves the object of scrutiny and debate, which is all to the good (see Horsley 1997; 2000; 2004; Stanley; McKnight and Modica 2013). It bears note, however, that these areas are not only concerned with the ways Paul is interpreted and appropriated for political purposes today. They also inform, and necessarily so, the investigation of Paul as a member of the Jewish Diaspora in the Roman world (Nanos and Zetterholm).

The Paradox of Reading Paul's Letters Today

Many, perhaps most, readers of Paul's letters come to them with religious interest. Paul's letters have long offered Christianity a rich resource for devotion and for theological reflection. As mentioned above, the letters are the most frequently encountered vein of Scripture in many churches. At least some of the more lyrical passages in them, such as Paul's assurance that nothing "will be able to separate us from the love of God in Christ Jesus our Lord" (Rom. 8:28-39) or his praise of love as the "better way" (1 Cor. 12:31—13:13), are among the most cherished passages of Scripture for many people. Metaphors that appear in Paul's arguments have exercised powerful and decisive influence in Christian theology: that of baptism as a "dying with Christ," for example (Rom. 6:3-11), or of the church as the "body" of Christ (Rom. 12:3-7; 1 Cor. 12:4-30), or the Lord's Supper as a proclamation of the death of Jesus (1 Cor. 11:17-34). Paul's use of an apparently preexisting Christian hymn in Philippians has shaped Christian understanding of the divinity of Christ as one who, though "in the form of God," "emptied himself" to accept "the form of a slave" and humbled himself even further, in obedience to God, to the point of "death on a cross" (Phil. 2:6-8).

This familiarity makes for a remarkable paradox: When we read these letters today, we do so with purposes Paul never imagined, and may grant them an importance they never enjoyed in Paul's own day. They are our primary source for understanding Paul; but that was not true for Paul's first readers, for whom he was not a "biblical author" to be "interpreted." The possibility of reading the letters anachronistically inevitably increases when they are incorporated into modern worship as "Scripture."

The Paradox of "Theological" or "Pastoral" Readings

It should strike us as curious that readers today approach even Paul's genuine letters to discover his "theology." After all, we do not have a sample of the message Paul initially proclaimed to gather a community (although many interpreters have tried to read Romans as such). Rather, all of the letters were written to assemblies some time *after* Paul—or, in the case of Romans, others—had founded them. In his letters, Paul sought to strengthen or, occasionally, as he saw it, to correct their adherence to Christ. As a consequence, the letters have a theological character, but they never spell out his convictions in any systematic way. Paul often leaves a key conviction unspoken, since he could presume his audience already had heard, or heard about, his proclamation. The letters are therefore problematic sources, at best, from which the premises and contours of "Paul's theology" might be constructed as an exercise of historical imagination.

The passage from Philippians cited above, for example, shows that Paul's understanding of the death of Jesus already depended on traditions he received from early assemblies that preceded him. He explicitly acknowledged as much when he wrote to the Corinthians, "I handed on to you as of first importance what I in turn had received: that Christ died for our sins in accordance with the scriptures" (1 Cor. 15:3). Note that Paul does not explain here which Scriptures he has in mind, or just what dying "for our sins" meant. In fact, Paul could describe the salvific value of Christ's death in different ways: as a "sacrifice of atonement" (*hilastērion*, Rom. 3:24-25), though Paul never elaborates a comparison with the ritual of the Day of Atonement (as does Hebrews); or as the slaughter (NRSV: "sacrifice") of a Passover lamb (1 Cor. 5:7)—a very different ritual!—or as deliverance from the "curse" of Deut. 21:23, though, again, this reference seems to have played no larger part in his thinking (Gal. 3:13). Surprisingly, amid these diverse and conflicting metaphors, Paul never offers even a rudimentary explanation of just *how* he understands Christ to have "died for our sins." He is more concerned, in Romans, to insist that those who have "died *with* Christ" in baptism (another dramatic metaphor that is simply asserted, not explained) can no longer live in sin, having been joined to Christ's obedience (Romans 5–6).

His purpose in these letters (and in the apostolic work of which they are occasional instruments) has been described as "pastoral." This might also strike us as curious, since Paul was not evidently interested in the sort of long-term spiritual accompaniment of individuals and families in settled congregations that we associate today with pastoral ministry. (Indeed, he seems intentionally to have left such work to others whom he described as his "coworkers," *synergoi*.) The "daily pressure" about which Paul complained to the Corinthians, caused by his "anxiety for all the assemblies" ("churches": 2 Cor. 11:28 NRSV), was less oriented to the self-fulfillment of individuals than to the sanctity in which they were to maintain themselves. ("Saints"—literally, "holy ones" [*hagioi*]—was Paul's preferred designation for members of his assemblies.) Looking at the non-Jewish world through the eyes of a Hellenistic Jew, Paul regarded the hallmarks of such holiness in the avoidance of the vices characteristic of that world—the worship of other gods, using tangible forms ("idolatry"), and a range of sexual transgressions to which he simply referred as "immorality" (*porneia*: see Gaca; Ruden)—and the maintenance of an ethos of affectionate mutual regard characteristic of the idealized Roman household. Paul sought to establish a sort of baseline of such holiness and then, on an ad hoc basis, to perform whatever corrections were needed to maintain it. We might consider Paul "pastoral," then, to the extent that he was an "advisor" who "counseled" his congregations "in order to be able to present them to Christ at his coming, which Paul expected in the near future" (Dahl, 73, citing Rom. 15:16; 1 Cor. 1:8; 2 Cor. 11:2; Phil. 1:10-11; 1 Thess. 3:13; 5:23).

He described his work to the Romans in terms of priestly service (*latreuein*, Rom. 1:9; *diakonos, leitourgos, hierourgōn*, 15:8, 16, terms associated with public ritual action). He sought to present to God "the obedience of the nations" (Rom. 15:17; see 1:5-6), represented in each city by the holy living of individuals on whom he called to present their bodies as "a living sacrifice, holy and acceptable to God" (Rom. 12:1-2), and on an international scale by the sanctified "offerings [*prosphora*] of the nations" (Rom. 15:16-17). The latter phrase rang with the language of the prophet Isaiah's vision in which the earth's nations streamed to Jerusalem, bearing tribute and joining in the worship of Israel's God (see Isaiah 60, and Paul's quotations in Rom. 15:8-13); but also with echoes of an imperial vision in which conquered peoples offered their gifts to Caesar (e.g., Virgil, *Aeneid* 8.720–23). More prosaically, it referred to the collection of money Paul had gathered from various assemblies in Achaia and Macedonia as "aid for the poor among the saints" in Jerusalem (Rom. 15:25-26). Paul hoped those funds would be received as more than relief, as evidence of a fulfillment of messianic prophecy.

It appears, then, that what might be called the "pastoral" aspect of Paul's work had a much nearer eschatological horizon than many church leaders acknowledge today as they plan decades-long ministerial careers. Even Paul's expression of concern for "all the assemblies" in 2 Corinthians comes at the end of a recital of dangers Paul had faced *in travels abroad* (11:23-27). His letters responded to situations that arose after Paul had *departed* from one city or another, usually after a relatively brief stay—just sufficient to inaugurate an assembly. (Paul's longest stays in a single place, according to the book of Acts, were eighteen months in Corinth and a little more than two years in Ephesus—hardly what many contemporary denominations would consider lengthy "pastorates.") Neither did Paul apply himself to what we might call "church growth." To judge from one admittedly conflictual but nonetheless telling situation, he gave thanks that during his initial stay in Corinth he had baptized only Crispus and Gaius, and the household of Stephanas (1 Cor. 1:14-16); the increase of the Corinthian congregation under the baptismal ministry of Apollos, and the lively competition of perspectives that increase generated, precipitated a crisis for him (1 Cor. 2:1—3:15). Paul seems to have regarded innovation with suspicion: his interventions were intended to preserve the assemblies in an initial, pristine state of "holiness" as they awaited the imminent return of Christ. This aspect of Paul's work shows him ever on the move, eager to establish fledgling congregations and then to move on. He looks back, through his letters or the efforts of his colleagues, to maintain the sanctity of a congregation over what he clearly believes will be the short term.

The culmination of Paul's story, however, was a series of disappointments bordering on the tragic. We cannot say whether his views immediately prevailed in controversies in Corinth or in Rome. We do know, however, that the anxiety he expressed concerning his last journey to Jerusalem, bearing the collection, was more than warranted. The story told in Acts 21 describes controversy in Jerusalem over Paul's allegiance to the Torah and the accusation—which Luke considers false—that Paul had brought some, at least, of his non-Jewish delegates into the precincts of the temple that were reserved for Jews alone (21:28-29). The riot that ensued set Paul on a narrative road that ends in Rome, whither he was sent on charges of civil unrest that he was compelled to appeal before the emperor (Acts 22–28).

The deep symbolic significance Paul attached to the collection, his reason for being in Jerusalem, goes unmentioned in Acts; so also, then, is any hint at the effect of its failure on him. Also missing is any account of Paul's subsequent hearing before Nero, or any reference to Paul's execution, on the emperor's authority, events reported in other sources (*Acts of Paul* 10.6; Eusebius, *Hist. eccl.* 2.25.5). Instead of these catastrophes, Luke offers the reader the triumph of Paul speaking the word of proclamation boldly before assembled philosophers in Athens (17:16-34); before the Roman procurators Felix and Festus and the Judean king Agrippa (chapters 24–26); and—for the first time in the narrative—before an unbiased synagogue audience, in Rome itself (28:17-22). These accomplishments fulfill Jesus' prophecy that his followers would take his word "before kings and governors" (Luke 21:12), and incorporate Paul's last days in Rome within Luke's theme of the inexorable spread of the word "to the ends of the earth" (Acts 1:8). But these triumphant notes come at the cost of what Luke must suppress. The reader will not learn from Acts how much hung, for Paul, on the journey to Jerusalem. Nor does Luke convey the purpose behind Paul's fervent attempts to conform the non-Jews in his assemblies to a life of holiness: namely, in order to impress upon his fellow Jews that they were living in the last days (see Romans 11).

It appears enough for Luke that Paul helped to inaugurate the church of Jews and non-Jews (though he is careful to stipulate that the important first steps were taken by Peter in Joppa, Acts 10). Just so, in the generation after Paul's death, another writer represented the core of Paul's gospel as the "mystery" that God intended Jews and non-Jews to worship together in the name of Christ (Eph. 3:1-6). But while Paul had hoped the "obedience of faith among the nations" would manifest the fulfillment of scriptural promises to Israel, the author of Ephesians understood the Pauline "mystery" to involve the dispensability of Torah itself, its having been "abolished" by Christ (*katargēsas*, Eph. 2:13-16)—an idea that was unthinkable for Paul himself (see Rom. 3:31).

The attention given to reading and interpreting Paul's letters today, especially in churches, may then be described as paradoxical. The paradox lies not just in the fact that these letters were manifestly written to others, centuries ago. It is also a matter of the letters being directed to achieve specific ends that made sense within an eschatological scenario that has not just been "delayed," but has manifestly failed. When Paul is read today simply as the champion of a law-free, "gentile"

Christianity, he is being read through the lens of Ephesians and Acts. But this is to impose onto Paul's letters the "perfect hindsight" that our place "downstream" from him allows us. The temptation for those of us who find our place in the current of gentile Christianity is to imagine that our religion is what Paul sought to found.

The Paradox of Paul's Authority

Some passages in the letters suggest that Paul may have not been the clearest of communicators. In places, Paul seeks to "correct" or manage what he considers his audience's mistaken apprehension of his own earlier teaching (see 1 Cor. 2:1-6; 5:9-13; 1 Thess. 4:13-18), or hints at obligations that were perhaps not explicit earlier (e.g., the master's "duty" in Philem. 8). He admonishes the Corinthians for grievously misunderstanding the nature of the Lord's Supper, though he had passed along to them traditions he obviously considered important (1 Cor. 11:17-34). He is "astonished" at how quickly the Galatians have deserted his teaching (Gal. 1:6-9), though he refers obliquely to having taught something else earlier (did he once "preach circumcision," 5:11? Is he now "building up" what he once "tore down," 2:18?). In none of these passages does Paul admit that he has changed his mind, or that he might not have spoken clearly in the first place—even when his advice appears to remain contradictory (compare his advice on food offered to idols in 1 Corinthians 8 and 10:14-22). Further, his readers may well have been confused when he took a different tack than what they may have heard from the tradition of Jesus' words—regarding questions of marriage and divorce, for example (1 Corinthians 7), or his refusal of the support to which apostles are entitled (1 Corinthians 9). They might have been as vexed by his sometimes cavalier attitude to the authority of other apostles (Gal. 2:11-14; 2 Cor. 11:1-6), or his fierce denunciations of "other" gospels (Gal. 1:6-9; 2 Cor. 11:4). If Paul had such difficulty communicating with his first hearers, perhaps the contemporary reader may be forgiven for not finding the meaning of his letters transparent!

Precisely because Paul's letters have been read, preached, cherished, annotated, and exposited over centuries of Christian practice, they present their contemporary readers with another paradox that we might call a "lexical illusion." Put simply, we *read* Paul, and more, we read Paul as a part of the Bible. We thus may think of him as an influential and articulate *writer*, picking up his pen to express sublime thoughts. This would have surprised many of Paul's contemporaries, however, for whom Paul was not, first of all, a writer. (Some adversaries in Corinth contemptuously declared that his letters were the weightiest aspect of his work, and even these were unimpressive: see 2 Cor. 10:9-10.) Nor would many of those who knew him best have regarded him primarily as a "thinker," and certainly not one whose authority was unquestioned. Indeed, one of the most vivid impressions one gets from these letters is that of an ardent and often scrappy polemicist. Paul appears frequently to argue for a viewpoint or a practice that he expects to be controversial, at least, and likely contested by at least a few of his hearers. The Corinthian correspondence shows that Paul faced considerable opposition from some of the more influential members of that assembly who found his arguments unconvincing. Paul's prominence in our New Testament hardly justifies the assumption that his voice normally prevailed in his own day.

It is a commonplace that as readers of Paul's letters, we are "listening in" on only one half of a conversation, but even this is putting the matter too simply. We are listening to an intensely opinionated correspondent! The reverence Paul is accorded in the Christian tradition for his role as paramount guide into the practices of new life "in Christ" is, in large part, the mirror image of the significance Paul claims for himself as he addresses "his" congregations. They may have many guides in Christ, but "not . . . many fathers," he tells the Corinthians in a characteristic claim (1 Cor. 4:15); he is an example to be imitated (Phil. 3:17). His letters often give a contemporary reader the sense of riding an emotional roller coaster. In the rhetoric of 1 and 2 Corinthians, for example, Paul alternates between assuring a community that the Spirit of Christ dwells among them, guiding them and guaranteeing their holiness, and shaming them for not living up to even the rudimentary standards of the pagan world (1 Cor. 5:1-8). To contemporary readers more accustomed to modern ideals of mutual respect and equality among persons, Paul's rhetoric may come across as authoritarian, perhaps even coercive or abusive.

It is the enduring gift of feminist scholarship to have clarified that in his letters (and, we may presume, in his initial face-to-face efforts as well), Paul might *claim*, but could never *presume*, his authority. Indeed, in correspondences such as the Corinthian letters, he appears to be scrambling to find the rhetorical ground from which to assert a right to a hearing. We must take into account, then, not only the existence of another "half" of a conversation but also the possibility that Paul's construal of one or another situation was a minority opinion and may even, on occasion, have been unintelligible to his readers. The point may seem subtle, but it is an important principle to which feminist interpretation calls much-needed attention. A view of biblical authority that *presumes* Paul's voice would have prevailed, simply because it was his, is anachronistic. It takes Paul's letters "out of the public domain where argument is in order and where Paul's strong arguments could have social impact." Careful attention to the way Paul argued shows that he never presumed his voice was sufficient to settle an issue. Rather, he hoped to gain the assent of his hearers to his arguments "*because they are convincing*" (Wire, 10, emphasis added). Today as well, when various and competing appeals are made to this or that passage in Paul's letters, the same principle suggests that mere resort to biblical authority is insufficient and inappropriate: thoughtful and ethical discernment remains our shared responsibility, within the churches no less than in the public square.

Seeing Paul through a Glass, Darkly

I have been dwelling on the challenges and complications of understanding Paul quite deliberately. Any hope that we will arrive at a single understanding of the apostle that will convince everyone must be tempered by recognizing the divergent responses Paul received in his own day and the significant variety of portrayals of Paul that have been cherished over the centuries—beginning with writings found in our New Testament.

The Pauls in the New Testament

We do not have all of Paul's letters to the assemblies: we do not have what he says he earlier wrote to the Corinthians, for example (1 Cor. 5:9). The reference in Col. 4:16 to a letter to the Laodiceans, not otherwise attested, prompted a Christian in the third or fourth century to produce one by patching together phrases from the available letters of Paul. We have Paul's letters, we may presume, because after they were first given the hearing for which Paul wrote them, some persons in the assemblies thought them worth preserving, exchanging with others (see Col. 4:16 again), and collecting. We should also presume that Paul wrote for the purposes that are evident in the letters themselves; the *subsequent* work of preserving, exchanging, and collecting was done for different purposes. The letter form became a popular device by which others disseminated the apostle's thought, *after* his own letters had won whatever (probably mixed) reception they were given. The *Epistle to the Laodiceans*, a third letter to the Corinthians, and correspondence with the philosopher Seneca are examples of letters written by other Christians, living long after the apostle's death, to achieve results for which Paul should hardly be held responsible (for texts discussed here, see Elliott and Reasoner; for further discussion, Pervo). The technical term for such "falsely signed" writing is *pseudepigraphy.*

Today, many interpreters are convinced that pseudepigrapha appear in our New Testament as well as outside it. The "Pastoral" Epistles (1 and 2 Timothy and Titus) are different enough in vocabulary, writing style, and mood, and seem to address so different a situation from the other letters, that they are the most widely considered to be pseudepigrapha. Ephesians is also widely questioned, and after it, Colossians and 2 Thessalonians (but see the entries on these letters). It is a principle of scholarship that judgments about Paul's own thought should be based first on the genuine (that is, the unquestioned) letters, Romans, 1 and 2 Corinthians, Galatians, Philippians, 1 Thessalonians, and Philemon, and that the other, possibly pseudepigraphic letters should be used only when they corroborate what has been found in the genuine letters. From the scholarly viewpoint, the appearance of some pseudepigrapha in our New Testament should not cloud this principle. After all, various writings that are now universally recognized as pseudepigraphic, like the *Acts of Paul* (in which *Laodiceans* and *3 Corinthians* appear), not only were once popular but also were frequently copied and regarded by some Christians as part of the New Testament. Hebrews was often copied after Romans in collections of Paul's letters, on the assumption (now almost universally rejected) that Paul wrote it; the *Epistle to Barnabas*, a pseudepigraphon bearing the name of Paul's erstwhile companion, was also included in some copies of the New Testament. Furthermore, while the shape of our New Testament gives the impression of continuity, leading some interpreters to describe the "canonical" pseudepigrapha (Colossians, Ephesians, and the Pastorals) as appropriate "adaptations" of Paul's legacy by faithful "Pauline churches" or a "Pauline school," there is no *external* basis for establishing only some pseudepigrapha as the creations of such "faithful" disciples of Paul, and rejecting others as deviations or betrayals (Elliott 1994, 25–54). The scholarly principle holds that each writing should be evaluated in terms of its own similarity to or difference from the genuine letters.

But letters were not the only way Paul's legacy was fashioned and refashioned in early Christianity. At one point in his controversy with some members of the Corinthian assembly, Paul wrote, "I have become all things to all people, that I might by all means save some" (2 Cor. 9:22). His immediate purpose was apparently to defend his refusal of financial patronage from wealthy members of the church; but today his words have floated free of their original context to become something of an emblem for what his sympathizers might consider his strategic skill, and what less charitable interpreters might consider an unscrupulous ambition. Even in the first few centuries of

Christianity, Paul seems, chameleon-like, to have taken on a wide variety of guises, depending on who held him in their gaze.

The Acts of the Apostles was only the first of several narratives that gave Paul, or one version of Paul, pride of place. Written decades after Paul's death, Acts purports to continue the authoritative account begun in the Gospel of Luke of "the things that were fulfilled among us" (Luke 1:1). The narrator is never identified. In some dramatic passages, the narrator suddenly shifts to the first-person plural ("we"), giving rise to the belief that the account is eyewitness testimony of a companion of Paul: traditionally, Luke, the "beloved physician" of Col. 4:14. But the abrupt use of the first-person was a stylistic device in Hellenistic historiography and novels, meant to convey the immediacy of past action. The narrator strikes a number of notes in describing Paul that are not found, or are in some tension, with Paul's own letters. In Acts, Paul is first named "Saul" (many Jews bore both Hebrew and Greek names), and identified as a native of Tarsus (9:11) and a student of Rabbi Gamaliel (22:3), who is revered in the Mishnah as well. Acts reports that Paul's actions as a persecutor of the followers of Jesus were authorized by the high priest (9:1-2). And Acts narrates—three times, twice in recitals by Paul himself!—the dramatic reversal in his course on the road to Damascus, where he is blinded by a bright light and hears the commissioning voice of the risen Jesus (chaps. 9, 22, 26). Here, Paul is also a Roman citizen, a piece of information that arises at a crucial plot point to deliver Paul from an angry mob in the temple and set him on the protracted course that ends in Rome (22:25-29).

All of these pieces of information appear only in Acts, and serve to present Paul dramatically as a faithful and observant Jew. Here he is also an indefatigable missionary, proclaiming Christ in cities in Syria, Cilicia, Galatia, Asia Minor, Achaia, and Macedonia, and at last, in chains, in Rome. In the adventurous style common to Hellenistic novels, his travels are recounted as accompanied by miraculous healings and deliverance from shipwrecks, imprisonments at the hands of corrupt magistrates, and attacks from jealous Jewish rivals, all of which give Paul occasions to make his case in eloquent speeches in synagogues, theaters, and the court of the temple, and before philosophers, governors, and kings (in explicit fulfillment of Jesus' words in Luke 21:12).

What is left unsaid in Acts is just as interesting. As mentioned above, although Acts narrates Paul's final visit to Jerusalem, we learn nothing of his collection or how it was received. Instead, hostile "Jews from Asia" stir up mob action by making a false accusation, that Paul has brought non-Jews into the temple itself (21:27-29). And Acts ends on a triumphant note: Paul has at last reached Rome and has opportunities freely to address the city's Jewish leaders without interference from his antagonists (28:21-22; perhaps mirroring Luke's own narrative purpose). Though living under Roman guard there for two years, he welcomes inquirers and preaches and teaches "without hindrance" (28:30-31). We know from other sources, and Luke's readers must have known, that Paul was martyred under Nero, probably in 64 CE, but that event has no place in the story Luke wants to tell.

Competing Memories

The multiplicity of portraits of Paul—which is to say, the multiplicity of "Pauls" effective in particular historical situations—did not end with the diversity in the New Testament; it was only sparked by that diversity. For example, the author of 1 Timothy assumed Paul's identity (though writing, most scholars agree, decades after his death) to exhort the subordination of women and to extol marriage (2:12-15; 4:1-4)—in some tension with Paul's own commendation of women colleagues (and superiors: Rom. 16:1-7), and his exhortation to the Corinthians that he wished all people could remain unmarried as he was (1 Cor. 7:1-7)! Whether Paul himself encouraged the silencing of women is a matter of still-unresolved controversy around the status of 1 Cor. 14:33-34 (are these lines genuine, or a later interpolation into the text?). Regarding marriage, 1 Timothy and 1 Corinthians seem to offer contradictory advice, but set together in the New Testament as equally letters of Paul, they provide a sort of ranked hierarchy: the ideal is celibacy; second-best, but still good, is a single, monogamous marriage. Other variations—suffering divorce and even remarrying, provided it is within the assembly—are acceptable, but clearly represent failures to achieve the ideal. The "biblical" Paul is effectively conformed to the moral expectations of the Roman household (see the entry on the Pastoral Epistles).

But a different memory of Paul persisted: perhaps a hundred years later, the anonymous author of the *Acts of Paul* described the apostle as teaching a "gospel of virginity" and leading the Iconian noblewoman Thecla, as she then led other women, to break off engagements and even leave husbands. Tertullian repudiated the *Acts of Paul* because it so clearly endorsed the ordained leadership of women, but could not declare the document a forgery (it does not claim to be written by Paul); instead, he attacked the impudence of its author. His attack shows us, however, that in the third century a priest was able to compile such a portrait and do so "out of love for Paul" (*Bapt.* 17). Nor did the *Acts* represent one man's idiosyncratic perspective: it appeared in manuscripts of the New Testament as late as the sixth century and was a widely popular text long afterward, to judge from the proliferation and variety of manuscripts of the writing.

Other such contrasts could easily be multiplied. (1) In the early second century, Marcion championed Paul as "*The* Apostle," who had rightly taught Christians to reject Jewish law and Jewish Scripture. Marcion was condemned as a heretic, but his claim regarding Paul is only a little more extreme than that of Ephesians, where we see formulated another early synthesis of Paul's gospel, now as the unification of Jews and gentiles into one people through the "abolishing" of the law through Christ's death (2:13-16). Decades later, the anonymous author of an early Christian novel apparently shared this basic understanding of Paul as an opponent of the law, but bitterly opposed it, casting a Paul-like figure as the wicked mortal enemy of the properly law-abiding apostles Peter and James in terms that evoke Paul's confrontation with Peter in Galatians 2 (*Ps.-Clem. Rec.* 1.70–71). According to Irenaeus, the Ebionites, too, repudiated the apostle, "maintaining that he was an apostate from the law" (*Adv. haer.* 1.26.2). Another writing, the *Ascents of James*, alleges that Paul was an impostor, a Greek who came to Jerusalem and accepted circumcision only to woo the high priest's daughter; when his prospective father-in-law spurned him, "he became angry and wrote against circumcision and against the Sabbath and the law" (Epiphanius, *Panarion* 16.6–9). Heated arguments about Paul's view of the law are not a recent innovation!

(2) The pseudepigraphic letters between Paul and Seneca depict warm mutual respect between the apostle and the emperor Nero's closest advisor, who even brings Paul's letters to the emperor's attention; they commiserate over the unfairness of Nero's blaming the Christians for the great fire

in 64. Paul counsels a policy of quiet life, rather in keeping with Rom. 13:1-7 and 1 Tim. 2:2. In the *Martyrdom of Paul*, however (which was incorporated in some versions of the *Acts of Paul*, but also traveled separately), the apostle speaks defiantly to the emperor, warning that his lord comes "to wage war upon the world with fire." After being put to death, Paul returns in a resurrected state to warn Nero that he faces eternal judgment; in terror, the emperor releases Paul's companions. The defiant tone stands in contrast to the perception among many contemporary readers of Rom. 13:1-7 as a quietist, even abject endorsement of governing authority as established by God. It is noteworthy, then, that the earliest reports of Christian martyrdoms—apparently composed and circulated to present an "ideal" protocol for extreme circumstances—portray Christians citing or quoting the apostle, indicating that "we have been taught to render honor . . . to princes and authorities appointed by God" (*Martyrdom of Polycarp*); "we give honor to our emperor" (*Acts of the Scillitan Martyrs*), even as they offer resolute defiance. (The site of Paul's own martyrdom and his tomb "outside the walls" were sites of Christian worship from very early on.) Romans 13:1-7 appears to have been read, at least by some Christians, as a script for respectful refusal to obey authority (Schottroff).

(3) Paul's oblique reference to a heavenly vision (2 Corinthians 12), his description of seeing Christ raised in a "spiritual" rather than a "physical" body (1 Cor. 15:50), and his insistence that "flesh and blood cannot inherit the kingdom of God" (1 Cor. 15:50) stand in contrast with the depiction in Acts of Paul's remarkable but clearly terrestrial audition of the heavenly Christ (Acts 9; 22; 26), and in even more pointed contrast with the terrestrial and quite tangible appearances of the risen Jesus to his disciples in Luke 24:36-43 or John 20:26-29 or 21:1-14. We know that some Christians took the language of Paul's own letters further because their opponents appropriated Paul's memory or voice to denounce them. In the *Acts of Paul*, men who declared "that there is no resurrection of the flesh, but that of the spirit only, and the human body is not the creation of God" come to Corinth and trouble Paul's church; the narrator includes a transcript of Paul's response as *3 Corinthians*, universally regarded today as a pseudepigraphon, in which Paul affirms not only the bodily life, death, and resurrection of Jesus but also his miraculous birth from Mary (something Paul never mentions in the unquestioned letters).

(4) As a final example, Paul's own comments on slavery are maddeningly brief and enigmatic. The two-word slogan in 1 Cor. 7:21 is characteristic: "if you can gain your freedom, *mallon chrēsai*"— alternatively translated, "take advantage of the opportunity!" and "make use of your present condition instead!" His letter to the owner of Onesimus is rhetorically powerful but cryptic (see the introduction to Philemon). Later writings sought to clear up the mystery by attributing to Paul a clear endorsement of the master-slave relationship, though tempered with Christian kindness (Eph. 6:5-9; Col. 3:18—4:1), and 1 Timothy went further, insisting that slaves in the churches should not "be disrespectful on the ground that they are members of the church: rather they must serve all the better since those who benefit by their service are believers and beloved" (6:1-2). (The author is also concerned to limit support for widows to only the impeccably worthy: 5:3-16.) The risk that slaves might consider their status changed once they stood alongside their masters in the assembly may have arisen from Paul's own language in Gal. 3:28: "there is no slave nor free . . . in Christ Jesus." Some early Christian communities did in fact practice the manumission of slave members (Hermas, *Mand.* 8.10; *Sim.* 12.8; *1 Clem.* 55.2). But Ignatius, bishop of Smyrna, who presented himself as an

ardent follower of Paul, specifically rejected the practice: "Do not be haughty to slaves, either men or women; yet do not let them be puffed up, but let them rather endure slavery to the glory of God, that they may obtain a better freedom from God. Let them not desire to be set free at the church's expense, that they not be found slaves of desire" (*To Polycarp* 4). Centuries later, John Chrysostom complained from the pulpit that Christian efforts to redeem slaves constituted "violence" against masters, "the subversion of everything." He cited "Paul"—that is, 1 Tim. 6:1—to denounce the practice as inciting "blasphemy" against Christianity (*Homily on Philemon*).

These examples suffice to show that throughout the early centuries of Christianity, Paul was remembered in different ways (Pervo). While a few of these memories have ended up in our New Testaments today, it is just as remarkable that the variety *persisted* so long: there simply was no single, "authoritative" version of Paul from whom all the alternatives could be imagined simply as divergences. Just as remarkable as the fact of diversity is the determination with which Christians have, in so many diverse ways, clung to a perceived continuity with Paul as an important warrant for their own actions. For every bishop like Chrysostom, whose homilies were gathered reverently and published in handsome volumes, we have indirect evidence for other, anonymous Christians (whom we would not know except for Chrysostom's protest!) who practiced the manumission of slaves, quite possibly in Paul's name and quite possibly aware that they were practicing an "alternative" Christianity opposed by their bishop!

Paul the Problem: Apostle of the Status Quo?

Our efforts to understand Paul's thought and work in his historical context and to wrestle with his legacy today are of importance far beyond the bounds of church life. Paul merits thoughtful attention wherever Christianity has played a role in shaping contemporary cultures. My goal here is not to resolve the numerous questions that continue to occupy Paul's interpreters—or even to name them all!—but to describe the most important patterns into which the answers continue to fall.

Many of the apostle's critics—and even a few of his champions, who appear to consider this a virtue—would agree that Paul was largely unconcerned with the social inequities and injustices of his age. To many contemporary ears, the New Testament letters that now appear under his name include some of the most offensively retrograde passages in Scripture. These letters are among the most cited parts of the Bible (and remain influential even when they are not cited!) when a variety of questions regarding civil rights, gender equality, economic justice, and other areas of public life are discussed today.

The Pauline Letters have played a dismal role in many of the most grievous episodes of modern history. For example, the nineteenth-century movement to abolish slavery in the United States faced steep challenges, not least because the Bible nowhere condemns slavery. To the contrary, letters appearing under Paul's name explicitly exhorted slaves to obey their Christian masters (Eph. 6:5-8; Col. 3:22-25; Titus 2:9-10), and not to assume that being members of the church together (literally, "brothers") constituted genuine equality with their masters (1 Tim. 6:1-2). At a time when questions about the authenticity of these letters were rare, the presumption that the apostle Paul condoned slaveholding was inevitably powerful, and for that reason, specific letters proved inestimably useful to slave owners in the US South who recruited preachers to indoctrinate their slaves regarding their spiritual "duties." But this woeful situation cannot be explained simply as resulting from a naive acceptance of letters that many scholars today consider pseudonymous. Even a century after the passage of the Thirteenth Amendment to the US Constitution, the civil rights movement faced fierce opposition among twentieth-century American Christians who read Paul as enjoining quiet submission even to fiercely segregationist government (see Rom. 13:1-7), and exhorting believers to "remain in the state in which [they were] called" (1 Cor. 7: 17-24 RSV). Martin Luther King Jr.'s "Letter from a Birmingham Jail," in which he challenged white clergy not to be "more devoted to 'order' than to justice" and lambasted appeals for Negro "patience," had as one of its targets just this legacy of Paul.

For another example, the women's suffrage movement in the United States faced tremendous obstacles in the clear and ostensibly Pauline admonitions that women should keep silence in the assembly and submit to their husbands (1 Cor. 14:34-35; Eph. 5:22-24; Col. 3:18; 1 Tim. 2:11-15). Almost a century after US women won the right to vote, these passages continue to exercise a baleful influence in the cultural "backlash" against women's ongoing struggle for equality. Advocates for women and their children who suffer violence at the hands of the men in their homes candidly point out that these passages are now woven into a culture of rape, silence, and terror (Faludi), yet Christian clergy are often reluctant to denounce these texts from their pulpits. Like the passages exhorting subordination of slaves, verses encouraging women's subordination continue to hold powerful sway through the presumption, alive and well in some corners of American society, that striving for equality between genders or among races somehow springs from an inordinate self-indulgence. Both these sets of passages are hard to square with Paul's own declaration that in Christ "there is neither slave nor free, neither male nor female" (Gal. 3:28). But this only intensifies the question: If Paul wrote all these passages, was he unaware of the tensions between them? Or (as some more conservative Christians today would have it) did Paul wisely see, from the first, that freedom and equality could properly be exercised only within straitened limits?

Paul presents other problems as well, to which I have already pointed. His retrospective comments about his "former life in Judaism" (Phil. 3:4-7; Gal. 1:11—2:10) have often been read as flat dismissals of an obsolete and ineffective religion ("loss," "rubbish"). Alongside Gospel narratives assigning blame for Jesus' death to the "crowds" or "people" of Jerusalem, these passages have provided impetus not just for Christian supersessionism but also for centuries of violence against Jews that came to a terrible climax under Nazism. Yet as the historical record shows, even some Christian pastors in Nazi Germany who recognized that their government was perpetrating grave evils were often reluctant actively to resist it, not only out of fear but also from an exaggerated concern to obey the apostle's admonition to "be subject to the governing authorities" (Rom. 13:1).

Those same words from Romans served to quell Christian resistance to apartheid in South Africa and to the national security regimes of Central America in the 1980s (Brown). They have been cited to deflect pacifism and conscientious objection to combat in every US war to date, and, with Paul's exhortations (as they are usually translated) to "remain in the life the Lord has assigned," the "condition in which you were called" (see 1 Cor. 7:17-24), have proven a powerful inhibition of Christian involvement in every progressive movement down to the present.

But Paul's legacy has not always been read in so monochromatic a way. S. Scott Bartchy has shown that the now-standard reading of those exhortations in 1 Cor. 7:21-24, in which the Christian's "calling" (*klēsis*) is understood as a calling *to a particular social location*, a "state" or "condition," is lexically and exegetically impossible: the Greek simply does not say what the English represents. In subsequent work, he has traced the decisive (mis)translation to the period of the Peasants' Revolt in Germany and Martin Luther's response to it—hardly a situation conducive of objective, dispassionate exegesis! But the translation persists, and exercises decisive control over the assumptions that modern readers bring to Paul. Indeed, we perceive a much narrower range of possible meaning in Paul's letters than our predecessors may have done. For example, some clergy were ranged with the poor in the fourteenth-century Peasants' Rebellion in England, including a bishop who publicly read Paul's declaration that "there are divisions of work, but all of them, in all men, are the work of the one Lord" (1 Cor. 12:6) as showing clearly that God did not intend disparities of wealth in creation (Thomas Brinton, *Sermon* 44). For another example, the words in 2 Thess. 3:10—"if any will not work, neither let them eat!"—have been quoted by right-wing pastors and politicians in order to vilify families seeking state-provided food or medical assistance, with such regularity that the verse has become a banner of what one journalist calls "poverty denialism" in government (Goldberg). But a century ago, Vladimir Lenin quoted the same verse as exemplifying "the prime, basic, and root principle of socialism: 'He who does not work, neither shall he eat.'" It was obvious to Lenin, just as it was to a number of anonymous Russians who made the slogan into banners plastered around Petrograd, that those who "would not work" were the bourgeois profiteers, who exercised monopoly control over grain markets and used their power to suffocate labor. "Every toiler understands that," said Lenin, and "in this simple, elementary and perfectly obvious truth lies the basis of socialism" (Lenin, 391-98).

Particular challenges to a received understanding of Paul's "social conservatism" have been posed especially from Latin American interpreters working in the context of the theology of liberation. One of the earliest in a line of philosophical interpreters of Paul, José Miranda read Romans in terms of the contemporary tension between justice and "law and civilization" (Miranda, 109–200; more recently, Jennings; Frick). Elsa Tamez has argued that "in societies where poverty and marginalization abound," evangelistic misreadings of the Protestant understanding of justification by faith "can be inappropriate and even violent" (Tamez, 23). Paul's thought, she continues, was in fact "markedly utopian: Paul longed for a society of equals where solidarity would reign" (49). Néstor O. Míguez has read 1 Thessalonians in terms of the strategies needed to keep hope vital in a situation of imperial oppression. Indeed, Luise Schottroff argued years ago that the pivotal theme of liberation theology, the preferential option for the poor, was simply an elaboration of Paul's conception of the *ekklēsia* (Schottroff, 249). One of the most important efforts on the part of a North American to synthesize a liberative theology of the New Testament relies on the Pauline language of "powers and principalities" to describe the need to name, engage, and unmask systems of domination in our own day (Wink 1984; 1992; 1993), and others have sought to describe a more emancipatory understanding of Paul's thought (Elliott 1994; Lopez; Zerbe 2012).

The Promise of a Critical Historical Imagination

Such widely divergent interpretations, or appropriations, of a text can leave many a reader perplexed: "but what did Paul really *mean*?" Were the busybodies rebuked in 2 Thessalonians the indolent recipients of some imaginary Roman antecedent of the modern welfare state, or were they people of means who could pursue lives of leisure, presuming that their social inferiors would attend to their needs? (The latter attitude is in fact well documented among the Roman aristocracy.) Was the Letter to Philemon most like the genre of the *amicus* ("friend") letter, which we know from a number of Roman examples, in which a social peer would appeal to an angry slaveholder to extend leniency to a slave who had disobeyed or run away, then had a change of heart? Or was it simply a request to "borrow" a slave's services for a time; or a carefully leveraged appeal to a master to fulfill an otherwise unspecified "duty" by granting a slave his freedom?

On these and many other points of interpretation, the *promise* of historical criticism is to describe a range of possible meanings that may be drawn, through inference, from the available data and, on occasion, to identify some as more or less probable (or even to rule some out as impossible). The *temptation* posed by historical criticism, however, is to exaggerate that promise: to imagine that once the right methods and instruments have been deployed, a single "right" interpretation, *what the text really meant*, can be determined. As the diversity of current interpretations of Paul shows, things rarely work out that way.

One reason is simply the limits of our evidence (and thus of the inferences we can draw from it). Another is that "we" contemporary readers do not agree on what should be done with whatever results might be achieved, because "we" actually encompass a variety of different subjectivities and purposes. Some of us presume the authority of Paul's voice because it is scriptural; we want to use historical-critical method to fix the single, authoritative meaning of his words. Others of us want to qualify or mitigate the consequences of one or another pronouncement in Paul's letters and use historical-critical method to circumscribe Paul as a man of his own age, *rather than* a transcendent voice of revelation, binding on all generations.

And many of us are frankly inconsistent about just when or how historical considerations should matter. For example, Paul is often cited most vociferously today by individuals who insist that *some* of his words, at least, enjoy timeless and universal authority. In the still-roiling debates over equal protection under law and marriage equality for same-sex couples, a few select passages (Rom. 1:24-27; 1 Cor. 6:9-10; 1 Tim. 1:8-11) are regularly invoked by some Christians to argue that God considers homosexuality, and even homosexual persons, an "abomination" (though that specific language is drawn from Leviticus, not Paul). My purpose here is not to adjudicate the issue but to point out that such appeals to Paul are necessarily selective: that is, most of these same Christians would presumably *not* argue analogously that the comments on slavery discussed above had an eternal validity, binding on twenty-first-century American society, any more than the other "abominations" mentioned in Leviticus might. Such appeals also necessarily avoid historical investigation. "Homosexuality" is a modern conception; we know, from abundant and intersecting data, that people in the ancient world did not recognize what we call "sexual orientation," and so Paul simply could not have commented on it (Nissinen). This has not stopped the appearance of some

recent Bible translations, however, where Paul's Greek is rendered—quite improbably—with interpretive paraphrases like "active and passive partners in homosexual relations." Whatever Paul *did*
mean to comment on in these passages (and this remains a matter of debate among scholars: see for
example Boswell; Scroggs; Martin, 37–64; Countryman; Ruden) is clearly abusive and outrageous.
But this means that equating Paul's target with contemporary same-sex couples who seek a church's
recognition of their love seems both exegetically dubious and morally gratuitous. Regrettably, with
regard to this unfinished debate, it seems that setting the Pauline Letters in their historical context
is the last thing some readers wish to do!

Some of us have used the historical-critical identification of Pauline pseudepigrapha to dis-
qualify certain letters, or verses in them, as tendentious adaptations of Paul's own voice, which in
contrast is more liberative than has usually been perceived (e.g., Elliott 1994; 2008; Lopez; Zerbe
2011; 2012). Others point out that the attempt to isolate the "genuine" voice of Paul only reinforces
the problematic and too-prevalent assumption of "the 'masculine' hegemonic voice inscribed in
kyriarchal Pauline or other ancient source-texts" (Schüssler Fiorenza 1999, 187), and the problematic aura of Paul himself as a "heroic" figure (Johnson-DeBaufre and Nasrallah). It is worth notice
that the plea to "decenter" Paul is based, in part, on a historical-critical argument that contextualizes Paul precisely as one voice among many on a crowded and complex Roman landscape (Wire).
Resistance to "kyriarchal" aspects of Paul's legacy involves recognizing the actual character of Paul's
own appeals for obedience, submission, and imitation as rhetoric—patterns that were reinscribed in
successive generations (Schüssler Fiorenza 1987; Castelli; Kittredge; Marchal).

Historical criticism, then, is neither a panacea that will reliably deliver us from the tyranny of an
oppressive text *or* an obsolete means of holding on nostalgically to the same text—though it can be
used for either purpose. The important consideration is what the interpreter's purposes are, for these
will determine just how one or another method of biblical study will be used. The twin virtues of
responsible interpretation are honesty with regard to the data (or lack of it) on a specific question,
and accountability with regard to the purposes toward which we invoke it. In this light, the scientific
mystique that the historical criticism of Scripture has long enjoyed has the effect of obscuring, or
effacing altogether, the actual role of the interpreter. More recent challenges to classical historical criticism, whether they have gone under the names "postmodern," "postcritical," "contextual,"
"deconstructive," or "minority" or "minoritized" interpretation, have sought to pull back the curtain
to reveal the interpreter's identity, standpoint, and intentions.

Such challenges are still mounted as exceptions to the status quo. Attention to the social location of the interpreter is most pronounced when members of a marginalized group seek to identify
the power relations inscribed in the dominant discourse of biblical scholarship. Greg Carey has
observed that in the history of biblical studies in the United States, a "commonsense" interpretation that privileged the biblical text as floating above ambiguity coincided with the culture of white
privilege. Thus, he observes, it remains the case today that "'minority' criticism is performed almost
exclusively by minorities," while the analysis of white interpreters is also performed, "well, almost
exclusively by minorities" (Carey, 7).

Nor is race the only modality in which questions of power relations are usually effaced by the
scholarly mainstream. For example, in his slender 2005 book on Paul, N. T. Wright discusses the

state of Pauline interpretation by identifying the social location of various alternative viewpoints. Narrative criticism precipitated, as naturally as dew, in "the postliberal and canonical air of New Haven"; secular Copenhagen gave rise, unsurprisingly, to readings of Paul "which owe little to traditional Jewish or Christian ideas and much to first-century pagan philosophy"; and political interpretation distilled, almost inevitably, from the context of "below-the-tracks university" life in Blue-State Massachusetts, where deep suspicion of American empire was presumably at home. Similarly, suspicion of the authenticity of Colossians and Ephesians derived from "a particular kind of German existentialist Lutheranism." But if those specific contexts produced the readings that Wright considers eccentric, social location has nothing to do, so far as he admits, with his own theological approach, except insofar as he speaks from "[his] own acquaintance with Paul." Wright attributes the same innocence to "the vast majority of Christians in the world today" who "read Paul with blissful ignorance" of those other, peripheral, situationally contingent "movements and counter-movements" (16–18).

Such comments would not deserve our attention if they were unusual. The point is that representations of interpretive innocence remain prevalent in biblical scholarship, and not surprisingly. Scholarship on the Bible is often sponsored by churches and church-affiliated educational institutions and continues to be shaped in large part by the interests of Christian ministry. Such sites are likely the context in which many readers will encounter this volume, and are assuredly the context in which many of its contributors work. But just here, many of the critical considerations discussed above run up against the prevalent routines of Christian theology. The habits that may be observed in many a Christian pulpit on a Sunday morning emphasize the unique saturation of the biblical texts with unitary and authoritative sacred meaning. Although some preachers may invite admiration for their virtuosic skill in extracting that meaning homiletically, it is just as important for a preacher to insist that the meaning he or she finds in the text is not their invention. The powerful ethos of "commonsense" interpretation requires that the preacher has only *discovered* the meaning that was somehow, supernaturally packed into the biblical text. Admitting that my own life experience helps to determine what I hear or see in the text suggests more than just that you may hear or see something different. The preceding discussion also shows that, historically, relations of unequal privilege and power have also determined the possibilities for which truths prevail as "common sense" in a particular society, at a particular time.

In contrast, the interpretation to which feminist, postcolonial, African American, and an array of other important voices call all of us will require habits of candid self-awareness. Alongside historical questions about the apostle Paul and lexical, exegetical, and rhetorical-critical questions about the range of possible meanings of his words, we will need to ask what is at stake for our engagement with the apostle and his legacy. In what ways do different parties "use Paul to think with"? What are the consequences of different claims, and why do the people raising those claims seek out the aegis of Paul's authority for them? Are there more direct and honest ways to think through interpreting Paul as a matter of public responsibility?

These questions have their true force only when they are joined with questions about the actual power relationships in our society, the nature of our participation in those relationships, and—to adopt the interpretive principle of the theology of liberation—the effect of those relationships on the poor. This mode of interpretation remains peripheral and contested in scholarship, and is practiced more or less sporadically in different faith communities, but it is avowed in the preparation of this volume and the structure of its various entries, including the entries on Paul's letters that follow. By attending to each letter as a text in an ancient historical context, these entries challenge the "commonsense" assumption that we can read the ancient texts with the directness of their contemporaries. By attending to the various ways one or another text has been heard, or contested, through history, and to the contours of contemporary debate as well, these entries are intended to erode the confidence that any part of the Bible simply "means one thing." But the loss of false confidence can be the occasion for new discovery and, when shared with others, new opportunity for mutual understanding.

Works Cited

Ashton, John. 2000. *The Religion of Paul the Apostle*. New Haven: Yale University Press.

Barrett, C. K. 1963. "Cephas and Corinth." In *Abraham unser Vater: Festschrift für Otto Michel*. Leiden: Brill.

Bartchy, S. Scott. 1971. ΜΑΛΛΟΝ ΧΡΗΣΑΙ: *First-Century Slavery and the Interpretation of 1 Corinthians 7:21*. Chico, CA: Scholars Press.

Boswell, John. 1980. *Christianity, Social Tolerance, and Homosexuality*. Chicago: University of Chicago Press.

Boyarin, Daniel. 1994. *A Radical Jew: Paul and the Politics of Identity*. Berkeley: University of California Press.

Brown, Robert McAfee. 1990. *Kairos: Three Prophetic Challenges to the Church*. Grand Rapids: Eerdmans.

Bultmann, Rudolf. 1953. *Theology of the New Testament*. Vol. 1. Translated by Kendrick Grobel. New York: Charles Scribner's Sons.

Carey, Greg. 2013. "Introduction and a Proposal." In *Soundings in Cultural Criticism*, edited by Greg Carey and Francisco Lozada, 1–15. Minneapolis: Fortress Press.

Castelli, Elisabeth A. 1991. *Imitating Paul: A Discourse of Power*. Louisville: Westminster John Knox.

Countryman, L. William. 2007. *Dirt, Greed, and Sex: Sexual Ethics in the New Testament and Their Implications for Today*. Rev. ed. Minneapolis: Fortress Press.

Dahl, Nils. 1977. *Studies in Paul: Theology for the Early Christian Mission*. Minneapolis: Augsburg.

Dunn, James D. G. 1983. "The New Perspective on Paul." *BJRL* 65:95–122.

———. 1998. *The Theology of Paul the Apostle*. Grand Rapids: Eerdmans.

Eisenbaum, Pamela. 2009. *Paul Was Not a Christian: The Original Message of a Misunderstood Apostle*. San Francisco: HarperOne.

Elliott, Neil. 1990. *The Rhetoric of Romans: Argumentative Constraint and Strategy and Paul's Dialogue with Judaism*. JSNTSup 45. Sheffield : JSOT Press.

———. 1994. *Liberating Paul: The Justice of God and the Politics of the Apostle*. Maryknoll, NY: Orbis.

———. 2008. *The Arrogance of Nations: Reading Romans in the Shadow of Empire*. Paul in Critical Contexts. Minneapolis: Fortress Press.

Elliott, Neil, and Mark Reasoner, eds. 2010. *Documents and Images for the Study of Paul*. Minneapolis: Fortress Press.

Faludi, Susan. 1991. *Backlash: The Undeclared War against American Women*. New York: Crown.

Fredriksen, Paula. 1988. *From Jesus to Christ: The Origins of the New Testament Images of Jesus*. New Haven: Yale University Press.

Frick, Peter, ed. 2013. *Paul among the Philosophers: The Apostle in the Grip of Continental Philosophy*. Paul in Critical Contexts. Minneapolis: Fortress Press.

Gaca, Karen L. 2003. *The Making of Fornication: Eros, Ethics, and Political Reform in Greek Philosophy and Early Christianity*. Berkeley: University of California Press.

Gager, John G. 1985. *The Origins of Christian Anti-Semitism*. New York: Oxford University Press.

Gaston, Lloyd. 1987. *Paul and the Torah*. Vancouver: University of British Columbia Press.

Goldberg, Michelle. 2013. "Poverty Denialism: According to Many in the GOP, the Poor Have It Easy." *The Nation* 297:21 (Nov. 25): 6, 8.

Horsley, Richard A., ed. 1997. *Paul and Empire: Religion and Power in Roman Imperial Society*. Harrisburg, PA: Trinity Press International.

———. 2000. *Paul and Politics: Ekklesia, Israel, Imperium, Interpretation*. Harrisburg, PA: Trinity Press International.

———. 2004. *Paul and the Roman Imperial Order*. Harrisburg, PA: Trinity Press International.

Jennings, Ted. 2009. *Transforming Atonement: A Political Theology of the Cross*. Minneapolis: Fortress Press.

Johnson-DeBaufre, Melanie, and Laura S. Nasrallah. 2011. "Beyond the Heroic Paul: Toward a Feminist and Decolonizing Approach to the Letters of Paul." In *The Colonized Apostle: Paul through Postcolonial Eyes*, edited by Christopher D. Stanley, 161–74. Paul in Critical Contexts. Minneapolis: Fortress Press.

Kahl, Brigitte. 2010. *Galatians Re-Imagined: Reading with the Eyes of the Vanquished*. Paul in Critical Contexts. Minneapolis: Fortress Press.

Kazantzakis, Nikos. 1960. *The Last Temptation of Christ*. New York: Simon & Schuster.

Kim, Seyoon. 2004. *The Origins of Paul's Gospel*. 2nd ed. Eugene, OR: Wipf & Stock.

Kittredge, Cynthia Briggs. 1998. *Community and Authority: The Rhetoric of Obedience in the Pauline Tradition*. HTS 45. Harrisburg, PA: Trinity Press International.

Lenin, Vladimir I. 1918. "On the Famine: A Letter to the Workers of Petrograd." *Pravda* 101 (May 24). ET: *Collected Works*, 391–98. 4th ed. Translated by Clemens Dutt. Edited by Robert Daglish. Moscow: Progress Publishers, 1972.

Lopez, Davina C. 2008. *Apostle to the Conquered: Reimagining Paul's Mission*. Paul in Critical Contexts. Minneapolis: Fortress Press.

Marchal, Joseph A. 2008. *The Politics of Heaven: Women, Gender, and Empire in the Study of Paul*. Minneapolis: Fortress Press.

Martin, Dale B. 2006. *Sex and the Single Savior: Gender and Sexuality in Biblical Interpretation*. Louisville: Westminster John Knox.

McKnight, Scott, and Joseph B. Modica, eds. 2013. *Jesus Is Lord, Caesar Is Not: Evaluating Empire in New Testament Studies*. Downers Grove, IL: InterVarsity Press.

Meeks, Wayne A. 1983. *The First Urban Christians: The Social World of the Apostle Paul*. New Haven: Yale University Press.

Meeks, Wayne A., and John T. Fitzgerald. 2007. *The Writings of Paul: Annotated Texts, Reception, and Criticism*. 2nd ed. New York: W. W. Norton.

Míguez, Néstor O. 2012. *The Practice of Hope: Ideology and Intention in 1 Thessalonians*. Paul in Critical Contexts. Minneapolis: Fortress Press.

Miranda, José. 1974. *Marx and the Bible: A Critique of the Philosophy of Oppression*. Translated by John Eagleson. Maryknoll, NY: Orbis.

Munck, Johannes. 1959. *Paul and the Salvation of Mankind*. Translated by Frank Clark. Richmond: John Knox.

Nanos, Mark D. 1996. *The Mystery of Romans: The Jewish Context of Paul's Letter*. Minneapolis: Fortress Press.

———. 2002. *The Irony of Galatians: Paul's Letter in First-Century Context*. Minneapolis: Fortress Press.

Nanos, Mark D., and Magnus Zetterholm, eds. 2014. *Paul within Judaism*. Minneapolis: Fortress Press.

Nissinen, Martti. 1998. *Homoeroticism in the Biblical World: A Historical Perspective*. Minneapolis: Fortress Press.

Peake, Arthur S. 1918. "The Quintessence of Paulinism." *BJRL* 4:285–311.

Pervo, Richard. 2011. *The Making of Paul: Constructions of the Apostle in Early Christianity*. Minneapolis: Fortress Press.

Portier-Young, Anathea E. 2011. *Apocalypse against Empire: Theologies of Resistance in Early Judaism*. Grand Rapids: Eerdmans.

Räisänen, Heikki. 1983. *Paul and the Law*. Philadelphia: Fortress Press.

Ruden, Sarah. 2011. *Paul among the People: The Apostle Reinterpreted and Reimagined in His Own Time*. New York: Image.

Ruether, Rosemary Radford. 1974. *Faith and Fratricide: The Theological Roots of Anti-Semitism*. New York: Crossroad.

Sanders, E. P. *Paul and Palestinian Judaism: A Comparison of Patterns of Religion*. Philadelphia: Fortress Press.

Schmithals, Walter. 1971. *Gnosticism in Corinth: An Investigation of the Letters to the Corinthians*. Translated by John E. Steely. Nashville: Abingdon.

Schottroff, Luise. 1992. "'Give to Caesar What Belongs to Caesar and to God What Belongs to God': A Theological Response of the Early Christian Church to Its Social and Political Environment." In *The Love of Enemy and Nonretaliation in the New Testament*, edited by Willard Swartley, 223–57. Louisville: Westminster John Knox.

Schüssler Fiorenza, Elisabeth. 1987. "Rhetorical Situation and Historical Reconstruction in 1 Corinthians." *NTS* 33:386–403.

———. 1999. *Rhetoric and Ethic: The Politics of Biblical Studies*. Minneapolis: Fortress Press.

Segal, Alan S. 1990. *Paul the Convert: The Apostolate and Apostasy of Saul the Pharisee* (New Haven: Yale University Press.

Smallwood, E. Mary. 1976. *The Jews under Roman Rule from Pompey to Diocletian*. Leiden: Brill.

Stanley, Christopher D., ed. 2011. *The Colonized Apostle: Paul through Postcolonial Eyes*. Paul in Critical Contexts. Minneapolis: Fortress Press.

Stendahl, Krister. 1976. *Paul among Jews and Gentiles*. Philadelphia: Fortress Press.

Stowers, Stanley K. 1994. *A Rereading of Romans: Justice, Jews, and Gentiles*. New Haven: Yale University Press.

Tamez, Elsa. 1991. *The Amnesty of Grace: Justification by Faith from a Latin American Perspective*. Trans. Sharon Ringe. Nashville: Abingdon.

Taylor, Walter F. 2012. *Paul, Apostle to the Nations: An Introduction*. Minneapolis: Fortress Press.

Theissen, Gerd. 1982. *The Social Setting of Pauline Christianity: Essays on Corinth*. Translated by John Schütz. Philadelphia: Fortress Press.

Wink, Walter. 1984. *Naming the Powers: The Language of Power in the New Testament*. Philadelphia: Fortress Press.

———. 1992. *Engaging the Powers: Discernment and Resistance in a World of Domination*. Minneapolis: Fortress Press.

———. 1993. *Unmasking the Powers: The Invisible Forces That Determine Human Existence*. Minneapolis: Fortress Press.

Wire, Antoinette Clark. 1990. *The Corinthian Women Prophets: A Reconstruction through Paul's Rhetoric*. Minneapolis: Fortress Press.

Wright, N. T. 2005. *Paul in Fresh Perspective*. Minneapolis: Fortress Press.

———. 2013. *Paul and the Faithfulness of God*. Christian Origins and the Question of God 4. Minneapolis: Fortress Press.

Zerbe, Gordon. 2011. "The Politics of Paul: His Supposed Social Conservatism and the Impact of Postcolonial Readings." In *The Colonized Apostle: Paul through Postcolonial Eyes*, edited by Christopher D. Stanley, 62–73. Paul in Critical Contexts. Minneapolis: Fortress Press.

———. 2012. *Citizenship: Paul on Peace and Politics*. Winnipeg, MB: CMU Press.

Zetterholm, Magnus. 2009. *Approaches to Paul: A Student's Guide to Recent Scholarship*. Minneapolis: Fortress Press.

ROMANS

Cynthia Briggs Kittredge

Introduction

The Letter to the Romans, the latest and longest of Paul's undisputed letters, was written from Corinth in about 55 CE to the church in Rome, the capital and center of the Roman Empire. Adapting the conventions of letter writing and employing ancient rhetorical techniques, Paul writes to those who share the faith of Jesus Christ, and throughout the letter he invokes a story of God, the Creator, and the people of Israel that is well known by those to whom he writes. In the argument of Romans, Paul displays dramatically the results and implications of Jesus Christ for the story of God and the people of God. As throughout the New Testament writings, the Scriptures of Israel are the primary fund for Paul's imagination and language in Romans. The first part of Romans (1–8) claims, presents, and elaborates the effects of the death and resurrection of Christ and participation in it through baptism. Romans 9–11 treats the question of the role of Jews and gentiles in the plan of God, and the third part (12–16) exhorts the congregation to a transformed pattern of life.

Another apostle evangelized and established the church in Rome. The first followers of Jesus interpreted his resurrection as God's vindication of a faithful human being and came to understand Jesus as Messiah. Gradually the community around Jesus, which had begun as a popular Jewish movement, spread the "good news" of the crucified Messiah to the cities of the Greco-Roman world, where the message was received by the gentiles. As faith in Jesus as the Messiah, the culmination of Israel's hopes, shifted from a Jewish sectarian context to a majority non-Jewish one, many questions about identity and practice arose. Central was the question of the role of the Torah, or Jewish law, for those in the new movement. The New Testament writings witness in different ways to the disputes and debate about observance of the law, relationships with governments, and organizations of households. Paul, as preacher and writer of letters, came to have a significant role in the ultimate resolution of these issues, both in his own time and in the decades that followed his ministry.

Paul writes the letter to the church at Rome, where he has not preached, to build and strengthen his ties with them as he prepares to deliver the collection of offerings from gentile churches to Jerusalem, the home of the church and the symbolic origin of the gospel. Paul seeks their support as he plans for his mission to Spain. The focus of energy in Romans is the relationship of gentiles and Jews in the plan of God, a subject central to Paul's understanding of his identity and his vocation, essential to the well-being of the community, and of ultimate significance for salvation.

Biblical scholars reconstruct the occasion of the letter and Paul's reasons for writing from clues within the letter itself, especially the information in the opening and closing (Rom. 1:8-15; 15:22-33). One ancient source outside the letter (Suetonius, *Life of Claudius*) appears to refer to the expulsion of the Jews from Rome under the emperor Claudius. On the basis of this passage, it is conjectured that perhaps the return of Jesus-believers of Jewish origin to the community of gentile believers, who now dominated in the Roman house churches, may have caused discord that Paul addressed in the exhortation to forbearance in Romans 14.

Paul, the writer of the letter to Rome, understands himself as an apostle, called to the work of preaching the gospel to the gentiles. (Paul describes his call in Gal. 1:11-12.) The "gospel" or "good news" (*euangelion*) is that Jesus, the Messiah, is the culmination of God's plan to bless all nations through Israel, to rescue the world from sin, and to re-create it to its original glory. The conviction that God, the Creator, was the God of all people originated in the exile and is expressed in the prophetic writings of Second Isaiah (Isaiah 40–54). Paul, a Pharisee who had previously been zealous to oppose those Jews who believed Jesus to be God's anointed one, was called to preach Jesus as Messiah.

At the same time, many others who followed Jesus read the Scriptures together and enacted the story of his death and resurrection in worship. Multiple strands of speculation about divine redeemer figures whom God would send to bring justice or to save the faithful are found in the Hebrew Bible and texts from the Second Temple period (Nickelsburg). However, the execution of the Messiah was not recognized as a conventional part of the script. In the patterns of death and resurrection and exile and restoration within Israel's Scriptures, believers in Jesus found metaphors and images to interpret their own lives and the lives of the nations. Jesus' faithfulness and his death as "sacrifice of atonement" (Rom. 3:25) come to represent the righteousness of God and God's promise of salvation for all. Understanding Romans in its ancient context requires placing it within the shared symbolic universe of the early Christian tradition, furnished with the stories and images from Israel's Scriptures. In order to appreciate the resonance of its language and concepts, it is also necessary to read it in dialogue with the political rhetoric of the Roman Empire, which also declared good news and the coming of rulers who promised peace.

Paul's Letter to the Romans in the Interpretive Tradition

Interpretation of Paul's Letter to the Romans has had enormous impact on Christian theology throughout history. Placed at the head of the canon of Paul's letters, theologians have read Romans as a systematic theology, as the singular apostle's last will and testament. Christian theologians and exegetes have read the dualistic rhetoric concerning Jews and gentiles in the letter as representative of real, historical Jews, as opposed to "Christians," those believers with whom Paul identifies. The antipathy toward "works righteousness," that is, the idea that one can "earn" salvation through effort, good works, or obedience to the law, is prominent in Christian theologies and finds its support in Romans (Rom. 4:1-25; 9:30-33). The polemic of the Reformers that caricatured the Jew, based on the language of Romans, as obsessed with "works righteousness" contributed to the antisemitism in Europe that was complicit in the Holocaust (Ruether; Carroll). Aware of the violent historical effects of the anti-Jewish reading of Romans and informed by more accurate depictions of Second Temple Judaism (Sanders), contemporary interpreters of Romans read the letter within the variegated landscape of Jewish practice and belief of the first century. Biblical scholars seek to interpret Romans with the categories of first-century thought and in terms of the shared cultural language of the time, rather than with anachronistic categories of Judaism and Christianity and concepts of individual salvation (Stowers). In Paul's context, they argue, the question of God's dealings with Jews and gentiles would have been in the foreground. Recent attention to the context of Romans in the Roman Empire has highlighted the ways Paul uses and subverts imperial language and patterns of thought (Wan 2000; Elliott 2008). When Romans is read intertextually with literature of the Roman Empire, new emphases and themes emerge. The rediscovery of the Roman Empire as a context for reading Romans coincides with a self-consciousness about the imperial context of North American biblical interpretation.

Romans in Contemporary Discussion

The transition from reading in the context of the "introspective conscience," that is, in terms of a modern psychological reading, to reading the letter in the historical context of Jewish and Christian self-definition has offered new ways for interpreters to engage with the rhetoric and politics of the letter (Stendahl 1963). Focus on Jews and gentiles, on *peoples* or *communities* with whom God is in relation, suggests analogies with "peoples" in the present with whom God is in relationship. How can Romans 9–11 be put into conversation with the conflicting faith claims in the world? Within Paul's wrestling with the fate of Israel and the nations in the comprehensive plan of God, is there a conviction about God's commitment to all peoples? Within the apocalyptic framework that sees the whole creation groaning as divine purposes work themselves out (Romans 8), there are resources for thinking theologically about ecology and the fate of the earth (McGinn). Paul's language about the power of sin over human beings and within systems is one powerful, first-century diagnosis of those who have been oppressed by sinful systems (Tamez). Paul's counsel to this community to live in a way that does not conform to the world but that requires transformation of values might be read as instruction to Christian people in the present who are negotiating life in a complex and pressured culture. The letter's focus on mission, the trajectory of the gospel to the whole world, and God's ultimate plan to save all people has been read in light of mission in the contemporary world (Jewett).

The attempt to read Romans in its historical context has been fruitful for theological reflection. It has identified the anti-Jewish impact of the previous tradition of interpretation and the limitations of an individualistic focus. At the same time, reading Romans with its own categories and concepts raises difficult questions about how to "translate" the vision of God and humanity from its social and historical context in the first century into a culture with radically different categories of thought and modes of imagination.

Romans 1:1-17: Paul Introduces Himself and the Gospel

▌ THE TEXT IN ITS ANCIENT CONTEXT

In densely packed phrases, Paul conveys how he understands his role. The "gospel of God," for which he is set apart, is continuous with the promises made by the prophets in the Holy Scriptures. Paul's own call is that of a "servant," or literally a "slave," of Jesus Christ. He quotes a traditional confession of faith that may have been valued by the church at Rome (1:3-4) that Jesus was "declared" or installed as Son of God at his resurrection. In tension with other statements in Paul's letters that assert that Jesus was equal to God from the time of creation (Phil. 2:6-11), this formula gives another perspective on Jesus' sonship—that it was revealed in his resurrection. The resonant term, "servant," connotes both humility and honor and evokes the suffering servant figure of Second Isaiah. Paul's purpose, given to him through Jesus Christ, is "to bring about the obedience of faith among all the Gentiles" (1:5). Although in the modern period faith has come to mean assent to a particular truth claim, here *pistis* describes an attitude and way of being that encompasses loyalty and trust. "Faithfulness" is a closer translation. Romans asserts God's faithfulness (3:3), cites the faithfulness of Jesus, and urges faithfulness as the path for gentile followers of Jesus. Those to whom he writes are also "called" to be God's holy people (Rom. 1:6-7).

After the greeting of "grace" and "peace," Paul thanks those in Rome, praises their faith, asserts his unceasing prayers, and expresses his wish to visit them. Just as he has reaped a harvest among the rest of the gentiles, so he wishes to proclaim the gospel to those in Rome. When he states that their faith is known throughout the world, Paul reflects the importance and centrality of Rome in the ancient empire. He explains his unfulfilled desire to visit in order to build a relationship as well as to recognize their independence from him. As he began his self-introduction with a summary of the gospel (Rom. 1:2-4), so he concludes his greeting to the church with another definition of the gospel (Rom. 1:16-17). This summary makes sense within the apocalyptic perspective of the letter: that in Jesus, God's plan for the fulfillment of history is nearing its finale. God's judgment is at hand. "Salvation" denotes the rescue of the world from negative judgment and death. God's rescue will encompass the Jew first and also the Greek.

For Paul and his contemporaries, the categories of Jew and gentile organized the world. Throughout Romans, Paul will argue for both the priority of the Jew and for the inclusion of the gentile. The word "gospel" (*euangelion*) is used in the prophets to speak of the coming of God (Isa. 40:9; 41:27; 52:7; 60:6; 61:1) and in political imperial rhetoric to refer to the victory of a ruler. The gospel reveals the "righteousness" of God, or God's "justice." The root of the Greek word translated "righteousness" is the word meaning "just," or "justice." Through Jesus Christ God is "making right" the relationship between humans and God. Faith, or faithfulness, is the criterion for salvation. Human faith reflects God's faithfulness. Using the conventional formula for citing Scripture, Paul quotes the prophet Habakkuk. In its original context in Hab. 2:4, faith expressed Jewish solidarity in the face of adversity (Nanos 2011). A better translation, noted in the NRSV margin, is "the one who is righteous by faith will live." Righteousness through faith makes life possible. The "righteous one" may also be an allusion to Christ, understood to be the ultimate example of faithfulness to God.

∎ THE TEXT IN THE INTERPRETIVE TRADITION

Beginning with Augustine and interpreted by Martin Luther, "faith" in 1:16-17 came to be understood as individual "belief." "Faith" was internal assent to a proposition about Jesus as Son of God. As such, faith was what defined a Christian and what was required for the individual to be "saved." This understanding of "faith" continues to dominate in Christian communities who characterize themselves as "evangelical" and who require an experience of "conversion." The sequence of "the Jew first and also the Greek" has been the basis for influential schemes of "salvation history." Dependent on the narrative in Luke-Acts, this construction of the story of the early church imagines that the gospel was offered to Jews first, who rejected it, then given to gentiles instead. The implication of this scenario—that the Jews have surrendered their role as the people of God in favor of the church—does not recognize Judaism as an ongoing religion of faithful people in relationship with God. Recent interpreters of Romans have disputed this conclusion and the exegesis on which it is based. Mark Nanos argues that Paul addressed Romans solely to gentiles and that for Paul, the covenant with God through Torah remained intact for Jews (Nanos 1996).

∎ THE TEXT IN CONTEMPORARY DISCUSSION

Contemporary interpreters of Romans have recontextualized Paul's language in the first-century discussion about Jewish and Christian identity and self-definition, rather than in terms of modern categories of faith and individual salvation. Within this first-century discussion, the obligation of Torah observance was the concrete expression of God's covenant with Israel and the definition of Israel's identity. As a nuanced understanding of the complexity of Judaism in the first century has grown, it has become more and more difficult to make easy analogies between categories in Romans and parties or positions in the time of the contemporary interpreter. Readers of Romans have been confronted with the distance between the ancient and contemporary contexts (Gager), and in some ways, this cultural gap has made interpretation more difficult. However, the recovery of the centrality and priority in the letter of the salvation of peoples, Jews and gentiles, rather than of individuals, has drawn renewed attention to the corporate nature of faith and the impact of the good news on society and nations. Rereading faith as "faithfulness" broadens the practical nature of faith into an orientation of one's whole being rather than a single act of assent. When "justice" is understood as the root of "justification," then the impact of the good news goes beyond the status of individuals and affects the network of relationships in society.

Romans 1:18—3:31: Human Wickedness and God's Justice through Jesus Christ

▌ THE TEXT IN ITS ANCIENT CONTEXT

In a highly structured argument, Paul illustrates how the gospel solves the deadly dilemma of human sin that is shared alike by Jew and gentile. Because sin would prevent any and every person from being declared just at the time of God's judgment, in order to be justified and therefore "saved" or "redeemed," God put forward Jesus Christ as "a place of atonement" (3:25, alternate NRSV reading). The effectiveness of Jesus Christ is compactly summarized in the climax of this section, 3:21-26. Leading up to the dramatic summary of the solution, Paul lays out an extended presentation of the problem: an exposition of the evil of gentiles and then of Jews. Paul and other Jews in the Hellenistic world understood that the law, given to the Jews by God as part of the covenant, was a powerful means of dealing with sin by offering a way to live righteously in accordance with the will of God (Stowers). As he does throughout Romans, Paul argues against the possibility that the law is an adequate solution for sin. He simultaneously wants to maintain the particular and unique relationship of the Jewish people with God and uphold the value of the law, while at the same time arguing that any reliance on the law or on religious identity in an exclusive way will result in failure.

Romans 1:18-32 depicts the evil of those gentiles who do not possess the law, but are able to know God through observation of the creation. Popular philosophers of Paul's time contended that God could be perceived through the natural order. Although they know better, gentiles do not honor God, but worship idols in the form of people and animals. Because of their idolatry, God "hands over" these people (the verb is used three times) to behavior that epitomizes lack of control and chaos, including to "lusts of their hearts" (1:24), "degrading passions" (1:26), and a "debased mind" (1:28). The epitome of disorder is the women's exchange of natural intercourse for unnatural and men's surrender of natural intercourse for passion for one another. In the construction of gender in the ancient world, sexual intercourse reflected the power relationship between male and female. In this arrangement, males were active and females passive (Brooten 1996). The asymmetrical pattern was built into "nature" and into God's creation. When humans fell into idolatry, wrong worship, the result is the violation of these gender patterns. The description of disorder and lack of control is meant to evoke horror.

Paul addresses a question to "you," a person who is judging others (2:1). Asking a rhetorical question to an imaginary opponent is a feature of the diatribe, a form of discourse used by Greek philosopher rhetoricians of Paul's time. Paul asserts that the self-righteous will be judged for their sinful deeds as well. Possession of the law, while a gift, does not prevent sin; it only makes it more visible. Because of sin, God's wrath and fury are the inevitable fate of all. A series of quotations from Scripture is the climax of Paul's portrait of universal sinfulness and its dire consequences (3:9-18). The portrayal of the inescapable plight reaches its turning point in 3:21. Now, without reference to the law, God's righteousness is "through faith in Jesus Christ for all who believe." The Greek genitive phrase translated to mean faith "in Jesus Christ" may also be translated to mean the faithfulness of Jesus, his trust in God exhibited in his life, which discloses God's righteousness. God has created a way for humans to be made right with God, justified, and judged righteous that is available equally to "all."

Images that describe how God's rescue is accomplished come from the worship and language of the early Jesus believers. "Redemption" is a metaphor that comes from the context of slavery and refers to the freeing of a person who is held hostage. God put forward Christ Jesus as a *hilastērion*, a "sacrifice of atonement" or "place of atonement" or "mercy seat." This term refers to an element in the ritual on the Day of Atonement (Lev. 16:3-15). In using this term, Paul alludes to a wider network of meaning that is not explained here but that makes a metaphorical connection between the death of Jesus and the ritual of atonement. While God overlooked sins committed in the past, at this present time, he shows himself to be righteous and makes righteous the one who has faith in Jesus or who has the faith of Jesus (3:26).

▌THE TEXT IN THE INTERPRETIVE TRADITION

Paul's affirmation that gentiles can know God through the "things he has made" expresses the belief, shared by Stoic popular philosophy, that the order that inheres in all created things reflects a divine order. In the history of interpretation and the development of doctrine these verses have been the locus for development of "natural theology," the idea that nature teaches the order of God. Paul's description of the consequences of idolatry, God's surrendering humans to the chaos of their passions and the exchange of what is natural for what is unnatural, continues to be read as the condemnation in Scripture of homosexuality for women and for men. The horror that the passage is meant to evoke in its ancient context echoes and amplifies the misunderstanding and suspicion of sexual relationships between same-sex couples that has been widespread in culture since that time. This passage gives cultural abhorrence of homosexuality scriptural legitimation. Caricatures of Jewish judgmentalism and hypocrisy as well as gentile debauchery and depravity have remained powerful and harmful throughout history. Paul's statement that "a person is a Jew who is one inwardly, and real circumcision is a matter of the heart—it is spiritual and not literal" (2:29) has led to the spiritualization of the identity of Jew and gentile as symbolic categories, rather than as real historical peoples. Influential theologies of the atonement that explain how Christ's death is a sacrifice for sin have been based in the language of *hilastērion* in this passage.

▌THE TEXT IN CONTEMPORARY DISCUSSION

Contemporary interpreters have grappled with how to translate the teaching and proclamation of these verses into the worldview and symbolic universe of the present. For example, many question the ancient understanding that the order of active male superiority and passive female subordination is woven into creation. Ideas about gender have changed over time in interaction with culture and religion. In more and more societies, equality of men and women is a fundamental value. Therefore, the logic of the text that understands same-sex intercourse to be a violation of this natural order and therefore an apt example of the consequences of idolatry is no longer accepted. For those who hold more traditional views about the relationship of male and female, its logic remains convincing.

Paul's argument depicts the universal sinfulness of all and the human need for salvation. He condemns self-righteousness and judgment of others on the basis that all sin. Just as sin is not limited to any one group of people, neither is God's salvation. Paul affirms that God's salvation is totally inclusive, of both Jew and gentile. As "justification by faith" came to mean that believing in Jesus was necessary for salvation, "faith" or lack of faith became the new dividing line between people and drew a boundary for God's mercy. However, when faith is reconceived as "faithfulness" and as "trust" modeled on the faithfulness of Jesus, it becomes a holistic orientation that might be mutually understood by Jews and Christians. Faithfulness comprises righteous action and works within the expanse of God's righteous judgment. In Rom. 1:18-32 idolatry is the chief cause of chaos and misery for human beings. While sexual immorality may be more easily recognized, idolatry is ultimately more destructive. Christian readers of this text might ask how to identify idolatrous worship in their own communities and reorient themselves to God.

Romans 4:1-25: Abraham Is Ancestor of Jews and Gentiles

▌ THE TEXT IN ITS ANCIENT CONTEXT

The story of Abraham (Genesis 12–17) provided Second Temple Jews with Scripture from which to draw lessons, preach, and on which to elaborate. In other Jewish writings from this period, Abraham represents a great hero of monotheism, the first Jewish convert from paganism, and the epitome of obedience to Torah. In the New Testament, the author of the Epistle of James extols Abraham as an exemplar of justification by works when he offered his son Isaac (James 2:21).

Paul interprets the Genesis story with his own questions in mind. Developing the question about Jewish identity and circumcision that he raised in 3:1, and offering additional support to his claim in 3:29 that the one God is the God of gentiles as well as Jews, Paul presents Abraham as a model of one who is justified by faith. In this argument, Abraham becomes the spiritual father or ancestor of the gentiles, the people who are symbolically incorporated into his lineage.

Paul employs conventional Jewish techniques of scriptural commentary and argument and builds his commentary around scriptural quotations: Gen. 15:6 (cited in Rom. 4:3, 22); Ps. 32:1-2 (Rom. 4:7-8); Gen. 17:5 (Rom. 4:17); and Gen. 15:5 (Rom. 4:18). He explores the text of Gen. 15:6 from different angles to illustrate the theme, "We know that a person is justified by faith apart from works prescribed by the law" (3:28). Paul plays on the word "reckoned" throughout this part of Romans, first using it in the context of payment to contrast righteousness that comes as wages with that which comes as a gift (3:28; see 3:24). Paul uses the verb "reckon" again in 4:6, citing Ps. 32:1-2 as a second corroborating scriptural support. Paul next argues that Abraham, the patriarch whose covenant with God was represented by the sign of circumcision, actually was "reckoned" righteous before his circumcision (4:9-10). The account of the sign of circumcision in Gen. 17:10-11 occurs after God's "reckoning" of righteousness to Abraham (in Gen. 15:6); therefore, Paul argues, Abraham was to be made the ancestor also of all who are not circumcised, but who follow his example of faith.

God's promise to Abraham that he would be made a great nation (Gen. 12:2) and "the father of many nations" (Gen. 17:5; Sir. 44:19-21) came through faith and rests on grace. The scriptural promise, "I have made you the father of many nations" (Gen. 17:5), is interpreted to mean that Abraham's descendants include all who share his faith. The God in whom Abraham believes, who "gives life to the dead and calls into existence things which do not exist," is the God of resurrection and creation. Abraham's faithful response to God's promise is elaborated in a short vignette portraying his "hoping against hope," his consideration of his own nearly dead body and Sarah's barren womb. He grows strong and gives glory, thus depicting the ideal heroic exemplar of faith. Paul's argument closes with the repetition of the thematic verse and a claim that the words of Scripture "it was reckoned to him" were written not only for his sake but for "ours also," referring to the audience of Romans. The concluding formula is likely an early Christian creedal statement summarizing the belief "in him who raised Jesus our Lord from the dead, who was handed over to death for our trespasses and was raised for our justification" (Rom. 4:24-25).

▌ THE TEXT IN THE INTERPRETIVE TRADITION

New Testament evidence shows Abraham to have been a major figure of exegetical and theological speculation for Christian writers (see James 2:21-23; 1 Pet. 3:6; and Hebrews, passim). Abraham's wife Sarah and slave Hagar figure in Paul's Letter to the Galatians as mothers of the slave and the free child, of Mount Sinai and Jerusalem (see Gal. 4:21-31). Later, Protestant theologians understood Abraham to be the representative of justification by faith in opposition to works righteousness, which they regarded as characteristic of the Roman Catholicism they opposed. John Calvin was concerned with questions about Paul's exegesis of the Abraham story that preoccupied his own forebears and contemporaries. These included how to reconcile Paul's portrait of Abraham's faith with his laughter in response to God's promise of a son (Gen. 17:7) and how to resolve the apparent contradiction between Paul's and James's exegesis of the Abraham story. As all exegetes do, the sixteenth-century interpreters looked to the biblical text to address their pressing theological questions (Steinmetz).

▌ THE TEXT IN CONTEMPORARY DISCUSSION

Contemporary scholarship sees Paul's argument here within the context of Jewish styles of biblical exegesis in the first century. Extrabiblical and legendary traditions about Abraham's adventures and virtues show the variety and fluidity of scriptural commentary. When Paul constructs the argument that Abraham is the father of both Jews and gentiles, we see theology built up out of story and patterns within God's activity. The presence of other versions and variations within the New Testament in James, Hebrews, and Galatians testifies to the creativity of early Christian theology. The emphasis of scholarly commentators is no longer to harmonize the statements of different New Testament authors or to arrive at one consistent reading of the accounts of Abraham in Genesis.

The negative contrast Paul sets up between being justified by works and justified by faith has been read by Christians to denigrate both ancient and modern Judaism. Recently scholars have corrected that historically inaccurate portrait of Jewish belief and practice. By reading Romans 4 within the context of Second Temple Judaism, contemporary scholarship understands that Paul is not arguing for the replacement of Israel by the church or contrasting grace and faith with the negative foil of the law. Rather, he is finding, within the story of God in Torah, grounds for gentiles being included in God's promises.

Keen awareness of the function of gender in the text and the role of gender in the culture causes some readers to note that Sarah does not play a role as an active agent of faith here in Romans as she does in Hebrews 11 and in Galatians 4 (Trible and Russell). God's sacrifice of his Son Jesus on the cross is able to rearrange genealogical relationships and make gentiles into the patrilineal line of Abraham (Eisenbaum).

Romans 5:1-21: Christ's Gift of Righteousness Brings Life

▌ THE TEXT IN ITS ANCIENT CONTEXT

In Romans 5–8, Paul elaborates the results of justification that were summarized in Rom. 3:21-26. The section begins and ends with an affirmation of the love of God (5:5; 8:39). Paul speaks of justification with the parallel images of "having peace with God" and "being reconciled to God," metaphors that have their meaning in the context of warfare and conflict. The audience of Romans would have recognized the echoes of imperial rhetoric that claimed the peace of the *Pax Romana* as the benefits gained by the emperor (Georgi). Here, however, the peace is gained not through the perpetration of violence. Rather it is Jesus' death ("through his blood"), not on behalf of the righteous, but on behalf of the unrighteous, that is the means of peace and the way to be saved.

In Paul's anthropology, boasting is a characteristic human activity. Boasting and being ashamed are part of the language of honor and shame typical of Greco-Roman culture (Jewett). For a Christian, it is what one boasts about, and on what basis, that matters. While Paul criticizes boasting in 2:17; 3:27; 4:2, here boasting is celebrated as positive and justified. Here the speakers, "we," who are made right with God through faith, as Abraham exemplified in the previous example, may boast in hope and because we are saved from God's wrath (5:3, 11). The phrase "glory of God" alludes to the story of Adam in Genesis (Gen. 1:26-28; Ps 8:5-8), whose transgression caused him to lose the glory of God that he possessed. The sequence of virtues, linked in a chain-like structure, culminates in God's love.

Paul explains how this salvation works through a comparison of Adam and Christ, two corporate figures, men who represent humanity. As a "type" of the one to come, Adam is parallel to Christ, who will rectify the damage caused by Adam's trespass. Paul retells the story of humanity as a sequence of reigns, each dominated by a different ruler. Each ruler personifies the quality of the age and tyrannizes his subjects, here as either death or life. While death, the result of Adam's sin, rules in Adam, through Christ those who have been given the gift of righteousness will rule in life. The verb to exercise dominion (*basileuein*) is translated in the NRSV as both "rule" and "reign." In extrabiblical literature, Adam is held responsible for human death (*4 Ezra* 3:7; Wis. 2:23-24). While Paul's Jewish contemporaries would have understood the giving of the law through Moses to rectify this deadly situation, in the story Paul tells, the law plays a role as a minor character (5:13, 20) that increases the trespass. While the two figures of Adam and Christ are parallel, and one's action cancels the other, Paul stresses how much greater is the gift of Christ. The increasing and abounding of grace leads to eternal life.

▌THE TEXT IN THE INTERPRETIVE TRADITION

Augustine found in Rom. 5:12 the locus of the doctrine of original sin that he developed from the phrase *eph' hō*, "in whom." Arguing against his theological adversaries the Pelagians and the Manicheans, Augustine diagnosed the fact of original sin in the human person as a child of Adam. Sin was propagated through Adam to all subsequent descendants, passed down by parents to their children. The baptism of infants, he argued, was necessary to cleanse them from sin. Luther radicalized Augustine's notion of original sin, elaborating that "all humanity sinned with Adam in Adam's sin." Original sin, according to Luther, is "complete lack of righteousness in all the parts of a person, and a predisposition to commit evil, a loathing of what is good, a delight in what is evil" (Reasoner, 49). Augustine and Luther's reading of this part of Romans has profoundly shaped church teaching and Western culture. On the other hand, historical-critical biblical scholars contend that, read in its context, Rom. 5:12 is an incomplete sentence that serves only as the basis for showing the parallel figure of Christ and the positive benefits of Christ's death for human beings to reign in life. As we have seen with other parts of Romans, the history of interpretation emphasizes one part of this passage strongly, while biblical scholars see Paul's emphasis elsewhere.

▌THE TEXT IN CONTEMPORARY DISCUSSION

Paul uses a variety of terms for salvation that are at home in different semantic settings. Here the metaphors for salvation, synonyms for justification, have their meaning in the setting of warfare and conflict. The rhetoric of this passage can be read as disguised commentary on the language of pacification and imposition of peace of the *Pax Romana* (Elliott 2008; Georgi). In the language of domination and rule, interpreters have seen an apt description of the way in which political and economic systems dominate human life in the present. Focus on imperial language in Romans has alerted interpreters to the contemporary imperial context of interpretation. Paul's mythological scenario might be translated into the present as analogous to global capitalism or globalization (Elliott 2008). The dramatic totalizing language of ruling, "exercising dominion," is apt for the reality of these systems of power. Attending anew to Paul's language of corporate connection and corporate identity can act as an antidote to commonplace assumptions about individualism in contemporary culture. The solidarity of sin in Adam is overcome by a parallel, yet superior "solidarity in grace" through Christ. Jesus "represents the weakness of God and thus the dominion of grace, the sole form of dominion befitting both humanity and God" (Georgi, 100).

Romans 6:1-23: United to Christ in Death and in Resurrection

▌THE TEXT IN ITS ANCIENT CONTEXT

The argument is advanced with a rhetorical question from an imaginary dialogue partner (6:1). The question appears to draw a conclusion from 5:20: if sin increases and grace abounds all the more, does that mean that one should continue to sin? Paul introduces and expands on narratives of baptism and enslavement to show that the free gift of justification does not give believers license to sin, nor does it cause sin to be impotent. Rather, sin still flourishes as a power with which to contend and not surrender. Paul personifies sin as a ruler, who exercises dominion, rules (*basileuein*), and who demands allegiance. Paul and his audience understand that those who undergo the rite of baptism into Christ are participating in the narrative of Christ's death and resurrection, a two-part movement of dying and rising. Death is in the past and resurrection is still in the future, a hope and expectation. The association of baptism and death is made also in Mark 10:38-40 in Jesus' response to the request of James and John for positions of honor. Jesus' response shows that early believers linked baptism with the death of Jesus. Paul connects the death in baptism to the destruction of the body of sin. He concludes that those he addresses are, just as Jesus, dead to sin and alive to God.

The language of life and death and of freedom and slavery organize this passage, and the categories shift and reverse in the course of Paul's argument. Death and slavery represent negative states that are reversed and overcome in the resurrection and baptism. The exception to this pattern is the conclusion of this passage, where slavery to righteousness is presented as the positive alternative to slavery to sin.

With the military imagery of weapons, Paul exhorts that bodies are to be employed as instruments of righteousness rather than as weapons of wickedness. As in 1:18-32, passions lead to danger and make one out of control. Sharp contrasts structure the argument: dead to sin/alive to God, not present to sin/present to God, not as instruments of wickedness/but instruments of righteousness, not under law/under grace.

In a response to another imaginary question (5:15), Paul uses the analogy of slavery to redescribe the human situation in relationship to Christ. The social world in which Paul lived was a slave society, and Paul used a familiar and extreme image to speak of the alternative between living in the rule of God or the rule of sin. Formerly slaves to sin, now those who are freed from it are slaves to righteousness. While slavery to sin means death (6:21), slavery to God means sanctification and eternal life. Here the alignment of freedom with life shifts to equate slavery to God with life.

▌THE TEXT IN THE INTERPRETIVE TRADITION

When slavery was a social institution thoroughly embedded in the fabric of society, as it was at the time of the writing of the New Testament, the instructions to slaves to obey their masters were read as Christian teaching about slavery. Because the Bible assumed the existence of slavery, readers who were not slaves concluded that slavery had divine support and approval. The prevalence of slavery in Christian Scripture and the fact that Paul and other authors did not unambiguously speak against it, made it possible to take slavery for granted and to see it as "natural." However, as criticism of the practice of slavery increased within society, readers sought to use the Bible itself to critique the slavery texts within it. When those who were enslaved and their descendants read these scriptural texts, they put their experience of oppression into dialogue with their faith and drew the conclusion that God did not intend for those made in God's image to be enslaved by others. The slave society offered the image of slavery, an apt metaphor for the tyrannical reign of sin (Tamez). On the basis of the conclusion of the passage in which "slaves of righteousness" is the positive alternative to "slaves of sin," some have argued that freedom is not freedom in the modern sense, but enslavement to the proper master. Because there was no alternative to a state of spiritual enslavement, human existence is inevitably some form of obedience (Cranfield, 323; Hays 1996, 38–39, 390).

▌THE TEXT IN CONTEMPORARY DISCUSSION

The Bible's historical role both to support slavery and to abolish it affects the way interpreters read the metaphors of slavery and their meaning in Romans 6. While slavery has been judged immoral by most contemporary societies, the enslavement of people by other human beings continues to be a political reality. "Human trafficking" and "sex trafficking" are the modern synonyms for slavery. Slavery is a state of "natal alienation" (Patterson) and remains the most extreme form of human mistreatment and violence. The spiritualization of slavery, its use as a metaphor, can direct attention away from its physical and bodily effects in real people's lives (Glancy). The reality of physical slavery is masked by the metaphor. On the other hand, to describe sin as an enslaving power highlights sin's total domination and indicates its evil results. The only effective opposition is "slavery" to God. While many interpreters have concluded from this passage that in a Christian perspective there is no state that is not obedience, others point to the images of freedom and equality in other parts of Paul's letters (Schüssler Fiorenza; Kittredge 1998). The concentration of slavery language in Romans 6 raises for readers the ethical question: How is it possible to use the language of "ruling" that so permeates Romans without adopting and reinforcing structures of domination and subordination in the present?

Romans 7:1—8:1: The Role of the Law

▌THE TEXT IN ITS ANCIENT CONTEXT

Paul asserts the holiness and goodness of the law and at the same time insists that it has no positive role in the life of those in Christ. He makes an analogy with marriage. The law of marriage no longer pertains to a woman whose husband has died. Just as Paul's analogies with slavery depend for their meaning on the existence of a slave society, so his use of marriage depends on the assumption of marriage in which the husband owns the wife and rules over her. A person "belongs" to Christ, as a wife "belongs" to her husband.

In denying that the law is sin (7:7), Paul employs the first-person pronoun to explain the relationship between sin and the law. With the "I," Paul is not telling his own story but is using the rhetorical form of a "speech in character" to tell the experience of a typical human being. The story echoes the story of Adam in Genesis 2, who transgressed God's commandment. Sin acts as the serpent (7:11). It alludes also to the story of the people of Israel who rebelled against God when they worshiped the golden calf (Grieb). Philo, a Jewish writer of the Second Temple period, wrote that covetousness or desire is the most basic sin, the source of all others. The dramatic description of the "I" who, because of indwelling sin, is unable to good, but only evil, has a parallel in the Dead Sea Scrolls: 1QS 3–4 identifies an evil impulse dwelling within the flesh that opposes God until God intervenes. Paul sees the person divided between mind and flesh and mind and members, one opposed to the other. In the scope of his argument, his statements about the law are subordinate in importance to the overall story of God's victory in Jesus Christ, and the statements about human slavery are preparatory to the affirmation of freedom and life. The positive turn comes in 8:1, and Paul summarizes the climax of the story in 8:3-4, that God did what the law could not do, by sending his son, to overcome sin.

▮ THE TEXT IN THE INTERPRETIVE TRADITION

The history of interpretation of Rom. 7:7-25 has focused on the identity of the speaker, the "I." Augustine, contesting with Pelagius, in early writings argued that the "I" was the person before he/she was in Christ, later that it was Paul himself, and finally that it was the person after conversion who still struggled with sin. For Augustine, the text denied the perfectibility of the human person. The history of reading Romans 7 as an example of the "introspective conscience of the West" (Stendahl) began with Augustine, who first identified the "I" with his own youthful self who was unable to do good on his own. Martin Luther then identified with Paul, interpreted through Augustine, and saw his own overzealous conscience in Paul's confession of helplessness over sin and the ineffectiveness of the law. The doctrine *simul iustus et peccator* ("at the same time justified and a sinner") summarized his reading of Rom. 7:14-20 as a description of the Christian's ongoing struggle with sin. Paul's description of the bondage of the will and its interpretation in Christian theology has shaped Western views of the human self as incapable of achieving good. Calvin's doctrine of "total depravity" is based on an interpretation of 7:14-21.

Interpreters have also made analogies between the "law" of Romans 7 and other aspects of human life: for Barth, the law was "religion" (Reasoner). When scholars began to read Paul with the cultural and religious milieu of his own time, rather than with the lenses of later Christian systematic theology, Romans 7 was read not as autobiographical but as "rhetorical reinforcement" of the larger argument of God's saving purpose for Jews and gentiles. Here Paul was offering an apology for Torah, a defense of its essential goodness, rather than a condemnation. With this approach, Paul's Letter to the Romans provided a New Testament model for imagining Christianity and Judaism, the descendants of the Torah-abiding Jews and Christ-believers in Romans, as both having a place in the purposes of God. Paul's vision in Romans created the basis for cooperative and appreciative relationships between Christians and Jews in the present.

▮ THE TEXT IN CONTEMPORARY DISCUSSION

Krister Stendahl and his followers succeeded in shifting scholars' interpretations of Romans away from the internal psychological reading to a reading that saw the subject of the letter as the relationship between peoples of the world, Jews and gentiles, in God's saving plan for the whole creation. In a world that had seen the murderous effects of antisemitism and hatred between peoples, the shift to a corporate understanding of Romans spoke eloquently and opened up avenues of dialogue and mutual understanding. However, the individualistic approach to Romans, that it is about the person's helplessness under sin and the need for inner assent and conversion to Christ, remains popular in evangelical Christianity and influential in Christian belief in general. Read as an autobiographical confession, Paul's story of "I do not do the good I want" resonates with contemporary people's own experience. Alcoholics Anonymous, for example, names powerlessness over alcohol as the first step of recovery. The power of sin, personified as a tyrant, describes and diagnoses a reality that many experience. Conversion to Christ within a Christian context or dependence on a "higher power" in Alcoholics Anonymous is effective in opposing and overcoming the force of sin. Others have read Paul's language about sin here to refer to systemic or corporate systems of oppression and enslavement that make "doing good" impossible. The challenge is how to translate the drama of Romans 7 into the contemporary context and find appropriate analogues to "sin," "law," the "good."

Romans 8:1—8:39: Life in the Spirit

■ The Text in Its Ancient Context

The argument that began in 5:1 culminates in 8:39, ending as it began on a note of "love." In the scriptural world that supplies the imagery in this passage, God's Spirit is present at creation, linked to the resurrection of Jesus, and given at baptism. History is envisioned as a battle between opposing forces, a struggle at the brink of its conclusion, which is the intervention of God. God's judgment is imminent. Here Paul claims that in the action of Jesus Christ, those who participate in his death and resurrection through baptism will not be condemned, but will become children of God. "Law," *nomos*, has various meanings here that range from the common, "rule," to the specific, "Torah." As in Romans 6–7, the primary opposition is between life and death, and secondarily between freedom and slavery.

In Rom. 8:3-4, Paul expresses how God succeeded in defeating sin, a task that the law failed to do, "by sending his own Son in the likeness of sinful flesh." After God's defeat of sin, the choice is between two ways of living, "according to the flesh" or "according to the Spirit." One is the way of life and the other the way of death. The ethical choice between two ways of behaving is modeled after Moses' challenge in Deut. 11:26-28 to choose between blessing and curse. Here the choices appear as two "spheres of influence," "reigns," "realms," or kingdoms. "Flesh" does not mean physical flesh, but is a term that signifies sin. The one who has faith has already been transferred from the realm of flesh/death to the realm of spirit/life because of the Spirit who dwells within the person. Romans 8:14-17 is a baptismal formula that uses the language of adoption and "sonship" to describe the relationship between God and those baptized/those believers/those in Christ. This relationship is opposed to the spirit of slavery, the antithesis of adoption and sonship. It allows the right of inheritance and the privilege of crying "Abba," the name given by a young child to a father. Traditions about the exodus undergird this passage—the people of Israel are considered children of God whom God creates, elects, and delivers from slavery in Egypt. The redemption in Christ is parallel with the delivery of Israel in the exile. The tradition of Israel's holy war funds these images of conquering and being children of God (Grieb).

Paul understands that the present time of suffering is part of the final struggle between the forces of good and evil that will culminate in victory for God. God's purposes include not only human beings but also the whole creation, described as groaning with labor pains. This culmination is near, but still in the future, a glory for which we "long" and "wait." Just as righteous Israel suffered in preparation for vindication by God, so those who are in Christ suffer as they await the "glory" about to be revealed. Paul's confidence that God will prevail is summarized in the assertion "those he called, he justified." In an allusion to Abraham's near sacrifice of Isaac, "who did not withhold his own Son," Paul connects God's giving up of Jesus with Abraham's giving up of Isaac.

■ THE TEXT IN THE INTERPRETIVE TRADITION

The overarching oppositions set up in this passage between the realm of the spirit and the realm of the flesh, characteristic of apocalyptic literature and deriving from "the two ways tradition" in the Deuteronomistic history, has been interpreted to denigrate the body and the material world in favor of the nonbodily and "spiritual." Appreciation of the origins of this oppositional language, and a nuanced understanding that what Paul means by "flesh" is not the physical body but is by definition the realm of sin, help readers to contextualize this dualism rather than universalizing or generalizing it. Romans 8:28-30 describes God's relationship with the elect people of God in a stair-step sequence of verbs. In these verses, Paul has transferred the scriptural terminology for Israel, "called," "chosen," "sons," onto those gentiles and Jews who follow Jesus (Reasoner, 86). While these verses originally referred to God's relationship with the people Israel, Luther and Calvin understood them to refer to God's choice of individuals for salvation. In the Protestant Reformation, theologians developed theologies of predestination of individuals from the verbs "predestined," "foreknew," and "called." Liturgically, the acclamation of the inseparability of the faithful from God's love is well known in burial services in both Protestant and Roman Catholic churches. Outside of their context in Paul's Letter to the Romans, these verses—"neither death, nor life, nor angels, nor rulers, nor things present, nor things to come"—have become an expression of faith for those who grieve the death of a loved one. For those who see Romans 1–8 as the theological center of Romans, this exultant affirmation of the love of God is the letter's "climax."

■ THE TEXT IN CONTEMPORARY DISCUSSION

The proclamation of freedom in Christ in Rom. 8:15-17 functions as a "canon within the canon" for many theologians of liberation. The inclusion of the whole creation in the cooperative struggle toward renewed relationship with God, described in poetic, apocalyptic language, provides a rich resource for readers who seek earth-affirming images in Scripture. The "groaning" of Rom. 8:22-23 evokes the cries of labor and the sounds of speaking in tongues (Stendahl 1976; McGinn). Feminist interpreters resist reading the language of flesh and spirit to create a mind-body or a male-female dualism. The transformation from "slaves" to "sons" and "heirs" describes the move from death to life and from slavery to freedom accomplished in baptism. The NRSV translation of *huioi* as "children" obscures its male referent and masks the patriarchal assumptions of the metaphors of adoption, sons, and heirs. At the same time, society's customs around adoption are not merely reflected by the text, but challenged, as indicated by the use of *teknoi*, "children"—male and female alike (McGinn; Kittredge 2012). Responding to the theological and ethical questions raised by readers after the Holocaust and in the economic and ecological crises at the close of the twentieth century, contemporary readers have turned away from focus on theologies of God's election of individuals and their promised salvation. Rather, interpreters have read Paul's affirmations of God's commitment to rescue the whole creation, and they have attempted to translate that faith into holiness of life in the present.

Romans 9:1-29: God's Promises to Israel Are Sure

◼ THE TEXT IN ITS ANCIENT CONTEXT

In Romans 9–11, Paul addresses the success of the gospel among gentiles and its rejection among the majority of Jews. The reversed relationship between Jews and gentiles calls into question the central role of God's elect people and threatens confidence in God's integrity. The stakes are high. In an extended argument that runs through these chapters, Paul draws on Scripture and on analogies from everyday life to speculate about what God is doing. In sending Jesus Christ, God has altered the overall plot of the story, but revised it in a way that makes sense with patterns of divine activity told in Scripture. The phenomenon of gentile acceptance of the gospel and Jewish rejection was an urgent and immediate challenge for Paul because it appeared to undermine the faithfulness of God. Paul's defense of God takes the form of a lament, colored by emotionally charged accusations, questions, challenges, expressions of doubt, and fury, alternating with thanksgiving and praise (Grieb; Hays 1989). Paul uses the "I" pronoun to refer to himself as he identifies with his own people and protests God's decisions. Paul affirms (9:4-5) that Israel possesses all the privileges and gifts of relationship with God and is the source of the Messiah.

In order to defend the word of God from an accusation of failure (9:6), Paul garners a series of arguments that depend on citation and analysis of different verses and images in Scripture. The first is that God specifies that it is through Sarah's child that God names true descendants. The second is that Jacob was chosen over Esau, and the third is that God raises up Pharaoh to show his power and proclaim God's name. The sovereign power of God to choose on whom to have mercy is asserted by this series of scriptural examples. Each one is tinged with irony, surprise, and reversal and emphasizes how God inexorably carries out God's purposes (9:11). Paul upholds God's justice and mercy (9:14) and at the same time asserts God's freedom to act without regard to human expectations. Employing the image of God as the potter (Isa. 29:16; 45:9; Jer. 18:1-11; Wis. 15:7; Sir. 33:13), Paul asks a series of questions (9:19-24) that imply the absurdity of the human creation arguing with the Creator. Citing the words of the prophet Hosea, who speaks of God's choosing Israel and calling her "my people" and "beloved," Paul applies this election to Jews and gentiles. He cites Isaiah's reference to a remnant and to "survivors" or "descendants." Paul's argument in 9:1—11:36 is a series of attempts to address the problem of God's change of plan, and its conclusion is not reached until the end of chapter 11.

◼ THE TEXT IN THE INTERPRETIVE TRADITION

When Romans was read as a treatise on Christian doctrine, it was Romans 1–8 that was considered the center of the letter while Romans 9–11 was considered a parenthetical topic of little importance for theologians (Reasoner). With the scholars of the new perspective, Romans 9–11 received renewed attention. While the question of the status of Israel had seemed settled and irrelevant for interpreters during the time when Christianity dominated as a sociopolitical force, it became a critical question in a new way for Christians after the Holocaust. Simultaneously, interest in the letter in its first-century context coincided with application to its contemporary context. Before the modern period, interpreters from Origen through Augustine and the Reformers were chiefly interested in the issue of election, "that God's purpose of election might continue." What is now understood in its historical context to have been an affirmation of God's relationship with a people was then interpreted as applying to individuals who were predestined to salvation or damnation. Interpreters read the "objects of wrath" and the "objects of mercy" as referring to two groups of people, each predestined to salvation or damnation. Augustine in his later work developed a strong predestinarian reading of the text. Karl Barth disputed rigid determinism and talked about God's purposes of election as being more general (Reasoner). Paul's rhetoric about the irony of God's choice and the stress on God's mercy was taken in an absolute and literal sense to speak about the predetermined fate of individuals and their inability to change that status. Commentators who have tried to put this passage into its historical context have read this passage as an argument among Jews about the role of Israel's covenant responsibility in God's overall purpose (Nanos 1996).

▓ THE TEXT IN CONTEMPORARY DISCUSSION

As the question of the ongoing status of the people of Israel was a critical theological issue for Paul, so the relationships between Christians and Jews after the Holocaust were urgent for biblical interpreters. Stendahl and others believed that Paul's argument in Romans 9–11 might give clues to understanding how Jews and Christians can be conceived to coexist within the mystery of God. As theologians grapple with pluralism of faith traditions, the way Paul uses Scripture and analogies with ordinary life may provide a model for how to reflect on what God is doing in the world. The manner in which Paul creatively engages with Scripture in a christological perspective, and in a way that seeks patterns within its narratives, can be used as a model for Christian preachers and theologians who interpret Scripture in the present (Hays 1989).

Although this passage's emphasis on the sovereignty of God appears to limit human choice and decision, the emphasis is not on human helplessness but on the mercy of God. While Paul mocks the idea that the pot would talk back to the potter, he himself is talking back to God out of an experience of anguish and making a bold and creative attempt to ascertain God's purposes.

Romans 9:30—10:21: Trying to Understand Israel and the Gentiles

▓ THE TEXT IN ITS ANCIENT CONTEXT

Opening the next stage of the argument with a rhetorical question, Paul contrasts gentile attainment of righteousness through faith with Israel's lack of success. Paul uses the opposition of faith and works to explain the paradox that gentiles who did not strive succeeded, while those who did strive did not. Behind this explanation lies the metaphor of the footrace in which two runners "chase" (*diōkein*), "strive" or compete. A "stumbling stone" has tripped up one contestant and allowed the other to overtake. A quotation that combines Isa. 28:16 and Isa. 8:14-15 refers to God who lays a stone in Zion. In 1 Cor. 1:23 the word *skandalon*, "stumbling stone," refers to Jesus Christ. Although the identity of the stone is left ambiguous here, Paul implies that Christ is the stone that is laid as an obstacle for Israel. The image of the footrace will be picked up again for further irony in 11:7-8.

In emotional language, appropriate for a lament ("heart's desire"), Paul expresses his wish that Israel be saved. Their "zeal," a quality Paul elsewhere attributes to himself (Phil. 3:6), misunderstands that righteousness through the law is not possible. "God's righteousness" comes through Christ, as the next verse asserts. In the statement "Christ is the end of the law," the word translated "end," *telos*, can mean either "termination" or "goal." "Goal" is the preferred interpretation: Christ is the "point" of the law as expressed in 3:21-26, "apart from the law" (3:21).

Employing a pesher style of scriptural interpretation in 10:5-13, Paul puts into opposition two quotations about the law, one from Lev. 18:5 and the other from Deut. 30:12-14. The text from Deuteronomy is used to interpret Leviticus. While Deuteronomy 30 in its original context asserts the nearness of the word so that the law could be done, here in Romans, by interspersing christological commentary into the quotation, Paul harnesses the original text to support the nearness of "the word of faith that we proclaim." The lips and heart of the quotation now speak of the requirement of assertion of faith with lips and in heart. Paul quotes two more verses from Scripture: Isa. 28:16 and Joel 2:32. Together these texts assert no distinction between Jew and Greek, their sharing of the same Lord, and the availability of salvation to "everyone" who calls on the name of the Lord.

The reference to calling on the name of the Lord leads Paul to address the possible objection that Israel has not been given the opportunity to call on the Lord and to believe. With a sequence of linked phrases in which the second of two becomes the first of a second pair, "believed," "heard," and "proclaimed," Paul presents a series of questions followed by scriptural quotations that demonstrate that God has provided Israel adequate opportunity to hear the good news. Isaiah 50–65 is the source of these quotations, passages where the prophet bewails the stubborn refusal of Israel to repent. Paul applies these prophetic critiques to the present situation of Jewish unbelief in Christ. Divine jealousy explains the current paradox. Deuteronomy 32:21 describes how the people's idolatry causes God to be jealous. In turn, God incites jealousy among his own people by taking on others. Paul attributes this motivation to God to account for Israel's unbelief.

◼ THE TEXT IN THE INTERPRETIVE TRADITION

Paul's reflection on the lack of success of his preaching of Jesus Christ to Israel, his own people, has been read by interpreters in their own historical context. They have understood Paul's words to describe and to diagnose their present. Reading *telos* to mean "end" rather than "goal," Marcion rejected the law as a whole. Others have cited this verse to support antinomianism. The Protestant opposition between faith and works, drawn from Paul and developed by Luther, has shaped Christian perceptions of Jews and Judaism as being motivated by "zeal" and focused on selfishness. Interpreted psychologically, this opposition is understood to be egoism and pathology. When this argument in Romans is read universally or timelessly, "Israel's unbelief" may be equated with ongoing Judaism, so that Judaism represents rejection of Jesus. For centuries, many churches derived from this interpretation of Romans 10 a mandate to convert Jews, but in the wake of the Holocaust many denominations worldwide have explicitly repudiated this view. So pervasive is this mapping of Paul's rhetoric in Romans onto contemporary Judaism that it is invisible and unconscious for many Christians (Levine). For example, Paul's christological interpretation of Deut. 30:12-14 has so defined the passage that Christian readers conclude that, for Jews, God is far away and must be sought across the seas, while for Christians, the word is near. The requirement of verbal confession and belief in the heart has become dominant in evangelical Protestantism as the necessary and critical action for conversion or salvation.

▮ THE TEXT IN CONTEMPORARY DISCUSSION

Contemporary interpreters grapple with the legacy of distorted and negative caricatures of Judaism built on Paul's rhetorical arguments about Israel and gentiles. Commentators see a sad irony that the portrait of Israel's unbelief presented by the prophet Third Isaiah to his own people, within their common tradition, to woo them back to faithfulness, has here been taken up by the lips of Paul, enshrined in Christian Scripture, and applied as Christian condemnation of Jews in the present. The agony of Paul's first-century commitment to his own people is lost in translation across history and context. Those who seek to read the letter in a way that honors its first-century context and still finds positive value as Christian Scripture attempt to understand Paul's scriptural interpretation as selective and tendentious; they place it within a wider conversation of interpretation of Scripture in the Second Temple period. At the same time, they try to read it sympathetically and find in it a model for reading Scripture. Richard Hays, for example, suggests that Paul's use of Scripture might provide a model of intertextual theological reflection for Christian readers (Hays 1989). Krister Stendahl developed the motif of "holy envy" to describe the ways that each religion envies the gifts of the other, and that envy is used by God for good (Landau).

Romans 11:1-36: The Restoration of Israel and the Inclusion of the Gentiles

▮ THE TEXT IN ITS ANCIENT CONTEXT

In the final stage of the argument of chapters 9–11, Paul refutes the conclusion that might logically be drawn from the portrayal of the people of Israel as "disobedient and contrary" (10:21). He completes his attempt to explain how God is keeping God's promises to Israel while drawing in the gentiles, by looking toward the future and imagining God's future action. He picks up and elaborates in turn on a series of images and metaphors from Scripture: the prophet Elijah's complaint and God's response, the motif of hardening, the dough, the olive tree, and the apocalyptic motif of previously unrevealed mystery.

The aim is to warn against arrogance of gentiles toward Israel, an attitude that ironically may have been provoked by earlier parts of Paul's argument. The lament continues with Paul citing himself and his own story. Implying a parallel between himself and Elijah, Paul recalls that God did not leave Elijah alone, but kept a remnant chosen by grace (1 Kgs. 19:18). This remnant is Paul's community of believers, who will have a role with regard to the salvation/fate of the rest. Citing from Isa. 29:10 and Ps. 69:22-23, Paul claims that God has hardened those who have not accepted the gospel. Returning to the image of stumbling in the footrace, Paul implies that the stumbling is temporary, not permanent, and will make Israel jealous. Here Paul uses again a "how much greater" argument (*pollō mallon*, see Romans 5) to predict the full inclusion of Israel that will be restated at the climax in 11:26. Again using himself as an example and employing the "jealousy" motif, Paul says that his role as apostle to the gentiles will, in a roundabout way, save some of his own. He invokes the images of the dough and roots to speak of the way that holiness "spreads" from the part to the whole. The word for "dough" is the same word as "lump," referring to clay, in 9:21. The image of root and branches leads into an elaborate argument whose central metaphor is the cultivation of an olive tree that is grafted with wild pieces, pruned, and regrafted. "Natural" (*kata physin*) is used to describe the original tree; "unnatural" (*para physin*), the wild branches. With this simile, Paul is able to speak of the relationship between peoples, Jews and gentiles, to speculate on shifting relationships between them, and to urge humility and forbearance toward Jews on the part of gentiles. Wild branches should realize their dependence on the roots. That some branches were broken off should serve as a warning against pride. In the final move, Paul imagines that in time, even the natural branches, formerly separated, will be grafted back in. As in Romans 9, where mercy is the last word, here kindness and mercy have the stress. Paul describes what God is doing using the word for a secret revealed by God: a "mystery." The "hardening" will last until "the full number of the Gentiles has come in. And so all Israel will be saved." The motif, known from the prophets, that the faith of Israel would lead all nations to God takes an unexpected twist: here the disobedience of Israel leads to mercy for one community first, and then for all. The section concludes with a doxology, or hymn of praise to God, that draws on language from Isaiah and from Job. The lament in which Paul complained and wrestled with the attempt to know God's ways and justify them to humans ends with an exclamation of wonder at the impossibility of knowing God or the "mind of the Lord."

■ THE TEXT IN THE INTERPRETIVE TRADITION

What was for Paul an urgent question in the first century, the ultimate fate of Israel in the plan of God, was not an issue for the church fathers and other early interpreters. In their view, the church had replaced Israel as the elect. It was ongoing Jewish practice and belief that posed a threat to them, and with which they disputed. Indeed, in much of its history, Paul's warning against gentile arrogance actually was used to fuel Christian triumphalism! Paul's hopeful conclusion about God's regrafting Israel into the tree did not hold a central place in their reading of Romans. Augustine focused on and developed Paul's negative statements about Israel. Luther understood that his contemporaries, the Jews and the Roman Catholics, exemplified those who lived as God's people by works rather than grace. Forcible conversion of Jews was one response to his reading of Romans 11. Karl Barth interpreted "all Israel will be saved" as speaking of the church. Among contemporary scholars, some interpret "all Israel" to refer to the church and Jesus-believing Jews, while Dunn and others understand it to include Christians and Jews (Reasoner).

■ THE TEXT IN CONTEMPORARY DISCUSSION

It makes sense that in the contemporary reality of religious pluralism, Paul's argument in Romans 9–11, and in Rom. 11:13-36 in particular, is taken up as a model for Christian theological reflection on God's surprising and unpredictable plans for the salvation of the whole world. While Paul claims in 11:34-35 the impossibility of human attempts to know the mind of God, it is exactly this effort that he makes in these verses. He approaches the task by searching for patterns in the Scriptures of Israel, even patterns that undermine traditional patterns of expectation. In addition to drawing on Scripture, Paul calls on images from everyday life—foot-racing, bread making, and horticulture—to attempt to imagine how God can demonstrate both faithfulness to the past and creativity for the future. Paul's surrender to the impossibility of the attempt after his extended effort in the exclamation of praise in the concluding doxology testifies to both human theological creativity and the merciful creativity of God.

Romans 12:1-21: Exhortation to Holy Living

▌ THE TEXT IN ITS ANCIENT CONTEXT

Paul appeals to the audience to practice a particular manner of life based on the argument of Romans 1–11. Several elements tie the content of this exhortation back to the images and stories earlier in the letter. "By the mercies of God" recalls the multiple examples of God's mercy demonstrated in the stories of Pharaoh and others in Romans 9. God's expansive vision of inclusion of the gentiles finds its concrete expression in the life of the community by the exercise of Christian virtues that echo the teaching of Jesus. Out of concern for the whole body, members are to practice forbearance toward the scruples and weaknesses of others (12:14). The language of baptismal renewal from Romans 6–8 recurs in the vocabulary of transformation and renewal (12:2) and of "one body" (12:4-5). Paul weaves together liturgical traditions from the early house churches, the preaching of Jesus, and the ethical teaching of the prophetic and wisdom traditions in Scripture. It is not possible to untangle these strands of teaching. The appeals appear to be general rather than to any specific behavior in the Roman church.

The image of sacrifice underlies the opening appeal "to present your bodies as a living sacrifice" and evokes the complex of meanings surrounding the sacrificial system in ancient Israel. As the drama of Rom. 6:12-19 described the members presented to slavery or to righteousness, here the presentation of the "body," the whole sentient being in community, is made to God. The "spiritual" worship (NRSV) might also be translated "rational" worship (*logikē*) or the worship one owes as a rational being (Byrne). The living sacrifice and the rational worship stand in sharp contrast to the corrupt and perverse worship of the creature rather than the Creator described in Rom. 1:18-32. Paul draws on the prophets who insist on the alignment of ritual and ethics (Isa. 1:10-20; Jer. 6:20; Hosea 8:11-13; Amos 5:21-27).

Believers are not to conform themselves to the current age, but are through baptism (6:4) to be transformed. Renewed minds enable discernment of God's will and, by implication, right decisions about how to live. The ideal of controlled rational discernment here corrects the picture of chaotic depravity in Rom. 1:18-32. Paul warns against arrogance and urges sober assessment of oneself "according to the measure of faith that God has assigned" (12:3). The stress on right proportion and differentiation resembles Stoic teaching about moderation and temperance. The measured tone contrasts with the apocalyptic drama portrayed elsewhere in the letter. The sequence of imperatives to love, zeal, joy, followed by the instruction to "bless," echoes the sayings from Jesus' teaching, particularly those found in the Sermon on the Mount in Matthew 5. The prohibition against taking vengeance cites a text in Deut. 32:35 that restricts the exacting of punishment to God. One feeds one's hungry enemies and gives water to those who are hostile in order to shame them. As in Prov. 25:21-22, "heap burning coals on their heads" (Rom. 12:20) may imply that they will experience remorse in response to one's good deed.

▌ The Text in the Interpretive Tradition

Paul's rationale for not taking vengeance—that one's forbearance to enemies would result in heaping "burning coals on their heads"—was interpreted in two directions by patristic commentators. John Chrysostom, on the one hand, understood Paul to mean that nonretaliation by Christians would have the effect of intensifying ultimate punishment by God toward enemies. Origen, Augustine, and Jerome, on the other hand, interpreted the heaping of burning coals to be a provocation to repentance, and hence to divine mercy for the enemies. Modern interpreters take parallel options, some taking the more generous approach: not taking vengeance gives enemies a chance to repent; and others taking the more severe one: that the righteous avoid vengeance so that God's vengeance on the unrighteous can be more severe.

▌ The Text in Contemporary Discussion

The potent mixture of Jewish wisdom and prophetic traditions and the inheritance of Jesus' teaching in this rhetorically eloquent exhortation demonstrates the close kinship of what later has been known as "Jewish" and "Christian" teaching. The conviction, held in common by prophets and early Christian writers, that right worship and right action are necessarily aligned, is a basis for ethical and liturgical decision making. Paul's imperative "do not be conformed to this world" (12:2) provides an antidote to the counsel of submission in Rom. 13:1-7 that follows. The apocalyptic sense that this present age is passing away provides leverage for Christians to critique and resist the powers that be in their political context. The exhortation to rational formation and decision making assumes the ability to reason on the part of human beings. Unlike those accounts in Romans that assert human incapacity for doing good (Rom. 7:14-26), here the outlook for human transformation is more hopeful. While a flesh/spirit dualism operates powerfully in other parts of the argument, the presentation of the body here presents a picture of bodily existence as integrated with physical, spiritual, and intellectual dimensions.

Romans 13:1-14: Subjection to Governing Authorities

▌ The Text in Its Ancient Context

Paul exhorts, "let every person be subject to the governing authorities." The address appears universal—the word translated "person" is literally "every soul." The tone is absolute as Paul claims that authorities on earth have a divine origin—they are appointed by God and have a purpose from

God. They are to be God's servants, to provoke fear of punishment and to execute God's judgment, symbolized by the sword. The language of the passage is replete with vocabulary of "order"—the roots *tasso-* and *tag-* mean "put," "place," "appoint," and the prefix *hyper* means "over." The symbolic universe assumed by these instructions is a hierarchical one in which human rulers rule with the authority of God, and the role of subordinates or citizens is to be ruled, to be subject, to take one's appointed place. "Fear," *phobos*, is the proper attitude to be shown by a subordinate to a superordinate. Elsewhere in the New Testament Epistles, commands to "be subject" are addressed to women, slaves, and children, who must behave as their appointed station requires (Col. 3:18—4:1; Eph. 5:21—6:9; Titus 2:1-10; 1 Pet. 2:18—3:7). The view of the world presented in Rom. 13:1-7 is closely paralleled in Hellenistic writings such as Wisdom and Josephus. God's judgment and wrath, which have played an important role in the narrative of the letter, are constructed as equivalent to the judgment of the authorities.

Historical-critical scholars have noted the tension, if not contradiction, between the perspective expressed here and Paul's view that the form of the world is passing away (1 Cor. 7:31) and that the rulers of the world are ignorant of the purposes of God (1 Cor. 2:6-8; 15:51-58). The counsel against resistance seems at odds with the exhortation not to conform to the world (Rom. 12:1-2). Some critics have evaluated the counsel to be so out of place that they judge that the passage is not a part of the original letter. Others try to conceive of a historical context in which such a counsel would have made sense. Within the context of imperial propaganda, Paul's instruction to pay taxes may have been made to ensure the safety of Jewish communities in Rome for whom tax revolts caused danger. Arguments about the historical context function to highlight Paul's statement as a historically specific and strategic instruction, rather than a generalizable principle about the relationship of church and state (Elliott 1997).

▌ THE TEXT IN THE INTERPRETIVE TRADITION

Discussion of this passage in the history of interpretation has been closely connected with the relationship of the interpreter's community with the political "authorities" of their own historical period. Most readers have had to grapple with the fact that although the text claims that there is an equivalence between the judgment of rulers and of God and that rulers are God's servants, this ideal is contradicted by experience—the experience of Christians under Roman rule in which martyrdom was the fate of many, the experience of blacks under apartheid in South Africa, African Americans under Jim Crow in the United States, and many others. Origen was disturbed by the claim that all governments are from God when some persecute believers (Reasoner, 130). He writes that "authority" can be misused and that God will judge those who violate the laws of God. Martyrdom is a means of overcoming evil governments. Since Luther identified Rom. 13:17 as the ultimate reference point for biblical teaching about the state and developed the doctrine of "two kingdoms," this text has been a center of controversy in theological discussion. For Luther, there were two ways for God's rule to be expressed: in the secular sphere, where the civic authorities ruled, and in the spiritual sphere, where the church ruled. On the basis of this passage, Luther opposed the peasant revolts in Germany. Karl Barth, on the other hand, rejected the equating of any political organization or ideology with the kingdom of God. For Barth, the state was evil, and all governments are under the judgment of God. Barth's insistence on the sovereignty of God above any civic authority appears to undercut the outward implication of the passage that civil authorities derive their legitimacy from God.

THE TEXT IN CONTEMPORARY DISCUSSION

The challenges raised by this text for contemporary interpreters come from the history of interpretation, particularly influenced by Luther, in which this text has been used to prohibit resistance or rebellion against state authority. In the "state theology" of South Africa in the time of apartheid, this text was the centerpiece of supporting and legitimizing apartheid and disallowing resistance (West). In order to dispute interpretations that read the text at face value for self-serving ends, engaged biblical scholars have employed different strategies to diffuse the text or to deploy its power in another direction. One strategy is to explain it as a realistic response to a dangerous political environment for Jews—to counsel quiescence for the sake of the safety of others. By contextualizing the text in a particular historical and social place, these readers relativize its absolute and universal-sounding claims. Another strategy is to place this counsel in the larger panorama of Paul's argument about nonretaliation, about overcoming evil with good (12:14-21), and within the wider framework of apocalyptic eschatology. For Christians living in contemporary situations of persecution, rather than being a text that prevents them from possible agency, the plea to be subject and the counsel that follows becomes a source of realism, caution, and hope in God's ultimate judgment against injustice (Tamez; Elliott 2008). Another approach is to recognize that the difficulty comes from the enormous distance between a worldview that sees the hierarchical political realm as a reflection of the hierarchical heavenly realm and a worldview built around democratic debate. Rather than affirming the exhortations to subordinates—citizens, wives, slaves, and children—to submit, readers will critique them on the basis of these democratic values.

Romans 14:1—15:13: Welcome One Another

THE TEXT IN ITS ANCIENT CONTEXT

Paul urges tolerance of diverse views and practices within the community by exhorting consideration of those whom he calls the "weak in faith." His rhetoric assumes that he counts himself among the "strong" (15:1), whom he urges not to pass judgment on those who take other positions about eating (15:2) and the observation of "days." It is not possible to identify precisely the early Christian parties or groups behind this dispute, nor is it certain whether Paul knows of specific disagreements about these matters in the church at Rome. One influential theory is that some believers returned to Rome who were more attached to the observance of Torah as part of Christian practice, and they came into conflict with those who did not practice dietary restrictions and other observances. However, vegetarianism, abstention from wine, and consideration of special "days" are not known to be part of Torah regulations. Those who reconstruct the disputes behind Paul's instructions here rely on controversies from other letters—over the eating of idol meat in 1 Corinthians 8–10, circumcision and feasts in Gal. 4:8-11 and Col. 2:20-23—although none of these provides a precise parallel.

Paul argues against judgmentalism on the basis of a series of theological rationales: that they should welcome one another because they have been welcomed by God, that the weak have the same lord/master as the strong (14:3-4), and that both groups do what they do out of full conviction and to honor the Lord (14:5-6).

The passage incorporates traditional elements from liturgical or wisdom settings; for example, 14:7-8 may be a hymn. The blessing/prayer wishes in 15:5-6, 13, 33, may also be traditional. Paul argues that the strong should refrain from eating or drinking in a manner that would injure another and destroy the "work of God," the community. One's own conviction, or one's "faith," makes the difference in discriminating what is sin. Paul cites Christ as a reason for tolerance, arguing that Ps. 69:9 refers to Christ's suffering rather than pleasing himself. Christ is the original source of "welcome" or acceptance. Returning to the theme of the reliability of God's promises and the story of Christ, Paul describes Christ as the servant of the circumcised whose ultimate purpose is the gentiles' glorification of God. A series of four scriptural quotations, from the Law, the Prophets, and the Writings (Ps. 17:50 LXX; Deut. 32:43 LXX; Ps. 117:1 LXX; Isa. 11:10 LXX), affirms Christ's purpose to bring gentiles to God. A prayer wish concludes the exhortation not to pass judgment, but to forbear, to act from faith, and to tolerate a range of diverse beliefs about matters of food and drink and calendar.

▌The Text in the Interpretive Tradition

Paul's appeal for tolerance, respect for the convictions of others, and inner commitment to one's own faith convictions in 14:1—15:13 has not been given the same attention in the history of interpretation that Romans 1–8 has received. Theologians who have been occupied with questions of predestination and free will have not found this moral exhortation to be of interest. The radical claims about faith in the earlier chapters of Romans appear to be compromised here with the focus on the needs of the "weak in faith." However, this section of the letter has received renewed attention because concern about how those with diverging opinions about Christian practice or belief can best live together is an urgent ethical issue in the current environment of diverse positions within the Christian community and without. In the context of the Roman Empire, this counsel of tolerance would have been an alternative value system (Elliott 2008).

▌The Text in Contemporary Discussion

Contemporary interpreters who read Romans as primarily occupied with the relationship between peoples in God's plan for salvation and with holy relationships within the community have developed the principles and theological rationales that are elaborated here. For example, Neil Elliott speaks of this passage as conveying an "ethic of solidarity" in tension with the Roman imperial system of hierarchy and patronage (Elliott 2008). Kathy Ehrensperger shows how a feminist ethic of relationships overlaps with the perspectives of Romans 14. She identifies an ethic of "mutuality and accommodation" rather than hierarchy. As theologians have focused on the relationship between "belief" and "practice," Paul's concrete practical counsel is valued as offering a way of living out the claims of the gospel in a complex and diverse world.

Analysis of the composition of this chapter out of fragments of liturgical and philosophical tradition demonstrates how the commonplace maxim "no one lives unto himself" is incorporated into a letter of Paul and in light of the overarching christological arguments takes on new depth and meaning (O'Neill). The anthropology implied in the exhortation here, with its emphasis on conviction and personal commitment, appears to give human beings more control and intention to their actions than does the anthropology of Rom. 6:12-19, in which every human serves a master. The language of thralldom and slavery seems in contrast to the more rational implications of this quasi-Stoic counsel. In the course of history, interpreters have been drawn to one or the other view more strongly. The choice to interpret one or the other anthropology as primary is a decision that is made on theological, ethical, or political grounds.

Romans 15:14-33: Paul's Reasons for Writing, Plans to Visit Rome, and Delivery of the Collection

▌ The Text in Its Ancient Context

These verses give information to reconstruct the "reasons for Romans" or the situation "behind" the letter. While appearing as informative "news" about his plans, the substance of this communication is highly symbolic and theological. Paul's travel and its rationale express his understanding of the relationship between Jews and gentiles and how he understands his identity and his purpose. Paul expresses confidence in the competence of the congregation. This friendship-strengthening rhetoric both reflects and fashions the relationship between the sender and receiver of the letter. At the same time as he underplays the letter as "writing rather boldly," Paul's self-description as a "minister of Christ Jesus to the Gentiles in the priestly service of the gospel of God, so that the offering of the Gentiles may be acceptable, sanctified by the Holy Spirit" (15:16) is a claim of unique status in God's mission. Using cultic language taken from the tradition of Israel's worship, Paul conveys his conviction that by his ministry, he is delivering the gentile believers in Christ as a holy offering to God. While he had begun the letter by saying that he is not ashamed, here Paul admits to having reason to "boast." As in 2 Cor. 2:12 and Gal. 3:5, the action of the Spirit in the community is accompanied by signs and wonders. The map of Paul's preaching extends in a full circle from Jerusalem to Illyricum on the east coast of the Adriatic Sea. The picture of the vast sweep of the gospel is less a reflection of Paul's own individual activity and more a theological portrayal of the inevitable progress of the good news.

Referring to his practice of not preaching where another person has begun the work of evangelism, Paul quotes from Isa. 52:15, words that refer to the work of the suffering servant. By borrowing the prophetic words to describe the recipients of his preaching who have "never been told" and "never heard," he makes an implied parallel between his ministry and that of the Servant of the Lord (Grieb). His missionary travels have occupied him until the present, when he will fulfill his long-held wish to visit them on his way to Spain. In ancient rhetoric, the expression "be sent on by you" may imply financial support. He speaks of his plan to deliver the collection from the churches of Macedonia and Achaia "with the poor among the saints at Jerusalem" (15:26).

The collection from the churches in Greece and its delivery and acceptance by the Jerusalem church represent economically the relationship between Jews and gentiles, the subject of the letter. By contributing to it, gentile churches demonstrate their gratitude to Jerusalem for the spiritual benefits that they have received, and by accepting it, the Jerusalem church acknowledges the rightful role of the gentile churches in God's promises. The successful delivery of the collection equals the confirmation and legitimization of Paul's own mission as apostle to the gentiles. He appeals for their prayers and asks that he be delivered from those unbelievers who would oppose him. Paul's letters refer to the collection for Jerusalem in 1 Cor. 16:1-4; 2 Cor. 8–9; and Gal. 2:10. The survey of Paul's plans concludes with a picture of the anticipated joyful union with the church at Rome.

THE TEXT IN THE INTERPRETIVE TRADITION

Before the advent of historical criticism, interpreters took the attribution of the letters to Paul at face value and accepted the presentation of Paul as chief apostle in all the letters and in Acts of the Apostles as factual. Paul's centrality and uniqueness was taken for granted. In the view of modern biblical criticism, the canon of the New Testament gives evidence that the figure of Paul was given increasing authority in the second century. The addition of pseudonymous letters, 1, 2 Timothy and Titus, and the Acts of the Apostles, Luke's theological history of the church, combined to create the persona of Paul. As the rhetorical character of Paul's letters has come to be better appreciated, Paul's own statements about his missionary practice or the views of his opponents or his relationship with the congregation to whom he writes have come to be understood as statements that do not just reflect reality but also contribute to shaping it. Tensions between theological perspectives in the undisputed letters, Ephesians and Colossians, and the Pastoral Epistles were recognized and interpreted as showing the development of the Pauline tradition, the positions that claimed Paul as their authoritative source. Paul's own self-understanding, which he expresses here, while it may have been more complicated or even contested in his own time, came to be accepted by the church. In reconstructing the reasons for Romans, scholarly scenarios develop one or more aspects of what Paul says here: need for support from the church at Rome, fear of the rejection of the collection, or the danger of the mission to Spain.

THE TEXT IN CONTEMPORARY DISCUSSION

Contemporary interpreters have given attention to the collection for the poor in Jerusalem as a concrete practice that expressed the solidarity (*koinōnia*) of the gentile churches with the mother church in Jerusalem. Within the structure of patronage in the Roman Empire, the collection functioned to communicate an alternative structure of relationship and accountability. Economic exchange and distribution shows the power of economic relations to embody relationships of justice. The collection for Jerusalem provides a model for practices of solidarity that subvert conventional values and create an alternative community. If the collection was a "symbol of resistance and subversion" (Wan, 196) in the context of the Roman Empire, what might be analogous practices of economic solidarity in the current globalized economy?

Romans 16:1-27: Paul Commends Phoebe and Greets His Coworkers

▌ THE TEXT IN ITS ANCIENT CONTEXT

The letter to the Romans concludes with greetings from Paul to members of the church at Rome (16:1-16), a warning against those who cause division (16:17-20), additional greetings, and a doxology (16:25-27). Critics have questioned whether these elements were part of the original Letter to the Romans or were added at later points in its composition. While all editions of Romans contain chapter 16, in some manuscripts the doxology comes after 15:33. In addition to textual evidence, readers have questioned how Paul could have known so many individuals by name in a community that he has not visited. The theory that Romans 16 was not an original part of the letter is no longer widely accepted. Paul's greetings to other leaders and his amplification of their association serve to strengthen the bonds with the community at Rome and to enhance Paul's own reputation and reception. The twenty-six leaders named here give insight into the makeup of the early Christian missionary movement, particularly the activity of other prominent missionaries, and the role of women as leaders. The terms "coworker," "beloved," "relative," and "in the Lord" convey the collaborative role of these individuals in the mission. The women named by Paul are named independently (Mary), paired with a man (Prisca, Junia), paired with another woman (Tryphaena and Tryphosa), or called "mother" (of Rufus) and "sister" (of Nereus). Paul's commendation of Phoebe names her as a deacon, a term that refers to offering service and that later became a formal office. She is a *prostatis*, a benefactor, who has provided Paul and others financial support. Phoebe is the one who delivers the letter to Rome. Prisca and Aquila, a missionary pair who are also mentioned in Acts 18, have demonstrated bravery that has earned the gratitude of all the churches of the gentiles. Andronicus and Junia receive high praise as "prominent among the apostles" and who were "in Christ before I was" (16:7). Paul greets these named coworkers and includes "all the other saints who are with them" (16:15). Paul asks them to greet one another with a holy kiss, a sign of love exchanged in the assembly. Critics disagree about whether the harsh warning that appears to interrupt the series of greetings is original to Romans or was added by a later writer. Its harsh tone appears to be out of place in Romans; however, other letters of Paul include severe warnings in their closing verses: Gal. 6:12-13; Phil. 3:2; and 1 Cor. 16:22.

There is widespread agreement that the doxology which concludes the letter is not original. Textual evidence shows it occurring in different positions (being omitted or included after chap. 14, after chap. 15, or in both positions). Its language concerning "strengthening you" and the disclosing of a "mystery" resembles the language of Ephesians (Eph. 1:9; 3:3-4, 6, 9; 5:32; 6:19). It may have been composed by a later writer who understood Romans itself as part of the "prophetic writings." At the time of the assembling of the canon, the doxology was added as an emphatic response and conclusion to a letter that had attained significance and esteem.

▌ THE TEXT IN THE INTERPRETIVE TRADITION

In the history of interpretation, Paul's centrality was accepted as a given. The presence of other evangelists, missionaries, or apostles, though clearly spelled out here, were not memorialized or celebrated by the ongoing tradition of the church. While Paul habitually greets, thanks, and refers to his coworkers, the singularity of Paul, his independence, and uniqueness are remembered most insistently by the tradition. That among these twenty-six names are recorded the names of nine women, some with titles—"deacon," "benefactor," "apostle,"—and some with epithets—"coworker," "sister"—may account for the fact that this series of coworkers has been overlooked in the history of interpretation and minimized in majority scholarship. Because the exclusion of women from leadership became an element of orthodox teaching, the names of the women here and their participation in the early Christian mission became invisible. The female name *Junia* was amended in the manuscript tradition to the otherwise unattested male name *Junias* to conform to the norm that no women were apostles (Brooten 1977). Phoebe, likely the one who delivered the letter to Rome, becomes a footnote in the story of the Letter to the Romans. In the contest over the authoritative interpretation of Paul in the canon, the position of 1 Timothy, which requires women to learn with all submission (1 Tim. 2:11-13), prevails. The memory of Paul's commendation of Phoebe, deacon of the church at Cenchreae, or Junia, prominent among the apostles and in Christ before Paul himself, fades into obscurity.

■ THE TEXT IN CONTEMPORARY DISCUSSION

As women have become conscious readers of Scripture and agents aware in the making of history, they have contributed to research into women in the Greco-Roman world and in Jewish and gentile Jesus movements. Readers have questioned the gender asymmetry encoded in Scripture and recognized its complicity in the maintenance of male superiority and female subordination in church and society. Reconstruction of early Christian history to include the presence and leadership of women has made it possible to read restrictive biblical texts differently and has recovered models and exemplars of women's leadership in the early period. Romans 16 gives rich evidence of a missionary movement of women and men in partnership, counters the view of the singular apostle, and nourishes the imagination for reenvisioning the *ecclesia* as a discipleship of equals (Kittredge 2012).

Works Cited

Briggs, Sheila. 1989. "Can an Enslaved God Liberate? Hermeneutical Reflections on Philippians 2:6-11."
     Semeia 47:137–53.
Brooten, Bernadette J. 1977. "Junia—Outstanding among the Apostles (Romans 16:7)." In *Women Priests:
     A Catholic Commentary on the Vatican Declaration*, edited by J. Leonard and Arlene Swidler. New York:
     Paulist.
———. 1996. *Love between Women: Early Christian Responses to Female Homo-eroticism*. Chicago: University
     of Chicago Press.
Byrne, Brendon J., SJ. 1996. *Romans*. Collegeville, MN: Liturgical Press.
Carroll, James. 2001. *Constantine's Sword: The Church and the Jews: A History*. Boston: Houghton Mifflin.
Cranfield, C. E. B. 1975. *The Epistle to the Romans*. Edinburgh: T&T Clark.

Eisenbaum, Pamela. 2004. "A Remedy for Having Been Born of Woman: Jesus, Gentiles, and Genealogy in Romans." *JBL* 123, no. 4:671–702.

Elliott, Neil. 1997. "Romans 13:1-7 in the Context of Roman Imperial Propaganda." In *Paul and Politics: Ekklesia, Israel, Imperium, Interpretation: Essays in Honor of Krister Stendahl*, edited by Richard A. Horsley. Harrisburg, PA: Bloomsbury T&T Clark.

———. 2008. *The Arrogance of Nations: Reading Romans in the Shadow of Empire*. Minneapolis: Fortress Press.

Ehrensperger, Kathy. 2004. *That We May Be Mutually Encouraged: Feminism and the New Perspective in Pauline studies*. New York: T&T Clark.

Gager, John G. 2000. *Reinventing Paul*. New York: Oxford University Press.

Georgi, Dieter. 1991. *Theocracy in Paul's Praxis and Theology*. Minneapolis, Fortress Press.

Glancy, Jennifer A. 2006. *Slavery in Early Christianity*. Minneapolis: Fortress Press.

Grieb, A. Katherine. 2002. *The Story of Romans: A Narrative Defense of God's Righteousness*. Louisville: Westminster John Knox.

Hays, Richard B. 1989. *Echoes of Scripture in the Letters of Paul*. New Haven: Yale University Press.

———. 1996. "The Moral World of the First Christians." *QR* 6, no. 4:13–30.

Jewett, Robert. 2007. *Romans: A Commentary*. Minneapolis: Fortress.

Kittredge, Cynthia Briggs. 1998. *Community and Authority: The Rhetoric of Obedience in the Pauline Tradition*. Harrisburg, PA: Trinity Press International.

———. 2012. "Feminist Approaches: Rethinking History and Resisting Ideologies." In *Studying Paul's Letters: Contemporary Perspectives and Methods*, edited by Joseph A. Marchal, 117–34. Minneapolis: Fortress Press.

Landau, Yehezkel. 2007. "An Interview with Krister Stendahl." *Harvard Divinity Bulletin* 35, no. 1: 29-31.

Levine, Amy-Jill. 2006. *The Misunderstood Jew: The Church and the Scandal of the Jewish Jesus*. San Francisco: HarperSanFrancisco.

McGinn, Sheila E. 2005. "Feminists and Paul in Romans 8:18-23: Toward a Theology of Creation." In *Gender, Tradition and Romans: Shared Ground, Uncertain Borders*, edited by C. Grenholm and D. Patte. New York: T&T Clark.

Nanos, Mark D. 1996. *The Mystery of Romans: The Jewish Context of Paul's Letter*. Minneapolis: Fortress Press.

———. 2011. "The Letter of Paul to the Romans." In *The Jewish Annotated New Testament: New Revised Standard Version Bible Translation*, edited by Amy-Jill Levine and Marc Z. Brettler. New York: Oxford University Press.

Nickelsburg, George W. E. 2003. *Ancient Judaism and Christian Origins: Diversity, Continuity, and Transformation*. Minneapolis: Fortress Press.

O'Neill, John Cochrane. 1975. *Paul's Letter to the Romans*. Baltimore: Penguin.

Patterson, Orlando. 1982. *Slavery and Social Death: A Comparative Study*. Cambridge, MA: Harvard University Press.

Reasoner, Mark. 2005. *Romans in Full Circle: A History of Interpretation*. Louisville: Westminster John Knox.

Ruether, Rosemary Radford. 1974. *Faith and Fratricide: The Theological Roots of Anti-Semitism*. New York: Seabury.

Sanders, E. P. 1977. *Paul and Palestinian Judaism: A Comparison of Patterns of Religion*. Philadelphia: Fortress Press.

Schüssler Fiorenza, Elisabeth. 2007. *The Power of the Word: Scripture and the Rhetoric of Empire*. Minneapolis: Fortress Press.

Steinmetz, David C. 1988. "Calvin and Abraham: The Interpretation of Romans 4 in the Sixteenth Century." *CH* 57, no. 4:443–55.

Stendahl, Krister. 1963. "Paul and the Introspective Conscience of the West." *Harvard Theological Review* 56:3, 199-215.

———. 1976. *Paul among Jews and Gentiles*. Philadelphia: Fortress Press.

Stowers, Stanley K. 1994. *A Rereading of Romans: Justice, Jews and Gentiles*. New Haven: Yale University Press.

Tamez, Elsa. 1993. *The Amnesty of Grace: Justification by Faith from a Latin American Perspective*. Translated by Sharon H. Ringe. Nashville: Abingdon.

Trible, Phyllis, and Letty Mandeville Russell. 2006. "Unto the Thousandth Generation." In *Hagar, Sarah, and Their Children: Jewish, Christian, and Muslim Perspectives*, edited by Phyllis Trible and Letty Mandeville Russell, 1–30. Louisville: Westminster John Knox.

Wan, Sze-Kar. 2000. "Collection for the Saints as Anticolonial Act." In *Paul and Politics: Ekklesia, Israel, Imperium, Interpretation. Essays in Honor of Krister Stendahl*, 191–215. Edited by Richard A. Horsley. Harrisburg, PA: Trinity Press International.

West, Gerald O. 2008. "Contending with the Bible: Biblical Interpretation as a Site of Struggle in South Africa." In *The Bible in the Public Square*, edited by Cynthia Briggs Kittredge, Ellen Bradshaw, and Jonathan Draper, 101–15. Minneapolis: Fortress Press.

1 CORINTHIANS

Laura S. Nasrallah

Introduction

First Corinthians is not the first letter that Paul and his coworkers wrote to those in Christ at Corinth (1 Cor. 5:9), but is part of a pattern of correspondence (7:1; 8:1; 12:1), oral reporting (1:11; 5:1), and visits from travelers (1:11; 4:7). This letter from Paul and Sosthenes to the community was penned from Ephesus (1 Cor. 16:8, 19) and dates to approximately 52 or 54 CE. The gift of the Corinthian correspondence, unique in the New Testament, is that it includes more than one authentic letter, allowing for historical reconstruction of a community's relationship with Paul over time. The letters collected in 2 Corinthians allow us to see that 1 Corinthians did not meet with universal success at Corinth. Second Corinthians 2:4, for example, mentions a letter of tears, and 2 Cor. 10:1—13:20 may be that letter of tears, in which Paul claims he has to act like a fool and boast. The passages 2 Cor. 2:14—6:13 and 7:2-4 together form an *apologia*, or defense, of Paul's apostleship. Because we have multiple letters to Corinth, we can glean more data and form a richer interpretation of productive struggle regarding ideas and practices over time between Paul and the Corinthians, between Paul and other traveling religious teachers, and, likely, among the Corinthians.

After nearly two millennia of study and commentaries on Paul's letters, the task of the commentator is more to curate what she or he thinks are important data and interpretations than to offer something new. But one contribution this commentary makes is that it joins other scholarly work that elucidates not what Paul meant in his communications with the Corinthians but the possible responses of the community in Christ. It considers what the participants in the *ekklēsia* had at hand in Roman Corinth theologically, religiously, politically, and socially. That is, what were the conditions out of which those in Christ developed their rituals and beliefs, made ethical and political choices, and evaluated Paul's critiques and suggestions?

Ekklēsia

If we move the focus away from Paul—ignoring the binary of whether he was a heroic apostle or a traitor to Christ's true message (the latter was Thomas Jefferson's view), and turn instead to the communities to which he wrote (Johnson-DeBaufre and Nasrallah), we must ask what *ekklēsia,* their word for themselves, may have meant. What did it signal about how their community worked or how they ideally envisioned themselves? Some have argued that the term is a translation of the Hebrew *qahal,* a congregation. Certainly, Jewish associations, which used the Greek term *synagōgē,* existed in the Diaspora and attracted gentile converts and allies. Some have argued that *ekklēsia* signals the similarity of these earliest communities in Christ to so-called voluntary associations—guilds of people who gathered based on their employment (a guild of textile workers, for instance)—whose community together included worship of a god, meals, and often financial contributions (Ascough et al.). Some have pointed out similarities to philosophical schools (Stowers 2011b). Recent scholarship has shown that many associations were quite small (Kloppenborg). We should not assume that those to whom Paul wrote understood themselves to be, or to be in the process of becoming, a tight-knit, unified community (Stowers, 2011c). Further, the common translation for *ekklēsia,* "church," risks picturing something anachronistic.

Those who heard the term *ekklēsia* in antiquity may have understood a range of meanings, but certainly a political, civic assembly would have been evoked in an urban context (to which Paul's letters are aimed, after all: Meeks 2003). The term in the classical period had referred to the democratic assembly of the city, usually made up of free adult male citizens. At the time of Paul's writings, political assemblies in Greek cities around the Roman Empire still bore the name *ekklēsiai,* or in the singular, *ekklēsia,* and still met to engage in democratic deliberation about what was best for their cities (Miller). Were the *ekklēsiai* to which Paul wrote places of democratic debate and deliberative discourse, of authoritative speeches and challenges to those speeches, of the busy roil of argument, struggle, and the testing of ideas (Schüssler Fiorenza 1987; 1993)?

In this short commentary, I use the term *ekklēsia* instead of church. I also avoid using the term "Christian," since applying it to Paul's letters would be anachronistic: the term was coined only approximately forty years after the writing of 1 Corinthians (see Pliny, *Ep.* 10.96; the statement in Acts 11:26 represents Luke's significantly later view). Moreover, while Paul had experienced an important change in identity, it was not to a known quantity called Christianity. Paul described himself as a Jew (e.g., Gal. 2:15)—a good Jew (Stendahl; Gager; Eisenbaum)—who had had a revelation of Christ and who was now called to communicate to "the nations" (NRSV: "Gentiles") about the righteousness of God that was available through faith (*pistis*) in this Christ (*christos,* the Greek translation of the Hebrew word that we render "Messiah" in English).

The Sociopolitical Context of Roman Corinth

To better understand the religious, political, and socioeconomic context within which the Corinthian *ekklēsia* developed their new identity in Christ, we must investigate Roman Corinth. In 146 BCE, the forces of the Roman general Mummius destroyed the city. It survived in a diminished form until Julius Caesar reestablished it as a Roman colony in 44 BCE, after which time it again emerged as a leader on the Peloponnesus. Corinth lay on a significant trade route in antiquity, on the isthmus connecting ancient Attica to the Peloponnesus. It nestled inland between its ports of Lechaion to the north and Kenchreai to the south, and near Isthmia, a town renowned for its quadrennial games. To transfer cargo from the Saronic Gulf to the southeast to the Gulf of Corinth to the northwest, ships had to negotiate with Corinth, unless they wanted to circumnavigate the Peloponnesus (Strabo, *Geog.* 8.6.20). Julius Caesar, Nero, and Herodes Atticus all attempted to dig a canal across the isthmus near Corinth, but failed, leaving it to Corinth to control a seven-meter-wide paved roadway (*diolkos*) that allowed oxen to drag ships or cargo across the narrow spit of land. Analysis of ceramic finds indicates Corinth's importance in trade (Slane).

Who made up the new, Roman Corinth? In literature of the first century BCE, the city is characterized by its tragic history and as a site of grief (Cicero, *Tusc.* 3.53; Nasrallah 2012). Some inhabitants remained in the region between 146 BCE and the city's refounding as a Roman colony in 44 BCE, but Corinth was largely resettled at that time. Unlike many Roman colonies, Corinth was repopulated not by military veterans but by ex-slaves. Numismatic evidence indicates that a mix of freedpersons—former slaves—and traders became leaders in Corinth upon the founding of the new colony (Spawforth). Although freedpersons were not usually eligible for magistracies, Caesar made exceptions for colonies he founded (Millis 2010; 2013; Williams). Thus some characterized the city as populated by "a mass of good-for-nothing slaves," in first-century-BCE poet Crinagoras's language (Harrill, 71; Spawforth, 169). Yet the rhetoric about low-status freedpersons may be precisely aimed to discredit the high-status freedpersons who emigrated to Corinth to take advantage of this commercial hub (Millis 2013).

Thus it may not be coincidental that in a letter to Corinth we find the only use in the New Testament of the technical term "freedperson" (*apeleutheros*, 7:22). Some freedmen in Corinth held high civic positions and the Forum was marked by the benefactions of ex-slaves. Paul's words "Let . . . those . . . who buy [be] as though they had no possessions, and those who deal with the world as though they had no dealings with it" (7:29-31) would have been particularly thought-provoking to Corinthians-in-Christ in an urban setting in which buying and dealings with the world were central to civic identity—and in which having been bought and later manumitted were part of the identity of local elites (Nasrallah 2013).

Ethnicity and Identity in Roman Corinth: The City and the *Ekklēsia*

Given this history, what about ethnicity in Roman Corinth? Paul writes as a Jew who both asserts and reframes his ethnicity (9:19-22) to a community that is largely gentile (e.g., 12:2). We should not be surprised that gentiles sometimes wished to affiliate with Jews and even to shift their ethnicity and to become Jewish (Lieu; Cohen). Although archaeological evidence of Jews at Corinth is late and meager (a poorly incised lintel that once read "Synagogue of the Hebrews"; an impost capital with three menorahs), Philo mentions Corinth as having a Jewish population (*Legat.* 281) and Josephus states that Vespasian sent six thousand Jews to Corinth to work as slaves in the canal across the isthmus that Nero was attempting (*J.W.* 3.540; Millis 2010).

Although those to whom Paul wrote at Corinth were mostly gentiles, their choice to affiliate with Jews in Christ meant a shift in their ethnicity. In 1 Cor. 10:1, Paul argues that "our fathers were all under the cloud," referring to the story of Moses leading them through the Red Sea, and thus writing gentiles into the story of Israel. Such shifts in, debates about, and reflections on ethnicity were not rare in Roman Corinth (Concannon); the historical and mythical prestige of the city's Greek past was highlighted, even in the Roman period, through monuments and through the dissemination of iconography associated with the myths of Corinth (Robinson). Yet the city's dominant Romanness is signaled by a vast majority of its public inscriptions that appear in Latin only (Millis 2010).

In 2 Corinthians, Paul fights opponents whom he mockingly calls "super-apostles," but in 1 Corinthians he struggles with the Corinthian community itself, or at least with some members of it. The cause of this struggle has been the subject of debate. A variety of theories have been presented regarding the theological-philosophical inclinations of these Corinthians in Christ and their interest in being "spiritual people." The thesis of F. C. Baur (1831) and others, of Judaizers or other Christian factions as outside opponents, has largely been left behind. In the mid-twentieth century, Walter Schmithals's theory that the Corinthian community tended toward "a pneumatic-libertine Gnosticism," which was at the same time Jewish, was popular. Hans Conzelmann qualified this by calling the Corinthians "proto-Gnostic," employed the label "Corinthian libertinism," and talked about their "enthusiastic individualism." More recent scholarship demonstrates that we cannot discover a pre-Christian "Gnosticism" that may have affected the Corinthians, as Schmithals maintained (Pétrement 1990; K. King).

Scholars have long characterized the Corinthians as gnostics, libertines, Judaizers, and especially individualists, concerned about their private spiritual success rather than that of the community. Such approaches assume that Paul's letter neutrally records events and that his viewpoint is normative (see Wire; Castelli; Schüssler Fiorenza 1999). Instead, 1 Corinthians should be investigated as part of a larger correspondence, some of which is lost to us, that provides data about a community that included men and women, poor persons and those at or above subsistence level, slaves and freedpersons and free, who sometimes accepted and sometimes resisted Paul's characterizations of them. The Corinthian correspondence indicates a context of deliberative debate as happened so often in the civic *ekklēsia*—of back and forth, of struggling together toward a better future. Paul's letters are written to particular communities about particular situations; they are not systematic theology or doctrine in their first instantiation. He uses his rhetorical arts to persuade the Corinthians, and we can use the letter to reconstruct vibrant debates at the very beginnings of what we have come to call Christianity.

Those debates were conducted as the appointed time was "growing short" (7:29-31; 15:51-57). Paul and the communities to which he wrote, like many who framed their lives in terms of Jewish apocalyptic thought, understood themselves to be awaiting the imminent end of the age and the *parousia* ("appearance") of Christ. Nonetheless, their attention is focused in this letter on things great and small: the resurrection of the body, what they should eat, whether they should have sex, to give a few examples.

Paul has been characterized as promoting faith over law and works. Readers often approach 1 Corinthians in light of Paul's emphasis on faith and as a letter enjoining early Christian morality.

Indeed, much of 1 Corinthians *is* about making ethical and practical choices in the world, and faith—faith in Christ, God's faithfulness, a concept that Paul explains in light of God's covenant with Abram (Gen 12:3; see Gal 3:6–18) and in the midst of a Jewish discussion about how God's faithfulness may or may not extend to "the nations," or gentiles—is central to Paul's letters. But when we look more closely, we realize that the binary of faith versus works may need dissolution and that the vague language of morality may not be adequate. Paul's writings about "morality" involve *practices* of communities in Christ, something we could even call "works." Is faith itself a matter of practice, or works? First Corinthians is, after all, very much about sex and eating, and even about whether Paul is owed a wage, as much as it is about things we might label more spiritual or faith-based: wisdom, spiritual gifts, and the resurrection.

The Text

The complex work of reconstructing the Corinthians in Christ is made somewhat easier because, other than some arguments about the place of 1 Corinthians 15 in the letter, most scholars agree that 1 Corinthians is a unified letter. In addition, it has few text-critical issues: its Greek text is remarkably uniform in various manuscripts (Fitzmyer, 63). It employs deliberative rhetoric (Conzelmann; Schüssler Fiorenza 1987; Mitchell 1991), the "political address of recommendation and dissuasion" that focuses on the future time as its subject of deliberation, urging audiences to pursue a course of action for the future, and often employs language of concord or harmony (Mitchell 1991).

Outline of the Letter

Chapters 1–4 of the letter contain the greeting and the *stasis*, or main point of the letter, and are characterized by a discussion of wisdom and an argument regarding how the Corinthians ought to think of themselves: they are not quite as spiritual as they thought themselves to be. In 5:1—11:1, Paul discusses particular case studies in ethical and theological practice, treating especially themes of sex and eating, as well as discussing the marital, ethnic, and social conditions in which persons may have been "called" to be in Christ. In 11:2—14:40, Paul treats further issues of practice in the *ekklēsia*, ranking the spiritual gifts the community experienced and seeking to control their use. Paul grounds these discussions in the political rhetoric of unity and "one body." In chapter 15, Paul turns to the topic of the resurrection of the dead, bringing together the cosmological hints about wisdom and the cosmos in chapters 1–4, together with concerns about the body's purity and practices in 5—11:1 and interest in the spiritual in 11:2—14:40. The epistolary closing comes in chapter 16.

Conclusions

According to the style of this volume, each section of my commentary on 1 Corinthians will be divided into three subsections: "the text in its ancient context," "the text in the interpretive tradition," and "the text in contemporary discussion." These divisions are heuristic. We should not think we have access to an ancient context that is pure data, neither disturbed nor enriched by our contemporary situations and by the long interpretative tradition. There is no true division between what the text meant and what it means today. Rather, we can use our locations of interpretation to open new questions about these ancient texts, and we can turn a critical eye to the limitations of our own locations. That is, we should approach the text with a *disciplined intimacy*, acknowledging the feeling of closeness that we may have with this text, whether as Christians, or because the text communicates important and recognizable ethical or political injunctions, or on account of the sheer pleasure of discovering something about ancient history. But we should also pursue the discipline of distance, acknowledging that the text was written in a time, language, and context not our own and that its values and injunctions, as well as the conditions of the social, political, and economic world in which it was produced, may surprise us.

1:1-17: Letter Writing and Community

▌ THE TEXT IN ITS ANCIENT CONTEXT

As is typical of ancient letters, 1 Corinthians begins with the *superscriptio*: "Paul, called to be an apostle of Christ Jesus by the will of God" (1:1). In other letters, Paul begins by introducing himself as "Paul, slave [*doulos*, sometimes translated more weakly as "servant"] of Jesus Christ" (Rom. 1:1, a letter in which he likely recommends himself to a community he doesn't know; see also Phil. 1:1) or "Paul, prisoner" (Philem. 1:1). The comparatively forceful *superscriptio* here introduces two key issues that follow in the letter. The first is the term *klētos*, "called" or "chosen." The letter uses this term and its cognates to talk about Paul's and the Corinthians' status. The addressees are described as "*chosen* holy ones" (1:2); "you were *called* into the fellowship of his [God's] son" (1:9). The issue of "calling" arises again in chapter 7. The second is the term *apostolos*, "one who is sent." As the letter ends, in 1 Cor. 15:9, Paul calls himself "least of the apostles," "unfit *to be called* an apostle," yet elsewhere in the letter he asserts his role as laying a foundation (3:10) and as a father (4:14-21), as well as his ability to shape-shift depending on audience (9:19-22).

If we look more closely at the *superscriptio* of this letter and others, we see that the majority are cowritten: Silvanus and Timothy are cowriters of 1 Thessalonians; Timothy again is cowriter of the Letter to the Philippians. Romans 16:22 reveals an amanuensis: "I, Tertius, the writer of this letter, greet you in the Lord." In addition, some delivered letters and traveled on behalf of Paul and various *ekklēsiai*, such as Timothy and Epaphroditus. First Corinthians is cowritten by Sosthenes, "brother." These are not just the letters of Paul; they invoke and evoke an entire network of writers, deliverers, and readers. The writing desk becomes crowded with coworkers and perhaps slaves and freedmen, former slaves, since people of such status were often responsible for penning and delivering letters (Mouritsen).

The extended sentence, which is also a statement of thanksgiving (1:4-8), reveals four key issues of the letter. *Charis* (v. 4), often translated "grace," also means "favor" or "delight." A form of this word appears again at verse 7, *charisma*, often translated "spiritual gift": the idea of gifts of God or God's grace, and the question of how these "gifts" should be used and ranked, become key issues in chapters 11–14. Second, the word *eploutisthēte*, "you were enriched," appears in verse 5; the letter will later challenge the Corinthians precisely on issues of spiritual and material wealth and poverty. Paul will characterize the Corinthians as "what is low and despised in this world" (1:28). Mention of hunger and of some who "have not" indicates that some within the Corinthian community are poor (11:22). Third, the phrase "in speech [*logos*] and knowledge [*gnōsis*] of every kind" (1:5) signals debates about lofty or lowly speech and about what truly constitutes knowledge (1 Corinthians 1–4; 13:2, 9, 12). Fourth, verse 8 signals the letter's concern with the end time (the "day of the Lord"), a theme that arises especially at 1 Cor. 7:29-31 ("time growing short") and in the discussion in 1 Corinthians 15 of material transformation and the last trumpet. Grace and gifts, poverty and wealth literal and metaphorical, word or speech and knowledge, and the coming day of the Lord: these four themes, introduced early in the letter in the traditional epistolary location for a prayer or thanksgiving, will weave their way throughout this letter.

The *stasis*, or main point of the letter, emerges at 1 Cor. 1:10: "Now I appeal to you, brothers and sisters, by the name of our Lord Jesus Christ, that all of you be in agreement and that there be no divisions among you, but that you be united [or "reconciled"] in the same mind and the same purpose." Some take this thesis statement as Paul's description of a historical fact and have attempted to outline various "factions" of the community, following on Paul's characterization of the community as stating "I belong to Apollos" or "I belong to Paul," based on whomever had baptized them. But we do not know if all the Corinthians would have accepted Paul's assessment, and indeed, it seems that Paul has to argue rather hard for his role as the one who "planted" the community (1 Cor. 3:4-23). His arguments may have met with little success, given his admission that others have successfully influenced the community at Corinth (2 Corinthians). Paul turns from this interest in baptism (which will appear elsewhere in the letter) to emphasize "the cross of Christ" and Paul's own preaching, which happens "not in persuasive words of wisdom but in a demonstration of spirit and power" (2:4).

▐ THE TEXT IN THE INTERPRETIVE TRADITION

John Chrysostom, a church leader from Antioch, was made archbishop of Constantinople in 397 CE. A well-known champion of Paul (Mitchell 2002), Chrysostom in some ways set forth what would become the mainstream Protestant understanding of a humble, suffering Paul among other apostles. Chrysostom focused on 1 Cor. 1:12 ("I belong to Paul . . .") and emphasized that Paul placed Peter last in this sequence to give Peter greater honor, despising any glory for himself. Chrysostom celebrated Paul's lack of eloquence in good homiletic fashion, with an anecdote: he once heard a "Greek" and a Christian arguing about whether Plato or Paul was superior. The Christian was wrong, Chrysostom argued, in trying "to establish that Paul was more learned than Plato." "For if Paul was uneducated and defeated Plato, the victory (as I have said) was glorious. . . . from this is it clear that his preaching has prevailed not by human wisdom but by the grace of God" (*Hom.* 3; Kovacs, 20–21). Chrysostom emphasizes the uneducated and common nature of early Christians, using Paul as a focal point to develop a well-known Christian trope, geographically widespread, that Christian identity was rooted in humble fishermen yet now elevated even women, fishermen, and the ignorant to a philosophical life (the Syrian Tatian, *Ad gr.* 32.1–3; the Carthaginian Tertullian, *De an.* 3; the Alexandrian Origen, *C. Cels.* 3.44, 50). Paul's rhetoric in 1 Corinthians concerning his own ineloquence and his inversion of wisdom and folly fit well with early Christian self-definition as simple and humble, yet triumphing over the sophistication of the world, even though the early

Christian men who used this trope were themselves quite sophisticated, educated, and powerful. Many Christians today, too, stand in an ambivalent relationship to certain forms of education and knowledge; it may be helpful to recognize that sometimes it is those who are well-educated who use the powerful persuasive trope of Christian simplicity and revelation.

THE TEXT IN CONTEMPORARY DISCUSSION

The Second Vatican Council's "Decree on Ecumenism, *Unitatis redintegratio*" alludes to 1 Cor. 1:13 at its beginning.

> The restoration of unity among all Christians is one of the principal concerns of the Second Vatican Council. Christ the Lord founded one Church and one Church only. However, many Christian communions present themselves to men as the true inheritors of Jesus Christ; all indeed profess to be followers of the Lord but differ in mind and go their different ways, *as if Christ Himself were divided*. ("Decree on Ecumenism, *Unitatis redintegratio* 1)

More recently, the World Council of Churches has declared as the theme for the "Week of Prayer for Christian Unity" the question, "Has Christ been divided?" (1 Cor. 1:1-17).

Paul's evaluation that the Corinthians were divided and his injunction that they must be unified in one body was powerful in the past and is powerful today. This letter's language of unity draws from common political tropes of its time. *Homonoia* in Greek and *concordia* in Latin were terms used by various cities of the Greek East, for example on their coins, to assert a harmony that was the hard-won result of civic power plays. Paul's rhetoric of "one body" takes part in a broader discourse of unity that we know from the political rhetoric of the early Roman Empire (Mitchell 1991). Yet, today, in reading this rhetoric of unity in 1 Corinthians both scholarly and Christian communities often take for granted that Paul's characterization of Corinthian schism was an accurate description of problems at Corinth and do not inquire whether the Corinthians might have disagreed. Rhetoric of schism and unity is powerful whether in antiquity or today; it can be used to affirm community, but it also can be used to exclude or shame those who disagree.

1 Corinthians 1:18—4:21: Spirit and Wisdom

THE TEXT IN ITS ANCIENT CONTEXT

The first four chapters of the letter move contrapuntally among the themes of Paul's role, the Corinthians' identity, spirit, and wisdom. The theme of wisdom was likely part of a long-standing conversation that was ongoing among the Corinthians in Christ; in this letter we find the term "wisdom" (*sophia*) seventeen times in contrast to its scant appearance elsewhere in Paul's genuine epistles (once in Romans and once in 2 Corinthians); so, too, *sophos* ("wise") appears eleven times in 1 Corinthians and four times in Romans, among the Pauline Epistles. Paul's letters reflect and discuss topics important to those to whom he wrote: obviously wisdom was a major theme among those at Corinth (Koester, 55–62). Paul takes an instructive tone in these chapters, one that might lead us to think that the Corinthians did not know much about wisdom or knowledge. Yet chapters 11–14 indicate that the Corinthians engaged in community practices that embodied and demonstrated their links to spirit and wisdom through "spiritual gifts." (I here leave the term "spirit" uncapitalized so that we do not read it through the lens of later Trinitarian ideas.)

Paul uses the rhetorical technique of developing his *ēthos*; that is, as Aristotle discusses it (*Rhet.* 1.2.1356a.4–12), the speaker describes himself in such a way as to make the audience sympathetic to him. Paul says that he did not come offering a testimony with lofty words or wisdom (2:1); he elaborates the common trope in which an orator talks about the simplicity and lack of education of his words over and against others—a simplicity and lack of education that then lends authenticity, truth, and power to his writing or speech. But Paul also may be making lemonade out of a lemon, since his opponents, it seems, characterize his person and speech in person as "weak" and "nothing" (2 Cor. 10:10). Paul places as central "Jesus Christ, and him crucified" (2:2), a "stumbling block" and weakness and scandal; Paul's juxtaposition of his own weakness with Christ's paradoxically elevates Paul: he is like Christ. In addition, with this language he may align himself with some in the community who are being called "weak," who are less educated and have concerns about being invaded by external, polluting forces.

First Corinthians 1:18—4:21 focuses on wisdom, yet questions what it (or she—the word is feminine in Greek: see below) truly is. Paul has just mentioned his role not as baptizer but as someone who preaches the gospel "not with wisdom," "lest the cross of Christ be emptied." Here the historical datum of the cross—a shameful criminal execution that predates the writing of this letter by only twenty years or so—is laid on a cosmological scale. It is understood to represent "the power of God" (1:18). Paul asserts—or perhaps admits—that the "word" (the term *logos* in Greek can mean "word," "speech," or "reason") of the cross is folly. The letter troubles the common sense that wisdom is good while folly is bad. The wisdom and folly of this world or universe (*tou kosmou,* 1:20, 28; also *kata sarka,* "according to flesh," 1:26; and *tou aiōnos toutou,* "of this age," 1:20, referring to the "debater") are contrasted to the wisdom and folly of God. The two are inversely related: God has made foolish the wisdom of this world (1:20); "what we preach" is in fact folly (*mōria,* 1:21).

Because of the emphasis on wisdom and knowledge (*gnōsis*), as well as the labels *sarkikoi* or *sarkinoi, psychikoi,* and *pneumatikoi*—that is, Paul's labeling certain people according to the terms "flesh," "soul," and "spirit"—in these early chapters of 1 Corinthians, twentieth-century scholars hypothesized either that the Corinthians were "gnostics" or that they were influenced by "gnostic" missionaries (Schmithals). But the language of wisdom and knowledge is not only found in materials we might label "gnostic"—for example, the texts found at Nag Hammadi and the points of view polemically treated by writers like Irenaeus and others—but also in Jewish texts that speculate about the creation of humans (esp. Gen. 2:7), divine inbreathing at creation, and the human potential for knowledge, wisdom, and being like God. Moreover, "Gnosticism" was not an established or unified school in the first century. The term itself is a later invention emerging from early Christian polemics, then reified in modern scholarship (K. King).

The language of wisdom at Corinth emerges in a context of many traditions that honored wisdom and knowledge in the ancient world, whether Jews, members of philosophical schools, or those who honored a goddess like Isis; it emerged in the context of rich philosophical debates and diverse stories about the creation of the world, including much debate over the interpretation of

Plato's *Timaeus*. Paul and the Corinthians perhaps had different understandings of the terminology of wisdom and knowledge, of flesh, soul, and spirit. But in their deployment of such language they stood in a conversation that preceded and would follow them about how creation happened and whether and how humans might know the divine in the present, as Jews and Christians alike debated the meaning and significance of a creation out of the clay or earth in Genesis 2 and reference to creation of the human in God's image in Genesis 1. Such Jewish and Christian debates about wisdom and knowledge, about flesh, soul, and spirit, happened in the context of a culture that produced images of the gods in human form, and happened in conversation with Greek philosophical texts and with the strong traditions of wisdom theology in Judaism, characterized by texts like Ben Sira and the Wisdom of Solomon, among many others.

Scholars have long situated 1 Corinthians within Hellenistic Jewish discourses on wisdom (e.g., Wilckens; Horsley; Sterling). There must have been at Corinth deep and rich debates about the nature of God and creation, about how God works and is manifest in the world, which drew from the wisdom theologies of Judaism. Proverbs 8:22 offers a famously clear statement of Wisdom personified as cocreator of the world with God (the Greek word *sophia* is grammatically feminine; see also Philo, *Cher.* 49 on God as "the husband of Sophia"). Other traditions, exemplified in the early-first-century CE Jewish writer Philo of Alexandria, seem to understand Sophia and Logos as related or interchangeable figures who are divine characters themselves; Philo talks about the Logos of God as the instrument by which God made creation (*Cher.* 127); elsewhere, the Logos is the image of God, in closest proximity to God, and the "charioteer" above all the other divine powers (*Fug.* 100; see also Philo, *Post.* 78; *Fug.* 97; Horsley 1979; Grabbe; Boyarin 2001).

Some (or many) within the Corinthian *ekklēsia* likely considered Sophia—Wisdom personified—to be a power of God that was significant for their theology and for their understanding of themselves. Jesus as Sophia or as a prophet of Sophia is well attested in earliest Gospel traditions (e.g., Luke 7:34-36; Lamp; Schüssler Fiorenza 1994; Johnson-DeBaufre). In 1 Cor. 2:9, we find a quotation that alludes to the Jewish Scriptures and bears a striking resemblance to *Gospel of Thomas* 17 (see also Q/ Lk 10:23-24; Koester, 58–59; Conzelmann, 63–64). Thus the Corinthians and Paul may have shared a source of Jesus sayings that involved wisdom, and perhaps they knew of theological traditions that employed terminology of hiddenness and revelation (see also 1 Cor. 2:7, 10; 3:13; 4:5; Koester, 55–56).

Indeed, the Corinthians may have understood Christ as Wisdom. Paul emphasizes Christ terminology instead and debates the meaning of *sophia*. For Paul, wisdom is not a divine power to be reckoned with, or a power that helps to perfect humans and render them friends of God, as she is depicted in the Wisdom of Solomon (from Alexandria, perhaps first century CE). Wisdom as cocreator of the world leaves only a faint trace in 1 Corinthians.

At Corinth, Wisdom is understood not only in terms of cosmology and theology but also in terms of sociology. The question of who has true wisdom and knowledge percolates throughout the letter. Paul extends a challenge: "Where is the one who is wise?" (1:20). In 1 Cor. 2:6, Paul renders wisdom into something he and others can impart, and only to the "perfect" or "initiates" (*teleioi*).

Paul discusses wisdom in ethnic terms in 1:22: *Ioudaioi* (which we can translate "Jews" or "Judeans"; see Cohen; Hodge) "ask for signs and Greeks seek wisdom." How might Paul's characterization of ethnicity have gone over in Roman Corinth, with its famed Greek heritage, its new Roman status? In this passage, Paul proposes an alternative mixed ethnicity for the *ekklēsia* in Christ at Corinth, aligning them with "those who are the called [*klētoi*], both Jews and Greeks" (1:24). Paul defines the identity of the *ekklēsia* at Corinth as a chosenness that brings Jews and Greeks together.

The community may have understood itself as wise, as "called," and also as *teleioi*, which can be translated "perfect" or "complete" and is also the term for "initiates." "Yet among the *teleioi* we do speak wisdom . . . God's wisdom, secret and hidden, which God decreed before the ages," Paul declares (2:6-7). A Corinthian hearing this might reasonably think that she or he is one of the "perfect" who has received the spirit from God, rather than the "spirit of this cosmos" or world (2:12). Later in the letter it becomes clear that Corinthians engaged in practices of *pneumatika*, spiritual things or spiritual gifts (1 Corinthians 12–14). But Paul introduces another label: the *psychikos*, the "soul" person, who doesn't discern things as the *pneumatikos*, or "spirit person," does (2:14-15). Certainly any reader or hearer of the passage would prefer to fall into the "perfect" and "spiritual" category. The news gets worse: Paul states that he had to address them as *sarkinoi*, "flesh people" (3:1), feeding them only milk. Not only was this true in the past, but also "you are still of the flesh" (3:3) because of "strife" and claims like "I am of Paul, I am of Apollos."

Paul's accusation of dissension because of Corinthian attachment to one apostle or another reprises the thesis of the letter and allows him to segue again to the issue of apostleship and leadership that he had raised earlier (1 Cor. 1:10-16). In 3:5—4:21, he continues to raise questions about the roles he and Apollos played in the community; he depicts himself and Apollos in the language of household managers (3:5: *diakonoi*; 4:1: *hypēretas* and *oikonomous*). These roles are often taken by high-status slaves or freedpersons who have risen in the ranks of a household, promoted by their masters to more authoritative roles (Martin 1990). The Corinthians are depicted as passive, as a field to be planted or as something to be built (Wire).

Paul goes on to depict active, suffering apostles in contradistinction to the Corinthians. The apostles are "as though sentenced to death, because we have become a spectacle to the world, to angels and to mortals" (4:9). The language of death sentence and spectacle reminds us of the very real Roman practice of putting people to death and of spectacle (Frilingos), yet Paul's image does not limit itself to the Roman imperial context; the image he gives is of cosmic battle (so also at 2:8, "rulers of this age"). He contrasts the apostles' role as "refuse of the cosmos" (4:13) to the Corinthians, who are enriched and have come to reign (4:8). The apostles are "fools for the sake of Christ, but you are wise in Christ" (4:10).

Given the language of reversal that has already occurred regarding true wisdom and God's foolishness, the Corinthians would do well to be suspicious of this seeming praise. Indeed, Paul makes it explicit that he speaks to them as "beloved children" in need of admonition and he suggests to them that he is their sole father in the midst of many guides (4:15), a father who might come "with a stick" rather than "with love" (4:21). From chapter 1 to the end of chapter 4, leadership and authority in the Corinthian community has been reduced from four examples of possible mystagogues or leaders ("I am of Cephas," "I am of Apollos," "I am of Paul," "I am of Christ") to two (Paul and Apollos), to one, in his framing of himself as the singular father.

▌THE TEXT IN THE INTERPRETIVE TRADITION

Later Christians often used and debated the meaning of the discussion in 1 Corinthians 1–4 of wisdom and knowledge, as well as the question of which humans could be "spiritual," which "psychic" (from the term *psychē*, "soul," not to be confused with our modern meaning of the term!), and which "fleshly" (or, later, "hylic" or "material"). In the decades and centuries after Paul wrote, Christians wished to be *gnostikoi*, which we could woodenly translate "gnostics," but given the historical misuse of that term, perhaps "in the know" is a better translation. They wished to be *pneumatikoi*, spiritual people. These were values common to the ancient world and indeed today.

In the late second century CE, Irenaeus, a Christian writer in Gaul, would accuse some Christians, whom he said were "followers of Valentinus" (a Christian philosopher-theologian who likely lived a few decades prior) of a kind of determinism that assigned people to a certain fixed category, that would gut any motivations for ethical behavior, and that would limit salvation (*Adv. haer.* 1.6.2). In a Christian text such as the *Tripartite Tractate*, found among the so-called gnostic materials at Nag Hammadi, we find the statement:

> Now, humanity came to be according to three essential types—spiritual, physical, and material—reproducing the pattern of the three kinds of dispositions of the Logos, from which sprung material, physical, and spiritual beings. The essences of the three kinds can each be known by its fruit. (*Tripartite Tractate* 118.14–29, in Kocar 2013)

While Irenaeus would accuse such Christians of a determinism that condemned some humans to a permanent state of ignorance of the Father and no possibility of salvation, closer investigation of the *Tripartite Tractate* or indeed Irenaeus himself shows that Paul's writings in 1 Corinthians 1–4 instead inspired a great deal of later theological controversy over what constituted correct Christian practice and thinking, and how one could attain to the status of being spiritual or "in the know," truly *gnostikos*.

We find further evidence of how 1 Corinthians inspired later debates about wisdom in Origen, for example, who in the late second century or early third century explained that what is meant by the "wisdom of the rulers of this world" are the secret and hidden philosophies, astrologies, and magi of various nations, which may lead to demonic invasion. Christians, in contrast, are purified by abstinence and pure practices and receive prophecy and gifts in this way (*De princ.* 3.3). In the early sixth century, someone who took up the name of Dionysius the Areopagite (according to Acts, a convert at Athens after he heard Paul's speech there) and used Paul's language of Greeks seeking wisdom to rehabilitate the truth of Greek philosophy for Christian purposes (Stang, 148–50). A variety of Christians found in 1 Corinthians' language of wisdom and knowledge a foundation from which to debate who could access such wisdom and knowledge and how.

▌THE TEXT IN CONTEMPORARY DISCUSSION

The November 1993 conference "Re-Imagining: A Global Theological Conference by Women: for Men and Women" was an ecumenical meeting largely organized by U.S. Protestant denominations as part of the World Council of Churches' larger "Ecumenical Decade: Churches in Solidarity with Women," begun in 1988. The repeated chant "Bless Sophia" at this conference, among other things, led to accusations of goddess worship. Organizers are said to have grounded their emphasis on Sophia through recourse to Scriptures in Proverbs, Luke, and 1 Corinthians. Accusations that Sophia rather than Jesus was set forth as a "divine revealer" and concerns that Sophia was elevated to a divine level indicate that some ancient communities in Christ were more flexible and expansive in their Christology and theology than modern communities. We can think, for example, of language of Jesus as "the Sophia of God" in 1 Cor. 1:24 or of the flexibility of ancient Jewish and Christian traditions that describe a Sophia who existed at the beginning of the world with God and created the world with God. An emphasis on Wisdom or Sophia can be controversial in any age, even if canonical texts present Sophia as cocreator with God or as attribute of God, as a figure who sends out prophets like Jesus, and as a divine figure instantiated by Jesus. A theology—thealogy, we could say, emphasizing the possibilities of thinking of a God who transcends gender and/or is sometimes thought of in feminine terms—that takes into account the traditions of Sophia can support two kinds of work. First, it can undergird the work of those theologians, whether ancient or contemporary, who point out that attempts to name God definitively as Father or Mother or to fix our idea of God too firmly are idolatrous. Second, taking into account ancient traditions of Sophia in Judaism and Christianity can aid those who argue for women's leadership in Christian communities.

1 Corinthians 5:1—6:11 Insiders, Outsiders, and Judgment

▌ THE TEXT IN ITS ANCIENT CONTEXT

Paul has introduced the idea that the Corinthians are not at the highest state of completion or initiation (*teleioi*) as spiritual people (*pneumatikoi*) and that he as father can correct them with love or with a stick (1 Cor. 4:21). In the pages that follow, Paul expands on the bad news that the Corinthians are not, in his opinion, at the level of spiritual or wise or perfected people. Paul treats particular examples of Corinthian practices that he seeks to correct.

He speaks against *porneia*, a broad term in the ancient world that the NRSV translates "immorality," but that among Jewish and Christian writings has tinges of sexual sin and of idolatry, which is often also sexualized as an improper relationship of a nation with a false god (see, e.g., Hosea 4:11; Revelation 17; Rom. 1:22-32). The theme of *porneia* echoes throughout the passage and reaches its apex in two vice lists at 5:9-11 and 6:9-10, lists that represent cultural understandings of disorder in the world and are typical discourse at the time, whether among those we would label Jews or those we would label Greco-Roman writers. On the one hand, Paul insists that the Corinthians were previously *pornoi* (NRSV: "fornicators") and idolaters (6:9); on the other hand, he describes them as "washed, made holy, made just [or righteous] in the name of the Lord Jesus Christ and in the spirit of our God" (6:11). This new state is called into question by the presence of some who are still *pornoi* among them, and the dangers of idolatry loom large in the following chapters.

Paul's first example is a man who "has" (a sexual euphemism) his father's wife, presumably his stepmother. This discussion of *porneia* reveals something larger about how Paul frames the community's identity. First, he roots the *ekklēsia* at Corinth in a Jewish identity by stating derogatorily that they have *porneia* among them that is not even found among "the nations" (5:1). Framing the man's sin as a contagion that can permeate the community like leaven that "puffs up" a lump of dough, he introduces the idea of Christ as Paschal sacrifice, indicating that he and/or those at Corinth followed early traditions (as in the Gospel of John) of Jesus as having been crucified on Passover. Paul's metaphor also assumes that the community will understand basic Passover practices. Second, Paul introduces explicitly the theme of insiders and outsiders. A quotation from Deut. 17:7, "Drive out the wicked person from among you" (5:13), not only shows that Paul expects the community at Corinth to make sense of references to Scripture, but also makes the point that it's God's business to worry about "those outside" and the Corinthians' business to worry about those "among" or "inside," a theme that will arise again with the question of outsiders' response to speaking in tongues (14:24-25). In 5:3-5, Paul suggests that when those in Christ at Corinth assemble, Paul's spirit is present and the community should deliver the man to Satan so that the man's flesh will be destroyed, but his spirit saved "in the day of our Lord" (5:5). What sort of ritual is imagined is unclear (perhaps even a death penalty? Gaca, 140), but the theme of spirit clearly carries through from the first four chapters into the rest of the letter, in which spiritual gifts are discussed as well as the idea of spiritual bodies.

From the case of the man with his stepmother emerges a larger point about judgment. Paul emphasizes that the Corinthians should be concerned with what is happening inside the community and with adjudicating—"judging"—things there. From the relatively mundane case at hand emerges a larger cosmological vision: the holy ones (*hagioi*, a term Paul and Sosthenes had applied to the Corinthians in 1:2) will judge the cosmos and the angels (6:2-3).

▌ THE TEXT IN THE INTERPRETIVE TRADITION

John Calvin's mid-sixteenth-century commentary on 1 and 2 Corinthians eruditely surveys early church fathers' interpretations of these epistles, as well as offering his opinion, which is marked by the rise of the Protestant Reformation, in which Calvin was a key figure. The insider-outsider language of 1 Corinthians is transferred to his contemporaneous situation of Protestant-Catholic relations and shows the malleability of Paul's text for various situations. Calvin notes that the passage about leaven and the true Passover "will also be of service for setting aside the sacrilege of the Papal mass. For Paul does not teach that Christ is offered daily, but that the sacrifice being offered up once for all, it remains that the spiritual feast be celebrated during our whole life" (Calvin, 189–90). Reference to the exclusion of the one called brother inspired Calvin momentarily to soften his antipapist tone, declaring that "no one may think that we ought to employ equally severe measures against those who, while at this day dispersed under the tyranny of the Pope, pollute themselves with many corrupt rites" (194). Inspired by Paul's line about not taking food with the brother who has offended, Calvin rails against "the Roman antichrist" that prohibits "any one from helping one that has been excommunicated to food, or fuel, or drink or any of the supports of life" (195). The way in which Calvin applies this passage to his own time reminds us of the larger history of interpretation of Paul's letters. Scholars and "lay" alike tend to define early Christianity over and against Jews (who have been characterized as particularistic and law-obsessed) and Catholics (who have been depicted as like "pagans" in their concern with works and ritual), as J. Z. Smith discusses in his *Drudgery Divine*. If we forget that Paul was a Jew and that many of his letters are concerned with very practical things, we may stand in danger of producing interpretations that read as anti-Jewish and anti-Catholic.

■ THE TEXT IN CONTEMPORARY DISCUSSION

Paul's use of strong language of insiders and outsiders has inspired scholars to discuss 1 Corinthians through the lens of anthropology and sociology, reminding us that contemporary interpreters of Paul's writings include those outside of confessional Christian circles who find the letters useful for comparison with other times and places.

Theissen (1982), for example, explains various theological and ritual stances at Corinth as linked to varieties of socioeconomic status there and suggests that scholars should be in the business of comparing early Christian literatures with other religious phenomena of the world. Taking up such a challenge, Jonathan Z. Smith (2004) and Richard DeMaris (1995) have used anthropological insights to understand 1 Corinthians in a *local* context. The former shows the way in which 1 Corinthians has influenced discussions of "commensalism" (namely, relations with other local religions) and Christian revivalism in the local context of Papua New Guinea. The latter elucidates Corinthian references to spirit in light of ancestor cults and familial practices, evidenced in the archaeological record at Corinth.

Many have found anthropologist Mary Douglas's expounding of how the individual body is controlled and regulated (or not) in relation to the social body (a group) helpful for an analysis of the various viewpoints that might stand behind 1 Corinthians (e.g., Neyrey). Might some members of the *ekklēsia* have perceived the body as dangerously permeable, and sought to control sex, eating, spirit-possession, and relations with outsiders, while some saw the body as less dangerously subject to pollution? Dale Martin (1995) addresses the important question of how these perceptions—theological and medical—of the individual body affected ideas of the communal body.

These comparisons and insights help us to sharpen our understanding that 1 Corinthians deserves close attention and comparison with other phenomena in the history of religions. Paul's letters are not written to "us," whatever our time and place, even if his injunctions about holiness and purity, as well as his exhortations to unity, might be used in church debates today, for example about sexuality or sex acts. There is no "commonsense" reading that respects the complexity of these letters. They require a contextualization in their own time, in light of religious practices and beliefs in the first century, before they can be appropriated today.

1 Corinthians 6:12—7:40: "All Things Are Permitted to Me" and "Stay as You Are"

■ THE TEXT IN ITS ANCIENT CONTEXT

Having insisted that those in Christ at Corinth were once, and in the present some still are, *pornoi*, Paul continues to treat the theme of immorality by quoting and questioning "slogans" that may be the Corinthians' own or that he assumes they will understand. In 6:12, we find "all things are permitted to me," met by Paul's commentary "but not all things are beneficial"; in 6:13, we find "food is meant for the stomach and the stomach for food," met by Paul's commentary "God will destroy both." With both verses, we find common structure; a rhetorical analysis shows the assertion of an idea, and then its qualification, which leads scholars to think that the assertion is an idea that the Corinthians have set forth, while the qualification is Paul's own response to the idea or slogan (Wire).

Paul takes the theme of his previous chapter and argues that the body (*sōma*) is not meant for *porneia* but for "the Lord" (6:13). *Sōma* in Greek signals the body proper; it signals the body politic (Mitchell 1991); it is also a term sometimes used for "slave." Throughout 1 Corinthians, the political force of the term *sōma* is deployed, as well as the frequent political rhetoric that the body should be unified. In Paul's thought, the Corinthians' bodies become members of, and come to constitute, the body of Christ (6:15), and so should communally maintain the purity of their body. The Corinthian community is also twice asked to think of itself as collectively "on the market," as if a slave body purchased by God. First Corinthians 6:19b-20 reads, "You are not your own; you were bought with a price. So glorify God in your body"; it is echoed by 7:23, "you were bought with a price; do not become slaves of humans." Participants in the *ekklēsia* at Corinth lived in a city steeped in the history of former slavery, refounded as it was by freedpersons; 1 Corinthians 7 makes clear that slaves are part of the community as well. Thus the language of *sōma* resonated at multiple levels, calling to mind the individual body and its morality, the slave body, and the communal body politic.

Paul argues that those to whom he writes should together "shun immorality," including associating with a prostitute. The conversation is framed toward a male audience that might "join" themselves (6:16) to a female. Jennifer Glancy interrogates the passage, wondering whether a slave would necessarily be excluded from the Corinthian body of Christ, since slaves were not able to control their bodies but could be subjected to *porneia* by their masters; ancient texts talk about slaves "used" by their masters as part of the "normal" operations of slavery, or a slave might be forced into prostitution (Marchal).

Paul reinforces his point about not joining one's body with a prostitute by using the metaphor of body as *naos*, or temple to the Lord. What temple is evoked? The Corinthians might be familiar with the kind of thought that Philo, for instance, exhibits when he interprets Genesis 2, describing Adam's body as a "shrine or sacred sanctuary" carrying within it the *agalma*, or "image," of the divine (*Opif.* 137). Given concerns expressed for a collection to be taken to Jerusalem (1 Cor. 16:1-4; 2 Corinthians 8–9), the temple in Jerusalem might be evoked. Given their location, one of the many temples of Corinth might be come to mind (Weissenrieder), each with its own *temenos*, or boundary, within which space is sacralized and only certain activities are allowed.

What are the appropriate practices of the individual body and the "body politic"? First Corinthians 7 extends this question to the circumstances of marriage, enslavement, and circumcision. The main theme of the chapter is to "remain as you are," which is elaborated in 7:17: "Only, let everyone lead the life which the Lord has assigned to him or her, and in which God has called him or her" (see Harrill). Here Paul reprises the significant theme of "call," which resounds throughout the letter and which was part of the unique ethnic and practical identity of the community at Corinth—recall that they are no longer Jews or Greeks, but "the called" (1:24). But this status as "the called" leads to an odd stasis rather than transformation: they may be called, but, depending on their place in society in Roman Corinth, the Corinthians may have been variously surprised, disappointed, or reassured to be told to remain as they are. Scholars still hotly debate the meaning of this passage, however, because of difficulties in understanding the Greek; Scott Bartchy has argued instead, for example, that Paul emphasizes that one's call in Christ is more significant than any social status, but that 1 Corinthians 7 does not encourage members of the community to remain enslaved. If we keep our attention on the question of the interpretation of those who first received the letter, we may reasonably surmise that they too debated the meaning of this section.

Some Corinthians likely understood their identity as "called" by Christ and the transforming ritual of baptism to lead to a present state of resurrection (Wire) and/or to upend the distinctions of a kyriarchal society—a term coined by Elisabeth Schüssler Fiorenza to point to intersecting structural injustices rooted in the rule of masters (*kyrioi*) over slaves, males over females. They might have disagreed with Paul's urgent call to remain in the state in which they had been called.

While marriage is a primary concern in chapter 7, we see all three of the socioeconomic and ethnic binaries of what is likely a pre-Pauline baptismal formula discussed here (marriage [male and female]: 7:1-16, 25-40; ethnicity [Jew nor Greek] in terms of circumcision as its sign: 7:18-20; slavery and manumission [neither slave nor free]: 7:21-24). We know that baptism was important to the community at Corinth (1:13-17) and that they practiced baptism on behalf of the dead (15:29). We can assume that the Corinthians used a standard pre-Pauline baptismal formula, since in 1 Cor. 12:13 Paul partially cites what are likely ritual words that we also know from Gal. 3:27-28: "As many of you as were baptized into Christ have clothed yourselves with Christ. There is no longer Jew or Greek, there is no longer slave or free, there is no longer male and female; for all of you are one in Christ Jesus."

The Corinthians likely had suggested to Paul that "it is good that a man not touch a woman," since he precedes this with "now concerning what you wrote." The Corinthians' practice may be rooted in expectations of an imminent end to time, or to larger cultural and philosophical discussions of desire and its extirpation; the popular philosophical idea of *enkrateia*, or self-control, is evoked in 7:9 with the word "they should control themselves." Philo, a Jew from Alexandria who was a near contemporary of Paul's, interpreted the entire Tenth Commandment as an injunction, "do not desire," and understood the Mosaic dietary laws as ascetic precepts that led to self-control (Svebakken), teaching how to keep the self inured to the buffets of outside attractions, whether of food or sex or prestige. Such philosophical practices as abstaining from sex and marriage might fly in the face of Augustan marriage laws. Later sources characterize the *Lex Julia de maritandis ordinibus* and the *Lex Julia de adulteriis coercendis* of 18–17 BCE as encouraging people to marry, enacting penalties for adultery, imposing financial penalties on unmarried men and women, and seeking to limit marriages so that those of senatorial status would not mix with those of lower status—thus a senator or his children were barred from marrying freedpersons, those involved in certain kinds of theater, and prostitutes (e.g., Dio Cassius, *Hist.* 54.16.1). These harsh reforms, which were presented as part of a family values campaign (Suetonius, *Life of Augustus* 34), were revised in 9 CE in the Lex Papia Poppaea, which used a carrot rather than a stick, preferring political candidates who had more children, allowing freedpersons who had more children substantial freedom from the patron-client relations with their former masters, and relieving from political responsibilities those who had a great number of children.

The discussion of marriage also reminds us that many at Corinth would hear these words in light of their own "mixed marriages" (Hodge), having to negotiate with or to be subject to a spouse who had different ethics and religious practices from their own. Paul's arguments indicate that he and perhaps the Corinthians shared some notion of an extended or communicable health or salvation (Hodge, 16): the one who is made holy can somehow extend that holiness to his or her spouse and render their children "saints" or "holy ones" (Hodge, 14).

Although chapter 7 focuses on marriage, Paul briefly treats circumcision and slavery, the two other categories of the pre-Pauline baptismal formula. He quickly argues that one should seek neither circumcision nor to remove the marks of circumcision. While Jewish men were not the only men to practice circumcision in antiquity, and while Jewish women were not circumcised, circumcision became a kind of metonymy for Jews (Cohen). In Galatians, Paul insists that circumcision is nothing, even though men in antiquity who affiliated with Judaism may have wished to participate fully in the covenants of Judaism, including circumcision: Paul instead offers an extended argument in Galatians that covenantal participation is possible without circumcision, since God brought Abra(ha)m into covenant with him before Abra(ha)m was circumcised.

Paul then proceeds to talk about slaves. Verse 20 asserts the larger theme of the chapter (Harrill), that "everyone should remain in the state in which he [or she] was called." It continues: "Were you a slave when called? Never mind. But if you can gain your freedom, rather use [it] [*mallon chrēsai*]." The last phrase is the subject of much controversy. The object of the Greek verb is unclear. Should they "use" their freedom? Their slavery? If we attend to the immediate grammatical context, we will conclude that they should use their freedom—that is, to seek manumission by some means. If we look at the overall message of chapter 7, with its banging repetition of "remain," we will conclude that we should supply "slavery." The grammatical uncertainty is not due to our weak grasp of first-century Greek: roughly three centuries after the writing of 1 Corinthians, John Chrysostom's community debated whether to supply "freedom" or "slavery" (*Hom. 1 Cor.* 19.5). The Corinthians who received this letter were likely as baffled as we. We may wonder whether they sought clarification from the carrier of Paul and Sosthenes's letter, who was likely a freedperson or slave; such letter carriers were often expected not only to deliver their masters' correspondence but also to voice and to interpret its contents (Mouritsen).

Many attempt to neutralize the passage's revolutionary idea of seeking freedom, on the one hand, or its horrifying quietism of staying enslaved, on the other, by reading the passage as "merely" eschatological or theological (e.g., Conzelmann; Horsley 1998). It is a reasonable choice after Paul's own phrasing in 7:29: "the appointed time has grown short" and the following passage, in which people are encouraged to live "as if not," with the conclusion that "the form of this cosmos [or world] is passing away" (7:31b). Many commentators impute to Paul (and thus to "his" churches) a disinterest in material conditions on account of expectation of an imminent *parousia* or appearance of Christ, but apocalyptic notions could equally lead to concrete political action such as the kind of revolutionary fervor Josephus mentions when he talks about Jewish prophets who led groups that opposed the Romans and were quashed. Others would argue that we should read Paul in light of popular philosophical movements like Stoicism that enjoin that gender and social status and economic opportunity should not matter if one rightly cultivates within oneself a philosophical lack of caring for external events (e.g., Philo, *Every Good Man Is Free*); Epictetus describes the slave who longs to be free, only to be freed and realize that he is enslaved by the need to supply himself with such things as food and clothes (*Diatr.* 4.1.33).

Such an approach misses the opportunity to think about material and social realities of slavery at Corinth (Nasrallah 2013). The Corinthians did not necessarily share Paul's argument to "remain as you are," and they may have debated what he meant by the elusive *mallon chrēsai*, "rather use." Perhaps they wished Paul had offered a clearer statement of social change in the present. Perhaps some of the Corinthians were aware of contemporaneous practices at Delphi and Kalymna, in which a slave was "sold" for freedom to a god and thus manumitted (Deissmann). Perhaps they preferred to think that baptism and their calling "in Christ" transformed ethnicity, gender, and social religions in the present, rather than accepting a present stasis followed by future transformation. Perhaps they found the divine to be inbreaking in the present, as evidenced in spiritual gifts or *pneumatika*, and understood their individual bodies and communal body alike to be based in a new calling rather than an old.

■ THE TEXT IN THE INTERPRETIVE TRADITION

Over the centuries, Christians have debated the merits of celibacy and marriage in clerical and lay life. While Paul prefers that people not marry, his injunctions in 1 Corinthians 7 allow for marriage, and even suggest that desire be recognized and channeled in marriage—thus that marriage exists not only for procreation but also as a locus of sexual morality. In 1523, Martin Luther wrote a treatise on 1 Corinthians 7, addressing it "to the August and honorable Hans Loser of Pretzsch," as a wedding gift, with the hopes that he will "no longer postpone your marriage" (Luther, 3). A pity for the bride, then, that Luther's treatise proper starts with the words "What a fool is he who takes a wife, says the world, and it is certainly true" (5). Of course, Luther goes on, like Paul, to point out the folly of this worldly wisdom, as well as to use Paul as a tool against the Roman Catholicism of his day. Luther states that he has taken on the task of interpreting 1 Corinthians 7 because "this very chapter, more than all the other writings of the entire Bible, has been twisted back and forth to condemn the married state and at the same time to give a strong appearance of sanctity to the dangers and peculiar state of celibacy" (3).

So too, in the ancient world, Paul's teachings on marriage were used in two opposing directions. Two examples will suffice to show how 1 Corinthians 7 was interpreted in radically different ways soon after it was written. First Timothy, written in Paul's name at the end of the first century or beginning of the second, insists that those who have the task of "bishop" should be married, although only once (3:2), and that "she" (whether Eve or women more generally is unclear) "will be saved through bearing children" (1 Tim. 2:15). The *Acts of Paul and Thecla*, a text embodying traditions circulating in the second century CE, insists that Paul blessed celibacy, and focuses on the story of a young woman, Thecla, who follows Paul and renounces her betrothal for a life of celibacy.

◼ The Text in Contemporary Discussion

The phrase "the appointed time has grown short" (7:29) has attracted recent attention by political philosophers and other scholars. Following on Walter Benjamin's *Theses on the Philosophy of History*, they expand on the idea of "messianic time" and find in Paul's writings a sense of crisis that has the potential to inspire new ways of thinking about being in the present. Giorgio Agamben is particularly interested in the use in 1 Cor. 7:29 of the term *synestalmenos* ("drawn together" or "shortened" like a sail) to discuss time (*kairos*) (Agamben, 62). Alain Badiou describes Paul as "poet-thinker of the event" and a "militant figure"; Paul is to Jesus as Lenin was to Marx (as Slavoj Žižek also argues). Even more than Jesus, Badiou argues, Paul marked a break in what he calls "evental time": that is, for Paul, the resurrection changed everything.

Paul's letters and the sort of apocalyptic thinking we find in 1 Corinthians 7 are worthy resources for political philosophy. But Badiou and others, in part because of their only cursory understanding of Paul's historical context, have misused and mischaracterized Paul as a hero of universalism. For example, while recognizing Paul as a Jew, Badiou has nonetheless supported anti-Jewish interpretation by emphasizing Paul as a universalist thinker above the particulars of Judaism (Badiou, 13, 23); despite his claimed interest in universality, Badiou sweeps Paul's statements about women under the carpet by seeing them as only "cultural" (103–4). Badiou and others have produced a Paul who is an "anti-philosophical theoretician of universality," who is uniquely right over and against the "opinions" of those to whom he writes; they have elaborated a Paul who in relation to messianic or "evental" time argues for a truth that is produced by the subject, without recognizing that the subject they celebrate looks awfully like a "rational," universal male (Dunning).

The transformative theological and political idea of the *eschaton* and "messianic time," which Agamben, Badiou, and others correctly see in Paul's letters, does not reach full potential in these contemporary philosophical conversations. Contemporary philosophers and cultural critics do not take into account the productive struggle over ideas that occurred between Paul and those to whom he wrote, and they assume that people's experience of an urgent expectation of the Parousia or appearance of Christ allowed for some sort of individualized spiritual transformation that nonetheless had no concrete social or political effects in the world.

1 Corinthians 8–10: Food Offered to Idols, Ethnicity, and Identity

◼ The Text in Its Ancient Context

Paul had said that the Corinthians are still "infants" (*nēpioi*) and "people of the flesh" (*sarkikoi* or *sarkinoi*, 3:1). Chapters 5–10 provide examples of the practical ethical outworkings of Paul's chastisement. While chapters 5–7 touched on issues of practices of the *sōma* that had particularly to do with sex and marriage, chapters 8–10 focus on practices regarding food and transformations in ethnic identity that occur for those in Christ.

In 1 Cor. 10:25, Paul uses the word *makellon*, a *hapax legomenon* (a word that appears only once) in New Testament literature (Cadbury): "Eat whatever is sold in the meat market without raising any question on the ground of conscience" (1 Cor. 10:25). The location of the *makellon* (an area primarily for selling meat and fish) in Roman Corinth is unclear, although fragmentary epigraphic evidence confirms that there was a *makellon* at Corinth (Cadbury, 139; Nabers; Kent, n. 321; West, n. 124; Nasrallah forthcoming). Although not all meat in antiquity was sacrificial meat, the markets were locations where trade and religion converged, along with the sale of meat (Ruyt). Divinities were honored there in the Roman imperial period, especially in the central, usually round building (Ruyt; Nabers).

In chapters 8–10, Paul offers somewhat contradictory advice about the eating of meat in sacred precincts or from the market. In chapter 8, on the one hand, he suggests that one shouldn't eat it (in particular not in sacred precincts, *en eidōleiō*), lest one offend the conscience of a "weak" brother or sister. In chapter 10, on the other hand, he indicates that one shouldn't ask about the origins of the sacrificial food (*hierothyton*)—one can go ahead and eat it. Two principles seem to dominate: first, a set of philosophical-theological slogans, likely the Corinthians' own: we know that there is one God, that idols don't really exist, and that the earth is the Lord's and everything in it; in sum: God trumps all, and it doesn't matter what you eat. Second, and in tension with the first, we find a social issue: think about your sibling's conscience, and don't offend your brother or sister by eating sacrificial food. With regard to eating and drinking in Corinth, we can also consider the question of the meals shared by those in Christ; we know that Paul considered these to be handled badly, and his comments indicate that some were likely poor and were certainly hungry (see below on 1 Cor. 11:17-34; e.g., Stowers 2011a). Debates about food in Gal. 2:11-13, in which Paul accuses Cephas of sitting at table with gentiles, then separating from them when some from James (brother of Jesus) came to visit, likely had to do with kashrut or Jewish dietary laws more generally, while the discussion in 1 Corinthians 8–10 seems to have to do more specifically with food associated with sacrifice and sacred precincts.

The Corinthians in Christ were familiar with the intimate connection between food, community, and cult. Meals were eaten in sanctuaries at Corinth. The Asklepieion near the Lerna Fountain at Corinth has some rooms that seem to have functioned for dining. In addition, excavations have revealed fish bones, lentils, and casserole dishes in the sanctuary of Demeter and Kore on the Acrocorinth, which had several structures for dining even in the Roman period (Bookidis and Stroud; Økland). Not only meat but also other sorts of food were sometimes sacrificial, and if not sacrificial, still sacralized by their consumption within sacred precincts (Ekroth), yet not all meat was sacrificial meat (Naiden). Yet Paul tries to convince the Corinthians that the commodity could be drained of its religious force (see discussions in Still; Gooch; Stowers 2011a).

If we ask how various participants in the Corinthian *ekklēsia* would have heard Paul's injunction to "eat whatever is sold in the meat market," we recognize, aided by archaeological materials, that the conditions in antiquity were such that slaves, free, or freedpersons entered into a market that was religiously marked to purchase goods that may or may not have been religiously marked. In addition, literary evidence often depicts slaves sent to the market to purchase food (e.g., *Life of Aesop*). Hearers of 1 Corinthians would have found it difficult to think of *hierothyton* as neutral food, or of their mandated or voluntary entrance into the meat market as religiously neutral. The commodity in question was tagged by religion, whether or not it is called *hierothyton* ("sacred offering") or *eidōlothyton* ("idol" or "image offering"). The food, the eating of it, and the market space are all marked by religious practice and affiliation.

Spliced into the conversations about food and idolatry in chapters 8 and 10 is Paul's own assertion regarding food, one's right (*exousia*), freedom, and his identity in chapter 9. (We also saw how
chapters 1–4 contrapuntally treat wisdom and Paul's role within the community.) "Am I not free?!"
Paul begins chapter 9. While Paul presents himself at the beginning of 1 Corinthians (and at its
end) as an apostle, not slave of Christ (as in Rom. 1:1), Paul here presents himself as analogous to
one "employed in the temple" (9:13). Such religious experts were not necessarily (only) high-status
priests but also temple slaves and/or public slaves in the employ of the temple (Shaner). Wondering
about his own finances, Paul refers to temple religious specialists eating from the altar. This image is
easily skimmed over as an odd metaphor, so that we can get to the meat (!) of Paul's self-description
in 9:19-23, but it is a crucial tie to the themes of chapters 7–8 and 10–11. In chapters 7–8, real slavery and freedom are at stake, as is the question of eating meat from the temple. In chapters 10–11,
eating *hierothyton* is again an issue, and by the end of chapter 11 the *ekklēsia* at Corinth is criticized
for how it does its eating and drinking.

What is at stake in these verses is Paul's identity as an apostle, what authority (*exousia*, 9:12b)
he has in the community at Corinth, and his wage (*misthos*, 9:18). Paul responds to this by proudly
stating that he is a shape-shifter. "For though I am free with respect to all, I have made myself a
slave to all, so that I might win more of them. To the Jews I became as a Jew . . . To those outside
the law I became as one outside the law . . . To the weak I became weak . . . I have become all things
to all people, that I might by all means save some" (9:19-22). The passage is confounding if we look
for Paul's biography or an insight into his psychology; we should read it instead as part of Paul's
ēthos—the rhetorical strategy by which a speaker both defines himself and does so in a way that he
hopes will draw the audience's sympathy.

Paul twice pauses in his arguments in chapters 8–9 to refer to Jewish Scripture. In 8:6, he offers
a remix of the Shema, the Jewish claim in Scripture and prayer that the Lord is one (Deut. 6:4),
expanded by a reference to "one Lord, Jesus Christ," perhaps quoting a common teaching of early
Christ-communities and perhaps also sparking, for the Corinthians, the idea of Stoic monotheism
(Thiselton, 635–37). That is, Jews were not the only ones in antiquity who argued for one God; some
who followed Greek and Roman religions also thought that there was one true God, and various
local manifestations or ways of imagining aspects of that God. In chapter 9, speaking of the issue
of wage, Paul offers an allegorical interpretation of Deut. 25:4, insisting, in what I think must be a
comic tone, that "You shall not muzzle an ox while it is treading out the grain" is a Mosaic statement
for "our sake": in the midst of a chapter about Paul's own identity, he briefly takes on the identity
of an ox. From these references and from the beginning of chapter 10, we can deduce that the Corinthians understood references to Jewish tradition and that they were a largely gentile community,
undergoing an ethnic-religious transformation toward a Jewishness rooted in faith in Christ.

At the beginning of chapter 10, Paul reprises the theme of food and idolatry using the exodus
story. "I don't want you to be ignorant, brothers and sisters," he writes—again, a reference to who is
in the know—"that our fathers were all under the cloud and all passed through the sea, and all were
baptized into Moses in the cloud and in the sea, and all ate the same spiritual food and all drank the
same spiritual drink. For they drank from the spiritual rock which followed them, and the rock was
Christ" (10:1-4). The passage was perhaps surprising to the Corinthians as they recalled their ethnic

change. It asserts that the paternity of those to whom Paul writes is derived from Moses, despite the fact that he later writes "when you were gentiles" (12:2)—that is, from the *ethnē*, or nations, that are precisely not Jews. The story of the exodus through the sea is framed in terms of baptism. This passage reminds us again that the Corinthians considered baptism to be a key ritual, perhaps one that transformed identity, community, and possibilities for present and future. Baptism, as we know from what is likely a pre-Pauline baptismal formula found in Gal. 3:28, included the phrase "neither Jew nor Greek." Here, as in Gal. 3:29, Paul reinforces the idea that baptism does not lead to an ethnically neutral state or to participation in a third or "new race," as some Christians would later assert (*Diogn.* 1.1; Buell), but to being incorporated within the stories, covenants, promises, and responsibilities of God's people, the Jews.

Here Paul offers a midrash on the exodus story that may trade on and shift other interpretations of exodus familiar to those at Corinth. In a roughly contemporaneous text, the Wisdom of Solomon, Wisdom herself leads the people through the sea.

> A holy people and blameless race wisdom delivered from a nation of oppressors. . . . She brought them over the Red Sea, and led them through deep waters; . . . wisdom opened the mouth of the dumb, and made the tongues of babes speak clearly. . . . When they thirsted they called upon thee [Wisdom], and water was given them out of flinty rock, and slaking of thirst from hard stone. (Wis. 10:15, 18, 21; 11:4)

The accounts in 1 Corinthians and the Wisdom of Solomon differ in various ways. The latter is a celebration of Jewish identity over against "the nations" and "the ungodly"; the former brings the nations into a Jewish lineage. The Wisdom of Solomon celebrates Wisdom; Paul may substitute Christ for Wisdom. The triumph of the story of the Wisdom of Solomon becomes a warning in 1 Corinthians: the latter tells the story of the exodus as a warning concerning idolatry, instruction, and trial or temptation, rather than a celebration as we find in the Wisdom of Solomon. Given what we learned in chapters 1–4 of the importance of wisdom/Wisdom to the Corinthian *ekklēsia*, we may reasonably wonder whether Paul is trying to shift the importance of this hypostatized figure in the community at Corinth.

▌ THE TEXT IN THE INTERPRETIVE TRADITION

In 10:26, Paul cites from Ps. 24:1 a kind of cosmological-philosophical slogan: "The earth is the Lord's, and everything in it." Such a way of thinking means that *anything*, even foodstuffs usually considered questionable, taboo, or forbidden due to dietary laws, is reframed as "the Lord's" and is thus acceptable. We find concern about this issue also in Gal. 2:11, framed in terms of Jews eating with gentiles. Written approximately fifty years later, Acts 10 reframes the fundamental insight in terms of dietary law and gives to Peter, not Paul, the vision (literally) that God says he may "kill and eat" all things (10:13). Acts adopts this probably earlier story to provide Peter with the insight that he can travel to the household of Cornelius the gentile, since "God has shown me that I should not call anyone profane or unclean" (10:28). Some recent scholars have argued that the canonical Acts of the Apostles knows Paul's letters and self-presentation, even if Acts presents Paul in quite a different light, as a tremendous speaker rather than one who is weak (Pervo). Acts 10 presents a *different* tradition from Paul's own in 1 Corinthians 8–10 with regard to eating and idolatry and relations with gentiles, so it is an "interpretive context" for Paul's letter in the loosest sense. But it is important to recognize that the community in Christ, whether in the time of Paul or in the century thereafter, picks up Jewish interpretive traditions that declare the Mosaic laws to be allegorizations of *people*, rather than literal injunctions about what to eat. For example, the *Letter of Aristeas* depicts a figure named Eleazar the high priest, who argues that Moses' true aim is *dikaiosynē* ("righteousness" or "justice"), and so Mosaic dietary law is to be interpreted with each animal as a symbol that corresponds to human ethical behavior (see Svebakken, 111–12).

First Corinthians 10:25 is used quite differently by Clement in second-century-CE Alexandria, who employs it in a larger section on eating, both to enjoin people not to "abolish social intercourse" but also to shun "daintiness . . . we are to partake of few and necessary things." A string of citations from 1 Corinthians leads Clement to mark his intended audience as fairly wealthy, since his conclusions have to do both with the host and with moderation at a luxurious table: "We are to partake of what is set before us, as becomes a Christian, out of respect to him who has invited us, by a harmless and moderate participation in the social meeting; regarding the sumptuousness of what is put on the table as a matter of indifference, despising the dainties, as after a little destined to perish" (*Strom.* 4.15). In the community at Corinth and elsewhere, food, status, economic access, and religious practice were intertwined issues. Maybe you aren't what you eat, but you are formed by those with whom you eat.

■ THE TEXT IN CONTEMPORARY DISCUSSION

Paul presents himself as a shape-shifter in 1 Corinthians 9, as "all things to all people." In other passages in his letters, he presents himself as nurse (1 Thess. 2:7), as father coming with a stick (1 Cor. 4:15-21), as someone having ecstatic experiences (2 Cor. 12:1-11), and as prisoner (Phil. 1:13-14), among many other self-portraits. Paul's presentation in 1 Corinthians, as well as these other self-portraits, has informed two responses. First, Paul offers a self so complex that students of his letters struggle to define his intention: Who *was* Paul? What was his frame of mind? This has led to a scholarly obsession with declaring Paul a hero (often a liberative or postcolonial hero, resisting the Roman Empire and bringing egalitarian community) or a betrayer of Christ's message (from the Pseudo-Clementine literature to Thomas Jefferson and beyond: Johnson-DeBaufre and Nasrallah). A better approach would be (1) to take into account the rhetorical nature of Paul's statements: he is not describing himself, but portraying himself to various communities for various reasons; (2) to consider whether our ideas of authorship and intention might not match those held in antiquity; and (3) to focus not only on Paul as hero but on the broad spectrum of early communities in Christ as well.

Second, some scholars of the past decades have interpreted Paul's shape-shifting in the context of the "new perspective" on Paul, placing Paul as a Jew negotiating his newly Jewish identity *in Christ* in the midst of the diversity within Judaism in the first century CE. They demonstrate that Paul has not invented a new religion, but stands alongside other Jews who try to make a way for gentiles to come into covenant with God.

11:2-34: Veiling and Eating

▌THE TEXT IN ITS ANCIENT CONTEXT

In chapter 9, Paul pointed to his own identity as shape-shifter; by the end of chapter 10, he emphasizes that his readers should do all to the glory of God and give no offense to "either Jew or Greeks or the *ekklēsia* of God," even as he himself seeks to please the many. Paul enjoins his audience here to "Be imitators of me, as I am of Christ" (11:1; see also 4:16). The pattern set up in this verse (Christ-Paul-participants in the *ekklēsia*) echoes throughout the following verses, even as the powerful political language of imitation echoes elsewhere in this letter and others (Castelli).

An initial commendation to the community for remembering him and what he has "handed down" quickly shifts to a correction of practices of prayer and prophecy. Paul begins by setting a hierarchy of "headship"—God, Christ, man, wife. This hierarchy undergirds his insistence that a man praying or prophesying should do so with head uncovered, while a woman doing so must cover her head. As Antoinette Clark Wire has shown, Paul then proceeds to offer several disparate logics for his insistence on such a practice. Although scholars have long tried to discover the causes of such an injunction—Does Paul promote Jewish women's practices of head-veiling? Does he criticize "pagan" women's loose hair and/or prophetic chaos leading to Dionysian-like abandon for women?—none is convincing, largely because we cannot know for certain the variety of veiling practices in Roman Corinth. We do know that Roman men *and* women covered their heads when engaged in pious practices, as we see in a statue of Octavian found at Corinth; were his right hand preserved, we would see it pouring a libation to the gods (see also Oster).

If we cannot fix a social context that explains Paul's injunction, we can glean several things about prayer and prophecy in the community at Corinth. First, men and women alike were praying and prophesying; as we think about the letter as a whole, we see that wisdom and spiritual gifts are key to the community (11:1-4, 12-14). Second, Paul wishes to change this practice in some way, perhaps especially through insisting on women's veiling and grounding this practice in a logic of women's subordination to men. Third, given the scattershot of logics he offers, it is likely that he is aware he faces a tough crowd, for whom only one reason for his argument will not suffice. Paul argues according to cosmology and creation: man as God's image and glory; woman as glory of the man; the Genesis 2 story that woman was made from man, with a concessive realization that men are born from women in verse 12. He argues according to "the angels," either indicating that the Corinthians understood angels to be present in their community practices and/or that he was alluding to the danger of angels' attraction to human women, as is hinted at in the biblical reference to angelic intercourse with female humans (Gen. 6:1-2; Wire; BeDuhn). Paul argues based on the logic of propriety (11:13), from nature (11:14), and from general practice in the *ekklēsiai* (11:16).

Paul proceeds to another practice that has to do with Corinthians' gathering (11:17-34): that of eating and drinking. When they gather to eat, he says, they do not engage in "the Lord's supper" (11:20). One concern, according to the text, is that "those who have nothing" (11:22) are humiliated. From Paul's perspective, something in meal practices has broken down. Scholars have speculated that perhaps this breakdown has to do with social status: some have access to food or the ability to come when they wish, leaving out or disregarding others with less status, such as slaves. Paul's final word is to "wait" lest condemnation fall (11:34).

Paul's discussion of what he "received from the Lord" about the supper is the earliest evidence we have of such a practice; although the traditions contained in the Gospels may be earlier, the Gospels themselves postdate the writing of Paul's letters. The meal is grounded with a historical etiology ("on the night he was handed over," 11:23): it is understood as a repetition of the practices of that first supper. The eschatological aspect of the meal is highlighted, as it is a proclamation of the death of the Lord "until he comes." For Paul, the Lord's Supper has potential dangers associated with it; interpreters influenced by the anthropology of religion have noted Paul's attribution of quasi-magical properties to the supper, since it can cause weakness, illness, and death if misused (11:30).

Those in Christ were not the only ones to gather at meals or to be warned about their behavior while doing so. Contemporaneous associations were well known for their practices of gathering to eat and to celebrate a god, and for regulating those gatherings. The second-century Iobacchoi inscription found in Athens, for instance, regulates participation and membership in their association to honor the god Bacchus (Dionysus) and states fines for poor behavior while in a gathering together (IG II^2 1368 = PHI 3584) as well as the financial contributions necessary to participate in the meal (Ascough, et al.).

Comments regarding meal practices in 1 Corinthians 11 should make us wonder not only about the ritual nature of the meal but also about food and hunger in the community. The majority of the population of the Roman Empire was poor (recent hypotheses extend from 68 to 99 percent), with poverty defined in this way by Peter Garnsey and Greg Woolf: "the poor are those living at or near subsistence level, whose prime concern it is to obtain the minimum food, shelter, and clothing necessary to sustain life, whose lives are dominated by the struggle for physical survival" (Garnsey and Woolf, 153; Meggitt). Various famines occurred in mid-first-century Greece and the Greek East, including perhaps one at Corinth in the early 50s CE (Winter, 6, 216–25). Corinth's economy depended on trade, and the city and its environs could not supply enough food for its urban population (Williams, 31–33, 38; Strabo, *Geog.* 8.6.23).

■ THE TEXT IN THE INTERPRETIVE TRADITION

Paul's assertion that women should be veiled when praying or prophesying and his arguments supporting this change in practice may have met with instant controversy. It also created controversy in the late second or early third century, as evidenced in the writings of Tertullian. The North African writer is famous for his pithy statement that "you [women] are the devil's gateway" (*On the Apparel of Women* 1.1). In *On the Veiling of Virgins*, Tertullian discusses 1 Corinthians 11 and the way in which it is being interpreted in his day. Some, he indicates, argue from 1 Corinthians 11 that, while women should veil while praying or prophesying, virgins should not; thus, virgins in those Christian communities in North Africa remain unveiled when they gather with others in church. These interpreters, Tertullian disgustedly says, ground their argument in Paul's statement about the unmarried woman being concerned about the affairs of the Lord, while the married woman worries about worldly affairs and how to please her husband (1 Cor. 7:34; Tertullian, *Virg.* 4.4).

Tertullian cites 1 Cor. 11:3 and its language of man as head of woman—a term in Greek that can also be translated "wife," but which Tertullian insists must be understood as a general classificatory term under which female virgin falls as a particular instance of "woman." He continues to argue that virgin women should also be veiled by appealing to the assertion in 1 Cor. 14:34-35 that women should be silent in the assembly. Is a virgin, he wonders acerbically, something of a third sex (*Virg.* 7.2), which can escape such regulations? In the end, he supports his argumentation by referring to a vision of a woman in his community to whom an angel appeared, rapping on her bare neck and sarcastically suggesting that she expose more of her body (*Virg.* 17.6). The issue of women and veiling in religious practice is a long-standing one, and some among earliest Christians argued strongly for women's veiling in religious community.

▌THE TEXT IN CONTEMPORARY DISCUSSION

Scholars today debate whether the Greek *kephalē* in 1 Cor. 11:3 should be translated "head" (as in RSV) or "source"; the latter might allow for a nonhierarchical interpretation of the passage, with the term "source" indicating the order of creation. At stake is the role of women in Christian community. Does 1 Corinthians provide a biblical foundation for the idea of women's subordination to men, especially with regard to women's roles in religious leadership in Christian ministry?

Mimi Haddad, president of Christians for Biblical Equality, along with many who participate in the organization, argues that 1 Corinthians 11 refers to the order of creation. Paul states in 1 Cor. 11:8-9, 11-12, that, despite the order of creation (man first, then woman, according to Genesis 2), men are now born from women. Haddad and others cite this as evidence of Paul's recognition of the roles of both sexes and the interdependence of men and women. She concludes: "Rather, in Christ both males and females are equal heirs of God's New Covenant community. Both are born of the Spirit, and both are gifted for leadership which is first and foremost service" (Haddad).

Haddad's perspective is one among many who debate whether Paul argued for women's egalitarian status in assemblies in Christ or argued for women's subordination (Elliott). Other feminist approaches would emphasize the clear role of women in the earliest Jesus movement, from accounts that Mary Magdalene was the first to greet Jesus after his resurrection to Paul's own list of women who were coworkers and even a woman apostle in Romans 16. Still others would add that the texts we associate with earliest Christianity, like all writing, are rhetorically constructed in order to persuade, and would ask why Paul here insists on a hierarchy that is in part gendered, while elsewhere in Paul's writings and other texts we find evidence of egalitarian tendencies in the early *ekklēsiai*.

1 Corinthians 12:1-26: Being the Body of Christ

▌THE TEXT IN ITS ANCIENT CONTEXT

Paul introduces the topic with the statement, "Now concerning spiritual gifts [or "spiritual things," *pneumatika*], brothers and sisters, I do not want you to be uninformed" (12:1). This statement may have been a surprise to those at Corinth who heard these words: with their interest in wisdom and knowledge, the Corinthians likely understood themselves to be quite well informed about spiritual gifts. The Corinthians, with their interest in *pneumatika*, were on the cutting edge of an emerging medical and philosophical debate in the first and second centuries, including medical debates over whether "spirit" runs through the blood and philosophical debates about the materiality of *pneuma*. From the fourth to the first centuries BCE, terms etymologically related to *pneumatika* are found approximately thirty-six times in extant literary writings. In writings from the first century CE, however, we find at least 104 uses of the term, and in the second century CE, a shocking 990 uses; a good many of these are Christian, emerging because of discussion of 1 Corinthians (Nasrallah 2003).

Nevertheless, even as Paul likely mirrors the Corinthians' own interest in and discussions of *pneumatika* and their participation in a broader cultural fascination with the topic of *pneuma*, he asserts that they do not understand spiritual gifts particularly well. He ranks spiritual gifts and seeks to reconfigure the importance of prophecy and glossolalia in the Corinthian community.

Paul embeds his ranking of spiritual gifts in a discussion of the body. First Corinthians is full of advice on the discipline and control of the individual body in relation to the "one body" of the *ekklēsia*. Paul uses the image of many members making up that one body (12:12-27). He uses the term *sōma* in two primary ways. The first is the *sōma* as the individual body, which can be transformed (1 Cor. 15:35-50) and, as we recall, can be bought (6:20; 7:23a). Paul folds this image of body into an image of "one body" as community ("For just as the body is one and has many members, and all the members of the body, though many, are one body, so it is with Christ," 12:12), joking that the foot shouldn't compete with the hand nor the ear complain that it isn't an eye. This language of one body derives from the political discourse of the day.

The image of "one body" and the idea of communal benefit are powerful tools of deliberative rhetoric, and present an argument that few would want to dispute. Who wants to damage the common body? The first-century-CE Stoic philosopher Epictetus enjoins: "you are a citizen of the world, and a part of it," and urges his hearers "to treat nothing as a matter of private profit . . . but to act like the foot or the hand, which, if they had the faculty of reason and understood the constitution of nature, would never exercise choice or desire in any other way but by reference to the whole" (*Diatr.* 2.10.1–4 [Oldfather, 275]. By the second century, the cities of Asia Minor aggressively minted coinage representing *homonoia*, the unity between these bodies politic, even as at the same time they fiercely competed with each other to secure Roman imperial attention and funds (Price; Kampmann).

Along with the rhetoric of one body, Paul employs the political language of "general benefit," often employed in deliberative rhetoric, to persuade the audience: all spiritual gifts must be for the general benefit (*to sympheron*, 12:7; Mitchell 1991). Paul's statement that all spiritual gifts are from the same spirit (12:11), moreover, further underscores his emphasis on unity and sameness over and against or in the midst of the diversity of spiritual gifts.

Paul's emphasis in chapter 12 on the common benefit and one body reorders and marginalizes those spiritual gifts that are connected to wisdom and knowledge, and that the Corinthians may have most valued. The general list of spiritual gifts in verses 8-10 is ranked in 12:28: "And God has appointed in the church first apostles, second prophets, third teachers; then deeds of power, then gifts of healing, forms of assistance, forms of leadership, various kinds of tongues." While 1 Cor.

12:14–26 argues for the significance of every member of the body, both the "weaker" and those given more "honor," this argument is undercut by the ranking and ordering of *pneumatika* in 12:28. This ranking erodes the emphasis on wisdom and knowledge—and concomitantly glossolalia and prophecy, gifts the Corinthians held dear. Paul admits the importance of prophets, but subordinates them to apostles; he also disaggregates prophecy from glossolalia, and ranks the latter last, perhaps as part of his strategy of challenging the Corinthians' understanding of Wisdom. After all, she was associated with eloquence and speech: "wisdom opened the mouth of the dumb, and made the tongues of babes speak clearly" (Wis. 10:21). Even infants (recall Paul's accusation in 3:1) benefit from Wisdom.

∎ The Text in the Interpretive Tradition

Christian communities have long struggled with questions of how the divine is manifest in different historical periods. Some early Christians believed that the Spirit and its gifts were relegated to a past time; the beginning of the *Martyrdom of Perpetua and Felicitas* (1.4) argues that new witnesses may still be found, and indeed may be greater than past ones: "Let those then who would restrict the power of the one Spirit to times and seasons look to this: the more recent events should be considered the greater, being later than those of old, and this is a consequence of the extraordinary graces promised for the last stage of time" (Musurillo). This is followed by a citation of Acts 2:17/Joel 2:28, which refers to the Lord pouring out "my spirit upon all flesh." The passage continues with allusions to ideas of Spirit, community benefit, and distribution of gifts also found in 1 Corinthians: "So too we hold in honour and acknowledge not only new prophecies but new visions as well, according to the promise. And we consider all the other functions of the Holy Spirit as intended for the good of the Church; for the same Spirit has been sent to distribute all his gifts to all, as the Lord apportions to everyone" (1.5; Musurillo).

In earliest Christianity, some groups celebrated new manifestations of the Spirit. This was certainly the case for those who edited and used the *Martyrdom of Perpetua and Felicitas*, a community that may have been associated with the prophetic renewal movement, sometimes called Montanism, that arose in Asia Minor in the late second century CE and flourished for some time around the Mediterranean basin. Of course, such prophetic renewal movements were not limited to ancient times, but can be found in a figure like Joachim of Fiore in the twelfth century or the movement, sparked at Azusa Street in Los Angeles in the early twentieth century, that came to be called Pentecostalism.

∎ The Text in Contemporary Discussion

We find a comparable phenomenon in the Shakers or the United Society of Believers in Christ's Second Coming, which began in the mid-eighteenth century and was characterized by women's leadership, ideas of the equality of the sexes, an understanding of an unfolding Parousia or appearance of Christ, and ecstatic experiences of spiritual gifts, including speaking in tongues. The community was known for "shaking" and speaking in tongues and prophesying. The 1816 biography of one key leader, Ann Lee, talks about the gifts of the Holy Ghost and the current time when people can be filled "with visions, revelations and gifts of God" (Bishop and Wells, v; 7). Although much of their understanding of revelation is grounded in interpretations of the book of Revelation, some Shaker writings combine references to Saul of Tarsus with reference to gifts (and 1 Cor. 2:11) in order to argue for a new, Spirit-filled dispensation (see the 1848 edition of *A Summary View of the Millennial Church, or United Society of Believers, Commonly Called Shakers* 5.5). The Spirit's working was sometimes manifest in "gift drawings" and in "gift music" (Morin).

Debate about dispensations of time and the Spirit have not ceased. Global Pentecostalism, in all its variegated forms, is a growing force in Christianity, especially in the so-called two-thirds world, while academic engagement with such ideas is ongoing (*The Journal of Pentecostal Studies*; J. K. A. Smith; Miller and Yamamori). Different Christian communities use the very same text, 1 Corinthians, to argue for the effervescence of the Spirit's inbreaking in community *and* to argue, to the contrary, that true Christian community gathers in a unified way in which all speech is comprehensible and the use of tongues is barred.

1 Corinthians 12:27—13:13: Love and the Ranking of *Charismata*

■ THE TEXT IN ITS ANCIENT CONTEXT

Chapter 13 seems like a digression because some of these materials are pre-Pauline, a kind of aretalogy of love derived from Jewish wisdom traditions (Conzelmann, 218). Yet its contents are intimately linked to the foregoing and following chapters on *pneumatika*: the themes of prophecy and tongues in particular, and the question of who is a spiritual person in general.

Chapter 13 begins by citing spiritual gifts significant at Corinth, but then relativizes their importance: "If I speak in the tongues of mortals and of angels, but do not have love, I am a noisy gong or a clanging cymbal. And if I have prophetic powers, and understand all mysteries and all knowledge, and if I have all faith, so as to remove mountains, but do not have love, I am nothing" (13:1–2). Paul emphasizes that these three things the Corinthians value (tongues, prophecy, faith) will all pass away, while "love never ends" (13:8). Returning to the theme of perfection (*to teleion*) raised in chapter 2, in which Paul contrasted the perfect person or initiate with the faulty Corinthians, Paul insists, "Our knowledge is imperfect and our prophecy is imperfect; but when the perfect comes, the imperfect will pass away" (13:9-10). Using the metaphors of being an infant and of gazing into a dim mirror, 1 Corinthians 13 emphasizes the immaturity and partialness of any sort of present knowledge and wisdom.

Verses 4-8a may present a pre-Pauline aretalogy—that is, a list of virtues or qualities—of love that is used to relativize the importance of wisdom in the Corinthian community. Aretalogies of Wisdom (as well as of Isis, who has qualities similar to Wisdom) are well known from the ancient world, and it is possible that the Corinthians knew these and celebrated Wisdom in their midst. First Corinthians 13 may seek to redirect the community's interest in wisdom by celebrating love instead, just as chapters 1–4 attempted to upend expectations about what true wisdom and knowledge are.

▌THE TEXT IN THE INTERPRETIVE TRADITION

Later Christian commentators connected Paul's comment, "If I deliver my body to be burned, but have not love, I gain nothing" (1 Cor. 13:3), to martyrdom. (Note that here lies one of the text-critical debates of 1 Corinthians: is the word "burn" or "boast" original to Paul's letter? They differ by only one letter in Greek.) In late second-century Alexandria, Clement argued: "You see that martyrdom for love's sake is taught" (*Strom.* 4.7). To celebrate the idea of the glory of a noble death, Clement cites Pindar, Aeschylus, Heraclitus, the words of Indian sages meeting Alexander the Great, and even Plato's *Republic*, among other sources. His discussion culminates with an argument about Christians displaying a true understanding of death for true love, a death that leads to glory, in a mix of Pauline verses from 1 Corinthians 13 about enduring love and 1 Cor. 4:9-13 about apostolic suffering. In heresiological debates, the verse is used to denigrate Christians with whom one disagrees. For instance, Tertullian argues that if Praxeas's body had been burned (in martyrdom)—Praxeas being another Christian whom Tertullian considered heretical—it would have profited him nothing since he did not have the love of God (*Prax.* 1.4).

First Corinthians 13 had a powerful afterlife as well in Augustine's *On Christian Doctrine*. All Scripture should be interpreted in light of "faith, hope, and love" while knowledge and prophecies fall away. Even a mistaken interpretation of Scripture, if it builds up love, argued Augustine, still goes in the right direction, even if the interpreter needs to be put correctly on the right path of interpretation (*On Christian Doctrine* 1.36–40). A person who has "faith, hope, and love" (1 Cor. 13:13) does not even need Scripture, except to instruct others (*On Christian Doctrine* 1.39). Dale Martin powerfully suggests that this principle of interpretation be applied to passages by Paul and those writing in his name that are used to condemn what some might today call homosexuality, especially in view of the quite different sex-gender system of the ancient world (Martin 2006, 49–50).

▌THE TEXT IN CONTEMPORARY DISCUSSION

In a sermon given on November 4, 1956, in Montgomery, Alabama, Martin Luther King Jr. delivered "Paul's Letter to American Christians." In it, "Paul" wonders at the "fascinating and astounding advances that you have made in the scientific realm" but states, "It seems to me that your moral progress lags behind your scientific progress" (M. L. King, 415), quoting Henry David Thoreau to support his argument. He offers an economic critique of capitalism's excesses, while arguing that America cannot turn to communism. He critiques American Protestantism, Roman Catholicism, and segregation in American society, particularly in the churches. He concludes by calling love the "most durable power in the world," and declares that it is "at bottom the heartbeat of the moral cosmos" (M. L. King, 420). He reaches this conclusion by interpreting 1 Corinthians 13, arguing that American Christians' "eloquence of articulate speech," "heights of academic achievement," and philanthropy are nothing if devoid of love: "I must bring my writing to a close now. Timothy is waiting to deliver this letter, and I must take leave for another church. But just before leaving, I must say to you, as I said to the church at Corinth, that I still believe that love is the most durable power in the world" (419). Martin Luther King, Jr., uses 1 Corinthians 13 to offer a cultural critique and to navigate the troubled waters of American politics by foregrounding a love that expels inequalities, whether of economics, race, or education.

1 Corinthians 14:1-40: Spiritual Gifts and Building up Community

▌ THE TEXT IN ITS ANCIENT CONTEXT

In 1 Cor. 14:1, Paul picks up the themes of the previous chapters and continues to work out his arguments about spiritual gifts, especially prophecy and glossolalia. "Pursue love," Paul insists, referring back to the contents of chapter 13; and "strive for the spiritual gifts," reminding his readers/hearers of chapter 12, "especially that you may prophesy." This last phrase reminds us that Paul highlights prophecy over against tongues. Paul may have invented this division; it is possible that the Corinthian community had not categorized and ranked the *pneumatika* received at baptism.

Paul offers a series of arguments that deconstruct the importance of tongues. These arguments hinge on the concepts of "building up" (*oikodomē*)—as we recall, a key term in political rhetoric of the first century—and intelligibility. In 1 Corinthians 14, by his own admission, Paul seeks to rein in tongues, which are a primary means of accessing the divine and divine knowledge: "For those who speak in a tongue do not speak to other people but to God; for nobody understands them, since they are speaking mysteries in the spirit" (14:2). Yet Paul admits in 1 Corinthians 14 that he too speaks in tongues. He thus asserts that he can match the high status of any Corinthian who exhibits glossolalia, but chooses not to. By the time of the writing of 2 Corinthians 12, Paul feels forced to argue again on the Corinthians' terms, especially over against the "super-apostles" with their spiritual gifts. Thus Paul circuitously talks about his own "visions and revelations" (2 Cor. 12:1). In his famous "fool's speech," Paul insists that the Corinthians' resistance to him has compelled him to enter into a sort of performance competition where he must demonstrate that he too has experienced rich charismatic experiences.

Because of passages like 1 Corinthians 12–14, because of Paul's discussion of his own ecstatic experience in 2 Corinthians 10–12, and because of Paul's references to bearing Christ's body or to having the spirit of God (7:40), some have understood Paul as a mystic (Schweitzer) or a shaman (Ashton). Others have pointed to spirit-possession as an important characteristic of the religious lives of Corinthians (J. Z. Smith; Mount).

▌ THE TEXT IN THE INTERPRETIVE TRADITION

First Corinthians 14:33b-34, with its comments on women (or, less likely, wives; the Greek *gynaikes* can mean either) being silent in the *ekklēsia*, clearly raised issues for later Christians. This can be seen from the way in which various manuscripts treat the verses. We have none of Paul's "autographs," or original manuscripts; thus variations from text to text in the manuscripts we do have often indicate early Christian interpretations of those now-lost origins. In several manuscripts, verses 34-35 are displaced to after verse 40; in other manuscripts, including the early P[46] (third century), these verses appear as following verse 33 (Thiselton, 1148). Some have hypothesized that because this text "wanders," it may not have been original, but a scribal gloss (Fee), but Wire demonstrates that the "wandering" nature of the passage traces back only to one manuscript, thus strengthening the argument that this is *not* an interpolation (Thiselton, 1148–49). While Paul mentions prominent women leaders in the earliest *ekklēsiai* (see Romans 16), in 1 Corinthians 11 he also offers a subordinationist logic for women's veiling. In addition, that passage, as well as 1 Corinthians 15, relies on the account in Genesis 2 of man's creation first, and woman's creation from man; it may be that the Corinthians (as with other, later Christian communities) relied instead on the idea in Gen. 1:27 that God created the human in God's image, "male and female God created them." We cannot know Paul's intentions, and his letters offer contradictory indications regarding the role of women in earliest Christian communities. What we can know is that Paul's letters indicate women's leadership and voice in earliest in-Christ communities, and both his support for and ambivalence about this phenomenon. His arguments for veiling and women's silence indicate that they were praying and prophesying in community unveiled, on the one hand, and that they were vocal in the community, on the other. Looking in 1 Corinthians and to other texts, especially Romans 16, we find a panoply of women in communication with Paul and leading in communities. Those who draw from Paul's letters the justification for subordinating women's leadership in worship have grounds to do so, and those who use Paul's letters to argue for women's leadership have grounds to do so as well.

The Text in Contemporary Discussion

The story of the origins of Pentecostalism at Azusa Street in Los Angeles, California, is replete with references to Acts 1–2 and the story of *heteroglossia*—speaking in other languages—in those passages. References to 1 Corinthians 12–14, with its emphasis on *glossolalia*, speaking in tongues, are puzzlingly less utilized, perhaps precisely because of how Paul cites his own speaking in tongues yet also downgrades and relativizes the importance of this spiritual gift among others.

One contemporary Pentecostal treatment of 1 Corinthians 14 comes in a sermon by Rev. David Yonggi Cho, pastor of the Yoido Full Gospel Church in South Korea (Myung and Hong). In 2007, this Pentecostal church claimed approximately a million members. In a sermon titled "The Benefits of Speaking in Tongues," preached on February 15, 2009, Cho began by narrating the origins of global Pentecostalism at Azusa Street. His sermon, grounded in 1 Cor. 14:18 ("I thank God that I speak in tongues more than all of you"), emphasizes the ongoing importance of this spiritual gift. Cho provides five reasons for speaking in tongues to encourage his audience to continue in the practice. He argues that speaking in tongues benefits the individual, who can pray in the spirit with the help of the Paraclete (the term used for the Holy Spirit in John's Gospel). It allows for prayers to well up when the person praying is sufficiently despairing that she or he cannot find a way to pray. It allows for all-night prayer vigils since, without the Holy Spirit, Christians would be unequal to the task of praying all night. Speaking in tongues, he asserts, can cast out a devil, and the Christian who speaks in tongues needs no psychologist as tongues have a healing function. Speaking in tongues, Cho further states, can calm nightmares and allows God to speak through humans. Finally, speaking in tongues is a privately edifying phenomenon that should be practiced *before* teaching or preaching a sermon; it leads to greater clarity and purpose in public speaking and preaching. Some Christian communities today continue to think of glossolalia as a powerful, expansive, and indispensable spiritual practice that can encourage, advocate, heal, and spur the growth of church ministry.

1 Corinthians 15:1-58: Transformations: From "Psychic Body" to "Spiritual Body"

■ THE TEXT IN ITS ANCIENT CONTEXT

Some have debated whether 1 Corinthians 15 belongs in this letter or is a segment of another writing with the theme of the resurrection. Most agree, however, that themes of the body, spirit, baptism, Christ's role, and the resurrection have been drawn from earlier in the letter and find their culmination in this, the final section of the body of the letter.

The chapter starts (vv. 1-11) with a defense and explanation of Paul's role in preaching the gospel, a role we know from Gal 1:11—2:10 was a matter of debate, even if the Acts of the Apostles solders into place Paul's authority in going to the gentiles (although not before giving Peter the primacy of place). Issues of Paul's identity and authority often surface in different ways in his letters—we need only to glance at the beginning of Galatians to see that he strongly defines his role as apostle with *no* connections to human authority there; in Romans, a community he does not know, he begins more cautiously with an unqualified self-designation as "apostle" and by describing himself more humbly as "slave of Christ." In 1 Cor. 15:1-11, Paul traces a proto-creedal statement that predates him (he uses a form of *paradidōmi*, a verb used to indicate the transmission of knowledge from a teacher, or by tradition, in his statement "what I in turn had received," 15:3) and links it to an authoritative line of transmission. Of "first importance" is that "Christ died for our sins in accordance with the scriptures, and that he was buried, and that he was raised on the third day in accordance with the scriptures" (vv. 3-4). Paul began his letter by emphasizing the crucifixion of Christ. Here, near the letter's end, he returns to the theme of Christ's death and elaborates on the theme of resurrection and the idea of death's overthrow.

Paul then traces the authoritative line of eyewitnesses, beginning with Cephas, then the Twelve, and the line continues "to all the apostles," then to James. Paul does not mention women in this list, though later sources would name Mary Magdalene and others. Paul states that he is "last of all": "as to one untimely born, [Christ] appeared also to me" (15:8). Paul locates his unfitness to be called an apostle *not* in the lack of ties he has to the historical Jesus or his lack of training in Jerusalem, but in his persecution of the *ekklēsia* of God. The proto-creedal statement recedes as Paul articulates that it does not matter whether it was "I or those" who preached and "so you believed," reprising the theme of various leaders at the beginning of his letter.

In verses 12 and following, Paul accuses the Corinthians of saying that "there is no resurrection of the dead" and argues the futility of this point of view (vv. 12-19) to those who are in Christ. We cannot know if the Corinthians actually claimed that there was no resurrection of the dead; indeed, this seems unlikely given that they baptize on behalf of the dead. Perhaps the Corinthians were emphasizing the power of resurrection in the present, even as they also emphasized Wisdom's power evidenced in their community through spiritual gifts. Paul then proceeds to defend the idea that Christ has been raised from the dead. He does so by turning to the story of creation and a typology that pairs Adam and Christ, with the first bringing death ("for as all die in Adam") and the second life ("so all will be made alive in Christ," v. 22).

Arguments from creation and arguments about Adam were commonplace at the time of Paul's writing of 1 Corinthians. Commentaries and philosophical debates over Plato's *Timaeus*, a story of the origins and structure of the cosmos, were penned; so, too, we find interpretations of Genesis that result in texts like the radical retelling of Genesis 1–2 in the *Hypostasis of the Archons* (perhaps second century CE). Jews contemporary with Paul engaged in debate over Genesis, sometimes with quite different interpretations, as we find in Philo's comment that all humans are a degeneration from the first human, who was "beautiful and good" and "lovely of body," compounded from the most pure and refined earthly substance (*Opif.* 137–40).

Portions of 1 Corinthians 15 remix 1 Thess. 4:13—5:11, with its eschatological themes. Here, as there, Paul offers an image of the Parousia or appearance of Christ in power (15:23). Paul employs language of the "reign of God" (15:24) and the destruction of "every ruler and authority and power." Given that the last of these to be destroyed is death, we can understand that, for the Corinthians hearing this letter, both temporal and cosmological rulers would be brought to mind, providing a coda to Paul's mention of "rulers of this age" crucifying "the Lord of glory" (2:8). Paul indicates that Christ's role should be understood in light of the Jewish Scriptures (Pss. 8:6; 110:1). Understanding this death-slaying Christ in relation to the psalmist's phrase "all things are put in subjection under his feet" might raise the question of whether he who subjected things is then superior or equal to God. Paul reassures the community that the Son is subject to God (15:28), dispelling any concerns or ideas that his theology involved "two powers in heaven," as did other, debated Jewish theologies of antiquity (Boyarin 2010; 2001).

Paul had begun this elaboration of the resurrection of the dead by stridently accusing the Corinthians of claiming there is no resurrection of the dead. He abruptly shifts back to them and to their practices, namely, baptism on behalf of the dead. This is the earliest and only reference in the Letters of Paul to such a practice, and it has raised many questions. The Corinthians may have been concerned about incorporating their ancestors into their new cult, and so baptism was a mechanism for initiating not only the living but also the dead (DeMaris). This practice becomes the grounds for Paul to insist on the truth of resurrection of the dead—not just of Christ but also of Christ as first evidence of a greater transformation.

In verse 35, Paul either paraphrases or caricatures a question from someone at Corinth: "How are the dead raised? With what kind of body do they come?" The answer is a full-scale blast in which Paul combines theories from religion and physics. Paul uses the metaphor of a kernel of grain, and argues that there are different kinds of flesh (*sarx*) and different kinds of bodies (*sōmata*), which themselves have different glories (*doxai*). We should think about this, as well as other aspects of 1 Corinthians, in light of scientific theories of the first century, a time when philosophical and theological speculation were often one and the same, and when theories from physics and medicine informed such speculation. For instance, while we may think of "spirit" as immaterial, Stoic philosophers of antiquity thought of it as a purer form of matter (Engberg-Pedersen).

This speculation from physics becomes the ground for further defining the "resurrection of the dead" and the particular problematic of the body. Paul lists a set of hierarchical binaries: weakness, power; physical, spiritual; first Adam, last Adam. Again, Paul argues from the creation story that the first Adam was a living soul, while the last Adam is a life-giving spirit. This language of *psychikon* versus *pneumatikon* echoes the hierarchical use of the terms in chapter 4 and may indicate some debate over the evolution or development of bodies from one kind of coarse matter to a finer kind of matter associated with spirit or *pneuma* (Engberg-Pedersen, 39–74). Certainly this language was quickly taken up and discussed by Paul's later interpreters. Origen tried to resolve the fact that Paul insisted the resurrected body was not flesh and blood, yet was a body (*De princ.* 2.10–11), while other early Christians, concerned about the continuation of the appetites after death, debated whether the resurrected body would have teeth or genitalia (Petrey).

Paul reprises and develops a vision of the end that he articulated in an earlier letter, 1 Thessalonians. This letter uses language of "putting on" (15:53) imperishability and immortality, imagery of clothing and unclothing, that probably called to mind baptismal practices (see 2 Cor. 5:1-5; Gal. 3:27).

■ THE TEXT IN THE INTERPRETIVE TRADITION

Paul's claim to have met Jesus "by revelation" (*apokalypsis* or cognates: Gal. 1:12, 16) and his lack of a familial or historical link to the earliest Jesus traditions or Jesus himself was a bone of contention among those in Christ in the first and second centuries and beyond. The Corinthians, among other communities, may have wanted to hear from an apostle who visited them a recital and confirmation of the "tradition" that Paul mentions in 1 Cor. 15:1-11; that is, they may have preferred someone who had known Jesus "in the flesh." Paul instead presents to them in writing "what I also received" (15:3) and explains how Christ appeared to him (15:6), using this revelation both to authorize his role as apostle and to present himself as called and chosen, echoing language of the Jewish prophets (Gal. 1:15)—not as a convert to a new religion (Stendahl).

This self-presentation would have many effects in the interpretive tradition. First, some would take up Paul's language of call, apocalypse, and visionary experience (see also 2 Cor. 12:1-13) and produce a text like the *Apocalypse of Paul*, found among the documents at Nag Hammadi, in which Paul is caught up into the heavens as he travels on his way to Jerusalem. Others, whose stance is represented in the Pseudo-Clementine literature (compiled in the fourth century CE but including sources that date to the second century CE), implicitly criticized Paul's claims as illegitimate, attributing to Jesus the saying that the "evil one" would also send apostles (*Clementine Hom.* 11.35.3). A fictional scene is set: The apostle Peter argues with "Simon"—a *magus*-figure whom Christians often evoked to represent their opponents—who is a lightly veiled stand-in for Paul. Peter challenges the truth of the sort of knowledge that comes through visionary experience, demonstrates that visions often occur to the impious rather than to the blessed, and finally spurts out: "So even if our Jesus did appear in a dream to you, making himself known and conversing with you, he did so in anger, speaking to an opponent. That is why he spoke to you through visions and dreams—through revelations which are external" (*Clementine Hom.* 17.19.1 [Meeks and Fitzgerald]). While it is clear that Paul's letters are very influential today, especially in Protestant Christianity, ancient texts also indicate a strong ambivalence about Paul's letters, on the one hand—letters that were, after all, much interpreted among Christians who would come to be called heretics (followers of Valentinus, for instance) as well as those who would come to be considered orthodox (John Chrysostom, for example). In addition, some ancient texts show a strong skepticism regarding claims for revelation, questioning whether a visionary experience of Christ (like Paul's) could be false. Many of those who heard Paul's message in antiquity were more skeptical of it than most Christians, and those who use Paul's thought for political theology, are today. Those who understand Christ primarily through the lens of Paul (some do call themselves Paulinists!) or who would argue, with Slavoj Žižek, that "There is no Christ outside Saint Paul," miss early Christian controversy and even rejection of Paul and his letters. The versions of Christianity prevalent today, especially in North American Protestantism, make it hard to picture what a Christian identity that rejects Paul would look like, or even to engage in the work of historical reconstruction of the voices of the Corinthians or others who may have debated or rejected Paul's teachings in the first century.

▌ The Text in Contemporary Discussion

Colossians 3:1-3, a pseudepigraphic text that claims to have been penned by Paul, offers the idea: "So if you have been raised with Christ, seek the things that are above, where Christ is . . . For you have died, and your life is hidden with Christ in God." As we have seen, some at Corinth may have understood themselves to have been living already, through the initiatory ritual of baptism, in a transformed, resurrected type of life. Colossians 3:1 takes up the themes of Paul's writings and transforms them more explicitly into the idea that Christians have already died and been raised with Christ, even in their present lives.

Karl Barth's 1924 *Die Auferstehung der Toten* decidedly rejects the idea that the resurrection occurs in the present: "It is not we who are the risen ones!" he exclaimed (Janssen, 65). Barth understood 1 Corinthians 15 as "the very peak and crown of this essentially critical and polemically negative Epistle" (Barth, 101) and "a clue to its meaning" (Barth, 5). It is a doctrine of last things, for Barth, which points to the gap between humans and God and the gap between now and then.

> Because it is *thus within* our existence, even our Christian existence, and must always be, however high we climb, because the "then" is really a *Then* and *There*, no Now and Here, the *reality* of the resurrection is exclusively the reality of the *resurrection*, the truth of Christianity is exclusively *God's* truth, its absoluteness is exclusively *God's* absoluteness. (Barth, 210–11)

In contrast, Rudolf Bultmann's appreciative 1926 response to Barth emphasizes that "our resurrection is reality, now that Christ is risen" (Janssen, 76). He explains: "in a certain sense, i.e. in so far as we belong to Christ, we are the resurrected, are the 'first fruits' . . . , are a 'new creation'" (Bultmann, 93–94). In this contrast between Barth and Bultmann we may see an echo of Paul's and some Corinthians' differing interpretations of the resurrection: Paul with Barth would insist on perfection or completion and resurrection as happening *then*, not now; think of his insistence, for example, in 1 Cor. 13:12: "For now we see in a mirror, dimly, but then we will see face to face." Some of the Corinthians, in contrast, may have delighted in spiritual gifts and in demonstrating the *now* of the new creation.

1 Corinthians 16:1-23: Epistolary Closing

▊ THE TEXT IN ITS ANCIENT CONTEXT

First Corinthians 15, with its crescendo of criticism of the Corinthians for their questions about the resurrection of the dead and compelling and varied arguments about the truth of the resurrection of the dead, its connection to the first and last Adam, and its ability literally to transform individuals and the cosmos, thundered at the end. Chapter 16, the closing of the letter, offers a quiet denouement and a glimpse of everyday life.

The letter first reminds its readers about the "contribution for the holy ones" (or "saints") and indicates that Paul has some expectation of equity among communities, since he has written the same to the *ekklēsiai* of Galatia. We also find, in 2 Corinthians 8 and 9, more letters about this contribution (see Georgi). We glimpse something of travel and social networks as Paul explains how to collect money and that he will send some emissary/ies, whom the Corinthians approve, with a letter—and funds—to Jerusalem.

Paul concludes with travel plans, as is typical of his letters, and reveals that he is likely in Ephesus as he writes. The social networks that Paul hints at or reveals earlier in the letter here arise again: the question of when Timothy and Apollos will visit Corinth is raised; the visit of Stephanas and Fortunatus and Achaicus to Paul, making up for the absence of the entire community, is mentioned, and their authority is enforced with the injunction to "be subject" to them and to "everyone who works and toils with them" (16:16). The epistle began with Paul's mention of Stephanas and "those in his household." The names Fortunatus and Achaicus hint at their servile or freedperson status, since one is nicknamed "fortunate," and the other is named after the region of his origin; we can wonder if they were Stephanas's slaves or freedpersons. Social networks are further highlighted as Paul offers greetings from *ekklēsiai* of Asia and mentions Aquila and Priscilla, whose names also appear in Romans 16.

Certain rituals and mechanics are exposed at the end of the letter. Perhaps like Romans—we know from Rom. 16:22 that the scribe Tertius wrote the letter—1 Corinthians was penned by a scribe, since Paul emphasizes his own writing at the end of the letter, probably in a note and signature, as was common in ancient letter writing.

▊ THE TEXT IN THE INTERPRETIVE TRADITION

Paul ends 1 Corinthians by reprising his mention of Stephanas and household at the beginning of the letter and names them "the first converts in Achaia." This may have aided in the invention of 3 Corinthians. This text is known from the Armenian Bible and the commentary of Ephrem; it also seems to have circulated as part of a larger *Acts of Paul* (Schneemelcher, 217). Third Corinthians consists of a fragmentary letter purporting to be from Stephanas "and the presbyters (or ambassadors) who are with him," and Paul's reply. The Corinthians' letter to Paul expresses concern about the teachings of two men in Corinth who are introducing new ideas, such as that one should not appeal to the prophets, that there is no resurrection of the flesh, that Christ was not born of Mary nor came in the flesh, that the creation is not God's work. A brief narrative element before "Paul's" reply claims that Stephanas's letter was delivered to Paul in Philippi, where he was in prison, and he sent a reply to the theological confusion introduced by these false teachers.

From the fictive correspondence of 3 Corinthians we see the staying power of certain names, like Stephanas's, in what became the Christian tradition. We also learn more of the ancient context in which early Christians wrote letters in Paul's name and imaginatively responded to new social and theological crises in "Paul's" voice. Such responses in Paul's name, but not by Paul, include New Testament writings like Colossians, Ephesians, and the Pastoral Epistles (1 and 2 Timothy, Titus), as well as "letters" to and from Paul, like 3 Corinthians. The epistle was a powerful literary tool not only among early Christians. This phenomenon, called "epistolary narrative" or "epistolary fiction" (Rosenmeyer), burgeoned in antiquity; letters of Plato, Socrates, and others were invented to provide biographical details or to tease out the philosophical importance of famous figures. In using pseudepigraphical letters to create new narratives, early Christians were taking part in a larger cultural phenomenon that we need not understand as forgery or deception. Rather, Christians (among others) were in their writings creating possible worlds in which a figure like Paul, even after his death, was wielded to support Christian communities' responses to theological difference with "his" authoritative voice. These pseudepigraphical letters represent the multiple and even opposing directions in which Paul's teachings could be taken.

▌THE TEXT IN CONTEMPORARY DISCUSSION

First Corinthians 16:2 discusses raising funds for a gift to be carried to Jerusalem: "On the first day of every week, each of you is to put aside and save whatever extra you earn, so that collections need not be taken when I come." The seeming conditional link between storing up money for the Jerusalem collection, on the one hand, and prosperity, on the other, makes the verse a possible source for those debating the "prosperity gospel."

Creflo Dollar, a famous pastor associated with the prosperity gospel, uses 1 Cor. 16:2, among other texts, to discuss the idea of prosperity in Bible study notes titled "The Secret Combination for True Prosperity" (Dollar). His Bible study notes argue that definitions of prosperity changed over time in biblical writings, and that 1 Cor. 16:2 is evidence of prosperity as "success in profitability and material gain." Although he reframes prosperity in terms of the total wholeness of the person, with money as only one aspect of prosperity, Dollar nonetheless reveals a larger debate going on among those who adhere to the prosperity gospel: which scriptural passages promise prosperity, and what do the same verses enjoin in terms of contributions (understood in contemporary churches as weekly tithes) that individuals may make?

This use of 1 Cor. 16:2 in the context of a broad range of biblical passages on "prosperity" reminds us, too, of how this strategy of interpretation is both fair use and misuse of Paul's letters. It is fair use because Paul's letters are indeed now part of a canon and as such can be juxtaposed with texts in a different language, from a different time period and context, in a creative theological way. But such a strategy is also misuse, because Paul's letters were in their first instantiation occasional, rather than works of systematic theology, to be picked over and juxtaposed with other "Scriptures." They were produced and received in an ad hoc, improvisational context by those who did not bear the name Christian, much less know that the letters would emerge into a canon of Pauline Letters or that some would put pen to papyrus to "imitate" Paul as he had enjoined (but perhaps not as he would have wished), writing letters in his name. The Letters of Paul were produced and received by those who could not imagine them embedded within a canon. It is our responsibility to pursue a letter like 1 Corinthians with a disciplined intimacy that calls us to see the text first as stranger, not at all written to us, or about us, and only later to see the text as intimate, as a fruitful interlocutor for the theological imagination, for political action, for religious practice today.

Works Cited

Agamben, Giorgio. 2005. *The Time That Remains: A Commentary on the Letter to the Romans.* Translated by Patricia Dailey. Stanford: Stanford University Press.

Ascough, Richard S., Philip A. Harland, and John S. Kloppenborg. 2012. *Associations in the Greco-Roman World: A Sourcebook.* Waco: Baylor University Press.

Ashton, John. 2000. *The Religion of Paul the Apostle.* New Haven: Yale University Press.

Badiou, Alain. 2003. *Saint Paul: The Foundation of Universalism.* Translated by Ray Brassier. Stanford: Stanford University Press.

Bagnall, Roger S., and Bruce W. Frier. 2006. *The Demography of Roman Egypt.* Cambridge: Cambridge University Press.

Bartchy, S. Scott. 1973. *Mallon Chrēsai: First Century Slavery and the Interpretation of 1 Corinthians 7:21.* Atlanta: Scholars Press.

Barth, Karl. 1933. *The Resurrection of the Dead.* Translated by H. J. Stenning. London: Hodder and Stoughton.

Baur, F. C. 1831. "Die Christuspartei in der korinthischen Gemeinde, der Gegensatz des petrinischen und paulinischen Christentums in der ältesten Kirche, der Apostel Petrus in Rom," *Tübinger Zeitschrift für Theologie* 4:61–206.

BeDuhn, Jason David. 1999. "Because of the Angels: Unveiling Paul's Anthropology in 1 Corinthians 11." *JBL* 118, no. 2:295–320.

Bishop, Rufus, and Seth Youngs Wells, eds. 1816. *Testimonies of the Life, Character, Revelation and Doctrines of Our Ever Blessed Mother Ann Lee.* Hancock, MA: J. Tallcott and J. Deming, Junrs.

Bookidis, Nancy, and Ronald S. Stroud. 1997. *Corinth XVIII, Part III: The Sanctuary of Demeter and Kore: Topography and Architecture.* Princeton: ASCSA.

Boyarin, Daniel. 2001. "The Gospel of the Memra: Jewish Binitarianism and the Prologue to John." *HTR* 94, no. 3:243–84.

———. 2010. "Beyond Judaisms: Metatron and the Divine Polymorphy of Ancient Judaism." *Journal for the Study of Judaism* 41:323–365.

Buell, Denise Kimber. 2005. *Why This New Race: Ethnic Reasoning in Early Christianity.* New York: Columbia University Press.

Bultmann, Rudolf. 1987. *Faith and Understanding.* Vol. 1. Translated by Louise Pettibone Smith. Edited by Robert W. Funk. Minneapolis: Fortress Press.

Cadbury, Henry J. 1934. "The Macellum of Corinth." *JBL* 53, no. 2:134–41.

Calvin, John. 1981. *Commentary on the Epistles of Paul the Apostle to the Corinthians.* Translated by John Pringle. Grand Rapids: Baker.

Castelli, Elizabeth A. 1991. *Imitating Paul: A Discourse of Power.* Louisville: Westminster John Knox.

Clement of Alexandria. 1994. "The Stromata, or Miscellanies." In *ANF* 2:299–568.

Cohen, Shaye J. D. 1999. *The Beginnings of Jewishness: Boundaries, Varieties, Uncertainties.* Berkeley: University of California Press.

Concannon, Cavan. 2014. *"When You Were Gentiles": Specters of Ethnicity in Roman Corinth and Paul's Corinthian Correspondence.* New Haven: Yale University Press.

Conzelmann, Hans. 1975. *1 Corinthians: A Commentary on the First Epistle to the Corinthians.* Hermeneia. Philadelphia: Fortress Press.

"Decree on Ecumenism, *Unitatis redintegratio.*" 1964. Documents of the II Vatican Council. http://www.vatican.va/archive/hist_councils/ii_vatican_council/documents/vat-ii_decree_19641121_unitatis-redintegratio_en.html. Deissmann, Adolf. 1908. *Licht vom Osten: das Neue Testament und die neuentdeckten Texte der hellenistisch-römischen Welt.* Tübingen: Mohr.

DeMaris, Richard E. 1995. "Corinthian Religion and Baptism for the Dead (1 Corinthians 15:29): Insights from Archaeology and Anthropology." *JBL* 114, no. 4:661–82.

Dollar, Creflo. 2006. "The Secret Combination for True Prosperity." *Creflo Dollar Ministries.* http://www.creflodollarministries.org/BibleStudy/StudyNotes.aspx?id=62.

Douglas, Mary. 1970. *Natural Symbols.* London: Barrie & Rockliff.

Eisenbaum, Pamela. 2009. *Paul Was Not a Christian: The Original Message of a Misunderstood Apostle.* New York: HarperCollins.

Ekroth, Gunnel. 2007. "Meat in Ancient Greece: Sacrificial, Sacred or Secular?" *Food and History* 5:249–72.

Elliott, Neil. *Liberating Paul: The Justice of God and the Politics of the Apostle.* Maryknoll, NY: Orbis, 1994.

Engberg-Pedersen, Troels. 2010. *Cosmology and Self in the Apostle Paul: The Material Spirit.* New York: Oxford University Press.

Fee, Gordon D. 1987. *The First Epistle to the Corinthians.* NICNT. Grand Rapids: Eerdmans.

Fitzmyer, Joseph A. 2008. *First Corinthians: A New Translation with Introduction and Commentary.* AYB. New Haven: Yale University Press.

Frilingos, Christopher A. 2004. *Spectacles of Empire: Monsters, Martyrs, and the Book of Revelation.* Philadelphia: University of Pennsylvania Press.

Gaca, Kathy L. 2003. *The Making of Fornication: Eros, Ethics, and Political Reform in Greek Philosophy and Early Christianity.* Berkeley: University of California Press.

Gager, John G. 2000. *Reinventing Paul.* New York: Oxford University Press.

Garnsey, Peter, and Greg Woolf. 1989. "Patronage of the Rural Poor in the Roman World." In *Patronage in Ancient Society*, edited by Andrew Wallace-Hadrill, 153–70. London: Routledge.

Georgi, Dieter. 1992. *Remembering the Poor: The History of Paul's Collection for Jerusalem.* Nashville: Abingdon.

Glancy, Jennifer A. 2002. *Slavery in Early Christianity.* Oxford: Oxford University Press.

Gooch, Peter David. 1993. *Dangerous Food: I Corinthians 8–10 in Its Context.* Waterloo, ON: Wilfrid Laurier University Press.

Grabbe, Lester L. 1997. *Guide to the Apocrypha and Pseudepigrapha.* Vol. 3, *Wisdom of Solomon.* Sheffield: Sheffield Academic.

Haddad, Mimi. 2013. "Male Rule a Biblical Ideal? Part Two." *CBE International.* http://www.cbeinternational.org/?q=content/2013-09-12-male-rule-biblical-ideal-part-two-arise-e-newsletter.

Harrill, J. Albert. 1995. *The Manumission of Slaves in Early Christianity.* Tübingen: Mohr Siebeck.

Hodge, Caroline Johnson. 2007. *If Sons, Then Heirs: A Study of Kinship and Ethnicity in the Letters of Paul.* Oxford: Oxford University Press.

Horsley, Richard A. 1979. "Spiritual Marriage with Sophia." *VC* 33:30–54.

———. 1998. *1 Corinthians.* ANTC. Nashville: Abingdon.

Janssen, Claudia. 2000. "Bodily Resurrection (1 Cor. 15)? The Discussion of Resurrection in Karl Barth, Rudolf Bultmann, Dorothee Soelle and Contemporary Feminist Theology." *JSNT* 79:61–78.

Johnson-DeBaufre, Melanie. 2005. *Jesus among Her Children: Q, Eschatology, and the Construction of Christian Origins.* Cambridge, MA: Harvard University Press.

Johnson-DeBaufre, Melanie, and Laura S. Nasrallah. 2011. "Beyond the Heroic Paul: Toward a Feminist and Decolonizing Approach to the Letters of Paul." In *The Colonized Apostle: Paul Through Postcolonial Eyes,* edited by Christopher Stanley, 161–74. Minneapolis: Fortress Press.

Kampmann, Ursula. 1998. "Homonoia Politics in Asia Minor: The Example of Pergamon." In *Pergamon, Citadel of the Gods: Archaeological Record, Literary Description, and Religious Development,* edited by Helmut Koester, 373–93. Harrisburg, PA: Trinity Press International.

Kent, J. H. 1966. *Corinth VIII, Part III: The Inscriptions, 1926–1950.* Princeton: ASCSA.

King, Karen L. 2005. *What Is Gnosticism?* Cambridge, MA: Harvard University Press.

King, Martin Luther, Jr. 1956. "Paul's Letter to American Christians." *The King Center.* http://www.thekingcenter.org/archive/document/pauls-letter-american-christians-0.

Kloppenborg, John. 2013. "Membership Practices in Pauline Christ Groups." *Early Christianity* 4, no. 2:183–215.

Kocar, Alexander. 2013. "'Humanity Came to Be According to Three Essential Types': Ethical Responsibility and Practice in the Valentinian Anthropogony of the Tripartite Tractate (NHC I, 5)." In *Jewish and Christian Cosmogony in Late Antiquity,* edited by Lance Jenott and Sarit Kattan Gribetz, 193–221. Tübingen: Mohr Siebeck.

Koester, Helmut. 1990. *Ancient Christian Gospels: Their History and Development.* Harrisburg, PA: Trinity Press International.

Kovacs, Judith L. 2005. *1 Corinthians: Interpreted by Early Christian Medieval Commentators.* The Church's Bible. Grand Rapids: Eerdmans.

Lamp, Jeffrey S. 2000. *First Corinthians 1–4 in Light of Jewish Wisdom Traditions: Christ, Wisdom, and Spirituality.* Lewiston, NY: Mellen.

Lieu, Judith. 2002. *Neither Jew Nor Greek? Constructing Early Christianity.* London: T&T Clark.

Luther, Martin. 1973. *LW* 28.

Marchal, Joseph A. 2011. "The Usefulness of an Onesimus: The Sexual Use of Slaves and Paul's Letter to Philemon." *JBL* 130, no. 4:749–70.

Martin, Dale B. 1990. *Slavery as Salvation: The Metaphor of Slavery in Pauline Christianity.* New Haven: Yale University Press.

———. 1995. *The Corinthian Body.* New Haven: Yale University Press.

———. 2006. *Sex and the Single Savior.* Louisville: Westminster John Knox.

Meeks, Wayne A. 2003. *The First Urban Christians: The Social World of the Apostle Paul.* 2nd ed. New Haven: Yale University Press.

Meeks, Wayne A., and John T. Fitzgerald. 2007. *The Writings of St. Paul: Annotated Texts, Reception and Criticism.* New York: Norton.

Meggitt, Justin J. 1998. *Paul, Poverty, and Survival.* Edinburgh: T&T Clark.

Miller, Anna C. 2013. "*Not with Eloquent Wisdom*: Democratic *Ekklēsia* Discourse in 1 Corinthians 1–4." *JSNT* 35:323–54.

Miller, Donald E., and Tetsunao Yamamori. 2007. *Global Pentecostalism: The New Face of Christian Social Engagement.* Berkeley: University of California Press.

Millis, Benjamin W. 2010. "The Social and Ethnic Origins of the Colonists in Early Roman Corinth." In *Corinth in Context: Comparative Studies on Religion and Society,* edited by Steven J. Friesen, Daniel N. Schowalter, and James C. Walters, 13–36. Leiden: Brill.

———. 2013. "The Local Magistrates and Elite of Roman Corinth." In *Corinth in Contrast: Studies in Inequality,* edited by Steven J. Friesen, Sarah A. James, and Daniel N. Schowalter, 38–53. Leiden: Brill.

Mitchell, Margaret M. 1991. *Paul and the Rhetoric of Reconciliation: An Exegetical Investigation of the Language and Composition of 1 Corinthians.* Tübingen: Mohr Siebeck.

———. 2002. *The Heavenly Trumpet: John Chrysostom and the Art of Pauline Interpretation.* Louisville: Westminster John Knox.

Morin, France. 2001. *Heavenly Visions: Shaker Gift Drawings and Gift Songs.* Minneapolis: University of Minnesota Press.

Mount, Christopher. 2005. "1 Corinthians 11:3-16: Spirit Possession and Authority in a Non-Pauline Interpolation." *JBL* 124, no. 2:313–40.

Mouritsen, Henrik. 2011. *The Freedman in the Roman World.* Cambridge: Cambridge University Press.

Musurillo, Herbert, trans. 1972. *The Acts of the Christian Martyrs.* Oxford: Clarendon Press.

Myung, Sung-hoon, and Yonggi Hong, eds. 2003. *Charis and Charisma: David Yonggi Cho and the Growth of Yoido Full Gospel Church.* Oxford: Regnum.

Nabers, Ned Parker. 1967. *Macella: A Study in Roman Archaeology.* Princeton: Princeton University Press.

Naiden, F. S. 2013. *Smoke Signals for the Gods: Ancient Greek Sacrifice from the Archaic through Roman Periods.* New York: Oxford University Press.

Nasrallah, Laura Salah. 2004. *An Ecstasy of Folly: Prophecy and Authority in Early Christianity.* Cambridge, MA: Harvard University Press.

———. 2012. "Grief in Corinth: The Roman City and Paul's Corinthian Correspondence." In *Contested Spaces: Houses and Temples in Roman Antiquity and the New Testament,* edited by David L. Balch and Annette Weissenrieder, 109–40. Tübingen: Mohr Siebeck.

———. 2013. "'You Were Bought with a Price': Freedpersons and Things in 1 Corinthians." In *Corinth in Contrast: Studies in Inequality,* edited by Steven J. Friesen, Sarah A. James, and Daniel N. Schowalter, 54–73. Leiden: Brill.

———. Forthcoming (2014). "Archaeology and the Pauline Letters." In *Oxford Handbook of Pauline Studies,* edited by Barry Matlock. New York: Oxford University Press.

Neyrey, Jerome. 1986. "Body Language in 1 Corinthians: The Use of Anthropological Models for Understanding Paul and His Opponents." *Semeia* 35:129–70.

Økland, Jorunn. 2010. "Ceres, Κόρη, and Cultural Complexity: Divine Personality Definitions and Human Worshippers in Roman Corinth." In *Corinth in Context: Comparative Studies on Religion and Society,* edited by Steven J. Friesen, Daniel N. Schowalter, and James C. Walters, 199–229. Leiden: Brill.

Oldfather, W. A., trans. 1925. *Epictetus: Discourses, Books 1–2.* LCL 131. Cambridge, MA: Harvard University Press.

Oster, Richard. 1988. "When Men Wore Veils to Worship: the Historical Context of 1 Corinthians 11.4." *NTS* 34, no. 4:481–505.

Pétrement, Simone. 1990. *A Separate God: the Christian Origins of Gnosticism.* Translated by Carol Harrison. San Francisco: HarperSanFrancisco.

Petrey, Taylor. 2010. "Carnal Resurrection: Sexuality and Sexual Difference in Early Christianity." ThD diss., Harvard University Divinity School.

Pervo, Richard I. 2008. *Acts: A Commentary.* Hermeneia. Minneapolis: Fortress Press.

Price, S. R. F. 1985. *Rituals and Power: The Roman Imperial Cult in Asia Minor.* Cambridge: Cambridge University Press.

Robinson, Elizabeth A. 2011. *Histories of Peirene: A Corinthian Fountain in Three Millennia.* Princeton: ASCSA.

Rosenmeyer, Patricia A. 2001. *Ancient Epistolary Fictions: the Letter in Greek Literature.* Cambridge: Cambridge University Press.

Ruyt, Claire de. 1983. *Macellum, marché alimentaire des romains.* Louvain-la-Neuve: Institut supérieur d'archéologie et d'histoire de l'art, College Érasme.

Schmithals, Walter. 1971. *Gnosticism in Corinth: An Investigation of the Letters to the Corinthians.* Nashville: Abingdon.

Schneemelcher, Wilhelm, ed. 1992. *New Testament Apocrypha.* Vol. 2, *Writings Relating to the Apostles, Apocalypses and Related Subjects.* Rev. ed. Cambridge: James Clarke & Co.

Schüssler Fiorenza, Elisabeth. 1983. *In Memory of Her: A Feminist Theological Reconstruction of Christian Origins.* New York: Crossroad.

———. 1987. "Rhetorical Situation and Historical Reconstruction in 1 Corinthians." *NTS* 33:386–403.

———. 1993. *Discipleship of Equals: A Critical Feminist Ekklesia-logy of Liberation.* New York: Crossroad.

———. 1994. *Jesus: Miriam's Child, Sophia's Prophet: Critical Issues in Feminist Christology.* New York: Continuum.

———. 1999. *Rhetoric and Ethic: The Politics of Biblical Studies.* Minneapolis: Fortress Press.

Schweitzer, Albert. 1931. *The Mysticism of Paul the Apostle.* Translated by William Montgomery. New York: Henry Holt.

Shaner, Katherine. 2012. "Religion and the Civic Life of the Enslaved: A Case Study in Roman Ephesos." ThD Dissertation, Harvard University Divinity School.

Shewring, W. H., trans. 1929. *The Passion of Perpetua and Felicity.* London: The Fleuron. Modernized translation by Paul Halsall. 1996. "Medieval Sourcebook: St. Perpetua: *The Passion of Saints Perpetua and Felicity* 203." Internet Medieval Source Book. Fordham University Center for Medieval Studies. http://www.fordham.edu/halsall/source/perpetua.asp.

Skogen, Dan. 2009. "The Battle Continues For Nebraska Church Formerly Affiliated With the ELCA." *Exposing the ELCA.* http://www.exposingtheelca.com/exposed-blog/the-battle-continues-for-nebraska-church-formerly-affiliated-with-the-elca.

Slane, Kathleen Warner. 2000. "East-West Trade in Fine Wares and Commodities: the View from Corinth." *RCRFActa* 36:299–312.

Smith, James K. A. 2010. *Thinking in Tongues: Pentecostal Contributions to Christian Philosophy.* Grand Rapids: Eerdmans.

Smith, Jonathan Z. 2004. "Re: Corinthians." In *Relating Religion: Essays in the Study of Religion,* 340–61. Chicago: University of Chicago Press.

Spawforth, A. J. S. 1996. "Roman Corinth: The Formation of a Colonial Elite." In *Roman Onomastics in the Greek East: Social and Political Aspects,* edited by A. D. Rizakis, 167–82. Paris: Diffusion de Boccard.

Stang, Charles M. 2012. *Apophasis and Pseudonymity in Dionysius the Areopagite: "No Longer I."* New York: Oxford University Press.

Stendahl, Krister. 1976. *Paul Among Jews and Gentiles and Other Essays.* Minneapolis: Fortress Press.

Sterling, Gregory E. 1995. "Wisdom among the Perfect: Creation Traditions in Alexandrian Judaism and Corinthian Christianity." *NovT* 37, no. 4:355–84.

Still, E. Coye, III. 2002. "The Meaning and Uses of *EIDOLOTHYTON* in First Century Non-Pauline Literature and 1 Cor 8:1—11:1: Toward Resolution of the Debate." *Trinity Journal* 23, no. 2:225–34.

Stowers, Stanley K. 2011a. "Kinds of Myth, Meals, and Power: Paul and the Corinthians." In *Redescribing Paul and the Corinthians*, edited by Ron Cameron and Merrill P. Miller, 105–50. Atlanta: Society of Biblical Literature.

———. 2011b. "Does Pauline Christianity Resemble a Hellenistic Philosophy?" In *Redescribing Paul and the Corinthians*, edited by Ron Cameron and Merrill P. Miller, 219–44. Atlanta: Society of Biblical Literature.

———. 2011c. "The Concept of 'Community' and the History of Early Christianity." *Method and Theory in the Study of Religion* 23, nos. 3–4:238–56.

Svebakken, Hans. 2012. *Philo of Alexandria's Exposition of the Tenth Commandment.* Atlanta: Society of Biblical Literature.

Theissen, Gerd. 1982. *The Social Setting of Pauline Christianity: Essays on Corinth.* Edited and translated by John H. Schütz. Philadelphia: Fortress Press.

Thiselton, Anthony C. 2000. *The First Epistle to the Corinthians.* NIGTC. Grand Rapids: Eerdmans.

United Society of Believers, Commonly Called Shakers. 1848. "A Summary View of the Millennial Church." *Pass the Word Services.* http://www.passtheword.org/shaker-manuscripts/Millennial-Church/mchrch4x.htm.

Weissenrieder, Annette. 2012. "'Do You Not Know That You Are God's Temple?' Towards a New Perspective on Paul's Temple Image in 1 Corinthians 3:16." In *Contested Spaces: Houses and Temples in Roman Antiquity and the New Testament*, edited by David L. Balch and Annette Weissenrieder, 377–412. Tübingen: Mohr Siebeck.

West, A. B. 1931. *Corinth VIII, Part II: Latin Inscriptions, 1896–1926.* Cambridge, MA: ASCSA.

Wilckens, Ulrich. 1959. *Weisheit und Torheit: Eine exegetisch-religionsgeschichtliche Untersuchung zu 1 Kor 1 und 2. BHTh*, 26. Tübingen: Mohr.

Williams, Charles K., II. 1993. "Roman Corinth as a Commercial Center." In *The Corinthia in the Roman Period (JRASup 8)*, edited by T. E. Gregory, 31–46. Ann Arbor: JRA.

Winter, Bruce W. 2001. *After Paul Left Corinth: The Influence of Secular Ethics and Social Change.* Grand Rapids: Eerdmans.

Wire, Antoinette Clark. 1990. *The Corinthian Women Prophets: A Reconstruction through Paul's Rhetoric.* Minneapolis: Fortress Press.

World Council of Churches. 2014. "Week of Prayer for Christian Unity." World Council of Churches. http://www.oikoumene.org/en/press-centre/events/week-of-prayer-for-christian-unity.

Žižek, Slavoj. 2000. *The Fragile Absolute: or, Why is the Christian Legacy Worth Fighting For?* London: Verso.

2 CORINTHIANS

David E. Fredrickson

Introduction

Second Corinthians has impressed itself on scholars as a collection of originally separate Pauline writings, a quilt made of several letter fragments. The integrity of the letter has so been put in doubt that even Paul's authorship in the case of one passage (6:14—7:1) has, for plausible reasons, been called into question. The letter as we read it today appears to have seams, to have been sown together at a time unknown by an editor unnamed. Note the abrupt and, by current standards, inexplicable transitions between 2:13 and 14; 6:13 and 14; 7:1 and 2; 7:16 and 8:1; 8:24 and 9:1; and 9:15 and 10:1. For many interpreters, these appear to be awkwardly stitched together texts hinting at a history of compilation. And so it is frequently said that 2 Corinthians lacks argumentative flow. The simplest explanation is that the letter never possessed rhetorical unity since it was not in the strict sense *a* letter penned by Paul. This is the dominant scholarly opinion today, and it renders naïve any questions about the meaning of the letter considered as a whole, either in the first century, in the history of interpretation, or for modern readers.

Yet there is another way of reading 2 Corinthians, one that is not alarmed when letters written in or near the first century shift from topic to topic or change tone without warning (for the "mixed" type of letter, see Malherbe 1988, 73, 81). This approach bolsters the case for integrity by highlighting the continuity of themes and key terms across the letter. Along these lines, we might observe that the contrast Paul draws between himself and his opponents over severity and gentleness in leadership style runs throughout the letter, from 1:12 to 13:10 to be precise. Most importantly, this alternative way of reading defers final judgment concerning the letter's unity until it reconstructs events and emotions between Paul's sending of 1 Corinthians and his composition of 2 Corinthians. This present approach *presumes* the letter's unity and uses passages throughout to imagine a complicated situation between Paul and the church at Corinth, which only a complex letter, appearing to some readers as having seams, could even hope to address.

It appears, then, that we have arrived at a method of reading the letter. First, there is a need to discern the situation and then observe what Paul has to say to it. But a word of warning is in order: not only must our reconstruction remain tentative and open to revision, but we must also admit that the story of Paul and the Corinthians is entirely a Pauline fiction. (Actually, it is my fiction about Paul's fiction.) That is, there is no way for us to see through the letter to "what really happened" between the two Corinthian letters. All we have is the way *Paul* wants his readers to see what happened and what it all means. A clear division between context and text or between occasion and rhetoric is therefore an illusion. Paul's construal of persons, events, and emotions is rhetorical from the very start. That does not make the backstory of 2 Corinthians narrated below any less interesting. It does demand, however, that any interpretation, and that certainly includes this essay, confess that it is a fiction, provisional, and risks being taken in unanticipated directions. I emphasize this demand at the beginning of the essay, since habits of the biblical commentary genre will induce me to write as if I had forgotten it.

So where to begin in *imagining* the events and emotions as Paul wants his first readers to think of them? Second Corinthians 1:8-9 tells a dismal tale of Paul's journey in Asia, one of melancholy and thoughts of suicide. Christian writers of the fourth century, perhaps alarmed at the sadness of the apostle, thought Paul was describing external events: his arrest, a court's death sentence, and the apprehension anyone would feel in such circumstances (see Fredrickson 2000). But the phrase "we ourselves in ourselves had the sentence of death" (here and below, my own translation) would more likely have been understood in the first century as self-condemnation, the feelings that overwhelm the soul with regret or remorse. Regret arose from the paradox of the stern judge and convicted offender inhabiting the same body.

What did Paul have to regret? In 2 Cor. 7:8, he speaks plainly about the matter: he had written a letter to the church powerful enough to induce pain in the readers. He refers to this letter in 2:3-4 as he denies that it was his intention to cause grief, thus, of course, reinforcing our sense that he did. This is the so-called letter of tears, which has puzzled interpreters for centuries. John Chrysostom thought this letter was 1 Corinthians itself. Today some scholars identify it as 2 Corinthians 10–13, although a third opinion, one the present essayist shares, holds that the letter is lost and not to be identified with any extant Pauline writing and therefore a bit of a mystery (see Furnish, 163–68). But thanks to Ps.-Libanius and Ps.-Demetrius, unknown authors of the two surviving ancient epistolary handbooks, there are some helpful clues (see Malherbe 1988, 30–41, 66–81). These handbooks gave instructions on how to write a grieving letter (*epistolē lypētikē*), and when the many actual letters of grief in antiquity (e.g., Ps.-Demosthenes, *Ep.* 2) are also consulted, we learn that a letter writer's grieving self-presentation was intended, and understood by recipients, as stinging moral reproof (see Fredrickson 2001). To paraphrase the critical portion of these letters: "The tears through which I write are evidence of the grief your behavior has caused me."

What did the church at Corinth do to cause Paul pain? Paul hints in 2:1 at an unplanned visit to Corinth. He made this trip presumably because 1 Corinthians, the letter carried by Timothy, did not have its desired effect of discouraging the elite from displaying their social status, the main problem addressed in that letter. During this impromptu visit, Paul was injured or treated unjustly by some member of the church (Barrett 1970). He alludes to this event tactfully in 2:5 and mentions the offender directly in 7:12 ("the one who injured"), though still without naming him. He refers to himself as "the one injured." Here is the point: the church, for its part, took no action against the one who had treated Paul unjustly during his unplanned visit. So Paul fled to Ephesus and from a distance wrote the "letter of tears," rebuking the community for its indifference to the injury he suffered. Titus took this epistle to Corinth.

As Paul tells this story, when the letter arrived in Corinth under Titus's care it had a double effect. On the one hand, it caused the Corinthian church grief, yes, but a "grief according to God," as Paul assures his readers, since the letter's severity issued in their repentance. That is, it aroused the readers' zeal for Paul (7:7, 11-12). On the other hand, the community's newfound resolve to discipline the offender was excessive; note the term "vengeance" (*ekdikēsis*) in 7:11. In its response to the letter of tears, then, it seems that the church swung around wildly from its former indifference to the offense committed against Paul. The harshness of their treatment of the offender is indicated in the term *epitimia*, which stands behind the English term "punishment" in 2:6. *Epitimia* held a special place in Greco-Roman moral exhortation. It was moral chastisement intended to cause shame, a particularly extreme measure in the honor-seeking society of the first century, especially if it was delivered in public (see Malherbe 1983). It was a commonplace worry for ancient moral guides in antiquity, except among harsh Cynics (see Malherbe 1989), that public reproof, particularly of young men, might result in suicide (see, e.g., Plutarch, *How to Tell a Flatterer from a Friend* 70F–71C). It is no wonder, then, that Paul expresses concern for the offender; he is liable to being "drunk down by excessive grief" (2:7), a euphemism for suicide.

The letter of tears had one more effect, though if we are to understand it, one more set of players in Corinth must be introduced. As if the relationship between Paul and the church were not complicated enough, missionaries critical of Paul's manner of ministry entered Corinth, most likely after his flight to Ephesus. In his absence, they competed with him (and with one another? see 2 Cor. 10:12) for the community's allegiance. Paul calls them "super-apostles" (2 Cor. 11:5 and 12:11) and characterizes them in terms reminiscent of harsh Cynic philosophers who sought to dominate those they led (Malherbe 1970). Again, it must be emphasized that this depiction of his rivals is Paul's: his portrayal of them as severe moralists accentuates his own image as conciliatory, gentle, and gracious. Yet the issue of Paul's free speech was far broader than Paul and his relationship with the Corinthians. A fundamental disagreement about the nature of frank speech raged (sometimes within the same author) from the Hellenistic period well into late antiquity: Was it to be viewed as the verbal expression of the wise man's moral independence, or was it to be regarded as a means to improve others in the context of friendly relations? (For a study in *parrēsia* as display of freedom and as the art of moral improvement, see John Chrysostom's encomium of Babylas, *De sancto hiero-martyre Babyla* [PG 50:541–46]).

What did these rival apostles think of the letter of tears? They praised it for its severity; but they also contrasted the letter's power at a distance with Paul's deficient physical presence and his ironic and deceptive spoken words. In what might be regarded as the earliest commentary on the Pauline Epistles, 2 Cor. 10:9-10 describes the characterization of Paul's own letters that he attributes to his rivals. The passage is saturated with terminology from ancient rhetorical handbooks and treatises. "To frighten," "weighty," and "strong" are the markers of "forcefulness" (*deinotēs*), a style of speaking in which orators, most notably in the ancient world Demosthenes (see Dionysius of Halicarnassus, *Demosthenes* 22), overwhelmed audiences. Two additional phrases indicate the super-apostles' familiarity with ancient rhetorical and literary criticism: "presence of the body" and "attenuated speech" (*ho logos exouthenēmenos*, my translation: see Fredrickson 2001). "They say" Paul's physical presence, a reference in rhetorical terms to oratorical delivery, is weak, and that he intentionally makes his speech less forceful than he could (as judged by the letters) and more like the utterings of persons of low esteem, much in the style of Socrates, whose ironic self-deprecation pricked holes in puffed-up dialogue partners. So the letter of tears was just one more piece of evidence that Paul in the church's presence was deceptive and lacked the frank speech, the quality of *deinotēs*, that marked true apostles. This charge of disparity between words and deeds Paul vigorously disputes in 10:10 and throughout the letter, as we will see below.

So here are the issues facing Paul on the eve of 2 Corinthians. First, Paul is in an impossible position. He must assert that he possesses frank speech, but the medium for his apology is a letter, and as he writes from a distance, he runs the risk of convicting himself of the very charges summarized in 10:9-10. This problem he takes up in 2 Cor. 2:14—4:6. Second, the individual who wronged Paul has been isolated from the community; Paul exhorts the community to bring him back in 2:5-11. Third, even though the church responded to the letter of tears positively by disciplining the offender, the grief (or was it resentment or vexation?) lingered on; Paul confronts this issue in 4:7—7:16 as he places his frank speech into the ancient tradition of friendship, stresses his love for the church, and appeals for reconciliation. To further assuage hard feelings, he accentuates his regret for ever having written the letter (1:8-9 and 7:8). The final purpose of 2 Corinthians, if the present reconstruction of the letter's occasion is at all plausible, is to dissuade the church from recognizing the legitimacy of the super-apostles and their harsh form of leadership; this he does sporadically in 2 Corinthians 1–7 and pointedly in chapters 10–13.

Nothing has yet been said about 2 Corinthians 8–9. These chapters deal with the collection for the saints in Jerusalem. In 1 Cor. 16:1-9, Paul had tailored his travel plans around his pivotal role in organizing a fund from the churches of Galatia, Macedonia, and Corinth for the relief of communities in Jerusalem. The problem for Paul was how to encourage the Corinthians to make good on their promise to contribute without reinforcing the patron-client ideology that permeated all charitable activities in the Roman period. Gift-giving in general symbolized the social difference between giver and recipient and announced the former's power and superiority while emphasizing the latter's neediness and obligation to repay the gift through public glorification of the giver. This is precisely the problem Paul attacks so energetically in 1 Corinthians. It also explains why Paul shuns the financial support of the Corinthian elite in 2 Corinthians 10–13: simply put, he doesn't want to be owned (see Marshall). Finally, it is worth considering that domination hidden in the gift-giving of ancient society and potentially, Paul fears, in the collection for the saints in Jerusalem resembles the sovereignty in disciplinary matters that the super-apostles exhibit. In other words, patronal power and super-apostle severity are two instances of domination. Paul's opposition to any form of lordship that is not inhabited by the crucified Messiah is a central feature in all of his letters and especially here in 2 Corinthians. This makes him a sharp, if indirect, critic of empire.

2 Corinthians 1:1-7: The Sound of P

◼ THE TEXT IN ITS ANCIENT CONTEXT

The Greek letter *pi* (*p*) is repeated twenty-six times in these verses. There is comfort in the repetition of sounds, as in the sincere utterance of "there, there." Each time the letter *pi* is pronounced, lips meet, puffing a bit of breath toward the other person. An intimacy adheres to these hesitant vocalizations, a gentle insistence of breath. *Parakalō* and its noun cognate *paraklēsis* together occur ten times. Perhaps Paul entreats, or does he exhort? *Parakalō* could mean either, and it is impossible to say with certainty which is meant here. Another word starting with *pi* in this passage is *pathēma*. This word bears a double character also: it meant suffering, but included both exterior and interior aspects. Thus it signifies pain inflicted on Paul from without (beatings or maltreatment, for example), or it could refer to emotions themselves, like love, or regret (cf. Rom. 8:18; Phil. 3:10). It, with its cognate *paschein* ("to suffer"), occurs four times.

Paul clearly departed from his usual practice of beginning a letter by thanking God for the very issues he addresses in the rest of the text (e.g., 1 Cor. 1:4-9; Phil. 1:3-11). Does this mean that 1:3-7 is unrelated to the rest of the letter? Not at all. *Parakalō* ("I exhort" or "entreat") in its second sense anticipates the grace, gentleness, and forgiveness in Paul's manner of leadership in contrast to the severity of the super-apostles. Yet the dueling meaning within the one word also anticipates the movement of Paul between the reproof of the letter of tears and his begging for reconciliation.

Note further that in 1:3 Paul links his manner of ministry to divine names: the father of compassionate feelings (*oiktirmos* suggests the vocalizations of ritual lament, "keening" in other words) and the God of all exhorting/entreating. The association of Paul's grace in ministry with God's grace is the primary form of Paul's apology through the letter (e.g., 5:18—6:2). Similarly, in 1:5, Paul and Christ are, insofar as emotions (*pathēmata*) are concerned, indistinguishable (cf. Phil. 1:8), and that goes a long way to defending his form of ministry. Paul develops the motif of his sharing of emotions/suffering with Christ throughout the letter and includes the Corinthians in 1:6-7. Finally, in verse 7, he states his hope about the community; this is yet another way of exhorting/begging. The content of his hope (there is, incidentally, another *pi* in the middle of *elpis*) is unstated at this point, but the position of *paraklēsis* at the end of the sentence suggests the church has its own comforting to do by restoring the offender (2:7) and continuing to mend fences with Paul (1:13-14; 4:14-15; 6:20—7:4).

◼ THE TEXT IN THE INTERPRETIVE TRADITION

Early Christian commentators took from these first verses clues to the nature of the whole letter and emphasized the "consolation" in the midst of suffering that Paul proclaims. Pelagius, however, focused on Paul's setting his name before his recipients, adopting "the custom of secular judges," because "he is an apostle who is writing to those who are accountable to him"; he thus emphasized the element of correction throughout the letter (*Commentary*).

It is also the case that commentators diminished the passionate side of many Pauline terms in this letter (e.g., see below on "weakness" in 13:4). Their treatment of *pathēmata* in 1:1-7 is no exception. I translated the word above as "emotions." The English "sufferings" expresses the view of early commentators that Paul has in mind things done to him, shipwreck or imprisonment for example, not stirrings within his soul difficult or impossible to control like grief or desire (see John Chrysostom, *In epistulam ii ad Corinthios* [*homiliae 1–30*, PG 61:579]; but for a combination of the inner and outer aspects see Theodorus Studites, *Epistulae* 252.15). A similar downplaying of passion can be seen in the case of *oiktirmos* (1:3). In the interpretive tradition, the word came to be defined by the benefactor and his *philanthropia* ("love for humanity"). This redefinition dulled the sharp edge of violent emotion conveyed by the word in the case, for example, of the widow or childless mother keening the death of her loved one (see John Chrysostom, *De corruptoribus virginum* [PG 60:744]). The New Testament itself is partly responsible for adding a sense of condescension to this term (see Luke 6:36), but beginning with Clement of Alexandria (*Protrepticus* 1.8.4), the Christian tradition substituted a philanthropic wish on God's part to save humanity and show it mercy for a divine desire for communion with humanity.

▌ THE TEXT IN CONTEMPORARY DISCUSSION

The "Father of all compassionate feelings and the God of all entreaties" (2 Cor. 1:3) is a weak and unsuitable God for those who, like the super-apostles, see church leadership in terms of issuing divine commands from a position of dispassionate invulnerability. The adequacy of the philosophical idea of impassibility for the representation of God in the Old Testament has been called into question by biblical interpreters (see, e.g., Fretheim). Christian theology's comfort with a self-constituting and self-sufficient God has been sharply critiqued by Jürgen Moltmann (1974) as he put a question to the tradition seldom asked in Christian theology: What did the death of the Son mean for the Father?

2 Corinthians 1:8-13: Reconciliation as Resurrection

▌ THE TEXT IN ITS ANCIENT CONTEXT

As previously noted, in 1:8-9 Paul uses the ancient rhetoric of regret to communicate to the church his turbulent emotional state after he sent the letter of tears but before he met up with Titus in Macedonia. Such self-disclosure might have itself been seen as a gesture of reconciliation (see Aristotle, *Nicomachean Ethics* 1110b 18–30), since Paul implies that he did not delight in criticizing the church. In fact, the uncertainty of his relationship with the community after he wrote severely weighs Paul down to the point of considering suicide, if his readers are to believe these self-revelations, as he makes his way through Asia.

Unlike those whose confidence is based on themselves (perhaps a dig at the super-apostles; see 3:5 and Phil. 3:2-4), Paul's boldness for life and ministry resides in his relationship to the church (see 1:14; cf. Phil. 4:1; 1 Thess. 2:19-20). For this reason, his report of rescue by the God who raises the dead is a theological interpretation of the Corinthians' change of heart reported by Titus (see 7:6-7). The church's (tentative?) steps toward Paul are portrayed as the working of God (cf. Phil 2:13), and in verses 10-11 he hopes for further rescue/reconciliation. Finally, it is significant that, located between two theologically rich understandings of the church as communion (1:11 and 14), we find the charge of "fleshly wisdom" leveled at Paul by the super-apostles. What Paul understands as a ministry growing out of the bonds of friendship, whose speech embodies "openness" and "sincerity" (both synonyms for *parrēsia*) and exhibits "the grace of God," his opponents characterize as rhetorical trickery. That fundamental tension between Paul and his rivals runs through 2 Corinthians from beginning to end.

▌ THE TEXT IN THE INTERPRETIVE TRADITION

Early Christian commentators took Paul at his word when he declares his sincerity (*eilikrineia*), a term that in conjunction with *haplotēs* ("frankness," NRSV) in rhetorical theory was a matter of straightforward and clear language in contrast to artificiality and the concealment of figured speech (see Smiley, 219–24). John Chrysostom praised Paul for this very reason (*Homilies in 2 Cor.* [PG 61:405–6]). Theodoret of Cyrus was likewise impressed: Paul "teaches only what he has been taught by the grace of God, adding nothing of his own to it. . . . The facts speak for themselves and prove that he is right" (*Commentary*). The fathers' enthusiasm for Paul's *eilikrineia* may have come from the central role this term played in ancient rhetorical handbooks, where it connoted the opposite of irony, flattery, and particularly the moral criticism carried out under cover of rhetorical figures (Fiore). In short, early interpreters thought Paul's sincerity was synonymous with his *parrēsia*.

▌ THE TEXT IN CONTEMPORARY DISCUSSION

One dramatic difference between early Christian commentary on Paul's letters and contemporary scholarship is the attention given in the latter to Paul's persuasive speech, that is, rhetoric. Rather than presuming, for example, that Paul really has despaired of life and seeking to identify the "affliction" he suffered (1:8), scholars ask about the rhetorical effect of such claims. While this approach has proven very fruitful, and is employed in this essay, it sometimes raises the question of whether Paul was manipulative, since today's readers often associate "rhetoric" with speech that gets its way dishonestly. That there is no easy response, or perhaps no response at all, to this modern doubt about Paul is indicated by the undeniable similarity between his self-revelations in 1:8 (and in 7:8-12) and the contemporary rhetoric of domestic violence: "I know I hurt you; it pains me that I hurt you; but I only wanted to show my love; I will harm myself if you do not forgive me." Rhetorical analysis cannot by itself determine whether Paul meant what he said, only how it *might* have been heard by a first-century audience.

2 Corinthians 1:15—2:4: If I Am a Flatterer, Then So Is God

▌ THE TEXT IN ITS ANCIENT CONTEXT

A pattern in Paul's argumentation is emerging. Paul's style of ministry mimics God's; his emotions are indistinguishable from Christ's. To fault him is to fault God. To oppose him is to oppose Christ.

In this passage Paul deflects the super-apostles' charge of flattery by implicating God in the same yes-saying that he, Silvanus, and Timothy make the core of their preaching (for the "light touch" in 1:17 as a sign of flattery see Plutarch, *How to Tell a Flatterer from a Friend* 65B; 71F). The topic of flattery here is not in question, since from Cicero (*De amicitia* 93) we learn that the phrase "Yes, yes and No, no" had broad circulation as early as the first century BCE. It was a proverbial expression for the flatterer's malleability and desire to please and had been lifted from its original literary context of a play by Terence. The flatterer is devious; he wins victims over by posing as a friend and telling them what they want to hear. Flatterers transform themselves into the ones they seek to please, a behavior Paul's adaptability in 1 Cor. 9:19-23 dangerously approaches. Paul, however, argues that his change of travel plans (1:15-16) is not evidence of flattery but proof of his desire to spare the church further grief, a point he reiterates in 1:23—2:4.

In 1:18-22, Paul presents himself and God not as flatterers, though they do say only "yes," but as friends, as the term *pistos* ("faithful") in verse 18 and the verb *bebaioō* (lit., "I make firm or constant") in verse 21 indicate. These two terms were commonly associated with the motif of friendship (see Xenophon, *Memorabilia* 2.6.20; and Lucian, *Toxaris* 6–7, 9, 20, 35, 63) and now in Paul's use define the relationship of God with the community and the community with Paul.

▌ THE TEXT IN THE INTERPRETIVE TRADITION

What did the early church make of Paul's letter of tears (2:4)? John Chrysostom made a proposal that persuaded many later commentators: the letter of tears is actually 1 Corinthians. Chrysostom thought the offender mentioned in 2 Cor. 2:5-11 was the same person singled out for discipline in 1 Cor. 5:1. While this solution has several obvious deficiencies, which modern commentaries do not fail to point out, one cannot keep from admiring its simplicity. But the chief problem with the proposal is this: in 1 Corinthians, Paul does not present himself as grieving. There is no reason to categorize it as a grieving letter (*epistolē lypētikē*).

▌ THE TEXT IN CONTEMPORARY DISCUSSION

Some scholars have suggested that we look no further than 2 Corinthians 10–13 to find Paul's "letter of tears" (see Watson). This would be a simple solution if it were not the case that in this portion of the letter Paul does not present himself as grieving, aside from the possibility of lament he mentions in 12:31. Furthermore, the "letter of tears" dealt with an individual's unjust act, but 2 Corinthians 10–13 concerns the super-apostles' rivalry with Paul. (For additional reasons to doubt identification of the "letter of tears" with chapters 10–13, see Amador.)

2 Corinthians 2:5-11: Shame and Satan

▌ THE TEXT IN ITS ANCIENT CONTEXT

This passage is the gateway to the rest of 2 Corinthians 1–7. Later arguments are anticipated as Paul seeks to persuade the community to forgive and accept the offender who had been disciplined and put to shame. Paul turns the injury from himself (2:5, 10) and stresses that now the community must forgive and confirm love. Here Paul is performing, and asking the church to enact, the inconsistency that the super-apostles perceive in Paul's ministry. A true apostle, they would assert, is severe (see 13:3), and the true church would enforce discipline without reprieve. But Paul detects the bullying and begrudging Satan (2:11) in such a one-sided approach to pastoral care. Paul sees the face of Christ, however, in the act of forgiveness (2:10). And then, in order to ground his ministry in Christ's lordship (which does not exclude weakness) and God's grace, Paul takes his readers on an extensive literary digression in 2:12—7:4, which echoes his painful procession to reunite with Titus in Macedonia.

THE TEXT IN THE INTERPRETIVE TRADITION

Paul's characterization of Satan as an envious bully (2 Cor. 2:11) would become a stock theme in early Christianity. Envy (!) entered the garden to corrupt Adam and Eve and their descendants (see Theophilus, *Ad Autolycum* 2.29; Epiphanius, *Panarion* 3.416.1; Antiochus Monachus, *Pandecta scripturae sacrae* 55). In this regard, there is an intriguing overlap in Christian and Hellenistic traditions as they grow and influence one another in late antiquity. Envy, understood as begrudging the happiness of another, was a prominent *theological* explanation among Greeks for human disappointment and loss (see Plutarch, *Consolatio ad Apollonium* 105B). In erotic relationships, personified Envy was blamed for separations (see Chariton, *Chareas and Callirhoe* 1.1.16; Nicetas Eugenianus, *Drosilla and Charicles* 1.52–53).

THE TEXT IN CONTEMPORARY DISCUSSION

Readers interested in connecting Paul's concern about the shaming and isolating effects of punishment with current criticism of the American criminal justice system might consult the recently adopted social statement of the Evangelical Lutheran Church in America (see "The Church and Criminal Justice: Hearing the Cries," at http://www.elca.org/en/Faith/Faith-and-Society/Social-Statements/Criminal-Justice). The complicity of some Christian beliefs in the needless worsening of offenders' lives is slowly coming into general consciousness. For centuries, Christians have promoted biblical texts that view the purpose of punishment to be the isolation and destruction of offenders (see, e.g., 2 Peter). Christians elect state and federal legislators who pass laws requiring or enabling mass incarceration, mandatory sentencing, the location of prisons far removed from families and other systems of support, solitary confinement, and other collateral punishments that work through the harsh logic of isolation. It is sobering to think that Paul regards the self-destructive results of enforced isolation as the work of Satan.

2 Corinthians 2:12—3:3: Topography of an Apostle's Heart

THE TEXT IN ITS ANCIENT CONTEXT

This is a provocative definition of the rhetorical unit since, as I noted above, many scholars detect a seam between verses 13 and 14. They suggest that 2:14—7:5 (with the possible exception of 6:14—7:1) was taken from another Pauline epistle and inserted into an opening created by cutting between 2:13 and what is now 7:5. Attractive as this theory might be (it accounts for what would otherwise be a delayed thanksgiving period in 2:14), there are thematic continuities that make the proposal of interpolation unnecessary. Note the place names in verses 12-13 (Troas and Macedonia) and Paul's reference to "every place" in verse 14. Along these lines, the term *thriambeuein* ("to lead in triumphal procession") suggests movement, while in verses 12-13 Paul discuss his travel in some detail. But the most striking connection between the writing before and after the conjectured seam is the resonance between Paul's having "no relief" at not finding Titus and the apostle's being led in a triumphal procession. A brief explanation of the Roman triumph, and of its adaptation by ancient erotic writers (primarily in poetry and ancient romance), is in order.

Roman generals had the practice of degrading foreign nobility captured in military campaigns by parading them as slaves through the streets of Rome. For poets and novelists, Eros conquered, enslaved, and forced the rejected lover, or the one uncertain of the beloved's response, to march in an equally humiliating procession (see Ovid, *Amores* 1.2.19–52; and Miller). Two other motifs, both of which figure prominently in 2 Corinthians, were often allied with the lover led in triumph. *Servitium amoris* (the slavery of love; see Murgatroyd) depicted the lover's paradoxical "voluntary slavery" (e.g., Plato, *Symposium* 184C), degrading loss of self-control (Zagagi), and lovesickness even to the point of death (Xenophon, *Symposium* 4.14; Achilles Tatius, *Leucippe and Clitophon* 1.7.2–3). Paul deploys the other popular motif, *Amor vincit omnia* ("Love conquers all"), in 2:14 and extensively in 2 Corinthians 10–13.

So, how does Paul turn the erotic connotations of the triumph motif to his rhetorical aim of conciliating the Corinthians to himself? The metaphor presents Paul suffering a lover's pain, the grief of separation from his beloved community, and, more significantly, apprehension over its response to his stinging reproof in the letter of tears. He presents himself suffering with self-accusation and worry, not unlike the unrequited lover of Latin elegy, whose every thought is about the beloved's rejection. Moreover, note that *God* leads Paul in this triumphal procession. This is striking not only because readers knew that Eros plays the part of conquering general in love poetry but even more because knowledge of God is apparent for all who see into Paul's experience, which he has been narrating since "our affliction" in 1:4. Some, of course, will smell nothing but the odor of death; presumably Paul wants readers to think of the super-apostles here. Paul's readers, however, *if and as they remain true to him*, will perceive the fragrance of life in his socially demeaning and soul-draining love for them.

▌ THE TEXT IN THE INTERPRETIVE TRADITION

For over a thousand years, "Love conquers all" lay dormant, but when it awoke in the Middle Ages it was applied to Pauline texts with vigor. Even God is vanquished by love for humanity, according to Bernard of Clairvaux (*Sermon* 64.10 [PL 183:1088]). Hadewijch of Antwerp thought so too.

> What seems to the loved soul the most beautiful encounter
> Is that it should love the Beloved so fully
> And so gain knowledge of the Beloved with love
> That nothing else is known by it

Except: "I am conquered by Love"
But he who overcame Love was rather conquered
So that he might in love be brought to naught
God the lover is victim of love. (*Poems in Stanzas* 8.71–77)

In the fourteenth century, the Byzantine theologian Nicholas Cabasilas, writing about the christo-logical topic of *kenosis* ("emptying"), likens the God emptied by *erōs* first to the "locked out lover," perhaps the most popular ancient cliché depicting the slave of love, and then to the "lover led in a triumphal procession" (*thriambeuein erastēn*: *The Life in Christ* 6.3). Even though it took over a thousand years, the erotic motif of triumph in 2 Cor. 2:14 opened a way into the passion of God that had been foreclosed by the philosophically inspired doctrine of divine impassibility.

2 Corinthians 3:1-18: Frank Speech and Moses' Face

▌THE TEXT IN ITS ANCIENT CONTEXT

This section is a carefully crafted argument resting to a great degree on Paul's playfulness with the Greek language, and therefore difficult to appreciate in English translation. Nevertheless, some points can be made. In 3:12, Paul claims to use the very *parrēsia* ("frank" or "free speech," not "boldness" as the NRSV translates; see Fredrickson 1996) that his opponents charge that he lacks. Paul's rhetorical predicament lies in the fact that he makes this claim at a distance, through a letter; for Paul simply to assert his free speech would be to confirm the criticism directed against him. His solution is this: rather than giving proof of his confidence based on his own power (3:5), Paul appeals to the Spirit, whose work was to inscribe the Corinthians in his heart (3:2-3; for the eroti-cism of such writing, see *Greek Anthology* 12.57).

The Spirit is life-making precisely in this way, by its deepening of *philia* ("friendship") to the point of love (*erōs* or *agapē*). *Parrēsia* of this kind is the language of friendship, as Plutarch once remarked (*How to Tell a Flatterer from a Friend* 51C), not the verbal expression of an individual's freedom attained through self-control and moral accomplishment, as many philosophers (and most likely the super-apostles) taught. If *parrēsia* is a function of friendship, Paul argues, then the new covenant (literally "new arrangement"), which is love and longing for communion kindled by gazing at another's face and being looked upon (cf. 1 Cor. 13:12), guarantees free speech to all, wherever the Spirit is. The covenant of death, though having a glory of its own, is the application of written laws and commands; it does not create friendship and is unable to kindle the gaze upon the face of another and experience the other in his or her singularity, as the sons of Israel discover (3:7).

Moses' face plays an equally important role in the second of the proofs of Paul's *parrēsia* (3:12-18). The argument here is structured according to the rhetorical technique of comparison (*synkrisis*), using negative and positive examples. Paul is not like Moses, who covered his face, a movement in Greek culture associated with shame. Moses veiled his face so that the "sons of Israel" might not gaze upon the *telos* ("end," in the sense of intended result) of "that which is being nullified," pre-sumably the old covenant. The shaming effect of that which is written on stone was alluded to in 3:9 in two ways. First, the word Paul uses to describe the end result of the new covenant, *glory*, was generally understood as the opposite of shame. Second, the old covenant is described as a ministry of condemnation. It is tempting to think that Paul is describing the situation of the disciplined offender in 2:5-11. He, Moses, the "sons of Israel" (3:14-15), and perhaps Paul himself—as he made his way through Asia to Macedonia, despairing of life over the alienation he feared his *grammata* ("letters") had worked on the Corinthian church—they are all caught up in the ministry of death.

But Moses' face does not remain veiled. Verse 16 should be translated, "whenever he [not "one"] turned to the Lord, the veil was taken away." The "he" is Moses in his role as positive example. Paul, indeed the whole church, is *just like* Moses, who in that moment of face-to-face intimacy with the Lord, an intimacy created by the Spirit, is free, and if free, then bold of speech, since the two words *eleutheria* and *parrēsia* were nearly synonymous. So once again Paul bases his free speech not on individual power or accomplishment but on a Spirit-made intimacy in which "we all" (3:18) are free in the moment of an uncovered face, as in the climactic instant of the ancient Greek wedding when the bride—her veil swept aside in the moment of *apokalypsis*—and groom gazed without shame on each other's face. The political consequences of 3:18 are staggering when contrasted with the ancient world's limitation of freedom and frank speech to elite male citizens. In the phrase "we all," Paul envisions a community of any and all persons, all equally free to speak their minds, as they simultaneously gaze upon one another as if in a mirror and in this way are transformed into what they see, Christ the image of God (cf. 4:4).

▊ THE TEXT IN THE INTERPRETIVE TRADITION

"For the letter kills, but the Spirit gives life" (3:6). No other Pauline phrase so profoundly set the course of Christian biblical interpretation and theology. Early on, Paul's distinction between letter and Spirit, in which he clearly prefers Spirit over letter, was interpreted as the difference between text and the author's intention (see Grant). At least three consequences flowed from this reading: first, it paved the way for the phonocentrism of Greek philosophy to overtake Christian theology. What is phonocentrism? Jacques Derrida has analyzed texts in the Western intellectual tradition, from Plato (see especially *Phaedrus* 275C–276E) to the twentieth century, and has pointed out the tradition's unjustified preference for voice over writing. Yet it is not Derrida's point simply to reverse the two by awarding to writing a privileged status over voice. Rather, he shows that what philosophers understand as the deficiencies (Derrida would not use this term) of writing affect the voice as well, but very few thinkers ever admit this. For example, it is generally agreed that writing inevitably destabilizes meaning, since the mortality of the author and that of the reader leave no enduring witness to what was meant when the text was composed. The move that characterizes phonocentrism is to claim that the everyday experience of hearing oneself think or the perceived immediacy of speaking one's thoughts proves that voice mitigates the danger of contaminating one's thoughts. The voice holds and protects the idea from contamination, so it is claimed in phonocentrism, as it travels from one's mind through the external world through another's ear and ultimately to his or her own interiority. In short, phonocentrism thinks of voice as a somewhat successful substitute for the thinking one does silently in one's head; but writing, in this view, as a phonetic system representing voice in the speaker's absence, is merely a substitute for a substitute and thus two steps removed from self-present thought (see Culler, 89–110). From the phonocentric perspective, then, the letter kills in the sense that it fails to live up to the voice's power to deliver the speaker's thoughts. Second, the misconstrued distinction between letter and Spirit enabled Christians to appropriate the allegorical method employed by Stoics (and others) in the interpretation of Homer and thus created a special class of spiritual persons who presumed they could read past the literal meaning of texts into God's mind. Third, the distinction between letter and Spirit contributes to animosity against Jews, who, according to the Christian interpretation of Paul's distinction, are incapable of knowing the meaning of their own Scriptures.

▌THE TEXT IN CONTEMPORARY DISCUSSION

Paul's reasoning from friendship and the face here bears an intriguing resemblance to recent approaches to ethics by writers influenced by Jacques Derrida and Emmanuel Levinas (see, e.g., Caputo 1993; for the related idea of *perichōrēsis* in recent trinitarian theology and ecclesiology, see Moltmann 2000). Nevertheless, Derrida's wariness of the reduction of friendship to brotherhood in Western political philosophy, which buys the communion of some at the price of excluding others, must be kept in mind (Derrida). Does Paul himself fall into the trap of building a community on the backs of others, that is, on the exclusion of "the sons of Israel" (3:7)? This question, which can only be raised here and not answered, is crucial in light of the comparison Paul makes between the two covenants in 3:4-18. It is not possible to rescue Paul from the charge of anti-Judaism simply by pointing out that it is the old covenant that is nullified (3:14) and not Judaism itself. Is there a difference between covenant and Judaism, or enough of a difference between the two so that Christ's nullification of the former does not mean the destruction of the latter?

2 Corinthians 4:1-6: Your Slaves

▌THE TEXT IN ITS ANCIENT CONTEXT

In 4:1-3, Paul reiterates his claim that he possesses all the boldness and openness necessary for an apostle of Christ, and if anyone (think super-apostles here) thinks his gospel is hidden or that he is playing tricks on the Corinthians with his talk of grace and forgiveness, then it must be that the god of this age (think Satan here) has blinded their minds. A word about the two major ancient theories of vision might be helpful at this point. One theory, which posits that very small bits of objects break off and pass through the air into the soul via the eyes, plays no role here. The other imagines a light in the soul or mind, burning like a lamp and sending out its rays through the eyes to illumine external objects. From this latter perspective, to be blinded is to have one's internal fire extinguished. That is what Paul says the god of this age has done to his opponents. They have no fire. In them, no beams of light proceed from an internal fire, and this suggests that they lack love or desire, which was also conceptualized as burning within the innards (cf. 1 Cor. 7:9; 2 Cor. 11:29). They do not love the Corinthians as Paul does; rather, Paul implies, they preach themselves as lords over the community (cf. 2 Cor. 1:24; 11:20).

In contrast, Paul preaches himself as the community's slave (4:5). Paul once more alludes to the *servitium amoris* motif so popular in the erotic literature of the ancient world (see comments on 2:14 above). He loves the Corinthians madly and without regard for his own dignity, and he does so in imitation of Jesus ("on account of Jesus"), who took the form of a slave (see Phil. 2:7).

■ The Text in the Interpretive Tradition

The Christian tradition by and large has suppressed Paul's vision of a lovesick, servile Christ who is here Paul's model for imitation. The authors of Colossians and Ephesians, for example, eliminated the motif of Christ as slave as they revised Paul's theology and substituted their philosophically influenced gospel of self-control. But there are moments in the tradition when poetry returns Christology to Paul's daring appropriation of the slavery motif, which we find in Phil. 2:7 as well. Guerric of Igny (1080–1157) is a good example of a writer turning Christ's slavery away from obedience to God the Father and toward humanity.

> "I will not serve," man says to his Creator. "Then I will serve you," his Creator says to man. "You sit down. I will minister, I will wash your feet. You rest; I will bear your weariness, your infirmities. Use me as you like in all your needs, not only as your slave but also as your beast of burden and as your property." (*Sermon* 29.1; Monks of Mount Saint Bernard Abbey, 2:55–56)

At the end of the thirteenth century or the beginning of the fourteenth, the Italian mystic Jacopone da Todi spoke to Jesus in a way that likely would not have displeased Paul.

> You went about the world as if you were drunk,
> Led by Love as if you were a slave . . .

■ The Text in Contemporary Discussion

Paul's introduction of slavery into his discourse about Christ and about his own ministry have not gone unnoticed by contemporary scholars. Some quite correctly criticize the way the idea of Jesus as a slave (to God, as it is almost always assumed) has legitimated various forms of domination within the church and in secular social institutions influenced by Christianity (Briggs). Recognition that the figure of the popular leader (demagogue) in ancient democracies was frequently described in servile terms (Martin 1990) goes some distance in undermining the oppressive potential of this motif. For many other scholars, however, Jesus' slavery to God is not at all problematic—quite the opposite, since they think his obedience as the "new Adam" reverses the disobedience of the first Adam, thereby offering salvation and a model of Christian behavior to the church (see Barth, 63–64).

The erotic motif of *servitium amoris* in 2 Cor. 4:5 and throughout the epistle has important consequences for the interpretation of Paul's Christology, understanding his hopes for the political culture of the churches he established and, ultimately, the contemporary appropriation of Pauline thought for contemporary Christianity. First, the "work of Christ" (a standard phrase used by theologians to speak of the role of Jesus in their theological systems) will have to include his passionate longing for communion, his slave-like devotion to humanity. Second, church leaders, who often claim to pattern themselves after Paul, would have to question the prevalent view of Paul as an authoritarian leader and imitate instead his imitation of Christ as a slave of love. Finally, ecclesiastical regimes of oppression that legitimate themselves by an appeal to Jesus' obedience to the Father, or in the case of secular institutions by obedience to higher authority, would have to be challenged (see Fredrickson 2013).

2 Corinthians 4:7—5:10: More Body

▌ THE TEXT IN ITS ANCIENT CONTEXT

To review: in the face of charges that he is a deceptive flatterer lacking courage to speak his mind, Paul asserts his *parrēsia* (3:12, 4:1), placing it in the context of friendship and love but also contrasting it with the speech of the super-apostles who, like the Cynics, are harsh moral critics. In 4:7—5:10, he further develops the idea of frank speaking based on friendship. In language that anticipates the weakness he will describe as his experience in the aftermath of his abduction into paradise in 12:1-10, Paul's hardships in 4:8-12 remind him that the power he possesses in excess is not the force of command but the enslaving power of love, which God has enkindled in his heart to illumine the glory of God that Paul sees on the face of Christ (4:6). The slavery motif is developed in 4:10-12, where the bearing of the master's death in one's own body goes to the heart of servitude, as verse 12 powerfully states. Paul's *servitium amoris* to Christ is inseparable from his slavery to the church in Corinth. It is out of this relationship with the church, not his own moral virtue, that his speech flows freely (4:13).

The topic of 4:14—5:10 is increased intimacy in the *parrēsia*-generating relationship Paul has with the Corinthians. He begins in 4:14-15 by repeating the topics of resurrection and transformation (see 1:10-11, 14, 21; 3:18). Abruptly, however, as if Paul had a conversion to the philosophic doctrine of the immortality of the soul, 4:16—5:1 introduces stock themes about the afterlife as it was described in Platonism and accepted by a few of the later Stoics. These themes include the inner and outer human being; the insignificance of present suffering in comparison with the soul's perfection; the eternality of things unseen; and, most significantly, the body as prison or temporary dwelling place of the soul (See Seneca, *Ep*. 102.23; 120.14). New Testament scholars have for decades pointed out the profound difference between immortality of the soul and resurrection of the body. So why has Paul conflated the two notions here? Quite possibly Paul speaks like a philosopher in 4:16—5:1 in order to undermine philosophy's commitment to the survival of the separated self that lives in unchanging and serene contemplation of the universe when the external influence of its body has been removed. By temporarily passing as a philosopher in 4:16—5:1, he gives his attack on philosophical reason all the advantages of stealth.

Having drawn his readers' attention to the isolated self-sufficiency of the wise man's soul (see 3:5), note in 5:2-5 how powerfully Paul rejects the philosophical idea of death as the soul stripped of flesh (see Seneca, *Ep*. 102.24–25). He groans and longs for more clothing, for more body, not less. Life after death for Paul is not the eradication of death (that is philosophy's delusion in the teaching of the immortal, bodiless soul), but the drinking down of death by life (NRSV "swallowing up," cf.

1 Cor. 15:53-57), an unimaginable event and an impossible possibility (5:4) rightly given over by Paul to the name of God, who gives the Spirit (cf. 1:20-22).

◼ THE TEXT IN THE INTERPRETIVE TRADITION

Interpreters up to the tenth century understood the "inner person" (4:16) as Paul's reference to the soul just as the "outer person" designated the body (Suda, *Lexicon* Epsilon 3170). Yet if it is the case, as discussed above, that Paul *plays* with the philosophical commonplace of body as the house (or prison, or crypt) of the soul in order to challenge the very notion of a bodiless soul, the interpreters of the early church and the Byzantine period mistook his rhetorical strategy in 4:16—5:1. They thought he was advocating asceticism as the path to spiritual perfection. In fact, with great regularity, they slightly misquoted the Pauline text as follows: "*as much as* the outer person is destroyed, *to this extent* the inner person is renewed" (emphasis mine: see Basil, *Quod deus non est auctor malorum* [PG 31:337]; Ephraem Syrus, *In sermonem, quem dixit dominus, quod: In hoc mundo pressuram habebitis, et de perfectione hominis* 335; Michael Choniates, *Epistulae* 2.132.269).

◼ THE TEXT IN CONTEMPORARY DISCUSSION

In recent years there has been a growing interest in possible intersections of Pauline thought and contemporary philosophy (see Caputo and Alcoff; Frick). Second Corinthians 4:16—5:10, in its complex engagement with Platonic themes, is a natural site for these modern conversations to take place. Three Pauline themes (there are certainly others) in this passage invite comparison with postmodern philosophy, which has its own complex engagement with Platonism that at least on some points runs parallel to Paul's. First, the thought of death swallowed down by life, discussed above, and the accompanying thought of resurrection did not fall on an unsympathetic ear in the case of Jacques Derrida (Kearney); indeed, for Derrida, dreaming the impossible is always the way to start any undertaking whatsoever, but especially in the case of philosophy, theology, and justice (see Caputo 1997, 20–26). Second, the famous Pauline phrase "for we walk by faith not by sight" (5:7) reads almost as a motto for some postmodern critiques of foundationalism (Caputo 1997, 41–48). Third, the eschatological desire for a future that cannot be known or described is indicated by the groaning, longing, and wishing of 5:2, and this passion correlates with the aim of deconstruction: to impassion a wish for something totally other in those of us whom tradition, theology, and social systems have trained not to expect the unexpected and not to welcome surprises (Caputo 1997, 134–49).

2 Corinthians 5:11-19: The Madness of Saint Paul

◼ THE TEXT IN ITS ANCIENT CONTEXT

In 5:13, Paul admits that he went insane (*exestēmen*), a moment of candor whose significance is not apparent. The present essay has stressed Paul's consistent description of the opponents' Cynic-like moral severity and their complaint against him that he is bold in letters but deceptively weak in the church's presence. If this is the situation, then 5:13 might be read as Paul's admission of inconsistency and his explanation of it. Going mad with violent emotion in rhetorical performance was, in fact, an important element in the style of speech called *deinotēs* (see the comments above on 2 Cor. 10:9-10; and Voit), and presumably the opponents would have approved of Paul's blast of anger in the letter of tears. The style of speech contrasting with *deinotēs* was known as "grace" (*charis*). To achieve this style, the speaker must do precisely what Paul says he did when he returned from his madness and is still doing as he writes: "we are temperate" (*sōphronoumen*: see Van Hook, 32). The purpose of this calm self-presentation was to persuade and win over (as Paul says he aims to do in 5:11) rather than to overwhelm hearers as in the case of *deinotēs*.

Following on Paul's confession of madness are two applications of the motif of friendship, one to Christ (5:14-17) and the other to God (5:18-19). In each instance, the point is to distance Paul's ministry from flattery and associate it as closely as possible with divine grace (cf. 1:12). The "love [*agapē*] of Christ" in 5:14 will be misunderstood if readers interpret it through the influential but problematic work of Anders Nygren's *Agape and Eros*, which rules out of order the porous border between *agapē* and *philia* running throughout the present commentary (for a trenchant critique of Nygren, see McGinn). There is one point about friendship in antiquity, however, that Nygren properly underlines: its exclusivity. There was in Paul's day the widespread opinion that friendship was dyadic; if anyone had more than one, or possibly two friends, that person might well be thought of as a flatterer and guilty of *polyphilia*, the vice of having many friends (see Plutarch, *On Having Many Friends* 93B–97B). Read against this aversion to *polyphilia*, the quasi-hymnic writing in 5:14-15 trades on the commonplace that "friends have all things in common" (how else would all die or all live unless all share all things with Christ?). There is a "new creation" (5:17) in which having many friends is the very nature of things, not a symptom of flattery and deception.

Paul shifts in 5:18-19 from a christo-logic to a theo-logic, but the point remains the same. The new, many-friended creature that Paul is legitimates his manner of ministry in which reconciliation (in the sense defined below) and forgiveness take center stage. This new creation applies to God also, although interpreters rarely notice this. The Greek word translated "reconcile" does not refer to a restoration of a previous relationship so much as the initiation of new friendship (see Fredrickson 1997, 171–74) in which all things are shared. God's yes-saying in Christ (1:18-20) is matched by God's having all things in common with the *kosmos* and placing in "us" (Paul? Paul and his cowriters? the readers, too? the world?) the *logos* (word? logic?) of reconciliation.

▌THE TEXT IN THE INTERPRETIVE TRADITION

Various commentators have wanted to protect Paul from the meaning of his own words. Typical is John Chrysostom, who rendered the sense of Paul's statement hypothetical: "What Paul means is that *even if* people think he is mad, everything he does is for the glory of God" (*Homilies on the Epistles of Paul to the Corinthians* 11.2, emphasis added). Other interpreters have construed Paul's madness as prophetic truth-telling, since they read *exestēmen* in 5:13 in light of Ps. 116:11: "I said in my consternation [*en tē ekstasei mou*] 'Everyone is a liar'" (see Eusebius, *Commentaria in Psalmos* [PG 23:353]). The latter reading supports the explanation given above. Finally, in the early church there was another interpretation of Paul's madness, and this one plays an important role in present-day discussions. It is that 2 Cor. 5:13 refers to Paul's vision of the Lord recounted in

12:1-10 (see Athanasius, *Expositiones in Psalmos* [PG 27:301]; and Cyril of Alexandria, *Expositio in Psalmos* [PG 69:1156]).

■ THE TEXT IN CONTEMPORARY DISCUSSION

Paul's madness (5:13) is difficult to understand. An influential explanation among today's scholarly readers is that Paul's opponents, influenced by Gnosticism or by the ideal of the "divine man," had accused him of *not* having ecstatic experiences, validations in their view of an apostle of Christ (Schmithals, 187–89; Georgi, 252, 280–83). This verse would thus be Paul's rebuttal. As we have seen, there is indeed support in the early church for one portion of this claim, Paul's possible allusion to visionary experience. Yet the larger assertion, that a demand had been placed on Paul, depends on our viewing the opponents as seekers of ecstatic visions or speaking in tongues, for which there is scant evidence in 2 Corinthians and silence in the interpretive tradition (see Barrett 1973, 166–67; Furnish, 324–25).

2 Corinthians 5:20—7:4 God Entreating through Us, Not Them

■ THE TEXT IN ITS ANCIENT CONTEXT

In a tender and urgent reminiscence of 1:3-7, where it was likewise not possible to distinguish between God's entreaty or exhortation and Paul's, so also in 5:20—6:2 Paul pleads for the community to be reconciled (in the full sense of the term) to him. If the Corinthians withhold forgiveness, then Paul's ministry itself becomes the cause of offense (6:2) in spite of the proof of its validity provided by the hardships he suffers (6:4-10). With an open mouth (6:11), an allusion to *parrēsia* (see Isocrates, *Oration* 12.96), he entreats the church, calling them by name ("Corinthians"). His heart is wide, a sign of joy and the holding of another in one's heart as in 3:2-3. Holding another in one's heart is a sign of friendship, according to John Chrysostom (PG 61:491), but the community's grief has narrowed (6:12) their souls (see Diogenes Laertius, *Lives of Illustrious Philosophers* 7.118) and forced Paul out of their "innards" (*tois splanchnois*). He pleads with them (6:13) to make room for him.

Paul then pleads with the church in Corinth not to align itself with the super-apostles. Scholars have correctly identified "mismatched" (*heterozygountes*) as nuptial imagery. Their assessment is confirmed by the terms denoting union, which follow in verses 15-16, especially *koinōnia*, which was widely employed; marriage was defined, in fact, as a *koinōnia* of bodies, wealth, and children. And yet the way the same scholars deal with *apistois* (translated by the NRSV as "with unbelievers") leads them to conclude that Paul here warns church members not to marry outside the community (cf. 1 Cor. 7:12-16 for a more complex view on the matter held by Paul himself). There is another way to read this text. The term *apistos* in 4:4 likely refers to the *disloyal* super-apostles. Moreover, not only did the yoke (*zygos*) function in marital contexts, but it was also a metaphor for the pulling together of friends. Paul uses it in Phil. 4:3 to persuade the readers of that letter to financially support the missionary work of Euodia and Syntyche as the church had supported him. Paul's plea, then, not to be "otherwise-yoked" with the unfaithful ones might be interpreted as his warning not to support the super-apostles.

■ THE TEXT IN THE INTERPRETIVE TRADITION

Interpreters in the early church sometimes found themselves in the uncomfortable position of making sense of texts that, from the perspective of the tradition's adherence to the *apatheia* (impassibility) of God, could not mean what they say. "The word *became* flesh" (emphasis added) in John 1:14 is a good example. Here the threat to the unchangeable, eternal Word comes not from heretical teaching but from the biblical text itself. The recourse of substituting "take on flesh" for "become flesh" was the preferred solution to this problem (see Theodoret of Cyrus, *Eranistes*, passim). Another famous example is Gal. 3:13, where we read that Christ "became a curse for us"; Jerome explained (*Commentarius in Epistolam S. Pauli ad Galatas* 2 [PL 26:387–88]) that this should not be taken literally—to Luther's irritation (*Lectures on Galatians* [*LW* 26:276]). This brings us to 2 Cor. 5:21, which Athanasius (*Oratio II contra Arianos* 47.2) recognized was as problematic as John 1:14 and Gal. 3:13. The stakes are high, however, since this verse undergirds Paul's plea for reconciliation in 5:20 and presents readers with a shocking idea: God made Christ "to be sin." Gregory of Nyssa (*Contra Celsum* 1.69) softened the offense by claiming that Paul wrote *sin* but meant *flesh*. Eutherius (*Confutationes quarundam propositionum* 4) took a different approach and applied what interpreters in the tradition had learned in dealing with John 1:14: Christ was not altered to be sin but "took our sin and caused it to disappear" (*aphanisai*). Theodorus Studites (*Parva Catechesis* 30) similarly emphasized that Christ "put on" human nature corrupted by sin.

■ THE TEXT IN CONTEMPORARY DISCUSSION

What do love (*agapē*, 5:14) and justice (*dikaiosynē*, 5:21) have to do with one another? This important question, especially in the context of Christian responses to the criminal justice system in the United States, has been sidelined by Nygren's approach to love and by translators insisting on using "righteousness" to represent *dikaiosynē*. Even when the question is asked, however, justice is often reduced to calculation or the equitable enforcement of rules, and love is reduced to mercy's smoothing the rough edges of justice. But Paul holds the two tightly together, each indeed as an example of the other, not only in 2 Corinthians 5 but also in Gal. 5:5-6 and, by extension through nuptial imagery, in Phil. 3:7-11. Justice and love share at least two things in Paul. First, each is constituted by openness to the future (see especially Gal. 5:5-6). Just as one would never say of a beloved, "I have loved enough," so justice forbids saying, "justice has been done." The second thing love and justice share is that they spring from the singularity of the other; it is always the face of *this one* that calls forth my love just as it is the call of *this one* that moves me to response. For these reasons, both love and justice are pure gifts.

2 Corinthians 8:1—9:15: By Poverty Enriched

■ THE TEXT IN ITS ANCIENT CONTEXT

In the ancient world, gift-giving displayed social status and obligated recipients to repay benefactors with gratitude and honor (see Danker). While Paul challenges the elite of the Corinthian church in these two chapters to contribute to the fund for the saints in Jerusalem, he nevertheless seeks to persuade them not to participate in a system of benefaction that would shame the poor in the Corinthian church (since they had nothing to give) and would establish the churches of Greece and Asia as patrons of the struggling client church in Jerusalem. Paul has a difficult task in front of him: to disrupt the circle of gift and gratitude without ruining the collection itself.

Paul shames the Corinthians by praising the generosity of the impoverished Macedonians (8:1-6). Yet there is more to it than this. First, an impossible logic about the Macedonian gift loosens, if not dissolves, the connection between giving and the display of social status. How so? In verse 2, the strange condition that makes gift-giving possible is "profound poverty." It is not the case, then, as it is with Corinth's wealthy elite, that the Macedonians give out of their fullness, as if their gift testified to their invulnerability. Like the widow in Mark 12:41-44, the Macedonians give out of their emptiness.

In 8:9, the "gift [*charis*] of our Lord Jesus Christ" follows the same unexpected pattern of giving out of poverty, in language that echoes the Christ hymn in Phil. 2:5-11. Paul writes, "by the poverty of that one you got rich." Next, in 8:13-15, Paul tries a second strategy, manipulating the well-known philosophical topic of proportional equality (Aristotle, *Nicomachean Ethics* 1130b–1132b). Instead of the expected notion of equality as distribution according to status (that is, equality is achieved when superior persons receive more), however, Paul implies that the very act of giving is the admission that one might one day be in need. Equality understood in this way exposes human frailty, even that of the elite, within any system of economic exchange.

To the ears of modern readers, chapter 9 simply repeats chapter 8. One prominent scholar has argued that the two chapters circulated independently before the final compilation of 2 Corinthians (see Betz). But to repeat oneself was not necessarily a fault in ancient letters (see Phil. 3:1). And although it is the case in chapter 9 that Paul again undermines the patron-client structure that had monopolized the act of giving in the ancient world, he does so in a different way, using a theological argument: God's justice *is* God's scattering, and this is good news for the poor, as the quotation of the Psalm in 9:9 suggests. Such a definition of justice (NRSV translates "righteousness") must have been shocking, since in the wake of Plato (*Republic* 433B–435B), justice was understood as a harmony of interests or a strict limitation on individuals to perform assigned roles within an unchallenged gradation of social power. In short, 2 Corinthians 8 and 9 does not credit God with preserving the patron-client relationship, but with deconstructing it. The wildly unaccountable dissemination in verses 10-11, just another instance of scattering, does indeed produce gratitude to God, but what is one to be grateful for (note the "indescribable gift" in 9:15) at the scene of such dispersion accomplished by God's giving? Might it be the generosity (*haplotēs*), made possible by God's grace, of shaking things loose? Thus, in the end, it is not gratitude that Paul imagines the poor in Jerusalem will feel toward the church in Corinth: it is longing for communion (vv. 13-14).

■ THE TEXT IN CONTEMPORARY DISCUSSION

Paul's probing of the ideology of the gift (*charis*), which might also be translated as "grace," bears a remarkable resemblance to recent philosophical and theological discussions of gift-giving (see

Horner; Walters) that have been inspired, at least in part, by Derrida's critical analysis of Marcel Mauss's 1925 anthropological study *The Gift: The Form and Reason for Exchange in Archaic Societies*. What is the connection between the first-century apostle and recent philosophers, at least the ones for whom the language of religion has proven indispensable? Very briefly stated, for Derrida, the gift in a pure sense is impossible: it refuses to let itself be intended by the giver or perceived by the recipient. In the moment that a gift either generates the expectation of repayment or a feeling of obligation, it ceases to be a gift. Thus the very possibility of a gift (for which there needs to exist a giver, a gift, and a recipient) also makes gift-giving impossible (see Caputo 1997, 160–64). This is not a mere word game, as Paul's ingenious and impassioned attempt to free the collection from the ancient system of benefaction shows. Christ's poverty, God's disseminative justice, and the gift's indescribability all reflect Paul's efforts to keep the elite from capitalizing on the collection and dominating the Corinthian church.

2 Corinthians 10:1-18: *Miles Gloriosus: Militia Amoris*

▌ THE TEXT IN ITS ANCIENT CONTEXT

In the first five words of 10:1, Paul manages to say "I" three times and to write "Paul" once for good measure. His audacity, mentioned in 7:16 but kept under wraps in chapters 8 and 9, now bursts forth: Paul is a warrior! But unlike the stock figure of the *miles gloriosus* of Roman comedy (see Plautus, *The Swaggering Soldier*), whose penchant for comparing himself to others and commending himself (see 10:12-18) sets the stage for Paul's appearance in chapters 10–12, and in whose image Paul creates the super-apostles, Paul is a soldier in Love's campaign. Rather than boasting in personal power, he swaggers in his weakness (10:10; 11; 21, 29, 12:9-10; 13:3-4, 9). This is not, however, weakness in a general sense, that is, an incapacity that could be remedied with extra effort or training. Rather, the erotic motifs woven into the discourse of these chapters suggest that Paul's weakness is the kind ancient love poets wrote about: desire for a communion that appears impossible. Second Corinthians 10–13 is a complex argument, ironies captured within ironies, a pretended and demented bragging about those desperate emotions about which no one but a crazed lover would ever boast. Paul's boasting in his weakness was intended to expose his opponents' severity and to commend Christ's gentleness and reasonableness that the apostle seeks to emulate.

Once again, the charge of duplicity rears its head: 10:1 incorporates into its own discourse the opponents' complaint that Paul is bold at a distance but *tapeinos* ("lowly," connoting, from the perspective of elites, marginalized persons of low social class) when present. Fighting words! Note the military terms marching forward: "I am bold" (10:2), "daring" (10:2), "wage war" (10:3), "weapons of our warfare" (10:4), "take down strongholds" (10:4) and "elevated heights" (10:5), "taking captive" (10:5), "obedience" (10:5,6), and "avenge disobedience" (10:6). Paul is conducting a campaign, to be sure, but first-century readers, especially those who remembered the motif of the triumphal procession in 2:14 and its association with the motif *servitium amoris*, would see the amatory point: Paul portrays himself as Eros taking captive and subjecting to servitude the high-minded, philosophical despisers of love, who in ancient amatory literature often reversed course and fell especially hard in love through Eros's avenging intervention (see the opening chapter of Xenophon of Ephesus, *An Ephesian Tale*; Philostratus, *Ep.* 12; *Greek Anthology* 5.294). Verse 6 marks a pause in the general campaign; only when the Corinthians' obedience to Christ (obedience of love, that is, another instance of *servitium amoris*) is complete will Paul turn to the others. Yet, lest anyone take his feigned belligerence in 10:1-6 seriously, in 10:8 he denies intent to pull anything or anyone down. He wouldn't want to frighten anyone (10:9)!

▌ THE TEXT IN THE INTERPRETIVE TRADITION

According to 10:9-10, Paul's letters written before 2 Corinthians had already entered an interpretive tradition of considerable sophistication. As I noted in the introduction, the super-apostles evaluated Paul's letters and speech according to the literary and rhetorical standards of the time; his speech in the presence of the community, they said (10:10), was "attenuated" (*exouthenēmenos*). The *Rhetorica ad Herennium* (4.11.16) equated attenuated speech with the simple style that employed everyday language and could, if handled skillfully, achieve elegance. If mishandled, however, it was debased and merely ordinary, and as Cicero noted (*De oratore* 20; see also Quintilian, *Institutio oratoria* 9.2.3), it was furthest from the forceful style (*deinotēs*). In short, we might infer the opponents charged that Paul in the presence of the church used irony (*eirōneia*), not in the modern sense of saying the opposite of what one means but in the ancient sense. That is, he talked the way poor people and slaves talked (cf. 1 Cor. 1:28), although he was capable of much more, and did so in order to ridicule others (see Dio Chrysostom, *Oration* 42.1-3). John Chrysostom (*In illud: Utinam sustineretis modicum* [PG 51:304]) had no doubt that Paul's opponents accused him of irony. In fact, Chrysostom's reading of 2 Cor. 10:9-10, and particularly his detailed explanation of Paul's "attenuated speech," lines up with the discussion of this topic in rhetorical handbooks and literary treatises (for a deep appreciation of Chrysostom as a Pauline interpreter, see Mitchell).

▌ THE TEXT IN CONTEMPORARY DISCUSSION

Such talk about lowliness, weakness, love, and slavery in Christian discourse forced Friedrich Nietzsche to cry out, "Bad air! Bad air!" (Nietzsche, 24). Hatred, revenge, envy—these terms taken together translate *ressentiment*, the word Nietzsche deployed against what he perceived to be the stench of Jewish and Christian souls deformed by the "revaluation of values." In a "slave revolt," he complained, the weak of the world seek "spiritual revenge" against the strong and their spontaneous affirmation of life; by promoting guilt, pettiness, and duties, the priestly class prevails by sullying the heroic embrace of life (Nietzsche, 19–33). This is not the place to assert or deny that Paul's weakness or the *servitium amoris* motif were examples of *ressentiment*, but the question might at least be raised whether the eroticism Paul weaves into his self-presentation and into his Christology entails a spontaneous and infinite affirmation of the other and thus even a slight chance for a rapprochement with Nietzsche's "yes-saying." (For a reading of the philosopher that might facilitate such an unexpected meeting of minds, see Caputo 1993, 42–68.)

2 Corinthians 11:1-4: Zealous to Preserve Christ's Marriage Bed

▌THE TEXT IN ITS ANCIENT CONTEXT

Here Paul raises the stakes on the church's flirtation with the super-apostles. He has married the Corinthians off to Christ; for them now to shift their allegiance to his rivals would be the same as abandoning their nuptial union with Christ. Paul makes a similar move in his letter to the Galatians (1:6-9), where a note similar to verse 4 can be heard.

▌THE TEXT IN THE INTERPRETIVE TRADITION

Paul, in unconscious cooperation with the Song of Songs, had perhaps no more profound influence on later doctrine than in the nuptial imagery he employs here for the relation of Christ and the church (for the early church, see Elliott; for a medieval example, see Gilbert of Hoyland, *Sermons* 2.5). Luther's notion of the "joyous exchange" comes out of this tradition (see, e.g., his *The Blessed Sacrament of the Holy and True Body of Christ and the Brotherhoods* [*LW* 35]).

▌THE TEXT IN CONTEMPORARY DISCUSSION

Unlike their medieval counterparts, today's readers are no doubt bewildered or put off by the conceptual framework of Christ as bridegroom and the church as bride. To be sure, definite risks accompany this way of imagining Christian doctrine and piety. First of all, there appears to be a bias toward heterosexual marriage that abets heterosexism in contemporary culture (on which see Jung and Smith). To counter this impression that Paul is a champion of heterosexual marriage, one need only read his tepid commendation of marriage in 1 Thess. 4:3-8 and 1 Corinthians 7 (see Martin 2006). Moreover, nuptial imagery actually has the potential of deconstructing the binary opposition of male and female—think of Corinthian manbrides! (See Fredrickson 2013, 129–49). Finally, a clear distinction must be made between Paul's use of nuptial imagery in his genuine epistles and that found in the pseudonymous letters (Colossians, Ephesians, and the Pastorals). In the former, Paul emphasizes the ritual of marriage, the wedding, and does so in the context of eschatological expectation. Furthermore, standard motifs of friendship (the theme of *koinōnia*, for example) define what it means to get married. In the pseudonymous letters, however, marriage is placed within the ancient Greek household (see Balch) and illustrates the same hierarchical relation that obtains between head and body and Christ and church, the very relations of power and authority that the genuine Paul says Christ is presently nullifying (see 1 Cor. 15:24; for the brazen misconstrual of this verse to legitimate hierarchy, see Eph. 1:20-23).

2 Corinthians 11:5—12:10: Dog Apostles, Hardships, and Weakness

▌THE TEXT IN ITS ANCIENT CONTEXT

As God is his witness, Paul loves the Corinthians (11:11). For that reason, they should take his refusal of financial support not as an insult but rather as witness of his affection. But there is more to his refusal than this. Paul is setting up an extended comparison between himself and the super-apostles in 11:12—12:13, just what he said in 10:12 he would not do. The comparison hinges on the opponents' Cynic-like behavior. In this connection, note in 11:9 that he refuses the Corinthians' aid in order that he might keep himself in every way "without weight" (*abarē*). The term "weighty" (*baros*) was often associated with Cynic philosophers (Malherbe 1970) whose harsh criticism was felt to be oppressive. Cynics also had the reputation of throwing their weight around in another way: by demanding lodging from the very people they rebuked. And then they ate them out of house and home (see 11:20: "preys upon you" might also be translated "eats up" or "devours"). Cynics, in short, had big jaws (see Billerbeck, 113).

Paul compliments himself perhaps too much (or is his sense of humor very dry?) when he explains the reason for this comparison with the super-apostles: he wants to prevent them from "being found as he is" (11:12). It turns out that Paul is a wreck, but before he enumerates his hardships (11:23-33) and exposes his weaknesses (12:8-10), he alludes in 11:13-15 and 20-21 to behavioral traits frequently associated with Cynic behavior. (The name "Cynic" is related to the Greek word for dog; for these traits, see Epictetus, *Diatr.* 2.12.24; 3.22.23–25, 45–50; 4.8.6–20; Lucian, *Fugitivi* 12–19; *Piscator* 31; Aelius Aristides, *Oration* 3.663–68, 671, 676, 682–83; Julian, *Oration* 6.201A.) He implies that the Corinthians ought to be horrified in discovering the super-apostles' real identity and ashamed not to have seen it before. Perhaps most important here is that the dog-like apostles are portrayed as minions of Satan (11:14-15), whom we have encountered before in this letter when severity threatens to drive an individual through shame to suicide (2:5-11).

Ancient philosophers listed their hardships for three reasons: to display their moral virtue; to describe training in moral virtue; and, less frequently, to show their kindly attitude (*philanthrōpia*) toward the ignorant masses they sought to improve (see Fitzgerald). In 11:23-33, Paul mimics the philosopher's occupational hazards; but in verses 28-29 he slips in sentiments illustrative not of a moralist's day-to-day troubles but of the emotions of those who care for and fret over a beloved, even to the point of burning (cf. 1 Cor. 7:9).

Second Corinthians 12:1-10 is a tour de force in which Paul makes the following point, representative of the entire letter, by having the Lord himself say it (12:9): weakness—the lover's sickness of body and soul when separated from the beloved—perfects divine power. The Lord should know of what he speaks, since he was crucified "out of weakness" (13:4). But why, from first-century perspectives, does Paul stage the event of his abduction into paradise in such dramatic terms? It is not an overstatement to say that in the ancient Greek world, anyone who had something important to say, especially about the great transitions of individual or community life, what anthropologists call liminality, told a story of erotic abduction. Consider Homer's *Iliad*, the founding of Europe, Zeus's love for Ganymede, Eos's desire for Tithonos, the educational experience of the young men of Sparta and Crete, the tolerance of forced marriages by abduction, and the bitterly protested marriages to Hades at death. It is not unreasonable to suppose that Paul could not have told the most important story of his life and of his ministry without narrating rapture into paradise (for erotic abduction and sexual violence in ancient culture, see Fredrickson 2013, 85–104). But in this mysterious event, this apocalypse, he refuses to boast. Of course, by saying that he won't talk about it, he speaks volumes.

◼ The Text in the Interpretive Tradition

The eroticism of these verses has faded from view in the modern period, but some readers, especially medieval mystics and monastics, experienced a reawakening of friendship in theology and in their communal life and treasured Paul's abduction (*harpagenta* in v. 2 and *hērpagē* in v. 4) into paradise, the unspeakable, wordless intimacy, and his disorienting and grief-filled return to earth. Paul's story matched their brief ecstasies and then the long and hollow periods of Christ's absence. There was a particular interest in Paul's experience of hearing "wordless words" (*arrēta rēmata*, 12:4), which was understood as erotic and an example of apophaticism (see John of Ford, *Sermons* 4.1; 45.2, 5; 94.9; 100.5).

◼ The Text in Contemporary Discussion

Apophaticism, or negative theology, is a kind of theological discourse that denies, inconsistently, that it is possible to speak about God. God is beyond being, it is claimed, and therefore to speak about God violates God, and yet this very impossibility impassions more and more words spoken and written about God. Robust in the medieval period, when Paul's loquacious silence about his encounter with Jesus in 2 Cor. 12:4 served as a kind of proof text, apophaticism is making a comeback in postmodern philosophy and theology thanks to the fascination the contradiction between speaking and not speaking held for Jacques Derrida. Derrida did not, however, share negative theology's confidence that it could *rest* in the God beyond being, beyond linguistic signification. Quite the opposite. In an uncanny and certainly unintended parallel to Paul's return to earth (12:7-10), where divine power happens in weakness, that is, in Paul's troubled, loving relation to the Corinthians, Derrida generalized the impossibility and passion of the speaking about God to the speaking about every other. "Deconstruction is rather the thought, if it is a thought, of an absolute heterogeneity that unsettles all the assurances of the same within which we comfortably ensconce ourselves. That is the desire by which it is moved, which moves and impassions it, which sets it into motion, toward which it extends itself" (Caputo 1997, 5).

2 Corinthians 12:11—13:10: A True Apostle

◼ The Text in Its Ancient Context

The letter is coming to an end. Paul must first extricate himself from his pretense of boasting and comparison with the super-apostles. This he accomplishes in 12:11-13 by shifting blame: the Corinthians themselves forced him to act the part of a bragging fool.

In 12:13-15, he deals one last time with the implications of his refusal of financial support. First, he seeks (the Greek term *zēteō* has erotic connotations and might also be translated "desires") them, not their things. Second, he is their parent (cf. 1 Cor. 4:14-15). The last reason (v. 15) can of course be read in terms of economics, but the words carry an erotic connotation as well, which should not be unexpected given the emphasis on love at the end of the verse. The words in question here are *dapanaō* and *ekdapanaō* (NRSV: "spend and be spent"). The first term might reasonably carry only economic meaning, but the fact that the second is used in the passive voice means that Paul himself is expended for their lives. There is continuity with the motif of *servitium amoris* running through-out the letter. Two obvious parallels are 1 Thess. 2:8 and Phil. 2:17. A more subtle parallel is Phil. 2:7, in which Christ is said to have "emptied himself." In Greek and Latin love literature, longing for communion with a beloved causes the lover to melt and then drain away, in other words to be poured out or expended (see Fredrickson 2013, 45–83; for a much later example of *dapanaō* used in this erotic sense, see Theodorus Prodromus, *Rhodanthe and Dosicles* 8.179: "the hearts of those who long are expended").

Before he bids farewell in a proto-trinitarian formula (13:13), which is itself significant in its repetition of Paul's emphasis throughout the letter on love, grace, and communion, Paul concludes the body of the letter with three final contrasts between himself and the super-apostles. First, in 12:20, as he returns to the ethical and social class issues he had addressed in 1 Corinthians (likely linked through elite male privileges), Paul makes a surprising turn: the church's bad behavior will be the occasion of God driving him once again into melancholy and causing him to lament. Reading verse 21 first and then going back to the first half of verse 20 raises a question: Is Paul suggesting that their finding him "not as they wish" means that they will find him weak and lacking in the severity of the super-apostles? Second Corinthians 13:3 hints that this was the case. The second contrast is the oblique criticism in 13:5-10 that Paul's rivals engage in moral exhortation in order to burnish their own reputations for frank speaking. Paul claims to have no stake in the Corinthians' progress other than their improvement. The final contrast, which ends the body of the letter, has Paul locating the purpose of his authority not in harsh criticism (the Greek phrase connotes "cut-ting") but in building up.

■ THE TEXT IN THE INTERPRETIVE TRADITION

In a stunning turn, the very weakness (*asthenia*) Paul seeks mightily to preserve in the face of the super-apostles' harshness, even to the point of his adopting the guise of a warrior, became an embar-rassment to the apostle's later interpreters. But Paul plainly *does* connect his weakness to Christ's in 13:4: "he [Christ] was crucified from weakness" and "we are weak in him." The subtle adjustments made to the first phrase by exegetes betray their nervousness over its dogmatic implication that weakness pertains to the whole Christ, a view that the fathers worried the uneducated reader might erroneously entertain (John Chrysostom, *In epistulam ii ad Corinthos* [PG 61:598–600]).

One solution to the perceived threat to the *apatheia* of God, a nonnegotiable point in Christian theology as soon as ancient philosophy was let in, was to assign the weakness mentioned in 13:4 to Christ's "human part" or "nature" or to his "flesh." His resurrection, power, and life were referred to the divine (see Gregory of Nyssa, *Contra Eunomium* 3.4.10). A related strategy was to deny any passivity in Christ. In Eusebius's words, "He himself made himself weak, not being conquered by another" (*Commentaria in Psalmos* 23.309). Christ's *voluntary* weakness made it not weakness in the usual sense (see Cyril of Jerusalem, *Catacheses ad illuminandos* 14.8). Finally, weakness might be understood simply as a matter of suffering persecution or plots (see John of Damascus, *Commentarii in epistulas Pauli* [PG 95:773]).

The Text in Contemporary Discussion

Second Corinthians begins (1:3) and ends (13:4) with divine suffering. The interpretive tradition's discomfort with Paul's straying outside the lines drawn for theology by the doctrine of the *apatheia* of God, a doctrine inspired by Greek philosophy, make Paul's weakness, his passions, all the more interesting. On several occasions in this essay, it was pointed out that Paul's subtle use and critique of Greek philosophical ideas make his writings a site of exploration for postmodern philosophers, especially those, like John Caputo, influenced by Jacques Derrida.

If we shift from God to Paul, a distinction that Paul himself obscures throughout the letter (see, e.g., 5:20-21), we note that the interpretive tradition generally characterized Paul's suffering as his endurance of hardships or opposition not unlike the wise man's training in virtue. Yet here are good reasons to think that his suffering was in fact the vulnerability opened up in him by loving the Corinthians: weakness, in other words. We have seen that Paul aligns himself with the weakness of Christ, and this leads him to a pastoral practice of adaptability, grace, and forgiveness, none of which compromises frank speech from Paul's perspective, as the harsh super-apostles charge, but that works in concert with truth-telling and justice. Paul insists on the "slavery of love" (*servitium amoris*) and related motifs drawn from erotic literature to unify the argument of the letter and persuade the Corinthians to accept his ministry and to reject that of his rivals. Finally, we observed how the letter's critique of the severe disciplinary practice that had the effect of isolating the individual who wronged Paul challenges the contemporary church to examine its understanding of punishment and the isolating practices of the American system of criminal justice.

Works Cited

Amador, J. D. H. 2000. "Revisiting 2 Corinthians: Rhetoric and the Case for Unity." *NTS* 46:92–111.

Balch, David L. 1981. *Let Wives Be Submissive: The Domestic Code in 1 Peter*. SBLMS 26. Chico, CA: Scholars Press.

Barrett, C. K. 1970. "Ο ΑΔΙΚΗΣΑΣ (2 Cor. 7.12)." In *Verborum Veritas: Festschrift für Gustav Stählin*, edited by Otto Böcher and Klaus Haacker, 149–57. Wuppertal: Rolf Brockhaus.

———. 1973. *A Commentary on the Second Epistle to the Corinthians*. HNTC. New York: Harper & Row.

Barth, Karl. 2002. *The Epistle to the Philippians*. Translated by James W. Leitch. 40th anniversary ed. Louisville: Westminster John Knox.

Betz, Hans Dieter, and George W. MacCrae. 1985. *2 Corinthians 8 and 9: A Commentary on Two Administrative Letters of the Apostle Paul*. Philadelphia: Fortress Press.

Billerbeck, Margarethe. 1978. *Epiktet: Vom Kynismus*. Philosophia Antiqua 34. Leiden: Brill.

Briggs, Sheila. 1989. "Can an Enslaved God Liberate? Hermeneutical Reflections on Phil 2:6-11." *Semeia* 47:137–53.

Caputo, John D. 1993. *Against Ethics: Contributions to a Poetics of Obligation with Constant Reference to Deconstruction*. Bloomington: Indiana University Press.

———. 1997. *The Prayers and Tears of Jacques Derrida: Religion without Religion*. Bloomington: Indiana University Press.

Caputo, John D., and Linda Martin Alcoff. 2009. *St. Paul among the Philosophers*. Bloomington: Indiana University Press.

Culler, Jonathan D. 1982. *On Deconstruction: Theory and Criticism after Structuralism*. Ithaca, NY: Cornell University Press.

Danker, Frederick W. 1982. *Benefactor: An Epigraphic Study of a Graeco-Roman and New Testament Semantic Field*. Saint Louis: Clayton.

Derrida, Jacques. 2005. *The Politics of Friendship*. New York: Verso.

Elliott, M. W. 2000. *The Song of Songs and Christology in the Early Church, 381–451*. Studien und Texte zu Antike und Christentum 7. Tübingen: Mohr Siebeck.

Fitzgerald, John T. 1988. *Cracks in an Earthen Vessel: An Examination of the Catalogues of Hardships in the Corinthian Correspondence*. SBLDS 99. Atlanta: Scholars Press.

Fiore, Benjamin. 1985. "'Covert Allusion' in 1 Corinthians 1–4." *CBQ* 47:85–102.

Fredrickson, David E. 1996. "*Parrēsia* in the Pauline Epistles." In *Friendship, Flattery, and Frankness of Speech: Studies on Friendship in the New Testament World*, edited by John T. Fitzgerald, 163–84. NovTSup 82. New York: Brill.

———. 1997. "The Presence of Jesus in 2 Corinthians 1–7." In *The Quest for Jesus and the Christian Faith*, edited by Frederick J. Gaiser, 163–74. Word and World Supplements 3. St. Paul: Word and World.

———. 2000. "Paul's Sentence of Death (2 Corinthians 1:9)." In *God, Evil, and Suffering: Essays in Honor of Paul R. Sponheim*, edited by Terence E. Fretheim and Curtis L. Thompson, 99–107. Word and World Supplements 4. St. Paul: Word and World.

———. 2001. "'Through Many Tears (2 Cor 2:4)': Paul's Grieving Letter and the Occasion of 2 Corinthians 1–7." In *Paul and Pathos*, edited by Thomas H. Olbricht and Jerry L. Sumney, 161–79. Atlanta: Society of Biblical Literature.

———. 2013. *Eros and the Christ: Longing and Envy in Paul's Christology*. Minneapolis: Fortress Press.

Fretheim, Terence E. 1984. *The Suffering of God: An Old Testament Perspective*. OBT 14. Philadelphia: Fortress Press.

Frick, Peter, ed. 2013. *Paul in the Grip of the Philosophers: The Apostle and Contemporary Continental Philosophy*. Minneapolis: Fortress Press.

Furnish, Victor Paul. 1984. *2 Corinthians*. AB. Garden City, NY: Doubleday.

Georgi, Dieter. 1987. *The Opponents of Paul in Second Corinthians*. Studies of the New Testament and its World. Edinburgh: T&T Clark.

Grant, Robert M. 1957. *The Letter and the Spirit*. London: SPCK.

Horner, Robyn. 2001. *Rethinking God as Gift: Marion, Derrida, and the Limits of Phenomenology*. Perspectives in Continental Philosophy 19. New York: Fordham University Press.

Kearney, Richard. 2005. "Deconstruction, God, and the Possible." In *Derrida and Religion: Other Testaments*, edited by Yvonne Sherwood and Kevin Hart, 297–308. New York: Routledge.

Jung, Patricia B., and Ralph F. Smith. 1993. *Heterosexism: An Ethical Challenge*. Albany: State University of New York Press.

Malherbe, Abraham J. 1970. "'Gentle as a Nurse': The Cynic Background to I Thess II." *NovT* 12:203–17.

———. 1983. "Exhortation in First Thessalonians." *NovT* 25:238–56.

———. 1988. *Ancient Epistolary Theorists*. SBLSBS 19. Atlanta: Scholars Press.

———. 1989. *Paul and the Popular Philosophers*. Minneapolis: Augsburg Fortress.

Marshall, Peter. 1987. *Enmity in Corinth: Social Conventions in Paul's Relations with the Corinthians*. WUNT 23. Tübingen: J. C. B. Mohr.

Martin, Dale B. 1990. *Slavery as Salvation: The Metaphor of Slavery in Pauline Christianity*. New Haven: Yale University Press.

———. 2006. *Sex and the Single Savior: Gender and Sexuality in Biblical Interpretation*. Louisville: Westminster John Knox.

McGinn, Bernard. 1996. "God as Eros: Metaphysical Foundations of Christian Mysticism." In *New Perspectives on Historical Theology: Essays in Memory of John Meyendorff*, edited by Bradley Nassif, 189–209. Grand Rapids: Eerdmans.

Miller, John F. 1995. "Reading Cupid's Triumph." *Classical Journal* 90:287–94.

Mitchell, Margaret. 2002. *The Heavenly Trumpet: John Chrysostom and the Art of Pauline Interpretation*. HUT 40. Louisville: Westminster John Knox.

Moltmann, Jürgen. 1974. *The Crucified God: The Cross of Christ as the Foundation and Criticism of Christian Theology*. New York: Harper & Row.

———. 1981. *The Trinity and the Kingdom: The Doctrine of God*. San Francisco: Harper & Row.

Monks of Mount Saint Bernard Abbey. 1970–1971. *Guerric of Igny: Liturgical Sermons*. 2 vols. Cistercian Fathers 8, 32. Spencer, MA: Cistercian.

Murgatroyd, Paul. 1980. "*Servitium Amoris* and the Roman Elegists." *Latomus* 40:589–606.

Nietzsche, Friedrich. 1998. *On the Genealogy of Morality: A Polemic*. Translated by Maudemarie Clark and Alan J. Swensen. Indianapolis: Hackett.

Smiley, Charles Newton. 1906. *Latinitas and Hellēnismos: The Influence of the Stoic Theory of Style as Shown in the Writings of Dionysius, Quintilian, Pliny the Younger, Tacitus, Fronto, Aulus Gellius, and Sextus Empiricus*. Madison: University of Wisconsin.

Schmithals, Walter. 1971. *Gnosticism in Corinth: An Investigation of the Letters to the Corinthians*. Nashville: Abingdon.

Stowers, Stanley K. 1986. *Letter Writing in Greco-Roman Antiquity*. LEC 5. Philadelphia: Westminster.

Van Hook, Larue. 1905. *The Metaphorical Terminology of Greek Rhetoric and Literary Criticism*. Chicago: University of Chicago Press.

Voit, Ludwig. 1934. ΔΕΙΝΟΤΗΣ: *Ein antiker Stilbegriff*. Leipzig: Dieterich.

Walters, Gregory. 2013. *Being Promised: Theology, Gift, and Practice*. Sacra Doctrina. Grand Rapids: Eerdmans.

Watson, Francis B. 1984. "2 Cor. X–XIII and Paul's Painful Letter to the Corinthians." *JTS* 35:324–46.

Zagagi, Netta. 1980. *Tradition and Originality in Plautus: Studies in the Amatory Motif in Plautine Comedy*. Hypomnemata 62. Göttingen: Vandenhoeck & Ruprecht.

GALATIANS

Brigitte Kahl

Introduction

Paul's epistle to the "assemblies [*ekklēsiais*] of Galatia" (1:2) is a circular letter dating from the early fifties CE. Its recipients are Pauline Christ communities in the Roman province of Galatia, a vast, multiethnic territory in central Asia Minor, whose inhabitants—among them a sizable Jewish population—were subject and tributary to Rome, collectively unified and naturalized as Roman Galatians. The terms *Galatians* and *Galatia* at Paul's time thus connoted a hybrid identity and location that, first and foremost, spelled out Roman victory and the power to name foreign nations and tribes (*ethnē*). More specifically, the common "surname" commemorates the successful subjugation and cooptation of the Celtic tribes, as the terms *Galatae/ai* ("Galatians"), *Galli* ("Gauls"), and *Keltoi* ("Celts") were widely synonymous in ancient Latin and Greek. Spread all over Europe, they had clashed with Rome for centuries and once even sacked the city itself (387 BCE). Greco-Roman political mythology and art stylized them as prototypical barbarians and archenemies of civilization, for example, in the Great Altar of Pergamon (Kahl 2010). In 279–278 BCE, three of their migrant tribes, after an assault on Delphi, had established the easternmost outpost of Celtic presence in the ancient Mediterranean by crossing over to Anatolia. They settled in what is today Turkey, around Ankyra. Following a century of severe clashes with Pergamon and a devastating Roman massacre in 189 BCE, they gradually changed from enemies to allies and power brokers of Rome. Ankyra in 25 BCE became the capital of the newly founded Galatian province, with a magnificent imperial temple to the goddess Roma and the god Augustus that featured a monumental Greek and Latin inscription of the emperor's worldwide achievements (the *Res Gestae*). Paul's Galatians could be either living in these northern tribal territories of the province, or further to its south, where Rome made its presence felt through roads (*Via Sebaste*), massive building activities, and numerous veteran colonies like Pisidian Antioch, Iconium, and Lystra (see Acts 13:13—14:23). Yet no matter which geographic or ethnic part of the province they inhabited, their identity was overlaid with a hybrid Romanized "Galatian-ness" and their everyday existence shaped by the imprint of colonization (Mitchell 1993a; Kahl 2010).

This Roman contextuality, although never explicitly addressed by Paul and entirely eclipsed in traditional interpretations, might be key to rethinking some of the most troublesome questions that Galatians—arguably Paul's most influential letter—raises for a twenty-first-century reading. In response to an acute crisis among his messianic communities, Paul tried to convince their non-Jewish Christ-followers that they should not adopt Jewish circumcision because they were fully legitimate Jewish children of Abraham already through Christ (3:1—4:31). This focal message was driven home as Paul recapitulated the formative events around Damascus, Jerusalem, and Antioch that established the coequality of circumcised and uncircumcised people "in Christ" (1:10—2:21). A new diverse commonality of oneness-in-difference was thus created that operated through love and mutuality (5:1—6:18). The uniformity of an all-circumcised *ekklēsia*, as demanded by Paul's opponents, was anathema (1:6-9).

From within this fervent confrontation between "foreskin" and "circumcision," Paul developed his signature theology of justification by grace and faith rather than by works of the law (Gal. 2:15-21), embedded in dramatic confrontations with the gospel-falsifiers (1:6-9; 5:12), "false brothers" (2:1-10), Peter (2:11-14), the allegorical "Hagar" (4:21-31), and the "stupid Galatians" themselves (3:1). This unrelenting antithetical force of Galatians has propelled its history of interpretation and often eclipsed Paul's great emancipatory manifesto about baptismal oneness across split-lines of race, religion, class, and gender (3:28), as well as his visionary statements about self and other reconciled through love and bearing one another's burdens (6:2). The polarization of "law versus gospel" and "faith versus works" prevailed, powerfully, not only molding Galatians into the core document of the Protestant Reformation but also helping to generate Christian anti-Judaism, patriarchal authoritarianism, and dogmatic policies of "zero tolerance" against others of all kinds—those (de) classified by wrong faith, inferior gender or status, or aberrant sexual orientation or social practice.

This standard reading of Galatians as the prototype of Christian conservatism and master script for the separation between Christianity and Judaism has been challenged over the past fifty years in the context of post-Holocaust, feminist, liberationist, womanist, empire-critical, and postcolonial approaches (Ehrensperger; Zetterholm). The "New Perspective on Paul" has entirely reconfigured the debate by pointing to the continuing Jewishness of Paul even after "Damascus" (Stendahl; Dunn; Wright 2005). Jewish scholars joined the discussion (Boyarin 1994; Nanos; Le Cornu and Shulam); feminist interpreters have either scrutinized Galatians for emancipatory traits (Gaventa; Osiek; Kahl 1999; Wiley; Lopez) or employed a hermeneutics of suspicion strongly critical of Paul (Fatum; Briggs; Schüssler Fiorenza 1999, 149–73); the native Anatolian context has been searched for hermeneutical clues (S. Elliott 2004; Arnold), and African American as well as African perspectives have been used for constructive rereadings (Braxton, Niang, Kamudzandu). Feminist Lutheran theologians have entered into the debate (Streufert). At the same time, empire-critical and postcolonial reconstructions have remapped the interpretational debates by pointing to the Roman rather than exclusively Jewish or Hellenistic contexts of Paul's theology (Horsley 1997; 2000; Stanley).

Right now, the interpretation of Galatians is shifting. The circumcision conflict at the heart of the letter appears as having been codetermined by Roman and civic pressures on the Galatians to conform to standard norms, apart from questions of the value or significance of the Torah itself (Winter, 124–43; Nanos, 257–71). The long-neglected phenomenon of Roman emperor worship, which was in fact massively present in provincial Galatia at the time of Paul (Hardin), points to the political idolatry of empire as potentially the primary target of Paul's polemics (Kahl 2010). And a new debate about the term "Christianity"—a term Paul himself never used—is emerging. Paul's messianic converts in Galatia defy our attempts at labeling or categorizing them (Boyarin 2004; Johnson Hodge; Campbell; Garroway), Instead of neatly categorized identities, we encounter here a messianic hybridity of multiply shaped identities, practiced as the commonality of love "in Christ." This hybridity mimics and mocks, summons and subverts the hybrid imperial identity imposed by Rome and her false gods.

At the beginning of the twenty-first century, appropriations of Galatians are being reoriented toward entirely new types of dialogue and interaction across all kinds of boundaries that dissect the body of humanity—and, for Christian interpreters, the body of Christ.

Galatians 1:1-9: The Other Gospel and the End of Otherness

▌ THE TEXT IN ITS ANCIENT CONTEXT

Tied into his signature greeting of "grace . . . and peace," Paul in the prescript of his letter highlights the key elements of the message he is entrusted with as God's ambassador (*apostolos*). The strong emphasis on a family-related terminology of God, Father, sonship, and siblinghood in Gal. 1:1-5 is noteworthy, as is the transition from the language of "I," "he," and "you" to the inclusive "we" and "our" over the first four verses, leading into the liturgical imperative collectively to worship and glorify "our" God and father (1:5). This concluding doxology is sealed by a participatory "Amen," to be pronounced in unison by the extended multiethnic family of God. The prominent placement of the resurrection event in 1:1 indicates that these new kinship affiliations are based on God's father-hood, made manifest in raising Jesus Messiah (= Christ) as his son "out of the dead" (cf. Rom. 1:4). As children of "our God and Father" (1:4), "we" are reborn as siblings of Jesus into God's diverse patchwork family of Jews and non-Jews together, a topic further explored in Galatians 3–4.

Read before the Roman backdrop, the political overtones of this ecumenical family construct are noteworthy. The establishment of empire-wide affiliations among diverse subject nations like Jews and Galatians, all of them united through a common fictive father (*pater patriae*), God (*divus*), son of God (*divi filius*), and Lord (*dominus*), was at Paul's time the prerogative of the emperor alone. It was he who claimed universal worship and fatherhood, especially in Galatia, where, around 50 CE, the lure of imperial religion was omnipresent as never before (Hardin). Furthermore, the liberation out of this "present evil age" (1:4) in the apocalyptic key of a new age lasting "forever and ever" (1:5), starkly clashed with the Roman ideology of a present "golden age"; it evoked a new exodus out of Roman slavery that was initiated when God's Son—*another* divine son, of a supreme God and Father other than Caesar—was resurrected from a Roman cross. In light of this Roman contextuality, the contours of a conflict between Paul's gospel of "grace . . . and peace" (1:3) and Roman peace (*Pax Romana*), between Christ-faith and imperial religion, are tangible from the outset, although Paul never addresses them directly—possibly in order to protect his addressees, whose names and locations he never discloses either (see Wright 2000; N. Elliott 2008, 25–43; Kahl 2010, 250–58).

What Paul makes more than explicit, however, is his stern disagreement with an "other gospel" that has gained ground in Galatia (1:6-9). Neglecting the most basic epistolary etiquette of his day, Paul abruptly moves from greeting to accusation as he indicts the Galatians of swift defection to this "other gospel." A double curse is hurled against anyone violating the integrity of the *euangelion* ("gospel") that Paul had preached to them (1:8-9). Full of hurt, anger, and sarcasm, Paul tries to disentangle the Galatians from whatever draws them toward those "who are confusing you and want to pervert the gospel of Christ" (1:7 NRSV).

Yet Paul is highly confusing himself. While he on the one hand anathematizes the proponents of an "other gospel," he simultaneously and with perplexing ambiguity declares this difference to be nonexistent. The Greek text of 1:6-7 says literally: "I am astonished that you are so quickly deserting . . . to a different gospel [*eis heteron euangelion*] which is not an other [*ho ouk estin allo*]." This sounds as if he is talking about two kinds of otherness, one that he fiercely contests, and one that he embraces as "not other." Nowhere else in the New Testament is the term *euangelion* so programmatically discussed as in Gal. 1:6—2:22. Is the "gospel according to Paul" thus *one*, or is it *one and other*? With this enigma, the whole interpretation of Galatians is at stake.

▌ THE TEXT IN THE INTERPRETIVE TRADITION

Traditionally, most translators and commentators have assumed that the "other gospel" was the Jewish gospel of circumcision that Paul wanted to leave behind. They thus saw fit to "correct" his paradoxical statement about difference and not-difference into an unambiguous rejection of the "other gospel" as being false or nonexistent: "I am astonished that you are so swiftly turning to a different gospel—*not that there is another*" (NRSV, emphasis added). With this, the "gospel of Christ" right from the beginning was cast into the "iron cage" of a binary construct that set Christianity off against the cursed other, whether Judaism or paganism or, in later centuries, heresy, or Islam, or other "opponents." During the Reformation, Luther redrafted the root binary in Galatians between Christ-gospel and the false circumcision gospel as the antithesis between Protestantism and Catholicism: his opposition of the "gospel" of faith righteousness to the "law" of works righteousness became foundational for Protestant and evangelical interpretations until today (Kahl 2010, 11–16).

But what if Paul contested, rather than (re)inscribed, this binary order, and what if he saw it primarily "at work" in Roman law rather than in Jewish Torah? What if his theology of the other is much more complex and subversive than our (falsely) simplified translations of Gal. 1:6-7 have led us to believe? Krister Stendahl, spearheading the New Perspective already in the 1970s, showed that the core of Paul's theology is not about excommunication of the other but community-building with the other—not about Christians versus Jews, rather about Jews together with gentiles (Stendahl, 1–7). More recently, J. Louis Martyn has done groundbreaking work regarding the apocalyptic "antinomies" or "pair of opposites" that were constitutive parts of the old cosmos but that were dissolved for Paul, through the Christ event, including the polarity of circumcision versus foreskin (Martyn 1997, 393–400). Thinking along these lines, we might regard Paul as criticizing the Galatians for applying an outdated binary model of otherness and oneness by moving toward circumcision; they act as if their difference (foreskin) still made them "other" to the Jews, or vice versa. This, the present entry proposes, is the basic deception of the "other gospel which is not another." The Galatians cannot be circumcised because this would reestablish the oppositional structure of the world as self over and against other. That opposition for Paul is the essence not of Torah (cf. 5:14), but rather of the worldwide "combat order" codified as Roman *nomos*. In this reading, the "other gospel" Paul rejects is essentially the Roman gospel of peace through war and victory, although it is disguised as "Jewish gospel" of strict obedience to the requirements of Torah, that is, circumcision. This issue of misleading appearance and of "hypocrisy"—making the deceptive claim to represent nothing but God's law while in reality following the logic of empire—is addressed throughout Galatians (e.g., 2:13; 6:12).

THE TEXT IN CONTEMPORARY DISCUSSION

Present-day examples abound for this dynamic of "othering," which, in the name of God, tacitly replicates the law of imperial or colonial domination. We might take a look at Africa, where HIV has become a pandemic that affects millions of people and tears the social fabric of communities apart. One of the aggravating factors is the attitude of many Christian churches that stigmatize people with HIV/AIDS as "sinners," rightly punished for their sexual promiscuity and needing to be cast out from churches, social life, and families to prevent further infection. In the name of Christ, taboos are imposed that not only cause enormous additional trauma for people with HIV but also prevent effective education about the spread of the disease and proper prevention. African theologians like Musa Dube and others have spoken up against the devastating self-righteousness in this "false gospel" that divides the body of Christ into a healthy and virtuous self over and against a sick and sinful other. This split, in fact, reproduces and reinscribes the law and logic of the colonial powers. Under the disguise of "rigorous Christianity," a distorted, moralistic understanding of human sexuality is perpetuated that was once preached by Western missionaries who condemned African sexuality as the evil other, to be colonized and civilized by the superior Christian self (Dube, 77–92; Mligo). As in Paul's day, the "other gospel" shape-shifts from allegedly proper faith to a law of domination, comparable to what Paul fiercely contested as irreconcilable with the coequal oneness and solidarity in God's universal family.

Galatians 1:10-21: Damascus: Defecting from the Culture of Enmity

THE TEXT IN ITS ANCIENT CONTEXT

As if he were acknowledging the confusion among his readers regarding the "otherness" of the messianic gospel, Paul declares that it is indeed alien to all human traditions and teachings. Nor is it accountable to any religious authority apart from the divine revelation (*di' apokalypseōs*) of Jesus

Christ (1:12). God's verification of Jesus as Messiah (*Christos*) struck Paul himself like a flash of lightning, unhinging his whole world. According to all human standards and norms, he had been impeccable and a model of religious superachievement, practicing Judaism flawlessly and with a competitive edge in his zeal for the "traditions of the fathers," violent in his conduct of holy warfare against dissidents like the Jesus-assemblies (1:13-14).

At this point, the divine intervention, or rather interruption, hit him. God not only revealed (*apokalypsai*) the persecuted other as "God's Son" to him but also charged Paul to proclaim (*euangelizōmai*) this "other" reality of God as "good news" (*euangelion* = "gospel") among the non-Jews: the sinners, gentiles, infidels whom he had previously seen as the irreconcilable other to God, to Judaism, and to himself (1:15-16). This was a complete transvaluation of all values and belief systems to which Paul had adhered. He had become a new, other-defined self and was in a vulnerable position now, unable to "consult with flesh and blood" about the nature of his transformation (1:16)—a different person unknown to his former allies and victims alike, and probably to himself too. Initially staying away from Jerusalem (1:17, 22), he visited Peter and James only after three years and for a brief period of fifteen days. Arabia, Damascus, Syria, and his native Cilicia were the places where he was "now proclaiming the faith that he once tried to destroy" (1:23). He was out among the gentile others, an other himself, proclaiming the one God of Israel who is with the other (Isa. 2:1-4).

▮ The Text in the Interpretive Tradition

"Damascus" over the millennia has become shorthand for the foundational event of Christianity and the beginning of the Christian world mission, which was all too often closely aligned with worldwide occidental colonialism and cultural imperialism. Once Paul's experience was understood as a "conversion" from Judaism to Christianity, a transition from a narrow-minded Jewish particularism to the wide-open, transethnic universalism of a new world religion, Christianity was framed in a binary way and turned into an inevitably anti-Jewish self-construct. Furthermore, Martin Luther's "tower experience" (*Turmerlebnis*) and search for a "gracious God," which occasioned his break with Catholicism, was often anachronistically collapsed with Paul's transformation from Jewish "Saul" to Christian "Paul." Following Krister Stendahl and the New Perspective, however, this antithetical view was challenged, reframing the "conversion" to another religion as a prophetic call *within* Judaism (Segal) and emphasizing the lasting Jewishness of Paul (Dunn, 341–60; Nanos; Eisenbaum).

Another question concerns the relationship between Paul's "firsthand" report of his "revelation" in Galatians and its noticeably divergent, later counterparts in Acts. Paul's famous "fall from his horse" is mentioned in neither Acts nor Galatians, and the name change from "Saul" to "Paul" occurs only in Acts 13:9 (and is unrelated to Damascus). Other facets of the different accounts are plainly incompatible and have led to perennial scholarly debates regarding the basic chronology and key coordinates of Paul's life and of early church history. Different from Paul's own more guarded account in Galatians, Acts makes his post-Damascus conflicts with the Roman order very explicit (e.g., Acts 17:6-7), while simultaneously trying to minimize their importance and to present Paul as a Roman model citizen (e.g., 16:37), inflating instead clashes with Judaism—an interpretive pattern that has been prevalent up to today (Kahl 2008).

▊ THE TEXT IN CONTEMPORARY DISCUSSION

"Damascus" in our language still stands for a profound life-changing experience. What happens if we realize that the whole construct we have used to validate ourselves while devalidating the other is no longer valid? Can strangers, aliens, competitors, adversaries, and even the fiercest enemies turn into neighbors? The terrorist attacks of September 11, 2001, on the World Trade Center and Pentagon, cost three thousand lives. For weeks afterward, New York City became a sanctuary of mourning and shared grief, while an international outcry against violence and a strong wave of sympathy reached out to the United States from all over the world. Yet what could have become a decisive turning point—a "Damascus" of sorts—toward sustainable global peace after the end of the Cold War was incinerated in the fire of retaliatory strikes and military counterviolence. In their book on restorative justice and peacemaking, Elaine Enns and Ched Myers report how members of the 9/11 family "made poignant pleas that violence not be done in their loved ones' names; instead, they turned their grief into actions for peace." Venturing on peace-building missions to countries like Afghanistan, they "transgressed the strictures of wartime's absolute demand for national loyalty by traveling to war zones to seek the human face of the 'enemy'" (Enns and Myers, 71–72).

What if a similar audacity "to defect from the culture of enmity" was at the core of Paul's Damascus experience, which demobilized him as a "holy warrior"? Prior to Damascus, he had seen the churches as compromising national and religious loyalty in the face of perpetual gentile (including Roman) onslaught against Israel. Might his post-Damascus "world mission" be described as journeying into the foreign "war zones" of otherness, not to plant "Christianity" in opposition to Judaism or paganism but to convey the Good News of Christ (*euangelizōmai auton en tois ethnesin*, 1:16) that deconstructs enmity and establishes viable peace? If so, then "Damascus" today could be taken not simply to mean the birth but rather the rebirth of Christianity as a comprehensive movement toward reconciliation with the enemy-other as the core of one's self-in-Christ.

Galatians 2:1-10: Peace Council at Jerusalem

▊ THE TEXT IN ITS ANCIENT CONTEXT

After many years of journeying, it took a second revelation (*apokalypsis*, 2:2) to make Paul finally return to Jerusalem. He returns as someone other from whom he was before, seeking the consensus of the Jerusalem leaders regarding "the gospel that I proclaim among the Gentiles"—clearly an "other gospel" in their eyes. Paul brings two mismatched "brothers" along, the Jew Barnabas and the Greek Titus (2:1). The textual hints at the drama surrounding their visit are cryptic, but clear enough to understand the key issue: From the standpoint of the Jerusalemites, the uncircumcised Titus (2:3) and the new mode of gentile-Jewish community he embodies are an anomaly threatening the integrity of the Christ proclamation. Conflicts pop up instantaneously. Paul mentions false brothers, infiltration of his communities, spying (2:4)—but he also passionately reports that eventually Titus was not forced to be circumcised and the "truth of the gospel" was preserved (2:3-5). Finally, in a somewhat miraculous reversal, the Jerusalem leaders concede the legitimacy of Paul's *other* gospel. Galatians 2:8-10 is a statement of groundbreaking importance: "On the contrary, when they saw that I had been entrusted with the gospel of the foreskin [*euangelion tēs akrobystias*], as Peter with the one of the circumcision [*tēs peritomēs*], . . . they gave to me and Barnabas the right hand of fellowship [*koinōnia*] . . . Only that we remember the poor" (my translation). The "gospel of Christ" (1:7) is authorized in two different versions that are applicable to two different groups, previously divided by an insurmountable boundary: Jews and gentiles. The "truth of the gospel" (2:5) is not uniformity but pluriformity; it reconfigures difference from enmity toward community and commonality (*koinōnia*). Yet this transformation is not encoded in a dogmatic statement, nor through erasing diversity (the foreskin of the male gentiles), but through concrete bodily and material practices of sharing—a handshake of solidarity and the collection of money from the gentile communities for the poor in Jerusalem, which became Paul's signature project.

∎ THE TEXT IN THE INTERPRETIVE TRADITION

In line with the dominant reading, which sees in Galatians the appearance of a new unified and distinct phenomenon, Christianity, most translators and interpreters have eclipsed the notion of the "one" gospel of Christ being two different gospels. The phrases "gospel *of* the foreskin" and "gospel *of* the circumcision" were rendered as "gospel *for* the Gentiles" and "gospel *for* the Jews" by the majority of translations, thus acknowledging only the difference between the audiences, but not the differentness within the gospel itself. Indeed, Hans Dieter Betz went so far as to assume that the notion of the two gospels was essentially un-Pauline and "may very well [have] come from an underlying official statement" (Betz, 97, 82). Most striking is Marcion's rendering in the second century, which simply omitted "gospel of the circumcision" from the text, as he saw it as an illicit compromise with outdated Jewish law-observance on Paul's side; therefore also the term "community" in 2:9 and the reference to the collection as "remembering of the poor" were removed (Riches, 103). Once the Jerusalem agreement became a merely tactical concession and the diversity of foreskin and circumcision that Paul envisioned was erased into the foreskin-only uniformity of gentile Christianity, the concrete practices of "difference-management" that integrated the diverse body of Christ lost their foundational importance as well. Not surprisingly, the importance of the collection as a church-founding antipoverty campaign is usually played down as a theologically irrelevant "kind of philanthropic gesture" (Betz, 101), although Paul mentions it as a primary act of economic and spiritual community-building, not only in Gal. 2:10 but also in 1 Cor. 16:1-4; 2 Corinthians 8–9; and Rom. 15:25-32 (Georgi 1992; 2005; Wan 2000; Longenecker).

∎ THE TEXT IN CONTEMPORARY DISCUSSION

Identifying the Jerusalem Council as the declaration of mutual acceptance (*koinōnia*) of formerly exclusive and hostile identities raises fascinating questions of unity and diversity in the early Jesus movement and today. Paul's radically inclusive messianic praxis of reconciling the nonuniform bodies of foreskin (gentileness) and circumcision (Jewishness) through concrete practices of solidarity "in Christ" might challenge contemporary notions of a uniform Christianity, to be defined over and against Judaism, Islam, Buddhism, or atheism. What would it mean for Christians to think

Christianity outside the binary opposition of self-versus-other that has shaped Christian theology and ecclesiology throughout the centuries? In the contemporary landscape, what might be new ways of embodying a sort of Christian "both/and" identity that might correspond to what Jared Garroway describes when he refers to Paul's "Jew-Gentiles" (Garroway, 1–10)?

Paul Knitter is one of the leading voices in interreligious dialogue today. Formerly a Catholic priest, trained at Rome during the Second Vatican Council, he identifies himself as both a Christian and a Buddhist. For him, Christ remains central in his spiritual practice, but this doesn't mean that Buddha is secondary. The Buddhist concept of the No-Self, for example, enabled him to understand Christ in a new way. Meditating on a regular basis, the traditional Christian practices of Eucharist, worship, and scriptural reflection have lost none of their importance for him. While he wants to share the message of the kingdom with non-Christians, he doesn't necessarily aim at "converting" them; rather, he understands the living, resurrected Christ to urge him to find the presence of the Spirit in others. Knitter frames his interreligious creed in the provocative book title *Without Buddha I Could Not Be a Christian*. Might the discussion above suggest that Paul of Tarsus could have pointed to Titus with an equally border-transgressive claim: "Without the gentiles I couldn't be a Jew true to Christ"? Does Paul's model of a bridge-identity through rigorous deconstruction of self and other contain new impulses to peace-building practices in the interreligious arena today that need to be unearthed?

Galatians 2:11-21: Eating (Dis)orders at Antioch and Justification by Faith

▌ THE TEXT IN ITS ANCIENT CONTEXT

The clash between Peter and Paul at Antioch was harsh and somewhat traumatic; again, concrete bodily markers and practices of community (*koinōnia*) were at stake. Jews including Peter had been eating together with the gentiles, but after the arrival of emissaries from James in Jerusalem, they withdrew from the common table "for fear of those from the circumcision." Boundaries were then reinstalled, visible to everyone (2:11-14). Paul calls this a collective hypocrisy of Peter and the Antiochene Jews (*synypekrithēsan*) and is shocked that even his companion Barnabas, witness of the Jerusalem agreement, joined them.

As his rebuke of Peter seamlessly leads into an extended exposition of justification theology, Paul links the Antioch table crisis with the present circumcision conflict in Galatia. The separation that originally set "us," Peter and Paul as "Jews by birth," apart from "gentile sinners" is no longer valid because sin is on "our" side as well (2:15). Doesn't Peter the Jew live like a gentile (i.e., as a sinner, too, betraying his Jewishness: 2:14)? It might well be that Paul here thinks in particular of the Roman order, which has made both Jews and gentiles/nations subservient to and compliant with global structures of injustice and power divinization, which from a radically Torah-based perspective is sin. In this situation, the whole hierarchical split between righteous selves and sinful others is made obsolete, no matter how carefully one tries to fulfill the requirements of Torah by doing "works of the law" (2:16). Paul fully concedes the challenge this commonality of both Jewish and gentile sin poses to the entire system of social categorization and distinction that provides status and recognition. The Antioch episode demonstrates how the temptation to "rebuild" the old, law-based divisions of "us" (righteous) versus "them" (sinful) is almost irresistible (2:17). Yet to actually put trust, or faith (*pistis*), in the righteousness of these new practices that reconfigure the relationship between self and other is what makes people just (or righteous) in their relations to both God and neighbor, according to Paul (2:16, 18).

This inevitably leads into social conflicts where these faith practices defy the required practices (*erga* = "works") of the established law (*nomos*) and turn the messianic communities into transgressors and "sinners" (2:16-17). In first-century Roman Antioch, the "mixed" table community of circumcised and uncircumcised, under the auspices of Jesus as Messiah, probably represented a political anomaly bordering on civil disobedience. It meant practicing an alternative *oikoumenē* among the conquered nations that acknowledged, not the triumphant Caesar, but his lawfully executed convict as supreme peacemaker, Lord, lawgiver, and divine presence. Since certain exemptions from the expectation of worship and subservience to Caesar were granted to Jews alone, Paul's Jewish antagonists in Antioch may well have been troubled by the blurring of boundaries as non-Jews joined with Jews at the common table. Would they be seen as inciting non-Jews to withdraw from normal civic honors to the emperor? Did they consequently either plead to avoid the common table (2:12) or seek to impose circumcision on the non-Jewish believers (2:14) as an "evasive action" to establish some minimal compliance with law and order (Winter, 141–42; Nanos, 257–71; Kahl 2011, 219–22)? Either explanation might make clearer the connection between the situation in Antioch and subsequent events in Galatia.

For Paul, this going back to "works of the law" means "nullifying" the grace of God and the crucifixion event (2:21)—a collective "hypocrisy" (2:13) that claims as Torah-obedience what, in fact, is subservience to *Caesar's* law, which has "hijacked" Torah. Jews and gentiles alike, formerly justified or unjustifiable by the criterion of law, are now together justified by Christ-faith, thus forging a new type of coequal community in tension with the established law of "divide and rule" that perpetually outlaws the other. There is no going back. Rather, the self has to accept its "death to the law" as death to itself, in an act of co-crucifixion with Christ that leads to an entirely new mode of life (2:19-20). Sin is overcome, not by law-works that set each one apart from the other, but by love-works of self-giving for the other that are embodied in Christ. This is the core of God's grace and of Paul's justification apart from the law (2:21).

▌ THE TEXT IN THE INTERPRETIVE TRADITION

One of the most perennial problems around Gal. 2:15-21 has been the theological split that detached the Protestant emphasis on justification by faith as core doctrine from the circumstances of the Antiochene incident itself. Paul's grand community manifesto was long read as an abstract theological declaration, without its concrete scriptural context. "Faith" became reduced to its vertical and personal component, as the individual act of belief "alone," while its horizontal and social dimension was eclipsed and often disqualified as "works of the law." The "dogmatic" and "conservative" Paul became the antagonist of the socially involved, liberating practice of Jesus. The seeming indifference of justification theology toward ethics led many Christians to question its theological relevance or to sidestep it as a "subsidiary crater" of Paul's theology (Schweitzer, 225). The following insights provided the decisive turning points in these debates: first, the Greek genitive *pistis Christou* could be translated either as "faith *in* Christ" or "faith *of* Christ," that is, pointing to the model faithfulness and obedience of Jesus (Hays); second, "works of the law" in Paul might not mean meritorious "good deeds," but rather exclusivist and boundary-marking practices to maintain a distinct status (Dunn, 140); third, "law" is not simply Torah but can also imply *nomos* in a more general sense, including Roman and civic *nomos* (Taubes, 24; Georgi 1997, 153); and, fourth, *nomos* can also be defined in terms of competition for honor and status (Jewett, 298), or of antithetical binaries (Martyn 1997, 406), or of the hierarchical antagonism between a dominant self and an inferior other (Kahl 2010, 23).

◼ THE TEXT IN CONTEMPORARY DISCUSSION

"Law" in this latter perspective is the normative order that systemically negates the worth of countless people on a global and local scale by "ranking" them, based on their economic or social status, their gender, ethnicity, religion, education, bodily (dis)ability, age, or other criteria. The poor, black, Hispanic, immigrant, indigenous, old, or underachieving part of humanity is disqualified as the loser and "undeserving," becoming dispensable or even disposable. Feminist liberation theologian Elsa Tamez, from Costa Rica, sees this "logic of alienation" and "out-casting" as the primary economic and social context for efforts to retrieve the transformative power of justification by grace and faith for today, efforts that mean affirming the humanity and dignity of those treated as "human trash." For Tamez, as for the Argentinian Néstor Oscar Míguez, the most powerful present-day embodiment of the "law" as an order of exclusion is the "law of competition" that is imposed globally by the neoliberal market economy and that justifies boundless self-interest and greed. "Sin" in this perspective is both personal and structural evil; it applies to us simultaneously as accomplices and as victims of injustice. Justification is inseparable from justice, opening a new logic of life and empowerment. It requires not only the renunciation of self-aggrandizement on the part of those in power but also the cessation of self-denigration on the part of those who see their marginalization as inevitable, natural, or God-willed punishment for their sin.

Galatians 3:1-29: "Queering" the Human Family

◼ THE TEXT IN ITS ANCIENT CONTEXT

The principal topic of Galatians 3, with 3:28 as its climactic statement, is the "genealogy" of the *ekklēsia* as messianic commonality that dismantles and reconfigures all established self- constructs emerging from exclusivist, hierarchical identity markers—like nation, race, class, or gender. The chapter starts with another angry rebuke of the Galatians. They have lost their messianic clear-sightedness for the meaning of "Christ crucified" and have gone back to "works of the law" (3:1-5).

If this means Christ-believing gentiles accepting circumcision to make them less prone to accusations of civil disobedience (compare the discussion of 2:11-21 above), Paul sees this seemingly Torah-based "accommodation" as entirely anti-Jewish.

Already in Gen. 12:3, the "proto-gospel" (*proeuēngelisato*, 3:8) had declared the Jewish progenitor Abraham as the future "body" incorporating God's transethnic blessing for every nation and tribe. One singular "seed" alone (*spermati*, *henos*) is carrying what might metaphorically be called the "genetic information" needed to generate this exceptional body of a collective self in communion with the other—"who is Christ [Messiah]" (3:16). This unique messianic seed was activated through the event of crucifixion and God's life-giving act of resurrection that claims life "out of the dead" (1:1; 3:13-14). The resurrected divine Son embodies God's universal fatherhood by granting new life in his own body to all those living in the shadow of Roman crosses, and a new identity as children of God and seed of Abraham. Becoming "one in Christ Jesus," Jews and non-Jews together are made heirs to Abraham's promise of a blessing that is color-blind, status-blind, and gender-blind (3:26-29).

The theological backbone of Paul's argument is a discourse of law and oneness that draws on the oneness of God as core-commandment of Torah (Exod. 20:1-5; Deut. 6:4). Oneness in the Messiah (3:28), however, is not the absence of diversity, but the contestation of an enslaving uniformity imposed by Caesar as the supreme "mediator" of the law, including Torah. Through his power to grant or revoke Jewish privileges, among them the privilege of nonparticipation in imperial cult, the emperor can bend Torah into a hybrid misrepresentation of God's will and oneness (3:19-20; Kahl 2010, 227). Although Rome did not suppress religious (including Jewish) diversity per se, it "united" all conquered nations and religions in a collective submission that prominently featured worship of Caesar as the one lord, God, son of God, and father in a kind of "imperial monotheism"—a horrendously idolatrous practice and anathema, from a Jewish perspective (Kahl 2010, 138–44). Despite their exemption from the expectation of emperor religion proper, Jews had to make every effort to show their subservience to and reverence for Caesar in other ways. However, accepting uncircumcised non-Jews who didn't worship Caesar, like Paul's messianic gentiles in Galatia, might have easily looked like making Judaism a hotbed of rebellion against Rome (Winter, 141–42; Nanos, 257–71). Ultimately, it was Caesar as "mediator of the law" (3:19) who determined that Paul's interpretation of Torah was "lawless."

"The mediator is not of the one [*henous ouk estin*], but God is one [*heis estin*]," Paul counters (3:20). His model of oneness radically challenges a construct of God and humanity that unifies the worldwide imperial "family" of the nations through oppressive imperial patriarchy and the idolatrous divinization of power. Contrariwise, the messianic family is derived from the (pro)creative power of a "seed" that generates life "out of the dead" (1:1) and is thus resistant to the dehumanizing, consent-producing power of Roman crosses. Baptism means reincorporation, through the generative power of the messianic "seed," that ends any form of patriarchal lineage. Humanity is no longer segregated into descendants of "our clan" or "their clan," highborn or lowborn, rich or poor fathers—or the absence of "documented" fathers altogether. In Paul's vision, the old, ghettoized self vanishes as humans are "reclothed" as new human beings in Christ: children of God and of Abraham, but siblings to one another and to Christ without any human father present, in this all-inclusive community where there is no longer Jew or Greek, slave or free, male and female, "for all of you are one in Christ Jesus" (3:26-28).

THE TEXT IN THE INTERPRETIVE TRADITION

As the climactic summary of Galatians 3, Paul's words in 3:26-28 constitute one of his most influential and controversial statements. There is a broad consensus that it originated from a pre-Pauline baptismal tradition, as attested elsewhere (1 Cor. 12:13; Col. 3:9-11; *2 Clem.* 12.2; *Gos. Thom.* 22; *Gospel of the Egyptians* 3.91; MacDonald). Its egalitarian implications, however, are matters of much debate. Does the "baptismal formula" mainly attest to emancipatory practices in the congregations prior to and at odds with Paul (Schüssler Fiorenza 1985, 208–11; Briggs)? Or is it exemplary of Paul's fear and erasure of difference in terms of "repressive sameness" or "coercive universalism" (Boyarin 1994, 234–35; Castelli, 124)? Would the baptismal oneness chiefly point to a future eschatological entity or a secluded spiritual reality "in Christ," without real-life implications, as much of the interpretational tradition has implicitly assumed? Is therefore the demand of subordination for women, children, slaves, and political subjects elsewhere in the (deutero-)Pauline letters (e.g., Eph. 5:21—6:9) compatible with Gal. 3:28; or, contrariwise, is the demand of subordination the "canonical betrayal" of Paul, that is, his conservative "gentrification" (N. Elliott 1994, 25–54)? In terms of "male and female," would Paul's oneness formula imply a primordial androgyny (Meeks), or the critique of the order of marriage and procreation (Schüssler Fiorenza 1985, 211), or might it rather signal severe "gender trouble" in Galatia due to Paul's deconstruction of dominant masculinity paradigms that were linked to circumcision as an established marker not just of Jewishness but also of maleness? (Kahl 1999; 2000; Wiley; cf. Lieu).

THE TEXT IN CONTEMPORARY DISCUSSION

How might Paul's baptismal oneness of Gal. 3:28 translate into today's society that is no longer split into "Jew" or "Greek/gentile," but into black and white, poor and rich, aliens and citizens, inmates and free people? Around eight million people in the United States are presently incarcerated, on probation, or on parole. Compared to the overall population, this is not only by far the largest number in any country of the world but also includes a disproportionally high number of poor people, African Americans, and immigrants. Two key markers of Gal. 3:28—race/ethnicity and social location in terms of class, the lingering heritage of slavery, and immigration status—are involved in creating a hierarchical division of society that separates "us" as the law-abiding citizens, preferably perceived as white, from "them" who are the righteously incarcerated lawbreakers: dangerous and dark "others." According to Mark Taylor, a part of the "surplus population" needs to be sacrificed to keep the others complacent and under control, and this sacrifice is enacted by a theatrical spectacle of control that keeps viewers both in fear and fascinated by state power (Taylor, 49, 60, 105–6; cf. Wacquant).

From Paul's perspective, this status quo might look like another version of the dehumanizing and therefore godless imperial model of "divide and rule" he was confronted with in his own day. The waters of baptism for him have "drowned" this entire system, washing away the distinction markers that give "us" (the nonimprisoned) a sense of self-righteousness and legitimate superiority, which is derived from the existence of unrighteous others: This is how for Bob Ekblad the Pauline theology of justification by faith rather than through works of the law starts to develop its transformative power. Ekblad reads Paul, including Galatians 3, with people in jail, in particular with undocumented immigrants at the US-Mexican border who know all too well the "curse of the law" (Gal. 3:10) that perpetually condemns them as illegal. For him, Jesus is the "Good Coyote" who crosses people over the border into the kingdom of God, against the law, despite the law. "In the waters of baptism into Jesus' death and resurrection the borders are brought down, and there are no longer distinctions between the law-abiding and criminal, US citizens and foreigners, legals and illegals, brown and white, chemically dependent and clean and sober, poor and rich, male and female—all are one in Christ. . . . We're all wetbacks, and must even count ourselves as fellow 'criminal aliens'" (Ekblad, 192).

Galatians 4:1-31: Mother Paul: Giving Birth to Messianic Solidarity

■ THE TEXT IN ITS ANCIENT CONTEXT

In chapter 4, Paul continues the messianic reconfiguration of family, genealogy, and identity. Consistent with the nonpatriarchal messianic "seed logic" of his midrashic discussion in Galatians 3, female concepts of mothering and birth-giving start to invade Paul's language with surprising consistency, making its gender dichotomies porous all throughout—most strikingly in Paul's "unmanly" depictions of himself as an inglorious missionary and a birth-giving mother in labor pains (4:12-20). In the subsequent allegory of the two competing archmothers (4:21-31), it is no longer Abraham's biological fatherhood, but an exclusively female differential—paradoxically spelled out as the "barren motherhood" of a childless and abandoned woman (4:27; Isa. 54:1)—that defines kinship and belonging, including citizenship in the metropolis ("mother city") of Jerusalem "above" (4:26, 31).

This highly irregular family construct is introduced in the opening section (4:1-7) by a strong appeal to "come of age" as children of God who recognize their adoption into an entirely new kin group, a transition tantamount to redemption from slavery. Collectively invoking God as *Abba*-Father (4:6), Paul says, "we" transition from slaves or minors to God's children (4:1). This change in legal status is achieved through God's Son, "born by a woman" and "under the law." His lawful death and his law-defying resurrection deflects the force of the law that defines people on the one hand as either Jew or Greek/gentile/Roman, and on the other as subservient/slaves to Rome, which in the common Roman perception "naturally" entails feminization and demasculinization (Lopez, 26–54). Persons are no longer confined by these attributions, nor by the codes of behavior (including circumcision) they entail. Rather, they are redeemed, that is, "bought out" (*exagorazein*), from "under the law" and its legal grip on their allegiance, conduct, and perception of themselves as opposed to others (4:4-5). It is noteworthy that in 4:1-7, "law" is equated with the "elemental spirits of the world" (*stoicheia tou kosmou*), which according to Martyn (1997, 393–406) are the (binary) "pairs of opposites" that antithetically constitute the cosmos as its basic building blocks and function as universal agents of enslavement for both Jews and gentiles ("us": 4:3, 5). This is strong evidence of the peculiar hybridity in Paul's law terminology, which excludes any clear alignment of *nomos* with Torah alone and rather points toward the worldwide governance through Roman law.

In 4:8-10, Paul admonishes the Galatians ("you") not to step back into their prior enslavement and underage status by resubscribing to the former gods that are "non-Gods." Recent scholarship has pointed out that in this passage Paul's antithetical stance against imperial religion, rather than Judaism and paganism in general, surfaces most visibly (Hardin, 116–47). The imperial gods that have co-opted all other civic deities are present among Roman subjects in a ceaseless sequence of "special days, and months, and seasons, and years" (4:10). These observances throughout the calendar year define civic time and space through a never-ending flurry of public festivals, processions, sacrifices, concerts, meals, benefactions, and rituals of all kinds (Mitchell 1993b, 10). Returning to at least minimal forms of participation on the side of the Galatians would restore political conformity as a matter of prudence; otherwise, they might imagine that they should take on a fully Jewish status through circumcision and thus hope to be excused from civic worship, as were the Jews.

Paul disagrees passionately. Rather than blending into the imperial *oikoumenē* of the imperial father and god on Caesar's terms, he tries to realign the Galatians with the generative body of Christ that brought them forth in the new shape of a humanity no longer split into two; that is, to *disalign* them from the destructive and all-devouring law of competition, combat, conquest that he sees embodied in the imperial idols who all claim falsely to be gods (4:8). His description of the birthing process that brought forth the new messianic (Christ-)identity among the Galatians and of the birth labors he himself is again enduring on their behalf (3:19) is one of the most moving passages in Paul's letters. He reminds the Galatians of their initial encounter, when they practically picked him up from the garbage pile of "human trash"—the embodiment of otherness in its plainest shape, as disposable and despicable nothingness (*exoutheneō*, "despise, regard as nothing," 4:14; cf. 1 Cor. 1:28). Yet it was precisely in this solidarity with the destitute human other, stripped of all human dignity, that the Galatians accepted the Messiah, the embodiment of an alternative world order (cf. Matt. 28:31-46). It is to this shape (*morphē*) of humanity as one alongside or in solidarity with another that Paul tries to rebirth his converts in his messianic labor pains (*ōdinō*): "My children with whom I am again in the pain of childbirth until Christ is formed [*morphōthē*] in you" (4:19).

It is only in this overall logic that the concluding passage (4:21-31) makes sense. All depends on taking seriously Paul's clues demanding a strictly "allegorical" and coded reading of "Hagar." Hagar is not a "real" woman, nor is she identical with her counterpart in Genesis 16 and 21. Rather, she represents what Paul "allegorically" attaches to her as a "correspondence" (*allegoroumenos, systoichei*): the blasphemous cooptation of the exodus-Torah ("Mount Sinai"), by the Roman law of colonial slavery, including the compliant birth of children into the enslaving master order as its subjects and soldiers (4:24-25). What Paul wants to "drive out" (*ekbale*, 4:30) is not Hagar the slave woman as a person, but on the contrary, "Hagar" as the mental and social imprint of Roman slavery on Jewish practices and mind-sets in Paul's time that she allegorically embodies as "Jerusalem now" (4:25). Hagar stands for the deceptive self-perception of those whom the Roman "father" claims as slaves, in continuous appellation to them as either *his* "children" or as subservient females who give birth to these children. The metaphorical Hagar's son, similar to the pre-Damascus Paul and the Antiochene Peter, personifies an enslaved body using aggressive self-assertion (*ediōken*, 4:29; 1:13; *anagkazeis*, 2:14) against other enslaved bodies. This delusional practice of "freedom" makes the conquered violently reenact against each other the law of conquest and combat that continues to enslave them all.

Hagar's allegorical counterpart is the "free woman." She is "our mother" (4:26)—the new body of one-with-another (3:28) that is generated out of "barren mothers" (like Paul), through the generative power of the messianic seed (3:16) and Abraham's transethnic blessing (3:8). This whole genealogical/birth narrative strongly draws on the theological deep structures of the Genesis accounts, with their entirely irregular construction of birthrights for second-born sons in opposition to existing patriarchal law. It brings all those parents not capable of bringing forth "proper" children together with all "other" children of God whom the law doesn't entitle to their share of the "inheritance" (4:31). Together, "we" are children of the promise like Isaac, citizens of the "Jerusalem above" as universal metropolis of peace and freedom (4:26). Yet "our" messianic reaffiliation requires clear dissociation (4:30) from the forces represented by "Hagar": forces that maintain the self-destructive and fratricidal binaries opposing "self" to "other" (Kahl 2004; 2013; Lopez, 153–63).

▋ THE TEXT IN THE INTERPRETIVE TRADITION

One of the biggest interpretational liabilities of Galatians has been the binary reading that took the Hagar allegory as a "proof text" for a violent and supersessionist Christian disalignment from the other of Judaism. This polarity is famously depicted in the defeated and blindfolded female body of the "Synagogue," opposed by the triumphant woman "Ecclesia," in many churches in Europe. In line with Genesis 16 and 21, Gal. 4:21-31 has been read as another "text of terror" (Trible) that canonized the "legitimate" oppression and exclusion of Hagar not only as "Jew" but also as the abused and traded woman, the exploited African American (sex) slave, the single mother, the disposable foreigner (Williams 1993; 2006; Briggs, 224). Furthermore, the equally relentless stance of Gal. 4:30 against Hagar's son Ishmael, who was according to Qur'an 2:121 the cofounder of the Kaaba in Mecca, could very well preconfigure contemporary anti-Islamism (Hassan). Without a Roman "reading lens," the harsh verdict against Hagar can indeed all too easily change into the epitome of Christian anti-Judaism, patriarchy, xenophobia, and "kyriarchal" social master codes as they are commonly attributed to Paul (Schüssler Fiorenza 1999, 163–65).

▋ THE TEXT IN CONTEMPORARY DISCUSSION

As a theological text, Galatians 4 is strikingly concrete in talking about able and defective human bodies. When the Galatians received and restored the weak, perhaps disfigured body of Paul as if he were Christ (*hōs Christon Iēsoun*, 4:14), rather than "spitting" (*exeptysate*) at him, they themselves became the "seed" (3:16) of the Messiah in his disabled and reenabled shape, as crucified and resurrected (4:12-15). This "form" and body of Christ is now in danger of being aborted (4:19) under the censorship of "standard" expectations regarding circumcised and noncircumcised bodies.

The pressure of normative body images in our contemporary society is strongly felt by people who don't conform to established standards of "ability." Bioethicist Adrienne Asch (1947–2013) was a pioneer in feminist disability studies who passionately spoke against prenatal testing as a means to detect disabilities in unborn children and terminate those pregnancies. Blind all her life and a passionate pro-choice advocate, she nonetheless strongly condemned such targeted abortions, arguing that life with disabilities was not "worthless" life (Parens and Asch). That might strongly resonate with Paul, who himself experienced the life-giving power of the messianic "seed" (3:16) in Galatia as a disabled, perhaps (vision)-impaired (cf. 4:15) missionary who received solidarity—and as the birth-giving mother of a human shape accused of being an intolerable misfit (4:12-20). His theology of the "body of Christ" suggests the integration (not necessarily the "mending") of broken and non-normative bodies in a healing, supportive community where they can thrive in their diversity. Could Paul's expulsion of the metaphorical body of "Hagar" be read, in a contemporary version, as the exorcism of compulsive, self-destructive (body) images of perfection and "normalcy" that we impose on ourselves and others? This "law" of accomplishment keeps people enslaved to the established master order by instilling constant anxiety, competition, and relentless "persecution" (cf. Gal. 4:29) of imperfection, in a never-ending race toward adequate performance and conformity. Ultimately, the "stigmatization of disability drives power mechanisms of capitalism" (Tataryn and Truchan-Tataryn, 14; cf. Isherwood).

Galatians 5:1—6:18: Old Cosmos and New Creation: The Ecology of Interdependence

▌THE TEXT IN ITS ANCIENT CONTEXT

The last section of Galatians shifts the emphasis to the concrete conflicts in Galatia. For the first time, the pressure to be circumcised is actually made explicit (5:3, 11; 6:11). And in candid language, Paul addresses issues of ethical norms and community rules that specifically target divisive behavior like "biting and devouring one another" or "competing against one another, envying one another" (5:15, 26). The catalog of vices and virtues in 5:19-23, though using a conventional pattern of ancient moral discourse, nonetheless is specifically tailored toward internal strife as signaled in eight out of the fifteen vices listed: enmity, rivalry, jealousy, anger, quarrels, dissensions, factions, envy. All of these for Paul reflect an inflated sense of self-entitlement that damages the relationship between oneself and the other.

In contrast, love is the first item in the list of virtues. These all uniformly emphasize community-building "fruits of the spirit" like joy, peace, patience, kindness, generosity, faithfulness, gentleness, self-control (5:22). The term "one another" (*allēlōn*), derived from *allos-allos* ("other-other"), occurs no less than seven times in the brief section (5:13—6:2), pointing to the messianic movement from self-against-other to self-with-another that dissolves all binaries and divisions. The "law of Christ" is to "bear one another's burdens" (6:2); this fulfills Torah, which is "summed up" (*peplērōthei*) in the *one* commandment of Lev. 19:18 to love your neighbor as yourself (Gal. 5:14). In all these ethical admonitions, "faith that 'works' through love" (*energoumenē*, 5:6) is the key concept: the indicative, that is, the Christ-reality of a new life "through the spirit," is inseparable from the imperative of "walking according to the norm of the spirit" (5:25).

"Spirit" in this context is the opposite of "flesh." The antithesis "spirit versus flesh" first came up in 3:2-3, together with the juxtaposition "works of power" or "faith" versus "works of the law" (3:5); it structures the whole passage, alongside the parallel polarity of "freedom versus slavery." The spirit-engendered life in conformity with the law of Christ/Spirit embodies the "freedom" of the Galatians to withdraw from their slavish allegiance to the dominant law. Chapter 5 starts with a passionate plea that the Galatians "stand firm" in their freedom and not "submit again to a yoke of slavery" (5:1). Slavery was linked to the allegorical Hagar and the flesh in the preceding passage— and to the imperial law of divisiveness and submission that Paul sees creeping up in the circumcision conflict as well as in other internal combats and competitions.

Does this strongly antithetical structure in fact reinscribe the old dichotomies as structuring principle and basic building blocks of the cosmos (*stoicheia tou kosmou*, cf. 4:3, 9)? Is the assertion of freedom for ourselves on its underside inevitably the affirmation of slavery for others? These are valid questions. Paul dispels them with a carefully worded paradox: Messianic freedom is enacted as mutual slavery. It is not the unrestricted pursuit of self-interest from a master position as licensed by imperial law; rather, it is that law's perpetual subversion by "serving as slaves (*douleuete*) to one another through love" (5:13). Unlike manumission by civic and imperial law, Christ-freedom thus is the undoing of slavery rather than its tacit reinscription as licit.

What if a member of the congregation fails to live according to the law of love? How should the community respond, without the backup of established law, "if anyone is detected in a transgression" (6:1)? One might think that at this point, finally, a strong hand is needed to restore order and accountability. Yet in the final section (6:1-10), Paul carefully avoids the recourse to any hierarchical authority (including his own) that judges, sanctions, and corrects misbehavior. Judgment and setting things right is strictly mutualized as task of the spirit-guided (*pneumatikoi*, 6:1) community. Any transgressor must be held accountable indeed, but in a "spirit of meekness." Mindfulness of the judge's own fallibility has to counterbalance the constant temptation to reestablish oneself in a master position over and against a sinful other (6:1). The "law of Christ" is not fulfilled through sanctioning the other's lapses, but through "bear[ing] one another's burdens" (6:2).

Paul here seems to be concerned about the judges more than the transgressor. The urge of the self to display its own righteousness before the dark foil of another's offenses is sarcastically derided: After examining their own works, those who want to be important (but are not) should acclaim their merits strictly to themselves alone (*pros seauton monon*, 6:4). They should avoid the sort of "competitive boasting" (Jewett, 296) that reproduces the whole falsehood and deception (*phrenapatā*, 6:3) of social status, distinction, and superiority. God is the only judge, and only in the final judgment will each one have to carry their "own burdens" (6:5). Yet investing one's life into the "Spirit" by "working for the good of all" (6:10) will reliably bring forth eternal life, whereas "sowing into the flesh" of self-obsession (and circumcision) will engender the harvest of death (6:8).

At the end, Paul adds a postscript in his own "large letters" (6:11-18). Circumcision in Galatia does not mean what it ordinarily does, namely, a seal of Jewish allegiance; its advocates are not really concerned about Torah (6:13). Rather, the "persecution" that they fear from the outside enforces the pressures to conform to established norms and identity markers (6:12; Winter, 123–43; Hardin, 85–115). At this point, Paul makes a final declaration: It is exactly this death-dealing conformity to a commonly accepted world order (*kosmos*) of divisive binaries that is dead through the cross. The universal logic that breeds violence, war, and subjugation, while claiming to be without alternative, has been deactivated. Paul is "crucified to the old *kosmos*" and the old *kosmos* to him (6:14). Yet the power of the resurrection emerges as the life-giving manifestations of the "new creation." It is not yet fully present, but tangible reality wherever the old antitheses of self versus other, or circumcision versus foreskin, are invalidated (6:15). This is the "canon" of peace and mercy (6:16). It continuously dissolves enmity and polarity (which continuously keep building up again) within a community practice of dynamic mutuality and peace-building propelled by the transformative power of the Spirit and "the grace of our Lord Jesus Christ/Messiah" (6:18). With this concluding testimony framed as a farewell greeting to his Galatian brothers and sisters followed by a final "Amen," Paul summarizes and closes his letter.

▌THE TEXT IN THE INTERPRETIVE TRADITION

Rather than being understood as the climax of Galatians, Paul's condensed reflection about love and community practice in Galatians 5–6 has often been disavowed as a mere afterthought to the letter, as it was seen as being in tension with its main theological thrust of "faith (alone)" versus "works" (see Barclay, 7–16). The question of how Paul's theology and ethics are related has been widely debated, including the complex issue of "indicative" and "imperative"—that is, the paradoxical relationship between justification as the state of already achieved freedom from sin on the one hand and the demand to actively "work" against sin in line with faith, love, and Spirit on the other, as expressed in Gal. 5:1, 5-6, 25 (Horrell, 10–15). Another disputed topic has been the opposition of "flesh" (*sarx*) versus "spirit" (*pneuma*). The term "flesh" was often falsely identified as the inferior and sinful materiality of the human body, specifically with regard to sexuality. On the opposite side, "spirit" came to be understood as the superior and immaterial sphere of the "soul" and of "spiritual discernment," defined in entirely individualistic categories. Instead, as has been rightly stated, "flesh" in Paul stands for the "radical inclination to self-centeredness," in conjunction with the general biblical notion of flesh as the sphere of sin, that is, "human existence [seen] from the aspect of its being hostile to God and other human beings because it is essentially turned in on self" (Byrne , 45).

▌THE TEXT IN CONTEMPORARY DISCUSSION

Galatians as Paul's probably most consequential letter has been discussed from a variety of perspectives, but rarely in light of the current ecological crisis. While the phenomenon of a global, life-threatening devastation of the earth's habitat didn't exist yet in the ancient world, and Paul certainly was not a "green" theologian, one might rightly ask whether the cosmic scope of his antidualistic thinking and the strong concern for the social, religious, and cultural other as key signatures of his messianic theology might have implications for the nonhuman other of nature as well. Does the "new creation" (*kainē ktisis*) in Gal. 6:15 as a condensed statement of the messianic transformation refer to humans alone, or is the conversion of ourselves in relation to the other of earth, water, and air implied?

As the *Sydney Morning Herald* reported in June 2013, a church in Queensland, Australia, has twenty-four solar panels bolted to its roof in the shape of a Christian cross. And a mosque in Bursa, western Turkey, is projected to have a vertical-axis wind turbine (without the big revolving blades) installed on a minaret. Should one read the "solar cross" on a Christian church as a crude trivialization, a fad, a blasphemous persiflage on Paul's august theology of the cross, or as one of its valid and urgent contemporary recontextualizations? The cross obviously features prominently all throughout Galatians, including the final handwritten postscript in 6:11-18. In 6:14-15, Paul boldly declares that he is crucified to the (old) *kosmos* and the *kosmos* to him, because the dichotomies on which the established world order (*kosmos*) rests (like the antithesis of circumcision/Jews versus foreskin/gentiles) have been dissolved and left behind. The cross thus opens up an ongoing transformation of self and other toward reconciliation and mutuality that clearly transcends the realm of humans. Paul is crucified to the entire *kosmos* with its multiple polarities, not just its faith-based, ethnic, and social divisions (Martyn 1985). Echoing the biblical creation accounts in Genesis 1–3 and Isa. 43:18-19; 65:17-25, the "new creation" in Gal. 6:15 that is born out of the cross, then, would be more than simply a new society or religion, it would rather comprise the entirety of the human and nonhuman world (Kahl 2010, 272–73).

The polar (dis)order that over the centuries has become formative for Western philosophy, theology, and civilization excludes and exploits not only the human other in terms of gender, race, religion, and class, but also the other of nature and earth. Paul's radical regard for the other and his messianic model of a "corporate solidarity" in Christ, as perceptively outlined by David Horrell (274), for our time thus inevitably have an ecological dimension as well—for example, where our mutual interdependence within overarching ecosystems and the rights of nonhuman species need to be acknowledged (Horrell, Hunt, and Southgate, 190–94). "Greening" Paul and his theology of faith-justification is one of the most cutting-edge tasks ahead for Pauline interpretation. And maybe the "solar cross" and the "wind energy minaret" mentioned above could allow us to envision a nonbinary creation (Gal. 6:15) as the forging of new coalitions toward a universally sustainable connectivity across all kinds of religious and other boundaries that was as vital to Paul's world as it is to ours.

Works Cited

Arnold, Clinton A. 2005. "'I Am Astonished That You Are So Quickly Turning Away!' (Gal 1:6): Paul and the Anatolian Folk Belief." *NTS* 51:429–49.

Barclay, John M. G. 1988. *Obeying the Truth: Paul's Ethics in Galatians*. Edinburgh: T&T Clark.

Betz, Hans Dieter. 1979. *Galatians*. Hermeneia. Philadelphia: Fortress Press.

Boyarin, Daniel. 1994. *A Radical Jew: Paul and the Politics of Identity*. Berkeley: University of California Press.

———. 2004. *Border Lines: The Partition of Judaeo-Christianity*. Philadelphia: University of Pennsylvania Press.

Braxton, Brad R. 2002. *No Longer Slaves: Galatians and African American Experience*. Collegeville, MN: Liturgical Press.

Briggs, Sheila. 1994. "Galatians." In *Searching the Scriptures*. Vol. 2, *A Feminist Commentary*, edited by Elisabeth Schüssler Fiorenza. New York: Crossroad.

Byrne, Brendan. 2010. *Galatians and Romans*. Collegeville, MN: Liturgical Press.

Campbell, William S. 2006. *Paul and the Creation of Christian Identity.* New York: T&T Clark.

Castelli, Elizabeth A. 1991. *Imitating Paul: A Discourse of Power.* Louisville: Westminster John Knox.

Dube, Musa, ed. 2007. *Theology in the HIV and AIDS Era Series: Reading the New Testament in the HIV and AIDS Contexts.* Geneva: World Council of Churches.

Dunn, James D. G. 2005. *The New Perspective on Paul: Collected Essays.* WUNT 185. Tübingen: Mohr Siebeck.

Ehrensperger, Kathy. 2004. *That We May Be Mutually Encouraged: Feminism and the New Perspective in Pauline Studies.* New York: T&T Clark.

Eisenbaum, Pamela. 2009. *Paul Was Not a Christian: The Original Message of a Misunderstood Apostle.* New York: HarperOne.

Ekblad, Bob. 2005. *Reading the Bible with the Damned.* Louisville: Westminster John Knox.

Elliott, Neil. 1994. *Liberating Paul: The Justice of God and the Politics of the Apostle.* Maryknoll, NY: Orbis.

———. 2008. *The Arrogance of Nations: Reading Romans in the Shadow of Empire.* Minneapolis: Fortress Press.

Elliott, Susan M. 2004. *Cutting Too Close for Comfort.* JSNTSup 248. Sheffield: Sheffield Academic.

Enns, Elaine, and Ched Meyers. 2009. *Ambassadors of Reconciliation.* Vol. 2, *Diverse Christian Practices of Restorative Justice and Peacemaking.* Maryknoll, NY: Orbis.

Fatum, Lone. 1989. "Women, Symbolic Universe and Structures of Silence." *ST* 43:61–80.

Garroway, Joshua D. 2012. *Paul's Gentile-Jews: Neither Jew Nor Gentile, But Both.* New York: Palgrave Macmillan.

Gaventa, Beverly Roberts. 1990. "The Maternity of Paul: An Exegetical Study of Galatians 4:19." In *The Conversation Continues: Studies in Paul and John in Honor of J. Louis Martyn,* edited by Robert T. Fortna and Beverly Roberts Gaventa, 189–210. Nashville: Abingdon.

Georgi, Dieter. 1992. *Remembering the Poor: The History of Paul's Collection for Jerusalem.* Nashville: Abingdon.

———. 1997. "God Turned Upside Down." In *Paul and Empire: Religion and Power in Roman Imperial Society,* edited by Richard Horsley, 148–157. Harrisburg, PA: Trinity Press International.

———. 2005. "Is There Justification in Money? A Historical and Theological Meditation on the Financial Aspects of Justification by Christ." In *The City in the Valley: Biblical Interpretation and Urban Theology,* 283–207. Atlanta: Society of Biblical Literature.

Hardin, Justin K. 2008. *Galatians and the Imperial Cult: A Critical Analysis of the First-Century Social Context of Paul's Letter.* Tübingen: Mohr Siebeck.

Hassan, Riffat. 2006. "Hagar in African American Biblical Appropriation." In *Hagar, Sarah, and Their Children: Jewish, Christian, and Muslim Perspectives,* edited by Phyllis Trible and Letty M. Russell, 149–67. Louisville: Westminster John Knox.

Hays, Richard. 1983. *The Faith of Jesus Christ: An Investigation of the Narrative Substructure of Galatians 3:1—4:11.* Chico, CA: Scholars Press.

Horrell, David G. 2005. *Solidarity and Difference: A Contemporary Reading of Paul's Ethics.* London: T&T Clark.

Horrell, David G., Cheryl Hunt, and Christopher Southgate. 2010. *Greening Paul: Rereading the Apostle in a Time of Ecological Crisis.* Waco, TX: Baylor University Press.

Horsley, Richard A., ed. 1997. *Paul and Empire: Religion and Power in Roman Imperial Society.* Harrisburg, PA: Trinity Press International.

———. 2000. *Paul and Politics: Ekklesia, Israel, Imperium, Interpretation: Essays in Honor of Krister Stendahl.* Harrisburg, PA: Trinity Press International.

Isherwood, Lisa. 2008. *The Fat Jesus: Christianity and Body Image.* New York: Seabury.

Jewett, Robert. 2007. *Romans: A Commentary.* Hermeneia. Minneapolis: Fortress Press.

Johnson Hodge, Caroline. 2007. *If Sons, Then Heirs: A Study of Kinship and Ethnicity in the Letters of Paul.* Oxford: Oxford University Press.

Kahl, Brigitte. 1999. "Gender Trouble in Galatia? Paul and the Rethinking of Difference." In *Is There a Future for Feminist Theology?* Edited by Deborah F. Sawyer and Diane M. Collier, 57–73. Sheffield: Sheffield Academic.

———. 2000. "No Longer Male: Masculinity Struggles Behind Galatians 3.28?" *JSNT* 79:37–49.

———. 2004. "Hagar between Genesis and Galatians: The Stony Road to Freedom." In *From Prophecy to Testament: The Function of the Old Testament in the New*, edited by Craig A. Evans, 219–32. Peabody, MA: Hendrickson.

———. 2008. "Acts of the Apostles: Pro(to)-Imperial Script and Hidden Transcript." In *In the Shadow of Empire: Reclaiming the Bible as History of Faithful Resistance*, edited by Richard A. Horsley, 137–56. Louisville: Westminster John Knox.

———. 2010. *Galatians Re-Imagined: Reading with the Eyes of the Vanquished.* Paul in Critical Contexts. Minneapolis: Fortress Press.

———. 2011. "Galatians and the 'Orientalism' of Justification by Faith: Paul among Jews and Muslims." In *The Colonized Apostle: Paul through Postcolonial Eyes*, edited by Christopher Stanley, 206–22. Minneapolis: Fortress Press.

———. 2013. "Krieg, Maskulinität und der imperiale Gottvater: Das Augustusforum und die messianische Re-Imagination von 'Hagar' im Galaterbrief." In *Doing Gender—Doing Religion*, edited by U. Eisen, C. Gerber, and A. Standhartinger, 273–300. WUNT 302. Tübingen: Mohr Siebeck.

Kamudzandu, Israel. 2013. *Abraham Our Father: Paul and the Ancestors in Postcolonial Africa.* Minneapolis: Fortress Press.

Knitter, Paul. 2009. *Without Buddha I Could Not Be A Christian.* London: Oneworld.

Le Cornu, Hilary, and Joseph Shulam. 2005. *A Commentary on the Jewish Roots of Galatians.* Jerusalem: Academon.

Lieu, Judith. 1994. "Circumcision, Women and Salvation." *NTS* 40:358–70.

Longenecker, Bruce W. 2010. *Remember the Poor: Paul, Poverty, and the Greco-Roman World.* Grand Rapids: Eerdmans.

Lopez, Davina. 2008. *Apostle to the Conquered: Reimagining Paul's Mission.* Minneapolis: Fortress Press.

MacDonald, Dennis R. 1987. *There Is No Male and Female: The Fate of a Dominical Saying in Paul and Gnosticism.* Philadelphia: Fortress Press.

Martyn, J. Louis. 1985. "Apocalyptic Antinomies in Paul's Letter to the Galatians." *NTS* 31:410–24

———. 1997. *Galatians: A New Translation with Introduction and Commentary.* AB. New York: Doubleday.

Meeks, Wayne A. 1974. "The Image of Androgyne: Some Uses of a Symbol in Earliest Christianity." *HR* 13:165–208.

Míguez, Néstor Oscar. 2004. "Galatians." In *Global Bible Commentary*, edited by Daniel Patte, 463–72. Nashville: Abingdon.

Mitchell, Stephen. 1993a. *Anatolia: Land, Men, and Gods in Asia Minor.* Vol. 1, *The Celts and the Impact of Roman Rule.* Oxford: Clarendon.

———. 1993b. *Anatolia: Land, Men, and Gods in Asia Minor.* Vol. 2, *The Rise of Christianity.* Oxford: Clarendon.

Mligo, Elia Shabani. 2011. *Jesus and the Stigmatized: Reading the Gospel of John in a Context of HIV/AIDS-Related Stigmatization in Tanzania.* Eugene, OR: Pickwick.

Nanos, Mark. 2002. *The Irony of Galatians: Paul's Letter in First-Century Context.* Minneapolis: Fortress Press.

Niang, Aliou Cissé. 2009. *Faith and Freedom in Galatia and Senegal: The Apostle Paul, Colonists, and Sending Gods*. Biblical Interpretation Series 97. Leiden: Brill.

Osiek, Carolyn. 1992. "Galatians." In *The Women's Bible Commentary*, edited by Carol A. Newsome and Sharon H. Ringe, 333–37. Louisville: Westminster John Knox.

Parens, Erik, and Adrienne Asch, eds. 2000. *Prenatal Testing and Disability Rights*. Washington, DC: Georgetown University Press.

Riches, John Kenneth. 2008. *Galatians through the Centuries*. Malden, MA: Blackwell.

Schüssler Fiorenza, Elisabeth. 1985. *In Memory of Her: A Feminist Theological Reconstruction of Christian Origins*. New York: Crossroad, 1985.

———. 1999. *Rhetoric and Ethic: The Politics of Biblical Studies*. Minneapolis: Fortress Press.

Schweitzer, Albert. 1931. *The Mysticism of Paul the Apostle*. London: Black.

Segal, Alan. 1990. *Paul the Convert: The Apostolate and Apostasy of Saul the Pharisee*. New Haven: Yale University Press.

Stanley, Christopher D., ed. 2011. *The Colonized Apostle: Paul through Postcolonial Eyes*. Paul in Critical Contexts. Minneapolis: Fortress Press.

Stendahl, Krister. 1976. *Paul among Jews and Gentiles, and Other Essays*. Minneapolis: Fortress Press.

Streufert, Mary J., ed. 2010. *Transformative Lutheran Theologies: Feminist, Womanist, and Mujerista Pespectives*. Minneapolis: Fortress Press.

Tamez, Elsa. 1993. *The Amnesty of Grace*. Nashville: Abingdon.

Tataryn, Myroslaw, and Maria Truchan-Tataryn. 2013. *Discovering Trinity in Disability: A Theology for Embracing Difference*. Maryknoll, NY: Orbis.

Taubes, Jacob. 2004. *The Political Theology of Paul*. Stanford: Stanford University Press.

Taylor, Mark Lewis. 2001. *The Executed God: The Way of the Cross in Lockdown America*. Minneapolis: Fortress Press.

Trible, Phyllis. 1984. *Texts of Terror: Literary-Feminist Readings of Biblical Narratives*. Philadelphia: Fortress Press.

Wacquant, Loic. 2009. *Punishing the Poor: The Neoliberal Government of Social Insecurity*. Durham: Duke University Press;

Wan, Sze-Kar. 2000. "Collection for the Saints as Anticolonial Act." In *Paul and Politics: Ekklesia, Israel, Imperium, Interpretation. Essays in Honor of Krister Stendahl*, 191–215. Edited by Richard A. Horsley. Harrisburg, PA.: Trinity Press International.

Wiley, Tatha. 2005. *Paul and the Gentile Women: Reframing Galatians*. New York: Continuum.

Williams, Delores. 1993. *Sisters in the Wilderness: The Challenge of Womanist God-Talk*. Maryknoll, NY: Orbis.

———. 2006. "Hagar in African American Biblical Appropriation." In *Hagar, Sarah, and Their Children: Jewish, Christian, and Muslim Perspectives*, edited by Phyllis Trible and Letty M. Russell, 171–84. Louisville: Westminster John Knox.

Winter, Bruce. 1994. *Seek the Welfare of the City: Christians as Benefactors and Citizens*. Grand Rapids: Eerdmans.

Wright, N. T. 2000. "Paul's Gospel and Caesar's Empire." In *Paul and Politics*, edited by Richard Horsley, 160–83. Harrisburg, PA: Trinity Press International.

———. 2005. *Paul: In Fresh Perspective*. Minneapolis: Fortress Press.

Zetterholm, Magnus. 2009. *Approaches to Paul: A Student's Guide to Recent Scholarship*. Minneapolis: Fortress Press.

EPHESIANS

Jennifer G. Bird

Introduction

It is important to keep in mind that, when the Letter to the Ephesians was written in the first century, many of its ideas might have been new and perhaps somewhat startling to the people who read or heard it. When we consider the letter's content from this angle, we can see not just what is unique to Ephesians but also how striking some of the letter's components are, despite the fact that the letter has become part and parcel of Christian thought.

We find a surprising array of topics and issues in the letter. Written near the end of the first century, Ephesians shows evidence of several components of what became Gnostic thought ("every spiritual blessing in the heavenly places," 1:3; "made known to us the mystery of his will," 1:9; "fullness of time," 1:10; "spirit of wisdom and revelation," 1:17; "fullness of him who fills all in all," 1:23; "mystery," "perceiving," and "understanding" language in 3:3-4; "renewed in the spirit of your minds," 4:23; dualistic language in 5:6-16). Here as well are traces of an internal struggle among the various strands of thought within Judaism regarding who belongs to the covenant and which observances are legitimate (1:3-14; 2:11-22). And here are marked distinctions from several ideas found in the genuine Pauline Letters, which contribute to some scholars labeling Ephesians as deuteropauline instead of genuine. (The various strands of thought in Judaism went beyond just what Josephus named as the "schools" of the Essenes, Pharisees, Sadducees, and Zealots. Jesus' own disciples were Jews, and some of them had some differences of opinion from what Paul was saying, for instance. Any time we see New Testament texts claiming that Christ is the fulfillment of God's true covenant, we can pause to consider how this stands in contrast with other Jewish beliefs at the time. At the very least, there were proponents of Jewish observances visiting some of Paul's churches offering different instructions than he did [Acts 15; 2 Corinthians 10–13; Galatians 1–2].)

Though there are significant topics throughout the letter, the overarching and most important aspect of it for us today is perhaps the focus on the spiritual realm. Not only does this focus foster beliefs in a literal and embodied devil as a spiritual evil being (6:10-16), but it also creates a worldview primarily interested in spiritual warfare and attending to people's souls or spirits more than addressing the needs of this physical world. This in turn can lead to a form of escapism, if not simply a seemingly depoliticized or apolitical perspective on the world. In the twenty-first century, we cannot afford to live such disinterested and disconnected lives. Rather, however spiritually we experience the world, we also need to be intimately involved in making it a more humane and just place to live.

That this heavenly realm is discussed, as we shall see, in terms suggesting a mirror or counter to the empire of this world raises significant questions for us in terms of how we ought to be reading this letter, or any such imperial language, today. The source of power and control within any kingdom draws on the elements of fear and highly rigid roles for a majority of the people. Thus we do well to pay attention to the relationship that is encouraged here between "citizens" and the lord or king in the spiritual kingdom of heaven. Similarly, the passage giving instructions to persons occupying different roles in the household, customarily called the "household code" (or *Haustafel*: 5:21—6:9), must be seen as making deliberate sociopolitical claims, which restrict and control at times or grant relative freedom to the various people within the household structure. In light of this element of the letter, members of the church today would do well to consider carefully how or whether to use this paradigm to help define family relationships.

Among the other topics to be addressed in discussing this letter are an at least partially realized eschatology (1:14), fully realized at times, meaning that the spiritual salvation available because of Christ is already at work in us (e.g., 1:7); the main New Testament references to predestination (1:3-11; 2:10); the imagery of the church as the bride of Christ (5:22-32); and fodder for the idea that followers of Christ are "soldiers for the Lord," which comes from the quasi-military rhetoric found here (6:10-17).

Ephesians plays a role in the stark distinction one sees between churches that focus on the "Christ of salvation" rather than the "Jesus of the Gospels." A focus on high Christology is underwritten by letters such as Ephesians, at the expense of potentially losing touch with the humanity of Jesus.

Ephesians 1:1—2:10: Spiritual Blessings and Riches in Christ

▌ THE TEXT IN ITS ANCIENT CONTEXT

Though we do not know who the original recipients were, as *en Ephesō* was likely added into the letter from a marginal notation, it was most likely written for a church in the vicinity of Ephesus. This opening section discusses the Christ in a way that Jesus himself might not have identified with (1:3-14; see also 2:11-22). Here, references to being chosen by God, to inheritance as sons, and to redemption through Christ's blood all resonate with aspects of Judaism's belief system as much as with Greco-Roman religious traditions. It is also a passage resplendent with the language of predestination. The author declares that God "chose us" before the foundation of the world (1:4); in love he "destined us" to adoption (1:5); our inheritance is according to his purpose (1:11); and there are good works prepared for us to accomplish in Christ (2:10). There is great comfort for the recipients in such promises and assurances.

Throughout, this letter resonates with elements of what would become Gnosticism. Terminology such as "riches" and "spiritual blessings"; "heavenly places," "mysteries," and "the mystery of God's will"; "fullness" and "fullness of time"; "spirit of wisdom"; "knowledge"; "enlightenment"; and "spiritual powers" are all later developed in Gnostic worldviews. It is somewhat striking to see such proto-Gnostic ideas in the canon, given both how different it is from the perspective of the genuine Pauline writings and that the Gnostic traditions would later come to be deemed heretical by church fathers. In another deuteropauline move, we see the idea of having *already* obtained the inheritance in Christ, what we now refer to as "realized eschatology." The "sealing with the Holy Spirit" (1:13) perhaps draws on the way emperors, rulers, or other people of great importance would "mark" a letter with their seal. This idea resonates with royal importance, though Christ, not the Roman emperor, is the "lord" whose seal is placed on these recipients.

▌The Text in the Interpretive Tradition

Ephesians 1:4-11, and to a much lesser degree 3:8-10, has played heavily in the church's discussion of predestination over the centuries. It was first made a significant focus in what is now referred to as the Pelagian controversy in the early fifth century. The basic beliefs promulgated by Pelagianism, all deemed heretical by the Council of Carthage (418), focus on the concept we have come to refer to as original sin and the early church's reading of the story of Adam and Eve in Genesis 2–3. Pelagius denied that there was ever a pristine state that is so often read into Genesis 2; he denied that there was a moment in time when sin entered into human actions, and thus that there was ever a time when humans were perfect and would have had immortality. He also insisted that our bodies dying is a natural event, and not something caused or brought about by "Adam and Eve" in the garden. Finally, his claim that we are born not in our full development, "but with a capacity for good and evil; we are begotten without virtue as much as without fault, and before the activity of the individual will there is nothing in humans other than what God has placed in them," suggests that he wanted to reject the idea of humans being born tainted. This is also backed up by his claim that newborn children need not be baptized, which is the second of his beliefs that was denounced at the Council of Carthage. Pelagius's ideas significantly downplayed the need for the Christ event, and placed a great deal of agency with humans instead of salvation stemming only from God and God's grace through Christ.

Church fathers, in particular Augustine, responded to Pelagius's ideas with claims that put the efficacy of salvation squarely on God and God's grace, though humans were thought to be called on to participate. For the early church fathers, giving humans any level of responsibility for salvation in this way was explained by the idea of divine foreknowledge of humans' actions, here drawing on Eph. 1:4-11. It was Augustine who made the obvious conclusion clear, that if one was chosen or elected to be a child of God, then one was also chosen or elected to salvation. As one might imagine, taking this idea to its next logical step would cause problems for later theologians of the church.

It was John Calvin who built on Augustine's idea of predestination to salvation to include the implied other component: predestination to sin and damnation as well. This idea, double predestination, was rejected by other Reformers, however. Still drawing on this passage in Ephesians, Huldrych Zwingli and Martin Luther focused on the chosenness in Christ, and God's goodness and righteousness. Within the Roman Catholic tradition, the discussion of predestination engendered two extremist positions, which were eventually both permitted by Pope Paul V. They are represented by Thomism and Molinism, beginning with grace and free will, respectively, with significant debate regarding the nature of grace, both as sufficient and as efficacious. Karl Barth (1957) interpreted this divinely predestined election as entirely focused on Christ, as we would expect from him: election to salvation is ascribed to humankind through Christ, and Christ took on himself the election to damnation. The "grace versus free will" discussion remains somewhat unresolved in many, perhaps all, Christian denominations.

The phrase "by nature, children of wrath" (2:3) also received attention over the centuries. In response to Pelagius's denial of original sin, this passage helped early church fathers formulate the belief in the inherent corruption of human nature, an essential component of the belief in original sin.

■ THE TEXT IN CONTEMPORARY DISCUSSION

In Eph. 1:7 we see the first reference to a realized redemption, as opposed to the idea espoused in the genuine Pauline Letters that it will be fulfilled at the Parousia. The metaphor for atonement used here, "redemption through his blood," is based on ideas about sacrifice that call for reconsideration. The redemption-through-blood metaphor is also used in 5:2, which refers to the pleasant aroma of an offering and sacrifice. This is, no doubt, one of the main reasons ancient peoples thought such offerings would be pleasing for their god(s). But the insistence on the necessity of the blood that comes from death, and the violence implied by it, in order to restore life or to bring about reconciliation between two parties, has been problematized by numerous theologians, in particular in the last few decades (Terrell; Weaver).

The idea that apart from Christ, all people live "in the lusts of [their] flesh, indulging the desires of the flesh and senses, and were by nature children of wrath" (2:1-4; see also 1:3) is one that warrants our thoughtful consideration. Though it may be familiar to many people, it does draw on a dualistic worldview, wherein the spirit is good, but all things to do with the body are bad. Many contemporary scholars of religion or biblical studies have commented on the detrimental effects of such dualisms on the ways we relate to others (see Ruether). What we see, specifically here in Ephesians, also underscores a belief that only in Christ can people be moral, disciplined people. There is very little in the adult world of continuums and variety that can be so simply labeled. Dualisms are necessary for children in order to help them establish good judgment and healthy, respectful behaviors, but these dualisms are best left behind as one matures in mind, body, and faith.

On the topic of predestination, suggested by 1:4-8 and 2:8-10, I offer a few caveats for the thoughtful reader today. First, the concept of predestination was originally only about being saved, where our souls would go after dying, contrasted with ideas of who or what we are "destined" to be in this life. As such, predestination came to be intimately connected to the idea of original sin. But the basic idea of "original sin," contrary to popular belief, is not an inherent component of Genesis

2–3; rather, it is a belief read *into* that passage that requires taking the narrative as a literal account instead of as it was intended: as a myth. There is much theological content of the early church that is based on a literal reading of this story, perhaps often to our detriment. The assertion of the reality of "original sin," and thus the manifold ways that have subsequently been developed to describe God's saving us from it, are among the most far-reaching ideas within Christian doctrine. The system of thought that has been built up around these texts, including the ideas of election to salvation, election to damnation, and total human depravity without Christ; that humans are by nature disobedient and that it is Adam and Eve's fault that we need salvation; how salvation is conferred to humans, even simply the preoccupation with the relation of divine grace to human free will—are all dependent on the early (mis)readings of Genesis 2–3. The early intense focus on the belief in human inadequacy, depravity, and disobedience, not to mention the disparagement of our bodies and anything that is natural to them, has left its mark on the collective consciousness of the church and its doctrine. One does not have to agree with these early, eager, earnest church leaders. There are more beneficial and life-supporting ways to read those biblical passages that do not end up denigrating the value and beauty of our bodies or our humanness itself.

The second caveat is directly related to the first. If the God who created us also gave us our minds to use, it is not a transgression of God's will or grace to suggest that the conversation regarding salvation, as debated and deliberated over the centuries, simply went painfully awry. Saying that God would create all humans, but would choose in advance some to be saved and others to receive eternal damnation, goes against all moral sensibility. Some people counter this claim by saying that God's ways are higher than ours. This response asserts that what seems unjust to us is somehow reasonable, given God's love for us and simultaneous need for justice in response to our sin.

It is the effort to make something unique of the Christ event that prepared the way for the early church writers to apply God's foreknowledge and "choosing" to salvation, now only in Christ. Prior to the Christ event, election was a matter of God's having chosen the Jews, through their ancestors the Israelites, which is represented in the covenant. Election and salvation are intertwined in the Jewish context, though the focus is on salvation in this life, not what happens after dying. "Salvation" has been understood in numerous ways within the church over the centuries, not to mention what it means to people of other faiths. Given how deeply rooted in dualistic thinking the traditional Christian ideas of salvation and predestination are, the reevaluation of it, to which a number of contemporary theologians call the church, will present a considerable, but perhaps beneficial, challenge.

Ephesians 2:11—3:21: Mystery, Power, and Oneness in Christ

▌ THE TEXT IN ITS ANCIENT CONTEXT

The writer here makes it clear that he is writing as a member of Israel to people who, while formerly gentiles, are now considered a part of the covenant promises given to Israel. The reference to two groups of people, those of "the uncircumcision" in contrast to those of "the circumcision," recalls the dilemma that Paul often addressed for the young communities: Do gentiles need to uphold the tenets of the law in order to be fully included in the covenant? Paul's consistent response was no: The law was Israel's means to the covenant; gentiles trying to uphold the law had missed the whole point. In Ephesians, however, we see Paul's idea taken one step further. The writer claims in 2:14-15 that Christ broke "down the dividing wall, that is, the hostility between us. He has abolished the law with its commandments and ordinances." Ephesians says that it is not simply that the law was only intended for Israel, as Paul suggested, but also that the law is what is causing the enmity between Jews and gentiles within the *ekklēsia*, and that because of Christ the law is abolished. One might imagine that this idea would not have sat well with some Jews in the first century.

Though it may seem reassuring to many today, in the author's claim that Christ "established peace" we perhaps ought to hear something more along the lines of the imposition of the *Pax Romana* by the Roman emperors. It would have been heard as abruptly as this by those who were not convinced by the gospel or who did not embrace gentiles within Judaism. Similarly, the author draws on "strangers and aliens" terminology, which would resonate with Israel's past, when the Israelites were strangers and aliens in Egypt. We see this label used in one other New Testament letter, 1 Peter. Both letters, written near the end of the first century, simultaneously draw on Israel's past and speak of how it is no longer needed or valid. For instance, in 3:9-10, there is a suggestion that God's wisdom had been kept hidden until the establishment of the church, even though this church is built on the "foundation" of Israel's prophets and the apostles. It is important to note that these claims were being made within the early church, in particular in light of what they imply about the people of Israel and the validity of their belief system.

The building imagery in 2:20-22 is perhaps an intentional move away from the body metaphors Paul so often uses (e.g., Romans 12; 1 Corinthians 12) to something more tangible and durable, even permanent.

Whether one sees 2:11-22 as similar to encomiums attributed to emperors (Perkins), or finds in 1:20—2:22 the application of the general structure of ancient Near Eastern divine warfare mythology (Gombis), in either case it is clear that praise and exaltation of rulers or other gods is being adapted here in praise of Christ. For instance, the latter passage includes an exaltation of the God or divine king (1:20-2), naming a threat (2:1-3), describing the battle or victory (2:4-7), ascribing lordship to the victor (mostly prior to this section, in 1:3-11; 2:6), and the building of a house or temple to the god (2:19-22), ending with a celebration. Since this paradigm already existed, applying it to Christ would place him in competition with the deified emperor in addition to other gods.

In 3:3-21, we see more ideas that diverged from genuine Pauline ideas. The author writes, "the mystery was made know to me by revelation," but here the previously undisclosed "mystery" is that "the Gentiles have become fellow heirs" with Jews (3:6). Paul himself regarded this as the clear message of scripture, however (e.g., Rom. 4:1-15), and used the language of "mystery" to refer to the paradoxical course that God's purposes had taken in the temporary "hardening" of Israel (Rom. 11:25-26). Those nuances are absent from Ephesians. Further, references to fullness (*plērōma*), knowledge, wisdom, and riches, all employed in this section, are used in ways that are foreign to the Pauline Letters. Through and through, Ephesians affirms the need for the spiritual knowledge that can only be revealed through Christ.

Interestingly enough, 3:20-21 sounds like a benediction, as we would expect at the end of such a letter. Thus some scholars suggest that this letter was, as many others in the New Testament are, pieced together from more than one source.

◼ THE TEXT IN THE INTERPRETIVE TRADITION

Ephesians 2:11-22 has been important throughout the centuries in terms of Jewish-Christian relations. It was a helpful passage for Tertullian to reference in denouncing one of the men he considered heretics, Marcion. Since Marcion believed the God of Jewish Scripture was a different God from the one of Christian Scripture (which meant, for him, a few of the writings we consider the New Testament), Tertullian and others emphasized the continuity between the "Old" and "New" Testaments and the belief that the two groups of people being brought together, Jews and gentiles, would be brought together under the same God (Tertullian, *Apology* 37, 50). Much has been made of this passage over the centuries, with interpretations ranging from maintaining Israel's place of prominence as God's chosen people (Barth) to a dismissal of Israel's relevance altogether for Christianity (Lindemann).

Luther used 2:20-22, the church as God's building, to speak against papal primacy. He suggested that the papacy is one part of the church, of which only Christ is the head. Thus all parts of the church are equal to each other, and final authority rests with Christ, not the pope.

◼ THE TEXT IN CONTEMPORARY DISCUSSION

A careful biblical theologian today will turn to Romans 9–11, in addition to Eph. 2:11-22, for textual support for the discussion of the relationship between the church and Israel. I wish to draw attention to supersessionism and the irrelevance of Israel or Judaism that several passages in Ephesians appear to endorse. Saying that Christ "abolished the enmity" between Jews and gentiles, the enmity that was the law of commandments (2:14-15), sets up the Scripture that is sacred to Jews as a problem that needs to be eradicated. The very belief espoused here, that God has extended the covenant to all people, is embraced by some Jews but certainly not all, both then and now. Thus any and all attempts to "make peace" between the church and Judaism today that do not take this point into account will ultimately be of no avail. But there can be no doubt that there is fodder in the texts of the New Testament to support both ideas: that the coming together of all Jews and gentiles in the covenant is God's will, and that there is only one special sect of Judaism that "counts" as the correct one of the covenant, which is the one that became what we know as Christianity.

Two striking developments in this section of Ephesians are worth consideration. The first is the change from the very human Jesus of Nazareth, who is the central character in the Synoptic Gospels and is seen mingling with and relating to the masses, to the elevated and mighty Christ, who is above all earthly powers and is enthroned in the heavenly realm. As such, he might appear out of reach of the people who need him (2:20-22). The other is the contrast between the kind of *ekklēsia* Paul's genuine letters describe and the communities as they are defined here. When Paul first employed the terminology to gatherings of followers of Jesus, an *ekklēsia* was an assembly or gathering of the *polis*, one that would address physical, daily concerns of the people allowed into the gatherings. In Ephesians, the realm in which their *ekklēsia* takes effect is the spiritual, cosmic realm. Perhaps both are needed, but a one-sided focus on the spiritual realm can lead to apathy in the face of the problems in the tangible world.

Another aspect of the spiritual or heavenly kingdom described in Ephesians is that while it may be seen to offer a counterempire or kingdom to the Roman Empire, all of the roles of dominance and subjectivity are maintained, but simply applied to a new ruler (Bird). For some, this idea of God as almighty ruler is comforting; certainly it has pervaded Christian thought, doctrine, and hymns for two thousand years. But that does not mean that understanding our world in those terms is the most beneficial way to conceive it. For instance, when we speak of the powers of this world being subject to Christ (1:20-22), we set up a system that turns the former oppressors into the oppressed, and vice versa. In other words, we imply a divine sanction of the cycle of domination of one power over another. Though Ephesians speaks of this in the "spiritual" realms, when a person is subject to this victorious Christ/ruler, one assumes either that only the next life or spiritual realm is important, or that claiming that Christ is above all justifies whatever action one undertakes in order to establish "peace" on his behalf. The former situation tends to lead to withdrawing from the world; the latter mind-set leads to tragedies such as the Crusades, but also to a sense that "might makes right."

Similarly, when we see the claim in Ephesians that the peace of Christ is established among his followers, we should consider how such things happen. Within the Roman Empire, the rule and reign of the emperor were established by means of terror, intimidation, and military action. What happens when we view the empire of God and the heavenly rule of Christ through the same lens? This perspective highlights a tension between *offering* the peace of Christ and *imposing* it on others. Those who, as members of the cosmic *ekklēsia*, presume to be members of this new empire may be reassured by the dominance and rule of Christ. But what fearsome implications for those "outside"! The image constructed of those who continue to live in disobedience and ignorance (4:17-22; 5:5-8, 11-12) does not encourage including them, but of distancing oneself and one's group from such others. The demonizing of the "other" continues in this new empire—as an act of intimidation, at the very least—and, as history has shown us again and again, can set the stage for violent military attacks once this *ekklēsia* is also embraced by worldly emperors. While many people today may enjoy the language in Eph. 3:18-19 about knowing the great extent of God's love and the love of Christ that surpasses knowledge, responsible handling of Scripture requires that we remember the context of such encouraging words.

Ephesians 4:1—5:20: Unity in the Body of Christ and Living Wisely

▌THE TEXT IN ITS ANCIENT CONTEXT

Clearly, 4:1-16 is concerned with creating unity, an issue alluded to in other parts of the letter as well. Here the issue seems to be that people spoke of things such as baptism or "faith" with different purposes, or as being symbolically meaningful in different ways, and that there is consequently some confusion regarding spiritual gifts. Thus the author asserts that there is only one God, from whom all these things (faith, baptism, hope, gifts, etc.) come to them. Having a common understanding of such important matters would have been crucial to the sustainability of the movement.

The next section of the letter, 4:25—5:20, resonates with much of the basic content of Paul's earlier letters, in particular charging people to do their own work, to help others in need, to speak only words of edification, to not be deceived by foolish or misguided beliefs, and to put away wrath and anger. There is also a significant presence of dualistic thought, making dark/light and foolish/wise distinctions, and referring to the recipients as "children of light."

Speaking of Jesus as the Christ who gave himself up for them, "a fragrant offering and sacrifice to God" (5:2), draws on the common practice of animal sacrifice that would have been a part of Jewish and pagan worship alike in the first century. Here the metaphor serves to highlight the execution of Jesus, symbolized as a "sacrifice," as the most important aspect of who he is and what he did for the church.

▌THE TEXT IN THE INTERPRETIVE TRADITION

In seeking to create unity, as the beginning of this section does, the author endorses the idea that there is only *one* way, *one* hope, *one* faith, *one* baptism, and so on. While we may see the importance of such unity, it has also led to divisions over the centuries, for example, in understanding the intention, meaning, and symbolic efficacy of Christian baptism. Though the diversity belies the claim, different traditions have and will continue to understandably identify their own practice with the "one baptism" to which the text refers.

The primary references in church fathers' writings to this part of the letter are to 4:7-16, which discusses specific roles and gifts, all given freely by Christ as a gift of grace (4:7). While early writers seemed content simply to note that various roles (apostles, prophets, evangelists, pastors, and teachers) are listed, and just as often referred to Acts 6:2 or 20:28 as to this passage for edification regarding how to be a Christian leader, for the sixteenth-century Reformers the distinction between different roles was of great importance. Their primary concern regarded where, within the hierarchy of the church, each role was intended. Most notably, the role of bishop is not mentioned in this list, yet the bishop held a position of primacy at that time; were some of the roles named in Ephesians to be identified with specifically episcopal duties? Also, if the then-current role and function of the papacy had been intended by Christ, why does this passage not even allude to it? Throughout the ages, there has been agreement on the idea that all spiritual gifts are intended to serve the Word, and to build up the congregation. In present-day ecumenical dialogues, Romans 12 and 1 Corinthians 12 feature more prominently than Ephesians in discussions of spiritual gifts and their relative importance.

▌THE TEXT IN CONTEMPORARY DISCUSSION

The generalized language in 4:17-24 serves to perpetuate the denigration or demonizing of people who are not in the fold. All descriptions suggesting that outside of Christ people are callous and constantly "give themselves over to sensuality," practicing every kind of impurity and greed, is dangerous for us today. The reference to people's being objects of God's wrath prior to their becoming members of the church, and to their being ignorant and foolish apart from Christ can lead to judgmental views of "others" on the part of Christians. We see this clearly in 4:17-19, which says that the gentiles "live, in the futility of their minds. They are darkened in their understanding, alienated from the life of God because of their ignorance and hardness of heart." Not only does this kind of talk belittle people outside of the church, but it also suggests that apart from Christ all people are incapable of being moral and loving. We should not be surprised, then, to hear that many Christians believe, for instance, that atheists are by definition immoral people. If Christians are teaching their children to see non-Christians in this way, there is very little space for understanding others and much precedent for judging.

While the concomitant charge to be renewed in the spirit of our minds (4:23) is lovely, it comes at a great cost. If we could frame the positive ideas about living well and being "children of light" without demonizing those who do not align with our worldview, we would make great strides toward productive dialogues within various segments of our world today. If, however, we continue to speak with language implying that "if you're not with us you're against us," we will continue to see our leaders and politicians struggling to "be right" instead of struggling to be understood and to understand others. The dualistic mind-set that undergirds this letter is not helpful for navigating the diversity of belief systems and worldviews of our global community.

Ephesians 5:21—6:9: Household Code

▌ THE TEXT IN ITS ANCIENT CONTEXT

This section is one of the three clear examples in the New Testament (see also Col. 3:18—4:1; 1 Pet. 2:18—3:7) of the "household codes" that appear in ancient Greek and Latin writings; Martin Luther called these *Haustafeln*, "tables" of household duties. It is worth noting that all three cases appear near the end of the first century, and that the implications for women and slaves stand in stark contrast to the words of encouragement Paul himself gave several decades earlier (Gal. 3:28; as well as Rom. 16:1-16, or even the implications of equality between husband and wife in 1 Cor. 7:1-16). We should not be surprised to see this move, however, since the household codes endorse the patriarchal Roman family ideals. Since the rules of the household were understood to undergird economics and politics within a city, the household is the key to sociopolitical control (Schüssler Fiorenza 1997; D'Angelo). While many scholars have argued that the household ideals were adapted in a way that is kinder toward women, children, and slaves than the non-Christian archetype, others have described this relative "kindness" as "love-patriarchalism" (MacDonald). The worldview endorses what is culturally expected, namely patriarchy; but the commands are laced with love or kindness, which, presumably, softens the harshness of the domination and control.

The *Haustafel* section begins with a call to the entire community to "be subject to one another out of reverence for Christ" (5:21). Similarly, the wives are to submit to their husbands, in all things, as they do to the Lord (5:33), and the slaves are to obey their human masters with fear and trembling (6:5). Though the other typical members of the household are also addressed, their exhortations are not buttressed by obedience out of fear as is the case for wives and slaves (the NRSV translates *phobētai* with "respect" in 5:33, but the Greek literally says "that the husband may be feared"; the word is a cognate of *phobos*, "fear," in 6:5). We do well to ask why such strong language is used for these two groups of people in particular. Not only were women and slaves central to the economic productivity of the household, and thus were essential in supporting the empire; but their sheer numbers also made their control by others important to maintaining the social order. To be sure, the freedom and empowerment that women and slaves had experienced in the early movement, which had been fully endorsed by Paul in his letters, might well have been perceived by outsiders as a threat to social and political order. The shrewd reader of New Testament writings can see political power plays at work in and behind them.

One striking comparison that is particular to the Ephesian *Haustafel* is that the Christian community is constructed in terms of two images: the body of Christ and the subject status of a wife (Osiek; Sampley). Thus the *ekklēsia* is seen as both Christ's body and Christ's bride, in contrast with Paul's use of just the body metaphor (Romans 12; 1 Corinthians 12). Perhaps neither surprising—as the endorsement of the married-with-children state would earn favor with Roman officials—nor new—we see in Hosea and elsewhere in Hebrew Scriptures references to Israel as the bride of Yahweh—the effect of claiming that the church is the bride of Christ is nevertheless far-reaching.

In spite of the focus on the heavenly realms throughout this letter, the *Haustafel* section is grounded in everyday life with its attendant sociopolitical concerns. Just as in the Roman Empire the married-with-children state was encouraged by legislation, now the married state is encouraged in the *ekklēsia* by this letter.

▌The Text in the Interpretive Tradition

Men from all ages of Christendom have found two components of this section of the letter important and useful. First is the striking comparison between a marriage between and man and a woman and the "union" of Christ and his bride, the church. Second is the related phrase "this is a great mystery" (5:32). Interpreters have questioned what, exactly, the author intended by the term *mysterion*; and because this term was translated into Latin as *sacramentum*, this became a key passage for the Scholastic and Reformation debates regarding the sacraments.

As to the first point, we must note that, with few exceptions, the church fathers read Gen. 2:24 as an indication that marriage itself was established by God, as a part of creation, and thus was something sacred and holy. Building on this assumption, then, there were various claims made regarding the unique importance of marriage, often implying that physical or sexual love within a marriage ought to be on par with a spiritual, holy love. Marriage between a man and a woman was declared a *typos*, or a visual example, of the union between Christ and the church. Given marriage's divine endorsement, Augustine and others were able to defend the goodness of marriage against those who generally saw anything to do with the "flesh" as evil and corrupt. Augustine countered his contemporaries in his claim that the marriage alluded to in Genesis 2 was a sexually active marriage, and that had there been no sin (in Genesis 3), then sexual desires within marriage today would be without lust, since Augustine deemed lustfulness to be shameful (*De nuptiis* 54).

As to the matter of marriage constituting a sacrament, since the belief developed that sacraments bring about what they indicate (Hugh of St. Victor, *de sacramentis* 9.2; Peter Lombard, *Sententiarum libri quatuor* 4.1.4, 2.1), Aquinas concluded that the way marriage brought about participation in grace was that entering into marriage was symbolic of belonging to Christ. We see in writings beginning with the Reformation, and as recently as the Pastoral Constitution of the Second Vatican Council, an interest in speaking of Christian marriage as a special form of the worldly institution, simply because Christians are connected to Christ through salvation.

The final section of this passage, Eph. 6:5-9, along with the similar passages of Col. 3:22—4:1 and 1 Pet. 2:18-25, have played a significant role historically in justifying the inhumane treatment of enslaved African people in the United States. First Peter's discussion of masters and slaves is lengthier and declared that suffering made a person Christlike. These elements made it more popular than Ephesians on this topic.

▌THE TEXT IN CONTEMPORARY DISCUSSION

The theme of being subject to God or Christ out of fear (5:21) deserves some reconsideration. While there is much within the sacred writings of the Jews, and no small amount within the New Testament, that refers to devotion to God in terms of "fear," which is typically defended as meaning "reverence," we may still ask whether the terminology is positive or helpful. Fear and control go hand in hand. Fearing the power of the emperor is one thing; (re)importing such fear into the religious realm is simply ascribing the same dominant, and thus oppressive, relationship with the deity that the people have with the emperor. These may be structures and relations people can understand, and thus they may be effective, but that does not mean that they are beneficial for us today.

Describing the *ekklēsia* in terms of both Christ's body and Christ's bride is problematic for many scholars today (Merz), in part because the images are mutually exclusive and thus confusing. Beyond that, however, calling the church the bride of Christ feminizes the church (as "she") in a way that cannot be undone. Based on the initial application of the label in a heteronormative, patriarchal setting, "she" must be led by a man, and "she" is fully subservient to her "husband," the Christ. It only follows, of course, that the same dominant/submissive roles would then be applied between men and women within the *ekklēsia*. It is important to consider how starkly different this image is from what we see in the genuine Pauline writings, where Paul urges his readers not to behave according to the social, familial, and cultural gender roles of the wider culture (Gal. 3:28). Seeing the author of Ephesians intentionally adopting the androcentric, patriarchal political ideals for men and women ought to give the reader pause. This move not only encourages the married state for all people in the church, as the Augustan legislation of the first century BCE did for the people of the Roman Empire, but also places extraordinary focus on women's married status. The patriarchal, heterosexual marriage becomes the ultimate, if not the only, representation of the church's relation to Christ (Merz). Further, only heterosexual marriages would be considered "normal" or approved of by God.

The purity required or implied in 5:27 may make sense in context, but it also serves to perpetuate a double standard between men and women in terms of purity, and ultimately makes a detrimental connection between sex and purity. If it is the bride who needs to be pure, then it is the woman in the male/female couple who is expected to be "pure" today. The early church fathers had no difficulty identifying sexuality as impure, and hanging the responsibility for sexual "impurity" on women. We have inherited several components of their way of thinking that are detrimental to the way we view and value our bodies, sexuality, and women in general.

The metaphor of a "marriage" between Christ and the church has also been wielded in conversations regarding sex before marriage. These conversations might be reframed once we note that in Eph. 5:31, Gen. 2:24 has been pulled out of context, both in the Christian tradition and in current English translations, and interpreted as implying that Adam and Eve were *married* in the Garden of Eden. The NRSV, for example, represents the Greek *gynē* with "wife" rather than "woman" (compare the translation of *anēr* as "man" rather than "husband"). In the context of Genesis, however, we are only told why two people who are drawn to each other are to go out from their parents and start their own family. There is no mention of "marriage," and the Hebrew terms used throughout this passage, *'îš* and *'iššâ*, can just as easily be translated "man" and "woman" as "husband" and "wife." Though subtle, the distinction has far-reaching implications. It is in part on the basis of the translation "wife," as well as the commands and suggestions made by Paul in 1 Corinthians 7 (especially 7:9), that some Christians today claim that sex before marriage is a sin. The special significance attributed to marriage here may inform the harsh judgment some Christians pass on divorce as a sin as well, and may help to underwrite a worldview that says marriage is to be only between a man and a woman. Remarkably, the analogy between marriage and the relationship between Christ and his church appears to break down when some churches assert that only *men* can be the leaders or representatives of the (feminized) church, which is (symbolically) married to Christ, a male.

This Ephesians passage is often read today and embraced without hesitation by men and women alike. Suggesting that a husband is to his wife as Christ is to the Church, however, puts an inordinate, entirely unfair pressure on men. For centuries, Christians have sought to embrace this "ideal," but in doing so have only perpetuated the social and cultural confusion of healthy gender roles. If Christ's self-sacrificial "love" for the church is the primary model for men in marriage, it would seem to follow that men must protect and provide for their wives to a potentially limitless extent. It should be no wonder, then, that so many people expect women to need to be cared for, or that men as "breadwinners" should receive higher salaries and earlier promotions than equally qualified women. Similarly, suggesting that women are to be as subordinate to their husbands as they are *to Christ* seems extraordinary, in that it is not balanced with a similar injunction to men; yet, again, because it is in Scripture, many people today seek to abide by it as a way of showing faithfulness to Christ, assuming that it is what God intended.

Moreover, there can be no question that the racial, economic, educational, emotional, and spiritual effects of four hundred years of slavery in the United States continue to this day. This reality permeates cultural and social realities in the United States to the point that people who are conscious of it do not know where to begin to address it, and people unaware of it can easily carry on with life as they know it, with clear consciences. Many people today also try to claim that slavery no longer happens in our world, a belief all the more stunning since so much of our global, political, and trade relations are dependent on child labor for the production of goods and on child and female bodies for support of the highly lucrative international sex slave trade. Some scholars even push us to reconsider the value we place on child-rearing and housework, since so much of it is done "for free," yet disproportionately by women and often at great expense to them in terms of their careers or influence outside of the home (Engels; Hartsock; Schüssler Fiorenza, 1987).

Ephesians 6:10-24: Spiritual Battle and Benediction

■ THE TEXT IN ITS ANCIENT CONTEXT

In 6:10-17 (see also 4:8), we see a specific parallel between serving in the military and living the Christian life, though one cannot miss that the comparison is entirely spiritualized through the reference to the "rulers," "cosmic powers of this present darkness . . . spiritual forces of evil in the heavenly places" (6:12). The author suggests that as a follower of Christ, one can count on being prepared for the "battle" ahead, fully clothed in God's spiritual protection. We may also see the author responding to early persecution, even the prospect of martyrdom, in referring to the "evil day" and "standing firm" in the face of it. The letter itself ends with a typical greeting and benediction.

■ THE TEXT IN THE INTERPRETIVE TRADITION

Because of the spiritualized language of struggles and battles in this section of the letter, we ought not be surprised at the wide range of interpretive contexts in which the church fathers applied it. In addition to evoking the context of gruesome battlefields, which made this a prime passage in the construction of *militia Christi* (military service for Christ), it was also adapted to discuss—and at times encourage—martyrdom, monastic lifestyles, and mysticism.

The struggle against one's own passions and "carnal desires" is perhaps the most common application of this spiritual battle into everyday life, intimately connecting an ascetic life with a moral one (Clement of Alexandria, *Strom.* 2.109–10; 7.20). The early fathers equated our passions and desires with the enemy, the ruler of the spiritual realm of evil that all Christians are to fight and conquer. Interestingly, several church fathers wrestled with the implications that there are many real battles that take place within the First (Old) Testament. Origen concluded that God commanded such physical battles, in books such as Joshua, in order to foreshadow the spiritual battles of Christians. Just as soldiers were expected to put their military service and performance in battle above their own lives and families, so too many church fathers (Tertullian, Clement, Origen) discussed the calling to be a disciple of Christ as something that deserved highest regard, even claiming that the Christian's battle serves Christ's message of peace. In this way, the *militia Christi* is well grounded. The connection between devotion to Christ and fighting a *spiritual* battle led to a view of martyrdom as the ultimate way to prove one's worth to Christ: since victory "consists in achieving that for which one has fought," that is, salvation, a Christian martyr is victorious (Tertullian). Erasmus of Rotterdam's *A Handbook for the Christian Soldier* (1501) makes clear that the Christian's daily battle is a spiritual one, which will best be fought with God's armor, with knowledge and prayer being the two primary weapons.

■ THE TEXT IN CONTEMPORARY DISCUSSION

The idea of the armor of God is simultaneously familiar to many Christians but somewhat offensive to some modern sensibilities. Though this armor is fully "spiritualized" and described in terms of beneficent and loving actions, it is nevertheless preparing the community *for battle*. They are to be prepared at all times to figuratively "slay" their enemies with the words of their God, knowing that because of God they are invincible. There is a divine sanction for violence and a conquering mentality; it is embedded in church liturgy and hymns because they draw on the language present in the texts of the Christian tradition (Russell). Just because the imagery is now deployed within the spiritual realm does not neutralize the violent, aggressive, and bloody battle imagery associated with being Christ's soldier. At the same time, many theologians over the centuries have suggested that the Christian is only to fight defensively.

While many websites today will offer content for vacation Bible schools based on the theme of the "Soldier for Christ," we do well to keep in mind that in Ephesians, this metaphor is significantly, if not primarily, framed as soldiers fighting against the "powers and principalities" within the spiritual realm. The exhortation to be "strong in the Lord" (6:10) can be helpful, in particular when people are up against persecution or an unrelenting "foe." The notion that there is a literal devil lurking out there, supported by his demons and evil spirits, all of which constitute the forces of darkness, is still embraced by some Christians today. The realistic quality of the popular Christian novels *This Present Darkness* and *Piercing the Darkness* (Peretti 1986; 1989) indicates that the predilection for waging "spiritual wars" continues to this day, and that people are willing to spend a great deal of time and energy focused on the heavenly realm instead of on the tangible world we all live in. While focusing on the spiritual realm can be a palliative for real, physical discomfort or oppression, it can also promote a seemingly depoliticized worldview, which can neutralize the motivation for social change.

With many of our governmental leaders being faithful Christians who endorse this way of thinking, is it any wonder that our governments tend toward military action more often than to peace talks? Again, according to Russell, "Those who live in nations that shape the principalities of our day cannot afford triumphal hymns" (Russell, 68). The ideals of one's faith will dictate how one behaves in the world.

When we see terminology used in Ephesians (or in the New Testament in general) that is adopted from imperial pronouncements, political labels and ideas, household code ideals, and even from the imagery of preparation for battle, we would do well to stop and consider the inherent political implications in that terminology instead of moving quickly to spiritualize it. There is no question that the author of Ephesians is speaking in highly spiritualized terms, but even those spiritual ideas about a heavenly realm will influence how people behave politically. These dimensions are intertwined, and it is our responsibility to be aware of the political implications of such commingling. It is time to take seriously the detrimental results of blind adherence to such biblical texts and to consider why we often conveniently try to overlook some aspects of them. For some readers today, theological responsibility means courageously declaring the ideal that the Word of God leads to life, fulfillment, and liberation from oppression; it must not be oppression's cause. This is where reason and thoughtful reflection meet. Perhaps by challenging a focus solely on the heavenly realm and the rhetoric of battle, we may be inspired toward loving mutuality and a spirituality that enriches the world in which we live.

Works Cited

Barth, Marcus. 1959. *Israel und die Kirche im Brief des Paulus an die Epheser*. Theologische Existenz heute. Munich: Kaiser.

Bird, Jennifer. 2009. "Ephesians." In *A Postcolonial Commentary on the New Testament Writings*, edited by R. S. Sugirtharajah and Fernando F. Segovia, 265–80. New York: T&T Clark.

D'Angelo, Mary Rose. 1993. "Colossians." In *Searching the Scriptures*. Vol. 2, *A Feminist Commentary*, edited by Elisabeth Schüssler Fiorenza, Ann Brock, and Shelly Matthews, 313–24. New York: Crossroad.

Engels, Frederick. 2001. *The Origin of the Family, Private Property and the State*. Translated by Ernest Untermann. Honolulu: University Press of the Pacific.

Gombis, Timothy G. 2004. "Ephesians 2 as a Narrative of Divine Warfare." *JSNT* 26, no. 4:403–18.

Hartsock, Nancy. 1983. *Money, Sex, and Power: Toward a Feminist Historical Materialism*. Boston: Northeastern University Press.

Lindemann, Andreas. 1975. *Die Aufhebung der Zeit*. Gutersloh: Gerd Mohn.

MacDonald, Margaret. 1988. *The Pauline Churches: A Socio-historical Study of Institutionalization in the Pauline and Deutero-Pauline Writings*. Cambridge: Cambridge University Press.

Merz, Annette. 2000. "Why Did the Pure Bride of Christ (2 Cor. 11.2) Become a Wedded Wife (Eph. 5:22-33)?" *JSNT* 79:131–47.

Osiek, Carolyn. 2002. "The Bride of Christ (5:22-23): A Problematic Wedding." *BTB* 32:29–39.

Peretti, Frank. 1986. *This Present Darkness*. Wheaton, IL: Crossway.

———. 1989. *Piercing the Darkness*. Wheaton, IL: Crossway.

Perkins, Pheme. 1997. *Ephesians*. ANTC. Nashville: Abingdon.

Ruether, Rosemary Radford. 2011. "Rejection of Dualism." In *Creating Women's Theology: A Movement Engaging Process Thought*, edited by Monica Coleman, Nancy Howell, and Helene Russell, 60–70. Eugene, OR: Pickwick.

Russell, Letty. 1984. *Imitators of God: A Study Book on Ephesians*. New York: General Board of Global Ministries, United Methodist Church.

Sampley, J. Paul. 1974. *"And the Two Shall Become One Flesh": A Study of Traditions in Ephesians 5:21-33*. London: Cambridge University Press.

Schüssler Fiorenza, Elisabeth. 1987. *Women, Work and Poverty*. Concilium: Religion in the Eighties. Edinburgh: T&T Clark.

———. 1997. "The Praxis of Co-Equal Discipleship." In *Paul and Empire: Religion and Power in Roman Imperial Society*, edited by Richard A. Horsley, 224–41. Harrisburg, PA: Trinity Press International.

Terrell, JoAnne Marie. 1998. *Power in the Blood? The Cross in the African American Experience*. Maryknoll, NY: Orbis.

Weaver, J. Denny. 2009. "Forgiveness and (Non)violence: The Atonement Connections." *Mennonite Quarterly Review* 83, no. 2:319–47.

PHILIPPIANS

Julia Lambert Fogg

Introduction

Paul's letter to the "saints in Christ Jesus who are in Philippi" (1:1, translations are the author's, unless otherwise indicated) is not a systematic treatise on theology, but rather a work of theological and pastoral reflection. The letter interprets the Philippians' friendship with Paul and one another as their participation in and partnership with Christ. Paul calls this embodied participation of shared community practices *koinōnia*. Through this *koinōnia* they are experiencing salvation (2:13). Paul shows the believers at Philippi that, together with himself and Timothy (1:1), they are practicing being Christ to each other in their shared ministry. In this way, they are "working out [their own] salvation" (2:12). Paul's rhetorical strategy for community building (literally a kind of bodybuilding to embody Christ), reveals Paul's understanding of salvation as corporate participation in the representative and resurrected body of Christ.

Paul writes to the Philippians from prison (1:13). But what city? We don't know much more about Paul's imprisonment than that he was more than a few days travel from Philippi (2:26-8), in a city with imperial guard (4:22), and that he had been away long enough for multiple trips and correspondence to take place (2:25-30) and for Paul's preaching to affect the local community (1:13-17). In the ancient world, prisons were spare holding tanks at best, and dungeons at worst. Paul would have had to use his own resources to eat, to write, or to bribe the guard for any favors. Paul's physical discomfort and suffering in prison are magnified by those who ridicule him on the outside (1:15-16), and by the uncertain outcome of his imprisonment (2:23). Timothy assisted Paul through this suffering (1:1; 2:19), and Paul expected to be released from prison "soon" (2:23) to see the Philippians again (2:24). Some scholars have proposed to identify the city of Paul's imprisonment, following one or another externally reconstructed chronologies that synthesize Paul's letters with matching events or geographical movements in Acts. This work yields three main hypotheses.

Philippians was written from Rome, accounting for multiple trips (2:19-30) and references to the imperial guard (1:13) and Caesar's household (4:22). Ephesus also fits these criteria. Another possibility is Caesarea. Such identifications based on Acts are problematic, however, because Acts, like Paul, has its own rhetorical strategy for choosing particular geographical locations to tell Paul's story, and because Acts leaves out so much of what Paul reports firsthand. For those reasons, other scholars are reluctant to specify either a city of origin or a date (ranging from the 50s to early 60s), and that is the approach taken here.

Philippians contains a pre-Pauline liturgical tradition in 2:5-11, often called the "Christ hymn." Paul may borrow this tradition because it illustrates Christ's humble and obedient character (2:8) and specifically refers to Christ's attitude—his "mind-set" and the way he "thinks" (2:6). Rather than seizing equality with God, he embodies a humble disposition and assumes the form of a servant or "slave" (2:7). Christ's character and way of thinking anchor Paul's exhortation to the Philippians to "think like Christ" and act out of Christ's dispositions in 2:5. Most scholars agree in the identification of this pre-Pauline liturgical piece, but disagree on how to interpret another seam, a change in tone or logic, at 3:1-2. Although this shift suggests an interruption in the text, it actually works rhetorically to highlight the series of exemplars in chapter 2 (Christ, Paul, Timothy, and Epaphroditus) in contrast with the anonymous and negative examples of missionaries Paul calls "dogs" in 3:2.

Philippians stands out among Paul's letters for its joyful tone (e.g., 1:18, 4:1-4) and its effusive affirmation of friendship. Studies of ancient friendship language and themes have demonstrated the coherence of the letter and illuminated Paul's unique relationship to the Philippians. Such friendship themes include partnership in ministry (1:5; 1:7; 1:25; 2:22; 4:2-3), a common attitude and mind (1:27; 2:2-5; 3:15; 4:2), a shared struggle (1:27; 4:14), shared love and joy (1:7, 16; 2:2, 17-18), exchange of help and goods (2:19, 25-30; 4:10, 15-18), the same enemies (1:27-28; 3:2-4), and a shared offering to God (2:17-18; 4:15-20). Other studies focus on the form of ancient friendship letters, which begin with the sender expressing longing for the recipient (1:3-11), updating them on the sender's affairs (1:12-26; 2:19—4:1), expressing an interest in the recipient's affairs (1:26; 2:19), and an exhortation to continue the mutual friendship (1:27—2:18; 3:2—4:1). To this epistolary form, Paul adds a celebration of God's work in their friendship, their *koinōnia*. The theme of mutuality additionally shapes the rhetorical structure of Paul's letter. As Paul shifts between news about himself and interest in the Philippians' affairs, he is interpreting their mutual longing, shared thinking, prayer, and service to one another as an imitation of Christ's character. In this way, Paul's Letter to the Philippians is a theological demonstration of how to embody Christ's mind in the community body. And, as they literally conform their friendship to the shape of Christ, they partake in God's saving work among them.

Paul's Letter to the Philippians does not appear very often in discussions of Paul's theology. This is partly because Paul does not expound here on traditional systematic topics (redemption, salvation, creation, sin), and partly because of the way contemporary discussions have defined theology. If theology is the logical presentation of key concepts in a fully developed system of thought, then Philippians is not theological. But if theology is a sustained reflection on and an articulation of the divine-human relationship, then Paul is one of the most profound theologians, and this letter is deeply significant for Christians struggling to faithfully understand what it means to live in an increasingly complex, interconnected, and technologically dependent world.

Philippians 1:1-11: Sharing in Thanksgiving with Joy

▌ THE TEXT IN ITS ANCIENT CONTEXT

Paul begins the Letter to the Philippians with a traditional but lengthy greeting (1:1-2), followed by an effusive thanksgiving (1:3-8) that leads into a pastoral prayer (1:9-11). Paul recognizes his cosender, Timothy, as well as the "holy" believers in Philippi and the leaders among them. Paul does not yet name Epaphroditus, the Philippians' own minister who has carried this letter from Paul (2:25, 4:18) and now reads the letter aloud to the gathered assembly in Philippi.

The effect of such a generous epistolary opening is to affirm Paul's long relationship with the Philippians in the past (1:5), their mutual support in the present (1:7), and God's ongoing work in them for the future (1:6). Paul highlights the Philippians' sharing in his practice of prayer and his work in the gospel through their support of his ministry (1:7), and he uses the language of Greek friendship between two equals, and then extends this friendship to the entire community and to Christ; it is "Christ's love" that Paul has for the Philippians (1:8).

In addition to the Greek topos of friendship, Paul also draws on the ancient understanding of virtue ethics, that the mind controls the passions and the actions of the body. "It is right," then, for Paul to think about the Philippians with thanksgiving, and to "long for" them with the "passion of Christ" (1:8) since they, too, share his "heart" for them (1:7). Following these affirmations of shared affection, Paul will show how his mind shapes the actions he takes in friendship with Christ, and with the Philippians. One action is sending this letter with Epaphroditus to encourage them. Paul's words remind them that "the one who began a good work among you" will also bring that work to completion (1:6). When Epaphroditus arrives in Philippi and reads the letter aloud, Paul's words in 1:9-11 put the rhetorical aim of the letter into action: "that your love abound more and more in all knowledge" (author's translation), to discern the things that matter most in Christ (1:9-10). Paul will next exemplify this discernment of love abounding in his active friendship (*koinōnia*) with the Philippians.

Finally, Paul's reflection on and interpretation of *koinōnia* functions to counteract his physical and mental suffering in prison. The richness of positive, emotional language communicates Paul's confidence in God, to whom he gives thanks, and also his confidence in the Philippians, that they are standing firm, sharing with Paul in his suffering (1:7; 4:10-11), as Paul shares Christ's suffering (1:13).

▌ THE TEXT IN THE INTERPRETIVE TRADITION

Many interpretations of Phil. 1:1-11 have focused on the development of early Christian governance, the role of "overseers" and "deacons" (1:1 NIV) in Paul's time. Ecclesiastical and denominational differences have influenced the variety of translations of this phrase: "bishops and deacons" appears in translations as varied as that of John Wycliffe, the Geneva Bible, the Douay-Rheims translation, and the NRSV; meanwhile, the Contemporary English Version renders the phrase "church officials and officers." The Greek *episkopoi*, literally "overseers," traveled into Latin (*episcopus*), Spanish (*obispo*), and English (*bishop*).

Other recent interpretations have questioned the unity of the letter, suggesting that Paul wrote multiple letters to the Philippians, portions of which have been combined into the existing canonical letter. This argument partly rests on the observation that Paul doesn't "thank" the Philippians for the gift they sent, but only briefly mentions the gift at the end of the letter (4:16-17) (Peterman 1991).

▋THE TEXT IN CONTEMPORARY DISCUSSION

Paul's Letter to the Philippians is known in churches today as the "joyful letter." From the first verses of thanksgiving, where he sets out the themes of "love" (1:7-9), "grace" (1:7), and "joy" (1:4), the language is bright and effusive. Paul affirms their friendship by recounting instances of shared reciprocity (1:5, 7). Recent scholarship has given special attention to the rhetorical function of friendship language here. As contemporary churches search for ways to be community in a culturally and politically diverse, and at times divisive, global context, Paul's letter to this most beloved, faithful, and unique church appears especially pertinent. Faith communities may find in Philippians a way forward through mutuality and humility in Christ (1:1). As individual members draw closer to each other by sharing each other's suffering and joy, progress and setbacks, loss and abundance, the letter suggests, they draw closer to Christ.

Philippians 1:12-26: Embodying the Mind of Christ: Paul's Example

▋THE TEXT IN ITS ANCIENT CONTEXT

Paul not only celebrates the Philippians' friendship in chapter 1 but also aims to anchor that friendship in Christ's example of humility and obedience in chapter 2. In 1:12-26, Paul prepares the Philippians to see Christ's perfect mind by demonstrating how he has shown forth Christ's mind in prison.

First, Paul identifies the Christlike motivation that follows from a Christlike mind-set. Those who think like Christ are Paul's "friends" who love Christ and preach the gospel out of love (1:16). Then, typical of friendship speech, Paul contrasts these friends with "enemies" who are competing with Paul and preach the gospel out of "envy and rivalry" (1:15 NRSV). This rhetorical move is similar to the use of polarizing language of friends and enemies in the Fourth Gospel and James. Each instance of friend and enemy language functions to unite "us" over against "them." Thus Paul reinforces the common practices and mind-set that he shares with the Philippians, his friends.

Second, it is critical to note that Paul, most known for his polemical stances and ad hominem arguments, does not condemn the enemies who seek to hurt him. Instead of matching their boastful words or competitive motivations, Paul demonstrates a humility of mind and willingly bears their "intentions to increase my suffering" (1:17). "So what?" asks Paul (1:18 NRSV reads "what does it matter?"). He will endure "false motives or true" as long as Christ is preached (1:18 NRSV). Then Paul grounds his humility in joy—celebrating the Philippians' humility in continuing to stand with

Paul. Putting the mind of Christ into action, Paul can also claim the powerful presence, or "supply" (NRSV reads "help") of "the Spirit of Jesus Christ" (1:19).

Next, Paul shifts from the friendship categories of "friends and enemies" to what many contemporary scholars have read as an existential choice. But this description misses the way Paul continues his rhetorical point: that the discerning, Christlike mind (2:5) operates with humility. Paul presents his impending court sentencing as a rhetorical choice: "to live or to die" (1:21-23). Then he shows the Philippians how to think like Christ when they are discerning such choices. Ultimately, in Paul's example, the criterion for discerning the best choice is not "what is best for me" (after all, both choices offer a benefit to Paul, for "to live is Christ and to die is gain," 1:21), or "what I most desire" (to be released and "be with Christ," 1:23), but "what is best for you all" (1:24). Paul puts his friends first. To think like Christ is to look to the concerns of the other. Thus the Christian process of discernment, according to Paul, is not about one's own "desires," but rather about what one's friends need most in Christ. Indeed, when Paul chooses "to remain and continue in the flesh" for the Philippians, Christ is glorified (1:26).

▌THE TEXT IN THE INTERPRETIVE TRADITION

One of the difficult questions in the long interpretive history of Philippians has been where Paul was imprisoned. This letter does not seem to fit any of the Acts chronology. Nor do the hints about the "praetorian guard" (1:13) or Caesar's household (4:22) help us to pinpoint Paul's location.

Another question arises because Paul seems overly optimistic in 1:12-26. He is in prison and unsure of the outcome (2:23), but believes Christ is "revealed in my chains" (1:13). He is hungry, thirsty, and suffering (4:11-12), yet he affirms that his situation is furthering the "progress of the gospel" (1:12). Yet, understood pastorally, Paul's epistolary optimism functions to reassure the Philippians and to encourage those who stand in solidarity with him through their financial and emotional support.

In the end, Philippians steps free of such historical questions aimed at understanding Paul's imprisonment. The letter has, again and again, lent itself more readily as a model for the letters of prisoners of faith who follow in Paul's footsteps. Letters from other martyrs and prisoners of faith have reflected theologically on suffering (Dietrich Bonhoeffer, imprisoned Quakers, Stephen Biko) and on injustice (Martin Luther King Jr., Oscar Romero), and have striven to comfort their friends as Paul also does in 1:12-13 and 1:24-26, 30. But Philippians is also a *public* letter from prison. And, like Dietrich Bonhoeffer's *Letters and Papers from Prison* and Martin Luther King's "Letter from a Birmingham Jail," Paul's letter "to all the saints in Christ who are in Philippi" is rhetorically constructed to model Christ's way of thinking and acting.

▌THE TEXT IN CONTEMPORARY DISCUSSION

In the end, Paul dismisses the power of his jailors and presumes that the choice of a life-or-death sentence is his—not because he necessarily thinks he is in control, but precisely to exemplify how one should regard one's situation, whether one is in control or not. Thus the rhetorical construction of a life-or-death choice is not a literal consideration of suicide, but a way to model Christ's humble regard for others. Paul humbles his own desire to be with Christ now (1:23) in order to put the Philippians' needs first (1:24), thus demonstrating how they, too, may embody Christ's way of thinking in the midst of affliction, and in solidarity with others who suffer.

To observe Paul's interpretation of his prison situation does not address the state of prison systems today. Paul's friends had access to him; he wrote letters, socialized with the civil servants, received guests and gifts. Today, prison inmates suffer prolonged stays in solitary confinement without visitors. Maximum-security prisons are designed to minimize human contact. In such a situation, there is little possibility of articulating, let alone sharing, one's suffering, despair, or mental deterioration. For Paul, human relationships modeled on Christ's example and participation in one another's lives are part of a saving process. Prison activists today are asking if isolating prisoners from human contact doesn't disconnect them from restorative social communion and even the possibility of healing the whole community, inside and outside of the cell.

Philippians 1:27—2:18: Embodying the Mind of Christ: Christ's Example

■ THE TEXT IN ITS ANCIENT CONTEXT

As Rome transitioned from a city-state to a world empire in the first century BCE, Roman soldiers colonized Philippi and citizenship became an important social distinction among residents. Some had the "green card" of belonging, either Roman citizenship or, at least, citizenship within the city. But other residents were not so privileged. The "saints in Philippi" (1:1) whom Paul addresses did not necessarily share the same social or political status with one another. To correct this imbalance, Paul levels the playing field. He challenges the Philippians' investment in their own sociopolitical status. Instead of competing for higher social and political recognition by Roman officials, they are to "be worthy citizens" (*politeuesthe*) of Christ (1:27). The Greek verb *politeuesthe* is related to our language of "politics" and, through Latin, the language of "civic" responsibility and therefore "citizenship." With this language, Paul reorients the Philippians' personal and community identity: they are not vying to be citizens of the empire on earth, but are "striving side by side with one mind for the faith of the gospel" (1:27) to be citizens of Christ in heaven (3:20). This "heavenly citizenship" defines their humble *koinōnia* through the practices of servant friendship, rather than political favors for social advancement. Thus Paul delivers the Philippians from the constant race for honorary titles and beneficial political affiliations. He anchors their social and political identity in christological friendship "with one another" and with Christ (1:27—2:4). Now, because of their *koinōnia* with Christ, the Philippians' citizenship credentials are even greater than the emperor's (2:10).

To further impress on the Philippians that Christ's character is one of humility that leads to emptying oneself of status, not seizing it, Paul introduces a liturgical hymn (2:5-11). Perhaps the assembly sang together before or after the reading of Paul's letter, thus connecting their worship of Christ to their ethical practice of Christ's humility and emphasizing the embodied experience of sharing Christ.

Paul closes the section with an expanded exhortation (2:12-18) to obedience (2:12) and reminds the Philippians that God is the one working in them (2:13, 1:28) to bring them to completion (1:6).

With this exhortation comes a warning from the exodus. The Philippians are not to "murmur and argue" (2:14) like God's people did in the wilderness. But when they strive to be "worthy citizens" (1:27), and to share Christ's sufferings (1:29), they will also share in Christ's cosmic glory (as Lord, 2:10-11) and "shine like stars" (2:15). Their honor thus comes from Christ's cosmic lordship, not their individual status in the Roman Empire.

■ THE TEXT IN THE INTERPRETIVE TRADITION

Catholics and Protestants have often debated Paul's stance on "faith and works." Catholic readings of Philippians therefore emphasize 2:12, where Paul writes, "work out your faith," while Protestant theologians emphasize verse 13, "for God is at work in you." For Paul, both theological points are true at the same time: Empowered by divine grace, the faithful must live out their faith by actively participating in divine grace.

Scholars have long perceived in 2:6-11 a Christ hymn, sometimes designated by the Latin phrase *carmen Christi* (Martin). Extracted from the letter, the hymn seems to point to a more ancient and traditional concept, perhaps Hellenistic, of a heavenly being who comes to earth and then returns to heaven. Scholars have continued to look for the social setting—*Sitz im Leben*—of this pre-Pauline Christology. The hymn also offers a glimpse into the liturgical life of the early church. Further examination suggests that Paul has emended the preexisting hymn in verse 8, by adding "until death on a cross." The reason for this emendation becomes clear in the letter's current form, when Paul presents Epaphroditus as imitating Christ's obedience "until death" (2:30). Additionally, Paul has recontextualized the hymn to illustrate Christ's way of thinking: "Have this mind among you" (2:5). Now it is Christ's way of thinking that enacts his humility and obedience (2:6-8), receives honorary titles from God (2:10), homage from earth (2:11), and ultimately results in God's glory (2:11). Thus Paul uses the hymn to connect Christ's character and behavior with Christ's "mind."

Philippians 2:6-11 has been a critical text for the development of the theology of *kenōsis*, or self-emptying, highlighted in verse 7. In kenotic theology, Christ empties himself of all divinity, taking on the lowest form of existence by becoming human, and then by taking the lowest human form in the ancient social hierarchy, a slave. Thus the divine's servant nature effects salvation, and therefore Christ's followers are to imitate this self-emptying, servant nature as they participate in God's saving work.

■ THE TEXT IN CONTEMPORARY DISCUSSION

Today kenotic theology offers a helpful contrast to consumerist approaches to life. Rather than amassing as much as possible, or buying into the consumer's arms race for more and better, kenotic theology, which is constantly "pouring out" rather than "taking in," offers an alternative for Christians in the world. It emphasizes a way of "being" over "having." Read this way, the Christ hymn is perhaps as countercultural today as it was in the first-century Roman Empire. Whereas Paul's first-century audience heard his challenge to relinquish human status in order to share in Christ's glorified servanthood, today's readers may hear a challenge to relinquish consumption and ownership of more "stuff" in order to share and preserve our increasingly limited resources.

Hearing the exhortation to share in the divine *kenōsis* and Paul's political discourse about citizenship may challenge churches today to reflect on the broken US immigration system. Those who wish to immigrate legally wait decades for permission. Others fleeing economic desperation arrive only to live in fear of being separated from their US-born children. Undocumented immigrants are often denied legal rights because of their limbo status—they don't belong here or there. And children who arrived at an early age grow up thinking they are "American" only to discover they don't have access to the same "firsts" as other teens—first job, first car, first generation to go to college. Paul is not writing political policy, but advising a church how to live in a state that values some residents over others. In Philippi, Paul levels the playing field—you are all citizens of Christ. Churches today must reflect on Paul's pastoral approach to holding a community of differently documented members together as one body of Christ.

Philippians 2:19—4:1: Examples of Embodying the Mind of Christ

▌ THE TEXT IN ITS ANCIENT CONTEXT

In the ancient Mediterranean world, letters were not the primary source of communication. Personal visits were. Because the ancients preferred to network and conduct business in person, they developed a philosophical understanding of the letter as the author's presence (M. Mitchell, 650; Malherbe 1988). Paul thus chooses and sends first Epaphroditus (carrying this letter, 2:25-30), and then Timothy (2:19-24), to be his ambassadors—his physical voice and presence in Philippi.

But Paul's recommendation of Timothy and Epaphroditus in 2:19-30 functions in another critical way: they exemplify Christ's pattern of living in the flesh. Ancient philosophers often used the concept of a mirror to focus their students' gaze on the character after which they would pattern themselves (Johnson 1988). Instead of looking at their own image in the mirror, students would focus on their teacher as a mirror and shape themselves according to the lived pattern their teacher embodied. For Paul, Christ is this mirror and pattern for how he and the Philippians should think and reason, with humility and obedience, before God. But the Philippians cannot "see" Christ in action. So Paul utilizes the philosopher-teacher's refrain of "imitate me" (3:17; 4:9) and focuses the Philippians' gaze on how he embodies Christ's pattern. Now that he is in prison, Paul points to Epaphroditus and Timothy, who will provide the Philippians additional mirrors (2:19-30).

Timothy embodies Christ by being "genuinely concerned for your [the Philippians'] welfare." Paul contrasts Timothy's selflessness with the others who "are seeking their own interests, not those of Jesus Christ" (2:20-21 NRSV). Simply by sending Timothy, Paul too demonstrates his humble concern for the Philippians, who are anxious about Paul's welfare. Epaphroditus is the Philippians' ambassador to Paul. When he falls ill on the journey, Paul likens him to Christ, offering himself "until death" in service to Paul and the Philippians. In this way, Epaphroditus, too, exemplifies the humility of "putting others' concerns first" (2:19-21). Now, when the Philippians "welcome [Epaphroditus] then in the Lord with all joy, and honor such people" (2:29 NRSV), they are embracing Christ in their midst.

Paul reinforces his point in 3:1-4. Once students have seen how their teacher embodies Christ, they, too, can discern the un-Christlike patterns in other teachers. Thus Paul's abrupt criticism of competing teachers in 3:2 (the "dogs"), like his own mock boasting in 3:4-6, negatively illustrates Christ's pattern of humility. Scholars have tried to reconstruct the identity of these teachers, but this is not necessary to understanding Paul's rhetorical point (Kurz).

Next, Paul demonstrates how embodying the mind of Christ leads to fellowship, or *koinōnia*, with Christ. He begins with his own example in 3:4-11. Like Christ (2:6a), Paul acknowledges that he could boast in his own "human form" and origin, "circumcised on the eighth day, of the people of Israel, of the tribe of Benjamin" (3:5) and could rightfully claim superior status over others (3:6). But, also like Christ, Paul refuses to seize hold of this status (2:6b-8; 3:7-8). By rejecting such "confidence in the flesh," Paul gains something far greater: fellowship with Christ. When Paul shares Christ's "sufferings" and his obedience in death (3:10), he is participating in Christ's faithfulness and righteousness (3:9) and hopes to know "the power of his resurrection" (3:10).

Finally, Paul turns to the Philippians in 3:15 and exhorts them to embody the mind of Christ with him. This is not a finished process, but a shared striving "toward the goal for the prize of the heavenly call of God in Christ Jesus" (3:14). God is at work in the community as they "join in imitating Paul, and observe all of those who live according to" Christ's example in Paul, Epaphroditus, and Timothy. In this way, the community of Christ is "conformed to the body of his glory" (3:21 NRSV).

▮ THE TEXT IN THE INTERPRETIVE TRADITION

For much of the modern interpretive history, Phil. 2:19—3:1 was understood as a "travel narrative," a common way for friends to tell their listeners where they have been and where they are going. Taking the passage at face value, scholars have worked to interpret it in relation to that other narrative of Paul's travels, Acts, removing the passage from its rhetorical context in this letter and comparing it to information gleaned from Acts regarding where Paul was imprisoned, for how long, and in what situation.

There is a sharp rhetorical break in 3:2, and on the premises of source-critical method many scholars posit that the travel narrative was inserted beside the exhortative material that begins in 3:2 (e.g., O'Brien, 352). Read this way, the letter seems to be, at worst, disparate pieces of a conversation stitched together from multiple letters, some time after Paul wrote them, and at best, an incongruent argument on the part of Paul himself, perhaps due to the arrival of another letter from Philippi, causing Paul to change his tone of voice here to address the problem of false teachers he calls "the dogs."

The latter possibility further led scholars such as Ronald Hock to argue that "the dogs" and the "circumcision" refer to competing missionaries like those who evangelized the Galatian churches. These "circumcision parties" may have wished to convert the Philippians to Judaism, or to a more strict form of Torah observance. While this interpretation does explain Paul's enumeration *and rejection* of his Jewish credentials, according to Torah, in favor of "knowing Christ" (3:8), it loses sight of the rhetorical context and tone of the letter as a whole. That is, rather than boasting in his own credentials in 3:4-6, Paul is again demonstrating the humility that shapes how one "regards," "considers," and "thinks" according to Christ's humility and pattern of "thinking" (2:5), also illustrated by Timothy and Epaphroditus in chapter 2 (see above).

Another important question for Paul's interpreters arises in 3:9. Does the Greek phrase *pistis Christou* mean that Christ is the object of faith (i.e., the Philippians' *faith in Christ*), or the subject of faith (*Christ's faithfulness* to God)? Most translators have favored the objective translation, putting the emphasis on human belief in Christ. This leads to a Christianity defined by individual assent that privileges personal belief. But Philippians concentrates not on what the community believes, but on how they live out Christ's example. In 3:8, immediately preceding the problematic phrase, Paul uses a parallel genitive construction that is also ambiguous. The phrase *gnōsis Christou Iēsou* could be translated "knowing Christ" (objective) or "Christ's way of knowing" (subjective). In this case, *both* phrases fit Paul's meaning. Paul wants the Philippians to develop Christ's mind—Christ's way of knowing, thinking, discerning. But Paul is also describing a relational way of "knowing Christ" by participating in Christ's humility, suffering, and obedience to God in relation to community. The interpretive question is not easily solved, since decades of Christian theology have depended on one translation or the other. Still, Paul is perhaps best read as a proponent of "both/and." (For a more extensive argument advocating the subjective reading, see Hays; Stegman.)

▌THE TEXT IN CONTEMPORARY DISCUSSION

To contemporary Christian communities, both local churches and national denominations, that are fragmenting over discussions of sexual identity, arguing about how to reach the next generation, and stalemating over environmental policies, Philippians may be read to address the toll that individualism is taking on the very idea of community. To this situation, Paul holds up the ideal of a dynamic, shared, saving body. Christian community is not about worshiping in a church on Sunday, simply believing in Christ, or even converting one's neighbors. For Paul, healthy Christian community cultivates humility and obedience to God so that members are transformed in relationship with one another and conformed to Christ.

Philippians also challenges contemporary discussions in some Christian churches about salvation. Does salvation begin the moment one accepts Jesus Christ as Lord and Savior? Is salvation a lived, present reality, or something realized only in the future? Do we participate in our salvation, and if so, how? What is the role of the individual, the community, creation? For Paul, salvation is not an end or a beginning: it is a complex, dynamic, corporate relationship—the process of being conformed to Christ through fellowship with others. Such complexity makes today's question, what would Jesus do? seem facile. Asking about Jesus' actions only in the moment when one is making a specific decision misses a central piece of Paul's argument in Philippians: character. In Philippians, following Christ is not a series of actions, but an immersion in Christ's character, attitudes, and experiences. In salvation, the question is not, what would Jesus *do*? but rather, *how* would Jesus do it?

Philippians 4:2-23: Embodying the Mind of Christ in Life and Worship

▌THE TEXT IN ITS ANCIENT CONTEXT

Philippians 4:2-9 contains Paul's final exhortations to the community in Philippi. He begins by publicly exhorting two high-profile women by name (4:2). In their disagreement, they are not exhibiting the humility and shared mind of Christ that Paul has just exemplified (3:15-17). Paul does not take sides in their disagreement, which may be disrupting the community. Instead, Paul recognizes that while disagreements occur among the saints, with Christ's humility, Euodia and Syntyche should seek God's revealed solution rather than victory in the argument. Syntyche and Euodia are to "imitate Paul" and those with Paul (3:17) so that their behavior unites rather than divides, exemplifying the mind of Christ.

In 4:10-20, Paul finally includes the Philippians themselves as examples of Christ's mind for their sharing a gift with Paul in his suffering (4:10). Paul refers to a gift that Epaphroditus carried from the Philippians, perhaps financial aid, clothes, books, or a blanket Paul might need in prison. In the logic of the ancient system of patronage, *do ut des* ("I give in order that you will give"), there is no "free" gift (Stowers 1994, 110, 115). But each exchange between people created a relationship of dependency. When Paul accepts the Philippians' gift, he is now in debt to them. Paul acknowledges that the gift was of great benefit, but refuses to be in their debt. Such a social debt would restrict Paul's claim to be "self-sufficient" (4:11) and to depend only on God (4:13). So Paul deflects the benefit of the gift from himself and attributes the benefit to the Philippians. That is, through their gift they share in his "affliction" (4:14). And by "giving and receiving" with him (4:15-16), they practice the ethics of *koinōnia*, or community fellowship, that leads to salvation in Christ.

Some scholars have argued that Philippians is a letter of "thankless thanks" (Peterman 1991; 1997). Others have argued that Paul is quite conscious of the social conventions of thanksgiving, and that he seems to be walking a fine line between affirming the Philippians' gift and incurring the social debt of reciprocity that comes with the gift (White). The position taken here is that Paul reinterprets the Philippians' gift as a practice of *koinōnia* or community fellowship in Christ (Fogg). He does this by quickly moving through three different characterizations of the gift. First, Paul begins with friendship language, which invokes the ancient conventions of reciprocity (4:15-16). Next, instead of reciprocating with a material gift in return, or thanking them in a conventional way and thereby acknowledging that he has incurred a debt, Paul interprets the Philippians' gift as a contribution to their heavenly account with God (4:17). This introduces financial banking language, "your account" (v. 17), and, "I have been paid in full . . ." (v. 18), from which Paul immediately moves to the language of worship, "now that I have received from Epaphroditus the gift you sent, a fragrant offering" (v. 18). Finally, having received the offering, Paul takes up the role of priest and presents the "sacrifice" to God (v. 18). In this way, Paul transforms the Philippians' financial gift *to him* into "a sacrifice acceptable and pleasing *to God*" (4:18). It is therefore not the Philippians' material gift that Paul celebrates, but rather the relationship with him that their material gift signifies. In other words, their communion with Paul and with each other becomes their corporate offering and worship of God. So Paul has written, "I am being poured out as a libation on the offering of your faith" (2:17-18). The result of this communion is shared joy in Christ (2:18; 3:1; 4:4) and glory to God (4:20).

▮ THE TEXT IN THE INTERPRETIVE TRADITION

Paul names only three members of the Philippian community: one man, Epaphroditus (2:25), and two women, Euodia and Syntyche (4:2). (He does, intriguingly, leave a fourth member unnamed in 4:3.) Paul recommends Epaphroditus, "my brother and coworker and fellow soldier, your messenger and minister to my need" (2:25). Then he recommends the women "who have struggled beside me in the work of the gospel" and "whose names are in the book of life" (4:3). What roles did these women have in Philippi? Are they founders of the church? Are they significant patrons of Paul's ministry? Are they local teachers whose divided leadership in the community might disrupt unity, as occurred in the Corinthian churches? Whatever their role, Euodia and Syntyche are important enough in their church community to require Paul's attention and, apparently, to lead the church by example to embody Christ's mind together.

THE TEXT IN CONTEMPORARY DISCUSSION

Philippians is consciously liturgical. Paul gives thanks to God (1:3-8), prays (1:9-11), quotes a hymn (2:6-11), exhorts the community, and closes with an offering to God (4:10-20). Paul conducts himself as a priest, officiating for the Philippians at God's altar (2:17; 4:18-19). This liturgical work both describes the Philippians' service to God and enacts their shared life in Christ. Such liturgical rhythms remind today's readers that ancient letters were read aloud in early church gatherings. What letters edify our communities today? How is contemporary worship woven into our common life? And where are congregations living out their shared Christology? In attempting to answer to these questions, emergent church communities may have much to offer.

The interdependence of Paul's vision for the body of Christ is especially challenging for today's church. On the one hand, our global society understands what it means to be deeply dependent on one another economically and to be intimately entwined electronically in the social marketplace. Yet on the other hand, we cling fiercely to our independence and self-determination. As we have seen above, Paul's own theological reflection on practice suggests a both/and approach that we might consider as we wrestle with this existential situation.

Finally, living Christ's pattern of humility and obedience is a community effort, not an individual one. One's relationship with God is "worked out" (2:12) precisely in the ways one embodies Christ to fellow believers, and to those outside the community. For Paul, the theologically weighted word *salvation* means being in fellowship with Christ through one's fellowship with members of Christ's body. As believers practice Christ's humility and obedience in their shared suffering, joys, afflictions, and trials, as well as their shared practices of friendship and proclamation of the gospel, they *together* participate in God's salvation. This salvation in which they participate is the very "work" that God is bringing to completion (1:6; 2:13) in the Philippians as they live out Christ's pattern of social and relational humility and obedience now. Paul's assertion that their salvation is already coming to completion is both their hope and their witness in the world (1:28; 3:17-21), until they "shine like stars" in the cosmos (2:15).

Works Cited

Alexander, Loveday. 1989. "Hellenistic Letter-Forms and the Structure of Philippians." *JSNT* 37:87–101.

Cassidy, Richard J. 2001. *Paul in Chains: Roman Imprisonment and the Letters of Saint Paul*. New York: Crossroad.

Croy, N. Clayton. 2003. "'To Die Is Gain' (Philippians 1:19-26): Does Paul Contemplate Suicide?" *JBL* 122, no. 3 (September 1): 517–31.

Fee, Gordon D. 1994. *God's Empowering Presence: The Holy Spirit in the Letters of Paul.* Peabody, MA: Hendrickson.

———. 1995. *Paul's Letter to the Philippians.* NICNT. Grand Rapids: Eerdmans.

Fitzgerald, John T. 1996. *Friendship, Flattery, and Frankness of Speech: Studies on Friendship in the New Testament World.* Leiden: Brill.

Fogg, Julia Lambert. 2006. "Koinonia Is Soteria: Paul's Theological Reading of Practices in His Letter to the Philippians." PhD diss., Emory University.

Fowl, Stephen. 1990. *The Story of Christ in the Ethics of Paul: An Analysis of the Function of the Hymnic Material in the Pauline Corpus.* Sheffield: JSOT Press.

Gorman, Michael J. 2009. *Inhabiting the Cruciform God: Kenosis, Justification, and Theosis in Paul's Narrative Soteriology.* Grand Rapids: Eerdmans.

Hays, Richard B. 2002. *The Faith of Jesus Christ: The Narrative Substructure of Galatians 3:1–4:11.* 2nd ed. Grand Rapids: Eerdmans.

Hock, Ronald F. 1980. *The Social Context of Paul's Ministry: Tentmaking and Apostleship.* Philadelphia: Fortress Press.

Hooker, Morna D. 2000. "The Letter to the Philippians." In *The New Interpreter's Bible.* Vol. 11, *2 Corinthians–Philemon*, edited by Leander E. Keck, 469–549. Nashville: Abingdon.

Johnson, Luke Timothy. 1986. *The Writings of the New Testament: An Interpretation.* Philadelphia: Fortress Press.

———. 1988. "The Mirror of Remembrance (James 1:22-25)." *CBQ* 50:632–45.

———. 1993. "The Social Dimensions of Soteria in Luke-Acts and Paul." *SBLSP* 32:520–36.

Karris, Robert. 2000. *Prayer and the New Testament.* New York: Crossroad.

Kurz, William. 1985. "Kenotic Imitation of Paul and of Christ in Phil 2 and 3." In *Discipleship in the New Testament*, edited by Fernando Segovia, 103–26. Philadelphia: Fortress Press.

Malherbe, Abraham J. 1987. *Paul and the Thessalonians: The Philosophic Tradition of Pastoral Care.* Philadelphia: Fortress Press.

———. 1988. *Ancient Epistolary Theorists.* Atlanta: Scholars Press.

———. 1996. "Paul's Self-Sufficiency (Philippians 4.11)." In *Friendship, Flattery, and Frankness of Speech*, edited by John T. Fitzgerald, 125–39. Leiden: Brill.

Martin, Ralph P. 1997. *A Hymn of Christ: Philippians 2.5-11 in Recent Interpretation and the Setting of Early Christian Worship.* Downers Grove, IL: InterVarsity Press.

Martin, Ralph P., and Brian J. Dodd. 1998. *Where Christology Began: Essays on Philippians 2.* Louisville: Westminster John Knox.

Meggitt, Justin J. 1998. *Paul, Poverty and Survival.* Edinburgh: T&T Clark.

Mitchell, Alan. 1997. "Greet the Friends by Name: New Testament Evidence for the Greco-Roman *Topos* on Friendship." In *Greco-Roman Perspectives on Friendship*, edited by John T. Fitzgerald, 225–62. Atlanta: Scholars Press.

Mitchell, Margaret. 1992. "New Testament Envoys in the Context of Greco-Roman Diplomatic and Epistolary Conventions: The Example of Timothy and Titus." *JBL* 111:641–62.

O'Brien, Peter Thomas. 1991. *The Epistle to the Philippians: A Commentary on the Greek Text.* NIGTC. Grand Rapids: Eerdmans.

Peterman, Gerald W. 1991. "Thankless Thanks: Philippians 4.10-20." *TynBul* 42:261–70.

———. 1997. *Paul's Gift from Philippi: Conventions of Gift-Exchange and Christian Giving.* Cambridge: Cambridge University Press.

Secret, Mosi. 2012. "Prisoners' Letters Offer a Window into Lives Spent Alone in Tiny Cells." *New York Times*, October 2, A25 of the New York edition.

Stegman, Thomas D. 2009. *Second Corinthians*. Catholic Commentary on Sacred Scripture. Grand Rapids: Baker Academic.

Stowers, Stanley Kent. 1986. *Letter Writing in Greco-Roman Antiquity*. Library of Early Christianity 5. Philadelphia: Westminster.

———. 1994. "Friends and Enemies in the Politics of Heaven: Reading Theology in Philippians." *Pauline Theology*. Vol. 1, *Thessalonians, Philippians, Galatians, Philemon*, edited by Jouette Bassler, 105–22. Minneapolis: Fortress Press.

White, L. Michael. 1990. "Morality between Two Worlds: A Paradigm of Friendship in Philippians." In *Greeks, Romans, and Christians: Essays in Honor of Abraham J. Malherbe*, edited by David L. Balch, Everett Ferguson, and Wayne A. Meeks, 201–15. Minneapolis: Fortress Press.

Wiles, Gordon P. 1974. *Paul's Intercessory Prayers: The Significance of the Intercessory Prayer Passages in the Letters of St. Paul*. Cambridge: Cambridge University Press.

COLOSSIANS

Sylvia C. Keesmaat

Introduction

The ancient city of Colossae was located in the Lycus Valley (modern-day Turkey), less than fifteen miles from the more prominent cities of Laodicea, an important imperial center, and Hierapolis, famous for its healing springs. Due to Roman resettlement and its location on a trade route, the population of Colossae was quite diverse, including a Jewish community. An earthquake destroyed Colossae between 60 and 64 CE, and it appears that the city was not rebuilt for some time.

The letter itself suggests that Epaphras was the founder of the community (1:7-8) and that Paul was not personally known to them. Although the opening of the letter indicates that Paul wrote the Letter to the Colossians, there is some debate among scholars as to whether he indeed did. Those who argue against Paul's authorship point out that the vocabulary and theological emphases of Colossians differ from the letters that are universally accepted as Pauline. Not only does Colossians seem to have a more exalted view of Christ, but there is also less of an emphasis on the Spirit, as well as a turn to a more authoritarian and hierarchical social structure. Those who argue in favor of Paul's authorship point out that the different circumstances of this community could have resulted in differences in vocabulary and emphasis; that an exalted Christology is also found in Philippians; and that the perception of a more hierarchical social structure is a misunderstanding of the text in its original context. Some scholars argue that the letter was written in the presence of Paul by an associate and that that this accounts for differences of style and theological emphasis.

Given the occasional nature of Paul's letters, and the diversity of vocabulary and theology found in his other letters (for instance, justification by faith is central in both Galatians and Romans, but not in Corinthians), differences of style and theology are not a sufficient argument against authenticity. In fact, the theology of Colossians fits squarely with that of the other Pauline letters. In addition, the rich theology, evocative poetry, and clear familiarity with both the Scriptures of Israel and wider imperial culture are overwhelmingly consistent with Paul's other writings and suggest that Paul was indeed the author of this letter.

Paul's reference to his chains in Col. 4:3 suggests that he was in prison at the time of writing. Possible locations for this imprisonment are Ephesus (inferred from 1 Cor. 15:32; 2 Cor. 1:8), Caesarea (Acts 24:27), and Rome (Acts 28:16). Traditionally, the "Prison Epistles" (Philippians, Ephesians, Colossians, and Philemon) were thought to have been written during Paul's imprisonment in Rome. More recently, others have suggested that Paul was imprisoned in Ephesus when he wrote Colossians, since the proximity of the two cities would have facilitated the presence of both Epaphras and Onesimus with Paul at the time of writing. However, it is not clear that Luke (referred to in Col. 4:14) was with Paul in Ephesus. Although arguments are strong for both Rome and Ephesus, the balance of the evidence is slightly stronger for Ephesus. This would mean that the letter was written between 52 and 55 CE.

A few scholars have suggested that the close connection between Philemon and Colossians could provide a specific context for the letter. The letter itself indicates that it was carried to Colossae by Tychicus and Onesimus (4:7-9). If the latter is the slave Paul discusses in the Letter to Philemon (see commentary on 4:9 below), this could provide the occasion for Paul's extended comments on the relationship between masters and slaves in Col. 3:22—4:1.

The Colossian community was undoubtedly shaped by the strongly hierarchical character of Roman society, particularly the household unit, structured under the control of the *paterfamilias* (literally, "the father of the family"). The paterfamilias had economic and moral authority over the women of the household, slaves, and his own children, even after they reached adulthood. As we shall see, Paul's comments on the role of masters, women, children, and slaves in 3:18—4:1 provide insight into how this community struggled with what it meant to be followers of Jesus while negotiating their identities in the context of the story and hierarchy of the Roman Empire.

The closing of the letter indicates that Paul expected it to be read in neighboring church communities (4:15-16). The corporate address suggests that while it contained advice specific to the Colossians, this letter was also more widely applicable to other believing communities. Since these communities lived, moved, and had their being in cities that were shaped architecturally, liturgically, and economically by the historical realities of the Roman Empire, the following reading of Colossians will draw on recent research to show the ways early believing communities negotiated their identity in light of imperial realities (Horsley; Walsh and Keesmaat; Maier). In addition, the story of Israel deeply shaped Paul's understanding of the work of Jesus and God in the world. Hence, Paul's many allusions to the Scriptures of Israel will also be highlighted in this reading.

It is important to note that Paul's imagery and metaphors in this letter are rooted in the stories and symbols of his world. The overarching story of Rome with its myths, symbols, and images provided a rich cultural context for both Paul and the believers in Colossae. In addition, the story of Israel was the primary symbolic world for Paul and perhaps some of this letter's recipients. It is no surprise, therefore, to discover throughout this letter not only the metaphors and imagery of Rome but also those of Judaism.

Colossians 1:1-14: Greeting and Description of the Colossians' Story

▮ THE TEXT IN ITS ANCIENT CONTEXT

At the outset of this letter, Paul roots the identity of the Colossian believers in the story of both Jesus and Israel. As people who lived under the powerful rule of Rome, the Colossians would have been aware of the need to be faithful to the emperor, Nero, a faithfulness rooted in the widespread hope that Nero's gospel would unite the whole of the known world under the civilizing influence of Roman culture and law. Paul, however, not only describes a different identity, one of faithfulness to Jesus, but also a hope in a different gospel, one that also bears fruit in the whole world (1:2, 5-6). In fact, the imagery of bearing fruit is a direct challenge to Rome, since the fertility and abundance of the empire was celebrated as a result not only of Roman rule in general but also of the new age inaugurated by Nero. Paul, in contrast, asserts that it is the gospel of Jesus Christ that is bearing fruit not only in the whole world but also in the life of this particular community (1:6, 10).

Paul describes this fruit in a number of ways: it is the love that the Colossians have in the Spirit (1:7); it is connected to growing in the knowledge and understanding of God (vv. 9-10); and it is the fruit of "good work" as they walk in ways that are holy to the Lord (v. 10). All of this will be unpacked as the letter unfolds.

Throughout Jewish Scriptures, not only is fruitfulness a sign of Israel's obedience, but Israel is also the one called to bear the good fruit of justice and righteousness (Isa. 5:1-7; 2 Kgs. 19:30 // Isa. 37:31; Hos. 9:10-17). This fruit, moreover, is the way in which Israel would be a blessing to the nations (Isa. 42:6; 49:6). Paul evokes that story not only in his reference to bearing fruit but also in verses 12-14, where he describes the actions of Jesus, the beloved Son, who has rescued the Colossians from the power of darkness and transferred them to his kingdom. By referring to inheritance, redemption, and forgiveness, Paul is alluding to the exodus, where Israel was redeemed from the powerful kingdom of Egypt and welcomed into an inheritance and redemption by God.

By the end of this introduction, the recipients of this letter have been grounded in love and called to wisdom, knowledge, and the fruit of good works, all shaped by the story of Jesus.

▮ THE TEXT IN THE INTERPRETIVE TRADITION

In a later time, when the early church was exploring the implications and parameters of Christian faith, both Tertullian and Augustine appealed to Col. 1:6 to emphasize the universal nature of the true gospel, in contrast to heresies that, they asserted, tended to be limited in both time (in that they were recent doctrinal innovations) and location (for instance, the Donatists in Africa: Gorday, 4).

John Calvin (148), writing in a context where the mediating presence of the church was understood to be required for salvation, noted Paul's emphasis on faith in Jesus Christ in verses 4 and 7, along with the redemption and forgiveness found in Jesus, the beloved Son (v. 14), as evidence of the need for Christ alone for salvation. These verses, then, constituted a challenge to the papacy, which, in Calvin's opinion, undermined the sufficiency of Christ.

THE TEXT IN CONTEMPORARY DISCUSSION

For much of church history, the emphasis on the all-sufficient character of Christ's salvation was comfort in the face of uncertain circumstances. In a postmodern context, however, the overwhelmingly masculine and all-encompassing nature of Paul's claims in these verses may evoke a totalizing character that is experienced as oppressive. If this letter is addressed to those who are faithful and who are holy, how can this letter speak to others who make no such claims to holiness or faithfulness? Similarly, is Paul not making a totalizing claim about the story of Jesus that rivals the totalizing hegemonic claims made by the Roman Empire? Does this story not then function in what is potentially a similarly oppressive way as any hegemonic metanarrative? (Walsh and Keesmaat, 17–18).

Other questions arise in light of recent research into the importance of slavery as a context for this letter. Do the references to being made strong and enduring everything with patience (v. 11) indicate that even those who are followers of Jesus in this community suffer not only at the hands of the wider culture but also at the hands of masters who may or may not be believers? Can the reference to sharing the inheritance of the saints (v. 12) nevertheless provide a word of hope for those who are enslaved to imperial powers, both in Paul's time and today?

Colossians 1:15-23: Who Is Lord: Jesus or Caesar?

THE TEXT IN ITS ANCIENT CONTEXT

The poem found in Col. 1:15-20 describes the "beloved Son" of verse 13, into whose kingdom the Colossians have been transferred. It begins with an allusion to both the story of Israel and the story of Rome: "He is the image of the invisible God." In keeping with the theme of creation that permeates this passage, these words echo the biblical creation account of humankind's being created in the image of God (Gen. 1:26-27), an echo Paul picks up again in 3:10, where he describes the new nature of the Colossian believers as "renewed in knowledge according to the image of its creator." Throughout Israel's history, the language of humanity's being created in the image of God carried polemical weight in the face of mythologies that portrayed humanity as slaves who do the menial labor of the gods (Middleton). In the Roman Empire, where the emperor embodied the glory of the gods and where the images of the emperor dominated public space, Paul's appeal to the story of Adam would have sounded a subtle challenge to the superiority of the emperor.

The references to creation in these verses find their context not only in Genesis but also in the wisdom traditions of Israel, where Wisdom is described as the image of God (Wis. 7:26), the first-born of creation (Prov. 8:22; Sir. 24:9), the one who designed all things and permeates all things (Wis. 7:24; Prov. 3:19-20; 8:22-30), and the one in whom all things are made new (Wis. 7:37). Paul has taken these rich wisdom traditions and applied them to Christ (Moule, 59–67; D'Angelo, 317–18). Later they become explicit in his argument (1:28; 2:3).

Paul's language concerning the powers is also rooted in Israel's Scriptures, where the terms "thrones" (*thronoi*), "dominions" (*kyriotētai*), and "powers" (*exousiai*) commonly referred to kings and their dynasties, their realms, and the power that they exercised. While "rulers" (*archai*) could be used to refer to spiritual entities, it also referred to earthly rulers (Wink, 11–18). There is some debate as to whether these verses refer to spiritual powers or earthly institutions. Paul, however, insists that he is talking about all things in heaven and *on earth, visible* and invisible, suggesting that "thrones or dominions or rulers or powers" cannot simply be a reference to "invisible" or "heavenly" realities; they must also have a visible and earthly reference. In the Roman Empire, thrones, dominions, rule, and powers referred above all to Rome; to her *ruler*, Caesar, on the *throne* established by the gods; to his *dominion* over all of the known world; to his military *power* and might. In a few short words, Paul draws deeply on Israel's traditions to undermine the whole mythic structure of the empire: its ruler, its throne, its dominion, its power. Jesus is the one who created these structures and holds them together.

For those surrounded by the imagery and symbolism of Rome, Paul's language continued to sound familiar themes in a jarring way. In a world where Caesar was the head of the body politic, the empire, Paul describes Jesus as the head of a new body politic, the church (1:18).

Paul brings these verses to a climax with the claim that in Jesus, all things in heaven and earth are reconciled, for he has made peace through the blood of the cross (1:20). Making peace is nothing new in the empire. In fact, making peace is the language used "in Roman political discourse to celebrate the universal *pax* or military pacification arising from imperial rule" (Maier, 333). In striking contrast to Rome, where peace was brought through violent military might, economic oppression, and cultural domination, Colossians proclaims a peace achieved through the bearing of violence. This is not the violent hegemony of Rome. This is the reconciliation of all things, even the things that wound by a self-sacrificial love.

This reconciliation continues in the lives of the Colossian believers, who have heard the gospel proclaimed to them as it was proclaimed to every creature under heaven. It is this good news to every creature that rounds out the creation language of the poem, and it is this good news for which Paul became a servant (1:23, 25).

▌THE TEXT IN THE INTERPRETIVE TRADITION

In the face of the Arian assertion that Christ was not preexistent with the Father, but was a creature who was later exalted, the fourth-century church fathers appealed to these verses as the basis for the eternal preexistence of Christ and, in the fifth century for the doctrine of the two natures of Christ. Later, Calvin (149) pointed out that because they had been struggling with Arianism, the church fathers had missed the chief point of this text, which is that the Father is made visible to believers in Jesus. In so doing, he shifted the focus from Jesus' relation to God to Jesus' relation to believers.

More recently, Paul's description of "thrones, dominions, rulers and authorities" in verse 16 has played a central role in the debate on the meaning of the principalities and powers. Some argue that this language refers to heavenly spiritual beings who are identified with the powers of darkness in verse 13 (Arnold, 251–55). Others argue that these powers also include human systems and structures (Wink; Sumney, 67), an argument that is convincing in light of the political overtones of "thrones, dominions, rulers and authorities" in the first century.

▌The Text in Contemporary Discussion

Colossians 1:15-20 has become a central text in discussions of environmental theology. In that context, Paul's allusions to the story of creation, the centrality of the wisdom tradition with its emphasis on creation, Paul's description of the reconciliation of all things, whether on earth or in heaven (v. 20), and the proclamation of the gospel to all creatures (v. 23) provide a basis for a message of good news and redemption for all of creation (Bouma-Prediger, 105–10; Wilson, 309). This stands in contrast to the creation-denying asceticism that Paul critiques in 2:16-23.

Postmodern and postcolonial readers might also question, however, whether in these verses Paul continues to reinscribe the violent and totalizing character of the Roman Empire itself. His description of Jesus appropriates imperial language so powerfully that it seems that Jesus functions like any other imperial ruler. This is reinforced by the repetition of the phrase "all" and "all things" throughout the passage (vv. 15-16 [×2], 17 [×2], 18, 19, 20), and by the language of Jesus triumphing over his enemies in 2:15.

Interpreters struggle with this dynamic. Some argue that a ruler who makes peace by bearing rather than inflicting violence is engaging in self-sacrificial love rather than violent hegemony. Others argue that by imitating the language of empire, the text provides a basis for the sort of hierarchical and authoritative control that has often characterized Christendom. In such a context, the nonviolent character of Jesus' actions has been lost in the oppressive dynamic of the language of the "kingdom."

Colossians 1:24—2:6: The Mystery of Christ

▌The Text in Its Ancient Context

In light of Paul's other letters, the assertion that Paul is "completing what is lacking in Christ's afflictions for the sake of his body, that is, the church" is an unusual concept, because it suggest that Paul's suffering adds to or completes the suffering of Christ. Some argue that because the identification of Christ and the church is so close, the suffering of believers is the suffering of Christ (MacDonald 2000, 79); others argue that Paul is referring to the messianic woes, the sum of suffering that God's people must fulfill before the end times; and others argue that Paul is referring to the tradition of noble death in Greco-Roman literature, where the death of martyrs vicariously provides an example for the benefit of others (Sumney, 101).

However it is interpreted, in the context of participation in the story of Jesus' death and resurrection, which runs throughout this letter (see 2:10-13; 3:1-4), this verse serves to root Paul's experience more deeply in the story of Jesus. By implication, any suffering that those in this community might be experiencing is also rooted in that story.

In the imperial story, the mystery that is revealed, and the glory that is celebrated, is that of the glorious rule of the emperor himself. Instead, Paul asserts that wisdom and knowledge are hidden in God's mystery, Christ, who is, in Roman eyes, a failed Messiah who died at Roman hands. For the Colossians, however, he is the hope of glory (1:27). This Messiah, Jesus, who is Lord (while the slogan of the empire is that *Caesar* is Lord), is the one in whom they should walk. The language of "walking in the Lord" is rooted in Torah observance, in the story of Israel. Moreover, the Colossians not only walk in him but also are rooted and built up in him. These are images from the empire, usually applied to the way in which Nero gives root to, binds together, and builds up the whole of Roman society (Maier, 328). Rather than Nero, however, the Colossians are rooted and built up in a different Lord.

THE TEXT IN THE INTERPRETIVE TRADITION

In light of Paul's assertion that his sufferings complete what is lacking in Christ's suffering, interpreters from the church fathers to the present have been concerned to defend the sufficiency of Christ Jesus' death for salvation. In the sixteenth century, the Catholic Church taught that the blood of the martyrs played a role in the expiation of sins, using this verse to argue that the suffering of the saints has redemptive power (Gorday, 36). In opposition to this, Calvin argued that the suffering of the saints had no redemptive role; rather, their suffering confirmed the faith of the church. Since Christ lived in Paul, his suffering is the suffering of Christ; as a result, Paul's suffering edifies the church, rather than redeems it (Calvin, 165–67).

THE TEXT IN CONTEMPORARY DISCUSSION

The question of the place and role of suffering in the life of believers continues to dominate the interpretation of this passage. In the North American context, where the church has been shaped by a theology of blessing and prosperity, what meaning does Paul's language of suffering carry? Do these verses suggest that the church in North America has something to learn from the suffering of believers in other parts of the world?

Furthermore, in light of the legacy of suffering inflicted by Christians, in contexts like residential schools for native peoples in Canada and the United States, is there a way theologically to interpret this suffering in light of the suffering of Christ? Moreover, if Christians are the ones inflicting this suffering, have they abandoned the story of Jesus?

Colossians 2:8—3:4: Paul's Challenge to Idolatry

THE TEXT IN ITS ANCIENT CONTEXT

What is at stake in this letter is the very freedom of the believers at Colossae. If, as we have suggested, this community is struggling with the roles of both masters and slaves, Paul's allusions and ethical exhortations in the next section suggest that life shaped by the story and structures of empire is fundamentally an experience of being taken captive. His argument begins by showing the Colossian believers that their story is rooted in the story of Jesus: they have come to fullness in him (2:10); they were spiritually circumcised in him (2:11); they were buried with him in baptism (2:12); they were raised with him (2:12, 3:1); and they were made alive with him (2:13). All of this was made possible because Jesus, the head of every ruler and authority, erased the legal record against them, setting it aside.

The irony is complete: Jesus was stripped by the Roman authorities and held up to contempt as they celebrated their triumph over him. Now the tables are turned. Those rulers and authorities who were known to conquer and take captive the peoples of the world were disarmed by Jesus on the cross and made a public example (2:15). First-century hearers would have discerned an allusion to the victory parades that formed part of Roman triumphal celebrations, where conquered peoples, now Roman slaves, were paraded as a public example of what happens to those who resist the benefits of Roman imperial rule (Wright, 116). Rather than violently triumphing over and then parading conquered and enslaved losers, Jesus triumphed over the rulers and authorities by *disarming* them on a *cross*. This nonviolent suffering is not only a challenge to Roman power but also a word of hope to those who were enslaved under this empire. Jesus is not someone who glories in violence and the demeaning humiliation of captives.

There is much debate about what sort of "philosophy" and "empty deceit" Paul is referring to in these verses, especially since in 2:16-23, he describes religious restrictions and practices that could relate to Judaism (festivals, new moons, Sabbaths [v. 16]; angelic visions [v. 18]; and food restrictions [v. 21]). Others have found references to pagan ascetic religious practices in these verses.

Some have suggested that Paul is not referring to any one specific problem in the Colossian community but rather that he has in mind a range of possible challenges that these new disciples could face (Hooker). Others have explored Paul's allusions in these verses to the prophetic critique of idolatry found in Israel's Scriptures (Walsh). Just as idolatry is worthless, vain, and nothing (Pss. 97:7; 115:4-7; 135:15-18; Isa. 44:9; 57:13; Jer. 2:5), so the philosophy to which Paul refers is described as "empty deceit" (2:8) and a shadow without substance (2:17). Just as idols are constructed by human hands (Ps. 115:4; Isa. 2:8; 41:6-7; 44:11; Jer. 10:1-10; Hosea 8:4, 6; 13:2; Hab. 2:18), so the philosophy is a human tradition (2:8), and a human way of thinking (2:18) that imposes human commands and teachings (2:20). Just as idolatry results in a deluded mind and a fundamental lack of knowledge (Isa. 44:18-20; Hosea 4:6) and just as an idol is a teacher of lies (Hab. 2:18), so the philosophy is puffed up without cause (2:18) and deceives people by employing supposedly plausible arguments (2:4, 8). Just as idolatry is impotent, without value, and does not profit (Pss. 115:4-7; 135:15-18; Isa. 4:20; 46:1-2; Jer. 2:11; Hosea 7:16; Hab. 2:19), so the philosophy is of no value in checking self-indulgence (v. 23). And just as idolatry is a matter of exchanging glory for shame (Ps. 106:20; Jer. 2:11; Hosea 4:7; 7:16; 13:1-3; Rom. 1:23), so the philosophy disqualifies, insists on self-abasement (2:18), and promotes severe treatment of the body (2:23).

Of course, in biblical tradition, the critique of idolatry is rooted in the confession that Yahweh is the creator of heaven and earth (Pss. 115:16; 135:5-7; Isa. 40:12-26; 44:9-28; 45:12, 18; Jer. 10:11-16; 51:15-19). Paul also grounds his critique of the philosophy in the assertion that Jesus is the one through whom and for whom all things were created (Col. 1:15-17). And, of course, Jesus triumphs over all rulers and authorities on the cross (2:15), just as Yahweh triumphs over other gods.

Throughout the Jewish Scriptures, it is when the people of Israel forget their story that they succumb to the idolatry of the surrounding peoples. Paul, too, frames this whole section with the story that provides a context for the life of the Colossian believers. Picking up the narrative thread of Col. 2:12 in 3:1, he continues: "If, then, you have been raised with Christ, seek the things that are above, where Christ is seated at the right hand of God." In an empire where the deified imperial rulers were considered to continue to rule with the gods after their death, Paul asserts that Christ—who has been raised to new life—is seated at the right hand of God. Paul is not advocating an otherworldly dualism, but rather raising the question of ultimate authority. Who is really in control? Is the whole body of the empire held together by the emperor who nourishes and upholds it, or by Jesus? In using the imagery of the body politic in 1:18 and 2:19, Paul has already challenged the rule of Caesar. By stating that the whole fullness of the deity dwells bodily in Jesus (2:9), and placing Jesus at the right hand of God (3:1), Paul has undermined the sacred canopy of Roman rule. Not only are the religious practices of paganism characterized as idolatry, but Paul is also reminding this community that throughout Israel's Scriptures, the religious practices of Judaism were considered idolatrous when they were used in service of injustice and captivity (i.e., Isaiah 58). Paul's language reminds the community at Colossae that their practices reveal whom they worship and the story of which they are a part.

■ THE TEXT IN THE INTERPRETIVE TRADITION

In a later context, where Christianity was engaged in differentiating itself from both Judaism and other religious and civic associations, the early church fathers emphasized how these verses undermined the rituals of both Judaism and pagan mystery religions. As time went on, these verses were also used to challenge the body-denying practices and beliefs of Gnosticism.

For those in Christian traditions who practiced asceticism and taught its importance as a form of Christian discipleship, however (for instance, the desert fathers), these verses were problematic because they appear to condemn the ascetic practices that shaped early monasticism. As a result, these commentators emphasized that it was not the ascetic practices themselves that were the problem but rather the *intention* of the practitioner, who must ensure that such discipline is grounded in Christ and reflects a reliance on grace rather than human achievement (Gorday).

Later, in the face of Catholicism, with its emphasis on the intervention of saints and martyrs for salvation, Calvin identified Paul's reference to the worship of angels not only with the worship of saints in his own time but also with the practice of relying on the mediating role of those who had died. He argued that these verses assert that no mediator other than Christ is necessary to approach God (Calvin, 194–96).

■ THE TEXT IN CONTEMPORARY DISCUSSION

Paul's critique of the practices of the Colossian community has raised a number of questions in the minds of readers. Most prominent is the question of whether Paul is engaging in a supersessionist strategy here, denigrating the practices of Judaism and equating them with the elemental spirits of the universe that have the appearance of wisdom. Given Paul's allusions to the prophetic critiques of idolatry, along with his allusions and echoes of Israel's story and Scriptures in this letter, supersessionism seems unlikely. There is no doubt, however, that these verses have lent themselves to antisemitic purposes in the past.

It is also difficult to discern the precise nature of the beliefs and practices that Paul is critiquing, given the fact that we have only Paul's allusions to them, and these may be pejorative and emotive rather than entirely accurate (Caird, 162). How much can we trust Paul's depiction of "the philosophy" here?

Some have also asked whether Paul is describing his opponents in ways that can be applied just as easily to his own teaching. He describes the opponents' belief as "human tradition" (2:8) and "simply human commands and teachings" (2:22). In short, he says, "Do not let anyone condemn you" (2:16), and then proceeds with his own words of condemnation. The text invites us to identify with Paul's perspective here. But what is it about Paul's teaching that makes it more acceptable than that of his opponents (Walsh and Keesmaat, 102–14)?

Colossians 3:5-17: Living as Image Bearers

■ THE TEXT IN ITS ANCIENT CONTEXT

In light of this story, how then are the Colossians to live? In light of the creation-affirming language in Col. 1:15-23, it is unlikely that Paul is referring to a dualist rejection of the body when he tells the Colossians to "put to death whatever in you is earthly" (3:5). Instead, he lists examples that include not only sexual sins (sexual immorality, impurity, passion, evil desire) but also sins that tear apart community: covetousness, greed, anger, wrath, malice, slander, abusive language, and lying (3:5, 8-9). Moreover, he explicitly links greed with idolatry, suggesting that it is the consumptive economic practices of the empire that reveal the idolatry at its very heart. Sexual immorality, impurity, passion, evil desire, and covetousness all demonstrate the way in which greed manifests itself, both sexually and more generally.

Paul's language here again links the story of the Colossian Christians with that of Jesus. The new self with which they are clothed is being renewed in knowledge according to the image of its Creator. This is the knowledge that Paul has been praying for this community since the outset (1:9-10; 2:2), a knowledge that causes the Colossians to look more like this image of God found in Jesus, who suffered the violence of the empire in order to bring peace.

Paul again challenges the claims of imperial rule to bring pacification to all the peoples of the world by asserting that in the renewal Jesus brings there is "no longer Greek or Jew, circumcised and uncircumcised, barbarian, Scythian, slave and free," but that "Christ is all and in all" (3:11). Even those most marginalized and oppressed in the far-flung reaches of the empire (barbarian, Scythian), the most marginalized and abused in the households of the Colossians along with those who control them (slave and free), and those most easily dismissed as unworthy by the other (Jews and gentiles) participate in the story of Jesus and are being renewed in his image. It is an audacious claim in a context where only the civilizing influence of Rome was thought to bring renewal to the world.

In the face of the community-destroying practices that the Colossians are to put to death, Paul calls the community to be clothed with those virtues that instead build up community: compassion, kindness, humility, meekness, and patience (3:12). Paul, however, also recognizes the need—particularly in this community, where people are just learning to negotiate their old power structures and relations in light of their new identity in Christ—to bear with one another and to forgive. Not only will love be needed, but also the peace of Christ, to make such forgiveness possible. The reconciliation that comes from self-sacrificial love is the only thing that is to rule them. Paul winds up these admonitions with a call to thankfulness that permeates all they do: teaching, admonishing, singing, and learning. Such love, forgiveness, peace, and gratitude will be necessary to negotiate the complicated relationships that Paul alludes to in the next section.

■ THE TEXT IN THE INTERPRETIVE TRADITION

The central debate over these verses has been whether Paul considers the body to be evil. More Platonic interpretations of this text throughout history have associated that which is "earthly" with the body and its passions. John Chrysostom and others have challenged that view, arguing that it is our moral choices that determine what is earthly. Following Platonism, gnostics argued that true spirituality meant an escape from the body; once again, the church fathers strove to affirm the goodness of the created order. This temptation to denigrate the body and its desires has continued to plague Christian tradition through the ages, right up until the present time. It is striking that the church fathers, surrounded by a culture that was permeated with otherworldly spirituality, continued their emphasis on the goodness of the created order (Gorday, 42).

■ THE TEXT IN CONTEMPORARY DISCUSSION

What does Paul's assertion that there is no longer Greek and Jew, circumcised and uncircumcised, barbarian, Scythian, slave and free mean in a world where identity is constantly being negotiated and renegotiated? In the Roman Empire, all races and people were to be brought under the all-encompassing sway of Roman culture. In our own world, where cultural identity is rapidly being erased by the pervasive nature of global technology and culture, what are the implications of cultural and social differences being erased "in Christ"? Is this a denial of cultural difference? Or does the language of reconciliation hint at a different kind of cultural equality in Christ?

Colossians 3:18—4:1: Submission and Inheritance— A Jubilee for Slaves

■ THE TEXT IN ITS ANCIENT CONTEXT

The household code, as Col. 3:18—4:1 is known, has been the focus of much recent scholarly work (other household codes are found in Eph. 5:21—6:9 and 1 Pet. 2:18—3:7). No longer interpreted as an unequivocally oppressive text, these verses—in particular their nuanced character and the socially complex context in which they were written—have received more attention than in the past. As a result, there is a growing acknowledgment that they contained a subversive and liberating message in their ancient context (MacDonald 2000; Standhartinger; Sumney; Walsh and Keesmaat).

In the first place, while the language of these verses appears to uphold the status quo in directing women to be subject to their husbands, children to be obedient to their parents, and slaves to be obedient to their masters, it also subtly undermines the absolute authority of the head of the household. Not only are women, children, and slaves addressed in these verses; but the husbands, fathers, and masters are also uncharacteristically given commands to love (3:12), forgo provocation and harsh treatment (3:19, 21), and act justly and fairly (4:1).

It is difficult, however, to know how these commands were heard in Colossae. Within the Colossian community, there were complex and overlapping identities: slaves may have been parents, wives may have been masters, children may have been freeborn or slave and may have had parents who were believers or not, or have been the product of a mixed marriage between a believer and a non-believer (MacDonald 2010). In addition, a child may have been the offspring of the master of the house and a slave (McDonald 2012). How these commands were heard would have varied widely amongst the hearers themselves.

Second, when slaves are told that they are to obey their *masters according to the flesh* (v. 22, translated often as "earthly masters"), a question arises. In Pauline writings, the flesh (*sarx*) often has negative overtones, referring to a way of being that is opposed to the Spirit of God. Are these negative overtones present here?

Moreover, the language of these verses plays on the Greek word for "lord" and "master" (*kyrios*). If we translate all occurrences of *kyrios* in these verses as "master," capitalizing those occurrences that refer to Christ (and are usually translated "Lord"), the sense is much clearer. Paul tells slaves that they are to fear the Master, and do their work as if it is done for the Master, not for their masters. He tells them that they serve the messianic Master (usually translated "the Lord Christ").

This last phrase is important, because it concludes a sentence where slaves are told that from the Master they will receive an inheritance (3:24). It was not normal in Roman law for slaves to expect to inherit. However, in Israelite tradition, there is a time when slaves are released to receive their inheritance. This was known as the year of Jubilee (Leviticus 25). In the shifting sands of Jewish messianic expectation, there were certainly those who linked the coming of the Messiah with Jubilee expectation. When the Messiah came to establish God's kingdom, debts would be forgiven and slaves would be freed. It may be that this reference to the messianic Master refers to that tradition (Walsh and Keesmaat, 207–8). In addition, masters are called to treat their slaves justly and with equality; this last word, *isotēs*, denotes the equality of different social groups before Roman law. It has been suggested that this verse is the key to the passage as a whole, undermining the dominant ethos of subordination (Standhartinger, 13).

This careful language with regard to slaves likely reflects the complexity of slave relationships in the first century. Slaves at this time, whether children, adolescents, or adults, were simply assumed to be sexually available to their masters (MacDonald 2007, 95). If some of the slaves listening to Paul's letter had masters who were unbelievers, the possibility of following Paul's commands to put off immorality (3:5) would have been difficult. Even if their masters were believers, it is not immediately clear that sexual use of their slaves would have ceased, given cultural assumptions (MacDonald 2007, 101–3). However, it has been suggested that the fact that Paul warns masters of their accountability before their Lord, and the fact that "the relinquishing of past patterns of life is an ethical priority in the work (cf. Col. 1:21-23; 2:20; 3:5-7)" (MacDonald 2007, 101) means that masters were to cease their use of slaves for sexual relations.

The fact that Paul has already referred to the cancellation of the debtor's bond in 2:14 would have subtly undermined Paul's commands in these verses. So would his reference to the way in which Jesus had triumphed over those who gloried in parading slaves and conquered men, women, and children from around the empire in 2:15. In addition, in an empire where slaves comprised mainly those people who had been conquered and taken from their own lands, Paul's assertion that there is no slave and free, alongside no Greek or Jew, barbarian or Scythian, would have painted a picture of a world where the structures of slavery were called into question (Sumney, 254).

■ THE TEXT IN THE INTERPRETIVE TRADITION

For much of the interpretive tradition, these verses have garnered relatively little attention, primarily because Paul's commands here were seen as self-evident in the predominantly patriarchal culture of Christendom. The church fathers acknowledged that Paul was merely describing the natural order in relation to husband and wives, fathers and children. On the vexing issue of slavery, some asserted that while slavery was an inequity, the wise person is always free, even when outwardly enslaved (Ambrosiaster, cited in Gorday, 53).

In the 1800s, both sides in the heated debate over slavery appealed to these verses as a justification for slavery on the one hand (since Paul does not here judge the institution of slavery) and as providing a challenge to it on the other (for if masters were to treat their slaves justly and fairly, slavery as we know it would disappear [Swartley]).

■ THE TEXT IN CONTEMPORARY DISCUSSION

For many, Paul's commands in these verses provide an interpretive crux for the letter as a whole. Is Paul here upholding the authority and power of the patriarchal household, and therefore upholding the power structures of the empire? Do these verses demonstrate that Paul's all-encompassing language about Jesus as the one with ultimate authority and power in 1:16-20; 2:9, 15; and 3:1 provide the basis for a model of totalitarian control that is founded on male authority and hierarchy?

These are important questions to bring to the text, not only because they force us to ask what the theology of the letter looked like in the actual lives of first-century believers (especially those who were most vulnerable) but also because they compel us to realize how our own contemporary assumptions can affect our reading. In the context of modern feminism, and in a culture where slavery is considered morally repugnant, these texts seem oppressive. When read in their own nuanced and complex circumstances, it is apparent that Paul is carefully attempting to speak a word of liberation and hope into a situation of complex power structures.

If this letter does indeed explore the difficulty of faithful living in complex circumstances, then questions of discipleship come front and center. What are the contexts in which followers of Jesus find themselves negotiating different power relationships as they strive to be faithful? On the one hand, how do Western Christians, who benefit from slave-like working conditions prevalent in the two-thirds world, read these texts? Is there a need to heed the call to justice and equality in Col. 4:1? What does the biblical call for Jubilee look like in contemporary contexts? On the other hand, how does an abused young man who has to sell his body to live on the streets hear this message of the renewal in Jesus in a way that can possibly be lived in his situation? What is the word of hope to those who find themselves working as sharecroppers for North American companies in Colombia, knowing that the working conditions will likely kill them? Or the women working in a maquila who must endure sexual abuse in order to feed their families? How can those who are powerless and at the mercy of those who control their lives be faithful followers of Jesus?

Colossians 4:2-18: The Shape of the Community

◼ THE TEXT IN ITS ANCIENT CONTEXT

The closing section of this letter provides insight into the social context of this letter. In the first place, it is clear that Paul is urging those in this community to be careful in their walk, particularly in relation to outsiders. By urging them to walk in wisdom (*sophia*), Paul is alluding to the beginning of the letter (1:9; 2:3); however, the reference to outsiders makes it clear that such wisdom requires discernment. Similarly, and in light of Paul's somewhat coded language throughout the letter, his call to gracious speech, seasoned with salt, indicates a need for appropriate speech in different contexts. This is strengthened by the fact that there is more for Tychicus and Onesimus to tell the community than what has been put in the letter (4:9), suggesting that there are some things that Paul did not want to entrust to writing.

Paul's language in 4:7-9 alludes to some of the central tensions in this community. It is clear from the content of Colossians that the issue of slavery has been front and center throughout, as seen in the reference to both Epaphras and Tychicus as fellow slaves (1:7; 4:7), the references to the philosophy as that which enslaves (2:8), the overturning of the patterns of slavery (2:15; 3:11; 3:24—4:1), and the clear linking in the last verses of this letter with the Letter to Philemon. The author suggests that this letter has been brought to the Colossian community by Tychicus and Onesimus. Onesimus is described as part of this community by Paul (v. 9); it is likely that this is a reference to Onesimus the runaway slave mentioned in Philemon (MacDonald 2000, 188; Sumney, 269; Thompson, 106; cf. Wilson, 296; Lincoln 2000, 580). This makes it all the more astounding that Paul describes both Tychicus and Onesimus as beloved and *faithful*. How can a runaway slave possibly be faithful? By describing Onesimus this way, Paul is suggesting that previous commitments have changed for Onesimus. He is faithful in serving another Master, and this faithfulness is more important than faithfulness to his earthly master. More than that, however, Paul describes Tychicus as both a brother and a fellow slave (*doulos*) in the Lord, while Onesimus, who is an actual slave, is described as a brother. If the hearers of this letter haven't realized before this point that the categories have shifted, Paul now makes it explicit.

The greeting to Nympha and the church in her house (4:15) suggests that Nympha was the leader of the Christian community in Laodicea, raising the interesting question of how the commands of 3:18—4:1 would have been heard in a context where a woman exercised leadership over the community. There is such a similarity between the Christian communities in Colossae and Laodicea that they are encouraged to read each other's letters.

Paul's last request, "remember my chains," reminds the Colossians not only to pray for Paul (see 4:3) but also to remember where this gospel can lead. Participation in the story of Jesus leads to the same suffering that Jesus endured (1:11, 24). Even in that context, Paul hopes for grace for this community: grace as they remember the story of which they are a part, and grace as they discern how to live out that story in the complexities of life in the empire.

∎ The Text in the Interpretive Tradition

Paul's presence in prison as he writes this letter has provided an important context for interpreting his words. The church fathers highlighted the importance of prayer in situations of suffering, particularly as a guard against sin and as a way to overcome adversaries. In a time when many Christians were facing persecution, it was acknowledged that prayer, rather than weaponry, was the way believers fought against their adversaries; through prayer, they acknowledged that God provided strength to bear suffering (Gorday, 55).

∎ The Text in Contemporary Discussion

In a postmodern context, which acknowledges the coded nature of language, Paul's reference to gracious, seasoned speech that seeks to be appropriate in context highlights our need to be attentive to the way in which Paul's language may be guarded in this letter (Walsh and Keesmaat, 209). In a situation of oppression, what might Paul have been careful about articulating? How might his context in prison have affected his ability to write freely? Might his allusions to Jubilee and equality in the household code, for instance, be embedded in seemingly usual commands for obedience because it was too dangerous for this vulnerable community to be perceived as undermining the social structures of imperial society? For those with ears to hear, the references to a new social structure are present in these verses and throughout the letter. For those who expect allegiance to accepted social codes, that language is present as well. In the same way, Paul is telling this community to be attentive to how their language will be perceived by those who have power over them.

In addition, when interpreting this letter, should readers perhaps privilege the hermeneutical insights of those who speak from a social location similar to Paul's? Should we question our own ability to interpret the letter well if we read from a position of privilege? Perhaps readers need to remember not only Paul's chains but also the chains of those in the present world before they can truly fulfill the task to which this letter calls them in the Lord (4:17).

Works Cited

Arnold, Clinton E. 1996. *The Colossian Syncretism: The Interface between Christianity and Folk Belief at Colossae.* Grand Rapids: Baker.

Bouma-Prediger, Steven. 2001. *For the Beauty of the Earth: A Christian Vision of Creation Care.* Grand Rapids: Baker Academic.

Caird, G. B. 1976. *Paul's Letters from Prison (Ephesians, Philippians, Colossians, Philemon) in the Revised Standard Version: Introduction and Commentary.* Oxford: Oxford University Press.

Calvin, John. 1860. *Commentaries on the Epistles of Paul the Apostle to the Galatians, Ephesians, Philippians, and Colossians.* Translated by John Pringle. Edinburgh: Calvin Translation Society.

D'Angelo, Mary Rose. 1994. "Colossians" in *Searching the Scriptures.* Vol. 2, *A Feminist Commentary,* edited by Elisabeth Schüssler Fiorenza. New York: Crossroad.

Francis, Fred O. 1962. "Humility and Angelic Worship in Col. 2:18." *Studia Theologica—Nordic Journal of Theology* 16, no. 2:109–34.

Gorday, Peter, ed. 2000. *Colossians, 1–2 Thessalonians, 1–2 Timothy, Titus, Philemon.* Ancient Christian Commentary on Scripture, New Testament 9: Downers Grove, IL: InterVarsity Press.

Hooker, Morna D. 1973. "Were There False Teachers in Colossae?" In *Christ and Spirit in the New Testament,* edited by Barnabas Lindars and Stephen S. Smalley, 315–31. Cambridge: Cambridge University Press.

Horsley, Richard A., ed. 1997. *Paul and Empire: Religion and Power in Roman Imperial Society.* Harrisburg, PA: Trinity Press International.

Lincoln, Andrew T. 1999. "The Household Code and the Wisdom Mode of Colossians." *JSNT* 74:93–112.

———. 2000. "The Letter to the Colossians." In *The New Interpreter's Bible.* Vol. 11, *2 Corinthians, Galatians, Ephesians, Philippians, Colossians, 1 and 2 Thessalonians, 1 and 2 Timothy, Titus, Philemon,* edited by Leander E. Keck, 553–669. Nashville: Abingdon.

Maier, H. O. 2005. "A Sly Civility: Colossians and Empire." *JSNT* 27, no. 3:323–49.

MacDonald, Margaret Y. 2000. *Colossians and Ephesians.* Sacra pagina. Collegeville, MN: Liturgical Press.

———. 2007. "Slavery, Sexuality and House Churches: A Reassessment of Colossians 3.18—4.1 in Light of New Research on the Roman Family." *NTS* 53:94–113.

———. 2010. "Beyond Identification of the Topos of Household Management: Reading the Household Codes in Light of Recent Methodologies and Theoretical Perspectives in the Study of the New Testament." *NTS* 57:65–90.

———. 2012. "Reading the New Testament Household Codes in Light of New Research on Children and Childhood in the Roman World." *SR* 41, no. 3:367–87.

Middleton, J. Richard. 2005. *The Liberating Image:* Imago Dei *in Genesis 1.* Grand Rapids: Brazos.

Moule, C. F. D. 1957. *The Epistles of Paul the Apostle to the Colossians and to Philemon.* Cambridge: Cambridge University Press.

Standhartinger, Angela. 2000. "The Origin and Intention of the Household Code in the Letter to the Colossians." *JSNT* 79:117–30.

Sumney, Jerry L. 2008: *Colossians: A Commentary.* Louisville: Westminster John Knox.

Swartley, Willard M. 1983. *Slavery, Sabbath, War and Women: Case Issues in Biblical Interpretation.* Scottdale, PA: Herald.

Thompson, Marianne Meye. 2005. *Colossians and Philemon.* Two Horizons New Testament Commentary. Grand Rapids: Eerdmans.

Walsh, Brian. 1999. "Late/Post Modernity and Idolatry: A Contextual Reading of Colossians 2.8—3.4." *ExAud* 15:1–17.

Walsh, Brian, and Sylvia Keesmaat. 2004. *Colossians Remixed: Subverting the Empire.* Downers Grove, IL: InterVarsity Press.

Wilson, R. McL. 2005. *A Critical and Exegetical Commentary on Colossians and Philemon.* ICC. London: T&T Clark.

Wink, Walter. 1984. *Naming the Powers: The Language of Power in the New Testament.* Minneapolis: Fortress Press.

Wright, N. T. 1986. *Colossians and Philemon.* TNTC. Grand Rapids: Eerdmans.

1 THESSALONIANS

Edward Pillar

Introduction

The Roman Empire was not a distant and inconsequential authority on the horizon of the Thessalonians' life. Having been founded in 316 BCE by the amalgamation of a number of small settlements, Thessalonica was defeated in battle by the Romans in 197 BCE and from then began its comprehensive imperialization. The Thessalonians drank freely of imperial ethos, philosophy, and culture, which together were a dominant influence on every aspect of their existence.

Thus, when Paul and his companions entered the city and began to proclaim the gospel concerning the Lord Jesus Christ, it is inevitable that the interpretative lens through which their message was heard and understood would have been one profoundly influenced by imperial ideas, ethos, and culture. It is this that we need to consider if we are to hear Paul as the Thessalonians heard him.

Moreover, we should allow the possibility that even if Paul did not directly intend to make references that might be understood as challenges to the imperial ethos and culture, the Thessalonians themselves, from where they stood in this extraordinary blend of Greek and Roman imperial culture, may well have drawn conclusions that engaged with their situation politically as well as spiritually.

At the heart of Paul's gospel, accepted by the Thessalonians, was the announcement that God had raised Jesus from the dead. The implications of this suggestion, more than any other, must be taken seriously if we are to appreciate the significance of this letter—the earliest Christian writing that we have. Emphasis on the resurrection should not simply be seen by readers in the twenty-first century as a precursor to the Parousia—the anticipated reappearance of Jesus Christ, but rather as bearing profound implications for how the Thessalonians were to live in the present and how they were to view and relate to their rulers, the imperial authorities.

1 Thessalonians 1:1-10: The Gospel in Thessalonica

■ THE TEXT IN ITS ANCIENT CONTEXT

Paul begins the letter with a foundational statement of how he sees the Thessalonians. First, he refers to them as the church, the *ekklēsia*. However, rather than the Athenian model of *ekklēsia* as essentially a forum for democracy, Paul seems to see the Thessalonian *ekklēsia* as a gathering to share what was common among them, to support, challenge, and encourage one another in their newfound discipleship of Jesus Christ. Nonetheless, there remains a political nuance in the very act of adopting the name *ekklēsia*, for the Thessalonians are joined together in a new anti-imperial assembly. Conversion to God would have involved massive social, cultural, and political reorientation. A strong, supportive, and encouraging *ekklēsia*, or "church," would have been vital for the survival of each convert. Paul makes clear that this new "church" is rooted in relationship to God the Father and to the Lord Jesus Christ. Paul's reference to God as Father may highlight the fact that this *ekklēsia* is no longer dependent on the imperial father—the emperor—as *Pater Patriae* ("father of the country"). In addition, the reference to the Lord Jesus Christ may be Paul's way of saying that the Lord of this *ekklēsia* is specifically not the emperor; the reference to Jesus as the Christ may hint at the fulfillment and priority of the narrative of Israel over against the imperial story.

Paul then reflects back to the Thessalonians three key elements essential to understanding the visit of Paul and Silas to Thessalonica. First, the gospel was announced in Thessalonica. Here, Paul adopts another imperial term—"gospel," normally reserved for good news concerning the emperor or the imperial family—as an encompassing description of his message. Paul's gospel comprised news of the resurrection of Jesus from the dead. The practical significance of the news of the resurrection for the Thessalonians is that the immense power of the empire—epitomized by crucifixion—has been usurped and upended by a greater power: that of the living and true God. Second, the gospel announcement included mention of the reappearance of Jesus (his Parousia, hinted at in 1:10 and made clear at 2:19; 3:13; 4:15; 5:23). Once again, Paul is taking up a term familiar in the imperial context, normally used, for example, at the appearance and entry of a king into a city. Third, Paul's gospel makes clear that Jesus will rescue the Thessalonians from or defend them against wrath.

A second key element is that of the suffering of the Thessalonians as they receive the gospel. It is clear from 1:6 that the Thessalonians have endured persecution in the process of accepting the gospel (cf. 2:14 and 3:3). It is also likely that Paul speaks about wrath (1:10) precisely because there was a readily perceived and present awareness of suffering. Moreover, the Thessalonians' own expectation of wrath, and thus of suffering, would be linked to the neglecting of the gods and idols inherent in their social, cultural, and political context. Thus, while the Thessalonians would interpret the wrath as having its origin in the anger of the pagan gods, its precise form may well encompass both official and informal harassment and persecution. While the Thessalonians anticipated that Jesus would rescue or defend them both in their present context of suffering but also as persecution continued, it is made clear that they suffered at the hands of their "own compatriots" (2:14). Paul later encourages the Thessalonians that they are not destined for wrath (5:9).

The response of the Thessalonians is highlighted by the welcome given to Paul and Silas (1:9) and their joyous reception of the gospel (1:6). Their confidence in the gospel is underscored by their willingness to reorient their lives away from idols and toward God while waiting for the appearance of Jesus, the resurrected Son. Paul's use of an unusual term to describe this "waiting" is one used by the Jewish historian Josephus to portray waiting for the emperor (*J.W.* 7.68, 71).

▌ THE TEXT IN THE INTERPRETIVE TRADITION

Scholars have seen 1:9-10 as an example of Paul's mission preaching, perhaps adopted from other evangelists before him or employed by Jewish apologists in their contacts with gentiles (although Friedrich considered it to be part of a baptismal hymn: Friedrich, 502–16). Georg Strecker agrees and points out that it contains two of the affirmations fundamental to Christian faith: (a) worship of the true God and (b) the expectation of the return of Jesus the Son of God, who had been raised from the dead (Strecker, 65). However, it is unlikely that Paul would have been bound by a previous kerygma and more likely would have announced a gospel relevant to and contemporary in each context (Hooker, 435). The "wrath to come" has often been assumed to originate with God (e.g., Calvin 1960a, 339; Best, 85; Fee, 50)—although the text does not support this. Moreover, while the wrath is often taken to be eschatological, Martin Luther argued that the destruction of Jerusalem by Vespasian and Titus and the subsequent expulsion of the Jews is sufficient evidence for the "ruthless wrath of God" (Luther 1971, 138). Robert Jewett (37–41) suggests massacres, famine, or expulsion may have been in view here.

▌ THE TEXT IN CONTEMPORARY DISCUSSION

The experience of the Thessalonians highlights the transformative challenges of the gospel for every cultural, social, and political context. The close relationship between church and state in contemporary democratic societies and the normalization of consumerism have often left the demands of the gospel as little more than the requirement of slight moral and ethical adjustment, while the changes required by the gospel in the Thessalonian context involved a radical social and political metamorphosis.

1 Thessalonians 2:1-12: Paul's Defense of his Ministry

▌ THE TEXT IN ITS ANCIENT CONTEXT

This section begins with the first in a series of reminders—"you know" (*oidate*)—perhaps alerting the Thessalonians to what Paul and Silas had taught them during their visit to the city. Paul wants to remind the Thessalonians of what he considers they know to be true. First, he takes up the theme of suffering and reminds them that he and Silas suffered for the gospel prior to arriving in Thessalonica. In this there is a clear attempt to identify himself with the Thessalonians' own situation and to show empathy. So begins Paul's defense. Why Paul feels he has to defend himself is not entirely clear, but most likely it relates to the struggle and suffering that the Thessalonians are presently experiencing, and may relate to the grief to which Paul later refers regarding the deaths among the group (4:13). Paul's defense entails reference to their relation to God, an appeal to the evidence of their character, refuting rumors about their motives, and repeated references to the gospel. However, at the end of this section Paul returns to the theme inherent in his gospel, that of the subversion and arrogation of all other powers and authorities as he reminds the believers of the call on their lives.

First, Paul stresses that he and his companions consider themselves approved by God (2:4); their priority in speaking is to please God (2:4); and he maintains that God has been their witness (2:5). Second, Paul highlights the character that was evident while they were with the Thessalonians. They were gentle, "like a nurse" (2:7), which points also to the fatherly relationship they had with them (2:11). They sought to engage deeply with the Thessalonians, sharing "our own selves" (2:8), and moreover worked hard in order not to be a burden to them (2:9), insisting that they were never less than pure, upright, and blameless (2:10).

Third, he challenges accusations that appear to have arisen among some in the believing community. Paul's insistence that they did not come to Thessalonica with deceit or impure motives (2:3), nor with words of flattery (2:5), nor with any pretext for greed (2:5) makes clear that suspicions and concerns had arisen with the believing community as to the authenticity of Paul's mission among them.

Finally, he emphasizes his own sense of responsibility to present the gospel to them. He and Silas had shown great courage in declaring the gospel (2:2), believing that it had been entrusted to them (2:4). They shared (2:8) and proclaimed (2:9) the gospel, all the while urging, pleading, and encouraging the Thessalonians to live a life worthy of God (2:12).

▌The Text in the Interpretive Tradition

John Huss, who after being accused of heresy was persecuted and burned at the stake, emphasized Paul's stress on integrity in the announcement of the gospel (Huss, 106), while Calvin considered that Paul reminds his readers of his integrity in order to stress the divine origin of their call to faith (1960a, 342).

▌The Text in Contemporary Discussion

At the heart of contemporary discussion is the validity of the gospel and those who proclaim it for every culture and context. The gospel concerning the resurrection of Jesus Christ from the dead continues to challenge and subvert structures that lay claim to power and authority over those called into God's kingdom. The gospel belongs to God and is founded on God's action in Jesus Christ. Those who proclaim his gospel are called to do so in the same humble and self-effacing spirit that was evident in Jesus himself. Moreover, Paul's own emphasis on how he and his companions lived their own lives as key aspects of the proclamation of the gospel is a timely call to authenticity and integrity for all to whom the gospel has been entrusted.

1 Thessalonians 2:13—3:11: Persecution, Suffering, and Wrath

▌The Text in Its Ancient Context

The theme of suffering persecution continues through this section. Paul and Silas give thanks to God for the way in which the Thessalonians received the word of God. First Thessalonians 2:13-14 echoes 1:6 in its reference to imitation. In 1:6, the Thessalonians are said to be imitators of Paul, Silas, and the Lord. The reference to "the Lord" is noteworthy and seems to suggest that the apostles and the Thessalonians share with the Lord the experience of receiving the word of God in the midst of suffering. In 2:13-14, they are described as receivers of the word of God in the midst of persecution, but on this occasion they are imitators of their Judean brothers and sisters.

The element of imitation Paul highlights is that of suffering at the hands of one's compatriots. Just as the Judean believers suffered persecution at the hands of their compatriots, so too the Thessalonians are experiencing persecution by their own neighbors. Moreover, Paul appears to suggest that suffering incurred from compatriots is becoming typical for followers of the Lord Jesus, for not only are the Lord's disciples being persecuted, but the Lord Jesus himself and the prophets before him also suffered in this way. In 2:15-16, Paul highlights how the Jews (*hoi Ioudaioi*) had apparently and unfortunately adopted this malevolent habit over many centuries (see below).

Paul then appears to suggest that the Jews were presently experiencing "wrath," although he elaborates neither on the source nor on the nature of the wrath. However, as wrath in the ancient world was normally associated with the neglect of appropriate cultic activity, then we may tentatively consider that Paul views the Jews' present experience of wrath to have its source in God, whom they neglect in their rejection of the Lord Jesus, the prophets, and the Christian disciples.

Although Paul had made clear that there would be persecution (3:3-4), the depth of Paul and Silas's concern over the Thessalonians becomes apparent. There is the concern that the Thessalonians' fledgling faith and the newly formed *ekklēsia* may have dissipated under the pressure of the suffering brought about by the persecutions.

The longing "with great eagerness" (2:17) that Paul expresses to travel again to Thessalonica and to strengthen and encourage the church arises out of this concern for the persecuted Thessalonians. Moreover, the profound personal investment that Paul and Silas have made in the Thessalonians is unmistakable in their description of the new church as "our glory and joy" (2:20) and additionally in their apprehension lest their labor had been in vain. Thus Timothy is sent to visit them. It is not made clear at this point why Timothy was able to make the journey while Paul was not, other than the enigmatic reference to Satan (2:18). Although some argue that Paul intends Satan and "the tempter" to be understood as one and the same (Fee, 120), Paul himself does not make the identity of "the tempter" clear, nor does he make the supposed link with Satan explicit.

Timothy's task in journeying to Thessalonica is at least twofold. First, he is to strengthen and encourage them (3:2). Clearly some of them have been disturbed by the persecutions and may even have begun to doubt the veracity of Paul's message to them. The extent of the persecutions may have led some to question Paul's teaching that Jesus would rescue or defend them against wrath (1:10). Additionally, the impact of the persecutions on the young church and possibly even Paul's awareness of it is made clear in two ways: First, in his expression of fear that the tempter had tempted them and all of Paul and Silas's hard work in the city had come to nothing (3:5); and second, in his saying again that he longs to see them face-to-face and to restore or to mend what is lacking in their faith (3:10). Such a comment would be superfluous unless it was evident that the Thessalonians' immature faith had in some measure been fragmented in the ongoing persecutions.

Timothy's second task was to bring an account to Paul and Silas of the condition of the Thessalonian church (3:5). Timothy's report involved good news. The Thessalonians still have kind memories of the apostles and also long to see them again (3:6). This positive report brings great encouragement to Paul and Silas, who respond with hopefulness. Paul's affirmation, "For we now live" (3:8) is cautiously optimistic. As long as the Thessalonians "continue" to stand firm, then Paul and Silas can assess that their work is bearing fruit.

Paul concludes this section of his letter with a blessing for abundance in love and strength in their lives of holiness as they look to the appearance of the Lord Jesus.

▌ THE TEXT IN THE INTERPRETIVE TRADITION

First Thessalonians 2:14-16 is among those passages "repeatedly used to demonize the Jewish people" (Hagner, 70). Thomas Aquinas clearly considered the Jews responsible for the killing of the Lord Jesus, and argues that they were also antagonistic, prohibiting and impeding the preaching to the gentiles, and that all this was by "divine permission . . . that they fill up the measure of their sins" (1969, 19). Luther was convinced that "this work of wrath is proof that the Jews, surely rejected by God, are no longer his people, and neither is he any longer their God" (1971, 139). Calvin comments here that God "strips the Jews of all honor, so as to leave them nothing but hatred and ill repute" (Calvin 1960a, 348).

▌ THE TEXT IN CONTEMPORARY DISCUSSION

While Raymond E. Brown raises the possibility that the polemic against the Jews may be an interpolation, as it resembles pagan polemic and is "scarcely characteristic of Paul" (Brown, 463), Ernest Best is an example of those who argue that Paul held "an unacceptable anti-Semitic position" (Best, 122), and F. F. Bruce considered that just because Paul himself was a Jew did not rule out the possibility of anti-Jewishness here (Bruce, 51). However, Ben Witherington III considers that Paul has in view here a "temporal and temporary judgment which has already come in full" on those who opposed the gospel in Judea. At most, Paul may well have seen the wrath come upon the Jews as "poetic justice" in the light of the execution of Jesus and the persecution of Jesus' earliest followers (Witherington, 87). Hatred and racism have no place in Paul or the contemporary church, but rather we can see this passage as deep encouragement for those suffering persecution.

1 Thessalonians 4:1-12: Sanctification as a Mark of Community

▌ THE TEXT IN ITS ANCIENT CONTEXT

There is considerable evidence for the presence of voluntary associations in Thessalonica established on the basis of professional or religious affinities (Ascough, 316). Each of these associations would obligate its members to a common ethos, values, and rules. Both the regularity and the content of the gatherings would differ from group to group. It seems likely that the *ekklēsia* in Thessalonica would have been recognizable as a voluntary association with its own distinctive ethos. In this section, Paul follows his words of blessing (3:13), which seek to encourage holiness among the believers, by reminding them of the values and ethos that he and Silas had insisted should mark the *ekklēsia* (4:1-2). As far as Paul is concerned, the Thessalonians know very well what these values are. Paul then makes reference to two key elements of the distinctive ethos of the Thessalonian *ekklēsia*.

The initial concern is for their sanctification. Here Paul reminds the believers of three specific elements, each regarding sexual purity. The first aspect is that they should abstain from fornication. Second, that they should all learn to discipline their sexual desires, controlling themselves in a manner worthy of God and of course adopting the values they were instructed in and that should be espoused by the group of believers themselves. Moreover, they should not reflect the values of those outside the group or in other associations. Third, Paul reminds them that they should not use sexuality as a tool of power or exploitation.

It may be that the believers previously belonged to groups where there was a degree of sexual freedom or where, as a generalized aspect of Roman culture, power and status were expressed through sexual dominance. Indeed, Paul's reminder may have been prompted by rumors of inappropriate activity, but that was not to be a mark of the Thessalonian Christian *ekklēsia*. Paul insists that rejecting the instruction to pure and holy behavior was a rejection of God's authority, perhaps hinting that this would lead to exclusion from the Christian association.

Paul's second reminder listed above seems to concern the impression made on outsiders by the loving nature of the group of believers. Having reiterated the primacy of love as the key aspect of their ethos, Paul then encourages them to ensure that the life they share together be marked by honesty and freedom from dependence on those who do not share their ethos and values. Rather than individualizing the instructions in 4:11-12, we should rather see them as admonishments intended to be understood corporately. In particular, Paul speaks of living together "quietly" (4:11). This is probably a reference to living without selfish ambition and without the striving for honors that may have prevailed in other associations that were profoundly influenced by values of the empire-inclined city. The group is to look after their own affairs and not be dependent on outsiders for their regulation and direction.

▌The Text in the Interpretive Tradition

Tertullian cited 1 Thess. 4:3-5 in arguing "in defense of modesty, of sanctity, of chastity: they all aim their missiles against the interests of luxury, and lasciviousness, and lust" (1870a, 101). Whereas Jerome references 1 Thess. 4:7 in his treatise questioning marriage, "for God called us not for uncleanness, but in sanctification" (1892, 1.16), Augustine spoke more positively of marriage for purposes of procreation, not "in the passion of lust like the Gentiles who do not know God" (1955, 13). Scholarly debate here has often centered on the meaning of *skeuos* (here translated "body") in verse 4, while almost equal weight throughout history has been placed on the translation "wife" as on "body." Both alternatives are theoretically possible, but the use of *ktasthai* ("control, acquire") seems to point to "body" as the preferred option.

▌The Text in Contemporary Discussion

In an era when the power of sexuality seems to prevail in public and private, religious and political arenas, this passage from Paul is a timely reminder of the robust challenge to followers of the Lord

Jesus to live lives that are defined by the values of Christ and not to be enslaved by the dominant ethos of the day.

1 Thessalonians 4:13—5:11: Confidence in the Gospel

▌ THE TEXT IN ITS ANCIENT CONTEXT

Paul elucidates the meaning of salvation in answer to profound concerns that have arisen among the Thessalonian believers. He then urges them to encourage one another (4:18; 5:11).

The first stimulus to mutual encouragement (4:18) is accompanied by a restatement of the gospel, "Jesus died and rose again" (4:14). However, while Paul's previous reiteration of the gospel in 1:10 was set in the context of courage, confidence, and hopefulness, here there is ignorance, grief, and hopelessness (4:13). It is likely that "those who have died" were killed during the substantial and ongoing persecution suffered by the Thessalonians from their compatriots. The expectation of the Thessalonians was that they would be rescued or defended against such wrath (1:10), and thus it appears that these bereavements have led to a serious reassessment of the veracity of Paul's teaching and perhaps even the gospel itself. Therefore, Paul has to reiterate the gospel on which their hope is based: "we believe that Jesus died and rose again" (4:14). Moreover, Paul then gives his confident assessment of what this gospel hope means for both the living and dead in Thessalonica and elsewhere. Because Jesus has been raised from the dead, he is Lord over against the claims of the emperor. Thus Paul anticipates that Jesus will appear as a conquering king in a manner reminiscent of the *parousia* of imperial victors. As with the familiar imperial custom, those who accept Jesus and accede to his lordship will go out to greet him—whether presently dead or alive. It is in no way necessary to insist that this was intended to be an exact prediction of the events that will accompany the appearance of Jesus, but Paul appears to blend imperial practice with war imagery from the Qumran community (1QM 1:4-17) and prophetic oracles from Zechariah 9 to paint a picture of a dramatic and decisive salvific event.

The second stimulus to mutual encouragement (5:11) again draws on the key aspects of the gospel: the death of Jesus leading to resurrection, "who died for us, so that . . . we may live with him" (5:10). However, 5:9 also appears to mirror 1:10. It goes perhaps to the heart of the motive for the letter, that of reassurance within a present experience of severe suffering under persecution and a restatement of the trustworthiness of the gospel and the deep hope that it provides, "For God has destined us not for wrath but for obtaining salvation through our Lord Jesus Christ."

Although Paul says, "you do not need to have anything written to you," he nevertheless considers it necessary to restate his teaching about "the times and the seasons" (5:1). From the perspective of awareness of the chronology of the narrative of God's people and the anticipation of the fulfillment of God's purposes, Paul sets up a direct challenge to the assertion of Roman imperial ideology that the empire can guarantee "peace and security." Rather, just as the Israelites were protected in Egypt against the angel of death, so the Thessalonians will be safe against the "sudden destruction," while those outside the *ekklēsia* will discover that "there will be no escape" (5:3). Paul then juxtaposes the lifestyle of the believers over against that of those who continue to live under the values and ethos of the empire: the believers are children of light over against those of the darkness; of the day over against the night; awake rather than asleep; and sober instead of drunk (5:4-7). Moreover, Paul appears to highlight once again the church/imperial contrast by adopting two elements of the dress of the soldier, who was commissioned to keep a contrived "peace and security" under the imperial banner. The Christian will put on the breastplate of faith and love and the helmet as the hope of salvation. Paul's final assertion here highlights his deep confidence that the destiny of the believer, whether presently alive or dead, is salvation through the death and resurrection of the Lord Jesus Christ.

Throughout this letter Paul has had his eyes on the anticipated appearance of the Lord Jesus. One element of his concern for the Thessalonian believers is that holiness might be the distinctive feature of their group. Paul's encouragement that this holiness should be maintained and strengthened in practical ways as the central ethos of the group is encapsulated in his final blessing (5:23). Previously he has spoken of sexual purity and mutual love as distinguishing marks (4:1-12). Now Paul highlights respectful internal relationships, thankful prayer, and openness to the Spirit. First, Paul emphasizes the need for a deep respect and profound love for those who have spiritual responsibility. Second, they are all to ensure peaceful relationships within the group. This peace has to extend to warning those who might be idle or cause trouble, strengthening those who are discouraged, and helping those who may be weak in the face of the persecutions. They are to be patient with one another. Third, thankfulness is to define their life together. Moreover, their continuous expression of prayer is to be distinguished by joy.

Finally, Paul expresses his desire that the Thessalonians should be open to the activity of the Holy Spirit among them and particularly that they cherish and appreciate prophetic words. It may be that hasty contempt has been shown when prophecies that might have strengthened or admonished the community have been shared. Rather, they are to test everything to make sure that nothing that might be profitable to their growth and strength is lost. Paul assures them all that God is faithful and will prepare them well for the appearance of Jesus.

▮ THE TEXT IN THE INTERPRETIVE TRADITION

Discussions around eschatology have inevitably dominated consideration of this passage. The early church appeared to be particularly concerned with the individual context of eschatology, countering suggestions that it is only the soul that survives death. Tertullian, for example, tackled the thorny issue of the decomposition of the body in the interval before resurrection, arguing for "the integrity of the whole substance of man" at the resurrection (1922, 57). Origen stressed the transformation of the body at the resurrection into a state of incorruptibility (*Against Celsus* 5.19), while Augustine considered the possibility that those who are alive at the resurrection might pass through death into immortality as they were "carried aloft" to meet Christ in the air (1963, 20.20). Calvin speaks of the transformation into "an entirely new nature" while reminding us of the inevitable judgment that awaits (1960b, 2:17). In more recent times, the dispensationalist views popularized by J. N. Darby and published in the Scofield Bible have dominated in some quarters. The rapture, interpreted from 1 Thess. 4:17, whereby the faithful were snatched away from the earth upon the Parousia of Jesus, became a central tenet in this belief system. Each interpretive strategy ultimately concerns the meaning of salvation: will it take place in the present or the future; is it for the individual or for a corporate body; does it involve apocalyptic destruction of creation or its restoration?

▮THE TEXT IN CONTEMPORARY DISCUSSION

N. T. Wright is among those who have critiqued the escapist rapture theologies prevalent among the evangelical wing of the church, as popularized by Hal Lindsey in *The Late Great Planet Earth* and by Tim LaHaye and Jerry B. Jenkins's *Left Behind* series. Wright has argued that such theologies' acceptance of the subsequent cataclysmic destruction of the earth deny the need to put things right in this world as it will all be destroyed anyway (Wright, 119). Helmut Koester emphasizes the significance of the believing community in the context of the Parousia (Koester, 159) and concludes, "Paul envisions a role for the eschatological community that presents a utopian alternative to the prevailing eschatological ideology of Rome" (166). The transformation of all creation is predicated on the resurrection of Jesus Christ from the dead. This in turn supports a robust understanding of the resurrection of all believers as life in community and cooperation with God putting things right on the earth as a more balanced and ecologically friendly view.

2 THESSALONIANS

Edward Pillar

Introduction

Although the Pauline authorship of this second letter is sometimes questioned, more often scholarship accepts its authenticity (Malherbe, 349–74). Scholars who observe differences in language, style, and theology do not always take into account the changed circumstances of the Thessalonians. The believing community based in Thessalonica continues to suffer considerable persecution and perhaps even a significant increase in persecution as they seek to live out their calling to be followers of the Lord Jesus Christ. Paul speaks specifically and carefully into the Thessalonian context at this precise time to encourage them. Their imperially dominated context seems to be a more acute backdrop for Paul than was the case in the first letter. The focus of encouragement for the believers is set against an awareness of the clash of kingdoms—God's and Caesar's. In order to affirm the believers' stance in the face of their suffering, Paul adopts apocalyptic imagery to inspire and to strengthen.

2 Thessalonians 1:1-12: Steadfastness in Suffering

▌ THE TEXT IN ITS ANCIENT CONTEXT

The greetings at the head of this letter are almost identical to the first letter, but there is emphasis in the repetition of "God our Father and the Lord Jesus Christ." There are three key elements here that may arise from a subtle countercultural stance Paul is taking and supporting in the church in Thessalonica. First, true peace has its source in God the Father contra Caesar as *Pater Patriae* ("father of the country"). Second, the true Lord is Jesus the Risen One. And third, the prevailing narrative is not the imperial story (e.g., Virgil's *Aeneid*), but God's story that finds its fulfillment in the Christ.

In the light of the evidently significant persecution of the Christians in Thessalonica, there is the possibility that Paul draws inspiration from the account of the suffering of the Jews in the face of the persecution at the hand of Antiochus IV Epiphanes. Two centuries prior to Paul, the Jewish people had been ordered to forsake their laws and traditions and to defile the temple in Jerusalem. Although their suffering was interpreted as discipline, their resistance and steadfastness in the face of tyrannical oppression was celebrated. Moreover, there was a clear belief that the Lord would punish the unrighteous to the full measure of their sins (2 Macc. 6:14). If indeed Paul is alluding to this account, then it is most likely that he is simply seeking to encourage the Thessalonians to remain faithful against whoever persecutes them.

Paul advocates the vengeance of God's kingdom over Caesar's kingdom. While Paul assures the Thessalonians of prayers in the face of their struggle against persecution, it is not clear whether he intends to affirm their accentuated suffering or their steadfastness and faith as signs of the judgment of God and as creative preparation of the believers for the kingdom of God (1:5). Moreover, Paul sees God's response to the suffering of the Thessalonians as decisive and definitive, affirming God's response as "just" (1:6). This goes so far as eternal punishment (1:9), hinting that Paul advocates an "eye-for-an-eye" rejoinder from God. Paul affirms his confidence that the coming of the Lord Jesus will be the conclusive day of judgment (1:9-10).

▌ THE TEXT IN THE INTERPRETIVE TRADITION

The apocalyptic nature of this passage was important for John Chrysostom, who passionately argued for the justice of God against the wicked. However, while he stressed, "Let us not remember the kingdom so much as hell. For fear has more power than the promise" (Chrysostom, 477) and "If we always think of hell we shall not soon fall into it" (476), he also counseled that believers should not rejoice at the punishment of others (475).

▌ THE TEXT IN CONTEMPORARY DISCUSSION

Just as those described in 2 Maccabees anticipated that resurrection would bring both vindication of the righteous and God's judgment whereby there would be a putting things to right, there is also a challenge here to actualize God's righteousness in the face of suffering. The impact of the insidious, life-sapping values evident in modern economic and militaristic empires must be countered with a confidence in God's ultimate conquest. However, those suffering persecution and seeking vengeance against the perpetrators should not deny the love, mercy, and justice that lie at the heart of God's kingdom.

2 Thessalonians 2:1-17: Avoiding Deception— the Day of the Lord

▌ THE TEXT IN ITS ANCIENT CONTEXT

This passage is ultimately about deception. Paul is concerned that the believers should not be deceived by those who say the day of the Lord has already come. Paul also speaks of the deception that clouds the perception of the unbeliever. Paul's intuition seems to be that the previous narrative of Israel under persecution is the template for what the Thessalonians should expect in the future. Just as Antiochus defiled the temple in his day, so Paul may also now be drawing on the account of Gaius Caligula, who promoted himself as divine and insisted upon setting up a statue to himself within the Jerusalem temple in 41 CE. However, while we might seek to interpret "the lawless one" as Antiochus or Caligula, Paul hints that neither their coming (*parousia*) nor any previous or present tyrant (2 Thess. 2:9) is necessarily direct evidence that they are the "lawless one," and the anticipated direct confrontation between the "lawless one" and the Lord Jesus has yet to take place. The momentous "day of the Lord" has not yet dawned. Nonetheless, we can at least surmise that, set within the Thessalonian imperial context, Paul does intend his readers to infer that an imperial tyrant is the target for annihilation at the magnificent splendor of the Lord's coming. Moreover, Paul assures the Thessalonians that their persecutors are operating under a powerful delusion—possibly that they refuse to accept the revelation of God in Jesus Christ—that will lead to their ultimate punishment.

Paul makes plain his desire to encourage the Thessalonians: they are loved and have been chosen. God called them, through a gospel that countered imperial claims, to serve the new Lord. And Paul is confident that their present experience of being tested will prepare them for salvation. Again Paul seems to hint at those who had suffered under Antiochus as they had resolutely held to their ancestral traditions, and he encourages the believers in Thessalonica to hold decisively to the traditions they had been taught (2:15) while offering a blessing that is steeped in the confident hope of the resurrection. Moreover, Paul references the elusive figure of the one who "restrains," but as Gordon Fee makes clear, "we can describe what it is they know, but with almost no insight as to what it meant to them" (Fee, 285).

▌The Text in the Interpretive Tradition

Following Tertullian's assertion that the "lawless one" of 2 Thess. 2:3 was the antichrist (Tertullian, 1870b, 463), scholars throughout history have presented various individuals as the antichrist. Among others, Calvin (1960b, 4.2.11) considered the pope to be a candidate, as did Luther, who also included "the Turk" in his designation (Luther 1857, 193). However, Augustine was a little more circumspect, suggesting something of a communal nature to the antichrist, referring to "all who are wicked . . . the multitude of men who belong to him" (1963, 20.19). Perhaps the earliest example of the identification of a living figure with antichrist may be found in the late first-century-BCE *Ascension of Isaiah* 3:13—4:22, where some have interpreted the language as code suggesting that Nero was antichrist (Charles 1900, li–lxxiii). Augustine considered this and also the hypothesis that the "restrainer" is the Roman Empire but finally concludes, "for myself, I confess, I have no idea what is meant" (1963, 20.19).

▌The Text in Contemporary Discussion

For a long time people have pulled together different elements of apocalyptic texts, including 2 Thessalonians, fusing the figure of the antichrist and the lawless one, seeking to identify them with present individuals in order perhaps to give these texts a sense of literal veracity and in addition to further particular viewpoints. This can be done clearly in service to imperial agendas, as when Saddam Hussein invaded Kuwait or when Osama Bin Laden was held responsible for the attacks on the United States in 2001. Such identification justified, for some, the American invasion of Iraq and latterly of Afghanistan. It's possible *in this way* for readers to be "deceived"; today and here we have some analogy with what Paul wants to say. The important thing is to remain focused on the establishment of God's kingdom in the midst of suffering and all the while holding firmly to the values, ethos, and traditions of the Lord Jesus.

2 Thessalonians 3:1-18: Warning the Idle

■ THE TEXT IN ITS ANCIENT CONTEXT

Just as Paul appeals for prayer for himself and his companions, he confidently asserts the faithfulness of the Lord. There are wicked and evil people from whom Paul and his companions need defending, and there is evil itself (literally "the evil one") from which they all need protection. The values of the kingdom to which the believers have been called are evident as Paul prays that they might be directed to the love of God and to the steadfastness of Christ—no doubt a reminder of Christ's patient endurance under suffering (note the Thessalonians' patient waiting in 1 Thess. 1:9).

Again, Paul is concerned that the believers should hold to the traditions they have been taught (3:6). There is to be a clear delineation between those who hold to the traditions and those who idly let things slip. It is not clear whether the idlers are casually awaiting the appearance of the Lord or whether they have given up working in anticipation of what they see as their inevitable demise at the hands of their persecutors. Certainly this latter case would be seen as a betrayal of a living confidence in God and a capitulation to the demands of their persecutors. The strength of Paul's reprimand denotes the seriousness with which he takes the need for all to continue working hard in the confident assurance of the appearance of the Lord Jesus.

Paul demonstrates his pastoral commitment to the church in Thessalonica once again as he encourages the believers to treat the idlers not as enemies but as fellow believers in need of warning and admonishment. The extent of the persecution suffered by the believers that is evident throughout this letter might easily divide the group and cause it to slowly disintegrate. However, Paul's encouragement to continue to treat those who have become lax as brothers and sisters is a clear sign of his pastoral determination to see this fledgling group shine radiantly as evidence of the power of the gospel to transform lives and communities. Paul's final salutation—repeated in 1 Cor. 16:21 and Col. 4:18—here both emphasizes his authorship of the letter and his concern noted in 2 Thess. 2:2 about false doctrine circulating in his name.

■ THE TEXT IN THE INTERPRETIVE TRADITION

Augustine critiqued those monks who refused to work and who insisted that "they must be free for prayer, chanting psalms, for reading and for the word of God" (1952, 362) and cited 2 Thess. 3:10 against them. Aquinas quotes Augustine and affirms "that religious are bound to manual labour" (Thomas Aquinas 1973, 2.2, 187.3). Luther, however, suggests that this passage had been quickly corrupted by "lay people" and prefers, "let the minister of the Word be more intent on godliness than on the work of his hands," and as far as eating is concerned, "let God worry about that" (Luther 1973, 324). Calvin argued that those who excused themselves from the "common rule" (of work) should forfeit their sustenance as the reward of their work (1960a, 418).

▌The Text in Contemporary Discussion

Bruce Winter suggests that the idle busybody might be a reference to those who have not yet moved on from being beholden to the benefaction of a patron but instead are politicking and all the while trying to influence the believing community in the favor of the patron. Those who might be in a position to support such an idle busybody should not do so (Winter, 57–58). Best indicates that the community may be tempted to eject the idle ones in order to purify it and "relieve themselves of an intolerable burden" (Best, 333), although Néstor Míguez highlights the possibility that there may have been a class of idle rich, the traders and landowners, in Thessalonica who did not need to work with their hands, but relied on their servants (Míguez, 67). Furthermore, it is striking that while Vladimir Lenin adopted, "He who does not work neither shall he eat" as a principle of socialism (Lenin, 85), this slogan is also heard on the lips of those representing the American right-wing movement such as US Representative Michele Bachmann (Volsky).

Works Cited

Ascough, R. S. 2000. "The Thessalonian Christian Community as a Professional Voluntary Association." *JBL* 119, no. 2:311–28.

Augustine. 1952. *The Work of Monks.* In *Treatises on Various Subjects*, 323–94. Edited by R. J. Deferrari. Translated by Mary Sarah Muldowney. FC 16. Washington, DC: Catholic University of America Press.

———. 1955. *The Good of Marriage.* In *Treatises on Marriage and Other Subjects*, 9–51. Translated by Charles D. Wilcox et al. FC 27. New York: Father of the Church.

———. 1963. *City of God.* Translated by J. W. C. Wand. London: Oxford University Press.

Best, Ernest. 1972. *A Commentary on the First and Second Epistles to the Thessalonians.* BNTC. London: Black.

Brown, Raymond E. 1997. *Introduction to the New Testament.* New York: Doubleday.

Bruce, F. F. 1982. *1 and 2 Thessalonians.* WBC 45. Waco, TX: Word.

Calvin, John. 1960a. *The Epistles of Paul to the Romans and to the Thessalonians.* Edited by D. W. Torrance and T. F. Torrance. Translated by R. Mackenzie. Edinburgh: Oliver and Boyd.

———. 1960b. *Institutes of the Christian Religion.* Edited by John T. McNeil. Translated by Ford Lewis Battles. Louisville: Westminster John Knox.

Charles, R. H., ed. 1900. *The Ascension of Isaiah.* London: Black.

Chrysostom, John. 1879. *Homilies on Thessalonians.* In *The Homilies of St. John Chrysostom, Archbishop of Constantinople: On the Epistles of St. Paul the Apostle to the Philippians, Colossians, and Thessalonians.* Oxford: James Parker.

Fee, Gordon D. 2009. *The First and Second Letters to the Thessalonians.* NICNT. Grand Rapids: Eerdmans.

Friedrich, G. 1965. "Ein Tauflied Hellenistischer Judenchristen, 1 Thess. 1:9f." *TZ* 21, 502-16.

Hagner, Donald A. 2000. "Anti-Semitism and the New Testament." In *Eerdmans Dictionary of the Bible.* Edited by D. N. Freedman, A. C. Myers, and A. B. Beck. Grand Rapids: Eerdmans.

Hooker, Morna D. 1996. "1 Thessalonians 1:9-10: A Nutshell—But What Kind of Nut?" In *Frühes Christentum*. Vol. 3, *Geschichte–Tradition–Reflexion: Festschrift für Martin Hengel zum 70*, edited by Hubert Cancik, Hermann Lichtenberger, and Peter Schäfer, 435–48. Tübingen: Mohr Siebeck.

Huss, John. 1953. *On Simony*. In *Advocates of Reform*, edited by M. Spinka, 196-278. London: SCM.

Jerome. 1892. *Against Jovinianus*. In *NPNF²* 6:346–86.

Jewett, Robert. 1986. *The Thessalonian Correspondence: Pauline Rhetoric and Millenarian Piety*. Philadelphia: Fortress Press.

Josephus. 1927–1928. *Jewish War*. Translated by H. St. J. Thackeray. 3 vols. LCL. Cambridge, MA: Harvard University Press.

Koester, Helmut. 1997. "Imperial Ideology and Paul's Eschatology." in *Paul and Empire*, edited by Richard A. Horsley, 158–66. Harrisburg, PA: Trinity Press International.

Lenin, Vladimir. 1992. *The State and Revolution*. London: Penguin.

Luther, Martin. 1857. "Of Antichrist." In *The Table Talk of Martin Luther*, 193–225. Translated and edited by W. Hazlitt. London: Bohn.

———. 1955. *The Catholic Epistles*. *LW* 30. H. T. Lehmann, ed. St. Louis: Concordia.

———. 1971. *The Christian in Society*. *LW* 47. F. Sherman and H. T. Lehmann, eds. Philadelphia: Fortress Press.

———. 1973. *Select Pauline Epistles*. *LW* 28. St. Louis: Concordia.

Malherbe, Abraham J. 2000. *The Letters to the Thessalonians*. AB 32B. New York: Doubleday.

Míguez, Néstor O. 2012. *The Practice of Hope: Ideology and Intention in 1 Thessalonians*. Paul in Critical Contexts. Minneapolis: Fortress Press.

Origen. 1965. *Contra Celsum*. Translated by Henry Chadwick. Cambridge: Cambridge University Press.

Strecker, Georg. 2000. *Theology of the New Testament*. Berlin: de Gruyter.

———. 1870a. *On Modesty*. In *ANF* 4:56–122.

———. 1870b. "On the Second Epistle to the Thessalonians." In *Against Marcion*. In *ANF* 3:269–476.

Tertullian. 1922. *Concerning the Resurrection of the Flesh*. Translated by A. Souter. London: SPCK.

Thomas Aquinas. 1969. *Commentary on Saint Paul's First Letter to the Thessalonians and the Letter to the Philippians*. Translated by F. R. Larcher and M. Duffy. Albany, NY: Magi.

———. 1973. *Summa Theologiae*. Vol. 47. Translated by J. Aumann. London: Blackfriars.

Volsky, Igor. 2011. "Michele Bachmann: 'If Anyone Will Not Work, Neither Should He Eat.'" *Thinkprogress.org*. November 7. http://thinkprogress.org/lgbt/2011/11/07/362845/michele-bachmann-if-anyone-will-not-work-neither-should-he-eat/

Winter, Bruce W. 1994. *Seek the Welfare of the City: Christians as Benefactors and Citizens*. Carlisle: Paternoster.

Witherington, Ben, III. 2006. *1 and 2 Thessalonians: A Socio-Rhetorical Commentary*. Grand Rapids: Eerdmans.

Wright, N. T. 2008. *Surprised by Hope*. San Francisco: HarperOne.

1 TIMOTHY

Deborah Krause

Introduction to the Pastoral Epistles

The Pastoral Epistles (PE) comprise a corpus of pseudepigraphical teachings attributed to the apostle Paul and ostensibly written to his closest followers, Timothy and Titus. These books were likely compiled in the early second century CE. Written several generations after the death of the historical Paul, the PE represent a part of the early church's interpretation of Paul. As an evangelist to the gentiles and leader of churches, the historical Paul saw his letters as a means to an end. As such, he likely did not think of himself predominantly as a "letter writer." By the second century, however, his letters (copied and redistributed) had become widely known, and his ministry (heroically recounted in Luke's Acts of the Apostles) had become legendary. First and Second Timothy and Titus take their place in relation to this period of remembering and reinterpreting Paul. As such, they pose as the Pauline voice of authority about matters related to church leadership (hence the name "Pastoral Epistles"), and they seek to define the Pauline legacy for the church in a particular direction. Importantly, they were but one venture in the struggle to define that legacy. Other writings, such as the canonical Acts of the Apostles and the noncanonical Acts of Paul, engaged in the interpretation of the Pauline tradition in remarkably different directions. Such divergent interpretations mark a moment in the contentious period of early Christian origins in which the Pauline legacy was deeply contested (e.g., 2 Pet. 3:16). In particular, the PE represent the effort to codify and manage the written teachings of Paul into a set of resources for guiding and directing not simply local communities but also the universal church.

Most historical scholars of early Christian literature argue that the PE were composed as a corpus. They do not appear in the earliest artifacts of the process of canonization (e.g., Marcion's list of early Christian writings, c. 144 CE, or the earliest extant manuscript of Paul's letters, P[46]), and thereby likely represent a singular performance of Paul's voice and insight as an intervention into early Christian disputes about the interpretation of Paul. As a corpus their likely original order would have concluded with 2 Timothy, the final writing offering a poignant glimpse of Paul as he provides his last testament to his entrusted colleague and friend. In this historical perspective, the corpus may have been composed to appear as a trove of recently (and miraculously) discovered Pauline insight and the key to the overall interpretation of Paul's occasional letters (i.e., 1 Thessalonians, 1–2 Corinthians, Philippians, Philemon, Galatians, and Romans).

One of the important elements of reading the PE in light of their likely historical origins is the awareness that they are not really letters. Their letter form is a part of their construction of a Pauline voice and authority. As such, the PE present perspectives on church order and governance in the guise of personal letters between Paul and his closest companions. Ironically, in attempting to direct Paul's wisdom more broadly for a diversifying and growing movement, the PE mimic a personal and privileged space of communication. Such layers of rhetoric make the interpretation of these writings a fascinating study in navigating the construction of authority in the interpretation of Paul and the early church.

While the historical-critical perspective on the PE described in this introduction has revolutionized their interpretation in the last century, it is important to remember that for the vast majority of the church's history, the authorship of the letters was not questioned. For that reason, for most of the church's history, 1 and 2 Timothy and Titus have not been distinguished as a particular interpretation of the Pauline tradition from the late or early second century. Rather, the writings have been seen as authentic communication between Paul and his closest companions in ministry—a continuation of Paul's correspondence. As such, these writings have been remarkably successful in achieving their original intent—to influence and direct the Pauline tradition as it has informed the life and ministry of the church. The form of this current commentary, with its emphasis on ancient, interpretive, and contemporary aspects of the text, offers an excellent opportunity to engage in an exploration of the PE in ways that honor their various contexts and perspectives of interpretation.

Introduction to 1 Timothy

The intimate tone struck by 1 Timothy prepares its readers/hearers for unfettered, trustworthy, and "genuine" access to Paul's thinking about the matters he is about to discuss with one whom the tradition (and Paul's historical letters) present as one of his most trusted coworkers in the ministry. Imagine how the gathered leadership would have responded upon the first reading of these writings! From a context several generations removed from Paul's ministry and in the midst of controversies about his teaching and the church, the reading of his communication to his friend Timothy would come across as a rare opportunity to overhear his voice and glean his perspective. No doubt, the gathered faithful were on the edge of their seats.

1 Timothy 1:1-2: Opening Salutation

■ THE TEXT IN ITS ANCIENT CONTEXT

The naming of writer and sender is a stock element of the greeting of the Greco-Roman letter. Such greetings are also characterized by a blessing. The naming of Paul as sender and Timothy as his "genuine child in the faith" frames the relationship of the sender and recipient as intimate.

■ THE TEXT IN THE INTERPRETIVE TRADITION

Paul's association with Timothy is certainly referenced in his likely historical writings where he is named as a cowriter (2 Cor. 1:1; Phil. 1:1; 1 Thess. 1:1; Philem. 1:1), an emissary (1 Cor. 4:17; 16:10; 1 Thess. 3:2), and a coprisoner (Phil. 2:19), but the connection became legendary within the Pauline interpretive tradition. For Luke, Timothy is narrated in the Acts of the Apostles as the child of a pious Jewish mother and a Greek (likely pagan) father (Acts 16:1). As such, his genealogy literally embodies the Pauline mission of the reconciliation of Jew and Greek. Additionally, Luke recounts that Paul circumcised Timothy prior to embarking on a missionary journey throughout Greece (Acts 16:3), an act that hardly seems to square with Paul's own boast regarding Titus's resistance to circumcision in Jerusalem (Gal. 2:3). Finally, the likely pseudonymous Pauline superscription at the conclusion of Hebrews references Timothy and his recent release from prison (Heb. 13:23).

■ THE TEXT IN CONTEMPORARY DISCUSSION

Much contemporary ecclesial interpretation of Timothy and Titus in relation to Paul focuses on the mentor-mentee relationship in developing leaders in ministry. The chapel of Concordia Seminary in St. Louis, Missouri, the flagship school for the ordained leadership of the Lutheran Church–Missouri Synod, is named for Timothy and Titus. Practical theologians refer to the PE as an example of Paul's careful stewardship of upcoming leaders for the church (e.g., Hoehl). Other scholars now question the authenticity of the canonical, legendary portrayal of Paul's relationship with Timothy and Titus. Some have advanced the hypothesis that Timothy and Titus (as referenced in Paul's historical letters) are the same person, an example of ancient heteronymity, the practice of ascribing multiple names to the same person (e.g., Fellows). Whatever the historical relationship of Timothy and Titus to Paul (or to one another), it is clear that the enduring interpretive tradition understands that they are linked in the act of imparting and receiving sound teaching and wisdom. Certainly the PE bear an important place in characterizing this relationship.

1 Timothy 1:3-11: Call to Proper Instruction

■ THE TEXT IN ITS ANCIENT CONTEXT

After its terse greeting, the writing takes up the context of interreligious conflict that may be the catalyst for the PE. The writer casts Paul in the role of instructing Timothy to remain in Ephesus in order to teach "certain people" not to teach "false teachings." The immediate preoccupation with the potential threat of "false teaching" and the caricature of it as "empty words" offers potential insight into the overall purpose of the PE, namely to establish an authoritative interpretation of Paul's teachings and set clear lines between correct and false instruction in the faith.

Within the ethos of the PE writer, proper instruction begins with proper interpretation of sacred tradition. Likewise, "false teachings" begin with misguided interpretation. For the PE writer as he performs Paul, this sacred tradition would be Israel's scriptural tradition. Far from being contrary to the law, the writer is chiding interpreters who miss the point of the law and "promote useless speculations." The particular malpractice in view in these verses arises out of what the writer characterizes as an overemphasis on "myths" and "endless genealogies."

▮ THE TEXT IN THE INTERPRETIVE TRADITION

While the historical context of this particular characterization has been difficult for historical scholars to label, it is noteworthy that other Greco-Roman rhetoricians (such as Plutarch and Philo) also warn against overly esoteric speculation on sacred or traditional origins (Wall, 63). While there is no way to know precisely what interpretations are in view in 1 Timothy, it is noteworthy that the canonical genealogical traditions in Matthew (1:1-17) and Luke (3:23-38) represent divergent interpretations of Israel's scriptural tradition for the sacred and salvation-historical origins of Jesus. Could it be that this kind of diversity was even further multiplied within the PE writer's context, and that such divergences and arguments about them bred conflict and division within the church?

▮ THE TEXT IN CONTEMPORARY DISCUSSION

Contemporary liberation theologian, poet, and activist Elsa Tamez has written a commentary on 1 Timothy in which she traces lines of connection between struggles for power at work between the PE writer and his opponents and the challenges of Roman Catholic women in the barrios of Costa Rica. Tamez argues that those who hold ecclesial, economic, and social power within the church often use rhetoric to disparage and demean those who threaten their power and authority. First Timothy offers her a ground from which to explore these contested relationships in the church and to validate the experience of women in her community who struggle every day to survive and to claim their God-given dignity in the midst of global socioeconomic and political oppression and ecclesial domination.

1 Timothy 1:12-20: Christ's Mercy—An Example from Paul's Biography

▮ THE TEXT IN ITS ANCIENT CONTEXT

The PE writer offers thanks to Jesus Christ for the merciful experience of his calling to Christ's service. This particular element of Paul's biography—whether it be characterized as a call to mission or a "conversion"—offers a powerful insight into the development of the PE writer's Christology.

In Paul's seven likely authentic letters (i.e., Romans, 1 and 2 Corinthians, Galatians, Philippians, 1 Thessalonians, Philemon), he often refers to his "revelation" (*apokalypsis*) as an event in which God is the agent, Jesus Christ is the subject ("God was pleased to reveal his Son in me"), and the content is a mission to proclaim the gospel of Jesus Christ among the gentiles (e.g., Gal. 1:15-16). The fact that Paul had persecuted the churches prior to this event is mentioned (Gal. 1:13), but it is not a part of the content or experience of his revelation. In the Acts of the Apostles, likely written at least forty years after Paul's own letters, Luke narrates this event (Acts 9:4) as one in which Jesus himself, after a flash of heavenly light, asks, "Saul, Saul, why do you persecute me?" The PE writer continues the characterization of the event in this vein. The writer describes Jesus, not God, as the source of the experience, and the primary content of the phenomenon is the dramatic reversal of Paul's work from persecuting the churches to proclaiming the gospel within them. No doubt Luke and the PE writer had much to do with the legendary characterization of Paul's "Damascus road" experience as a "conversion" more than, in his own words, a theological "revelation." In the interpretive trajectory of Luke and the PE writer, Paul's primary connection is with Jesus (in contrast to God), and the content of the experience is not so much a theological vision of how Paul's mission to the gentiles relates to God's saving purpose for the world, but rather how he has been mercifully saved from his "unbelief" (1:13). Furthermore, Paul is portrayed not so much as a collaborator with God in the mission to the gentiles, as an example of Christ's mercy and redemption for those who are to believe in him (1:16). He has become the chief sinner whose own salvation is the proof that "Christ came into the world to save sinners" (1:15).

▌THE TEXT IN THE INTERPRETIVE TRADITION

The characterization of Paul as the first or chief among sinners has captured the imagination of the Christian interpretive tradition. One prominent interpreter of this motif, Augustine, noted that Paul's conversion was powerful testimony to Christ's saving power precisely because the devil held him so tightly. As Augustine notes, "the enemy is more overcome by wringing a man from him of whom he had more hold" (St. Augustine's Confessions I, 8.4, The Loeb Classical Library, 423). No doubt the personal appeal of the Pauline example inspired Augustine in his own journey toward conversion, and offered him an archetype for understanding and teaching the process of conversion in general.

▌THE TEXT IN CONTEMPORARY DISCUSSION

The topic of whether the historical Paul "converted" to a new faith tradition (i.e., "Christianity") or responded to a theological calling consistent with his own Jewish belief and practice is a prominent subject of debate within the contemporary critical scholarly engagement of the historical Paul in the "Newer Approaches to Paul." At stake in this debate is the question of whether Paul understood himself to remain a Jew in his experience of his revelation or changed his religious identity in response to it. Pamela Eisenbaum summarizes the historical research that informs this debate, and well outlines her sense of how the characterization of Paul's "conversion" from his Jewish faith has had tremendously negative ethical and moral consequences in terms of anti-Judaism within

Christian theology. No matter where one stands in this debate in Pauline scholarship, one must acknowledge the formative role of the PE in representing Paul as a converted sinner who identifies his life prior to his religious experience as "unbelief."

1 Timothy 2:1-15: The Call to a Quiet Life

▌ THE TEXT IN ITS ANCIENT CONTEXT

The PE are well known for their promotion of a proto-orthodoxy. Throughout the corpus, the writer calls for adherence to "sound doctrine" and for guarding the "deposit of faith." The opening instructions of 1 Timothy identify the danger of "false teachings" (1 Tim. 1:3) in the church. Overall, however, the PE corpus seems preoccupied more with orderly behavior (i.e., orthopraxy) than belief. In this vein, 1 Tim. 2:1-15 takes up the call to challenge the church leadership to promote a "peaceful and quiet" life.

The opening verses of this section relate to offering prayers, intercessions, and thanks on behalf of all people, kings and all who are in authority (2:1-2). In relationship to those in political authority, the goal of a "peaceful and quiet life" is characterized by acknowledging the hierarchies of power that frame the social experience of the churches. In this sense, the opening verses of this section offer an implicit call for the readers and hearers of the PE to know their place within the sociopolitical order, and as leaders of the churches, to do what is necessary to ensure ongoing peace and harmony between those in governing authority and the church. As the section goes on to address the behavior of men and women in worship (2:8-15), the writer continues with the theme of "proper" behavior within the social hierarchy for the good of the community. Throughout the section, images of speaking and language continue to tie back to the initial goal of a peaceful and quiet life.

While the writer addresses both the behavior of men and women in worship, the majority of the discussion is devoted to women. This imbalance is telling regarding the PE writer's energy for instruction and reproof. While the behavior of men can be generally addressed, women, it seems, require more specific and repeated calls to "learn in silence" (v. 11), "not to teach or have authority over men" (v. 12), and "to keep silent" (v. 12). Some scholars argue that this focus on the prevention of women's speech likely signals a context in which women were already actively at work teaching and leading in the church. It is, in other words, prescriptive rather than descriptive rhetoric (e.g., Schüssler Fiorenza, 310).

The writer summarizes his prohibition of women's speech and leadership within the community with an argument based on a midrashic interpretation of Genesis 2–3. As the PE writer applies the story of Adam and Eve to his prohibition of women's teaching and leadership, he offers Eve as the prototypical woman who is easily deceived (ostensibly, by the serpent). One explanation for this is that the author focuses on deception in the Genesis text in order to speak to the deceptive teachings at work in the community, where women are particularly susceptible to such teachings (2 Tim. 3:6-7; see Bassler, 60). This interpretation helpfully contextualizes the prohibitions and mitigates concerns about how the author's appeal to "origins" seems to imply that all women are inherently untrustworthy.

▌The Text in the Interpretive Tradition

Early church interpreters of 1 Tim. 2:15-16 discerned a christological claim in this text's connection between childbearing and salvation. Given that the term "childbearing" is preceded in 1 Tim. 2:15 by the definite article ("the"), interpreters such as Justin Martyr and Ignatius of Antioch argued that the singular act of Mary's childbearing of Jesus Christ reversed the curse of Eve's original transgression (Witherington, 240). This messianic interpretation has not endured in the church. By and large, the technical matter of the presence of the definite article has been taken to mean childbearing in general as interpreters have promoted an understanding of the text as an ontological statement on the secondary and untrustworthy nature of women, and their consignment to positions within the church and household in which they are supervised and controlled.

▌The Text in Contemporary Discussion

The prohibition in this text of women's teaching and leadership has served as a key proof text in the church's structural exclusion of women from leadership in general and from offices that include ordination in particular. While the call to silence and the relegation of women to positions of submission within the community may sound antiquated, it is remarkable to see how broadly this text is cited as an authority in current manuals of church administration and polity, for example in the teaching of the Roman Catholic Church, the Lutheran Church–Missouri Synod, and the Southern Baptist Convention (Krause, 50–52).

1 Timothy 3:1-16: Qualities for Church Leadership

▌The Text in Its Ancient Context

The list of qualities for bishops (*episkopoi*) and deacons (*diakonoi*) found in 1 Tim. 3:1-13 provide the corpus of 1 and 2 Timothy and Titus with the traditional characterization of "pastoral" letters. Namely, they are concerned with matters of church leadership and administration. From a historical-critical perspective, this emphasis locates the writings within the realm of an administrative discourse on leadership and how it is ordered properly within the church. In this sense, these writings stand apart from the rest of the Pauline canon as they are framed as an intramural discussion, by leaders and for leaders, rather than the address of a leader to a given community or set of communities. The two lists, while separate (first bishops, then deacons), are coordinated by the rhetorical use of "likewise" in 1 Tim. 3:8. While each office requires different characteristics, they are like one another in anticipating the most exemplary elements of Greco-Roman moral virtue—the highest quality of character imaginable.

In this sense, the lists seem to be framed ideally and perhaps in contrast to false teachers within the midst of the community. Indeed, several of the qualities of bishops and deacons are framed negatively (e.g., "not a drunkard, not violent, not quarrelsome, no lover of money," v. 3; or "not double-tongued, not addicted to much wine, not greedy," v. 8). This element may support the understanding that this portion of the writing is not simply a manual on leadership but also a way of framing the conflict besetting the church regarding leadership. The list makes plain that not all leaders are created equally, and the current crisis over competing leaders ("false teachers") within the church provides the opportunity to set the standards and expectations of the church's leadership high while simultaneously maligning its opponents.

▌ THE TEXT IN THE INTERPRETIVE TRADITION

The intramural leadership emphasis of the PE was attractive to generations of church leaders into the third and fourth century. Early church fathers offered commentary and sermonic amplification of the corpus (e.g., Clement, Polycarp, Theodore of Mopsuestia, and Chrysostom: Witherington, 168). While the text of the PE shies away from offering a "job description" for bishops and deacons and concentrates instead on characteristic virtues of the positions, there is a sense in which the PE represent a developmental step in defining offices of leadership (bishop, elder, deacon) rather than mere functions of different leaders in the community (oversight, teaching, and service). The emphasis on virtues rather than duties for leaders no doubt proved valuable to generations of church leaders who followed in different contexts and circumstances.

▌ THE TEXT IN CONTEMPORARY DISCUSSION

In the midst of the list of qualities for deacons, there is an enigmatic passage that is of particular interest to contemporary interpreters within settings where the leadership and ordination of women is debated. First Timothy 3:11 marks an abrupt change in the flow of the PE writer's list of expectations for deacons. Until this point, the list does not identify whether men or women are in view. Suddenly, at verse 11 the writer states that "women" (Greek *gynai*, translated "wives" in a few translations such as the NIV) are "likewise" expected to behave virtuously. When this verse is understood to refer to women (rather than wives) it stands as a testimony to the presence of women within the designated (and likely financially compensated) offices of the early church. While there is a great deal of evidence for the leadership of women in the seven likely authentic letters of Paul (e.g., Rom. 16:1), and in other traditions of the early Jesus movement (e.g., Mark 15:41), the fact that these late first- or early second-century writings of the church reference women's leadership challenges all forms of the church today to acknowledge that women's leadership in the church is not a recent mark of human progress but an original expression of the church's vision for community.

1 Timothy 4:1-16: Sound Teaching

▌ THE TEXT IN ITS ANCIENT CONTEXT

This portion of the writing draws on the mentor-mentee relationship between Paul and Timothy. The writer evokes the wisdom and experience of Paul as he encourages Timothy to "let no one despise your youth" (v. 12). The pseudepigraphical and pseudepistolary framework (mimicking the form of a letter) of the writing's composition offers the chance to see this relationship as paradigmatic of a problem within the late first- and early second-century church. The historical Paul would likely not have been in much of a position to encourage his mentees in the command of authority and respect, given his own particular struggles in attaining these things for himself (e.g., 2 Corinthians 10–12). However, by the early second century, Paul's leadership had been lauded in both the reinterpretation and use of his teaching and in legendary traditions found in the Acts of the Apostles and the *Acts of Paul*. In this sense, the church leaders of the PE corpus no doubt faced the anxiety of establishing the authority of a new generation of leaders and teachers of the tradition. The call to claim one's authority within the rising generation, and to lead with conviction and purpose, resonates with the structural institutional developments at work within the second-century church. One striking element of the genius and innovation of the PE corpus is that it positions this call in the person and voice of the legendary leader himself.

THE TEXT IN THE INTERPRETIVE TRADITION

One poignant element of the mentor-mentee relationship drawn in this unit is the challenge to carry on the work of ministry and the life of the church in the midst of Paul's absence. In verse 13, the writer states: "Till I come, attend to the public reading of scripture, to preaching, and to teaching." These are practices of ministry as they relate to corporate worship. Such practices have parallels within the worship practices of early Judaism. Early church fathers such as Justin demonstrate that this list of activities continued to describe much of the shape of corporate Christian worship into the second and third centuries, and liturgies of the Western and Eastern traditions and the Reformation show that such practices are prominent elements of corporate worship even to the present day.

THE TEXT IN CONTEMPORARY DISCUSSION

In outlining the contours of "sound teaching," the text also characterizes the false teachers' practices. The identification of the "liars" with those who "forbid marriage and abstain from certain foods" (v. 3.) is somewhat surprising in light of common practices of a celibate clergy and fasting within parts of the contemporary church. Importantly, Paul's likely authentic letters reflect positively on the gift of celibacy within the life of the church (e.g., 1 Cor. 7:1, 8). In light of these discrepancies with both the historical Paul and the contemporary church, it is clear to see that the PE corpus defines orthopraxy and orthodoxy at times more narrowly than can be seen within either more ancient or contemporary expressions of the church.

1 Timothy 5:1—6:3: Clarifying Roles and Responsibilities

THE TEXT IN ITS ANCIENT CONTEXT

In this section, the writer addresses roles within the church and homes in on widows, elders, and slaves. It is not clear why these three groups are treated together and why elders, for instance, are not discussed earlier in chapter 3 along with the qualifications for bishops and deacons. One clue to the connection between widows, elders, and slaves in this unit is the common use of the term "honor" (meaning financial payment) in each case. Widows, on the one hand, are discussed in terms of limiting their draw on the financial resources of the community. Elders, on the other hand, are recommended for a significant raise (a double portion). Slaves are reminded that their service to their masters benefits beloved believers. In sum, compensation for widows is curtailed, while that for elders is raised. Slaves, whose labor is uncompensated, are called to regard their masters as "worthy of all honor." Far from an equitable distribution of resources among all groups (such as is envisioned by Luke in Acts 2:44-45 and Acts 4:32-35), this writer calls for a redistribution of the financial resources of the community toward a particular constituency (elders), and away from others (widows and slaves).

The writer's process of identifying "authentic" or "real" widows is instructive. Where the practice of the church had become that of providing for all women whose husbands had died, the letter writer is redirecting the responsibility for care back to private family units and away from the church (1 Tim. 5:16). In this process, the writer calls for the community to honor (compensate financially) those widows who are "real," that is, who meet criteria that would ensure that there was no private familial community of support, as well as those widows who would be considered beyond the age of remarriage. Given the limits the writer sets (over the age of sixty, the wife of only one husband, who has raised children, but has none that can financially support her), one might wonder if any widow in the ancient world would be considered "real," or if the only "real" widow in the eyes of the writer might be a dead widow! Certainly, the position of widow as the writer has constructed it is populated by women who would have very little social power (few familial relationships and no access to financial resources other than the support received from the church). In this sense, the writer's agenda may be seen as surpassing simply trimming the budget and more along the lines of consolidating and managing relations of power within the church. Such a perspective on the social dynamics of this text helps to clarify that, far from a natural evolution in Paul's thought, the claims of 1 Timothy represent a marked reorientation of power in the church, and a striking reinterpretation of Paul's legacy.

▌ THE TEXT IN THE INTERPRETIVE TRADITION

Most of the history of the church's interpretation of this passage has read these instructions regarding widows, elders, and slaves as the teaching of the apostle Paul. In this perspective, interpreters have argued that Paul, by the time of this writing, has seen the unsustainable nature of the vision of the church he upheld in places such as 1 Thess. 5:14; Gal. 3:28; and 1 Cor. 11:17-22. Moreover, he has seen the error of his commitment to "preach the gospel free of charge," and not to collect on his right as an apostle to compensation (1 Cor. 9:18). On this reading, in 1 Timothy, Paul advocates for the professional compensation of elders (1 Tim. 5:17-18) even while he argues for the church's financial support of widows to be curtailed. What such theories miss is that far from a linear development of Paul's thought and practice, the PE writer's instructions involve a complete reorientation of Paul's priorities. Scholarship that takes seriously the pseudepigraphic nature of the writing offers an understanding of how this writing has appropriated Paul's persona and authority to structure the church in remarkably alternative ways to his vision of community found in the likely authentic letters of the Pauline corpus. These ways centralize power and financial resources in the newly constructed offices of bishops, elders, and deacons, and limit the authority of other classes within the church that have grown in significance in the community (such as widows and slaves).

▌The Text in Contemporary Discussion

In many contemporary contexts of the church, the rhetoric of 1 Tim. 5:1—6:3 appears to be complicit with histories of the subjugation of women and slaves and the marginalization of certain classes from professional ministry. In particular, the writer's attack on the character of women in his community as "idlers, gossips, and busybodies" (5:13) and his paternalistic chide for slaves not to disrespect their masters (6:2) place him on the wrong side of movements for human liberation and struggles for justice within the church and world. Once again, an appreciation of the pseudepigraphical nature of this writing helps to locate this rhetoric not in the natural evolution of Paul's thought and the growth of the church but rather in late first- and early second-century struggles to determine the social construction of the church in the world. The rhetoric of the PE writer offers insight into how those struggles transpired. Women increased in stature and presence within the church, and other elements of the church resisted. The text's misogyny and paternalism do not need to be seen as prescriptive of contemporary church polity but as descriptive of the kinds of struggles that arose in the face of the social mobility of the early church. In these descriptions, we certainly hear the perspective of the letter writer; however, we also learn that women and slaves were enough of a concern in their emerging roles to merit the writer's concern and calls for their submission. Far from needing to honor all the writer's expectations, contemporary readers can appreciate that the writing contains witnesses to those women and slaves who dared to network socially and resist the confines of traditional households in order to pursue their vocations and engage in ministry.

1 Timothy 6:4-19: False Teaching and the Call to Guard the Good Confession

▌The Text in Its Ancient Context

One of the remarkable challenges to Paul's apostolic identity and leadership was that he did not know the historical Jesus. In his correspondence with churches, Paul references this embarrassing datum as being "untimely born" (1 Cor. 15:8). While he affirms his own religious authority as immediate and from God, as opposed to human teaching (Gal. 1:12), it is clear that his opponents capitalized on this fact and insinuated that his apostolic identity was not legitimate (2 Corinthians 11–12). In this light, it is powerful to witness how the PE writer develops the Pauline tradition to clarify and originally authorize the church's leadership (e.g., Timothy) in relation to the historical Jesus. In verse 12, the writer presents Paul connecting Timothy's good confession at his ordination to the "good confession" Jesus Christ made in his trial before Pontius Pilate. In this sense, the PE writer (much like Luke in his Acts of the Apostles) has solved for the Pauline tradition what for Paul was an enduring challenge in his ministry—suspicion about the source of his authority. Connecting Timothy's confession at his ordination with that of Jesus in his trial before Pilate provides an original and indisputable ground of authority, identity, and purpose for the leaders of the church.

◼ THE TEXT IN THE INTERPRETIVE TRADITION

The connection between the confession of church leaders at ordination and the confession of Jesus at his trial before Pontius Pilate provided the early Christian martyrological tradition the opportunity of calling leaders to stand firm in their faith in times of religious persecution. Jerome Quinn notes the connection between 1 Tim. 6:12 and the late second-century North African text of the *Acts of the Scillitan Martyrs* (Quinn and Wacker, 542–43). The leader of the twelve Christians in this text, Speratus, testifies in his hearing using language similar to the claims of the dominion and sovereignty of God (as opposed to the emperor) in doxological affirmation of 1 Tim. 6:16: "he alone is immortal and dwells in unapproachable light, whom no one has seen or can see, to him be honor and eternal dominion."

◼ THE TEXT IN CONTEMPORARY DISCUSSION

This unit of text bears an aphorism that has had a long interpretive history and is broadly referenced in North American popular culture. In verse 10, the PE writer states, "love of money is the root of all evil." The most widely referenced version of this saying is shortened in popular rhetoric to "Money is the root of all evil." Needless to say, there is an important distinction between the *love* of money (in Greek, *philargyria*) and money itself (*argyria*). Nonetheless, Christian faith has often been characterized, on account of this misquotation, as promoting an impossible standard in practical worldly terms. Moreover, defenders of capital have chided that the institution of the church is hypocritical, because it obviously needs money to operate. One prominent example of the defense of money against this misquotation is Ayn Rand's presentation of Francisco D'Anconia's apologia for money in the novel *Atlas Shrugged*. In the novel, D'Anconia passionately outlines Rand's philosophy of "capital" as far from "evil," but rather the source of all creativity, power, and good in the world. Ironically, while the PE writer may represent an early church leader with whom Rand might have some affinity regarding values of self-sufficiency, this treatise would illustrate the essential problem of the "love of money," which is indeed maligned in the text. As the PE writer sees it, the problem with the *love* of money is the elevation of human productivity above a theological framework that would identify God as the source of all goodness and creative power.

2 TIMOTHY

Deborah Krause

Introduction

Second Timothy takes a different form than 1 Timothy. Rather than a simple continuation of instructions for church leadership, 2 Timothy is structured as a final testament from Paul to one of his most trusted emissaries. As such, the writing presupposes Paul's imprisonment in Rome rather than his Aegean travels and ministry as envisioned in 1 Timothy and Titus. In this light, scholars of the corpus have proposed that the canonical order may not have been the original design of the corpus, but rather that Titus and 1 Timothy would have preceded the poignant last testament of Paul to Timothy in 2 Timothy.

2 Timothy 1:1-18: The Good Treasure Entrusted to You

◼ THE TEXT IN ITS ANCIENT CONTEXT

Overall, the opening verses of 2 Timothy build a sense of poignancy by referring to Paul as one who "suffers" for his calling as preacher, apostle, and teacher, with the implication that those who lead in his stead should and will do the same.

The writing opens with words of affirmation for Timothy in his faith and with a reminder of the deep bond between Timothy and Paul in light of Paul's authorization of Timothy through the laying on of hands (v. 6).

◼ THE TEXT IN THE INTERPRETIVE TRADITION

Luke presents the story of Paul's meeting of Timothy in Lystra and adds a detail of his lineage, namely, that he is the son of a Jewish mother and a Greek father (Acts 16:1). For Luke, this tradition of Timothy's Jewish and Greek ethnic heritage makes him an ideal companion of Paul as he carries the gospel of Jesus Christ into Macedonia, literally embodying the reconciliation of Jew and Greek. For the PE writer, the mixed ethnic heritage is not as important as the enduring (multi-generational) faithfulness of Timothy's family, encompassing both his mother and his grandmother. As such, he is a model of steadfast faithfulness for which the PE writer is calling throughout the PE corpus. In both interpretive contexts (Luke and the PE), Timothy lives as a model of faithfulness, and his heritage is claimed in support. How that heritage is characterized offers insight into what in particular is being valued about Timothy's faith in each interpretive context.

Later interpreters of the Pauline tradition, such as John Chrysostom, continued to make theological meaning out of Timothy's foreign biological heritage and the PE writer's representation that he is Paul's "beloved son." In his *Homily 19 on Romans* 11.7 Chrysostom notes that if Paul could call Timothy (of Lystra) his "son" (which Paul also claims in 1 Tim. 1:2), then all people of faith have the capacity to be God's children. As such, claims to ethnic heritage as either a point of privilege or dishonor have no place in the life of faith.

▌THE TEXT IN CONTEMPORARY DISCUSSION

The PE writer presents Paul encouraging Timothy in his faith with these words: "for God did not give us a spirit of timidity but a spirit of power and love and self-control." In their ancient context, these words served as a challenge to church leaders to stand firm on the foundation of the faith and to claim the authority of their ordination and leadership to guide the church. Not surprisingly, however, the call to courage has been found useful by rhetoricians in many different contexts. Far from the confines of challenging church leaders, President Barack Obama used this text as a rallying cry to console and encourage the citizens of Boston and the United States at a memorial service after the Boston Marathon Bombing on April 18, 2013. Toward the end of his address, speaking directly to the yet unknown perpetrators of the violence, the president noted that their goal may have been to spread terror, but "our fidelity to our way of life, to our free and open society, will only grow stronger. 'For God did not give us a spirit of timidity but a spirit of power and love and self-control.'" As these words from the Pauline tradition were reanimated for the encouragement and hope of a city and a nation, the hundreds of attendees of the memorial service rose to a standing ovation.

2 Timothy 2:1-26: Dedication to Service and Sound Teaching

▌THE TEXT IN ITS ANCIENT CONTEXT

In chapter 2, the PE writer presents Paul directly charging Timothy and other leaders with him to be strong and to share in suffering (presumably with Paul, and foremost with Jesus Christ). In addition to using Paul's own biography and circumstances to compel and to inspire to greater dedication, the PE writer draws on three models of Greco-Roman masculinity in the persons of the soldier, the athlete, and the farmer. The purpose of these brief and somewhat enigmatic portraits is to challenge church leaders to be trustworthy in their tasks. The lessons seem to call listeners to focus wholly on the work of ministry. They are to avoid outside entanglements (like a good soldier), follow the rules (like a victorious athlete), and work hard (like a successful farmer). On the one hand, this call to focus and discipline seems to challenge leaders to function as "professional" ministers (in contrast to the tent-making historical Paul). On the other hand, the work of the clergy is cast in comparison to secular pursuits, and the expectations of church leaders can be identified in the Greco-Roman cultural mainstream values of hard work, discipline, and integrity.

◼ THE TEXT IN THE INTERPRETIVE TRADITION

The conclusion of the chapter raises the question of how we should characterize an apparent heretical teaching about the resurrection within the church. In 1 Corinthians 15, Paul himself battled with what he considered a misunderstanding of the resurrection: the denial of the efficacy of a general resurrection of the dead following, and separate from, Christ's resurrection. It is clear that a similar denial may have been present decades later, in the PE writer's context in the late first or early second century CE. Quinn and Wacker comment on the tenacity of this heretical teaching over this period, and in the following decades of early patristic interpretation and leadership as well: for example, Origen was compelled to argue for a "double resurrection," that is, of Jesus and of the faithful in general, in his commentary on Rom. 5:9. As Quinn and Wacker note, such a double understanding of the resurrection—apparently a very early development in Christian belief, though never receiving wide acceptance in Judaism—was an offense against the intellect of the Greco-Roman world. Moreover, the expectation of a judgment of all humankind on the "day of the Lord" offered a sin-focused eschatology that was difficult to square with the proclamation of a gospel in which the death and resurrection of Christ were proclaimed as the good news that sin had been forgiven (Quinn and Wacker, 683). Seen in this light, the challenges of understanding the resurrection in the PE are merely a way station between Paul's original challenge in Corinth and Origen's enduring challenge to maintain the general resurrection. What these three moments have in common is the purpose of reinforcing how God's work in the death and resurrection of Jesus relates to God's sovereign plan to save the world.

◼ THE TEXT IN CONTEMPORARY DISCUSSION

At the end of chapter 2, the PE writer returns to the overarching theme of challenging church leaders to carry out their ministries with discipline and care. The disposition of peacemaking is attributed to leaders. In verses 23-25, the writer declares that a servant of the Lord must not be quarrelsome, must be kindly to everyone, an apt teacher, patient, correcting opponents with gentleness. This list of expectations places the work of church leadership in the realm of navigating difficult (conflicted) social relationships. While much of the PE corpus has the ring today of antiquated structures and outdated paradigms, this call for ministers to lead with charity and openness to others is rhetoric straight out of many contemporary "boundary training" and conflict resolution seminars for clergy. When it comes to ministry, the PE writer seems to embrace that sound teaching and doctrine can only go so far. Often what is most important in the formation of faithful Christian communities is the capacity for leaders to show and be shown compassion, and to embrace ways of serving that make for peace.

2 Timothy 3:1-17: Avoid the Unholy and Adhere to Paul's Example

■ THE TEXT IN ITS ANCIENT CONTEXT

Commentators have long struggled to identify the particular beliefs and practices of the opponents who are in view in the PE. Whether they should be characterized as "Gnostic," antinomian, libertine, and so on is difficult to determine from the PE writer's rhetoric. This opacity of theological and social problems is hard to understand in the PE. If the writer were targeting particular opponents, why would not their errant beliefs and practices be enumerated clearly for church leadership to see and understand? Several options are possible. It may be that the PE writer and his audience are completely aware of the theological and ethical specifics of the opponents' beliefs and practices and therefore do not need to rehearse them. On the other hand, it may be that the PE writer has crafted the PE to characterize ecclesial and social ills more generally, so that the corpus will have more of an enduring role in guiding the ministry of the church in a variety of contexts and situations.

The vice list that opens 2 Tim. 3:1-9 seems to support the thesis that the PE writer has intentionally framed the opponents in generic terms. Here the eschatological framework of the "last days" sets up the expectation that people will fall into numerous social ills. The list of vices is extensive (superseded in the New Testament only by Rom. 1:28-32, which may serve as a base of tradition for the present list). Together they offer an overwhelming rhetorical demonstration that in the "last days" one can expect the world "to go to hell." Importantly, the vices listed provide the opposite extreme of the idealized virtues of the soldier, athlete, and farmer of 2 Tim. 2:4-6. As such, the PE writer offers broad cartoons of good and bad men among whom his churches' leaders can easily locate themselves and their opponents.

■ THE TEXT IN THE INTERPRETIVE TRADITION

In contrast to the generic portrait of bad leaders in 2 Tim. 3:1-9, the PE writer presents a portrait of Paul's suffering and persecution in 2 Tim. 3:10-17. The legend of Paul's suffering is one that finds broad appeal in the interpretive tradition. Luke, in the Acts of the Apostles, narrates the obstacles, angry crowds, trials, torture, and shipwrecks that Paul encounters. Likewise, the early Christian noncanonical writing the *Acts of Paul* presents Paul (and companions like Thecla) facing imprisonment, mob violence, wild beasts, and persecution (Taussig, 337–44). Luke's characterization serves to draw Paul into a line of "witnesses" (including Jesus) who suffer on behalf of the way of the gospel. The *Acts of Paul* characterizes Paul as a model of chaste devotion who eschews the trappings of culture and devotes himself wholly to the preaching and teaching of the Word. The PE writer's characterization of Paul's suffering offers a model of leadership with which to challenge and encourage the leaders of the church. Overall, the original call of Paul to "imitate me as I imitate Christ" (1 Cor. 11:1) is well heard in the interpretive tradition, and Paul's various commitments are reflected in its multifaceted expressions.

▐ The Text in Contemporary Discussion

One element of the PE writer's characterization of his opponents that does not bear a generic tone is his description of those, among the perpetrators of various vices, who "make their way into households and captivate silly women, overwhelmed by their sins and swayed by all kinds of desires, who are always being instructed and can never arrive at any knowledge of the truth" (2 Tim. 3:6-7). No doubt this rhetoric is filled with hyperbole; however, the subject of women and their particular vulnerability to doctrinal error is present at several points in the PE corpus (e.g., 1 Tim. 2:12-14; 5:13). While scholars debate the historical circumstances that gave rise to this rhetoric, contemporary feminist biblical critics have challenged that the writer's characterizations of women bear a misogynistic tone—in particular, demeaning women's activities and ways of knowing as frivolous, weak, and untrustworthy. Critics have countered to the PE writer, if these women are of such little account, why do their words and activities preoccupy so much of your concern?

2 Timothy 4:1-22: Presenting Paul's Final Requests

▐ The Text in Its Ancient Context

In many ways, the source of much of the rhetorical power of the overall PE corpus is lodged in the closing words of this chapter. While this trove of writings, presented to church leaders as lost letters of Paul, would no doubt have had profound impact within the late first- and early second-century church, that impact could only be compounded by the framing of the letters as personal correspondence between Paul and two of his most trusted emissaries in ministry, and furthermore as the last words of Paul written from prison prior to his death in Rome. The conclusion of 2 Timothy provides the forum for this presentation of Paul. He knows his death is imminent (4:6), and in this position he is able to dispassionately model the kind of leadership he is calling for from others. Needless to say, this is a compelling setting from which to impart wisdom to the church's leadership: "proclaim the message; be persistent whether the time is favorable or unfavorable; convince, rebuke, and encourage, with the utmost patience in teaching" (2 Tim. 4:2); "be sober, endure suffering, do the work of an evangelist, carry out your ministry fully" (2 Tim. 4:5).

▐ The Text in the Interpretive Tradition

The particulars of Paul's death are a shadowy mystery in Christian origins. The canon of the Christian New Testament does not record the event of his death. Luke chooses to conclude the Acts of the Apostles with Paul under arrest in Rome and yet preaching openly to the close of the story. The only other canonical reference to Paul's Roman imprisonment and impending death come in these verses of 2 Timothy. In the mid- to late second century, Ignatius of Antioch in his *Letter to the Ephesians* refers to Paul's death as a martyrdom in chapter 12, where he lionizes Paul as "the holy, the martyred, the most deservedly happy" (The Ante-Nicean Fathers, vol. 1, 55). Beyond these few specifics, other sources hold that Paul was beheaded (in contrast to Peter's more brutal upside-down crucifixion).

■ The Text in Contemporary Discussion

In the midst of the heroic portrait of Paul and the gentle admonishing of Timothy in his leadership, the PE writer manages to get in one last parting shot at those within the community who are susceptible to false teaching. It is in this sense that the PE likely originated as the parts of an intramural manual on leadership in ministry and have endured as such throughout much of church history. Only among teachers does such lampooning of bad teaching make sense. It emerges from the camaraderie of shared struggle. Acknowledging the "last days," the PE writer speaks to the condition of "itching ears" among the members of the church who seek teachers who will tell them what they want to hear. In the contemporary interpretation of this passage within twenty-first-century North American Christianity, this concept of itching ears has been used to characterize a progressive attitude toward tradition. In the midst of a culture and church polarized around issues of human sexuality, women's rights, environmental degradation, and the relationship of church and state, some church leaders appeal to the rhetoric of the PE writer as a demonstration that the "last days" are upon us and that "fundamentals" of the Christian faith, such as the authority of Scripture, the virgin birth, the bodily resurrection, and other tenets are "under negotiation" by those who have "itching ears" and who seek teachers who will tell them what they want to hear instead of the truth. In such contexts of rhetoric, it is important to recall that the PE themselves were forged in the midst of the early church's struggles over leadership, theology, and social structure. As such, their deployment to characterize one expression of ecclesial structure, belief, or practice as in error as opposed to another tends more to mirror their rhetorical origins than accomplish a definitive statement of orthodoxy.

TITUS

Deborah Krause

Introduction

While the canonical shape of the PE corpus places Titus at the end (being the shortest of the writings), it is quite likely that the corpus was originally intended to conclude with what is now called 2 Timothy, which takes the form of a final testament from Paul before his death (see above).

Titus 1:1-16: Opening Words of Paul to Titus

▌THE TEXT IN ITS ANCIENT CONTEXT

Titus parallels the scenario envisioned in 1 Timothy; Paul is writing during the period of his Aegean ministry (prior to his departure to Rome) to one of his trusted emissaries, in this case Titus on the island of Crete.

▌THE TEXT IN THE INTERPRETIVE TRADITION

Titus plays a prominent role in Paul's own recounting of the origins of his relationship with the Jerusalem church and his ministry to the gentiles. Paul notes that his second journey to Jerusalem was in the company of Barnabas and Titus. What is remarkable about Titus, as Paul describes it, is that he was a gentile and uncircumcised. During the visit to Jerusalem, he was not compelled to be circumcised, and through this detail Paul seems to want to communicate that the Jerusalem church leadership were at this point convinced of the authority of his calling and understanding of the gospel (Gal. 2:1-3). Elsewhere, Titus plays a significant role in serving as an intermediary and negotiator of Paul's unraveling relationship with the Corinthian church. At several points in that correspondence, Paul references Titus and his reconciling role (2 Cor. 2:13; 7:6, 13; 8:6, 16,

23). Finally, Paul seems to imply that Titus may have more credibility with the church than Paul himself (2 Cor. 12:18). Given his significance to Paul, both as an archetype of the faithful Greek and as an effective emissary, it is remarkable that Luke does not mention Titus in the Acts of the Apostles. While the PE writer clearly reanimates the place of Titus in the Pauline legacy through the PE corpus, Luke and other Pauline interpreters are more likely to reference the role of Timothy as trusted emissary of Paul.

▮THE TEXT IN CONTEMPORARY DISCUSSION

Along with Timothy, Titus has come to represent the church in the generations after Paul. While Paul found them to be important partners in his ministry in the Aegean, the PE corpus solidified their role in the Christian imagination as the torchbearers of the ongoing tradition. During Paul's historical ministry, Timothy and Titus bore the message of the gospel and stood in Paul's stead to strengthen and encourage the churches when he could not. After his death, and as Paul's legend and interpretation developed, they stand as examples of those faithful followers who uphold the tradition and pass it on to the next generation. In this sense, Timothy and Titus stand for those leaders who work to keep the church alive as it moves forward and finds its shape and purpose in each succeeding generation.

Titus 2:1-15: Enforcing the Social Order

▮THE TEXT IN ITS ANCIENT CONTEXT

As mentioned above, much of the traditional material found in 1 and 2 Timothy is also present in Titus. While this may appear to be the PE writer "repeating" himself, it is a device by which to reiterate the important message of the corpus and the relevancy of the same message for various contexts. As such, it is a means of underlining the universal applicability of the Pauline tradition. One element of the traditional material in Titus 2 is the "household code," in which the expectations of social order common in the Greco-Roman milieu are outlined. In contrast to Paul's use of the metaphor of the "body of Christ" to say that everyone in the community, no matter their role, has a place (1 Corinthians 12), the PE writer in Paul's name establishes a clear social hierarchy in Titus 2 (parallel to 1 Tim. 5:3—6:3), in which the overarching message is that everyone in the community should know his or her place.

▮THE TEXT IN THE INTERPRETIVE TRADITION

The representation of the Pauline tradition as one that establishes the theological basis and ecclesiological command for the social hierarchy of the household code has had significant consequences in numerous contexts. One powerful consequence has been a widespread ambivalence toward Paul in the African American Christian heritage. The teaching in Titus 2:9, "tell slaves to be submissive to their masters and give satisfaction in every respect: they are not to talk back" (an eerie echo of the mandate for women's silence in 1 Tim. 2:12), has played a role in casting all of Paul's teachings in a negative light. The great twentieth-century North American theologian Howard Thurman recounts the story that his grandmother (who was enslaved as a child) would ask him to read the Scripture to her, but rarely asked for the writings of Paul. When Thurman asked why, she noted that the slave master's preacher would often remind the slaves that Paul said slavery was God's will and several times a year would quote, "slaves should submit to and honor their masters" (Thurman, 30–31).

■ THE TEXT IN CONTEMPORARY DISCUSSION

Feminist interpreters work to excavate the rhetorical tactic in the PE writer's use of household codes. In the *Women's Bible Commentary*, Joanna Dewey engages Titus with historical-critical analysis to unveil the anxiety that underlies the PE writer's maintenance of the household code in the corpus. Dewey notes, for instance, that a driving force behind the PE writer's rigid social order is the sense that God, who is imagined as the paternal overlord of this hierarchal social structure, could be discredited by the misbehavior of his subjects (Titus 2:5). One particular strategy of the PE writer in Titus 2 that Dewey uncovers is the conscripting of older women to "encourage" younger women in their submission to this patriarchal social order and their subordinate role within it (Titus 2:3-5; see Dewey, 361). This strategy has a long history in the implementation of patriarchy. Often, within women's struggle for equality in ecclesial structures over the course of the twentieth and twenty-first centuries, some of the most vociferous and effective opponents of women's ordination have been powerful women in the existing structures of church hierarchy. No doubt, power manifests itself complexly in social organizations of the church and society. The struggle for women's full inclusion in church leadership (which in spite of advances in different quarters continues to this day) offers insight into the complexity of power at work in the midst of a hierarchically ordered and transforming social structure.

Titus 3:1-15: Avoiding Controversy for the Whole Church

■ THE TEXT IN ITS ANCIENT CONTEXT

The PE writer's concern for "the quiet life" continues into chapter 3 with a call for members of the church to be "subject to rulers and authorities, to be obedient, to be ready for every good work, to speak evil of no one, to avoid quarrelling" (Titus 3:1-2). The call to be subject to governing authorities echoes Paul's from Rom. 13:1-7. While the historical authenticity of that text has been debated, it provides a more robust theological justification for the connection between those with human sovereignty and God. The rhetoric of Titus 3:1-2 stands as shorthand of the earlier argument of Rom. 13:1-7. Given that the PE writer was likely addressing a group of leaders already familiar with Paul's teachings, it may be that the broader theological justification can be assumed between the writer and his audience. This context of the representation of Paul in the PE provides a helpful insight into why the PE overall seem to present such an abbreviated, and less nuanced, form of instruction than that found in Paul's likely authentic letters. Given that all the correspondence now resides within a canonical context under the label of "Paul," however, the work of interpretation involves the challenging step of attending to the differences between texts like Rom. 13:1-7 and Titus 3:1-2, and allowing the particularities of their rhetoric to be heard even in the midst of the similarities of their themes.

◼ THE TEXT IN THE INTERPRETIVE TRADITION

In the midst of the call for obedience among church members both to governing and familial leaders, the PE writer challenges his audience to positively "devote themselves to good works," to "avoid stupid controversies, genealogies, dissensions, and quarrels about the law," and "to have nothing more to do with anyone who causes divisions" (Titus 3:9-10). Note that the writer does not deny the existence of such controversies and divisive ideas, but he nonetheless calls his readers to avoid such things. In this sense, the writing stands within the church's tradition of promoting ecumenical engagement even in the midst of acknowledging doctrinal differences. The concept is captured well in the phrase (often attributed to Augustine) "in necessary things, unity; in unnecessary things, liberty; in all things, charity."

◼ THE TEXT IN CONTEMPORARY DISCUSSION

Titus 3 offers a glimpse into what has become a debate in contemporary Christianity regarding the nature of salvation. In Paul's similar historical correspondence, the concept of salvation is articulated as the work of God (in and through Jesus Christ), and is most often cast within a global context. God's saving work, in other words, is articulated as the work of redeeming all creation. Paul articulates his ministry to the gentiles as one component of this overarching plan of God for the salvation of the world (Romans 9–11). In Titus 3, the PE writer articulates a view of salvation that is more personal. In fact, the PE writer, writing in the name of Paul, proclaims that when he was "saved" (something that, as a pious Jew, the historical Paul would not have imagined he needed), he was delivered from involvement in division, argument, and controversy (Titus 3:3-7). Theological differences over the global and personal dimensions of soteriology continue to this day. What is captured in the Pauline interpretive tension between Romans 9–11 and Titus continues to be a tension at the heart of contemporary faith and practice. In this sense, the interpretive expression of Paul in the PE is an impetus still at work in Christian faith and practice.

Works Cited

Augustine. 1912. *Confessions.* Book 1. LCL. edited by T. E. Page and W. H. D. Rouse. New York: Macmillan.

Bassler, Jouette M. 1996. *1 Timothy, 2 Timothy, and Titus.* Nashville: Abingdon.

Dewey, Joanna. 1992. "1 Timothy, 2 Timothy, and Titus." In *The Women's Bible Commentary,* edited by Carol A. Newsom and Sharon H. Ringe. Louisville: Westminster John Knox.

Eisenbaum, Pamela. 2009. *Paul Was Not a Christian: The Original Message of a Misunderstood Apostle.* San Francisco: HarperOne.

Fellows, Richard G. 2001. "Was Titus Timothy?" *JSNT* 81:33–58.

Hoehl, Stacy. 2011. "The Mentor Relationship: An Exploration of Paul as Loving Mentor to Timothy and the Application of This Relationship to Contemporary Leadership Challenges." *Journal of Biblical Perspectives on Leadership* 3:34–47.

Ignatius. 1999. "Letter to the Ephesians." *Ante-Nicene Fathers,* vol. 1., edited by Alexander Roberts and James Donaldson. Peabody, MA: Hendrickson.

Krause, Deborah. 2004. *1 Timothy.* New York: T&T Clark.

Pervo, Richard I. 2010. *The Making of Paul: Constructions of the Apostle in Early Christianity*. Minneapolis: Fortress Press.

Quinn, Jerome, and William Wacker. 2000. *The First and Second Letters to Timothy*. Eerdmans Critical Commentary. Grand Rapids: Eerdmans.

Schüssler Fiorenza, Elisabeth. 1998. *In Memory of Her: A Feminist Theological Reconstruction of Christian Origins*. 2nd ed. New York: Crossroad.

Tamez, Elsa. 2007. *Struggles for Power in Early Christianity: A Study of 1 Timothy*. Translated by Gloria Kinsler. Maryknoll, NY: Orbis.

Taussig, Hal, ed. 2013. *A New New Testament: A Bible for the 21st Century Combining Traditional and Newly Discovered Texts*. New York: Houghton Mifflin Harcourt.

Thurman, Howard. 1949. *Jesus and the Disinherited*. Nashville: Abingdon.

Wall, Robert. 2012. *1 and 2 Timothy and Titus*. Two Horizons New Testament Commentary. Grand Rapids: Eerdmans.

Witherington, Ben, III. 2006. *Letters and Homilies for Hellenized Christians*. Vol. 1, *A Socio-Rhetorical Commentary on Titus, 1–2 Timothy and 1–3 John*. Downers Grove, IL: IVP Academic.

PHILEMON

Eric D. Barreto

Introduction

The twenty-five verses of Philemon have had an outsized influence on our culture and history. Curiously, its influence has been perhaps most resonant beyond the walls of the church rather than within, as this diminutive correspondence became a site of contestation over the morality of slavery in the United States. Philemon has unfortunately been too frequently and tragically misread. At the same time, this correspondence is a powerful witness of the ways the gospel demands we reimagine how we relate to one another, especially in light of wider societal pressures to embrace destructive hierarchies.

The shortest of Paul's letters, Philemon appears to be full of practical and personal matters but not much theological reflection, especially in comparison to a letter like Romans. Such initial impressions are incorrect, for in this short letter we discover the epitome of Paul's pastoral and theological work. The letter is a vivid illustration of the careful cultural negotiations people of faith must grapple with in a complex world. Most importantly, however, this letter revolves around a critical theological question. If God has drawn people together into communities of faith, how then are we to relate to one another when the dictates of the wider culture lead us toward division and social stratification rather than toward unity and equality?

The letter deals with a seemingly personal matter, which nonetheless evokes deep theological and communal questions. Somehow, Philemon's slave Onesimus has come to be in Paul's presence and provided succor to him in his time in prison. The letter itself does not make clear how Onesimus and Philemon came to be separated. Most interpreters have theorized that Onesimus escaped his master's house and yet somehow ended up becoming a Christian under the tutelage of Paul, Philemon's friend. Perhaps more likely is that Philemon himself sent Onesimus to Paul as a helper during his imprisonment. Prisoners in antiquity relied on the kindness of the free—whether friends or family—to provide for their daily needs. There was no cafeteria or commissary in an ancient prison. One's provisions came from those faithful friends who deigned to visit one in prison (see Matt. 25:36).

In light of Onesimus's kind service to Paul as well as Paul's deep affection for him as a believer (v. 10), Paul sends Onesimus back to his master's household with this letter. What does Paul hope for his dear "child" Onesimus?

The whole letter will be explored as one sense unit, though the section on the letter's "ancient context" does provide an outline based on sections of the letter.

▌ THE TEXT IN ITS ANCIENT CONTEXT

No exegetical question about Philemon is more important than determining what precipitating event led Paul to write this letter. What are the relational dynamics among Paul, Philemon, and Onesimus? How this question is answered often predetermines a great deal of the conclusions interpreters will reach about the import of this letter for contemporary Christians.

The difficulty is that the letter itself provides few solid clues about the nature of the conflict Paul seeks to address. Key to the background of this letter are four verses, though they each prove difficult to interpret: verses 11, 15, 16, and 18.

First, verse 11 notes that Onesimus appeared to Philemon to be "useless," while he has now proven "useful" to Paul and thus to Philemon too. That is, Paul intimates that Onesimus's utility has shifted in Philemon's eyes. But how exactly has this shift occurred? Second, Paul recounts in verse 15 that some separation has grown between Philemon and Onesimus, a separation Paul now hopes to help heal. However, what is the nature of this separation? Third, Paul seems to allude to Onesimus's status as a slave (*doulos*) in verse 17. Despite the importance of Onesimus's identification as a slave in the history of this letter's interpretation, this is the only time that the word is used in the whole letter. Why? Last, verse 18 seems to allude to some debt Onesimus may owe Philemon. And yet, what exactly is the nature of this debt?

From these few strands of data, interpreters have long sought to reconstruct the background to this letter. Most common has been the conclusion that Onesimus was a runaway slave who somehow came into Paul's circle of influence. Onesimus thus became a Christian, but Paul is now sending him back to his owner, Philemon. Paul seeks to reconcile these conflicted individuals who are now brothers in Jesus. This interpretation can be found throughout Christian tradition, starting with John Chrysostom and continuing through Reformers like Luther and Calvin and the majority of modern study Bibles and commentaries.

Challenges to this regnant conclusion have emerged. For instance, Allen Dwight Callahan has contended that Philemon and Onesimus were actually brothers caught in a bitter rivalry. Moreover, Philemon is now being reexamined by a growing number of African American scholars in particular (see Johnson, Noel, and Williams). These are important critiques of the traditional interpretation, though the view that Onesimus was a runaway slave remains influential.

Behind all these interpretive questions lies an ethical query. Did Paul hope that Philemon would liberate Onesimus? Did Paul in this letter question slavery at its core? Did Paul take the gospel to its liberative end and declare—even if subtly—that the ownership of humans has no place in the church? Often, interpreters have highlighted Paul's willingness to abide by the status quo of antiquity. There were laws regulating slavery, and Paul fully abided by them, these interpreters insist, even sending a runaway slave back to his owner. His submission to the status quo is often seen as commendable, something Christians should imitate. This view depends in significant part on the view that passages enjoining slaves' subordination to masters in other letters (Ephesians, Colossians, 1 Timothy, Titus) are genuine epistles of Paul, a judgment seriously challenged today (see the introductions to those letters and the essay "Situating the Apostle Paul in His Day and Engaging His Legacy in Our Own"). Others, however, have argued that a more robust rejection of slavery resides in Paul's rhetoric. How then do we make sense of these disparate possibilities?

In the end, the best interpretation of Philemon may lean on an ancient tradition of interpretation as more recent scholarship has questioned and reframed it. That is, Onesimus probably was Philemon's slave. He was likely sent to Paul by Philemon to care for Paul's needs in prison; Paul now sends Philemon back to Onesimus. In his letter, however, Paul develops a subtle but no less powerful rationale for reconfiguring how Christian community is conceived. He thus forwards a theological argument that could, if embraced, collapse the all-too-frequent oppressions that mar our world still today. Onesimus returns to Philemon no longer as a slave but a sibling, no longer a piece of property but a beloved brother. Their relationship has been irretrievably changed by the gospel.

Slavery Then and Today

Also critical to the interpretation of Philemon is the very practice of owning another person for economic gain. It would be incorrect simply to equate the practice of slavery in antiquity with its many modern forms today and in the recent past. The commodification of human bodies has taken a wide number of forms throughout history. Two errors ought to be avoided. Modern slavery does not coincide precisely with ancient slavery. Neither is it true that these forms of slavery are wholly distinct.

Several key differences are evident when studying slavery in antiquity and in the history of the United States. First, slavery in antiquity was not based on phenotype, skin color, or other visible identity markers. Peoples were not lumped together as slaves simply because of their cultural attachments or their race. Instead, a variety of misfortunes such as debt or defeat in military conflict could imprison individuals in long-term though not necessarily lifetime servitude. Second, therefore, slavery was not an inevitable and inescapable condition of a particular people. Emancipation was possible, and slavery was not necessarily seen as an inheritance passed from generation to generation.

At the same time, there are some commonalities that ought to be noted. First, both systems converted people into commodities, products that could be owned and used for the benefit of an owner. The dehumanization present in such economic systems is inescapable, no matter the other rationales tied into these systems of slavery. Second, both systems lean on the stratification of a hierarchical society in which some are owners and others are slaves. Some are inherently superior, and others must defer to them. Such hierarchy is antithetical to the gospel as enunciated by Paul in Philemon.

Ancient and modern practices of slavery are not identical. Despite differing practices and assumptions governing and justifying it, slavery remains a theological and ethical scandal. Thus interpretations of Philemon cannot dwell solely on Paul's character or matters of abstract dogma about freedom. At its core, this letter is about how we structure our relationships to one another and how the gospel must shape and reshape these webs of belonging.

Introductory Matters (vv. 1-7)

Like many of Paul's letters, the opening provides a number of interpretive clues for hearers. First is Paul's self-identification as "a prisoner of Christ Jesus" (v. 1). In this way, Paul casts his lot with the broken and despised of the world and thus approaches Philemon not as a spiritual superior but as a dedicated servant of Christ and a friend. Rhetorically, Paul is establishing his equality with Philemon, a sense of equality he will nonetheless use as leverage in the body of the letter.

Moving from the sender to the recipient of the letter, we discover that this epistle is misnamed. Though Philemon was certainly the primary recipient, the addressees include a certain Apphia and Archippus (who may have been the wife and son of Philemon) but also the whole church that gathers in his home. That is, this is not just a personal but a communal letter. Paul makes a request of Philemon but calls on the witness of the whole community to ensure the proper result. The contents of this letter do not include only matters of personal business between the apostle Paul and Philemon the head of his household but a mutual discourse among all of God's children in this congregation.

The thanksgiving section (vv. 4-7), however, returns to a second-person singular address. Paul turns to Philemon in particular, though the opening makes clear that there is a wider audience for this message. In these verses, Paul praises Philemon's faithfulness and witness to the gospel and begins to suggest that there may be something that he might do in order to share in "all the good that we may do for Christ" (v. 6). This initially cryptic reference takes form in the body of the letter.

The Body of the Letter (vv. 8-21)

Paul continues to emphasize not his power over Philemon but the relationship they share. But notice that Paul continues to point glancingly to his power even as he *says* he is subsuming it. Thus, for example, Paul states that he could demand Philemon's compliance (v. 8), and yet he appeals to a brother in the faith, not an inferior person (v. 9). We learn in verse 10 the primary concern of Paul's letter: he is interceding on behalf of Onesimus, who has become like a son to Paul. As noted above, however, it is not immediately clear what the backstory is between Onesimus and Philemon. There is clearly a profound relational tie between Paul and both Onesimus and Philemon. His concern seems to be to align the relationship between the latter two.

In verse 11, a pun in the Greek is lost in English translation. When Paul distinguishes that Onesimus was "useless" but is now "useful" to Philemon, he plays on Onesimus's name, which in Greek means "useful" or "beneficial." In short, the rules by which Philemon relates to Onesimus have changed; his worth, as Paul will detail later, is not based on his utility but on the kinship these followers of Jesus now share. Paul follows this language of persuasion with language of adoption.

This new relationship is embodied by Paul's description of Onesimus as "my own heart." Though he was certainly a help to Paul during his imprisonment (v. 13), Paul's love for Onesimus extends beyond the service he provides. In subtle language, Paul is exhorting Philemon to receive Onesimus in the same spirit, to inhabit this "good deed" (see v. 6). After all, it was Onesimus who had stood in the gap for Philemon, serving an imprisoned Paul in his stead.

But why was Onesimus with Paul in the first place? In verse 15, Paul seems to allude to a period of separation between Philemon and Onesimus. Why were they separated? Was it because Onesimus happened to flee his captivity? Was it because Philemon and/or the church who met in his home sent Onesimus to care for Paul's needs while in prison (see v. 13)?

It seems most likely that Onesimus was not a runaway slave. The encounter of a runaway Onesimus and an imprisoned Paul seems all too serendipitous. What are the chances that they would meet and develop a close relationship only to discover that Paul knew Onesimus's aggrieved master? Such a striking coincidence would certainly need to be mentioned in the letter. Instead, Paul assumes that Philemon knew Onesimus was in his presence. Paul never explains how he came to know Onesimus. Thus it seems most likely that Onesimus was sent by Philemon to care for him in prison. During that time, Paul has to come see Onesimus in a new way. Now Paul invites Philemon to do the same.

Verses 15-16 mark the transformation of Onesimus and a reinvention of the relationship between him and Philemon. Paul theorizes in verse 15 that Onesimus's separation from Philemon (whatever the reason) was a divine initiative so that their bonds would be extended but also transformed. Onesimus is much more than a slave now, Paul tells Philemon; he has become your brother, your kin, a part of you (v. 16).

Just as Onesimus previously stood in Philemon's stead, Paul now asks Philemon to receive his erstwhile slave as if Paul himself were his guest (v. 17). When Philemon sees Onesimus, he ought to imagine the face of Paul. Paul offers to fulfill any debt he might have incurred, even taking the scribe's pen in his own hand to state this (v. 19). And yet, the very next verse is an even more powerful rhetorical stroke: "I say nothing about your owing me even your own self." In saying nothing of this indebtedness, Paul nonetheless raises it. In these renewed communities of faith, it seems, debt is ever present, never discharged, but its payment also never demanded.

Perhaps the debt Paul offers to repay in Onesimus's place is not a straightforward offer. Previous interpreters have suggested that these debts may have been the reason for Onesimus's slavery or that he incurred a debt in running away from his master. But what if the mention of the debt is rhetorical? Between brothers and sisters in faith, no such thing could exist. It may be that, in light of how verse 19 concludes, the debt Paul speaks about is figurative.

As the body of the letter draws to a close starting in verse 20, Paul once again alludes to Onesimus's name by asking Philemon to provide him this "benefit" (*onaimēn*). And when he refers to having "his heart" refreshed, Paul must be pointing back to verse 12. Caring for Onesimus is caring for Paul himself. Here, a powerful model of mutual belonging is present. Paul concludes with words of confidence of Onesimus's "obedience" (v. 21). Paul's rhetoric of persuasion hits its peak here. Paul is not forcing Philemon's hands, but neither is he leaving this critical matter to chance. The witness of the community and the clarity of the good news require a new form of community and belonging.

Final Greetings (vv. 22-25)

These closing words of greeting are not just appendages to the letter. Though we know little about the people Paul names in these closing verses, the rhetoric of persuasion is clearly still evident. The letter is bracketed both in its opening and closing with language of mutuality. Thus, for instance, Paul refers in verse 1 to Philemon as a coworker (*synergos*) and in verse 2 to Archippus as a "fellow soldier" (*systratiōtēs*). Both words share a common Greek prefix (*syn*). That same prefix reemerges again in these closing verses when he refers to Epaphras, "my fellow prisoner" (v. 23, *synaichmalōtos*) and a list of other companions as "fellow workers" (v. 24, *synergos*). Mutual belonging is thus the primary rhetorical stance of the letter of Philemon. There is a flattening of hierarchies. At the same time, Paul is more than willing to deploy the power he has over Philemon. After stating that he is "confident of [his] obedience," Paul follows this note of surety with a not-so-subtle reminder in verse 22. When he asks Philemon to make his household ready for a visit, Paul is not just making necessary travel arrangements or being a polite guest. He is promising to visit this household of sisters and brothers to ensure their community reflects the gospel in all its fullness. Even in this brief letter, the rhetoric of persuasion is consistent and at the center of Paul's argumentation.

■ THE TEXT IN THE INTERPRETIVE TRADITION

Because of its brevity and the seemingly personal nature of the correspondence, Philemon has suffered from scholarly and exegetical neglect. As detailed above, most interpreters of Philemon have reconstructed the letter's background around a runaway slave and his aggrieved owner. This interpretation was advocated as early as John Chrysostom in his *Homilies on Philemon* in the fourth century. Near unanimity has prevailed ever since. So, in nearly every study Bible and commentary available today, Onesimus is assumed to be a runaway slave whom Paul is returning to his proper master. In many cases, Paul's decision is read as acquiescence to the status quo of his day. According to these interpreters, the letter does not contain a full embrace of ancient slavery, but neither does it seem to oppose it in a full-throated way.

Demetrius K. Williams (12) has argued that when scholars have paid attention to the letter, three primary interpretive questions have guided the tradition. First, interpreters posit what the letter reveals about Paul, not Philemon or Onesimus. In this way, Paul himself becomes an exemplar of humble and measured leadership.

Second, interpreters have had to grapple with the ethical and theological implications of slavery both in antiquity and today. Some found in Paul's subtle rhetoric sanction to continue modern forms of slavery, while others read in the letter a call for liberation. Proponents of slavery saw in Philemon a commitment to a cultural status quo. If Paul did not explicitly condemn slavery, they averred, why should we? In fact, if Paul was willing to send back a fugitive slave to his owner, ought not good citizens to have done the same in the antebellum United States? In contrast, slavery's detractors dwelled on the transformed status of Onesimus in the letter. As Paul himself concludes, Onesimus is "no longer as a slave but more than a slave, a beloved brother" (v. 16).

Last, Philemon has become embroiled in questions about Colossians and its authenticity as a composition of Paul himself because of the reference to Archippus in Col. 4:17 (see also Fitzmyer, 8–9).

Most recently, Philemon has reemerged as a critical instance of the destructive power that flawed exegesis can work and also of how readings from diverse social locations can reveal theological blind spots. Reading from the perspective of Onesimus and privileging the perspective of the enslaved reveal an entirely new way to understand this letter. In short, such a fresh reading can open up new possibilities. As a recent book concluded, "We are interested in hearing from Onesimus and reading from his marginalized position and find that the newer reading perspectives give him voice and agency. However, these newer readings and interpretations will not traverse the same worn and tired territory that has kept Onesimus enslaved and silent. To liberate Onesimus, Paul's letter to Philemon must be read anew or reread from this totally different basis and perspective" (Johnson, Noel, and Williams, 7).

■ THE TEXT IN CONTEMPORARY DISCUSSION

Reading Philemon in light of this interpretive history and today's pressing questions requires that we reinterpret Paul's rhetorical strategy in Philemon and its continued significance in theological reflection. Specifically, the composition and theology of Philemon ought to be set alongside the purported heights of Paul's other correspondence. Philemon is likely an exemplar of the kind of pastoral work Paul engaged in on a daily basis. Such quotidian conflicts probably absorbed most of Paul's attention. Philemon thus exemplifies the merging of a particular theology with a particular mode of belonging in community. If we have caught a glimpse of God's character in Jesus, how then ought we live together in faith? This is the question that resonates in Philemon and Romans alike, and the response Philemon provides is no less vital in our world today.

We might begin by asking how we understand Onesimus's role in this triangle of relationships. Interpreters have often focused largely on the relationship between Paul and Philemon, between the great apostle and the slave master, thus excluding from consideration the one individual whose life would be most affected by the outcome of this correspondence. Onesimus's very life and identity are at stake in the rhetorical negotiation Paul outlines. Of course, we can know very little about Onesimus's perspective on these matters. His voice is never directly heard in the letter.

But what we can glimpse are the difficult but necessary ways that Paul sought to stitch together communities composed of all kinds of people: poor and rich, powerful and weak, free and slave. In a hierarchical and highly structured culture, Paul sought to create small spaces of belonging, where these conventions might not hold absolute sway. Perhaps these small, largely powerless communities could not change the political status quo of the day. Perhaps they could not overturn the moral and cultural logics that ruled their society. Perhaps they could not even escape these basic assumptions about the functioning of human civilizations. However, in this letter, Paul invites Philemon and the church around him to imagine a new way to relate to one another. Thus Paul's mode of instruction here is not primarily by dictate or merely listing a new set of rules for everyday life; instead, he posits a theological imagination around kinship and belonging, the implications of which he invites Philemon and the church to embody in their own community. In short, what does it mean to receive one another as beloved sisters and brothers? What effect does this mutual reception have on the ways in which our culture marks us as superior or inferior?

Key to such interpretive efforts will be questioning received assumptions about this letter. Though the notion that Onesimus was a runaway slave has long been sanctioned by interpreters of the letter, recent studies have demonstrated ably how critical it is to revisit even this seeming consensus. Such seeming unanimity often imports unquestioned assumptions into interpretations that too easily become destructive and discordant with the text itself. Onesimus's story may have yet to be told because regnant assumptions have limited exegetical possibilities.

In short, Philemon is an exhortation to communities of faith to bond as kin, to embrace one another as children of God. The gospel reconstitutes our relationships and our communities at a fundamental level. The gospel also calls us, then, to give ear to those who are normally voiceless in our midst. Our communities must have wide boundaries and an eagerness to invite other voices to speak along with an equal yearning to listen carefully to these marginalized voices.

In light of these new relational ties, Philemon ought to propel its readers to rethink slavery again, both its historical legacies and contemporary iterations. Philemon's history of interpretation should remind us of the great harm that can be wielded by the exegete. Today, we ought to remain humble about our own interpretations of Scripture but also prophetic as we strive to invite the liberating reign of God in our midst.

How then do we live in the light of this witness today? How do we resist the siren calls of our own highly structured and demarcated social structures? How do we develop new lines of kinship even as so much of the wider culture draws us toward isolation and homogeneity? The Letter to Philemon suggests that the gospel has reordered our societal structures even as we live within them. Even as we feel the constraints of the ways we relate to one another, God has declared a new order in which the primary way we relate to one another is not based on inferiority and superiority but kinship, sisters and brothers adopted by a loving and just God. This was true for Philemon and Onesimus, no matter their relationship and conflicts. The same remains true for us today.

Works Cited

Callahan, Allen Dwight. 1997. *Embassy of Onesimus: The Letter of Paul to Philemon. The New Testament in Context*. Valley Forge, PA: Trinity Press International.

Fitzmyer, Joseph A. 2000. *The Letter to Philemon*. AB 34C. New York: Doubleday.

Johnson, Matthew V., James A. Noel, and Demetrius K. Williams, eds. 2012. *Onesimus Our Brother: Reading Religion, Race, and Culture in Philemon*. Paul in Critical Contexts. Minneapolis: Fortress Press.

Williams, Demetrius K. 2012. "'No Longer as a Slave': Reading the Interpretation History of Paul's Epistle to Philemon." In Johnson, Noel, and Williams, 11–45.